The Structure of Typed Programming Languages

Foundations of Computing
Michael Garey and Albert Meyer, editors

Complexity Issues in VLSI: Optimal Layouts for the Shuffle-Exchange Graph and Other Networks, Frank Thompson Leighton, 1983

Equational Logic as a Programming Language, Michael J. O'Donnell, 1985

General Theory of Deductive Systems and Its Applications, S. Yu Maslov, 1987

Resource Allocation Problems: Algorithmic Approaches, Toshihide Ibaraki and Naoki Katoh, 1988

Algebraic Theory of Processes, Matthew Hennessy, 1988

PX: A Computational Logic, Susumu Hayashi and Hiroshi Nakano, 1989

The Stable Marriage Problem: Structure and Algorithms, Dan Gusfield and Robert Irving, 1989

Realistic Compiler Generation, Peter Lee, 1989

Single-Layer Wire Routing and Compaction, F. Miller Maley, 1990

Basic Category Theory for Computer Scientists, Benjamin C. Pierce, 1991

Categories, Types, and Structures: An Introduction to Category Theory for the Working Computer Scientist, Andrea Asperti and Giuseppe Longo, 1991

Semantics of Programming Languages: Structures and Techniques, Carl A. Gunter, 1992

The Formal Semantics of Programming Languages: An Introduction, Glynn Winskel, 1993

Hilbert's Tenth Problem, Yuri V. Matiyasevich, 1993

Exploring Interior-Point Linear Programming: Algorithms and Software, Ami Arbel, 1993

Theoretical Aspects of Object-Oriented Programming: Types, Semantics, and Language Design, edited by Carl A. Gunter and John C. Mitchell, 1993

From Logic to Logic Programming, Kees Doets, 1994

The Structure of Typed Programming Languages, David A. Schmidt, 1994

The Structure of Typed Programming Languages

David A. Schmidt

The MIT Press
Cambridge, Massachusetts
London, England

This book was typeset by the author and was printed and bound in the United States of America.

Library of Congress Cataloging-in-Publication Data

Schmidt, David A.
 The structure of typed programming languages / David A. Schmidt.
    p.   cm. — (Foundations of computing)
 Includes bibliographical references and index.
 ISBN 0-262-19349-3
 1. Programming languages (Electronic computers) I. Title.
 II. Series.
 QA76.7.S345 1994
 005.13'1--dc20   93-39912
                    CIP

Contents

Series Foreword

Theoretical computer science has now undergone several decades of development. The "classical" topics of automata theory, formal languages, and computational complexity have become firmly established, and their importance to other theoretical work and to practice is widely recognized. Stimulated by technological advances, theoreticians have been rapidly expanding the areas under study, and the time delay between theoretical progress and its practical impact has been decreasing dramatically. Much publicity has been given recently to breakthroughs in cryptography and linear programming, and steady progress is being made on programming language semantics, computational geometry, and efficient data structures. Newer, more speculative, areas of study include relational databases, VLSI theory, and parallel and distributed computation. As this list of topics continues expanding, it is becoming more and more difficult to stay abreast of the progress that is being made and increasingly important that the most significant work be distilled and communicated in a manner that will facilitate further research and application of this work. By publishing comprehensive books and specialized monographs on the theoretical aspects of computer science, the series on Foundations of Computing provides a forum in which important research topics can be presented in their entirety and placed in perspective for researchers, students, and practitioners alike.

Michael R. Garey
Albert R. Meyer

Preface

Although few programmers ever design a programming language, all programmers should understand the structuring techniques that a designer uses. Working from developments in lambda calculus and type theory, this textbook presents one such set of techniques. The book uses the techniques in a rational reconstruction of existing programming languages and in the design of new ones. This lets the reader see why existing languages are structured as they are and how new languages can be built as variations on standard themes.

As the book's title suggests, the focus rests upon typed programming languages. Recent research on type theory suggests that types can play the central role in structuring a language, so the text scripts the story in this way, in the process consolidating a variety of results found only in the research literature. Typing structures for binding are emphasized, because the history of programming language design roughly parallels the succession of answers one gives to the question, "What phrases can be named in a program?" This motivates the study of lambda calculus, polymorphism, and intuitionistic type theory. The last topic has special value, for it reveals that a programming language is a logic, where its typing system defines the propositions of the logic and its well-typed programs constitute the proofs of the propositions.

Contents of the Book

Chapter 1 presents the syntactic and semantic tools for the design and analysis of a core programming language, where the core language consists of fundamental data values, operations, and control structures. The tools include abstract syntax definitions, static type checking laws in inference rule format, and elementary denotational semantics. The related induction proof techniques are presented. The tools are applied to an example while-loop language, which is extended in subsequent chapters.

Chapter 2 introduces the *abstraction principle*, which is a technique for introducing naming devices—declarations—into a language. Procedures, functions, consts, modules, and classes all arise from the abstraction principle. Evaluation strategies are examined, and the impact of variable declarations on the structure of the language gets close scrutiny.

Chapter 3 defines the *parameterization principle*, which allows the various forms of abstractions to receive parameters. The semantics of parameter transmission receives close attention, and its relationship to the semantics of abstraction is summarized in the *correspondence principle*, which suggests that the two should coincide.

Chapter 4 presents the *qualification principle*, which adds encapsulation constructs—blocks—to the language. Associated semantic questions lead to a study of scope, extent, encapsulation, objects, subtyping, and inheritance. By this point, the while-loop core language has been extended to an Ada/Modula-2 variant.

The language extension principles from Chapters 2–4 are summarized in Chapter 5 as being just record and lambda abstraction constructions, and the typing laws for the extensions are just the typing laws for the product and function space constructions in set theory, or for that matter, the inference rules for conjunction and implication in propositional logic. Thus, a programming language can be understood as a typed language core extended by a simply typed lambda calculus (with products). This motivates a study of the lambda calculus in Chapter 6, where standard results are surveyed.

Chapter 7 succinctly repeats the development of Chapters 2–5 for a core functional language. In this setting, the types that appear in the type checking laws make natural components for abstractions, parameters, and blocks, and this necessitates a study of types-as-values. Next, unification-based, ML-style type inference is presented, and finally Prolog is presented as a core language of booleans and unification extended by abstraction and parameterization.

Chapter 8 formalizes the issues related to types-as-values within a variety of higher-order lambda calculi, like the second-order lambda calculus, Fω, and the **type:type** calculus. Barendregt and Hemerik's Generalized Typing Systems are used as a common framework for the calculi, and issues regarding dependent product and dependent sum typing are discussed.

The final two chapters of the text introduce Martin-Löf's intuitionistic type theory, where a programming language's types are propositions and its programs are proofs in a logic. Propositional logic-typed languages are studied in Chapter 9, and predicate logic-typed languages are examined in Chapter 10. The former roughly correspond to the Pascal-typed imperative languages and the monomorphic functional languages, and the latter match the polymorphic imperative and functional languages. Chapter 10 places special emphasis on the viewpoint that types are really specifications and a well-typed program is one that satisfies its input-output specification. Inductively defined data types motivate proofs by induction.

Organization of a Course

The text is meant to be read from first chapter to last, but an instructor can choose to emphasize imperative language structure or functional language structure. In the former case, Chapters 2–6 form the heart of a course, and in the latter Chapters 6–10 move to the forefront. Chapters 9 and 10 can form the background for a course on specification and validation of (functional) programs.

An understanding of both syntax and semantics is crucial, but an instructor might prefer to discuss semantics issues informally and not delve into denotational semantics. To do this, an instructor should avoid those sections with the terms "semantics" and "soundness" in their titles. The occasional odd line containing the "$[\![\cdot]\!]$" brackets should also be skipped.

Students gain appreciation for language design by analyzing existing languages. An instructor should devote part of the course to an analysis of an imperative language, such as Ada, Eiffel, or Modula-3, or a functional one, such as Miranda, Scheme, or Standard ML. A significant programming project, for example, a compiler or interpreter, is recommended as well. When I teach the course, I present Standard ML in tandem with Chapter 7 and ask the students to implement a subset of Standard ML in itself.

Suggested Reading and Exercises

Near the end of each chapter is a short list of references for additional reading. References are identified by the last name of the author(s) and year of publication, for example, Schmidt 1986. References are alphabetized, for example, Reynolds 1981a, if an author possesses multiple references for a given year.

Each chapter concludes with an exercise set. The exercises are grouped and numbered by section, for example, for Chapter k, Exercise $m.n$ names the nth exercise for Section $k.m$. Difficult exercises are starred.

Acknowledgements

This text was inspired by five research papers: Hemerik and Barendregt 1990, Mosses 1983, Nordström 1981, Reynolds 1981a, and Tennent 1977. Although the end result does not utilize action semantics, the topic, summarized in Mosses 1992, influenced the entire text. In addition, Tennent 1981 and 1991 stand as the book-length precursors of the present work.

Olivier Danvy and Anindya Banerjee carefully read several drafts, implemented portions, and contributed many stimulating suggestions. Conversations, consultations, and casual chat with Stuart Anderson, James Bieman, Wim Bohm, Kim Bruce, Kyung-Goo Doh, Susan Even, Adrian Fiech, Michael Huth, Robert Harper, John Hatcliff, Neil Jones, Sergey Kotov, Dean Lass, Dave MacQueen, Karoline Malmkjær, Peter Mosses, Flemming Nielson, Hanne Riis Nielson, Michael O'Donnell, Peter O'Hearn, John Reynolds, Dave Rogers, Colin Stirling, Allen Stoughton, Bob Tennent, David Toman, Mitchell

Wand, and David Watt proved crucial to the final result. A special thanks is due to Mojmir Kretinsky and the other organizers of the 1990 SOFSEM Winter School in Janské Lázné, Czechoslovakia, for letting me present much of the material in a week of lectures. The hospitality of the computer science departments at Copenhagen, Edinburgh, and Glasgow is also appreciated. Closer to home, my department's head, Virgil Wallentine, is thanked for reducing my lecturing duties during what was supposed to be the final year of writing. Financial assistance from the U.S. National Science Foundation and the British Science and Engineering Research Council is gratefully acknowledged. Finally, Robert Prior, Jenya Weinreb, Yasuyo Iguchi, Ed Freedman, and the reviewers for MIT Press are thanked for their interest and suggestions.

The list of personal acknowledgements could easily be a section of its own, but I will try to summarize in just a few lines: For helping me to recover from this project, I thank Dr. Terry Pfannenstiel; for supplying good cheer, I thank Masaaki Mizuno; and for serving as my safety net, I thank my family and friends from Hays, Kansas. *Ad astra per aspera*.

The Structure of Typed Programming Languages

1 The Programming Language Core

Every programming language possesses a "core" of values and operations that establishes the fundamental capabilities of the language. For example, a language that has numeric values but not string values in its core might be useful for numerical calculation but not for text editing. A general purpose programming language owns a core that proves useful for as many applications as possible.

No one can say precisely how to design a language core. Nonetheless, the concept is helpful, because it gives a language designer a starting point. Given a language core, a designer can write sample programs and can study the computational powers (and weaknesses) of the language. Once the core meets the designer's expectations, it can be extended by conveniences like subroutines, modules, and the like.

In this chapter, we study the nature of the programming language core. Since core language design is an artistic activity, we cannot give a precise methodology. Nonetheless, we outline one possible structure for a language core and study an example in depth.

1.1 A Core Imperative Language

It is simplest to learn about the structure of core programming languages via an example, so we begin with the classical while-loop language. The syntax of the language appears in Figure 1.1. The definition is structured into four "levels," called *syntax domains*. Each syntax domain presents a distinct concept or aspect of the programming language. Here, numerals, storage locations, expressions, and commands are distinct concepts and are used in distinctly different ways.

Each syntax domain has its own syntax rule, which states how to build phrases of the domain. Let's examine the syntax rule for Expression:

$$E ::= N \mid @L \mid E_1 + E_2 \mid \neg E \mid E_1 = E_2$$

The letters N, L, and E are *nonterminals*; they represent previously constructed numeral, location, and expression phrases, respectively. For example, the construction @L builds an expression phrase from a previously constructed location phrase: if loc_1 is a location phrase, then $@loc_1$ is an expression phrase. The symbols @, +, $\neg$, and = are

---

C ∈ Command
E ∈ Expression
L ∈ Location
N ∈ Numeral

$C ::= L{:=}E \mid C_1;C_2 \mid$ **if** E **then** C_1 **else** C_2 **fi** $\mid$ **while** E **do** C **od** $\mid$ **skip**
$E ::= N \mid @L \mid E_1{+}E_2 \mid \neg E \mid E_1{=}E_2$
$L ::= loc_i, \quad$ if $i > 0$
$N ::= n, \quad$ if $n \in Integer$

Figure 1.1 _____

---

terminals. They represent operations, here, dereferencing, addition, negation, and equality, respectively. The set of expressions consists of exactly those phrases built by the five constructions in the syntax rule. The syntax rule is an *inductive definition*; this is developed in Section 1.3.

The "phrases" of a syntax domain are actually trees. Figure 1.2 shows the syntax tree for the Command phrase $loc_1{:=}0;$ **while** $@loc_1{=}0$ **do** $loc_2{:=}@loc_1{+}1$ **od**. A syntax tree displays the precise structure of a phrase. Indeed, a program's linear representation is just an abbreviation of the tree. Of course, a linear representation of a program might cause confusion about the tree's structure, for example, $loc_1{:=}1{+}2{+}3$. In this case, we introduce brackets to make the structure clear: $loc_1{:=}(1{+}2){+}3$.

The definition in Figure 1.1 is an *abstract syntax definition*. It defines the trees in a language, but it does not indicate how to map ambiguous linear representations (like $loc_1{:=}1{+}2{+}3$) into trees. This issue is formalized by a separate *concrete syntax definition*. For example, the concrete syntax definition for the Expression domain follows:

$E ::= E{=}T \mid T$
$T ::= T{+}F \mid F$
$F ::= N \mid @L \mid \neg E \mid (E)$

Extra syntax rules are added to state that equality and addition are left associative and that addition binds more tightly than equality. The extra rules resolve the ambiguities in linear representations, but they generate trees that have many superfluous nonterminals. Details about concrete syntax definitions can be found in any text on compiling.

Finally, a crucial issue is the *meaning* of a program. The while-loop language was chosen for this chapter because its constructions are well known. Although one's intuitions often suffice for understanding programs written in a simple core language, a formal

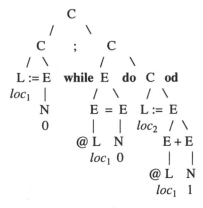

Figure 1.2

method for assigning meanings to programs proves helpful for precise analyses. Section 1.6 presents such a method.

1.2 Typing Rules

The abstract syntax definition in Figure 1.1 gives us firm intuitions about the structure of the imperative language, but it does *not* define the language's well-formed programs. The reason is that the syntax rules admit some malformed phrases, for example, (0=1)+2 is a malformed expression because addition, which is represented by the + terminal, cannot add a boolean to an integer.

We resolve this problem by refining the abstract syntax definition. There are, in fact, two types of expressions: integer ones and boolean ones. We could define two distinct syntax domains, Int-expression and Bool-expression, but we find it more convenient to leave the Expression domain as it is and add typing annotations (*type attributes*) to the expressions and all the other phrase forms of the language. A syntax tree is well formed (*well typed*) if type attributes can be attached to all of its nonterminals; the result is called an *attributed syntax tree*. For example, the tree in Figure 1.2 is well typed and its attributed syntax tree appears in Figure 1.3. The type attributes are affixed to the nonterminals by colons. In contrast, the syntax tree for (0=1)+2 cannot be assigned type attributes.

Obviously, we require some rules for attaching type attributes to programs. We use an inference rule format. The *typing rules* for the core imperative language are presented in Figure 1.4. There is a typing rule for each construction of each syntax rule. The

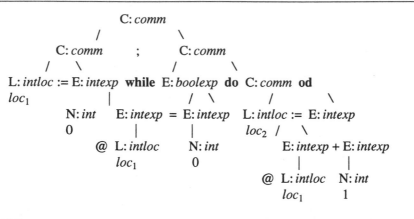

Figure 1.3 _____

typing rules state the conditions under which the constructions are well typed. Consider the construction, N ::= *n*, and its typing rule:

n: *int*,   if $n \in Integer$

Numerals are leaves in the syntax trees, and the rule states that a well-typed numeral tree is attributed by *int*. For example, this tree (leaf) is well typed:

N: *int*
2

Next, say that a numeral tree is used as an expression; this corresponds to the construction, E ::= N. The typing rule

$$\frac{N: int}{N: intexp}$$

says if the numeral tree, N, has type attribute *int*, then the expression tree consisting of N has type *intexp*. An example follows:

E: *intexp*
|
N: *int*
2

A more interesting example is C ::= L:=E and its rule:

For Command:

$$\frac{\text{L}: intloc \qquad \text{E}: intexp}{\text{L}:=\text{E}: comm} \qquad \frac{\text{C}_1: comm \qquad \text{C}_2: comm}{\text{C}_1;\text{C}_2: comm}$$

$$\frac{\text{E}: boolexp \qquad \text{C}_1: comm \qquad \text{C}_2: comm}{\textbf{if } \text{E} \textbf{ then } \text{C}_1 \textbf{ else } \text{C}_2 \textbf{ fi}: comm} \qquad \frac{\text{E}: boolexp \qquad \text{C}: comm}{\textbf{while } \text{E} \textbf{ do } \text{C} \textbf{ od}: comm} \qquad \textbf{skip}: comm$$

For Expression:

$$\frac{\text{N}: int}{\text{N}: intexp} \qquad \frac{\text{L}: intloc}{@\text{L}: intexp} \qquad \frac{\text{E}_1: intexp \qquad \text{E}_2: intexp}{\text{E}_1+\text{E}_2: intexp}$$

$$\frac{\text{E}: boolexp}{\neg\text{E}: boolexp} \qquad \frac{\text{E}_1: \tau exp \qquad \text{E}_2: \tau exp}{\text{E}_1=\text{E}_2: boolexp} \qquad \text{if } \tau \in \{\, int, bool \,\}$$

For Location: For Numeral:

$loc_i: intloc,$ if $i > 0$ $n: int,$ if $n \in Integer$

Figure 1.4

$$\frac{\text{L}; intloc \qquad \text{E}: intexp}{\text{L}:=\text{E}: comm}$$

If subtrees L and E are annotated with *intloc* and *intexp*, respectively, then the tree L:=E is annotated with *comm*, meaning that the assignment is well formed. An example is the tree for $loc_1 := 2$:

```
            C: comm
          /        \
   L: intloc  :=  E: intexp
     loc₁             |
                   N: int
                     2
```

Finally, notice that the typing rule for E ::= $\text{E}_1=\text{E}_2$ allows both integer expressions and boolean expressions to be compared.

Now, you should reexamine Figure 1.3 and verify that the type attributes are attached correctly. You should also write an algorithm that takes as its input a syntax tree and outputs the tree annotated with type attributes (when the tree is well formed).

To save space, we will often write the annotated syntax trees in linear form, displaying the type attributes as superscripts. The program in Figure 1.3 is written as follows:

$$((loc_1^{intloc} := (0^{int})^{intexp})^{comm}; (\textbf{while } ((@loc_1^{intloc})^{intexp} = (0^{int})^{intexp})^{boolexp}$$
$$\textbf{do } (loc_2^{intloc} := (((@loc_1^{intloc})^{intexp} + (1^{int})^{intexp})^{intexp})^{comm})^{comm})^{comm}$$

But the usual abbreviation for a well-typed tree is to show just the type for the root, like this:

$$loc_1 := 0; \textbf{ while } @loc_1 = 0 \textbf{ do } loc_2 := @loc_1 + 1 : comm$$

If there is a type attribute for the tree's root, this implies that all the subtrees have type attributes as well. The abbreviation $U:\tau$ can be read as an ''assertion'' or ''judgement'' from logic, so when we say $U:\tau$ *holds*, we are asserting that tree U is well typed.

The typing rules define a *static typing* for the language. The term ''static'' is used because the type attributes for a program can be calculated without evaluating the program. (The alternative is *dynamic typing*, where a program must be evaluated in order to calculate all its type attributes. An example is: **read**(loc_1); **if** $@loc_1 = 0$ **then** $loc_2 := \textbf{true}$ **else** $loc_2 := 1$; **write**$(@loc_2)$, where the type of $@loc_2$ is unknown until run-time.) Static typing is valuable because the type attributes predict the meaning of phrases, for example, if $@loc_1 : intexp$ holds, then we expect $@loc_1$ to evaluate to an integer. A language with static typing is *strongly typed* if no well-typed program produces run-time incompatibility errors. (An *incompatibility error* is an incorrect combination of operator and operands, for example, adding a boolean to an integer.) The language in Figure 1.3 is strongly typed, as we will verify in Section 1.8.

The addition of the typing rules raises two important questions: (i) Can a syntax tree be well typed in multiple ways? (ii) In what sense are the typing rules sensible (*sound*) in their assignment of type attributes to phrases? These questions are addressed in the next sections.

1.3 Induction and Recursion

An abstract syntax definition is an example of an *inductive definition*. An inductive definition defines a set of objects through a well-controlled method of self-reference. For example, the syntax rule:

$$E ::= \textbf{true} \mid \neg E \mid E_1 \& E_2$$

defines a set of trees, Expression, such that

(i)   **true** is in Expression;

(ii)   if a tree, E, is in Expression, then so is ¬E;

(iii) if the trees, E_1 and E_2, are in Expression, then so is $E_1 \& E_2$.

and no other trees are in Expression.

   We can effectively generate all the trees in Expression in stages:

- $stage_0 = \varnothing$;
- $stage_{i+1} = stage_i \cup \{true\} \cup \{\neg E \mid E \in stage_i\} \cup \{E_1 \& E_2 \mid E_1, E_2 \in stage_i\}$
      for all $i \geq 0$

and declare Expression $= \bigcup_{i \geq 0} stage_i$. That is, Expression is the set of all trees built by applying steps (i)–(iii) a finite number of times. This set is the syntax domain of expressions.

   Inductive definitions are crucial to proving properties of programming languages, because we can use a proof technique, called *structural induction*. The idea is, if we wish to prove that all trees in a language satisfy a property, P, we show that all the possible constructions for building trees must build trees with property P. When we try to prove that a particular construction builds a new tree with property P, and we see that the construction uses previously built trees to build the new one, then we can assume that the previously built trees already have property P to show that the newly constructed one has it as well. For example, to show that $P(t)$ holds for all trees, t, in Expression, it suffices to show

(i) $P(\mathbf{true})$ holds;

(ii)   for an arbitrary tree, E, in Expression, if $P(E)$ holds, then $P(\neg E)$ holds;

(iii) for arbitrary trees E_1 and E_2 in Expression, if $P(E_1)$ and $P(E_2)$ hold, then $P(E_1 \& E_2)$ holds.

The "if clauses" in (ii) and (iii) are called the *inductive hypotheses*.

   We now give an example. We define the *rank* of a tree in Expression by this definition:

- $rank(\mathbf{true}) = 0$
- $rank(\neg E) = rank(E) + 1$
- $rank(E_1 \& E_2) = max\{rank(E_1), rank(E_2)\} + 1$

For example, $rank((\neg\mathbf{true}) \& (\neg(\mathbf{true} \& \mathbf{true}))) = 3$. You should convince yourself that every tree has a unique rank—indeed, this is no accident; any definition coded like *rank*'s, that is, based on the structure of an inductive definition, is well defined. Such a definition is called a *recursive definition*.

   We now prove the following "obvious" property:

1.1 Proposition

Every tree has a rank greater than or equal to 0.

Proof: We use structural induction. There are three possible constructions:

(i)   The tree is **true**: By the definition, *rank*(**true**) = 0, which is greater than or equal to 0.

(ii) The tree is ¬E: The inductive hypothesis states that *rank*(E) = *k*, where $k \geq 0$. This means *rank*(¬*E*) = *k*+1, which is clearly greater than or equal to 0.

(iii) The tree is $E_1 \& E_2$: The inductive hypothesis states that that *rank*(E_1) = k_1, where $k_1 \geq 0$, and *rank*(E_2) = k_2, where $k_2 \geq 0$. So, *rank*($E_1 \& E_2$) = (*max*{k_1, k_2})+1, which which is clearly greater than or equal to 0.

Since all the constructions have the property, the proof is complete. □

We apply structural induction in the next section to prove that every syntax tree in the language of Figure 1.1 is well typed in at most one way.

1.4 Unicity of Typing

A language has the *unicity of typing* property if every syntax tree has at most one assignment of typing attributes to its nodes; that is, for every phrase, P, if P: τ holds, then τ is unique. Unicity of typing is a valuable property so we now show that the language in Figure 1.1 has the property. We build to the result in stages.

1.2 Proposition

For all N ∈ Numeral, *if* N: τ *holds, then* τ = *int.*

Proof: There is only one typing rule for numerals in Figure 1.4, and it makes N: *int* hold. □

1.3 Proposition

For all L ∈ Location, *if* L: τ *holds, then* τ = *intloc.*

Proof: Like the proof of Proposition 1.2. □

1.4 Proposition

Unicity of typing holds for the syntax domain Expression.

Proof: We use structural induction on the definition for Expression; there are five possible cases:

(i) N: By Proposition 1.2, N: *int* holds. Since there is only one typing rule in Figure 1.4 for an expression consisting of N, and it requires N: *int*, it must be that only N: *intexp* holds.

(ii) @L: Similar to case (i).

(iii) E_1+E_2: The inductive hypothesis, states, if $E_1:\tau_1$ and $E_2:\tau_2$ hold, then they hold for unique values for τ_1 and τ_2. There is only one typing rule for E_1+E_2 in Figure 1.4, and it requires that $E_1:$ *intexp* and $E_2:$ *intexp* hold. In the case that $\tau_1 = \tau_2 = intexp$, then $E_1+E_2:$ *intexp* holds. If either τ_1 or τ_2 is not *intexp*, then E_1+E_2 has no typing. In summary, if $E_1+E_2:\tau$ holds, then $\tau = intexp$.

(iv) $\neg E$: Similar to case (iii).

(v) $E_1=E_2$: Similar to case (iii). □

1.5 Theorem

Unicity of typing holds for the syntax domain Command.

Proof: The structural induction proof has five cases:

(i) L:=E: By Proposition 1.3, only L: *intloc* holds; by Lemma 1.4, if $E:\tau_1$ holds, then it holds for a unique value of τ_1. There is only one typing rule for L:=E in Figure 1.4, and it requires that $\tau_1 = intexp$. If that is the case, then L:=E: *comm* holds. If τ_1 is not *intexp*, then L:=E cannot be typed. In summary, if L:=E: τ holds, then $\tau = comm$.

(ii) $C_1;C_2$: By the inductive hypothesis, if $C_1:\tau_1$ and $C_2:\tau_2$ hold, then they hold for unique values for τ_1 and τ_2. There is only one typing rule for $C_1;C_2$ in Figure 1.8, and it requires that $C_1:$ *comm* and $C_2:$ *comm* holds. If this is indeed the case, then $C_1;C_2:$ *comm* holds. If either τ_1 or τ_2 is not *comm*, then $C_1;C_2$ has no typing. In summary, if $C_1;C_2:\tau$ holds, then $\tau = comm$.

(iii) **if** E **then** C_1 **else** C_2 **fi**: Similar to case (ii): Lemma 1.4 is used to reason about the typing of E, and the inductive hypothesis is used to reason about the typing of C_1 and C_2.

(iv) **while** E **do** C **od**: Similar to case (iii).

(v) **skip**: Easy. □

The above proof was structured in four stages, since there were four syntax domains. If a property must be proved about several syntax domains where the syntax rules are mutually recursive, then the structural induction proof should proceed on the syntax domains *simultaneously*, that is, as if the syntax rules were one big rule.

1.5 The Typing Rules Define the Language

Since only the well-formed programs are of value, it is really the set of typing rules—and not the abstract syntax rules—that define a language. The programs in a language are exactly the well-typed trees. The significance of the unicity of typing property is that a linear, untyped representation of a program, like $loc_1 := @loc_1 + 1$, can be safely used, since it represents (at most) one program.

If we are pedantic, or if our language lacks the unicity of typing property, we should derive our programs directly from the typing rules. As an example, say that we wish to derive the program in Figure 1.3 with the rules in Figure 1.4. We start with the rules $loc_1 : intloc$ and $0 : int$. The latter implies that $0 : intexp$ holds, so we have $loc_1 := 0 : comm$. At this point, we have derived the following tree:

$$0 : int$$
$$|$$
$$loc_1 : intloc \quad 0 : intexp$$
$$\setminus \quad /$$
$$loc_1 := 0 : comm$$

Of course, this is just the left subtree, inverted, of Figure 1.3. When we complete the deduction, we discover the tree in Figure 1.5.

If we treat the typing rules in Figure 1.4 as a *logic*, that is, as a set of axioms and inference rules, then the trees we derive are proofs in the logic. For this reason, we call the (inverted) trees *proof trees*. This notion is developed in Chapters 9 and 10.

Another important point is that the typing rules in Figure 1.4 constitute an inductive

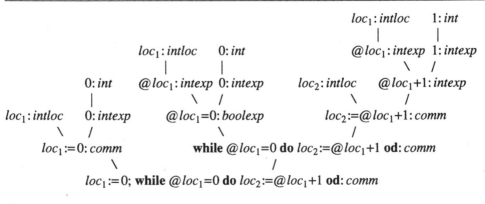

Figure 1.5

definition for generating well-typed trees. (Think of each typing rule as a "construction" for a language of proof trees.) For example, the rule

$$\frac{L:\textit{intloc} \qquad E:\textit{intexp}}{L:=E:\textit{comm}}$$

states: if t_1 is a proof tree whose root is labeled by a location, L, and *intloc*, and t_2 is a proof tree whose root is labeled by an expression, E, and *intexp*, then t_1 and t_2 can be joined into a new proof tree of the following form:

$$
\begin{array}{cc}
t_1 & t_2 \\
L:\textit{intloc} & E:\textit{intexp} \\
\diagdown & \diagup \\
\multicolumn{2}{c}{L:=E:\textit{comm}}
\end{array}
$$

At the beginning of this section, we noted that the unicity of typing property lets us write programs in untyped, linear representations. But some programming languages lack unicity of typing. For example, say that we add to Figure 1.4 these rules for coercion and real addition:

$$\frac{E:\textit{intexp}}{E:\textit{realexp}} \qquad \frac{E_1:\textit{realexp} \qquad E_2:\textit{realexp}}{E_1+E_2:\textit{realexp}}$$

Now, $0+1:\textit{realexp}$ can be derived two different ways:

$$
\begin{array}{cccc}
0:\textit{int} & 1:\textit{int} & 0:\textit{int} & 1:\textit{int} \\
| & | & | & | \\
0:\textit{intexp} & 1:\textit{intexp} & 0:\textit{intexp} & 1:\textit{intexp} \\
\diagdown & \diagup & | & | \\
0+1:\textit{intexp} & & 0:\textit{realexp} & 1:\textit{realexp} \\
| & & \diagdown & \diagup \\
0+1:\textit{realexp} & & 0+1:\textit{realexp} &
\end{array}
$$

We can argue that these two proof trees are two distinct programs, with possibly distinct meanings, but this is a bit harsh, since the coercion rule probably represents a coercion from fixed-point to floating-point arithmetic, and the end result should be the same. We require a *coherence* property: All derivations of some $E{:}\tau$ should yield the same meaning. Coherence is a natural property but not one that automatically holds. Chapter 4 considers the issue further.

1.6 The Semantics of the Core Language

A well-designed programming language will have a well-designed syntax, but syntax is not an end in itself. A purpose of a well-designed syntax is to guide the programmer to understanding the language's semantics. The imperative programming language has a well-structured syntax: Locations and numerals (apparently) represent themselves, expressions represent integers and booleans, and commands represent state transformation operations. But these intuitions should be formalized and confirmed.

We use *denotational semantics* to formalize the language's semantics. A denotational semantics is a recursive definition that maps well-typed derivation trees to their mathematical meanings. Figure 1.6 shows the meaning sets and operations that we use for the imperative language.

The *Bool* set consists of the two meanings, *true* and *false*; operation *not* is logical negation and *equalbool* compares two booleans for equality, for example, *equalbool*(*false*, *false*) = *true*. *Int* is the set of integers; its operations are addition and equality check. The *Location* set has no operations. Finally, *Store* is the set of m-tuples of integers. The elements of *Store* are storage vectors. The operations *lookup* and *update* use location numbers to index and insert values into storage vectors. The *if* operation selects a store based on the result of a test.

The meaning of a well-typed program is given by a recursive definition, $[\![\cdot]\!]$, on the typing rules. See Figure 1.7. The clauses have a regular, recursive structure. For example, since the typing rule

$$\frac{\text{L}: intloc \qquad \text{E}: intexp}{\text{L}:=\text{E}: comm}$$

says how to build a command tree, L:=E, from a well-typed location subtree, L, and a well-typed expression subtree, E, then the meaning, $[\![\text{L}:=\text{E}: comm]\!]$, is calculated in terms of the meanings of the two subtrees:

$$[\![\text{L}:=\text{E}: comm]\!] \cdots = \cdots [\![\text{L}: intloc]\!] \cdots [\![\text{E}: intexp]\!] \cdots$$

The term *compositional* is often used to describe a semantics definition in this style. A second, key feature of the semantics definition is *referential transparency*: If two phrases are the same meaning, then they can be used interchangeably. This is why, for example, we can simplify *plus*(*plus*(2, 3), 4) to *plus*(5, 4): *plus*(2, 3) and 5 are the same meaning.

We will read Figure 1.7 from the last line to the first. The meaning of a well-typed numeral is just the corresponding integer, for example, $[\![2: int]\!] = 2$. (Read $[\![\cdot]\!]$ as "the meaning of.") Similarly, the meaning of a well-typed location number is just itself, for example, $[\![loc_1: intloc]\!] = loc_1$.

Unlike numerals and locations, the meanings of expressions are dependent on the storage vector. For example, if location 1 contains a 3, then the meaning of $@loc_1+1$

$Bool = \{\, true, false \,\}$

Operations:

    $not\colon Bool \rightarrow Bool$

        $not(false) = true,\quad not(true) = false$

    $equalbool\colon Bool \times Bool \rightarrow Bool$

        $equalbool(m, n) = (m{=}n)$

$Int = \{\, \ldots, -1, 0, 1, \ldots \,\}$

Operations:

    $plus\colon Int \times Int \rightarrow Int$

        $plus(m, n) = m{+}n$

    $equalint\colon Int \times Int \rightarrow Bool$

        $equalint(m, m) = (m{=}n)$

$Location = \{\, loc_i \mid i > 0 \,\}$ (no operations)

$Store = \{\, \langle n_1, n_2, \ldots, n_m \rangle \mid n_i \in Int,\ 1 \le i \le m,\ m \ge 0 \,\}$

Operations:

    $lookup\colon Location \times Store \rightarrow Int$

        $lookup\,(loc_j, \langle n_1,, n_2, \ldots, n_j, \ldots, n_m \rangle) = n_j$

            Note: if $j > m$, then $lookup\,(loc_j, \langle n_1, \ldots, n_m \rangle) = 0$

    $update\colon Location \times Int \times Store \rightarrow Store$

        $update\,(loc_j,\, n,\, \langle n_1, n_2, \ldots, n_j, \ldots, n_m \rangle) = \langle n_1, n_2, \ldots, n, \ldots, n_m \rangle$

            Note: if $j > m$, then $update\,(loc_j,\, n,\, \langle n_1, \ldots, n_m \rangle) = \langle n_1, \ldots, n_m \rangle$

    $if\colon Bool \times Store_\perp \times Store_\perp \rightarrow Store_\perp$ (Note: $Store_\perp = Store \cup \{\, \perp \,\}$)

        $if(true, s_1, s_2) = s_1$

        $if(false, s_1, s_2) = s_2$

Figure 1.6 _____

For Command:

$\llbracket L{:=}E{:}\,comm \rrbracket(s) = update(\llbracket L{:}\,intloc \rrbracket, \llbracket E{:}\,intexp \rrbracket(s), s)$

$\llbracket C_1{;}C_2{:}\,comm \rrbracket(s) = \llbracket C_2{:}\,comm \rrbracket(\llbracket C_1{:}\,comm \rrbracket(s))$

$\llbracket \textbf{if } E \textbf{ then } C_1 \textbf{ else } C_2 \textbf{ fi} \rrbracket(s) = if(\llbracket E{:}\,boolexp \rrbracket(s), \llbracket C_1{:}\,comm \rrbracket(s), \llbracket C_2{:}\,comm \rrbracket(s))$

$\llbracket \textbf{while } E \textbf{ do } C \textbf{ od} \rrbracket(s) = w(s)$

      where $w(s) = if(\llbracket E{:}\,boolexp \rrbracket(s), w(\llbracket C{:}\,comm \rrbracket(s)), s)$

$\llbracket \textbf{skip}{:}\,comm \rrbracket(s) = s$

For Expression:

$\llbracket N{:}\,intexp \rrbracket(s) = \llbracket N{:}\,int \rrbracket$

$\llbracket @L{:}\,intexp \rrbracket(s) = lookup(\llbracket L{:}\,intloc \rrbracket, s)$

$\llbracket E_1{+}E_2{:}\,intexp \rrbracket(s) = plus(\llbracket E_1{:}\,intexp \rrbracket(s), \llbracket E_2{:}\,intexp \rrbracket(s))$

$\llbracket \neg E{:}\,boolexp \rrbracket(s) = not(\llbracket E{:}\,boolexp \rrbracket(s))$

$\llbracket E_1{=}E_2{:}\,boolexp \rrbracket(s) = equalbool(\llbracket E_1{:}\,boolexp \rrbracket(s), \llbracket E_2{:}\,boolexp \rrbracket(s))$

$\llbracket E_1{=}E_2{:}\,boolexp \rrbracket(s) = equalint(\llbracket E_1{:}\,intexp \rrbracket(s), \llbracket E_2{:}\,intexp \rrbracket(s))$

For Location:

$\llbracket loc_i{:}\,intloc \rrbracket = loc_i$

For Numeral:

$\llbracket n{:}\,int \rrbracket = n$

Figure 1.7 _____

should be 4. We formalize the dependency of an expression on the store by parameterizing the meaning of an expression on the store. Thus, the meaning of an expression is a function from *Store* to *Int* or *Bool*. Consider:

$\llbracket @L{:}\,intexp \rrbracket(s) = lookup(\llbracket L{:}\,intloc \rrbracket, s)$

The equation says that the meaning of a well-typed expression, @L, is calculated by a *lookup* operation, using s, the store, and the meaning of the subtree, L: *intloc*. For example, for input store $\langle 3, 4, 5 \rangle$, the meaning of $@loc_1$ is: $\llbracket @loc_1{:}\,intexp \rrbracket \langle 3, 4, 5 \rangle = lookup(\llbracket loc_1{:}\,intloc \rrbracket, \langle 3, 4, 5 \rangle) = lookup(loc_1, \langle 3, 4, 5 \rangle) = 3$. Similarly, the meaning of a well-typed addition expression is the sum of the meanings of the subtrees with respect to the current store. An example is: $\llbracket @loc_1{+}1{:}\,intexp \rrbracket \langle 3, 4, 5 \rangle = plus(\llbracket @loc_1{:}\,intexp \rrbracket \langle 3, 4, 5 \rangle, \llbracket 1{:}\,intexp \rrbracket \langle 3, 4, 5 \rangle) = plus(3, \llbracket 1{:}\,int \rrbracket) = plus(3, 1) = 4$.

    The meaning of a command is also calculated with respect to the store; the result is a new store. (A command "changes" the store into a new one.) Thus, the meaning of a command is a function from the set *Store* to *Store*. For example: $[\![loc_3 := @\,loc_1 + 1 : comm]\!]\langle 3, 4, 5\rangle = update([\![loc_3 : intloc]\!], [\![@\,loc_1 + 1 : intexp]\!] \langle 3, 4, 5\rangle, \langle 3, 4, 5\rangle) = update(loc_3, 4, \langle 3, 4, 5\rangle) = \langle 3, 4, 4\rangle$. The meaning of command composition is just the composition of the respective store transformation functions for C_1 and C_2. An example follows:

$[\![loc_3 := @\,loc_1 + 1;\ \textbf{if}\ @\,loc_3 = 0\ \textbf{then}\ loc_2 := 1\ \textbf{else skip}: comm]\!]\langle 3, 4, 5\rangle$

$= [\![\textbf{if}\ @\,loc_3 = 0\ \textbf{then}\ loc_2 := 1\ \textbf{else skip}: comm]\!]([\![loc_3 := @\,loc_1 + 1 : comm]\!]\langle 3, 4, 5\rangle)$

$= [\![\textbf{if}\ @\,loc_3 = 0\ \textbf{then}\ loc_2 := 1\ \textbf{else skip}: comm]\!]\langle 3, 4, 4\rangle$

$= if([\![@\,loc_3 = 0 : boolexp]\!]\langle 3, 4, 4\rangle,\ [\![loc_2 := 1 : comm]\!]\langle 3, 4, 4\rangle,\ [\![\textbf{skip}: comm]\!]\langle 3, 4, 4\rangle)$

$= if(false,\ [\![loc_2 := 1 : comm]\!]\langle 3, 4, 4\rangle,\ [\![\textbf{skip}: comm]\!]\langle 3, 4, 4\rangle)$

$= [\![\textbf{skip}: comm]\!]\langle 3, 4, 4\rangle = \langle 3, 4, 4\rangle$

The semantics of **while** E **do** C **od** should give pause; it defines the loop as a recursively defined function, w. It is beyond the scope of this text to give the foundations of this form of recursion, but we can understand w in terms of this family of functions:

$w_0(s) = \bot$, where $\bot$ stands for "undefined" or "looping"

$w_1(s) = if([\![E: boolexp]\!](s),\ w_0([\![C: comm]\!](s)),\ s)$

$w_2(s) = if([\![E: boolexp]\!](s),\ w_1([\![C: comm]\!](s)),\ s)$

$\cdots$

$w_{i+1}(s) = if([\![E: boolexp]\!](s),\ w_i([\![C: comm]\!](s)),\ s)$

$\cdots$

A function w_i represents a weakened version of the loop that can execute at most i iterations before becoming exhausted. The semantics of the while-loop itself, that is, function w, is characterized by: for all store vectors, s and s', $w(s) = s'$ if and only if there is some $k \geq 0$ such that $w_k(s) = s'$. (It is crucial here that $w_k(s) = s'$ implies $w_j(s) = s'$, for all $j \geq k$.) This property justifies the unfolding (i.e., "recursive call") of a recursively defined function in a calculation; an example follows:

$[\![\textbf{while}\ @\,loc_1 = 0\ \textbf{do}\ loc_1 := @\,loc_1 + 1 : comm]\!]\langle 0, 0\rangle$

$= w\langle 0, 0\rangle$

$= if([\![@\,loc_1 = 0 : boolexp]\!]\langle 0, 0\rangle,\ w([\![loc_1 := @\,loc_1 + 1 : comm]\!]\langle 0, 0\rangle),\ \langle 0, 0\rangle)$

$= if(true,\ w([\![loc_1 := @\,loc_1 + 1 : comm]\!]\langle 0, 0\rangle),\ \langle 0, 0\rangle)$

$= w([\![loc_1 := @\,loc_1 + 1 : comm]\!]\langle 0, 0\rangle)$

$= w\langle 1, 0\rangle$

$= if([\![@\,loc_1 = 0 : boolexp]\!]\langle 1, 0\rangle,\ w([\![loc_1 := @\,loc_1 + 1 : comm]\!]\langle 1, 0\rangle,\ \langle 1, 0\rangle)$

$= \langle 1, 0\rangle$

An output store is produced by w exactly when it can be produced in a finite number, k, of unfoldings, that is, exactly when w_k produces the same output store. Note that $[\![\textbf{while } 0\text{=}0 \textbf{ do skip od}]\!](s) = \bot$, for every possible input store, s.

Remember that $\bot$ is *not* a store but is "looping." We say that $\bot$ is an *improper meaning*; in contrast, truth values, numbers, location numbers, and storage vectors are *proper meanings*. A command, C, cannot proceed with an improper meaning, and we legislate that $[\![C\!: comm]\!](\bot) = \bot$ and call $[\![C\!: comm]\!]$ a *strict function*.

We can also study the semantics of a program independently of the specific meaning of the storage vector; let s stand for any store that contains at least two integers:

$[\![loc_2\!:=1; \textbf{if } @loc_2\text{=}0 \textbf{ then skip else } loc_1\!:=@loc_2\text{+}4 \textbf{ fi}: comm]\!](s)$

$= [\![\textbf{if } @loc_2\text{=}0 \textbf{ then skip else } loc_1\!:=@loc_2\text{+}4 \textbf{ fi}: comm]\!]([\![loc_2\!:=1: comm]\!](s))$

$= [\![\textbf{if } @loc_2\text{=}0 \textbf{ then skip else } loc_1\!:=@loc_2\text{+}4 \textbf{ fi}: comm]\!]update(loc_2, 1, s)$

$= if([\![@loc_2\text{=}0: boolexp]\!]update(loc_2, 1, s), [\![\textbf{skip}: comm]\!]update(loc_2, 1, s),$
$\qquad\qquad [\![loc_1\!:=@loc_2\text{+}4: comm]\!]update(loc_2, 1, s))$

$= if(false, [\![\textbf{skip}: comm]\!]update(loc_2, 1, s), [\![loc_1\!:=@loc_2\text{+}4]\!]update(loc_2, 1, s))$

$= [\![loc_1\!:=@loc_2\text{+}4: comm]\!]update(loc_2, 1, s)$

$= update(loc_1, [\![@loc_2\text{+}4: intexp]\!]update(loc_2, 1, s), update(loc_2, 1, s))$

$= update(loc_1, 5, update(loc_2, 1, s))$

The calculation hinges on the reasoning that $[\![@loc_2: intexp]\!]update(loc_2, 1, s) = 1$, regardless of the store that takes the place of s. This is why we require that s stand for a store that holds at least two integers, else the equality would fail. This issue is pursued in the exercises.

The semantics definition can also be used to prove program equalities and justify program transformations. For example, we might wish to show that $[\![loc_2\!:=1;$ $\textbf{if } @loc_2\text{=}0 \textbf{ then skip else } loc_1\!:=@loc_1\text{+}4 \textbf{ fi}: comm]\!] = [\![loc_1\!:=5; loc_2\!:=1: comm]\!]$. Since both commands represent functions on the store, it suffices to prove the result by *extensionality*, that is, for all store arguments, s, that hold at least two integers, the answers produced by the two functions are the same. The calculation for the left-hand side is given above. For the right-hand side, we have that: $[\![loc_1\!:=5; loc_2\!:=1: comm]\!](s) =$ $[\![loc_2\!:=1: comm]\!]$ $([\![loc_1\!:=5: comm]\!](s)) = [\![loc_2\!:=1: comm]\!]$ $(update(loc_1, 5, s)) =$ $update(loc_2, 1, (update(loc_1, 5, s))$. Now, we must ask, is $update(loc_1, 5, update(loc_2,$ $1, s))$ the same meaning as $update(loc_2, 1, (update(loc_1, 5, s))$? Since s must be a vector of the form, $\langle n_1, n_2, \ldots \rangle$, the answer is yes—the order of the updates does not matter.

1.7 Soundness of the Typing Rules

In the previous section, we calculated meanings for just well-typed programs. Ill-typed programs, like $loc_1 := (0=1)+2$, do not have meaning. In this section, we validate that the typing rules are *sound* in that every well-typed program has a meaning. To formalize the result, we must first formalize the type attributes for the language:

$$\tau ::= int \mid bool$$
$$\theta ::= intloc \mid \tau exp \mid comm$$

Next, we give a recursive definition, $[\![\cdot]\!]$, that maps each type attribute to its intended set of meanings:

$[\![int]\!] = Int$ $\qquad\qquad\qquad [\![bool]\!] = Bool$

$[\![intloc]\!] = Location$ $\qquad\qquad [\![\tau exp]\!] = Store \rightarrow [\![\tau]\!]$

$[\![comm]\!] = Store \rightarrow Store_\perp$

> where $A \rightarrow B$ denotes the set of functions from set A to set B,
>
> and $A_\perp$ denotes $A \cup \{\perp\}$

Our goal is:

1.6 Theorem

For all well-typed phrases, $P: \theta$, $[\![P: \theta]\!] \in [\![\theta]\!]$.

Proof: The proof is by induction on the typing rules in Figure 1.4. Since there are thirteen typing rules, there are thirteen cases in the proof. We show four and leave the rest as exercises.

- The phrase is $n: int$: Then $[\![n: int]\!] = n$, and $n \in Int = [\![int]\!]$.
- The phrase is $@L: intexp$: By the inductive hypothesis, we have that $[\![L: intloc]\!] \in [\![intloc]\!] = Location$. Now say that $[\![L: intloc]\!] = l$. Then, for every $s \in Store$, we have that $[\![@L: intexp]\!](s) = lookup(l, s)$, which must be a value in Int, since the arity of the *lookup* function is $Location \times Store \rightarrow Store$. This implies $[\![@L: intexp]\!] \in Store \rightarrow Int = [\![intexp]\!]$.
- The phrase is $C_1;C_2: comm$: By the inductive hypothesis, both $[\![C_1: comm]\!]$ and $[\![C_2: comm]\!]$ are elements of $Store \rightarrow Store_\perp$. For every $s \in Store$, we have that $[\![C_1;C_2: comm]\!](s) = [\![C_2: comm]\!]([\![C_1: comm]\!](s))$. By the inductive hypothesis for $[\![C_1: comm]\!]$, $[\![C_1: comm]\!](s) = s_1 \in Store_\perp$. If $s_1 = \perp$, then $[\![C_2: comm]\!](\perp) = \perp$, which is an element of $Store_\perp$. On the other hand, if $s_1 \in Store$, then the inductive hypothesis on $[\![C_2: comm]\!]$ lets us conclude that $[\![C_2: comm]\!](s_1) \in Store_\perp$. Hence, $[\![C_1;C_2: comm]\!] \in Store \rightarrow Store_\perp = [\![comm]\!]$.
- The phrase is **while** E **do** C **od**: $comm$: By the inductive hypothesis,

$[\![E\colon boolexp]\!] \in Store \to Bool$ and $[\![C\colon comm]\!] \in Store \to Store_\perp$.   Recall   that
$[\![\textbf{while } E \textbf{ do } C \textbf{ od}\colon comm]\!](s) = w(s)$, where $w(s) = s'$ iff there is some $k \geq 0$ such
that $w_k(s) = s'$. An easy proof by mathematical induction shows, for all $k \geq 0$, that
$w_k \in Store \to Store_\perp = [\![comm]\!]$. This means $w \in [\![comm]\!]$ as well. $\square$

1.8 Operational Properties of the Semantics

A denotational semantics maps a program to its mathematical meaning. This is convenient, because reasoning techniques such as function extensionality can be used to
prove program equivalence. But such reasoning might not reveal the computational patterns within a program. For this reason, we might also provide an *operational semantics*,
which displays the computation steps undertaken when a program is evaluated to its output. Some forms of operational semantics are interpreter-based, with instruction
counters, data structures, and the like, and others are inference rule-based, with proof
trees that show control flows and data dependencies.

Rather than introduce a second, new, operational semantics, we adapt the denotational semantics to our purposes, since the calculations in Section 1.6 already possess an
operational flavor. Here is an example from the previous section, written as if it were a
sequence of operational semantics computation steps:

$[\![loc_3\colon=@loc_1+1\colon comm]\!]\langle 3, 4, 5\rangle$

$\Rightarrow update([\![loc_3\colon intloc]\!], [\![@loc_1+1\colon intexp]\!]\langle 3, 4, 5\rangle, \langle 3, 4, 5\rangle)$

$\Rightarrow update(loc_3, [\![@loc_1+1\colon intexp]\!]\langle 3, 4, 5\rangle, \langle 3, 4, 5\rangle)$

$\Rightarrow update(loc_3, plus([\![@loc_1\colon intexp]\!]\langle 3, 4, 5\rangle, [\![1\colon intexp]\!]\langle 3, 4, 5\rangle), \langle 3, 4, 5\rangle)$

$\Rightarrow update(loc_3, plus(lookup([\![loc_1\colon intloc]\!], \langle 3, 4, 5\rangle), [\![1\colon intexp]\!]\langle 3, 4, 5\rangle), \langle 3, 4, 5\rangle)$

$\Rightarrow update(loc_3, plus(lookup(loc_1, \langle 3, 4, 5\rangle), [\![1\colon intexp]\!]\langle 3, 4, 5\rangle), \langle 3, 4, 5\rangle)$

$\Rightarrow update(loc_3, plus(3, [\![1\colon intexp]\!]\langle 3, 4, 5\rangle), \langle 3, 4, 5\rangle)$

$\Rightarrow update(loc_3, plus(3, [\![1\colon int]\!]), \langle 3, 4, 5\rangle)$

$\Rightarrow update(loc_3, plus(3, 1), \langle 3, 4, 5\rangle)$

$\Rightarrow update(loc_3, 4, \langle 3, 4, 5\rangle) \Rightarrow \langle 3, 4, 4\rangle$.

Each stage of the computation represents a machine configuration containing the instruc-
tions that remain to be computed. (If the multiple copies of the storage vector look "uno-
perational," then replace them by "pointers" to a global store variable.) We no longer
care about mathematical meanings; instead, we push symbols about and observe the patterns that result. In this way, we use the denotational semantics definition in Figure 1.7
plus the definitions of the operations in Figure 1.6 as an operational semantics for the
imperative language.

Since the purpose of an operational semantics is to evaluate program text plus an input data value to an output data value, we must formalize what we mean by a "Value." For *Bool*, the Values are *true* and *false*. (Thus, the textual phrase *not(false)* is not a Value, but *true* is, even though the two mean the same.) For *Int*, the Values are the numerals. (Again, *plus*(1, 2) is not a Value, but 3 is.) For *Location*, the location numbers, loc_i, are Values. For *Store*, the Values are the vectors, $\langle n_1, n_2, \ldots, n_m \rangle$, where each n_i, $1 \le i \le m$, is a Value from *Int*. (So, *update*$(loc_1, 2, \langle 1, 2, 3 \rangle)$ is not a Value, but $\langle 2, 2, 3 \rangle$ is.)

Next, we treat each equational definition, $f(x_1, x_2, \ldots, x_n) = v$, in Figures 1.6 and 1.7 as a computation rule, $f(x_1, x_2, \ldots, x_n) \Rightarrow v$. A computation rule is applied to a phrase, p_0, if p_0 contains a subphrase of the form, $f(e_1, e_2, \ldots, e_n)$, and all e_i, $1 \le i \le n$, are Values. The subphrase is called a *redex*. The redex $f(e_1, e_2, \ldots, e_n)$ is replaced by v', where v' is v with the e_is replacing the x_is. This produces a new phrase, p_1, and we write $p_0 \Rightarrow p_1$, a *computation step*. (The only exception to this technique is the *if* operation in Figure 1.6: Only the first of its three arguments need be a Value; the reason should be obvious.) In order to make the process deterministic, we always rewrite the leftmost redex in p_0.

A *computation* is a sequence of computation steps $p_0 \Rightarrow p_1 \Rightarrow \cdots \Rightarrow p_n$, for $n \ge 0$, and we write $p_0 \Rightarrow^* p_n$ for short. If p_n is a Value, then the computation *terminates*. The calculation shown at the beginning of this section is a terminating computation. You should study it and verify that at each stage of the computation the leftmost redex is rewritten. Normally, a computation starts with some special form of p_0, called a *program*. For the imperative language, a program is a phrase $[\![C: comm]\!]s_0$, for store value s_0.

An operational semantics should possess several key properties:

(i)   *subject reduction*: If p has an underlying "type" or "domain," τ, and $p \Rightarrow^* p'$, then p' has type τ as well.

(ii) *soundness*: If p has the underlying mathematical meaning, m, and $p \Rightarrow^* p'$, then p' means m as well.

(iii) *strong typing*: If p is well-typed and $p \Rightarrow^* p'$, then p' contains no operator-operand incompatibilities.

(iv) *computational adequacy*: A program p's underlying meaning is a proper meaning, m, iff there is a Value, v, such that $p \Rightarrow^* v$ and v means m.

All of these properties hold when we use the denotational semantics definition as an operational semantics: (ii) follows from the observation that a computation step, $\Rightarrow$, in the operational semantics is an equality substitution, $=$, in the denotational semantics; (i) follows from the previous observation and Theorem 1.6; and (iii) results from an induction proof that examines all the computation rules.

A proof of adequacy takes some work, but we do it to illustrate several useful proof techniques. First, we define a predicate, $comp_\theta$, (for "computable") on the type attributes $\theta ::= intloc \mid \tau exp \mid comm$.

- $comp_{intloc}p$ holds iff if p means a proper $l \in Location$, then $p \Rightarrow^* v$, and Value v means l.
- $comp_{\tau exp}p$ holds iff for all store Values, s, if $p(s)$ means a proper $n \in [\![\tau]\!]$, then $p(s) \Rightarrow^* v$, and Value v means n.
- $comp_{comm}p$ holds iff for all store Values, s, if $p(s)$ means a proper $s' \in Store$, then $p(s) \Rightarrow^* v$, and Value v means s'.

1.7 Proposition

For all well-typed phrases, $U: \theta$, $comp_\theta[\![U: \theta]\!]$ *holds.*

Proof: The proof is by induction on the typing rules. We consider three cases and leave the remainder as exercises.

- $loc_i: intloc$: Clearly, $[\![loc_i: intloc]\!] = loc_i \in Location$, a proper meaning. The operational semantics says $[\![loc_i: intloc]\!] \Rightarrow loc_i$, a Value.
- $E_1 + E_2: intexp$: For a Value, s, assume $[\![E_1 + E_2: intexp]\!]s = n \in Int$, a proper meaning. The denotational semantics states $[\![E_1 + E_2: intexp]\!]s = plus([\![E_1: intexp]\!]s, [\![E_2: intexp]\!]s)$, implying that $[\![E_1: intexp]\!]s$ and $[\![E_2: intexp]\!]s$ are proper, too. Now, the operational semantics says $[\![E_1 + E_2: intexp]\!]s \Rightarrow plus([\![E_1: intexp]\!]s, [\![E_2: intexp]\!]s)$. Since $comp_{intexp}[\![E_1: intexp]\!]$ holds, we have that $[\![E_1: intexp]\!]s \Rightarrow^* n_1$ and therefore $plus([\![E_1: intexp]\!]s, [\![E_2: intexp]\!]s) \Rightarrow^* plus(n_1, [\![E_2: intexp]\!]s)$, where n_1 is a Value. A similar argument holds for $[\![E_2: intexp]\!]s \Rightarrow^* n_2$. Finally, $plus(n_1, n_2) \Rightarrow n_3$, a Value that must be n, by soundness.
- **while E do C od**: *comm*: For store Value, s, if $[\![$**while E do C od**$: comm]\!]s = s' \in Store$, a proper meaning, then the denotational semantics of **while E do C od** states there is some minimal $k \geq 0$ such that $w_k(s) = s'$. We introduce a new language phrase, Ω, and say that $\Omega: comm$ and $[\![\Omega: comm]\!]s = \bot$. (Actually, Ω is **while 0=0 do skip od**.) Next, we define the family of programs wh_i as: (i) wh_0 is Ω; (ii) wh_{i+1} is **if E then** C; wh_i **else skip fi**. It is easy to prove that $[\![wh_i: comm]\!] = w_i$ and $comp_{comm}[\![wh_i: comm]\!]$ holds, for all $i \geq 0$. Hence, $[\![wh_k: comm]\!]s \Rightarrow^* v$, where Value v means s'.

    We finish with the aid of a useful abbreviation: We write $c_1 \sqsubseteq c_2$ to state that $[\![c_1]\!]s \Rightarrow^* v$ implies $[\![c_2]\!]s \Rightarrow^* v$. We can prove: (i) $\Omega \sqsubseteq$ **while E do C od**; (ii) if $c_1 \sqsubseteq c_2$, then **if B then** C; c_1 **else skip fi** $\sqsubseteq$ **if B then** C; c_2 **else skip fi**; and therefore: (iii) for all $i \geq 0$, $wh_i \sqsubseteq$ **while E do C od**. In particular, $wh_k \sqsubseteq$ **while E do C od**, and this implies $[\![$**while E do C od**$: comm]\!]s \Rightarrow^* s'$. $\Box$

Computational adequacy follows from the soundness of the typing rules, the soundness of the operational semantics and the above proposition. An important consequence of adequacy is a contrapositive: If the operational semantics of $[\![C: comm]\!]s_0$ fails to terminate, then $[\![C: comm]\!]s_0 = \bot$, since $\bot$ is the only improper meaning in $Store_\bot$. Thus, the operational semantics loops only when it should.

The version of operational semantics that we use is called a *subtree replacement system* and is studied in detail in Chapter 6.

1.9 The Design of a Language Core

As stated at the beginning of this chapter, the design of a programming language core is an artistic activity, often driven by a variety of (sometimes contradictory) design objectives. We might desire a language that

- is oriented to a specific problem area, such as real-time systems, data base systems, programming in the large, or graphic interaction.
- is general purpose.
- is user friendly, as seen in a pleasant user interface and well-written documentation.
- is efficient in its implementation, as realized by a compact, fast compiler that generates fast object code.
- is extensible, so that a user can add new language features to match particular applications.
- is secure against run-time programming failures, thanks to typing rules and compile-time type checkers.
- is orthogonal, in that the language is built from a few fundamental principles that are applied without unnecessary syntactical or semantical restrictions.
- has a simple syntax and semantics.
- has environmental support by means of editors, compilers, debuggers, and monitors.
- has logical support by means of a program validation logic.
- is portable to a variety of architectures.
- exploits specific architectural features, for example, has constructs for parallel programming on multiprocessor architectures.

Once the primary design objectives are selected, the core language can be designed.

A generally accepted slogan for language design is "consolidation, not innovation" (Hoare 1973); that is, a designer should utilize constructions and principles that have worked well in earlier projects and experiments. Then, the task of design boils down to verification that the constructions and principles coexist peacefully within the same language—the features do not interfere with one another. The adjective *orthogonal* describes a language feature whose behavior is understandable without reference to other language features and whose behavior does not conflict with the behavior of other language features. The subsequent chapters of this book present principles for introduction of orthogonal language features.

Denotational semantics emphasizes that a programming language can be understood in terms of sets of meanings and operations on the meanings. If we apply a "denotational semantics methodology" to core language design, we take the following steps:

1. Define the sets of meanings and their operations.
2. Give syntactic representations to the meanings and operations.
3. Organize the representations into an abstract syntax definition.

In the case of the core imperative language, the crucial features of the language are captured by the *Int*, *Bool*, *Location*, and *Store* sets. The operations for these sets define the computational capabilities for the language. For example, Figure 1.6 makes clear that the imperative language supports arithmetic on integers but not on locations. String manipulation is not provided.

Next, the sets and operations must be given syntactic representations: 0 for zero, + for addition, @ for *lookup*, and so on. Store elements get no syntax representation, since the imperative language maintains at most one store value at a time, and the value can be implicit.

The syntactic representations are grouped into syntax rules. The notion of syntax domain comes from grouping together those constructions that produce answers from the same set(s). For the imperative language, those operations that produce stores as answers are grouped into the syntax rule for the Command syntax domain. Similarly, those operations (and elements) that produce integers and booleans are grouped into the Expression domain.

With this methodology, the rationale for type attributes and typing rules becomes clear: A type attribute predicts the set where a phrase's meaning lives. Type attributes prevent operator-operand incompatibility errors and remind the user of the semantics of the language.

The above description says nothing about control structures. *Control* is the ordering of evaluation of a program's phrases, and a *control structure* orders the evaluation. The *if* operation in Figure 1.6 is a control structure, and so is the composition operation on functions that one gets automatically when one uses denotational semantics. Control structures are given syntactic representations as well, here, **if-then-else-fi** for *if* and ; for composition. The recursive definition of a function is another form of control structure, and in the imperative language one form of recursion is represented by **while-do-od**.

The definition of *if* in Figure 1.6 is not dependent at all upon the domains of its second and third arguments; it is easy to define a family of *if* operations of the form *if*: $Bool \times D \times D \to D$ for any set, D, whatsoever. Thus, we might have a conditional control structure for *Int*, *Bool*, *Location*, and so on. For example, this assignment command uses conditional control on both locations and integers:

(**if** $@loc_1=0$ **then** loc_1 **else** loc_2 **fi**) := (**if** $@loc_1=@loc_2$ **then** 0 **else** $@loc_2+1$ **fi**)

The generalization of a control structure is a useful idea, and in its general form, it is called the *type completeness principle*: No operation should be artificially limited in the type of arguments that it receives.

In the denotational semantics methodology, a data structure is a set of values. Consider arrays—an array is a vector of elements, and the *Store* set is a special form of array with its own *lookup* and *update* operations. What one normally calls an "array" in an imperative programming language is a vector of locations with a *lookup* operation. (Array "updating" is an assignment to the cell named by one of the array's component locations; the array itself is unaltered. That's why one uses ordinary assignment, for example, $A[2]:=@A[1]+1$, to do array updates.) Since the notions of array, *lookup*, and *update* are independent of the domain of the array's components, the type completeness principle suggests that we can create arrays of integers, booleans, and so on. The full blown result is APL-like, and its development is left as an interesting exercise.

A beautiful, unifying theory of control and data structures is given within *action semantics*; the references that follow provide additional information.

Suggested Reading

The core imperative language has a long history; some perspective is provided by Gelernter and Jagannathan 1990, Kamin 1990, MacLennan 1987, Marcotty and Ledgard 1986, Sethi 1989, Tennent 1981, and Watt 1990. Syntax issues are studied in every compiling text; two of many possibilities are Aho, et al. 1986 and Barrett, et al. 1979. Abstract syntax is mentioned in both, but see Schmidt 1986 and Mosses 1992 for nontrivial treatments. The notions of static and strong typing are treated informally in much of the literature, but Cardelli and Wegner 1985 attempt a formalization. See also Fokkinga 1981. Gelernter and Jagannathan 1990 describe different degrees of strong typing, and Thatte 1990, Cartwright and Fagan 1991, and Lee and Friedman 1993 describe middle ground between static and dynamic typing.

Inductive definitions are nicely introduced in van Dalen 1983. Denotational semantics can be studied from Meyer 1990, Nielson and Nielson 1992, Schmidt 1986, Stoy 1977, and Tennent 1991. Hennessy (1991) and Nielson and Nielson (1992) give useful introductions to modern varieties of operational semantics. Gunter (1992) provides a thorough treatment of the relationship of operational to denotational semantics.

Papers on the topic of programming language design are rare, but Hoare 1973 and Wirth 1974 and 1977 are important exceptions. Horowitz (1983) and Wexelblatt (1980) provide background material. The textbooks Tennent 1981, Ghezzi and Jazayeri 1987, Harland 1984, Loudon 1993, and Watt 1990 contain short presentations on design. The type completeness principle was proposed by Reynolds (1970) and is developed in Reynolds 1981, Tennent 1981, and Watt 1990. Harland 1984 uses type completeness to motivate a programming language with dynamic typing. A comprehensive theory of language structure is presented by action semantics. The standard reference is Mosses

1992, but related, useful papers are Mosses 1983 and 1989, Mosses and Watt 1987, Watt 1991, and Even and Schmidt 1990.

Exercises

1.1. Use Figure 1.1 to draw syntax trees for these programs:

    a. $loc_1:=0$; **while** $\neg(@loc_1=0)$ **do** $loc_1:=@loc_2+1$ **od**

    b. **if** $\neg2$ **then** $loc_1:=\neg(2=1)$ **else skip fi**

1.2. Write the complete concrete syntax definition for Figure 1.1.

2.1. Use the typing rules in Figure 1.4 to attach type attributes to the trees drawn for Exercise 1.1.

2.2. Revise Figures 1.1 and 1.4 so that

    a. Booleans can be assigned to locations, for example, $loc_1:=(0=1)$ is well-typed;

    b. Commands can be assigned to locations, for example, $loc_1:=(\textbf{skip})$; $@loc_1$ is well-typed;

    c. Locations (''pointers'') can be assigned to locations.

2.3. Add vectors to Figures 1.1 and 1.4: $vec_{i..j}$ represents a vector consisting of locations numbered from i to j. (Hint: It is best to create a new type attribute, *intloc exp*.) The syntax rule follows:

$$L ::= loc_i \mid vec_{i..j}[E]$$

A command like $vec_{1..3}[3]:=@vec_{1..3}[2]+1$ should be well typed. Is $vec_{1..3}[4]:=0$ well typed?

3.1. For Figure 1.1, use structural induction to prove

    a. Every $E \in$ Expression has at least one occurrence of a numeral or a location number in it;

    b. For every $E \in$ Expression, the occurrences of location numbers and numerals outnumber the occurrences of + symbols;

    c. For every $C \in$ Command, the number of occurrences of **if** equals the number of occurrences of **fi**.

3.2. a. Encode Figure 1.4 as a recursive definition: For each syntax rule in Figure 1.1, write a recursive definition, *type-of*, which maps a phrase to its type attribute. For example, for the syntax rule for Numeral, *type-of*$(n) = int$. Ill-typed phrases map to *error*, for example, *type-of*$(\neg 0) = error$.

    b. Prove, for all $C \in$ Command, that *type-of*$(C) \in \{ comm, error \}$.

   c. Prove, if *type-of*(C) = *comm*, then the syntax tree for C is well typed according to the rules in Figure 1.4. Also, prove the converse. Explain why this result implies Theorem 1.5.

4.1. Give a set of typing rules for Figure 1.1 such that unicity of typing does not hold.

4.2. Prove unicity of typing for the typing rules you defined in Exercise 2.3.

5.1. Use Figure 1.4 to draw proof trees for the well-typed programs in Exercise 1.1.

5.2. Since Figure 1.4 is an inductive definition, define a recursive definition, *strip*, which removes all the type attributes from a proof tree, for example, $strip(0: int) = 0$. Prove that *strip* translates proof trees into syntax trees; that is, for all proof trees C: *comm*, $strip(C: comm) \in$ Command.

6.1 Use Figure 1.7 to calculate the meanings of the following programs with the input store $\langle 0, 0, 0 \rangle$:

   a. $[\![loc_1 := 2;\ loc_2 := @loc_1 + 1;\ \textbf{skip}: comm]\!]$

   b. $[\![\textbf{while}\ @loc_1 = 0\ \textbf{do}\ loc_1 := 1\ \textbf{od}: comm]\!]$

   c. $[\![\textbf{while}\ 1 = 1\ \textbf{do}\ loc_1 := 1\ \textbf{od}: comm]\!]$

Next, calculate the meanings of the above programs but without an input store; that is, each program denotes a function from an input store to an output store (or looping).

6.2. Use Figure 1.7 to prove the following:

   a. $[\![C_1;\ (C_2;\ C_3): comm]\!] = [\![(C_1;\ C_2);\ C_3: comm]\!]$

   b. $[\![\textbf{if}\ E\ \textbf{then}\ C_1\ \textbf{else}\ C_2\ \textbf{fi};\ C_3: comm]\!] = [\![\textbf{if}\ E\ \textbf{then}\ C_1;\ C_3\ \textbf{else}\ C_2;\ C_3\ \textbf{fi}: comm]\!]$

   c.* $[\![\textbf{while}\ E\ \textbf{do}\ C_1\ \textbf{od};\ C_2: comm]\!]\ =\ [\![\textbf{while}\ E\ \textbf{do}\ C\ \textbf{od};\ \textbf{if}\ E\ \textbf{then}\ C_1\ \textbf{else}\ C_2\ \textbf{fi}: comm]\!]$

6.3. The denotational semantics definition is a recursive definition on the inductive definition in Figure 1.4. Write a denotational semantics as a recursive definition on the inductive definition in Figure 1.1. (Hint: Add a new meaning, *error*, to each of the sets in Figure 1.6. Ill-typed programs have the meaning *error*.)

6.4. If you worked Exercise 2.3, proceed. Define the denotational semantics of vectors. (Note: as in the previous exercise, you will probably need *error* meanings.)

6.5. (Reynolds) Pretend that the structure of storage vectors is unknown— all we know is that there is some set called *Store*. Next, say that the operations on *Store* are grouped into two families: $Acceptor = \{ a_i: Int \times Store \rightarrow Store \mid i \geq 0 \}$ and $Expression = \{ e_i: Store \rightarrow Int \mid i \geq 0 \}$. The intuition is that an *Acceptor* operation, a_i, can update the ith component of the store and an *Expression* operation, e_i, can lookup the value of the ith component of the store. Note that the notion of location is absent from the semantics; all we have are acceptor and expression operations. We now alter Figure 1.1, replacing the rule for Location by the following:

L ::= var_i

In this way, we have added *variables* to the language. The semantics of a variable is an acceptor, expression pair:

$[\![var_i: intvar]\!] = (a_i, e_i)$.

a. Revise Figures 1.4 and 1.7 to accommodate variables.

b. Say that the *Store* set is revealed to be the usual set of tuples, like that in Figure 1.6. Give definitions for a_i and e_i, and try to prove this "goodness" property: For all $s \in Store$, $[\![@var_i: intexp]\!]$ $([\![var_i:=E: comm]\!] s)$ = $[\![E: intexp]\!](s)$. Under what conditions does goodness hold?

c. Once again, pretend that the structure of the store is unknown. We say that a variable, L, is *good* if the goodness property holds: For all $s \in Store$, $[\![@L: intexp]\!]([\![L:=E: comm]\!](s))$ = $[\![E: intexp]\!](s)$. Show that the axiom: $e_i(a_i(n, s)) = n$ suffices to prove that var_i is good. Give additional axioms so that the calculations in Exercise 6.1 can be undertaken with good variables.

d. If you worked Exercise 6.4, proceed. A vector, $vec_{i..j}$, is now a tuple of variables from i to j. The syntax is:

L ::= var_i | $vec_{i..j}$[E]

Is $vec_{1..3}[1]$ a good variable? Is $vec_{1..3}[@vec_{1..3}[1]]$? In general, is $vec_{1..3}[@vec_{1..3}[E]]$ a good variable?

e. Say that we add a conditional expression to the syntax of variables:

L ::= var_i | **if** E **then** L$_1$ **else** L$_2$ **fi**

If the conditional expression has the expected semantics, are all well-typed variables in this syntax good variables?

f. Since type attributes reflect the structure of the semantics, consider this typing for variables:

V: *intvar*	V: *intvar*	V: *intacc* E: *intexp*
V: *intacc*	@V: *intexp*	V:=E: *comm*

That is, a variable is decomposable into its acceptor and expression subparts. With this idea in mind, give the typing rules, semantics, and pragmatics of this new construction for building variables from acceptors and expressions:

V ::= ... | ⟨A, E⟩, where A is an acceptor and E is an expression

6.6. Prove that every C∈ Command has at most one meaning with respect to $[\![\cdot]\!]$.

6.7. Say that $[\![C_0:comm]\!]s_0$ is *well formed* if, for every loc_i in C_0, the value of i is less than or equal to the number of integers held by s_0. Now, remove the two "Notes" from the definitions of *lookup* and *update* in Figure 1.6 so that the two operations are partial functions, for example, $lookup(loc_2,\langle 1\rangle)$ has no meaning. Prove: If $[\![C_0:comm]\!]s_0$ is a well-formed configuration, then it has a meaning.

7.1. Return to Figure 1.6 and remove the two "Notes" to the definitions of *lookup* and *update* so that they are partial functions, for example, $lookup(loc_3, \langle 0,1\rangle)$ has no meaning.

a. Give an example of a well-typed program that has no meaning.

Repair the problem as follows. First, define the family of sets, $Store_w = \{\langle n_1, n_2, \ldots, n_w\rangle \mid for\ 1 \leq i \leq w,\ n_i \in Int\}$. Thus, $Store = \bigcup_{w \geq 0} Store_w$. Do the same for locations: $Location_w = \{loc_i \mid i \leq w\}$; $Location = \bigcup_{w \geq 0} Location_w$. Next, define the predicate, *size*, on the types in the language:

$size_{w,\tau}v$ iff *true*
$size_{w,intloc}l$ iff $l \in Location_w$
$size_{w,\tau exp}f$ iff for all $k \geq w$, for all $s \in Store_k$, $f(s) \in [\![\tau]\!]$
$size_{w,comm}c$ iff for all $k \geq w$, for all $s \in Store_k$, $c(s) \in (Store_k)_\perp$

So, $size_{w,\theta}e$ holds true when e manipulates locations $\leq w$ and stores $\geq$ size w.

b. Define a new set of typing rules so that $C:comm_w$ holds when C manipulates locations $\leq w$ and stores $\geq$ size w. Prove: $size_{w,comm}[\![C:comm_w]\!]$ always holds. From this, conclude that all well-typed commands have meaning.

7.2. If you worked Exercise 6.3, proceed.

a. Prove a soundness theorem for the semantics for Exercise 6.3: For all $C \in Command$, if $C:comm$ holds, then $[\![C]\!] \in [\![comm]\!]$. (Recall, $[\![comm]\!] = Store \rightarrow Store_\perp$.)

b. Does this "completeness" property hold: If $[\![C]\!] \in [\![comm]\!]$, then $C:comm$ holds?

7.3. If you worked Exercise 6.4, proceed. Extend the soundness theorem for the language with vectors. Comment on the worth of your result.

8.1. Calculate the operational semantics of the examples in Exercise 6.1.

8.2. An important property that relates a denotational semantics to an operational semantics is the *full abstraction* property. Here is a variant of it for the imperative language. A *context* is a syntax tree with zero or more missing subtrees. Here is a precise definition of the command contexts:

$X ::= [\ ] \mid L:=E \mid X_1;X_2 \mid$ **if** E **then** X_1 **else** X_2 **fi** $\mid$ **while** E **do** X **od** $\mid$ **skip**

The "[ ]" marks the "holes" in the tree. We write $C[\ ]$ to denote a context. When a command, C_0, is inserted to fill the holes in the tree, we write $C[C_0]$.

Two commands, C_1 and C_2, are *operationally equivalent*, written $C_1 \equiv C_2$, when for all Values $s \in Store$, for all contexts $C[\,]$, we have $[\![C[C_1]: comm]\!](s) \Rightarrow^* s'$ iff $[\![C[C_2]: comm]\!](s) \Rightarrow^* s'$, for Value s'. That is, C_1 and C_2 have identical behavior in all contexts.

A denotational semantics, $[\![\cdot]\!]$, is *fully abstract relative to* an operational semantics, $\Rightarrow$, when for all commands, C_1 and C_2, $[\![C_1: comm]\!] = [\![C_2: comm]\!]$ iff $C_1 \equiv C_2$. That is, semantic equality and operational equivalence coincide.

a. Prove that the denotational semantics in Figure 1.7 is fully abstract relative to the operational semantics in Section 1.8.

b.* Prove for the imperative language that the above definition of full abstraction is equivalent to: For all contexts, $C[\,]$, $[\![C[C_1]: comm]\!] = [\![C[C_2]: comm]\!]$ iff $[\![C_1: comm]\!] = [\![C_2: comm]\!]$.

The proof of Part a is straightforward only because the imperative language is very simple. Indeed, the full abstraction property *fails* for the imperative language with procedures and parameters and the usual denotational semantics. See Gunter 1992 for background.

8.3. A computation $p_0 \Rightarrow^* p_n$ is *single threaded* in its store if for all p_i, $1 \leq i \leq n$, the store Values in p_i are identical. A single-threaded computation can be implemented with a global store variable. Prove, for the operational semantics in Section 1.8, for all well-typed programs, that all computations are single threaded in the store.

8.4. A *structural operational semantics* is an operational semantics where each computation step is a proof tree. Here are the inference rules for deriving a computation step:

$[\![L:=E: comm]\!]s \ \triangleright \ s'$,
  where $[\![E: intexp]\!](s) = n$, $[\![L: intloc]\!] = l$, and $s' = update(l, n, s)$

$$\frac{[\![C_1: comm]\!]s \ \triangleright \ [\![C_1': comm]\!]s'}{[\![C_1;C_2: comm]\!]s \ \triangleright \ [\![C_1';C_2: comm]\!]s'}$$

$$\frac{[\![C_1: comm]\!]s \ \triangleright \ s'}{[\![C_1;C_2: comm]\!]s \ \triangleright \ [\![C_2: comm]\!]s'}$$

$[\![\textbf{if } E \textbf{ then } C_1 \textbf{ else } C_2 \textbf{ fi}: comm]\!]s \ \triangleright \ [\![C_1: comm]\!]s$, if $[\![E: boolexp]\!](s) = true$

$[\![\textbf{if } E \textbf{ then } C_1 \textbf{ else } C_2 \textbf{ fi}: comm]\!]s \ \triangleright \ [\![C_2: comm]\!]s$, if $[\![E: boolexp]\!](s) = false$

$[\![\textbf{while } E \textbf{ do } C \textbf{ od}: comm]\!]s$
   $\triangleright \ [\![\textbf{if } E \textbf{ then } (C; \textbf{while } E \textbf{ do } C \textbf{ od}) \textbf{ else skip fi}: comm]\!]s$

$[\![\textbf{skip}: comm]\!]s \ \triangleright \ s$

A computation is a sequence of computation steps.

    a. Calculate the computations for the programs in Exercise 6.1.

    b. The above structural operational semantics treats expression evaluation as primitive. (That's why the denotational semantics definition for expressions appears in the rules.) Add structural operational semantics rules to show the computation steps in the evaluation of expressions.

    c. Prove that the structural operational semantics is sound, that is, If $[\![C: comm]\!]s \triangleright s'$, then $[\![C: comm]\!]s = s'$ in the denotational semantics.

    d. Prove that the structural operational semantics is adequate. In what sense does this mean that the structural operational semantics is "equivalent" to the operational semantics in Section 1.8?

8.5. A *natural semantics* is an operational semantics that encodes an entire computation into a single proof tree. Here are the inference rules:

$$[\![L:=E: comm]\!]s \triangleright s'$$
$$\text{where } [\![E: intexp]\!](s) = n, \ [\![L: intloc]\!] = l, \text{ and } s' = update(l, n, s)$$

$$\frac{[\![C_1: comm]\!]s \triangleright s_1 \quad [\![C_2: comm]\!]s_1 \triangleright s_2}{[\![C_1;C_2: comm]\!]s \triangleright s_2}$$

$$\frac{[\![C_1: comm]\!]s \triangleright s'}{[\![\textbf{if } E \textbf{ then } C_1 \textbf{ else } C_2 \textbf{ fi}: comm]\!]s \triangleright s'} \quad \text{if } [\![E: boolexp]\!](s) = true$$

$$\frac{[\![C_2: comm]\!]s \triangleright s'}{[\![\textbf{if } E \textbf{ then } C_1 \textbf{ else } C_2 \textbf{ fi}: comm]\!]s \triangleright s'} \quad \text{if } [\![E: boolexp]\!](s) = false$$

$$[\![\textbf{while } E \textbf{ do } C \textbf{ od}: comm]\!]s \triangleright s, \text{ if } [\![E: boolexp]\!](s) = false$$

$$\frac{[\![C: comm]\!]s \triangleright s_1 \quad [\![\textbf{while } E \textbf{ do } C \textbf{ od}: comm]\!]s_1 \triangleright s_2}{[\![\textbf{while } E \textbf{ do } C \textbf{ od}: comm]\!]s \triangleright s_2} \quad \text{if } [\![E: boolexp]\!](s) = true$$

$$[\![\textbf{skip}: comm]\!]s \triangleright s$$

Repeat Parts a–d of Exercise 8.4 for the natural semantics definition. Next, explain how to use a denotational semantics to *generate* a natural semantics. In what ways do the two semantics methods differ?

8.6. Yet another semantics for the imperative language operates on logical predicates, rather than storage vectors. It is called an *axiomatic semantics* or a *Hoare logic* (Apt 1981). We write $\{E_1\} C \{E_2\}$ to state that if boolean expression E_1 holds true prior to the computation of C, and C terminates, then boolean expression E_2 must hold true. An example of such a formula is: $\{@loc_1 > 0\} loc_1 := @loc_1 + 1 \{@loc_1 > 1\}$. Here are the rules for the imperative language:

$$\{[E_2/@L]E_1\} \ L:=E_2 \ \{E_1\} \qquad \frac{\{E_1\}C_1\{E_2\} \quad \{E_2\}C_2\{E_3\}}{\{E_1\}C_1;C_2\{E_3\}}$$

$$\frac{\{E_1 \wedge E_2\}C_1\{E_3\} \quad \{E_1 \wedge \neg E_2\}C_2\{E_3\}}{\{E_1\} \text{ if } E_2 \text{ then } C_2 \text{ else } C_2 \text{ fi}\{E_3\}}$$

$$\frac{\{E_1 \wedge E_2\}C\{E_1\}}{\{E_1\} \text{ while } E_2 \text{ do } C \text{ od}\{E_1 \wedge \neg E_2\}} \qquad \frac{E_1 \supset E_2 \quad \{E_2\}C\{E_3\} \quad E_3 \supset E_4}{\{E_1\}C\{E_4\}}$$

The phrase "$[E_1/@L]E_2$" stands for the substitution of E_1 for all occurrences of @L in E_2; for example, $[1+2/@loc_2](@loc\,1 > @loc_2 + 1)$ is $@loc_1 > (1+2)+1$. Draw proof trees for these formulas:

a. $\{@loc_1 > 0\}$ if $@loc_2 = 1$ then $loc_2 := 2$ else $loc_2 := @loc_1$ fi;
    $loc_2 := @loc_2 + 1 \; \{@loc_2 > 2\}$

b. $\{@loc_1 = 3 \wedge @loc_2 = 0\}$ while $@loc_1 > 0$ do $loc_2 := @loc_2 + 1$;
    $loc_1 := @loc_1 - 1$ od $\{@loc_2 = 3\}$

c. $\{\neg(@loc\,1 = 0)\}$ while $\neg(@loc_1 = 0) do loc_2 := 1$ od $\{@loc_2 = 2\}$

d.* Prove the soundness of the logic with respect to the denotational semantics in Figure 1.12: If $\{E_1\}C\{E_2\}$ can be proved, then for all $s \in Store$, if $[\![E_1 : boolexp]\!]s = true$ and $[\![C : comm]\!]s \neq \bot$, then $[\![E_2 : boolexp]\!]([\![C : comm]\!]s) = true$.

9.1. For your favorite programming language, identify its core. That is, select a minimal subset of the language that has the same computational power as the full language. Write the abstract syntax of the core, list the underlying sets and operations, and if the language is typed, describe the type attributes.

9.2. For each application below, design a core programming language: List the underlying data sets and their operations (including control structures), write an abstract syntax definition, and if necessary, formulate a set of typing rules.

   a. A hand-held calculator for students in a beginning math logic class. The students study propositional logic and build truth tables to determine the validity of propositional formulas.

   b. A line-oriented file editor. A user must be able to open and close files, locate lines and words, and enter and delete lines and words.

   c. A programmable video cassette recorder (VCR). A user should be able to write programs that make the VCR switch on and off at certain times, record shows, switch television channels, and so forth.

   d. A simple data-base manager. The system must be initialized by a "schema" (that is, a data structure declaration) so that users can insert, delete, and query data that is schema-shaped.

   e. A simple graphics manager for a video display unit. The manager must have the capability to maintain a bit map, draw and erase points and lines, and manage a cursor.

2 The Abstraction Principle

We now examine the role that names play in programming language development. Although names are not essential to a programming language (consider a hand-held calculator or a Turing machine), a nontrivial task is easier to handle if it is decomposed into named subtasks. Names are such a fundamental feature of programming languages that we take them entirely for granted. In this chapter we study the systematic introduction of names into a language.

Names are introduced by the *abstraction principle*.

The Abstraction Principle:

The phrases of any semantically meaningful syntactic class may be named.

This short statement holds a lot of power: It implies that we might name virtually any construct in a programming language. Here is a short list of constructs that are typically named and what we call the named entities:

Location: alias*
Numeral: const
Expression: function
Command: procedure
Declaration: module
Type structure: class (or ''type'')

We will encounter each of these in this chapter.

A named value is called an *abstraction*. An abstraction is defined by a *definition*, which typically looks like

define I = V

where I is the *name* and V is the *body*. The association of I to V is called a *binding*.

---

* We also study *variable declarations*, which are related to, but are different from, aliases.

An abstraction is invoked by mentioning its name, and for readability a keyword sometimes prefixes the *invocation*:

I   **invoke** I   **call** I

For example, in the case of command abstractions ("procedures"), the definition form is
proc I=C, and the invocation form is **call** I. We introduce a new syntax domain of
names, called Identifier. Also, the definition constructs are typically grouped together
into a new syntax domain, called Declaration.

We spend this chapter applying the abstraction principle to the imperative language
in Chapter 1.

2.1 Expression Abstractions

We begin our investigation with expression abstractions, commonly called "functions."
Figure 2.1 extends the imperative language with functions. As promised, we have added
the syntax domains Declaration and Identifier. A new syntax domain, Program, is
introduced so that the function definitions can be grouped at the beginning of a program.
A function is defined by the form **fun** I=E and is invoked by mentioning its name.
Function invocations can appear anywhere that expressions can, as indicated by the invocation construct, I, in the syntax rule for Expression. For example, the definition
fun A=1+@loc_1 makes loc_1:=A+2   well   formed;   this   is   sensible,   since
loc_1:=(1+@loc_1)+2 is well formed.

Functions complicate the language's typing structure. Like an expression, a function

---

$P \in$ Program $L \in$ Location
$D \in$ Declaration $N \in$ Numeral
$C \in$ Command $I \in$ Identifier
$E \in$ Expression

$P ::= D$ **in** C
$D ::=$ **fun** I=E $\mid D_1,D_2 \mid D_1;D_2$
$C ::=$ L:=E $\mid C_1;C_2 \mid$ **if** E **then** C_1 **else** C_2 **fi** $\mid$ **while** E **do** C **od** $\mid$ **skip**
$E ::= N \mid$ @L $\mid E_1+E_2 \mid E_1=E_2 \mid \neg E \mid I$
$L ::= loc_i,\ i>0$
$N ::= n,\ n \in Int$

Figure 2.1 _____

Let $\pi_1 = \{A\!:\!intexp,\ B\!:\!boolexp\}$

```
                                    ⊢ P: comm
                              /                    \
                ∅ ⊢ D: π₁ dec                              π₁ ⊢ C: comm
              /            \                              /          \
∅⊢D:{A:intexp}dec, ∅⊢D:{B:boolexp}dec  while π₁⊢E:boolexp  do π₁⊢C:comm od
      |                  |                     |              /        \
fun I= ∅⊢E:intexp  fun I= ∅⊢E:boolexp   π₁⊢I:boolexp   π₁⊢L:intloc := π₁⊢E:intexp
   A    |           B    /    \             B           loc₁      /        \
     ∅⊢N:int        ∅⊢E:intexp = ∅⊢E:intexp          π₁⊢E:intexp + π₁⊢E:intexp
       1               |             |                     |             |
              @ ∅⊢L:intloc  ∅⊢N:int              π₁⊢I:intexp   π₁⊢N:int
                   loc₁        0                       A            2
```

Figure 2.2 _____

has a type attribute, which is established when the function is defined. The type of a function must be communicated to the commands and expressions that use the function. To do this, we collect together the type attributes for all the function definitions into a new attribute, called a *type assignment*, which is a set of identifier, type attribute pairs. For example, the type assignment that results from the declarations:

    fun $A = 1 + @loc_1$,
    fun $B = @loc_1 = 0$

is the set $\{A\!:\!intexp,\ B\!:\!boolexp\}dec$. That is, A has type *intexp* and B has type *boolexp*. A type assignment will be represented by the symbol, π. We work with only those type assignments that represent (partial) functions; that is, for any identifier, I, there is at most one pair $(I\!:\!\theta) \in \pi$. For example, the compound declaration **fun** $A = 1 + @loc_1$, **fun** $A = @loc_1 = 0$ is not well formed, since the identifier A is defined twice.

A type assignment like $\pi_1 = \{A\!:\!intexp,\ B\!:\!boolexp\}$ is transmitted to the commands and expressions that invoke the functions. For example, with the assistance of π_1 we can verify that $loc_1\!:=\!A+2$ is a well-typed command, and to express this, we write $\pi_1 \vdash loc_1\!:=\!A+2\!:comm$. Thus, each node of a syntax tree is annotated with two attributes: a type assignment and a type. The annotated tree for the program **fun** $A=1$, **fun** $B=@loc_1=0$ **in while** B **do** $loc_1\!:=\!A+2$ **od** is given in Figure 2.2. Notice how the type attribute for a function definition is the name of the function and its type. The types of the functions are unioned together to form the type assignment, π_1. The type assignment is then copied to the subtree for the while-loop.

Let's consider the typing rules that assign the attributes to syntax trees. The first, important rule is the one for function definition:

$$\frac{\pi \vdash E: \tau exp}{\pi \vdash \textbf{fun } I=E: \{\, I{:}\tau exp\,\}dec}$$

This rule says, if E is a well-typed expression with type τexp, then **fun** $I=E$ is a well-typed declaration with type $\{I{:}\tau exp\}dec$. The π-attribute represents the (global) declarations that are visible to the function definition. The example in Figure 2.2 had no such global definitions; hence π was the empty set, $\varnothing$.

Individual declarations are unioned together by the construction, D_1,D_2. The typing rule reflects the union and imposes the restriction that the functions declared in D_1 do not clash with those in D_2:

$$\frac{\pi \vdash D_1:\pi_1 dec \qquad \pi \vdash D_2:\pi_2 dec}{\pi \vdash D_1,D_2:(\pi_1 \cup \pi_2)dec}$$

where $\pi_1 \cup \pi_2 = \pi_1 \cup \pi_2$, if $\{I \mid (I{:}\theta_1) \in \pi_1\} \cap \{I \mid (I{:}\theta_2) \in \pi_2\} = \varnothing$; else it is undefined. That is, the identifiers in π_1 are disjoint from the ones in π_2.

A more common way of combining declarations is through a sequencing operation, $D_1;D_2$, where the bindings in D_1 are visible for D_2's use. An example is: **fun** $A = @loc_1$; **fun** $B = A{+}1$. This typing rule enforces sequential declarations:

$$\frac{\pi \vdash D_1:\pi_1 dec \qquad \pi \cup \pi_1 \vdash D_2:\pi_2 dec}{\pi \vdash D_1;D_2:(\pi_1 \cup \pi_2)dec}$$

The typing of D_1 is calculated first, producing its type, $\pi_1 dec$. π_1 is then unioned to π, giving the type assignment for D_2.

When all the declarations are processed, they can be used by the command part of a program. This is expressed by the following:

$$\frac{\varnothing \vdash D:\pi dec \qquad \pi \vdash C: comm}{\vdash D \textbf{ in } C: comm}$$

Read the rule as saying: To annotate the syntax tree, D **in** C, give the D-tree an empty type assignment, $\varnothing$. Annotate the D-tree and obtain its type attribute, πdec. Give the C-tree π for its type assignment and annotate C. If the C-tree has type *comm*, then annotate D **in** C with type *comm*. (It is simplest to reuse *comm* as the type attribute for programs; Chapter 4 shows why.)

The typing rules for commands and expressions must be revised to accommodate the type assignments. For example, the rule for assignment now reads as follows:

$$\frac{\pi \vdash L: intloc \qquad \pi \vdash E: intexp}{\pi \vdash L{:=}E: comm}$$

This rule says, to annotate $L{:=}E$, start with a type assignment, π, and give it to the L- and C-subtrees. If the resulting type attributes for the subtrees are *intloc* and *comm*, respectively, then annotate $L{:=}E$ with *comm*.

There is one last, new rule—the one for function invocation:

$$\pi \vdash I : \tau exp, \quad \text{if } (I : \tau exp) \in \pi$$

The function invocation is well typed if I is bound in the type assignment. Of course, this rule is the reason why the type assignment, π, must be copied to all the nodes of the syntax tree.

A complete listing of the typing rules for the imperative language with functions is presented in Figure 2.3. To save space, we will sometimes write well-typed trees in linear form, with the type assignments as subscripts and the type attributes as superscripts. The linear form of the tree in Figure 2.2 is:

$$((\textbf{fun } A = (1_{\varnothing}^{int})_{\varnothing}^{intexp})_{\varnothing}^{\{A:intexp\}dec},$$
$$(\textbf{fun } B = (((@\,loc_1{}_{\varnothing}^{intloc})_{\varnothing}^{intexp} = (0_{\varnothing}^{int})_{\varnothing}^{intexp})_{\varnothing}^{boolexp})_{\varnothing}^{\{B:boolexp\}dec})_{\varnothing}^{\pi_1 dec}$$
$$\textbf{in } (\textbf{while } B_{\pi_1}^{boolexp} \textbf{ do } (loc_1{}_{\pi_1}^{intloc} := (A_{\pi_1}^{intexp} + 2_{\pi_1}^{int})_{\pi_1}^{intexp})_{\pi_1}^{comm} \textbf{ od})_{\pi_1}^{comm})^{comm}$$

where $\pi_1 = \{A : intexp, B : boolexp\}$

As usual, we write $\pi \vdash U : \theta$ to assert that the tree, U, uses a type assignment, π, to have type attribute, θ. Read $\pi \vdash U : \theta$ as, "within context π, U has type θ." An example is $\pi_1 \vdash loc_1 := A + 2 : comm$.

You should verify that the above tree is correctly annotated. You should also write an algorithm that takes as its input a syntax tree in the language of Figure 2.1 and produces as its output an annotated tree (if the tree is well formed). You will find that the algorithm is a left-to-right, postorder tree traversal, which attaches type assignments to the nodes while it descends the tree to the leaves and then attaches type attributes to the nodes while it ascends to the root. If you are familiar with attribute grammars, you will recognize that the type assignments are *inherited attributes* and the type attributes are *synthesized attributes*. A typical text in compiling gives details about attribute grammars. Finally, you should also redraw the tree in Figure 2.2 as a "proof tree," that is, as a tree drawn directly from the typing rules in Figure 2.3 (cf. Figures 1.3 and 1.5).

2.2 The Semantics of Abstractions

The semantics of the imperative language is significantly extended by the addition of abstractions. In this section we analyze the denotational semantics of functions.

Recall from Section 1.6 that the meaning of a command is a function from the current value of the store to a new store; that is, $[\![C: comm]\!] \in Store \to Store_{\perp}$. Similarly, the meaning of an expression is a function from the current value of store to an integer or boolean; that is, $[\![E: \tau exp]\!] \in Store \to [\![\tau]\!]$. This changes when declarations are added; the function definitions must be saved in a structure called the *environment*, and like the store, the environment must be supplied to expressions and commands. An environment

For Program:

$$\frac{\varnothing \vdash D: \pi dec \quad \pi \vdash C: comm}{\vdash D \textbf{ in } C: comm}$$

For Declaration:

$$\frac{\pi \vdash E: \tau exp}{\pi \vdash \textbf{fun } I=E: \{I:\tau exp\} dec} \qquad \frac{\pi \vdash D_1: \pi_1 dec \quad \pi \vdash D_2: \pi_2 dec}{\pi \vdash D_1, D_2: (\pi_1 \cup \pi_2) dec}$$

$$\frac{\pi \vdash D_1: \pi_1 dec \quad \pi \cup \pi_1 \vdash D_2: \pi_2 dec}{\pi \vdash D_1; D_2: (\pi_1 \cup \pi_2) dec}$$

For Command:

$$\frac{\pi \vdash L: intloc \quad \pi \vdash E: intexp}{\pi \vdash L:=E: comm} \qquad \frac{\pi \vdash C_1: comm \quad \pi \vdash C_2: comm}{\pi \vdash C_1; C_2: comm}$$

$$\frac{\pi \vdash E: boolexp \quad \pi \vdash C_1: comm \quad \pi \vdash C_2: comm}{\pi \vdash \textbf{if } E \textbf{ then } C_1 \textbf{ else } C_2 \textbf{ fi}: comm}$$

$$\frac{\pi \vdash E: boolexp \quad \pi \vdash C: comm}{\pi \vdash \textbf{while } E \textbf{ do } C \textbf{ od}: comm} \qquad \pi \vdash \textbf{skip}: comm$$

For Expression:

$$\frac{\pi \vdash N: int}{\pi \vdash N: intexp} \qquad \frac{\pi \vdash L: intloc}{\pi \vdash @L: intexp} \qquad \frac{\pi \vdash E_1: intexp \quad \pi \vdash E_2: intexp}{\pi \vdash E_1 + E_2: intexp}$$

$$\frac{\pi \vdash E_1: intexp \quad \pi \vdash E_2: intexp}{\pi \vdash E_1 = E_2: boolexp} \qquad \frac{\pi \vdash E: boolexp}{\pi \vdash \neg E: boolexp} \qquad \pi \vdash I: \tau exp, \text{ if } (I:\tau exp) \in \pi$$

For Location: For Numeral:

$\pi \vdash loc_i: intloc$ $\pi \vdash n: int$

Note: $\pi_1 \cup \pi_2 = \pi_1 \cup \pi_2$, if $\{I \mid (I:\theta_1) \in \pi_1\} \cap \{I \mid (I:\theta_2) \in \pi_2\} = \varnothing$, else undefined

Figure 2.3

is a set of identifier, meaning pairs; we will see examples momentarily.

Now, the meaning of a command is a function of the environment and the store: $[\![\pi \vdash C: comm]\!] \in Environment \rightarrow Store \rightarrow Store_\perp$. Let e represent an environment and s represent a store; as an example, the semantics of assignment becomes the following:

$$[\![\pi \vdash L:=E: comm]\!]e\ s = update([\![\pi \vdash L: intloc]\!]e,\ [\![\pi \vdash E: intexp]\!]e\ s,\ s)$$

The environment, e, is used by the components of the assignment to resolve identifier references, mimicking the distribution of the type assignments in the typing rules.

Similarly, the semantics of an expression is based on the values of the environment and the store: $[\![\pi \vdash E: \tau exp]\!] \in Environment \rightarrow Store \rightarrow [\![\tau]\!]$. An example follows:

$$[\![\pi \vdash @L: intexp]\!]e\ s = lookup([\![\pi \vdash L:intloc]\!]e,\ s)$$

The crucial clause is the one for function invocation:

$$[\![\pi \vdash I: \tau exp]\!]e\ s = v(s), \quad \text{where } (I=v) \in e$$

Function invocation causes an environment lookup: If I is bound to v in e, then v is extracted and used as the meaning of the invocation.

Even though all the pieces are not yet in place, we consider an example. Say that **fun** $A = @loc_1$ was declared and is used in the command, $loc_1:=A$. The function definition is saved in the environment $e_1 = \{A = f_1\}$, where $f_1(s) = lookup(loc_1, s)$. (Of course, f_1 is the meaning of A's body: $f_1(s) = [\![\varnothing \vdash @loc_1: intexp]\!]\varnothing\ s$.) Then, for type assignment $\pi_1 = \{A: intexp\}$, environment e_1, and store $\langle 2, 3, 4 \rangle$, we have the following:

$$[\![\pi_1 \vdash loc_2:=A: comm]\!]e_1\ \langle 2, 3, 4 \rangle$$
$$= update([\![\pi_1 \vdash loc_2: intloc]\!]e_1,\ [\![\pi_1 \vdash A: intexp]\!]e_1\ \langle 2, 3, 4 \rangle,\ \langle 2, 3, 4 \rangle)$$
$$= update(loc_2, f_1\langle 2, 3, 4 \rangle,\ \langle 2, 3, 4 \rangle)$$
$$= update(loc_2, lookup(loc_1, \langle 2, 3, 4 \rangle),\ \langle 2, 3, 4 \rangle)$$
$$= update(loc_2, 2, \langle 2, 3, 4 \rangle) = \langle 2, 2, 4 \rangle$$

Notice how the environment is distributed to the subtrees of the assignment, so that the function call can be processed. Also, the meaning of function A is *not* an integer, but a mapping from the current store to an integer. This is no accident; when we code a program, such as

$$\textbf{fun } F = @loc_1+1 \textbf{ in } loc_1:=0;\ loc_1:=F;\ loc_2:=2+F$$

we expect that the two invocations of F yield different results, since the store has changed.

Now we consider the semantics of function definitions. The meaning of a function definition is the binding of the function's name to the (meaning of) its body. We write this as follows:

$\llbracket \pi \vdash \textbf{fun } I {=} E \colon \{ I \colon \tau exp \} dec \rrbracket e\ s = \{ I = f \}, \text{ where } f(s') = \llbracket \pi \vdash E \colon \tau exp \rrbracket e\ s'$

I is bound to the meaning of E, creating an environment with one binding in it. Notice that E is *not* evaluated with *s*, the current value of the store—a store is supplied when the function is invoked.

The semantics of a compound declaration, $D_1;D_2$, is the union of the environments built by the two:

$\llbracket \pi \vdash D_1 ; D_2 \colon (\pi_1 \cup \pi_2) dec \rrbracket e\ s = e_1 \cup e_2$
   where $e_1 = \llbracket \pi \vdash D_1 \colon \pi_1 dec \rrbracket e\ s$ and $e_2 = \llbracket \pi \cup \pi_1 \vdash D_2 \colon \pi_2 dec \rrbracket (e \cup e_1)\ s$

Notice how the environment used by D_2 contains the bindings made by D_1. This matches the pattern established by the type assignments in the corresponding typing rule. In general, the meaning of a declaration is a function that maps the current values of environment and store into an environment that holds the bindings made by the declaration $\llbracket \pi \vdash D \colon \{ i{:}\theta_i \}_{i \in I} dec \rrbracket \in Environment \rightarrow Store \rightarrow \{ i{:}\llbracket \theta_i \rrbracket \}_{i \in I}$. Finally, we see the following:

$\llbracket \vdash D \textbf{ in } C \colon comm \rrbracket s = \llbracket \pi \vdash C \colon comm \rrbracket e_0\ s, \text{ where } e_0 = \llbracket \varnothing \vdash D \colon \pi dec \rrbracket \varnothing\ s$

That is, the environment built by the declarations is supplied the command part of the program.

The complete semantics definition for the language in Figure 2.3 is given in Figure 2.4. The meaning of the program in Figure 2.2 with the input store $\langle 0, 2, 4 \rangle$ is calculated in Figure 2.5.

Recall from Section 1.8 that we can use a denotational semantics definition as operational semantics. The first few operational semantics computation steps for the example in Figure 2.5 go like this:

$\llbracket \textbf{fun } A{=}1, \textbf{fun } B = @loc_1{=}0 \textbf{ in while } B \textbf{ do } loc_1{:=}A{+}2 \textbf{ od} \colon comm \rrbracket \langle 0, 2, 4 \rangle$
$\Rightarrow \llbracket \pi_1 \vdash \textbf{while } B \textbf{ do } loc_1{:=}A{+}2 \textbf{ od} \colon comm \rrbracket e_1\ \langle 0, 2, 4 \rangle$
      where $e_1 = \llbracket \varnothing \vdash \textbf{fun } A{=}1, \textbf{fun } B{=}@loc_1{=}0 \colon \pi_1 dec \rrbracket \varnothing\ \langle 0, 2, 4 \rangle$
$\Rightarrow \llbracket \pi_1 \vdash \textbf{while } B \textbf{ do } loc_1{:=}A{+}2 \textbf{ od} \colon comm \rrbracket e_1\ \langle 0, 2, 4 \rangle$
      where $e_1 = e_{11} \cup e_{12}$
      where $e_{11} = \llbracket \varnothing \vdash \textbf{fun } A{=}1 \colon \{ A \colon intexp \} dec \rrbracket \varnothing\ \langle 0, 2, 4 \rangle$
      and $e_{12} = \llbracket \varnothing \vdash \textbf{fun } B{=}@loc_1{=}0 \colon \{ B \colon boolexp \} dec \rrbracket \varnothing\ \langle 0, 2, 4 \rangle$
$\Rightarrow \llbracket \pi_1 \vdash \textbf{while } B \textbf{ do } loc_1{:=}A{+}2 \textbf{ od} \colon comm \rrbracket e_1\ \langle 0, 2, 4 \rangle$
      where $e_1 = e_{11} \cup e_{12}$
      where $e_{11} = \{ A = f \}, \text{ where } f(s') = \llbracket \varnothing \vdash 1 \colon intexp \rrbracket \rrbracket \varnothing\ s'$
      and $e_{12} = \llbracket \varnothing \vdash \textbf{fun } B{=}@loc_1{=}0 \colon \{ B \colon boolexp \} dec \rrbracket \varnothing\ \langle 0, 2, 4 \rangle$
$\Rightarrow \llbracket \pi_1 \vdash \textbf{while } B \textbf{ do } loc_1{:=}A{+}2 \textbf{ od} \colon comm \rrbracket e_1\ \langle 0, 2, 4 \rangle$
      where $e_1 = \{ A = f \} \cup e_{12}$

For Program:

$\llbracket \vdash D \textbf{ in } C: comm \rrbracket s = \llbracket \pi \vdash C: comm \rrbracket e_0 \ s, \text{ where } e_0 = \llbracket \varnothing \vdash D: \pi dec \rrbracket \varnothing \ s$

For Declaration:

$\llbracket \pi \vdash \textbf{fun } I = E: \{I:\tau exp\} dec \rrbracket e \ s = \{I = f\}, \text{ where } f(s') = \llbracket \pi \vdash E: \tau exp \rrbracket e \ s'$

$\llbracket \pi \vdash D_1, D_2: (\pi_1 \cup \pi_2) dec \rrbracket e \ s = e_1 \cup e_2$

 where $e_1 = \llbracket \pi \vdash D_1: \pi_1 dec \rrbracket e \ s$ and $e_2 = \llbracket \pi \vdash D_2: \pi_2 dec \rrbracket e \ s$

$\llbracket \pi \vdash D_1; D_2: (\pi_1 \cup \pi_2) dec \rrbracket e \ s = e_1 \cup e_2$

 where $e_1 = \llbracket \pi \vdash D_1: \pi_1 dec \rrbracket e \ s$ and $e_2 = \llbracket \pi \cup \pi_1 \vdash D_2: \pi_2 dec \rrbracket (e \cup e_1) \ s$

For Command:

$\llbracket \pi \vdash L := E: comm \rrbracket e \ s = update(\llbracket \pi \vdash L: intloc \rrbracket e, \llbracket \pi \vdash E: intexp \rrbracket e \ s, \ s)$

$\llbracket \pi \vdash C_1; C_2: comm \rrbracket e \ s = \llbracket \pi \vdash C_2: comm \rrbracket e \ (\llbracket \pi \vdash C_1: comm \rrbracket e \ s)$

$\llbracket \pi \vdash \textbf{if } E \textbf{ then } C_1 \textbf{ else } C_2 \textbf{ fi}: comm \rrbracket e \ s$

 $= if(\llbracket \pi \vdash E: boolexp \rrbracket e \ s, \llbracket \pi \vdash C_1: comm \rrbracket e \ s, \llbracket \pi \vdash C_2: comm \rrbracket e \ s)$

$\llbracket \pi \vdash \textbf{while } E \textbf{ do } C \textbf{ od}: comm \rrbracket e \ s = w(s)$

 where $w(s) = if(\llbracket \pi \vdash E: boolexp \rrbracket e \ s, \ w(\llbracket \pi \vdash C: comm \rrbracket e \ s), \ s)$

$\llbracket \pi \vdash \textbf{skip}: comm \rrbracket e \ s = s$

For Expression:

$\llbracket \pi \vdash N; intexp \rrbracket e \ s = \llbracket \pi \vdash N: int \rrbracket e$

$\llbracket \pi \vdash @L: intexp \rrbracket e \ s = lookup(\llbracket \pi \vdash L: intloc \rrbracket e, \ s)$

$\llbracket \pi \vdash E_1 + E_2: intexp \rrbracket e \ s = plus(\llbracket \pi \vdash E_1: intexp \rrbracket e \ s, \llbracket \pi \vdash E_2: intexp \rrbracket e \ s)$

$\llbracket \pi \vdash E_1 = E_2: boolexp \rrbracket e \ s = equal(\llbracket \pi \vdash E_1: intexp \rrbracket e \ s, \llbracket \pi \vdash E_2: intexp \rrbracket e \ s)$

$\llbracket \pi \vdash \neg E: boolexp \rrbracket e \ s = not(\llbracket \pi \vdash E: boolexp \rrbracket e \ s)$

$\llbracket \pi \vdash I: \tau exp \rrbracket e \ s = v(s), \text{ where } (I = v) \in e$

For Location:

$\llbracket \pi \vdash loc_i: intloc \rrbracket e = loc_i$

For Numeral:

$\llbracket \pi \vdash n: int \rrbracket e = n$

Figure 2.4 _____

$\llbracket \vdash \textbf{fun } A{=}1, \textbf{fun } B{=}@loc_1{=}0 \textbf{ in while } B \textbf{ do } loc_1{:=}A{+}2 \textbf{ od}: comm \rrbracket \langle 0, 2, 4 \rangle$

$= \llbracket \pi_1 \vdash \textbf{while } B \textbf{ do } loc_1{:=}A{+}2 \textbf{ od}: comm \rrbracket e_1 \; \langle 0, 2, 4 \rangle$

    where $\pi_1 = \{A: intexp, B: boolexp\}$

    and $e_1 = \llbracket \varnothing \vdash \textbf{fun } A{=}1, \textbf{fun } B{=}@loc_1{=}0: \pi_1\, dec \rrbracket \varnothing \; \langle 0, 2, 4 \rangle$

        $= (\llbracket \varnothing \vdash \textbf{fun } A{=}1: \{A: intexp\}\, dec \rrbracket \varnothing \; \langle 0, 2, 4 \rangle)$

            $\cup (\llbracket \varnothing \vdash \textbf{fun } B{=}@loc_1{=}0: \{B: boolexp\}\, dec \rrbracket \varnothing \; \langle 0, 2, 4 \rangle)$

        $= \{A = f, B = g\}$

            where $f(s) = \llbracket \varnothing \vdash 1: intexp \rrbracket \varnothing s = 1$

            and $g(s) = \llbracket \varnothing \vdash @loc_1{=}0: boolexp \rrbracket \varnothing \; s$

                  $= equalint(lookup(loc_1, s), 0)$

$= w \langle 0, 2, 4 \rangle$

$= if(\llbracket \pi_1 \vdash B: boolexp \rrbracket e_1 \; \langle 0, 2, 4 \rangle, w(\llbracket \pi_1 \vdash loc_1{:=}A{+}2: comm \rrbracket e_1 \; \langle 0, 2, 4 \rangle), \langle 0, 2, 4 \rangle)$

$= if(g \langle 0, 2, 4 \rangle, w(\llbracket \pi_1 \vdash loc_1{:=}A{+}2: comm \rrbracket e_1 \; \langle 0, 2, 4 \rangle), \langle 0, 2, 4 \rangle)$

$= if(equalint(lookup(loc_1, \langle 0, 2, 4 \rangle), 0), w(\llbracket \pi_1 \vdash loc_1{:=}A{+}2: comm \rrbracket e_1 \; \langle 0, 2, 4 \rangle), \langle 0, 2, 4 \rangle)$

$= if(true, w(\llbracket \pi_1 \vdash loc_1{:=}A{+}2: comm \rrbracket e_1 \; \langle 0, 2, 4 \rangle), \langle 0, 2, 4 \rangle)$

$= w(\llbracket \pi_1 \vdash loc_1{:=}A{+}2: comm \rrbracket e_1 \; \langle 0, 2, 4 \rangle) = \cdots = w \langle 3, 2, 4 \rangle$

$= if(\llbracket \pi_1 \vdash B: boolexp \rrbracket e_1 \; \langle 3, 2, 4 \rangle, w(\llbracket \pi_1 \vdash loc_1{:=}A{+}2: comm \rrbracket e_1 \; \langle 3, 2, 4 \rangle), \langle 3, 2, 4 \rangle)$

$= \cdots = \langle 3, 2, 4 \rangle$

Figure 2.5 _____

        where $f(s) = \llbracket \varnothing \vdash 1: intexp \rrbracket \varnothing \; s$

        and $e_{12} = \llbracket \varnothing \vdash \textbf{fun } B{=}@loc_1{=}0: \{B: boolexp\}\, dec \rrbracket \varnothing \; \langle 0, 2, 4 \rangle$

  $\Rightarrow \cdots \Rightarrow^* \langle 3, 2, 4 \rangle$

A key notion in the operational semantics is the computation of a textual phrase to a Value. In Section 1.8, the Values for *Bool*, *Int*, *Location*, and *Store* are specified. Now, we must state what the Values are for *Environment* and for those functions that are the meanings of expression abstractions:

- For environments, the phrase $\{i = v_i\}_{i \in I}$ is a Value.
- Every function, f, defined $f s = \cdots$, is a Value.

Notice that the components, v_i, of an environment Value need not be Values themselves. More will be said about this in Section 2.6. The properties of subject reduction, soundness, strong typing, and computational adequacy are preserved, and we leave their proofs for the Exercises.

2.3 Soundness of the Typing Rules for Abstractions

The addition of the type assignment attributes to the typing rules and the environment arguments to the semantics should make us wonder if the typing rules and the semantics are well formed. Indeed, it is crucial that the environment, e, used to calculate the meaning of a tree, $\pi \vdash U: \theta$, is consistent with the type assignment, π.

Here's how we formalize this. The current syntax of type attributes is:

$$\theta ::= \tau exp \mid intloc \mid comm \mid \pi dec$$
$$\tau ::= int \mid bool$$
$$\pi ::= \{ i: \theta_i \}_{i \in I}, \quad \text{where } I \subseteq \text{Identifier is a finite set}$$

Each type has an intended set of meanings:

$$[\![\tau exp]\!] = Store \rightarrow [\![\tau]\!] \qquad\qquad [\![intloc]\!] = Location$$
$$[\![comm]\!] = Store \rightarrow Store_{\perp} \qquad\quad [\![\pi dec]\!] = Store \rightarrow [\![\pi]\!]$$
$$[\![int]\!] = Int \qquad\qquad\qquad\qquad\; [\![bool]\!] = Bool$$
$$[\![\{ i: \theta_i \}_{i \in I}]\!] = \{ i: [\![\theta_i]\!] \}_{i \in I}$$

In the last definition, $\{ i: [\![\theta_i]\!] \}_{i \in I}$ names the set of environments of the form $\{ I_1 = v_1, I_2 = v_2, \ldots, I_n = v_n \}$, where $I = \{ I_1, I_2, \ldots, I_n \}$ and each $v_i \in [\![\theta_i]\!]$.

Now we proceed to the proof that the typing rules are sound. Environment, e, is *consistent with type assignment* π if $(I: \theta) \in \pi$ exactly when $(I=v) \in e$ and $v \in [\![\theta]\!]$. Let Env_{π} be the set of all environments that are consistent with π. The soundness theorem follows:

2.1 Theorem

For the language of Figure 2.3, if $\pi \vdash U: \theta$ and $e \in Env_{\pi}$, then $[\![\pi \vdash U: \theta]\!]e \in [\![\theta]\!]$.

Proof: As usual, the proof is by structural induction on the set of typing rules, and we display two typical cases. (The remainder are left as exercises.) For an identifier, I, say we have $\pi \vdash I: \theta$ and $e \in Env_{\pi}$. Then, $(I=v) \in e$; thus $[\![\pi \vdash I: \theta]\!]e = v$, where $v \in [\![\theta]\!]$, by the definition of consistency. For $\pi \vdash L := E: comm$ and $e \in Env_{\pi}$, the typing rule for assignment demands that $\pi \vdash L: intloc$ and $\pi \vdash E: intexp$ both hold. By the inductive hypothesis, $[\![\pi \vdash L: intloc]\!]e \in Location$ and $[\![\pi \vdash E: intexp]\!]e \in Store \rightarrow Int$. Hence, $[\![\pi \vdash L := E: comm]\!]e \, s = update([\![\pi \vdash L: intloc]\!]e, [\![\pi \vdash E: intexp]\!]e \, s, s) \in Store$, implying $[\![\pi \vdash L := E: comm]\!]e \in Store \rightarrow Store_{\perp}$. $\square$

2.4 Lazy Evaluation and the Copy Rule

A function definition can be evaluated *lazily* (call by name-style) or *eagerly* (call by value-style). Lazy evaluation for abstractions is the norm. This means the body of the abstraction is not computed until the abstraction is invoked. Consider this example:

fun $F = @loc_1+1$ **in** $loc_1:=0;\ loc_1:=F;\ loc_2:=F+2$

With lazy evaluation of F, the answer produced by $@loc_1+1$ is computed each time F is invoked. So, if the starting storage vector is $\langle 2, 3\rangle$, that is, loc_1 holds a 2 and loc_2 holds a 3, then at the program's conclusion, the storage vector is $\langle 1, 4\rangle$, because the first invocation of F evaluates to 1 and the second evaluates to 2.

   Lazy evaluation is natural because it supports an equational law, the *copy rule*, which states that the program

$\cdots$ **fun** $I = E \cdots$ **in** $\cdots I \cdots$

should be understood as having the same meaning as the program

$\cdots$ $\cdots$ **in** $\cdots E \cdots$

That is, the body of function I is copied into its places of invocation. (This is an example of referential transparency, cf. Section 1.6.) For example, the meaning of the above program should be the same as the meaning of this core language program:

$loc_1:=0;\ loc_1:=@loc_1+1;\ loc_2:=(@loc_1+1)+2$

This suits our intuitions that an abstraction is merely an abbreviation—a convenience. If F stands for $@loc_1+1$, then all uses of F are just abbreviations for $@loc_1+1$.

   If we study programs that use just D_1, D_2 as their only control construct for declarations, the copy rule is easy to state. Let **define** $I=V$ be an abstraction form; we write

define $I_1=V_1$, **define** $I_2=V_2, \ldots,$ **define** $I_n=V_n$ **in** U $\Rightarrow$ $[V_1/I_1, V_2/I_2, \ldots, V_n/I_n]$U

to state that the bodies, $V_1, V_2, \ldots, V_n$ are substituted for the invocations of $I_1, I_2, \ldots, I_n$ in the program U. Here, $[V_1/I_1, V_2/I_2, \ldots, V_n/I_n]$U represents the simultaneous substitution, for all $1 \le j \le n$, of expressions V_j for occurrences of identifiers I_j in U. We always assume that the identifiers $I_1, I_2, \ldots, I_n$ are distinct. Here is an example:

fun $A=1,$ **fun** $B=@loc_1=0$ **in while** B **do** $loc_1:=A+2$ **od**
$\Rightarrow [1/A,\ @loc_1=0/B]$**while** B **do** $loc_1:=A+2$ **od**
$=$ **while** $@loc_1=0$ **do** $loc_1:=1+2$ **od**

Since the copy rule performs the simultaneous substitution of abstraction bodies for their invocations, we should make precise the notion of "simultaneous substitution." For the syntax rules

$$C ::= L:=E \mid C_1;C_2 \mid \cdots$$
$$E ::= N \mid @L \mid E_1+E_2 \mid \cdots \mid I$$
$$L ::= loc_i$$
$$N ::= n$$

we define substitution by a recursive definition. For brevity, we write $[V_j/I_j]U$ to abbreviate $[V_1/I_1, V_2/I_2, \ldots, V_n/I_n]U$. Here is the definition:

$$[V_j/I_j]L:=E = [V_j/I_j]L:=[V_j/I_j]E$$
$$[V_j/I_j]C_1;C_2 = [V_j/I_j]C_1;[V_j/I_j]C_2$$

$\cdots$

$$[V_j/I_j]@L = @[V_j/I_j]L$$
$$[V_j/I_j]E_1+E_2 = [V_j/I_j]E_1+[V_j/I_j]E_2$$

$\cdots$

$$[V_j/I_j]I_k = V_k, \quad \text{if } I=I_k, \text{ for some } 1\le k\le n$$
$$[V_j/I_j]I = I, \quad \text{if } I\ne I_j, \text{ for all } 1\le j\le n$$
$$[V_j/I_j]loc_i = loc_i$$
$$[V_j/I_j]n = n$$

Now, the substitution done in the small example above can be precisely justified:

$[1/A, @loc_1=0/B]$**while** B **do** $loc_1:=A+2$ **od**
$=$ **while** $[1/A, @loc_1=0/B]B$ **do** $[1/A, @loc_1=0/B](loc_1:=A+2)$ **od**
$=$ **while** $@loc_1=0$ **do** $[1/A, @loc_1=0/B]loc_1:=[1/A, @loc_1=0/B](A+2)$ **od**
$=$ **while** $@loc_1=0$ **do** $loc_1:=[1/A, @loc_1=0/B]A+[1/A, @loc_1=0/B]2$ **od**
$=$ **while** $@loc_1=0$ **do** $loc_1:=1+2$ **od**

Substitution into $D_1;D_2$ cannot be understood as simply as that for D_1,D_2, and it is best to introduce a second copy rule for declarations:

(**define** $I_1=V_1,\ldots,$ **define** $I_n=V_n$); D
$\Rightarrow$ **define** $I_1=V_1,\ldots,$ **define** $I_n=V_n, [V_1/I_1, \ldots, V_n/I_n]D$

This translates $D_1;D_2$ into D_1,D_2 by explicitly propagating the bindings of D_1 into D_2.* A bit of care must be taken when we substitute expressions into declarations. For simplicity, we define simultaneous substitution on this syntax:

---

* This rule does *not* hold when declarations contain side effects, for example, the allocation of storage cells. See Section 2.9.

D ::= **define** I = U | D_1,D_2

$[V_j / I_j]$**define** I = U = **define** I = $[V_j / I_j]$U
$[V_j / I_j]D_1$,D_2 = $[V_j / I_j]D_1$,$[V_j / I_j]D_2$

We will not consider substitutions into declarations of form D_1;D_2, so we will avoid embarrassing questions about examples like $[@loc_1/A]$(**fun** $A=@loc_2$; **fun** $B=A+1$), which we might incorrectly write **fun** $A=@loc_2$; **fun** $B=@loc_1+1$. Here is a small example:

fun $A=@loc_2$; **fun** $B=A+1$ **in** $loc_2:=A+B$
$\Rightarrow$ **fun** $A=@loc_2$, $[@loc_2/A]$(**fun** $B=A+1$) **in** $loc_2:=A+B$
= **fun** $A=@loc_2$, **fun** $B = [@loc_2/A](A+1)$ **in** $loc_2:=A+B$
= **fun** $A=@loc_2$, **fun** $B = @loc_2+1$ **in** $loc_2:=A+B$
$\Rightarrow$ $[@loc_2/A, @loc_2+1/B]loc_2:=A+B$
= $loc_2:=(@loc_2)+(@loc_2+1)$

An important property of substitution is that it preserves the typing of a phrase:

2.2 Theorem

For the language of Figure 2.3, if $\pi_1 \cup \pi_2 \vdash U:\theta$, where $\pi_1 = \{j:\theta_j\}_{j \in I}$ and $\pi_2 \vdash V_j:\theta_j$, for all $j \in I$, then $\pi_2 \vdash [V_j/I_j]U:\theta$.

Proof: The proof is by induction on the typing rules. The crucial case is for an identifier, I, where we have the typing $\pi_1 \cup \pi_2 \vdash I:\theta$. The typing rule for I requires that $(I:\theta) \in \pi_1 \cup \pi_2$. First, if $(I:\theta) \in \pi_2$, then $\pi_2 \vdash I:\theta$ holds. But $[V_j/I_j]I = I$, so we have $\pi_2 \vdash [V_j/I_j]I:\theta$. Second, if $(I:\theta) \in \pi_1$, then I is some I_j, $j \in I$, and $[V_j/I_j]I = V_j$. By hypothesis, $\pi_2 \vdash V_j:\theta$ must hold; this gives the result. The other cases in the proof are routine, such as the one for L:=E, where we have the typing $\pi_1 \cup \pi_2 \vdash L:=E: comm$. By the typing rule for assignments, we have $\pi_1 \cup \pi_2 \vdash L: intloc$ and $\pi_1 \cup \pi_2 \vdash E: intexp$. By the inductive hypothesis, we know that $\pi_2 \vdash [V_j/I_j]L: intloc$ and $\pi_2 \vdash [V_j/I_j]E: intexp$ both hold. By the typing rule for assignment, we can infer $\pi_2 \vdash [V_j/I_j]L:=[V_j/I_j]E: comm$, which is just $\pi_2 \vdash [V_j/I_j]L:=E: comm$. $\square$

A corollary of the theorem is that the copy rules preserve typing; thus, we need type check a program only once. The theorem is not a surprise, because the type assignment in the language's typing rules "predicts" the substitutions that will be performed when the bodies of abstractions are copied into the body of a program.

A copy rule can be seen as a "computation rule" for the source language. But it is much more than that: It is a device for understanding programs with abstractions in terms of corresponding programs in the core language. We can uncover the meaning of a program with abstractions by applying copy rules to eliminate the abstractions and then using the semantics of the core language to get the meaning of the program. For example, we can prove that $[\![\vdash \textbf{fun } A = @loc_2; \textbf{fun } B = A+1 \textbf{ in } loc_2 := A+B : comm]\!]$, as defined by the semantics in Section 2.2, is the same meaning as $[\![A = @loc_2; \textbf{fun } B = A+1 \textbf{ in } loc_2 := A+B : comm]\!]$, as defined by the semantics in Chapter 1. We justify this argument in Section 2.6, where we show that the copy rule is *sound*; that is, it preserves meaning.

2.5 Eager Evaluation

If functions are evaluated eagerly (call by value-style), the copy rule fails. An eager evaluation of a function definition makes the function's body evaluate to an answer at the time the definition itself is evaluated. If we reconsider the example

$$\textbf{fun } F = @loc_1+1 \textbf{ in } loc_1 := 0;\ loc_1 := F;\ loc_2 := F+2$$

from the previous section, again with the input store $\langle 2, 3 \rangle$ but with eager evaluation, we see that F binds to 3. Both invocations of F yield a 3, and the final storage vector is $\langle 3, 5 \rangle$. The function definition is, in fact, a "const" definition.

The copy rule fails for eager evaluation, so a semantics definition must be consulted to determine the precise meaning of eagerly evaluated abstractions. (The next section gives details.)

A programming language could conceivably have both lazily and eagerly evaluated forms of abstractions (here, in the case of expression abstractions, we would have both "function" and "const" definitions), since the two forms serve two different purposes. A programming language designer must weigh the tradeoffs between such generality and the economy of the language's design.

2.6 Semantics of Lazy and Eager Evaluation

Figure 2.4 gave the semantics of lazily evaluated functions. The key to lazy evaluation in the imperative language is that the body of the function is given a store only when the function is invoked. The store is a "trigger" for "firing" the function. The semantics format for a lazily evaluated abstraction is

$$[\![\pi \vdash \textbf{define } I = U : \{ I : \theta \} dec]\!] e\ s = \{ I = f \}, \text{ where } f\ s' = [\![\pi \vdash U : \theta]\!] e\ s'$$
$$[\![\pi \vdash \textbf{invoke } I : \theta]\!] e\ s = f\ s, \text{ where } (I = f) \in e$$

We use Figure 2.4 to prove that the copy rule of Section 2.4 is sound.

2.3 Theorem

$[\![\vdash \textbf{define } I_1 = V_1, \ldots, \textbf{define } I_n = V_n \textbf{ in } C \colon comm]\!] = [\![\varnothing \vdash [V_j / I_j]C \colon comm]\!] \varnothing.$

Proof: We must show, for all $s \in Store$, that $[\![\vdash \textbf{define } I_1 = V_1, \ldots, \textbf{define } I_n = V_n \textbf{ in } C \colon comm]\!] s = [\![\varnothing \vdash [V_j / I_j]C \colon comm]\!] \varnothing s$. First, $[\![\vdash \textbf{define } I_1 = V_1, \ldots, \textbf{define } I_n = V_n \textbf{ in } C \colon comm]\!] s = [\![\pi_1 \vdash C \colon comm]\!] e_1 s$, where $\pi_1 = \{ I_j \colon \theta_j \}_{j \in I}$ and $e_1 = \{ I_j = [\![\varnothing \vdash V_j \colon \theta_j]\!] \varnothing \}_{j \in I}$. We obtain the result by proving the more general claim $[\![\pi_1 \vdash U \colon \theta]\!] e_1 = [\![\varnothing \vdash [V_j / I_j]U \colon \theta]\!] \varnothing$, for U being a command, expression, location, or numeral. The crucial case is for an identifier, I, where $[\![\pi_1 \vdash I \colon \theta]\!] e_1 = [\![\varnothing \vdash V_k \colon \theta_k]\!] \varnothing$, where $I = I_k$, for some $k \in I$. But $[\![\varnothing \vdash V_k \colon \theta_k]\!] \varnothing = [\![\varnothing \vdash [V_j / I_j]I_k \colon \theta_k]\!] \varnothing$.

The other cases are routine, such as the one for L:=E, where $[\![\pi_1 \vdash L \colon =E \colon comm]\!] e_1 s = update([\![\pi_1 \vdash L \colon intloc]\!] e_1, [\![\pi_1 \vdash E \colon intexp]\!] e_1 s, s) = update([\![\varnothing \vdash [V_j / I_j]L \colon intloc]\!] \varnothing, [\![\varnothing \vdash [V_j / I_j]E \colon intexp]\!] \varnothing s, s)$, by the inductive hypotheses for L and E. This equals $[\![\varnothing \vdash [V_j / I_j]L \colon =E \colon comm]\!] \varnothing s$. Since the argument, s, was arbitrary, we have $[\![\pi_1 \vdash L \colon =E \colon comm]\!] e_1 = [\![\varnothing \vdash [V_j / I_j]L \colon =E \colon comm]\!] \varnothing$. $\square$

Also, we can prove that the denotational semantics in Figure 2.4 gives the same meaning to a program as does the copy rule and the denotational semantics in Figure 1.7, Chapter 1, for the core language. For the next two results, let $[\![\cdot]\!]_c$ represent the core language semantics from Chapter 1, and let $[\![\cdot]\!]_a$ represent the semantics in Figure 2.4.

2.4 Lemma

If C contains no identifiers, then for all $e \in Env_\pi$, $[\![C \colon comm]\!]_c = [\![\pi \vdash C \colon comm]\!]_a e$.

Proof: An easy proof by structural induction, left as an exercise. $\square$

2.5 Theorem

$[\![\vdash \textbf{define } I_1 = V_1, \cdots, \textbf{define } I_n = V_n \textbf{ in } C \colon comm]\!]_a = [\![[V_j / I_j]C \colon comm]\!]_c.$

Proof: By Theorem 2.3 and Lemma 2.4. $\square$

The payoff from Theorem 2.5 is that we can uncover the meaning of a program (with lazily evaluated abstractions) by first applying the copy rule to eliminate the abstractions and then interpreting the resulting core language program in the semantics of the core language. This methodology proves valuable in the later chapters of this book, where we study languages whose abstractions have denotational semantics that are too mathematically sophisticated to be simply described. It is simpler to use the copy rule. This approach is sometimes called "copy rule semantics." It is based on the semantics of

Algol-60, which uses lazily evaluated bindings.

Now it is time to examine the denotational semantics of eager evaluation of functions. The key differences lie in the semantics of definition and invocation:

$$[\![\pi \vdash \mathbf{fun}\ \mathrm{I}{=}\mathrm{E}{:}\ \{\,\mathrm{I}{:}\tau exp\,\}\,]\!]e\ s = \{\,\mathrm{I}{=}[\![\pi \vdash \mathrm{E}{:}\ \tau exp]\!]e\ s\,\}$$

The store that is available at the point of definition is supplied to the function's body. Thus, the function's name binds to a fixed integer (or boolean). This forces the semantics of function invocation to become the following:

$$[\![\pi \vdash \mathrm{I}{:}\ \tau exp]\!]e\ s = v, \quad \text{where}\ (\mathrm{I}{=}v) \in e$$

Here is an example of eager evaluation semantics:

$$[\![\ \vdash \mathbf{fun}\ A{=}1, \mathbf{fun}\ B{=}@loc_1{=}0\ \mathbf{in\ while}\ B\ \mathbf{do}\ loc_1{:}{=}A{+}2\ \mathbf{od}{:}\ prog]\!]\langle 0, 2, 4\rangle$$
$$= [\![\pi_1 \vdash \mathbf{while}\ B\ \mathbf{do}\ loc_1{:}{=}A{+}2\ \mathbf{od}{:}\ comm]\!]e_1\ \langle 0, 2, 4\rangle$$
$$\text{where}\ \pi_1 = \{A{:}\,intexp, B{:}\,boolexp\,\}$$
$$\text{and}\ e_1 = [\![\varnothing \vdash \mathbf{fun}\ A{=}1, \mathbf{fun}\ B{=}@loc_1{=}0{:}\ \pi_1\,dec]\!]\varnothing\ \langle 0, 2, 4\rangle$$
$$= ([\![\varnothing \vdash \mathbf{fun}\ A{=}1{:}\ \{A{:}\,intexp\,\}dec]\!]\varnothing\ \langle 0, 2, 4\rangle)$$
$$\cup ([\![\varnothing \vdash \mathbf{fun}\ B{=}@loc_1{=}0{:}\ \{B{:}\,boolexpdec]\!]\varnothing\ \langle 0, 2, 4\rangle)$$
$$= \{A = 1, B = equalint(lookup(loc_1, \langle 0, 2, 4\rangle), 0\,\}$$
$$= \{A = 1, B = true\,\}$$
$$= w\langle 0, 2, 4\rangle$$
$$= if([\![\pi_1 \vdash B{:}\,boolexp]\!]e_1\ \langle 0, 2, 4\rangle, w([\![\pi_1 \vdash loc_1{:}{=}A{+}2{:}\,comm]\!]e_1\ \langle 0, 2, 4\rangle), \langle 0, 2, 4\rangle)$$
$$= if(true, w([\![\pi_1 \vdash loc_1{:}{=}A{+}2{:}\,comm]\!]e_1\ \langle 0, 2, 4\rangle), \langle 0, 2, 4\rangle)$$
$$= w([\![\pi_1 \vdash loc_1{:}{=}A{+}2{:}\,comm]\!]e_1\ \langle 0, 2, 4\rangle)$$
$$= \cdots = w\langle 3, 2, 4\rangle$$
$$= if([\![\pi_1 \vdash B{:}\,boolexp]\!]e_1\ \langle 3, 2, 4\rangle, w([\![\pi_1 \vdash loc_1{:}{=}A{+}2{:}\,comm]\!]e_1\ \langle 3, 2, 4\rangle), \langle 3, 2, 4\rangle)$$
$$= if(true, w([\![\pi_1 \vdash loc_1{:}{=}A{+}2{:}\,comm]\!]e_1\ \langle 3, 2, 4\rangle), \langle 3, 2, 4\rangle)$$
$$= \cdots = w\langle 3, 2, 4\rangle = \cdots = \perp$$

Since B is a "const" definition, the loop never converges, and the result is undefined.

The above example makes clear that the copy rule is unsound for eager evaluation semantics, but as an exercise, you should try to adapt the proof of Theorem 2.3 for eager evaluation and see where the proof fails. Without a copy rule, we must rely on the denotational semantics to explain the semantics of function definition and invocation.

The standard format for an eagerly evaluated abstraction follows:

$$[\![\pi \vdash \mathbf{define}\ \mathrm{I}{=}\mathrm{U}{:}\ \{\,\mathrm{I}{:}\theta\,\}dec]\!]e\ s = \{\,\mathrm{I}{=}[\![\pi \vdash \mathrm{U}{:}\ \theta]\!]e\ s\,\}$$
$$[\![\pi \vdash \mathbf{invoke}\ \mathrm{I}{:}\ \theta]\!]e\ s = v, \quad \text{where}\ (\mathrm{I}{=}v) \in e$$

A key is that the store is supplied immediately to the body of the abstraction, but there is a second, important issue: An improper meaning for the abstraction's body causes an improper meaning for the entire program. An example makes this point clear. Say that the syntax of Expression includes a phrase, **loop**, such that

$$[\![\pi \vdash \mathbf{loop}: intexp]\!]e\ s = \bot$$

The eager evaluation of functions demands that the meaning of the program **fun** A=**loop in skip** is $\bot$. (In contrast, lazy evaluation of the function would allow the program to perform the **skip** operation and terminate.) To enforce the correct semantics of eager evaluation, we require that the semantic binding operation, $\{I{=}v\}$, be *strict*: $\{I{=}\bot\} = \bot$. Thus:

$$[\![\pi \vdash \mathbf{fun}\ A = \mathbf{loop\ in\ skip}: comm]\!]\ s$$
$$= [\![\{A:intexp\} \vdash \mathbf{skip}: comm]\!]e_0\ s,$$
$$\qquad \text{where } e_0 = \{A = [\![\varnothing \vdash \mathbf{loop}:intexp]\!]\varnothing\ s\} = \{A = \bot\}$$
$$= [\![\{A:intexp\} \vdash \mathbf{skip}: comm]\!]\bot\ s,$$
$$= \bot$$

The last line of the calculation is justified because we legislate that $[\![\pi \vdash U: \theta]\!]\bot\ s = \bot$, that is, no proper meaning can result from an improper environment. A consequence of this change is that the union operation on bindings is strict as well: $e \cup \bot = \bot \cup e = \bot$.

2.7 Other Standard Abstractions

The function construct has established a pattern for abstraction definition and invocation that can be repeated. For a syntax domain, U, the syntax of a U-abstraction is **define** I = U, and the syntax for invocation is **invoke** I. The formats for the typing rules follow:

$$\frac{\pi \vdash U: \theta}{\mathbf{define}\ I{=}U: \{I{:}\theta\}dec} \qquad\qquad \pi \vdash \mathbf{invoke}\ I: \theta, \quad \text{if } (I{:}\theta) \in \pi$$

where θ represents a legal type for a U-construct. The key feature of the syntax is that the type of the invocation construct must match the type of the definition construct.

In one fell swoop, we now add command abstractions, numeral abstractions, and location abstractions to the language in Figure 2.1. This gives us the following:

P ::= D **in** C
D ::= **fun** I=E | **proc** I=C | **const** I=N | **alias** I=L | D_1,D_2 | $D_1;D_2$
C ::= L:=E | $C_1;C_2$ | **if** E **then** C_1 **else** C_2 **fi** | **while** E **do** C **od** | **skip** | **call** I
E ::= N | @L | $E_1{+}E_2$ | $E_1{=}E_2$ | ¬E | I
L ::= loc_i | I

N ::= *n* | I

The language now admits programs like this one:

(const $A=1$, **alias** $X=loc_1$); **fun** $F = @X+A$; **proc** $P = X:=F$
in call P; $X:=A$; **call** P

The alias abstraction is not a variable declaration; it is merely a name for a location number.

Like functions, procedures use lazy evaluation. Const and alias definitions do not depend on the store, so the question of lazy vs. eager evaluation is moot. Therefore, we can apply the copy rule to the above example, uncovering the core language program: $loc_1:=@loc_1+1$; $loc_1:=1$; $loc_1:=@loc\,1+1$.

A procedure is evaluated lazily because its purpose is to alter the store each time the procedure is called. Its semantics fits the pattern for lazy evaluation:

$[\![\pi \vdash \textbf{proc } I=C: \{I:comm\}dec]\!]e\ s = \{I = p\}$, where $p(s') = [\![\pi \vdash C: comm]\!]e\ s'$
$[\![\pi \vdash \textbf{call } I: comm]\!]e\ s = p(s)$, where $(I=p) \in e$

In contrast, an eagerly evaluated procedure would calculate a store value at the point of definition and retain it for future use. Such a device allows backtracking of a computation to the point of procedure definition. For example, the call to the eagerly evaluated procedure, P, in the program **proc** $P = \textbf{skip in } loc_1:=1$; **call** P undoes the assignment to loc_1. This idea is verified by the semantics of eager evaluation:

$[\![\pi \vdash \textbf{proc } I=C: \{I:comm\}dec]\!]e\ s = \{I = s'\}$, where $s' = [\![\pi \vdash C: comm]\!]e\ s$
$[\![\pi \vdash \textbf{call } I: comm]\!]e\ s = s'$, where $(I=s') \in e$

The concept is neat, but the implementation overhead is high. Another concern is looping: If a procedure is eagerly evaluated and looping occurs, this prevents the program from completing, even if the procedure is never called.

The denotational semantics of consts and aliases are easy. Here is one equation; the remainder are left as exercises.

- $[\![\pi \vdash \textbf{const } I = N: \{I:int\}dec]\!]e\ s = \{I = n\}$, where $n = [\![\pi \vdash N: int]\!]e$

2.8 Recursively Defined Abstractions

The typing rules implicitly disallow recursively defined abstractions. For example, the definition of P in

proc $P = $ **if** @$loc_1{=}6$ **then skip else** $loc_1{:=}$@$loc_1{+}1$; **call** P **fi in** $\cdots$

is ill typed, because P's binding is not visible to its own body. This can be remedied:

$$\frac{\pi \cup \{ \text{I}{:}comm \} \vdash \text{C}{:}\, comm}{\textbf{rec-proc } \text{I}{=}\text{C}{:}\, \{ \text{I}{:}comm \} dec}$$

with the understanding that, in the body of I, all references to I denote I's own body.

The usual repetitive control constructs can be simulated by recursive definitions. Here are two examples for commands: (i) **while** E **do** C **od** abbreviates **call** W, where **rec-proc** $W = $ **if** E **then** C; **call** W **else skip fi**; (ii) **repeat** C **until** E abbreviates **call** R, where **rec-proc** $R = $ C; **if** E **then skip else call** R **fi**. A language designer could conceivably introduce repetitive control structures into a new language by first designing a language core, adding abstractions, and then observing what structure of recursive abstractions are most often used in the solution of typical problems. The most commonly used patterns of recursive programming would be made into control structures.

The semantics of a recursively defined abstraction reflects the structure of its typing rule:

$$[\![\pi \vdash \textbf{rec-proc } \text{I}{=}\text{C}{:}\, \{ \text{I}{:}comm \} dec]\!] e \; s = \{ \text{I}{=}p \}$$
$$\text{where } p(s') = [\![\pi \cup \{ \text{I}{:}comm \} \vdash \text{C}{:}\, comm]\!] (e \cup \{ \text{I}{=}p \}) \; s'$$

As with the while-loop in Chapter 1, we can understand the recursively defined value, p, by means of a family of approximations:

$$p_0 \, (s) = \bot$$
$$p_1 \, (s) = [\![\pi \cup \{ \text{I}{:}comm \} dec \vdash \text{C}{:}\, comm]\!] (e \cup \{ \text{I} = p_0 \}) \; s$$
$$\cdots$$
$$p_{i+1} \, (s) = [\![\pi \cup \{ \text{I}{:}comm \} dec \vdash \text{C}{:}\, comm]\!] (e \cup \{ \text{I} = p_i \}) \; s$$

The value p_i represents a weakened version of p that can perform i calls before becoming exhausted. The meaning of p is characterized by: for all $s, s' \in Store$, $p(s) = s'$ if and only if there is some $k \geq 0$ such that $p_k(s) = s'$.

Although we have focused on recursively defined procedures, the concepts stated here apply to other forms of recursively defined abstractions as well.

Since a recursive abstraction is evaluated lazily, there is a variation of the copy rule that we can use to understand the recursion. First, we treat a recursive abstraction, **rec-proc** I = C, as an abbreviation for **define** I = (**rec** I:*comm*. C), where **rec** is a new constructor, and we introduce an *unfolding rule*:

(**rec** I:*comm*. C) $\;\Rightarrow\;$ [(**rec** I:*comm*. C)/I]C

We put the unfolding rule to work on this example:

(**alias** $A = loc_1$, **alias** $B = loc_2$);
rec-proc ADD = **if** $@A = 0$ **then skip else** $B := @B + 1$; $A := @A - 1$; **call** ADD **fi**
   in $A := 2$; $B := 3$; **call** ADD

We write the recursive program in its new form and begin:

(**alias** $A = loc_1$, **alias** $B = loc_2$);
proc ADD = (**rec** ADD:*comm.* **if** $@A = 0$ **then skip**
           else $B := @B + 1$; $A := @A - 1$; **call** ADD **fi**)
   in $A := 2$; $B := 3$; **call** ADD

$\Rightarrow$ **alias** $A = loc_1$, **alias** $B = loc_2$,
   proc ADD = (**rec** ADD:*comm.* **if** $@loc_1 = 0$ **then** *skip*
            else $loc_2 := @loc_2 + 1$; $loc_1 := @loc_1 - 1$; **call** ADD **fi**)
   in $A := 2$; $B := 3$; **call** ADD

$\Rightarrow$ $loc_1 := 2$; $loc_2 := 3$; (**rec** ADD:*comm.* **if** $@loc_1 = 0$ **then skip**
            else $loc_2 := @loc_2 + 1$; $loc_1 := @loc_1 - 1$; **call** ADD **fi**)

The definitions have been removed, but the recursive binding remains. But we can apply the unfolding rule and obtain the following:

$\Rightarrow$ $loc_1 := 2$; $loc_2 := 3$;
   if $@loc_1 = 0$ **then skip else** $loc_2 := @loc_2 + 1$; $loc_1 := @loc_1 - 1$;
                (**rec** ADD:*comm.* **if** $@loc_1 = 0$ **then skip**
                    else $loc_2 := @loc_2 + 1$; $loc_1 := @loc_1 - 1$; **call** ADD **fi**) **fi**

The rule exposes the body of the recursive binding. A copy of the recursive binding has been embedded into the code, in case there is need for another invocation of it. The semantics of the new program is identical to the semantics of the original, since the unfolding rule preserves meaning. This game can be continued, and we do so just one more time:

$loc_1 := 2$; $loc_2 := 3$;
   if $@loc_1 = 0$ **then skip else** $loc_2 := @loc_2 + 1$; $loc_1 := @loc_1 - 1$;
      if $@loc_1 = 0$ **then skip else** $loc_2 := @loc_2 + 1$; $loc_1 := @loc_1 - 1$;
         (**rec** ADD:*comm.* **if** $@loc_1 = 0$ **then** *skip*
            else $loc_2 := @loc_2 + 1$; $loc_1 := @loc_1 - 1$; **call** ADD **fi**) **fi fi**

Applications of the unfolding rule will not make the recursive binding disappear, and without running the program, no one can predict how many unfoldings will suffice for termination of the program. Despite this, we can claim that the unfolding rule plus the semantics of the core language lets us understand the semantics of a program with recursive abstractions, because we can always unfold the recursive abstraction when needed to expose code written in the core language. It is easy to see this behavior in the above example: if we evaluate the program, three applications of the unfolding rule suffice to give loc_2 value 5.

2.9 Variable Declarations

An alias abstraction names an already allocated location. This differs from a *variable declaration*, which allocates a fresh, anonymous location in the store, perhaps initializes it, and binds it to an identifier. The core imperative language uses explicit location numbers, but these prove troublesome in a fully developed, general-purpose language, so it is time to replace them by variable name declarations.

Since a variable declaration is part command and part abstraction, it is difficult to classify. It can be understood as a core language construct (in this case, variables are *not* identifiers in the sense of this chapter), or it can be understood as a form of eagerly evaluated abstraction. (This is developed in the following sections.) Perhaps the ultimate nature of the variable declaration is a "red herring," so we postpone discussion of the issue and add this simple form of variable:

$$D ::= \cdots \mid \textbf{var } I$$
$$C ::= L{:=}E \mid C_1;C_2 \mid \cdots$$
$$E ::= N \mid @L \mid \cdots$$
$$L ::= I$$

The construct allocates a location and binds it to I; we use it in programs like this one:

   var X; **var** Y; **proc** $P = Y{:=}@X{+}1$ **in** $X{:=}0$; **call** P

Of course, the copy rule cannot be applied to variable declarations, since location numbers are now anonymous. At best, we might devise a rule that copies the lazily evaluated abstractions and leaves the variable declarations in place. Then, the previous example is equivalent to this:

   var X; **var** Y **in** $X{:=}0$; $Y{:=}@X{+}1$

The variables remain behind in the underlying core language program. The formulation of such a copy rule is left as an exercise.

2.10 Semantics of Variables

The addition of variables forces a profound change upon the semantics of the programming language—declarations can now alter the store. This is clear from the denotational semantics of the variable declaration:

$$\llbracket \pi \vdash \mathbf{var}\ I\text{:}\ \{I\text{:}intloc\}dec \rrbracket e\ s = (\{I{=}l\}, s')$$
$$\text{where}\ (l, s') = allocate(s)$$
$$\text{and}\ allocate\text{:}\ Store \rightarrow (Location \times Store)$$
$$\text{is defined}\ allocate\ \langle n_1, n_2, \ldots, n_m \rangle = (loc_{m+1}, \langle n_1, n_2, \ldots, n_m, init \rangle)$$
$$\text{where}\ init\ \text{is some arbitrary integer, for example, } 0$$

The variable declaration is part abstraction (it makes the binding $I = l$) and part command (it updates s to s'). So, a pair—a binding and an updated store—form the meaning produced by a variable declaration. For uniformity, the semantics definitions for the other declarations must be revised to return binding, store pairs as well. The semantics of a lazily evaluated abstraction becomes

$$\llbracket \pi \vdash \mathbf{define}\ I{=}U\text{:}\ \{I\text{:}\theta\}dec \rrbracket e\ s = (\{I = f\}, s), \text{ where } f\ s' = \llbracket \pi \vdash U\text{:}\theta \rrbracket e\ s'$$

Since the abstraction does not alter the store, s, the answer consists of the binding and s. The semantics of a program changes slightly:

$$\llbracket D\ \mathbf{in}\ C\text{:}\ comm \rrbracket s = \llbracket \pi \vdash C\text{:}\ comm \rrbracket e_1\ s_1, \text{ where } (e_1, s_1) = \llbracket \varnothing \vdash D\text{:}\ \pi dec \rrbracket \varnothing\ s$$

The environment and store built by the declarations are used to evaluate the body of the program. The changes to the semantics are summarized in Section 2.15.

2.11 Type-Structure Abstractions

A variable declaration is part abstraction and part command, and it is illuminating to separate these two components in the syntax of the language:

D ∈ Declaration
T ∈ Type-structure
    D ::= $\cdots$ | **var** I:T
    T ::= **newint**

The new syntax domain, Type-structure, represents command-like constructs that allocate storage. Think of a type-structure construct as a "storage allocation routine": Each time **newint** is invoked, it allocates a fresh storage location and returns the name of the location. (**newint** is just the *allocate* operation from the previous section.) The declaration, **var** I:T, activates T and binds the value generated by T to I. Remember, **newint** is not the type attribute for I—it is a storage allocation routine.

It is worthwhile to contrast variable declarations with procedures. A procedure declaration, **proc** I=C, alters the storage vector only when it is invoked; that is, it is evaluated lazily. In contrast, a variable declaration, **var** I:T, activates T and alters the storage vector when the variable is declared, that is, it is evaluated eagerly. This point proves important later.

Since T is command-like, it is a small step to making variable declarations with initializations, for example, **var** A:**newint**:=0, or even with full-fledged commands, but we save these extensions as exercises.

The Type-structure domain will prove surprisingly rich. First, we consider type-structure abstractions. We call the new abstraction a *class* and use the following syntax:

D ::= $\cdots$ | **var** I:T | **class** I=T
T ::= **newint** | I

The Pascal-like languages use the syntax **type** I=T for type-structure abstractions, but we use the keyword **class** to make the point that Simula-style classes and objects evolve from type-structure abstractions (see Chapter 4). We can write

    class M = **newint**;
    var $A:M$; **var** $B:M$; **var** C:**newint**
    in $A:=0; B:=@A+@C$

Variables A and B bind to distinct locations, even though both invoke M. The reason is that lazy evaluation is used with type-structure abstractions—the body of M is evaluated each time it is invoked. For this reason, the copy rule applies, and the definition of M in the previous example can be copied for its invocations, giving the following:

    var A:**newint**; **var** B:**newint**; **var** C:**newint**
    in $A:=0; B:=@A+@C$

Consider again the syntax of the variable declaration; for the moment, say that we change it to **var** I=T. Now, it looks almost identical to a class definition, and we have only the semantics to distinguish between the two. We conclude that *a class is a type-structure abstraction that evaluates lazily, and a variable declaration is a type-structure abstraction that evaluates eagerly.* Although we do not state this claim categorically, it does provide a useful perspective for future analyses.

Classes are more interesting when they have Simula-style *record structure*:

D ::= $\cdots$ | **var** I:T | **class** I=T
T ::= **newint** | I | **record** D **end**

When activated, **record** D **end** allocates storage and returns a (declaration) value. Like **newint,** a record structure is activated when it is invoked by a variable name declaration. For example, four locations are allocated in the program:

class R = **record var** X : **newint, var** Y : **newint end**;
var $A:R$; **var** $B:R$ **in** $\cdots$

Our version of record structure can contain functions, procedures, and so on. Here is a sample:

var A : **newint**;
class R = **record var** C : **newint**; **proc** $P = (C := @A + 1)$ **end**;
var $F:R$; **var** $G:R$
in $\cdots A \cdots F.C \cdots$ **call** $F.P \cdots G.C \cdots$ **call** $G.P \cdots$

Storage cells are allocated for A, $F.C$, and $G.C$. When procedure $F.P$ (respectively, $G.P$) is invoked, it updates $F.C$ (resp., $G.C$).

The introduction of record structures into the language is not as arbitrary as it might seem. A compound declaration is in fact a record, and the mechanisms for type checking and giving semantics to record structures are already in place, because they are used to type check and give semantics to declarations. What we have done here is allow records to appear in a role other than just as declarations. If we wished to pursue this issue further, we might allow records to appear as expressions (this is common to functional languages) or even as commands (the result is a form of "case" statement), but we leave these ideas as useful exercises. In Section 2.14 we will rephrase the abstraction principle as a form of "record introduction principle."

Records are used by indexing, and this impacts the syntax of the language. We introduce a syntax domain of "identifier expressions":

$X \in$ Identifier-expr
X ::= I | X.I

and we modify all invocation constructs to use identifier expressions:

$$C ::= L:=E \mid C_1;C_2 \mid \cdots \mid \textbf{call } X$$
$$E ::= N \mid @L \mid \cdots \mid X$$
$$\cdots$$

$$L ::= X$$
$$X ::= I \mid X.I$$

The typing rules for type structures, variable declarations, and identifier expressions are straightforward:

$$\pi \vdash \textbf{newint}: intloc\ class \qquad\qquad \frac{\pi \vdash D: \pi_1\, dec}{\pi \vdash \textbf{record } D \textbf{ end}: \pi_1\, class}$$

$$\frac{\pi \vdash T: \delta class}{\pi \vdash \textbf{var } I:T: \{I:\delta\} dec} \qquad\qquad \frac{\pi \vdash T: \delta class}{\pi \vdash \textbf{class } I=T: \{I:\delta class\} dec}$$

$$\pi \vdash I: \theta, \quad \text{if } (I:\theta) \in \pi \qquad\qquad \frac{\pi \vdash X: \pi_1}{\pi \vdash X.I: \theta} \quad \text{if } (I:\theta) \in \pi_1$$

but note the differences in the typing of **var** and **class**. Figure 2.6 shows the typed version of the program seen earlier in this section.

2.12 Semantics of Type Structures

A type structure has a semantics that is command-like: When evaluated with the current environment and store, it alters the store and returns a value that can be bound to an identifier. That is, $[\![\pi \vdash T: \delta class]\!] \in Env_\pi \to Store \to ([\![\delta]\!] \times Store)$. Before we present the semantics, we must clarify the range of type attributes that a type structure can assume:

$$\delta ::= intloc \mid \pi$$
$$\pi ::= \{i:\theta_i\}_{i \in I}, \quad \text{where } I \text{ is a finite set, and } I \subseteq \text{Identifier}$$
$$\theta ::= \tau \mid \tau exp \mid comm \mid \delta \mid \delta class \mid \pi dec$$
$$\tau ::= int \mid bool$$

The set represented by $\delta class$ is $[\![\delta class]\!] = Store \to ([\![\delta]\!] \times Store)$. (See Section 2.3 for the sets represented by the other type attributes.) Here are the semantics definitions for the constructs related to the previous section:

$(((\textbf{var } A : \textbf{newint}_{\varnothing}^{intloc\ class})_{\varnothing}^{\pi_1 dec}$;

$(\textbf{class } R = (\textbf{record}$

$\quad\quad\quad (\textbf{var } C : \textbf{newint}_{\pi_1}^{intloc\ class})_{\pi_1}^{\pi_2 dec}$;

$\quad\quad\quad\quad (\textbf{proc } P = (C_{\pi_1 \cup \pi_2}^{intloc} := (@A_{\pi_1 \cup \pi_2}^{intloc})_{\pi_1 \cup \pi_2}^{intexp})_{\pi_1 \cup \pi_2}^{comm})_{\pi_1 \cup \pi_2}^{\pi_3 dec}$

$\quad\quad \textbf{end})_{\pi_1}^{\pi_2 \cup \pi_3 class})_{\pi_1}^{\pi_4 dec}$;

$((\textbf{var } F : R_{\pi_1 \cup \pi_4}^{\pi_2 \cup \pi_3 class})_{\pi_1 \cup \pi_4}^{\pi_5 dec}$,

$(\textbf{var } G : R_{\pi_1 \cup \pi_4}^{\pi_2 \cup \pi_3 class})_{\pi_1 \cup \pi_4}^{\pi_6 dec})_{\pi_1 \cup \pi_4}^{\pi_7 dec})_{\varnothing}$

$\textbf{in } \cdots A_{\pi_7}^{intloc} \cdots F.C_{\pi_7}^{intloc} \cdots \textbf{call } F.P_{\pi_7}^{comm} \cdots G.C_{\pi_7}^{intloc} \cdots \textbf{call } G.P_{\pi_7}^{comm})^{prog}$

where

$\pi_1 = \{A : intloc\}$ $\quad\quad\quad\quad\quad\quad$ $\pi_5 = \{F : \pi_2 \cup \pi_3\}$

$\pi_2 = \{C : intloc\}$ $\quad\quad\quad\quad\quad\quad$ $\pi_6 = \{G : \pi_2 \cup \pi_3\}$

$\pi_3 = \{P : comm\}$ $\quad\quad\quad\quad\quad\quad$ $\pi_7 = \pi_1 \cup \pi_4 \cup \pi_5 \cup \pi_6$

$\pi_4 = \{R : (\pi_2 \cup \pi_3) class\}$

Figure 2.6 _____

For Program:

$\quad [\![D \textbf{ in } C : comm]\!]s = [\![\pi_1 \vdash C; comm]\!]e_1 \, s_1$, where $(e_1, s_1) = [\![\varnothing \vdash D : \pi_1 dec]\!]\varnothing \, s$

For Declaration:

$\quad [\![\pi \vdash \textbf{define } I = U : \{I : \theta\} dec]\!]e \, s = (\{I = f\}, s)$,

$\quad\quad$ where $f s' = [\![\pi \vdash U : \theta]\!]e \, s'$ and $U \in \{E, T, C\}$

$\quad [\![\pi \vdash D_1 ; D_2 : (\pi_1 \cup \pi_2) dec]\!]e \, s = (e_1 \cup e_2, s_2)$

$\quad\quad$ where $(e_1, s_1) = [\![\pi \vdash D_1 : \pi_1 dec]\!]e \, s$

$\quad\quad$ and $(e_2, s_2) = [\![\pi \cup \pi_1 D_2 : \pi_2 dec]\!](e \cup e_1) \, s_1$

$\quad [\![\pi \vdash \textbf{var } I : T : \{I : \delta\} dec]\!]e \, s = (\{I = v\}, s')$, where $(v, s') = [\![\pi \vdash T : \delta class]\!]e \, s$

For Type-structure:

$\quad [\![\pi \vdash \textbf{newint} : intloc\ class]\!]e \, s = allocate(s)$

$\quad\quad$ where _allocate_ is defined in Section 2.10

$\quad [\![\pi \vdash \textbf{record } D \textbf{ end} : \pi class]\!]e \, s = [\![\pi \vdash D : \pi dec]\!]e \, s$

$[\![\pi \vdash X \colon \delta class]\!] e \; s = p(s)$

  where $p = [\![\pi \vdash X \colon \delta class]\!] e$, as defined by the semantics of Identifier-expr

For Identifier-expr:

$[\![\pi \vdash I \colon \theta]\!] e = v$, where $(I{=}v) \in e$

$[\![\pi \vdash X.I \colon \theta]\!] e = v$, where $r = [\![\pi \vdash X \colon \pi_1]\!] e$ and $(I{=}v) \in r$

The semantics of the record structure, **record** D **end**, is interesting because it is so simple: the meaning is the environment that the record structure builds (plus the altered store). Therefore, a record variable is a named environment; that is, **var** I: **record** D **end** builds an environment that holds D's bindings and binds it to I. Record indexing extracts specific bindings from the named environments; for example, *A.B* extracts the value bound to *B* in *A*. This notion of environment-as-value is useful, and it motivates the next section, where we consider modules.

2.13 Declaration Abstractions

Declarations can themselves be abstracted; we call the abstraction a *module*:

  D ::= $\cdots$ | **module** I={D} | **import** I

(The braces around the module's body are added only for clarity.) We will say that a module is "imported" when it is invoked. Here is a small example:

  module M = { **class** K = **newint**; **var** $A \colon K$; **proc** $P = A{:=}0$ };
  var B: **newint**;
  import M
  in call P; $B{:=}@A$

The declarations within module M are not visible to the rest of the program until M is imported; without M's importation, the command **call** P; $B{:=}@A$ would not be well typed.

  The typing rules follow the usual pattern:

$$\frac{\pi \vdash D \colon \pi_1 \, dec}{\textbf{module } I{=}\{D\} \colon \{\, I \colon \pi_1 \, dec \,\} dec} \qquad \pi \vdash \textbf{import } I \colon \pi_1 \, dec, \quad \text{if } (I \colon \pi_1 \, dec) \in \pi$$

The rules suggest that a module declaration binds an identifier to a record of bindings. This is confirmed by the semantics:

$$\llbracket \pi \vdash \textbf{module } I = \{D\}: \{ I: \pi_1 dec \} dec \rrbracket e \ s = (\{ I = f \}, \ s)$$
$$\text{where } f(s') = \llbracket \pi \vdash D: \pi_1 dec \rrbracket e \ s'$$
$$\llbracket \pi \vdash \textbf{import } I: \pi_1 dec \rrbracket e \ s = f(s), \quad \text{where } (I = f) \in e$$

This is the usual, lazy evaluation semantics for an abstraction. A key consequence of lazy evaluation is that the storage cells for a module's variables are not allocated until the module is imported. For example, only one location is allocated for the program:

> **module** M = { **var** A: **newint** }; **module** N = { **var** B: **newint** };
> **import** M **in** $A := 0$

The alternative, eager evaluation, allocates storage for a module's variables when the module is defined. In the above example, two locations would be allocated. The semantics of eager evaluation is

$$\llbracket \pi \vdash \textbf{module } I = \{D\}: \{ I: \pi_1 dec \} dec \rrbracket e \ s = (\{ I = e_1 \}, \ s_1)$$
$$\text{where } (e_1, s_1) = \llbracket \pi \vdash D: \pi_1 dec \rrbracket e \ s$$
$$\llbracket \pi \vdash \textbf{import } I: \pi_1 dec \rrbracket e \ s = (e_1, s), \quad \text{where } (I = e_1) \in e$$

If we allow indexing of the components of a module, as is common to most module-based languages, for example,

> **module** M = { **class** K = **newint**; **var** A: K; **proc** P = $A := 0$ };
> **var** B: **newint**;
> **in call** $M.P$; $B := @M.A$

then eager evaluation of the module definition is essential. (Also, the typing rule for module definition should be changed to that in Exercise 13.3.) In the example, eager evaluation ensures that the storage for A is allocated and ready when M.P is called. It is a challenge to give a proper semantics of module indexing when modules are evaluated lazily, and this is left as an exercise.

Another benefit of eager evaluation semantics is that a module can be *shared* by other modules. For example, perhaps we wish to code a module, S, that is shared by modules M and N. We might write this:

> **module** S = { **var** A: K; **fun** $F = @A + 1$ };
> **module** M = { **import** S; **proc** $INIT = A := 0$ };
> **module** N = { **import** S; **proc** $SUCC = A := F$ };
> **in call** $M.INIT$; **call** $N.SUCC$

The intent is that modules M and N share the same location for A. Eager evaluation of S makes this happen. Notice that our present version of typing rules would not allow the following:

> **module** S = { $\cdots$ };
> **module** M = { **import** S; $\cdots$ };
> **module** N = { **import** S; $\cdots$ };
> **import** M; **import** N
> **in** $\cdots$

The reason is that S would be imported twice—once through M and once through N—causing a redeclaration error. A redeclaration error seems reasonable when modules are evaluated lazily but not when they are evaluated eagerly. You are left with the challenging exercise of formulating a sound set of typing rules that support eager evaluation and reimportation.

Modules are essential to languages for programming-in-the-large because they support the development of large programs in parts—individual modules can be coded and compiled separately and linked together later. But how can a program that invokes external modules be type-checked? The following example depends on an external module M:

> **var** A: **newint**, **import** M **in** A :=@B +1

If M contains a declaration for variable B, then the program is well typed, but more information is necessary to verify this. Here is a hypothetical syntax:

> **var** A: **newint**,
> **import external** M: { B: *intloc*, C: *comm* }
> **in** A :=@B +1

External module M is a "parameter" to the program, and the additional information gives the "type" of the formal parameter. (This idea is explored in the next chapter.) Another solution is to require that the compiler consult a library of modules and locate M's definition there.

Our **import** construct resembles Ada's **use** construct, but it differs from Modula-2's **import** construct in a key way: In Modula-2, **import** can be used to make any declaration—not just a module—visible to another module. In Modula-2, **fun** F=1; **module** M = { **import** F **in fun** G=F +1 } makes F's definition visible to the body of M. Details are left for the exercises.

Modules look like classes, and a number of widely used "modular" languages include one construct in its most general form but not the other. There is a reason for this. Both modules and classes are named compound declarations. A module is an eagerly evaluated compound declaration, whereas a class is a lazily evaluated one. If a language has classes but not modules, then a module declaration, **module** M=D, is simulated by coding a class, **class** K=D, and activating it by **var** M:K. (But module sharing is not so easy to simulate!) Conversely, if a language has modules but not classes, then a class, **class** K=**record var** V_1: $\cdots$; **var** V_i; **proc** P_1= $\cdots$; **proc** P_j= $\cdots$ **end**, and its activations, **var** I_1:K, $\cdots$, **var** I_k:K, are simulated with modules by first declaring global variables to hold the data parts: **var** I_1:**record var** V_1: $\cdots$; **var** V_i **end**, $\cdots$, **var** I_k:**record var** V_1: $\cdots$; **var** V_i **end**, and then declaring a module, **module** M ={ **proc** P_1= $\cdots$; **proc** P_j= $\cdots$ }, to hold the procedures that manipulate the global variables. Of course, the procedures must be parameterized on the global variables. This simulation is unpleasant, and module-based languages support *opaque types* to ease the pain (see Chapter 4).

2.14 The Abstraction Principle Is a Record Introduction Principle

The principle of abstraction says that phrases of any "semantically meaningful syntactic class" may be named. So, we gave names to *intexp*-typed expressions, *boolexp*-typed expressions, *comm*-typed commands, and so on. In general, every type attribute, θ, names a "semantically meaningful syntactic class," namely, the well-formed phrases of type θ. So, the abstraction principle says we can construct the well-formed declaration $\pi \vdash \mathbf{define}\ I = U: \{I:\theta\}dec$ when $\pi \vdash U:\theta$ holds.

The type attribute, $\{I:\theta\}dec$, is telling: It shows that a declaration builds a phrase that is a binding of a name to a value. This notion is confirmed by the denotational semantics, where $[\![\pi \vdash \mathbf{define}\ I = U: \{I:\theta\}dec]\!]e\ s$ builds a singleton set consisting of the binding of I to the meaning of U. Similarly, a compound declaration is a set of bindings of distinct identifiers to their values, written $\{I_1=v_1, I_2=v_2, \ldots, I_n=v_n\}$. Such a set is an environment, but it is also a *record*. Since the semantics of a declaration is a record, and declarations are introduced into the language because of the abstraction principle, we can treat the abstraction principle as a "record introduction principle." The record introduction principle might say: Phrases of any semantically meaningful syntactic class may be components of records.

The fundamental operation upon records is indexing: for a record, x, its indexing, $x.I$, extracts the value that is bound to identifier I within x. Of course, this is the indexing operation, X.I, that is used upon modules and record variables, which are named records:

> **var** A : **record var** B : **newint end**;
> **module** M = { **const** K=0; **proc** P = $A.B$:= K }
> **in call** $M.P$

Although the language in this chapter allowed indexing just upon named records, it is reasonable to allow unnamed records to be used within commands:

> **var** A : **record var** B : **newint end**;
> **in call** { **const** K=0; **proc** P = $A.B$:= K } $.P$

There is a "multiple indexing" operation, the *with* expression, that makes visible all the bindings within a record: If record x is $\{I_1=v_1, I_2=v_2, \ldots, I_n=v_n\}$, then the expression *with* x *do* e makes I_1, I_2, $\ldots$, I_n visible to e. For example, for $x_0 = \{A=0, B=loc_1\}$, we can write *with* x_0 *do* B:=A+2 rather than $x_0.B$:=$x_0.A$+2. The Pascal-like languages support *with* expressions for record variables.

The *with* expression is important, because it suggests that a program, D **in** C, is actually the expression *with* D *do* C. The next, obvious generalization is to allow *with* expressions within the body, C, of the program. This is saved for Chapter 4.

2.15 Summary

Here is a summary of the programming language developed from the abstraction principle. Variables and identifier expressions are included. Locations have been dropped. The abstract syntax definition is

P ∈ Program   L ∈ Variable
D ∈ Declaration   N ∈ Numeral
T ∈ Type-structure X ∈ Identifier-expr
C ∈ Command   I ∈ Identifier
E ∈ Expression

> P ::= D **in** C
> D ::= D_1,D_2 | D_1;D_2 | **fun** I=E | **const** I=N | **proc** I=C | **var** I:T
> | **class** I=T | **module** I={D} | **import** X
> T ::= **newint** | **record** D **end** | X
> C ::= L:=E | C_1;C_2 | **if** E **then** C_1 **else** C_2 **fi** | **while** E **do** C **od** | **skip** | **call** X
> E ::= N | @L | E_1+E_2 | E_1=E_2 | ¬E | X
> L ::= X
> N ::= n | X
> X ::= I | X.I

The scheme for typing rules for U-abstraction definition and invocation reads as follows:

$$\frac{\pi \vdash U: \theta}{\textbf{define } I=U: \{I:\theta\}dec} \qquad \pi \vdash \textbf{invoke } I: \theta, \quad \text{if } (I:\theta) \in \pi$$

Here are the type attributes and typing rules for the above language:

$$\theta ::= \tau \mid \tau exp \mid comm \mid \delta \mid \delta class \mid \pi dec$$
$$\tau ::= int \mid bool$$
$$\delta ::= intloc \mid \pi$$
$$\pi ::= \{j:\theta_j\}_{j \in J} \quad \text{where } J \text{ is a finite set, and } J \subseteq \text{Identifier}$$

For Program:

$$\frac{\varnothing \vdash D: \pi dec \qquad \pi \vdash C: comm}{\vdash D \textbf{ in } C: comm}$$

For Declaration:

$$\frac{\pi \vdash D_1: \pi_1 dec \qquad \pi \vdash D_2: \pi_2 dec}{\pi \vdash D_1, D_2: \pi_1 \cup \pi_2 dec} \qquad \frac{\pi \vdash D_1: \pi_1 dec \qquad \pi \cup \pi_1 \vdash D_2: \pi_2 dec}{\pi \vdash D_1; D_2: \pi_1 \cup \pi_2 dec}$$

$$\frac{\pi \vdash N: int}{\pi \vdash \textbf{const } I=N: \{I:int\}dec} \qquad \frac{\pi \vdash E: \tau exp}{\pi \vdash \textbf{fun } I=E: \{I:\tau exp\}dec}$$

$$\frac{\pi \vdash C: comm}{\pi \vdash \textbf{proc } I=C: \{I:comm\}dec} \qquad \frac{\pi \vdash T: \delta class}{\pi \vdash \textbf{var } I:T: \{I:\delta\}dec}$$

$$\frac{\pi \vdash T: \delta class}{\pi \vdash \textbf{class } I=T: \{I:\delta class\}dec} \qquad \frac{\pi \vdash D: \pi_1 dec}{\pi \vdash \textbf{module } I=\{D\}: \{I:\pi_1\}dec}$$

$$\frac{\pi \vdash X: \pi_1 dec}{\pi \vdash \textbf{import } X: \pi_1 dec}$$

For Type-structure:

$$\pi \vdash \textbf{newint}: intloc\ class \qquad \frac{\pi \vdash D: \pi_1 dec}{\pi \vdash \textbf{record } D \textbf{ end}: \pi_1 class} \qquad \frac{\pi \vdash X: \delta class}{\pi \vdash X: \delta class}$$

For Command:

$$\frac{\pi \vdash L: intloc \quad \pi \vdash E: intexp}{\pi \vdash L:=E: comm} \qquad \frac{\pi \vdash C_1: comm \quad \pi \vdash C_2: comm}{\pi \vdash C_1; C_2: comm}$$

$$\frac{\pi \vdash E: boolexp \quad \pi \vdash C_1: comm \quad \pi \vdash C_2: comm}{\pi \vdash \textbf{if } E \textbf{ then } C_1 \textbf{ else } C_2 \textbf{ fi}: comm}$$

$$\frac{\pi \vdash E: boolexp \quad \pi \vdash C: comm}{\pi \vdash \textbf{while } E \textbf{ do } C \textbf{ od}: comm} \qquad \pi \vdash \textbf{skip}: comm \qquad \frac{\pi \vdash X: comm}{\pi \vdash \textbf{call } X: comm}$$

For Expression:

$$\frac{\pi \vdash N: int}{\pi \vdash N: intexp} \qquad \frac{\pi \vdash L: intloc}{\pi \vdash @L: intexp} \qquad \frac{\pi \vdash E_1: intexp \quad \pi \vdash E_2: intexp}{\pi \vdash E_1 + E_2: intexp}$$

$$\frac{\pi \vdash E_1: intexp \quad \pi \vdash E_2: intexp}{\pi \vdash E_1 = E_2: boolexp} \qquad \frac{\pi \vdash E: boolexp}{\pi \vdash \neg E: boolexp} \qquad \frac{\pi \vdash X: \tau exp}{\pi \vdash X: \tau exp}$$

For Variable:

$$\frac{\pi \vdash X: intloc}{\pi \vdash X: intloc}$$

For Numeral:

$$\pi \vdash n: int, \quad \text{for } n \in Int \qquad \frac{\pi \vdash X: int}{\pi \vdash X: int}$$

For Identifier-expr:

$$\pi \vdash I: \theta, \quad \text{if } (I: \theta) \in \pi \qquad \frac{\pi \vdash X: \pi_1}{\pi \vdash X.I: \theta} \quad \text{if } (I: \theta) \in \pi_1$$

Recursively defined U-abstractions, **rec-define** I=U, have this typing:

$$\frac{\pi \cup \{I: \theta\} \vdash U: \theta}{\pi \vdash \textbf{rec-define } I=U: \{I: \theta\} dec}$$

Here are the sets of values that the type attributes denote:

$$[\![int]\!] = Int \qquad\qquad\qquad [\![bool]\!] = Bool$$
$$[\![\tau exp]\!] = Store \rightarrow [\![\tau]\!] \qquad [\![comm]\!] = Store \rightarrow Store_\perp$$
$$[\![intloc]\!] = Location \qquad\quad [\![\delta class]\!] = Store \rightarrow ([\![\delta]\!] \times Store)$$
$$[\![\pi dec]\!] = Store \rightarrow ([\![\pi]\!] \times Store) \qquad [\![\{\,i\colon\theta_i\,\}_{i\in I}]\!] = \{\,i\colon[\![\theta_i]\!]\,\}_{i\in I}$$

The lazy evaluation semantics of abstractions is:

$$[\![\pi\vdash\mathbf{define}\ I{=}U\colon\{\,I\colon\theta\,\}dec]\!]e\ s = (\{\,I{=}f\,\},\ s)$$
$$\text{where } f\,s' = [\![\pi\vdash U\colon\theta]\!]e\ s'$$
$$[\![\pi\vdash\mathbf{invoke}\ I\colon\theta]\!]e\ s = f\,s,\ \text{ where } (I{=}f)\in e$$

The soundness of the typing rules ensures us that $[\![\pi\vdash U\colon\theta]\!] \in Env_\pi \rightarrow [\![\theta]\!]$. Here is the semantics of the imperative language developed in this chapter:

For Program:

$$[\![\ \vdash D\ \mathbf{in}\ C\colon comm]\!]s = [\![\pi\vdash C\colon comm]\!]e_1\ s_1$$
$$\text{where } (e_1, s_1) = [\![\varnothing\vdash D\colon\pi dec]\!]\varnothing\ s$$

For Declaration:

$$[\![\pi\vdash D_1,D_2\colon(\pi_1\cup\pi_2)dec]\!]e\ s = (e_1\cup e_2,\ s_2)$$
$$\text{where } (e_1, s_1) = [\![\pi\vdash D_1\colon\pi_1 dec]\!]e\ s$$
$$(e_2, s_2) = [\![\pi\vdash D_2\colon\pi_2 dec]\!]e\ s_1$$
$$[\![\pi\vdash D_1;D_2\colon(\pi_1\cup\pi_2)dec]\!]e\ s = (e_1\cup e_2,\ s_2)$$
$$\text{where } (e_1, s_1) = [\![\pi\vdash D_1\colon\pi_1 dec]\!]e\ s$$
$$(e_2, s_2) = [\![\pi\cup\pi_1\vdash D_2\colon\pi_2 dec]\!](e\cup e_1)\ s_1$$
$$[\![\pi\vdash\mathbf{fun}\ I{=}E\colon\{\,I\colon\tau exp\,\}dec]\!]e\ s = (\{\,I{=}f\,\},\ s),\ \text{ where } f\,s' = [\![\pi\vdash E\colon\tau exp]\!]e\ s'$$
$$[\![\pi\vdash\mathbf{const}\ I{=}N\colon\{\,I\colon int\,\}dec]\!]e\ s = (\{\,I = [\![\pi\vdash N\colon int]\!]e\,\},\ s)$$
$$[\![\pi\vdash\mathbf{proc}\ I{=}C\colon\{\,I\colon comm\,\}dec]\!]e\ s = (\{\,I{=}p\,\},\ s),\ \text{ where } p\,s' = [\![\pi\vdash C\colon comm]\!]e\ s'$$
$$[\![\pi\vdash\mathbf{var}\ I\colon T\colon\{\,I\colon\delta\,\}dec]\!]e\ s = (\{\,I{=}v\,\},\ s'),\ \text{ where } (v, s') = [\![\pi\vdash T\colon\delta class]\!]e\ s$$
$$[\![\pi\vdash\mathbf{class}\ I{=}T\colon\{\,I\colon\delta class\,\}dec]\!]e\ s = (\{\,I{=}p\,\},\ s),\ \text{ where } p\,s' = [\![\pi\vdash T\colon\delta class]\!]e\ s'$$
$$[\![\pi\vdash\mathbf{module}\ I{=}\{D\}\colon\{\,I\colon\pi_1\,\}dec]\!]e\ s = (\{\,I{=}e_1\,\},\ s_1)$$
$$\text{where } (e_1, s_1) = [\![\pi\vdash D\colon\pi_1 dec]\!]e\ s$$
$$[\![\pi\vdash\mathbf{import}\ X\colon\pi_1 dec]\!]e\ s = (e_1,\ s)$$
$$\text{where } e_1 = [\![\pi\vdash X\colon\pi_1]\!]e,\ \text{as defined by the semantics of Identifier-expr}$$

For Type-structure:

$$[\![\pi\vdash\mathbf{newint}\colon intloc\ class]\!]e\ s = allocate(s)$$
$$\text{where } allocate \text{ is defined in Section 2.10}$$

$[\![\pi \vdash \textbf{record } D \textbf{ end}: \pi class]\!]e \ s = [\![\pi \vdash D: \pi dec]\!]e \ s$

$[\![\pi \vdash X: \delta class]\!]e \ s = p(s)$

   where $p = [\![\pi \vdash X: \delta class]\!]e$, as defined by the semantics of Identifier-expr

For Command:

$[\![\pi \vdash L{:=}E: comm]\!]e \ s = update([\![\pi \vdash L: intloc]\!]e, \ [\![\pi \vdash E: intexp]\!]e \ s, \ s)$

$[\![\pi \vdash C_1;C_2: comm]\!]e \ s = [\![\pi \vdash C_2: comm]\!]e \ ([\![\pi \vdash C_1: comm]\!]e \ s)$

$[\![\pi \vdash \textbf{if } E \textbf{ then } C_1 \textbf{ else } C_2 \textbf{ fi}: comm]\!]e \ s$

   $= if([\![\pi \vdash E: boolexp]\!]e \ s, \ [\![\pi \vdash C_1: comm]\!]e \ s, \ [\![\pi \vdash C_2: comm]\!]e \ s)$

$[\![\pi \vdash \textbf{while } E \textbf{ do } C \textbf{ od}: comm]\!]e \ s = w(s)$

   where $w(s) = if([\![\pi \vdash E: boolexp]\!]e \ s, \ w([\![\pi \vdash C: comm]\!]e \ s), \ s)$

$[\![\pi \vdash \textbf{skip}: comm]\!]e \ s = s$

$[\![\pi \vdash \textbf{call } X: comm]\!]e \ s = p(s)$

   where $p = [\![\pi \vdash X: comm]\!]e$, as defined by the semantics of Identifier-expr

For Expression:

$[\![\pi \vdash N: int]\!]e \ s = [\![\pi \vdash N: int]\!]e$

$[\![\pi \vdash @L: intexp]\!]e \ s = lookup([\![\pi \vdash L: intloc]\!]e, \ s)$

$[\![\pi \vdash E_1{+}E_2: intexp]\!]e \ s = plus([\![\pi \vdash E_1: intexp]\!]e \ s, \ [\![\pi \vdash E_2: intexp]\!]e \ s)$

$[\![\pi \vdash E_1{=}E_2: boolexp]\!]e \ s = equalint([\![\pi \vdash E_1: intexp]\!]e \ s, \ [\![\pi \vdash E_2: intexp]\!]e \ s)$

$[\![\pi \vdash \neg E: boolexp]\!]e \ s = not([\![\pi \vdash E: boolexp]\!]e \ s)$

$[\![\pi \vdash X: \tau exp]\!]e \ s = f(s)$

   where $f = [\![\pi \vdash X: \tau exp]\!]e$, as defined by the semantics of Identifier-expr

For Variable:

$[\![\pi \vdash X: intloc]\!]e = l$

   where $l = [\![\pi \vdash X: intloc]\!]e$, as defined by the semantics of Identifier-expr

For Numeral:

$[\![\pi \vdash n: int]\!]e = n$

$[\![\pi \vdash X: int]\!]e = v$

   where $v = [\![\pi \vdash X: intloc]\!]e$, as defined by the semantics of Identifier-expr

For Identifier-expr:

$[\![\pi \vdash I: \theta]\!]e = v$, where $(I{=}v) \in e$

$[\![\pi \vdash X.I: \theta]\!]e = v$, where $r = [\![\pi \vdash X: \pi_1]\!]e$ and $(I{=}v) \in r$

The semantics of recursively defined abstractions, as exemplified by recursively defined procedures, is

$$[\![\pi \vdash \textbf{rec-proc}\ I{=}C\colon \{\,I{:}comm\,\}\,dec]\!]e\ s = (\{\,I{=}p\,\},\ s),$$
$$\text{where}\ \ p(s') = [\![\pi \cup \{\,I{:}comm\,\} \vdash C\colon comm]\!](e \cup \{\,I{=}p\,\})\ s'$$

and $p(s) = s'$ iff there is some $k \geq 0$ such that $p_k(s) = s'$, where

$$p_0(s) = \bot$$
$$p_{i+1}(s) = [\![\pi \cup \{\,I{:}comm\,\}\,dec \vdash C\colon comm]\!](e \cup \{\,I{=}p_i\,\})\ s$$

Suggested Reading

The abstraction principle originates from Landin 1965 and 1966, Strachey 1968, and Reynolds 1970, but the principle in its present form was stated by Tennent (1977a). Tennent 1981 and Watt 1990 show further developments. The research by Kohlbecker (1986) and Kohlbecker, et al. (1986) on hygienic macro expansion is also relevant. The denotational semantics of abstractions is due to Strachey (1968); see also Milne and Strachey 1976, Stoy 1977, and Schmidt 1986. The origin of the copy rule is the Algol-60 report by Naur (1963); the rule is studied in depth by Wegner (1972) and Reynolds (1981b). The semantics of lazy and eager evaluation is presented in Winskel 1993.

Exercises

1.1. Using Figure 2.3, (attempt to) draw attributed syntax trees for
    a. **fun** $A{=}1$, **fun** $B{=}@loc_1$ **in** $loc_1{:}{=}A{+}B$
    b. **fun** $A{=}@loc_1$; **fun** $B{=}A{+}1$ **in while** $A{=}0$ **do** $loc_1{:}{=}B{+}A$ **od**
    c. (**fun** $A{=}0$; **fun** $B{=}A$), **fun** $C{=}A$ **in skip**

1.2. Given Figure 2.3, prove
    a. $\pi \vdash C\colon comm$ and $\pi \subseteq \pi'$ imply $\pi' \vdash C\colon comm$.
    b. If $\pi \vdash C\colon comm$, then there is a minimal set, π_0, such that $\pi_0 \subseteq \pi$ and $\pi_0 \vdash C\colon comm$.

1.3. Prove that Figure 2.3 has the unicity of typing property (see Section 1.4).

2.1. a. For the well-formed programs in Exercise 1.1, calculate the meanings of the programs with the input storage vector $\langle 0, 1 \rangle$.
    b. Next, calculate the meanings of the programs without an input store; that is, calculate the functions of form $Store \rightarrow Store_\bot$ that the programs denote.

2.2. Prove the following equalities:

   a. $[\![\pi \vdash D_1, D_2 : \pi_1 dec]\!] = [\![\pi \vdash D_2, D_1 : \pi_1 dec]\!]$

   b. $[\![\pi \vdash D_1; D_2 : \pi_1 dec]\!] = [\![\pi \vdash D_1, D_2 : \pi_1 dec]\!]$, if no identifier defined by D_1 appears in D_2

   c. $[\![\pi \vdash (D_1; D_2); D_3 : \pi_1 dec]\!] = [\![\pi \vdash D_1; (D_2; D_3) : \pi_1 dec]\!]$

2.3. Extend the adequacy proof in Section 1.8 to the language in Figure 2.3 and 2.4. The type attributes have been expanded to

$$\theta ::= comm \mid intloc \mid \tau exp \mid \pi dec$$
$$\pi ::= \{ i : \theta_i \}_{i \in I}$$

First, extend the predicate $comp_\theta$ by

   (i) $comp_{\pi dec}p$ holds iff for all store Values, s, $comp_\pi p(s)$ holds.

   (ii) $comp_{\{i : \theta_i\}_{i \in I}}p$ holds iff (p means a proper $e \in \{ i : [\![\theta_i]\!] \}_{i \in I}$ implies $p \Rightarrow^*$ $\{ i = v_i \}_{i \in I}$, and for all $i \in I$, $comp_{\theta_i} v_i$ holds).

Now, prove: If $\pi \vdash U : \theta$ holds, then for all environments, e, $comp_\pi e$ implies $comp_\theta([\![\pi \vdash U : \theta]\!]e)$.

3.1. a. Add to the structural operational semantics in Exercise 8.4 of Chapter 1 the rules for declarations, functions, and function invocation. Prove soundness. (Hint: Add an environment argument to the semantics.)

   b. Add to the natural semantics in Exercise 8.5 of Chapter 1 the rules for declarations, functions, and function invocation. Prove soundness.

4.1. Apply the copy rules to the programs in Exercise 1.1.

4.2. In Section 2.4, the substitution $[V_j / I_j]D_1; D_2$ was not defined. If we did define $[V_j / I_j]D_1; D_2$, what should it be?

4.3.* Prove, if $\vdash D$ in C : $comm$ holds, then D in C rewrites to a core language program after at most a finite number of applications of the copy rules.

5.1. Give the pragmatic benefits and drawbacks of eagerly evaluated functions in an imperative language.

6.1. Prove the soundness of the copy rule for $D_1; D_2$ for lazy evaluation semantics.

6.2. a. Prove that the semantics of eager evaluation makes the typing rules in Figure 2.3 sound.

   b. Based on your work in Part a, explain why this typing rule for functions might be more appropriate:

$$\frac{\pi \vdash E : \tau exp}{\pi \vdash \textbf{fun } I = E : \{ I : \tau \} dec}$$

6.3. Say that eager evaluation is used for functions. This impacts the operational semantics and requires a new proof of computational adequacy. First, make the Values for environments be those phrases $\{i = v_i\}_{i \in I}$ such that all v_i, $i \in I$, are Values. Next, alter $comp_\pi p$. (Remember, meanings saved in the environment have already been calculated with respect to a store.) Now, reprove adequacy.

7.1. For the two typing rules at the beginning of Section 2.7, prove that the rules are sound with respect to the "usual" lazy evaluation semantics; do the same for the "usual" eager evaluation semantics.

7.2. Consider this core language:

K∈ Completion
C∈ Command
    K ::= C; K | **stop**
    C ::= L:=E | C_1;C_2 | **while** E **do** C **od** | K

A program is a *completion*, that is, a sequence of commands followed by a **stop**.

a. Add completion abstractions to the language: **label** I=K and **goto** I. Define a set of typing rules. Why are the keywords **label** and **goto** appropriate ones?

b. Give the denotational semantics of the language and prove the soundness of the typing rules for the language.

7.3. What is the difference between a location abstraction and an identifier abstraction? Give a (useful) example of an identifier abstraction. Say that the language has arrays. Explain why the alias abstraction **alias** $X = A[I, J]$ can prove useful.

8.1. Use the typing rule for **rec-proc** to draw attributed syntax trees for the following:

a. **rec-proc** $P = $ **if** $@loc_1 = 0$ **then skip else** $loc_2 := @loc_2 + 1$; **call** P **fi**
    in $loc_1 := 3$; $loc_2 := 4$; **call** P

b. **rec-proc** $P = $ **call** P **in call** P; **skip**

8.2. Here is a denotational semantics for the **rec** construct:

$[\![\pi \vdash \mathbf{rec}\ I: comm.\ C: comm]\!]e\ s = p\ s$
    where $p(s') = [\![\pi \cup \{I:comm\} \vdash C: comm]\!](e \cup \{I=p\})\ s'$

a. Prove the soundness of the typing rule for recursively defined abstractions.

b. Prove the soundness of the unfolding rule.

c. Prove that $[\![\pi \vdash \mathbf{rec\text{-}proc}\ I = C: \{I:comm\}dec]\!] = [\![\pi \vdash \mathbf{proc}\ I = \mathbf{rec}\ I:comm.\ C: \{I:comm\}dec]\!]$.

d. Prove adequacy of the **rec** construct by proving $comp_\pi e$ implies $comp_{comm}[\![\mathbf{rec}\ I:comm.\ C:comm]\!]e$.

8.3. a. Say that we desire mutually recursive procedures, for example,

proc $P = \cdots$ **call** $Q \cdots$, **proc** $Q = \cdots$ **call** $P \cdots$. Design an abstract syntax and typing rules. Define the semantics and prove the typing rule sound.

b. Analogous to **rec** I:*comm*. C from Section 2.8, here is a phrase for defining a set of mutually recursive abstractions:

$$\textbf{rec}\ \{\ I_1\!:\!\theta_1,\ \ldots,\ I_n\!:\!\theta_n\ \}.\ \{\ \textbf{define}\ I_1 = U_1,\ \ldots,\ \textbf{define}\ I_n = U_n\ \}$$

Give the typing rule and denotational semantics. State and prove sound an unfolding rule.

8.4. If you worked Exercise 7.2, proceed. Say that we allow recursively defined completion abstractions. In what way does this permit "backwards gotos"? Discuss the semantics of this construction.

8.5. If you worked Exercise 2.4, proceed. Extend that language with recursively defined procedures and extend the adequacy proof. You will need the technique used on Proposition 1.7 to prove the adequacy of **rec**.

10.1. If you worked Exercise 7.1 of Chapter 1, proceed. Extend the definition of the *size* predicate by

$size_{w, \pi dec} d$ iff for all $k \geq w$, for all $s \in Store_k$, $d(s) = (e, s')$, $s' \in Store_{k'}$, and
$\quad size_{k', \pi} e$ holds
$size_{w, \{i:\theta_i\}_{i \in I}} e$ iff for all $(i = v_i) \in e$, $size_{w, \theta_i} v_i$ holds

Prove, for the programming language with variable declarations and without location constants, that for all $w \geq 0$, for all $\pi \vdash U\!:\!\theta$, if $e \in Env_\pi$ and $size_{w, \pi} e$ holds, then $size_{w, \theta} [\![\pi \vdash U\!:\!\theta]\!]e$ also holds. Use this result to deduce that every well-typed program has a meaning.

10.2. Add array variable declarations: **array var** I[N]. Give the typing rule and semantics.

11.1. Say that the syntax of a variable declaration is altered to read **var** I:T:=E, so that initialization is possible. What are the merits and drawbacks?

11.2. The mix of the eagerly evaluated variable declaration with the other, lazily evaluated abstractions complicates the copy rules for the language. Consider this syntax:

P ::= D **in** C
D ::= **define** I=U | $D_1;D_2$

(Treat **var** I:T as an eagerly evaluated abstraction **var** I=T.) Here are some program transformation rules for copying lazily evaluated abstractions:

$(D_1;D_2); D_3 \ \Rightarrow\ D_1; (D_2;D_3)$
$D_1; (D_2;D_3) \ \Rightarrow\ (D_1;D_2); D_3$
define I=W; D $\ \Rightarrow\ $ [W/I]D; **define** I=W,

      if **define** I=W is evaluated lazily and no identifier in W is defined in D
D; **define** I=W **in** C $\Rightarrow$ D **in** [W/I]C, if **define** I=W is evaluated lazily

a. If you have not worked Exercise 4.2, then define [W/I](D_1;D_2). Next, apply
the transformation rules to this example:

      class K = **newint**; **var** B:K; **proc** P = B:=0;
      var C:**record var** B:K; **var** K:**newint**; **fun** F=@K **end**
      in call P

b. State the conditions under which a lazily evaluated abstraction, **define** I=W,
can be eliminated from a program D_1; **define** I=W; D_2 **in** C. Prove this. Generalize your results, stating the conditions under which all lazily evaluated
abstractions can be eliminated from a program.

c.* Expand the syntax of declarations to be: D ::= **define** I=U | D_1;D_2 | D_1,D_2.
Add additional transformation rules and repeat Part b.

12.1. Some languages with record variables allow assignment of one record to another
when the type attributes of the two records match. An example follows:

      class R = **record var** X:**newint**; **var** Y: **newint end**;
      var A:R; **var** B:R **in** A:=B

Give the typing rule and semantics for assignment extended to record variables.
What problems, if any, arise when functions, procedures, etc., are components of a
record variable?

12.2. Prove the soundness of the transformation rules in Exercise 11.2.

12.3.* Give the denotational semantics of array type structures:

      T ::= $\cdots$| **array** [N] **of** T

12.4.* Formulate and discuss the semantics of this example:

      rec-class *BIN-TREE* = **record**
          var *ROOT*: **newint**; **var** *LEFT*: *BIN-TREE*; **var** *RIGHT*: *BIN-TREE*
          end
      var A: *BIN-TREE*;
      rec-proc *TRAVERSE* = $A.ROOT$:=0; A :=@$A.LEFT$; **call** *TRAVERSE*
      in $A.RIGHT.ROOT$:=1; **call** *TRAVERSE*

13.1. Are these programs well typed? Give semantics to those that are.

a. **module** M = { **fun** F = @A+1 }; **var** A:**newint**; **import** M **in** A:=F

b. **var** A:**newint**; **module** M = { **fun** F=1 }; **import** M; **fun** G = F **in** A:=G+F

c. **module** M = { **var** M:**newint** }; **import** M **in** M:=1

13.2. Say that modules are evaluated lazily; thus, the copy rule can be applied. Next, say that indexing is allowed. Define a typing rule for module indexing so that the example:

$\cdots$ **module** $M = \{\textbf{fun } F = @A+1\}$ $\cdots$ **in** $A:=M.F$

rewrites to $A:=@A+1$. What complications arise in the type checking? In the semantics?

13.3. Say that modules are evaluated eagerly. Explain why this typing rule is more appropriate than the one in the text:

$$\frac{\pi \vdash D: \pi_1 \, dec}{\pi \vdash \textbf{module } I = \{D\}: \{I: \pi_1\} \, dec}$$

13.4. a. In Modula-2, *internal modules* restrict which bindings are visible to a module's body. For example, in

alias $A = loc_1$; **fun** $F = A+1$;
module $M = \{\textbf{visible } F \textbf{ in fun } G = F+2\}$; $\cdots$

only F's definition (and not A's) is visible to the body of M. (Note: Modula-2 uses the keyword, **import**, rather than **visible**, but we wish to avoid confusion with the examples in the chapter.) Give the syntax, typing rule, and semantics for this variant of module.

b. In Modula-2, internal modules limit which declarations are exposed when the module is imported, for example, for: **module** $M = \{\textbf{export } G \textbf{ in fun } F = 1$; **fun** $G = F+2\}$, when M is imported, only G's definition is visible. Give the syntax, typing rule, and semantics for **export**.

c. In Modula-2, internal modules are "automatically imported" at the beginning of the evaluation of the body of a program, for example,

module $M = \{\textbf{export } F \textbf{ in fun } F=2\}$ **in** $loc_1:=F$

is well typed. Define the typing rule and semantics for this.

13.5. a. Give the typing rules and semantics for this syntax of external module importation:

D ::= $\cdots$ | **import external** I: {F}
F ::= I:θ | F_1,F_2
θ ::= τexp | *comm* | *intloc* | πdec
τ ::= *int* | *bool*

b. Modify your answer to Part a so that the components of a module can be renamed on importation to avoided an unwanted identifier clash, for example, for external module $M = \{\textbf{alias } A=loc_1, \cdots\}$ and the program

fun $A = 0$, **import external** M: {$B=A$:*intloc*} **in** $B:=A$

the result is a program that assigns 0 to loc_1.

c.   If you are familiar with Modula-2 or Ada, comment on the similarities and differences for external module importation to that displayed in Parts a and b.

14.1.   Say that we add a **with** command to the language in Figure 2.5:

       C ::= $\cdots$| **with** D **do** C

a.   Define the typing rule and semantics.

b.   How does the **with** construct compare to the **import** construct in Section 2.13? To the **from** $\cdots$ **import** $\cdots$ statement in Modula-2?

c.   Say that **with** statements are added to all the other syntax domains, for example, E ::= $\cdots$ | **with** D **do** E. Explain why record indexing, for example, E.I, is redundant. Describe the pragmatics of **with**.

d.   Say that records have lazy evaluation semantics. What is the appropriate copy rule for **with**?

15.1.   Pick a core language, say, one designed as an answer to Exercise 9.1 or 9.2 from Chapter 1 and apply the abstraction principle. Justify why you included (and omitted) the various forms of abstractions.

3 The Parameterization and Correspondence Principles

Abstractions gain utility if they can be applied in a variety of situations. *Parameters* make this possible. In this chapter we study the introduction of various forms of parameters into a programming language. We call this the *parameterization principle*.

The Parameterization Principle:

Phrases from any semantically meaningful syntactic class may be parameters.

Like the abstraction principle, the parameterization principle wields great power; we can consider numerals, expressions, locations, declarations, commands, type-structures, and more, as potential parameters.

In its most general form, the parameterization principle suggests that any construct can be parameterized, but in this chapter we parameterize just abstractions. (Chapter 5 considers the general form.) For arbitrary syntax domains, U and V, the definition of a parameterized V-abstraction appears:

define $I_1(I_2:\theta) = V$

Its invocation with a U-parameter also appears:

invoke $I_1(U)$

I_2 is the *formal parameter*, and U is the *actual parameter*. (Later, we consider *parameter lists*.) The definition uses θ, a type attribute, to specify the type of the formal parameter, rather than a type-structure value, that is, rather than **define** $I_1(I_2:T) = V$. Our reason is that the Type-structure syntax domain lists the structures of just variables, and we plan to use constant values (integers, booleans, commands, etc.) as parameters as well.

The typing rules for a V-abstraction parameterized on a U-phrase are

$$\frac{\pi \uplus \{I_2:\theta_1\} \vdash V:\theta_2}{\pi \vdash \textbf{define } I_1(I_2:\theta_1) = V: \{I_1:\theta_1 \to \theta_2\} dec} \qquad \frac{\pi \vdash U:\theta_1}{\pi \vdash \textbf{invoke } I(U):\theta_2} \text{ if } (I:\theta_1 \to \theta_2) \in \pi$$

$\pi \vdash I:\theta, \quad$ if $(I:\theta) \in \pi$

where $\pi_1 \uplus \pi_2 = \pi_2 \cup (\pi_1 - \{(I{:}v) \mid (I{:}w) \in \pi_2 \ and \ (I{:}v) \in \pi_1\})$. The first typing rule says that the type attribute of I_1 is $\theta_1 \to \theta_2$; that is, I_1 requires an actual parameter of type θ_1 to produce a result of type θ_2. Notice that V, the body of I_1, uses a type assignment that holds the global identifiers and their types plus the formal parameter and its type. The formal parameter, I_2, cancels any global identifier that has the same name. (This is noted by the type assignment $\pi \uplus \{I_2{:}\theta\}$.) An example follows:

> **var** X:**newint**; **const** A=1;
>
> **proc** $P(A{:}boolexp) =$ **if** A **then** X:=0 **else skip fi**

The type assignment used by P's body is $\{X{:}intloc, A{:}int\} \uplus \{A{:}boolexp\} = \{X{:}intloc, A{:}boolexp\}$. Within P's body, uses of A refer to the formal parameter, which is *boolexp*-typed.

The second rule gives the typing of an invocation, where the type of the actual parameter must match the type of the formal one, and the third rule states the typing of a formal parameter reference.

The above example shows that a formal parameter is referenced the same way that an abstraction is invoked: by mentioning its name. It is simplest to use the same syntactic construct, the identifier, for both formal parameter reference and abstraction invocation. (Keywords like **call** and **import** are "syntactic sugar"; that is, they are used for readability and have no semantic content—treat "**call** P" and "P" the same.) This suggests that the semantics of both parameter reference and abstraction invocation should be the same and forewarns us of the *correspondence principle*, detailed in Section 3.7.

We now extend the language in the previous chapter with parameter forms. All the varieties of abstractions—procedures, functions, modules, classes, and so on—are eligible for parameters. We do not have the space to show all of the possibilities for all of the abstractions, so we focus upon parameters for procedures. The ideas we develop apply uniformly to the other abstractions.

The parameter format specific to command abstractions follows:

$$\frac{\pi \uplus \{I_2{:}\theta\} \vdash C{:}comm}{\pi \vdash \textbf{proc } I(I_2{:}\theta) = C{:} \{I_1{:}\theta \to comm\}dec} \qquad \frac{\pi \vdash U{:}\theta}{\pi \vdash \textbf{call } I(U){:}comm} \ \text{if } (I{:}\theta \to comm) \in \pi$$

We now consider the various possibilities for U and θ.

3.1 Expression Parameters

When expression parameters are used, the U-phrase becomes an E-phrase, and θ becomes τexp, where $\tau \in \{int, bool\}$. Definition, invocation, and parameter reference appear as follows:

$(((\textbf{var}\ A: \textbf{newint}_{\varnothing}^{intloc\ class})_{\varnothing}^{\pi_1 dec};$

$(\textbf{proc}\ P(M:intexp) = (A_{\pi_2}^{intloc} := M_{\pi_2}^{intexp})_{\pi_2}^{comm})_{\pi_1}^{\pi_3 dec})_{\varnothing}^{\pi_4 dec}$

$\textbf{in}\ (\textbf{call}\ P_{\pi_4}^{intexp \rightarrow comm} (@A_{\pi_4}^{intloc})_{\pi_4}^{intexp})_{\pi_4}^{comm})^{comm}$

where $\pi_1 = \{A:intloc\}$, $\pi_2 = \pi_1 \uplus \{M:intexp\} = \{A:intloc, M:intexp\}$,

$\pi_3 = \{P:intexp \rightarrow comm\}$, $\pi_4 = \pi_1 \cup \pi_3$

Figure 3.1 _____

D ::= $\cdots$ | **proc** $I_1(I_2:\tau exp) = C$ where $\tau \in \{int, bool\}$

C ::= $\cdots$ | **call** I(E)

E ::= $\cdots$ | I

Figure 3.1 shows the linear form of the attributed syntax tree for the program **var** A: **newint; proc** $P(M:intexp) = A:=M$ **in call** $P(@A)$. The program holds no surprises; $@A$ is an expression parameter and is typed *intexp*. An invocation like **call** $P(0=1)$ is unacceptable, because expression $0=1$ has type *boolexp*. Also, note the difference between the program in the figure and **var** $A:\textbf{newint};$ **proc** $P(M:intloc) = M := @M+1$ **in call** $P(A)$. Here, the formal parameter has type *intloc*—the actual parameter is in fact a variable parameter, rather than an expression parameter. Beginning programmers often miss the distinction between so-called ''value'' parameters and ''reference'' parameters. Here, the distinction is syntactic, because ''value'' parameters are members of the Expression syntax domain, whereas ''reference'' parameters are members of the Variable domain.

In this example, **fun** $F(X:intexp) = X+1$, **fun** $G(Y:intexp \rightarrow intexp) = G(1)$ **in** $\cdots G(F) \cdots$, is F an expression parameter? Strictly speaking, the answer is no, because expressions have type attributes of only *intexp* and *boolexp*. But parameterized functions make useful parameters, and the collection of phrases of type *intexp* $\rightarrow$ *intexp* form a ''semantically meaningful syntactic class,'' so we will allow them as parameters.

A crucial issue regarding expression parameters is the evaluation strategy. There are two obvious possibilities:

1. Evaluate the actual parameter immediately at the point of invocation. This is eager evaluation, known as *call-by-value*.
2. Delay evaluation of the actual parameter until the point of its use in the body of the abstraction. This is lazy evaluation, known as *call-by-name*.

Consider this example:

> **var** A: **newint**; **proc** P (M :*intexp*) = A:=M; A:=M
> **in** A:=1; **call** P (@A+1)

If the actual parameter, @A+1, is eagerly evaluated, a 2 is bound to M, and the two uses of M in P denote 2. If @A+1 is lazily evaluated, however, then (a representation of) @A+1 is bound to M, and the net effect is the same as copying @A+1 for the uses of M in P, giving A:=@A+1; A:=@A+1. Thus, the first use of M evaluates to 2 and the second evaluates to 3.

As for lazily evaluated abstractions, there is a copy rule (given in Section 3.3) for lazily evaluated parameters; it states that the semantics of

$$\cdots \textbf{define } I_1 (I_2 : \tau) = U \cdots \textbf{ in } \cdots \textbf{invoke } I_1 (V) \cdots$$

is the same as the semantics of

$$\cdots \quad \cdots \textbf{ in } \cdots [V/I_2]U \cdots$$

In principle, the copy rule should make lazy evaluation easy to understand, but in practice, difficulties arise. Perhaps it is our training from algebra, but if we examine just the code for procedure P, namely, **proc** P (M :*intexp*) = A:=M; A:=M, we tend to assume that M is a constant integer value, and we conclude that the second instance of A:=M is redundant. Eager evaluation is consistent with this conclusion, since M will be bound to a constant integer value. For this reason, eagerly evaluated parameters are more ''predictable'' than lazily evaluated ones.

This conceptual difficulty with lazy evaluation is due to: (i) the change in the store as a procedure evaluates, and (ii) the aliasing of a location by two different names. (In the example, once @A+1 binds to M, both A and M reference the same location.) If either (i) or (ii) is absent, lazily evaluated parameters are predictable. Indeed, Chapter 7 shows that lazily evaluated parameters work well within functional languages, which lack store. You are given the challenging and important exercise of writing the imperative language's typing rules so that they prevent the aliasing of a location by two different names within a procedure. (See Donohue 1977, Reynolds 1981b, and Tennent 1991 for background.)

Most languages use eager evaluation of expression actual parameters; several, notably Algol-60, Miranda, and Haskell, use lazy evaluation. Finally, note that an actual parameter that is itself parameterized, for example, a parameterized function actual parameter, is normally transmitted by lazy evaluation.

3.2 Semantics of Parameter Transmission

The semantics of eager and lazy evaluation of expression parameters bears strong resemblance to the semantics of eager and lazy evaluation of expression abstractions. Since we are studying expression parameters to procedures, we will assume that the procedure is evaluated lazily, which is the norm. We begin with eagerly evaluated parameters.

A parameterized procedure, $\pi \vdash \textbf{proc } I_1(I_2:\tau exp) = C: \{I_1:\tau exp \to comm\}dec$, has as its meaning a function that requires the environment, the value of the actual parameter, and the store to compute a new store. That is, I_1 denotes a function $p \in Env_\pi \to [\![\tau]\!] \to [\![comm]\!]$. The semantics is

$$[\![\pi \vdash \textbf{proc } I_1(I_2:\tau exp) = C: \{I_1:\tau exp \to comm\}dec]\!]e\ s = (\{I_1 = p\}, s)$$
$$\text{where } p\ v\ s' = [\![\pi \uplus \{I_2:\tau exp\} \vdash C: comm]\!](e \uplus \{I_2=v\})\ s'$$

and $e \uplus \{I=u\} = \{I=u\} \cup (e - \{(I=v) \mid (I=v) \in e\})$; that is, $e \uplus \{I=u\}$ is the environment that contains the pair $(I=u)$ and all the other pairs in e (less the one for I, if any). The invocation of the procedure forces the evaluation of the actual parameter:

$$[\![\pi \vdash \textbf{call } I_1(E): comm]\!]e\ s = p\ ([\![\pi \vdash E: \tau exp]\!]e\ s)\ s, \text{ where } (I_1 = p) \in e$$

The actual parameter, E, is evaluated with the environment and store to an integer (or boolean). The semantics of formal parameter reference looks like the semantics of an eagerly evaluated abstraction invocation:

$$[\![\pi \vdash I_2: \tau exp]\!]e\ s = v, \text{ where } (I_2=v) \in e$$

Figure 3.2 shows the semantics of the example in the previous section with an empty storage vector and eager evaluation of the actual parameter. The figure shows clearly a potential ambiguity: If the language uses eagerly evaluated expression parameters but uses lazily evaluated functions (expression abstractions), then the semantics for identifier lookup depends upon whether the identifier denotes a parameter or a function. In such a case, parameter and function names must be distinguished, say, by assigning distinct typing attributes, for example, $I:\tau exp$ to a function and $I:\tau param$ to a formal parameter. The details are left as an exercise.

A second issue is nontermination of the evaluation of the actual parameter. If actual parameter evaluation would loop, then so would the invocation. For example, say that $[\![\pi \vdash \textbf{loop}: intexp]\!]e\ s = \bot$. Then, $[\![\pi \vdash \textbf{call } I_1(\textbf{loop}):comm]\!]e\ s = p \bot s$, and we legislate that $p \bot s = \bot$. We say that p is a *strict* function of its actual parameter.

Next, we consider lazy evaluation. Here, the actual parameter is evaluated with the store only when the corresponding formal parameter is referenced. Thus, a procedure, $\pi \vdash \textbf{proc } I_1(I_2:\tau exp) = C: \{I_1:\tau exp \to comm\}dec$, requires the environment, an actual

$\llbracket \vdash \textbf{var } A \textbf{: newint}; \textbf{ proc } P\,(M:intexp) = A:=M; A:=M \textbf{ in } A:=1; \textbf{call } P\,(@A+1): comm \rrbracket \langle\rangle$

$= \llbracket \pi_2 \vdash A:=1; \textbf{call } P\,(@A+1): comm \rrbracket e_2\ s_2$

     where $\pi_2 = \{A: intloc, P: intexp{\to}comm\,\}$

     and $(e_2, s_2) = \llbracket \varnothing \vdash \textbf{var } A \textbf{: newint}; \textbf{ proc } P\,(M:intexp) = (A:=M; A:=M): \pi_2 dec \rrbracket \varnothing\ \langle\rangle$

       $= (\{A = loc_1, P = p\,\}, \langle 0\rangle),$

         where $p\,v\,s' = \llbracket \pi_1 \vdash A:=M; A:=M: comm \rrbracket(\{A = loc_1, M = v\,\})\ s'$

         and $\pi_1 = \{A: intloc, M: intexp\,\}$

$= \llbracket \pi_2 \vdash \textbf{call } P\,(@A+1): comm \rrbracket e_2\ (\llbracket \pi_2 \vdash A:=1: comm \rrbracket e_2\ \langle 0\rangle)$

$= \llbracket \pi_2 \vdash \textbf{call } P\,(@A+1): comm \rrbracket e_2\ \langle 1\rangle$

$= p(\llbracket \pi_2 \vdash @A+1: intexp \rrbracket e_2\ \langle 1\rangle)\ \langle 1\rangle$

$= p(plus(lookup(loc_1, \langle 1\rangle),\ 1))\ \langle 1\rangle\ =\ p\,2\,\langle 1\rangle$

$= \llbracket \pi_1 \vdash A:=M; A:=M: comm \rrbracket e_3\ \langle 1\rangle,\ \text{where } e_3 = \{A = loc_1, M = 2\,\}$

$= \llbracket \pi_1 \vdash A:=M: comm \rrbracket e_3\ (\llbracket \pi_1 \vdash A:=M: comm \rrbracket e_3\ \langle 1\rangle)$

$= \llbracket \pi_1 \vdash A:=M: comm \rrbracket e_3\ (update(loc_1,\ \llbracket \pi_1 \vdash M: intexp \rrbracket e_3\ \langle 1\rangle,\ \langle 1\rangle))$

$= \llbracket \pi_1 \vdash A:=M: comm \rrbracket e_3\ (update(loc_1, 2, \langle 1\rangle))$

$= \llbracket \pi_1 \vdash A:=M: comm \rrbracket e_3\ \langle 2\rangle\ = update(loc_1, \llbracket \pi_1 \vdash M: intexp \rrbracket e_3\ \langle 2\rangle,\ \langle 2\rangle)$

$= update(loc_1, 2, \langle 2\rangle)\ =\ \langle 2\rangle$

Figure 3.2 _____

parameter *function*, and the store to produce a new store. That is, I_1 denotes a function $p \in Env_\pi \to \llbracket \tau exp \rrbracket \to \llbracket comm \rrbracket$. We have the following:

     $\llbracket \pi \vdash \textbf{proc } I_1\,(I_2:\tau exp) = C: \{I_1: \tau exp \to comm\,\}dec \rrbracket e\ s = (\{I_1 = p\,\}, s)$

       where $p\,f\,s' = \llbracket \pi \uplus \{I_2:\tau exp\,\} \vdash C: comm \rrbracket(e \uplus \{I_2 = f\,\})\ s'$

     $\llbracket \pi \vdash \textbf{call } I_1\,(E): comm \rrbracket e\ s = p\,f\,s,\ \text{where } (I_1{=}p) \in e$

       and $f\,s' = \llbracket \pi \vdash E: \tau exp \rrbracket e\ s'$

     $\llbracket \pi \vdash I_2: \tau exp \rrbracket e\ s = f\,(s),\ \text{where } (I_2{=}f) \in e$

The crucial feature is the semantics of identifier reference, which supplies the current store to the formal parameter. This matches the semantics of lazy evaluation of expression abstractions. Figure 3.3 recalculates the meaning of the example with lazy evaluation.

     The typing rules can be proved sound with respect to either eager evaluation or lazy evaluation semantics. First, here is the present syntax of type attributes:

$[\![\vdash \textbf{var } A\!:\!\textbf{newint}; \textbf{proc } P\,(M\!:\!intexp) = (A:=M; A:=M) \textbf{ in } A:=1; \textbf{call } P\,(@A+1)\!:comm]\!]\langle\rangle$

$= [\![\pi_2 \vdash A:=1; \textbf{call } P\,(@A+1)\!:comm]\!]e_2\, s_2$

   where $\pi_2 = \{A\!:\!intloc, P\!:\!intexp\!\to\!comm\,\}$

   and $(e_2, s_2) = [\![\varnothing \vdash \textbf{var } A\!:\!\textbf{newint}; \textbf{proc } P\,(M\!:\!intexp) = (A:=M; A:=M)\!:\pi_2 dec]\!]\varnothing\,\langle\rangle$

      $= (\{A = loc_1, P = p\}, \langle 0\rangle),$

      where $p\, f\, s' = [\![\pi_1 \vdash A:=M; A:=M\!:comm]\!](\{A = loc_1, M = f\})\, s'$

      and $\pi_1 = \{A\!:\!intloc, M\!:\!intexp\,\}$

$= [\![\pi_2 \vdash \textbf{call } P\,(@A+1)\!:comm]\!]e_2\, ([\![\pi_2 \vdash A:=1\!:comm]\!]e_2\, \langle 0\rangle)$

$= [\![\pi_2 \vdash \textbf{call } P\,(@A+1)\!:comm]\!]e_2\, \langle 1\rangle$

$= p\, f_1\, \langle 1\rangle,$ where $f_1(s') = [\![\pi_2 \vdash @A+1\!:intexp]\!]e_2\, s'$

$= [\![\pi_1 \vdash A:=M; A:=M\!:comm]\!]e_3\, \langle 1\rangle,$ where $e_3 = \{A = loc_1, M = f_1\}$

$= [\![\pi_1 \vdash A:=M\!:comm]\!]e_3\, ([\![\pi_1 \vdash A:=M\!:comm]\!]e_3\, \langle 1\rangle)$

$= [\![\pi_1 \vdash A:=M\!:comm]\!]e_3\, (update(loc_1, [\![\pi_1 \vdash M\!:intexp]\!]e_3\, \langle 1\rangle, \langle 1\rangle))$

$= [\![\pi_1 \vdash A:=M\!:comm]\!]e_3\, (update(loc_1, f_1\langle 1\rangle, \langle 1\rangle))$

$= [\![\pi_1 \vdash A:=M\!:comm]\!]e_3\, (update(loc_1, ([\![\pi_2 \vdash @A+1\!:intexp]\!]e_2\, \langle 1\rangle), \langle 1\rangle))$

$= [\![\pi_1 \vdash A:=M\!:comm]\!]e_3\, (update(loc_1, 2, \langle 1\rangle)) = [\![\pi_1 \vdash A:=M\!:comm]\!]e_3\, \langle 2\rangle$

$= update(loc_1, [\![\pi_1 \vdash M\!:intexp]\!]e_3\, \langle 2\rangle, \langle 2\rangle)$

$= update(loc_1, ([\![\pi_2 \vdash @A+1\!:intexp]\!]e_3\, \langle 2\rangle), \langle 2\rangle)$

$= update(loc_1, 3, \langle 2\rangle) = \langle 3\rangle$

Figure 3.3

$\theta ::= \tau \mid \tau exp \mid comm \mid \delta \mid \delta\, class \mid \pi dec \mid \theta_1 \to \theta_2$

$\tau ::= int \mid bool$

$\delta ::= intloc \mid \pi$

$\pi ::= \{j\!:\!\theta_j\}_{j\in J}$ where J is a finite set, and $J \subseteq$ Identifier

As stated in Section 2.15, each type attribute, θ, names a set of values, $[\![\theta]\!]$. For sets S and T, let $S \to T$ be the set of functions that map arguments from S to answers in T. For the case of lazy evaluation semantics, we say that $[\![\theta_1 \to \theta_2]\!] = [\![\theta_1]\!] \to [\![\theta_2]\!]$. (Thus far, θ_2 has been *comm*, but θ_2 can be different when functions, modules, etc., are given parameters.) For example, $[\![intexp \to comm]\!] = [\![intexp]\!] \to [\![comm]\!] = (Int \to Store) \to (Store \to Store_\perp)$.

Now, the typing rules can be proved sound with respect to the lazy evaluation semantics. (See Chapter 2, Section 2.3.) We must prove $[\![\pi \vdash U\!:\!\theta]\!] \in Env_\pi \to [\![\theta]\!]$.

The key to the result is to prove, for $e \in Env_\pi$, that

$$[\![\pi \vdash \textbf{define } I_1(I_2{:}\theta_1) = U{:}\{I{:}\theta_2\}dec]\!]e \in [\![\{I_1{:}\theta_1 \to \theta_2\}dec]\!]$$

and this means we must prove, for every $v \in [\![\theta_1]\!]$, that $[\![\pi \uplus \{I_2{:}\theta_1\} \vdash U{:}\theta_2]\!]$ $(e \uplus \{I_2{=}v\}) \in [\![\theta_2]\!]$. But this follows from the inductive hypothesis for U, since $e \uplus \{I_2{=}v\} \in Env_{\pi \uplus \{I{:}\theta_1\}}$.

When eager evaluation semantics is used, the soundness proof is more complex because the definition of $[\![\theta_1 \to \theta_2]\!]$ is more complex. For example, $[\![\tau exp \to comm]\!]$ must be $[\![\tau]\!] \to [\![comm]\!]$. The appropriate definition for $[\![\theta_1 \to \theta_2]\!]$ and the soundness proof for eager evaluation semantics is left as an interesting exercise.

3.3 A Copy Rule for Lazily Evaluated Parameters

We observed earlier that there is a copy rule for lazily evaluated parameters; a program of the form

$$\cdots \textbf{define } I_1 (I_2{:}\tau) = U \cdots \textbf{ in } \cdots \textbf{invoke } I_1(V) \cdots$$

has the same meaning as

$$\cdots \qquad \cdots \textbf{ in } \cdots [V/I_2]U \cdots$$

We now formalize the copy rule, and in doing so, uncover a program transformation law that lies at the heart of this book.

Rather than define a copy rule specifically for parameterized abstractions, we find it more convenient to retain the copy rule from Chapter 2 and augment it with a rule for parameter binding. The intuition is that a parameterized abstraction is, first of all, an abstraction. To make this point as strongly as possible, we revise the syntax of a parameterized abstraction from

$$\textbf{define } I_1 (I_2{:}\theta) = U$$

to

$$\textbf{define } I_1 = \lambda I_2{:}\theta.\, U$$

That is, I_1 names a U-phrase that is parameterized on I_2. The parameterized phrase, $\lambda I_2{:}\theta.\, U$, is called a *lambda abstraction*. (The use of the ''λ'' and ''.'' are for historical reasons; read the symbols as mere separators between the formal parameter and the body of the abstraction.) For the record, the typing rule for the lambda abstraction is

$$\frac{\pi \uplus \{ I{:}\theta_1 \} \vdash E{:}\theta_2}{\pi \vdash (\lambda\, I{:}\theta_1.\, E){:}\theta_1 \rightarrow \theta_2}$$

and its semantics is

$$[\![\pi \vdash \lambda I{:}\theta_1.\, E{:}\theta_1 \rightarrow \theta_2]\!]e = f,$$
$$\text{where } f\,v = [\![\pi \uplus \{ I{:}\theta_1 \} \vdash E{:}\theta_2]\!](e \uplus \{ I{=}v \})$$

Now, it is clear that the copy rule from Chapter 2 can be applied to an example like

var A:**newint**; **proc** $P = \lambda X{:}intexp.\, A{:}{=}X$ **in call** $P(@A{+}1)$

giving

var A:**newint in** $(\lambda X{:}intexp.\, A{:}{=}X)(@A{+}1)$

So, we require a rule that binds the actual parameter, $@A{+}1$, to the formal parameter, X. We use this *parameter copy rule*:

$$(\lambda I{:}\theta.\, U)V \;\Rightarrow\; [V/I]U$$

where $[V/I]$ stands for the syntactic substitution of V for occurrences of I in U. The parameter copy rule lets us transform the previous example into this:

var A:**newint in** $[@A{+}1/X](A{:}{=}X) =$ **var** A:**newint in** $A{:}{=}@A{+}1$

Now that the lambda abstraction construct has been introduced, we must take great care with substitution into lambda abstractions, that is, with $[V/I](\lambda I'.\, U)$. Consider this example:

var A: **newint**;
fun $F = @A{+}1$; **fun** $G = (\lambda A\,{:}intexp.\, A{+}F)$
in $\cdots$

Recall that a sequential declaration, **define** $I{=}U;D$, can be transformed by the copy rule from Chapter 2: **define** $I{=}U;D \Rightarrow$ **define** $I{=}U, [U/I]D$. If we eliminate the second semi-colon in the example, we must substitute into the lambda abstraction:

$\Rightarrow$ **var** A: **newint**; (**fun** $F{=}@A{+}1$, **fun** $G = [@A{+}1/F](\lambda A\,{:}intexp.\, A{+}F))$ **in** $\cdots$

It seems we should substitute $@A{+}1$ for the occurrence of F in the body of G, but we obtain an incorrect result:

var A: **newint**; (**fun** $F = @A+1$, **fun** $G = (\lambda A\ :intexp.\ A+(@A+1)))$ **in** $\cdots$

The problem is that the body of F, that is, $@A+1$, contains a reference to a *free* (nonlo-
cally defined) identifier, A, that clashes with G's formal parameter, A. The proper way
of performing substitution is: If an expression, V, that contains a free identifier, I, is
substituted into $(\lambda I{:}\theta.\ U)$ (note that the formal parameter is the same I), then the
lambda abstraction must be rewritten so that the occurrences of I are renamed to some
fresh identifier. Then the substitution is made. In the above example, if G's formal
parameter is renamed to, say, B, then we have the following:

var A: **newint**; (**fun** $F = @A+1$, **fun** $G = [@A+1/\ F\ ](\lambda B\ :intexp.\ B+F))$ **in** $\cdots$
$= $ **var** A: **newint**; (**fun** $F = @A+1$, **fun** $G = (\lambda B\ :intexp.\ B+(@A+1)))$ **in** $\cdots$

The change of the formal parameter name from A to B does not affect the semantics of
G, and it allows the substitution to complete.

We can formalize this by the following definition of substitution into lambda
abstractions. (For simplicity, we consider just single substitution, $[V/I](\lambda I'{:}\theta.\ U)$. The
definition of simultaneous substitution, $[V_1/I_1, V_2/I_2, \ldots, V_n/I_n](\lambda I'{:}\theta.\ U)$, is left as as
a stimulating exercise.) The definition is given in three clauses. The first says that no
substitution occurs when the parameter name, I, matches the I that should be replaced:

$[V/I]\lambda I{:}\theta.\ U = \lambda I{:}\theta.\ U$

The second clause states the conditions under which a normal substitution is undertaken.
(The definition of "free" is given below.)

$[V/I]\lambda J{:}\theta.\ U = \lambda J{:}\theta.\ [V/I]U$, if $I \neq J$ and J is not free in V

The third clause states that the formal parameter, J, and all its uses must be renamed to
some new identifier, K, if there is a reference to a nonlocal J in V:

$[V/I]\lambda J{:}\theta.\ U = \lambda K{:}\theta.\ [V/I]\ [K/J]U$
    if $I \neq J$, J is free in V, and K is a fresh identifier

The definition of "free" can be formalized by a recursive definition. Say that we
use this syntax:

$D ::= $ **proc** $I{=}A \mid $ **var** $I{:}T \mid D_1,D_2$
$A ::= \lambda I{:}\theta.\ C$
$T ::= $ **newint**
$C ::= L{:}{=}E \mid C_1;C_2 \mid $ **call** $I(E)$
$E ::= N \mid @L \mid E_1{+}E_2 \mid I$
$L ::= I$
$N ::= n$

An identifier, I, is *free in* U if $I \in FV(U)$, where $FV(U)$ is defined:

$$FV(\textbf{proc } I = A) = FV(A) \qquad FV(C_1;C_2) = FV(C_1) \cup FV(C_2)$$

$$FV(\textbf{var } I{:}T) = FV(T) \qquad FV(\textbf{call } I(E)) = \{I\} \cup FV(E)$$

$$FV(D_1,D_2) = FV(D_1) \cup FV(D_2) \qquad FV(@L) = FV(L)$$

$$FV(\lambda I{:}\theta.\, C) = FV(C) - \{I\} \qquad FV(E_1+E_2) = FV(E_1) \cup FV(E_2)$$

$$FV(\textbf{newint}) = \varnothing \qquad FV(I) = \{I\}$$

$$FV(L{:=}E) = FV(L) \cup FV(E) \qquad FV(n) = \varnothing$$

(Note: "*FV*," the traditional name of this definition, stands for "free variables.") Substitution is defined in the usual way:

$$[V/I]\textbf{proc } I = A = \textbf{proc } I = [V/I]A$$

$$[V/I]\textbf{var } I{:}T = \textbf{var } I{:}[V/I]T$$

$$[V/I]D_1,D_2 = [V/I]D_1, [V/I]D_2$$

$$[V/I]\lambda I{:}\theta.\, C = \lambda I{:}\theta.\, C$$

$$[V/I]\lambda J{:}\theta.\, C = \lambda J{:}\theta.\, [V/I]C, \text{ if } I \neq J \text{ and } J \text{ is not free in } V$$

$$[V/I]\lambda J{:}\theta.\, C = \lambda K{:}\theta.\, [V/I]\,[K/J]C$$

$$\qquad \text{if } I \neq J,\ J \text{ is free in } V,\ \text{and } K \text{ is a fresh identifier}$$

$$[V/I]\textbf{newint} = \textbf{newint}$$

$$[V/I]L{:=}E = [V/I]L{:=}[V/I]E$$

$$[V/I]C_1;C_2 = [V/I]C_1; [V/I]C_2$$

$$[V/I]\textbf{call } I(E) = V([V/I]E)$$

$$[V/I]\textbf{call } I'(E) = \textbf{call } I'([V/I]E), \text{ if } I \neq I'$$

$$[V/I]@L = @[V/I]L$$

$$[V/I]E_1+E_2 = [V/I]E_1+[V/I]E_2$$

$$[V/I]I = V$$

$$[V/I]I' = I', \text{ if } I \neq I'$$

$$[V/I]n = n$$

Like the copy rule from Chapter 2, the parameter copy rule preserves the typing of a phrase, and this follows from the preservation of typing by substitution: If $\pi \uplus \{I{:}\theta_1\} \vdash U{:}\theta_2$, and $\pi \vdash V{:}\theta_1$, then $\pi \vdash [V/I]U{:}\theta_2$. In principle, the proof of this claim goes like the proof of Theorem 2.2. But substitution into a lambda abstraction raises difficulties when the formal parameter must be changed. Rather than tackle the proof now, we defer it to Chapter 6, where lambda abstractions are studied in depth.

The meaning of a phrase is also preserved by the parameter copy rule, since meaning is preserved by substitution: $[\![\pi \uplus \{I{:}\theta_2\} \vdash U{:}\theta_1]\!](e \uplus \{I = [\![\pi \vdash V{:}\theta_2]\!]e\}) = [\![\pi \vdash [V/I]U{:}\theta_2]\!]e$. The proof is delayed until Chapter 6.

Thanks to the soundness of the copy rules, a core language that is extended by lazily evaluated abstractions and parameters can be given a correct semantics via the semantics for the core language plus the copy rules for abstractions and parameters: We apply the copy rules to the program to rewrite it to a core language program and we utilize the core language semantics to give meaning.

3.4 Other Varieties of Parameters

The parameterization principle lets us create numeral parameters, command parameters, declaration parameters, variable parameters, and so on. Here is an example that uses the first two varieties:

> **const** $K=2$; **var** A: **newint**;
> **proc** $P(M:comm) = A := K+1$; M;
> **proc** $Q(X:int) = A := X$
> **in call** P (**call** Q (2)); **call** P(**call** P(**call** Q (K))); **call** P ($A := K$)

The first two invocations of P resemble those found in Pascal; the last, **call** $P(A := K)$, is startling but is syntactically acceptable. (If the **call** keywords confuse you, delete them all—they are just "syntactic sugar.")

Lazy evaluation is the norm for a command parameter—the command is evaluated only when the corresponding formal parameter is referenced. In contrast, an eagerly evaluated command parameter is evaluated when it is bound to the formal parameter; this can be used to define a backtracking point. For example,

> **var** A: **newint**;
> **proc** $P(M: comm) = \cdots$ **if** *"error"* **then** M **else** $\cdots$ **fi**
> **in** $\cdots$ **call** $P(A := 0)$

The eager evaluation of $A := 0$ causes a store value to be bound to M. (Recall the eager evaluation semantics: $[\![\pi \vdash \textbf{call } \text{I}(\text{C}): comm]\!]e\ s\ =\ p\ ([\![\pi \vdash \text{C}: comm]\!]e\ s)\ s$, where $(\text{I}=p) \in e$.) If, during the evaluation of P's body, *"error"* holds true, M is referenced and this extracts the store as it appeared when P was called but with A set to 0. The current store is discarded and replaced by the store named by M, effectively undoing P's actions. Of course, an implementation would need a more efficient way of implementing the backtracking than saving a copy of the store.

Declaration parameters can be used by modules to build bigger modules, for example,

module *COUNTER* $(M : \{ X : intloc, INIT : comm \} dec) =$
   $\{ \textbf{import } M; \textbf{ proc } P = (\textbf{call } INIT; X := @X+1) \};$
module $N = \{ \textbf{var } X : \textbf{newint}; \textbf{ proc } INIT = X := 0 \};$
import *COUNTER* (**import** N) **in** $\cdots$

The typing attribute of the formal parameter, M, makes it possible to type check and understand the body of the *COUNTER* module. Also, it is syntactically legal to write, say, **import** *COUNTER*(**var** X : **newint**; **proc** $INIT = X := 2$).

Finally, we consider variable parameters. This includes not only integer variables but also record variables, so we can write:

class $K = $ **record**
      var A : **newint**;
      proc $P (B : intloc) = A := @A + @B$
   end;
var $R : K$;
proc $Q (Y : \{ A : intloc, P : intloc \rightarrow comm \}) = $ **call** $Y.P (Y.A)$
in $A := 0$; **call** $Q (R)$

We observe in the example that the type of formal parameter Y is descriptive but wordy. It would be convenient to abbreviate it by the name K, since K has a corresponding type $\{ A : intloc, P : intloc \rightarrow comm \} class$, and write: **proc** $Q (Y : K) = $ **call** $Y.P (Y.A)$. But a drawback to using class names as formal parameter types is that it misleads the programmer about the nature of type structures, which are first and foremost storage allocation routines and *not* type attributes. Indeed, if we are using type structures as type attributes, we can write **proc** $P (A : \textbf{newint}) = \cdots$. This looks wrong, because A is not freshly allocated nor is it to be bound to a storage allocation routine. The abuse of type structures as type attributes is motivated by type equivalence issues, which we now examine.

3.5 Type Equivalence

Type equivalence is crucial to parameterized abstraction invocation—the type attribute of the actual parameter must match the type attribute of the formal. In the case of *intloc*- or *intexp*-typed actual parameters, type equivalence is easy to check. But consider:

> **class** R = **record var** X: **newint, var** Y: **newint end**;
>
> **var** E: R,
>
> **var** F: **record var** X: **newint, var** Y: **newint end**,
>
> **var** G: **record var** Y: **newint, var** X: **newint end**,
>
> **proc** $P(Q: \{X{:}intloc, Y{:}intloc\}) = \cdots$

Which of E, F, and G can be actual parameters that bind to Q? The typing rules in Section 2.15 state that all three have the same type attribute, and all of them can bind to Q. The typing rules enforce *structural type equivalence*, because the underlying structure of a value determines its type.

An alternative to structural type equivalence is *name equivalence*, also known as *occurrence equivalence*. In principle, in name equivalence typing, each class definition names a new type, distinct from all others. Two values have the same type if their typing information stems from the same class definition or from the same built-in type. But in practice, the typing is more complex: Primitive types (for example, *intloc*) are treated as equivalent, regardless of whether they are named by class definitions or not, but each occurrence of a compound type structure (for example, **record** or **array**) is treated as a new type, whether it is named or not. Occurrence equivalence is used when type structures are used in place of type attributes in procedure definitions. For the above example, say that we recode P as **proc** $P(Q{:}R) = \cdots$. With occurrence equivalence typing, only E is an acceptable actual parameter for Q. Indeed, all of E, F, and G have different types, because they were declared with different occurrences of type-structure expressions.

An implementation of occurrence equivalence typing attaches a unique "occurrence tag," called a *brand*, to each compound type-structure expression. The idea can be summarized by a revised typing rule for the record structure:

$$\frac{\pi \vdash D: \pi_1\, dec}{\pi \vdash \textbf{record } D \textbf{ end}: occ\, \pi_1\, class} \qquad \text{where } occ \text{ is a unique counter or address value}$$

Since the value of occ is unique for each record structure, we obtain these typings for the above example:

> R : $0\{X{:}intloc, Y{:}intloc\}class$
>
> E : $0\{X{:}intloc, Y{:}intloc\}$
>
> F : $1\{X{:}intloc, Y{:}intloc\}$
>
> G : $2\{X{:}intloc, Y{:}intloc\}$
>
> P : $0\{X{:}intloc, Y{:}intloc\} \to comm$

Occurrence equivalence typing is favored because it supports a form of "encapsulation": Procedures that are parameterized on one brand of record structure cannot be abused by being given another. Occurrence equivalence is also straightforward to implement. Structural equivalence checking is favored because it has a natural logic (for example, our typing rules), and it supports the linking of a program to external files or modules, a situation where the sharing of a single brand is often impossible. Most languages support just one form of typing equivalence, but Modula-3 allows the user some flexibility in choosing the appropriate typing equivalence.

The denotational semantics developed so far suits structural equivalence, but there is no harm in imposing a more restrictive equivalence such as occurrence equivalence. The semantics of programs stay the same, just fewer programs are given semantics.

3.6 Type-Structure Parameters

Type-structure parameters can be used to build different versions of classes. For example, different implementations of a "stack" structure can be used with class K in

> **class** *STACK1* = **record var** A: **newint; proc** *PUSH* = A := 0 **end**;
> **class** *STACK2* = **record var** A : **newint; proc** *PUSH* = A := 1 **end**;
> **class** K = (T: { A :*intloc*, *PUSH* :*comm* }*class*) =
>   **record var** S :T; **proc** *PUSH2* = **call** *S.PUSH*; **call** *S.PUSH* **end**;
> **var** X: K(*STACK1*); **var** Y: K(*STACK2*)

The type-structure parameter makes K "generic" in the data structures it handles, yet compile-time type checking is preserved.

Lazy evaluation is the proper way to transmit a type-structure parameter. The semantics of eager evaluation (namely, $\llbracket \pi \vdash \mathbf{invoke}\, \mathrm{I(T)}: \theta \rrbracket e\ s = p\ v\ s'$, where $(v, s') =$ $\llbracket \pi \vdash \mathrm{T}: \delta class \rrbracket e\ s$ and $(\mathrm{I}{=}p) \in e$) would activate the actual parameter and bind the allocated storage to the formal parameter, making it behave much like the "value parameter" in Pascal.

More general formats for type-structure parameters have been proposed. Ada allows its modules to be parameterized on type structures whose type attributes are unknown, for example,

> **module** M(T: Type-structure) = { **var** A: T; **proc** *SAVE*(X:T) = A := @X }
> $\cdots$ **import** M(**newint**) $\cdots$ **in call** *SAVE*(A)

It is crucial that all uses of T in the body of M are independent of the actual value bound to T. Unknowns in the type attributes make typing rules challenging to define. In the example, M's type attribute is apparently $\Delta class \rightarrow \{A{:}\Delta,\ SAVE{:}\Delta{\rightarrow}comm\}dec$, where Δ is an unknown. The typing of **import** M(**newint**) instantiates Δ by *intloc*, since the type attribute of **newint** is *intloc class*. Thus, **import** M(**newint**) has type $\{A{:}intloc,\ SAVE{:}intloc{\rightarrow}comm\}dec$.

The complications in the typing rules reflect complications in the semantics: Type attributes are values in the semantics. This raises serious questions about soundness, as we now see. (If you are not interested in such matters, please skip to the end of this section.) In the above example, M denotes a function whose arguments are the type attribute of its actual parameter, the value of its actual parameter, and the current store. We might define this as follows:

$$[\![\pi \vdash \textbf{module } I_1(I_2:\text{Type-structure}) = D: \{I_1:\Delta class \rightarrow \theta(\Delta)\}dec]\!]e\ s = (\{I_1 = m\}, s)$$
$$\text{where } m(\delta class)\ v\ s' = [\![\pi \uplus \{I_2:\delta class\} \vdash D: \theta(\delta)]\!](e \uplus \{I_2=v\})\ s'$$

We write $\theta(\Delta)$ for the type attribute that has occurrences of the unknown, Δ, in it. $\theta(\delta)$ is the type attribute when the Δ is instantiated by δ. Notice that the above definition is *not* a recursive definition, in the sense of Section 1.3, because $[\![\pi \uplus \{I_2:\delta class\} \vdash D: \theta(\delta)]\!]$ uses δ rather than Δ. Worse yet, to show soundness, we must prove $[\![\pi \vdash \textbf{module } I_1(I_2:\text{Type-structure}) = D: \{I_1:\Delta class \rightarrow \theta(\Delta)\}dec]\!] \in Env_\pi \rightarrow [\![\{I_1:\Delta class \rightarrow \theta(\Delta)\}dec]\!]$, but it is not clear what this even means, since Δ is an unknown.

The semantics of invocation is:

$$[\![\pi \vdash \textbf{import } I(T):\theta(\delta)]\!]e\ s = m\ (\delta class)\ ([\![\pi \vdash T:\delta class]\!]e)\ s,\ \text{where } (I=m) \in e$$

If we attempt to write the argument structure of m, we discover that $m \in (\delta class \in \textit{Type-attribute}) \rightarrow [\![\delta class]\!] \rightarrow Store \rightarrow ([\![\theta(\delta)]\!] \times Store)$. That is, the argument structure of m depends on the *value* of m's first argument. (Also, if the δ is instantiated with a type attribute, δ', containing unknowns, the value of the set $[\![\delta'class]\!]$ is far from trivial to calculate!) This is our first exposure to a *dependent type*, and we will postpone further study of this situation to Chapter 8.

3.7 The Correspondence Principle

Figure 3.4 summarizes the development of parameters for U-abstractions. Given the myriad of parameter forms, a language designer would benefit from a criterion for judging whether the extensions mesh smoothly with the original language. One such criterion is the *correspondence principle*: It suggests that the suitability of parameter forms can be judged by comparing them to the abstraction forms in the language.

The Correspondence Principle:

For every abstraction form, **define** $I_2 = U$, there may be a corresponding parameterization form, **define** $I_1(I_2:\theta) = \cdots$ **in** $\cdots I_1(U)$, (and vice versa) such that the semantics of binding I_2 to U is the same in both.

D∈ Declaration

U∈ Any-syntax-domain

A∈ Actual-parameter

> D ::= $\cdots$ | **define** $I_1(I_2 : \theta) = U$
>
> U ::= $\cdots$ | **invoke** I(A)
>
> A ::= N | E | C | L | D | T

(Note: we will not consider Actual-parameter parameters!)

Figure 3.4 _____

The primary consequence of the correspondence principle is that the semantics of a free (that is, nonlocal) identifier is independent of the way in which the identifier was bound. Thus, all identifiers can be understood in the same way, and components of a large program can be read more easily. A secondary consequence is that the correspondence principle clears the way for uniformly extending a programming language: if a certain form of abstraction already exists in the language (for example, command abstractions), then addition of the corresponding parameter form (for example, command parameters) adds no extra complications to the language and in fact unifies the language's treatment of bindings of the form (for example, commands). By and large, the development in the previous two chapters has followed this pattern, but a few anomalies will be considered momentarily.

When correspondence fails, problems can arise. For example, it is tempting to evaluate functions lazily but expression parameters eagerly. Consider

> **var** A: **newint**; **fun** $F = @A+1$;
>
> **proc** $P(X : intexp) = A := X+F$; $A := X+F$ **in** $\cdots$

Both X and F are *intexp*-typed identifiers, and both were validated by the typing rule $\pi \vdash I : \theta$, where $(I : \theta) \in \pi$, yet one denotes an integer and the other denotes a function from the current store to an integer (cf. Section 3.2). We have lost the relationship between the appearance of a phrase and its meaning, and a consequence is that procedure P cannot be understood without reading the program that encloses it. If the situation is left unchanged, some distinction should be made between expression abstraction identifiers and expression formal parameters. The distinction can be as subtle as different type attributes—*intexp* for F and *intparam* for X—or as explicit as a keyword, for example, $A := X + (\textbf{eval}\,F)$. Neither solution is ideal.

Another issue is the presence of one form of binding and the absence of the other. For example, the imperative language developed so far has numeral abstractions but lacks numeral parameters. For the case of numeral parameters, we noted that they are subsumed by expression parameters, since every numeral can be an expression. But the same argument could be made for numeral abstractions, since **const** I=N is subsumed by the expression abstraction **fun** I=N. If you have experience with Pascal-style const definitions, you may well be upset with their removal, because the **const** form serves the valuable purpose of naming a numeral that a compiler can use to improve the target code it produces. In contrast, a function definition is evaluated at run time, so a compiler cannot use it. Perhaps numeral abstractions should remain. A similar argument can be made for numeral parameters: A compiler can bind them to their formal parameters and create so-called *specialized abstractions*. An example of this is Tennent's notion of *static function*:

> **static-fun** $F(X:int) = X+1$,
> **var** A: **newint** **in** $A:=F(1)+F(3)$

which a compiler can simplify to

> **var** A: **newint** **in** $A:=2+4$

The numeral parameters are examples of *static parameters*. Actual parameters that must be evaluated at run time are *dynamic parameters*. An abstraction that takes a mixture of static and dynamic parameters might be simplified by a compiler by binding just the static parameters, creating a specialized abstraction. An example is

proc $SORT(LENGTH:int, VECTOR:list\text{-}of\,int) = \cdots LENGTH \cdots VECTOR \cdots$
in $\cdots$ **call** $SORT(3, [4,2,6]) \cdots$ **call** $SORT(4, [0,1,3,2] \cdots$ **call** $SORT(3, [4,3,2]) \cdots$

which is simplified to two specialized procedures:

proc $SORT\,3(VECTOR:list\text{-}of\,int) = \cdots 3 \cdots VECTOR \cdots$
proc $SORT\,4(VECTOR:list\text{-}of\,int) = \cdots 4 \cdots VECTOR \cdots$
in $\cdots$ **call** $SORT\,3([4,2,6]) \cdots$ **call** $SORT\,4([0,1,3,2] \cdots$ **call** $SORT\,3([4,3,2]) \cdots$

This exploitation of static parameters is developed into an art form in partial evaluation theory, where a theory of compiling and compiler generation is based on specialized abstractions. See Bjørner, et al. 1988, Consel and Danvy 1993, Jones, et al. 1993, and Launchbury 1992 for additional information.

3.7.1 The Semantics of Correspondence

Denotational semantics can justify when correspondence holds between an abstraction form and a binding form. Consider the lazy evaluation semantics of functions:

$$[\![\pi \vdash \mathbf{fun}\ I_2 = E\colon \{\,I\colon \tau exp\,\} dec]\!]e\ s = (\{\,I_2 = f\,\}, s),\ \text{where}\ f(s') = [\![\pi \vdash E\colon \tau exp]\!]e\ s'$$
$$[\![\pi \vdash I_2\colon \tau exp]\!]e\ s' = f(s'),\ \text{where}\ (I_2 = f) \in e$$

and the semantics of expression parameters:

$$[\![\pi \vdash \mathbf{define}\ I_1(I_2\colon \tau exp) = U\colon \{\,I_1\colon \tau exp \to \theta\,\} dec]\!]e\ s = (\{\,I_1 = g\,\}, s)$$
$$\text{where}\ g\,f\,s' = [\![\pi \uplus \{\,I_2\colon \tau exp\,\} \vdash U\colon \theta]\!](e \uplus \{\,I_2 = f\,\})\ s'$$
$$[\![\pi \vdash \mathbf{invoke}\ I_1(E)\colon \theta]\!]e\ s = g\,f\,s,\ \text{where}\ (I = g) \in e$$
$$\text{and}\ f\,s' = [\![\pi \vdash E\colon \tau exp]\!]e\ s'$$
$$[\![\pi \vdash I_2\colon \tau exp]\!]e\ s' = f(s'),\ \text{where}\ (I_2 = f) \in e$$

To prove the correspondence between the two, we must show that the same meanings result when E is bound to I_2 with the use of store s:

$$[\![\mathbf{fun}\ I_2 = E\ \mathbf{in}\ \cdots\colon \theta]\!]e\ s = [\![\mathbf{define}\ I_1(I_2\colon \tau exp) = \cdots\ \mathbf{in}\ \mathbf{invoke}\ I_1(E)\colon \theta]\!]e\ s$$

where I_1 is fresh. First, we note that $[\![\mathbf{fun}\ I_2 = E\ \mathbf{in}\ \cdots\colon \theta]\!]e\ s = [\![\pi_2 \vdash \cdots\colon \theta]\!](e \uplus \{\,I_2 = [\![\pi \vdash E\colon \tau exp]\!]e\,\})\ s$, where $\pi_2 = \pi \uplus \{\,I_2\colon \tau exp\,\}$. Next, we see that

$$[\![\mathbf{define}\ I_1(I_2\colon \tau exp) = \cdots\ \mathbf{in}\ I_1(E)\colon \theta]\!]e\ s$$
$$= [\![\pi_1 \vdash I_1(E)\colon \theta]\!]\ e_1\ s,\ \text{where}\ \pi_1 = \pi \uplus \{\,I_1\colon \tau exp \to \theta\,\},\ e_1 = e \uplus \{\,I_1 = g\,\},$$
$$\text{where}\ g\,f\,s' = [\![\pi_2 \vdash \cdots\colon \theta]\!](e \uplus \{\,I_2 = f\,\})\ s'$$
$$= g\,f_1\,s,\ \text{where}\ f_1\ s' = [\![\pi_1 \vdash E\colon \tau exp]\!]\ e_1\ s'$$
$$= [\![\pi_2 \vdash \cdots\colon \theta]\!](e \uplus \{\,I_2 = f_1\,\})\ s$$

But $f_1\ s' = [\![\pi_1 \vdash E\colon \tau exp]\!]e_1\ s' = [\![\pi \vdash E\colon \tau exp]\!]e\ s' = f_2\ s'$, since I_1 does not appear in E:

$$= [\![\pi_2 \vdash \cdots\colon \theta]\!](e \uplus \{\,I_2 = f_2\,\}\ s$$
$$= [\![\pi \vdash \mathbf{fun}\ I_2 = E\ \mathbf{in}\ \cdots\colon \theta]\!]e\ s$$

This proof adapts to eagerly evaluated functions and expression parameters, and for that matter, lazy or eager evaluation of other abstraction and parameter forms. This is left as an exercise.

3.8 Parameter Lists

The correspondence principle emphasizes that parameter transmission and abstraction definition are both instances of binding a value to a name. If we desire parameter lists, we must bind multiple values to multiple names. The traditional way to implement a parameter list is the tupling form

> **define** $I(I_1:\theta_1, I_2:\theta_2, \ldots, I_n:\theta_n) = U$

(the I_j's are distinct) along with an invocation form

> **invoke** $I(V_1, V_2, \ldots, V_n)$

that simultaneously binds the actuals V_j to the formals I_j. Here is a sample syntax:

> D ::= $\cdots$ | **define** I(FL)=U
> FL ::= I:θ | I:θ, FL
> U ::= $\cdots$ | **invoke** I(AL)
> AL ::= A | A,AL
> A ::= as in Figure 3.4

The syntax is accurate but cumbersome (try writing its typing rules), so we seek an alternative. The correspondence principle suggests that the binding of multiple actual parameters to multiple formal parameters should correspond to multiple definition bindings, that is, to a compound declaration. With this idea in mind, we produce a revised syntax for parameter lists:

> D ::= $\cdots$ | **define** I(F)=U
> F ::= I:θ | F_1,F_2
> V ::= $\cdots$ | **invoke** I(D)

with the associated typing rules

$$\frac{\pi \uplus \pi_1 \vdash U:\theta}{\pi \vdash \textbf{define } I(F)=U:\{\,I:\pi_1 \to \theta\,\}\,dec} \qquad \frac{\pi \vdash D:\pi_1\,dec}{\pi \vdash \textbf{invoke } I(D):\theta}\ \text{if } (I:\pi_1 \to \theta) \in \pi$$

where $\pi_1 = \textit{type-attrs}(F)$, $\textit{type-attrs}(I{:}\theta) = \{I{:}\theta\}$, and $\textit{type-attrs}(F_1,F_2) = \textit{type-attrs}(F_1) \cup \textit{type-attrs}(F_2)$. Here is an example:

> **var** A:**newint**;
> **proc** $P(W{:}intexp,\ X{:}intloc,\ Y{:}comm,\ Z{:}comm{\to}comm) = X := W;$ **call** $Z(Y)$;
> **proc** $Q = A := 0$
>   **in call** $P(\textbf{fun } W = @A + 2,\ \textbf{proc } Y = \textbf{call } Q,\ \textbf{alias } X = A,\ \textbf{proc } Z(C{:}comm) = \textbf{call } C)$

This format for parameter passing appears in Ada: Actual parameters are labeled by formal parameter names, and the order of the actual parameters is unimportant. (Of course, Ada allows a programmer to omit the labels from the actual parameters; then, the order in which the actual parameters are listed implies the names of the identifiers to which they bind.) The example shows that parameterized commands (for example, *Z*) can be parameters and that the **alias** abstraction is the proper way to bind a location parameter (for example, *X*). If **var** *X*: **newint** was used in the latter case, a fresh location would be allocated for *X*.

The semantics of parameter lists comes from the semantics of declarations:

$[\![\pi \vdash$ **define** $I(F)=U: \{ I{:}\pi_1 \rightarrow \theta \} dec]\!]e\ s = (\{ I{=}p \},\ s)$

    where $p\ e_1\ s_1' = [\![\pi \uplus \pi_1 \vdash U{:}\theta]\!](e \uplus e_1)\ s_1,$ and *type-attrs*(F) $= \pi_1$

$[\![$**invoke** $I(D){:}\theta]\!]e\ s = p\ e_1\ s_1'$

    where $(e_1, s_1) = [\![\pi \vdash D{:}\pi_1 dec]\!]e\ s,$ and $(I{=}p) \in e$

The second semantics equation is crucial. Upon invocation of I, the store at the point of invocation is supplied to the actual parameters. If abstractions are evaluated lazily, then the store is ignored by the actual parameters, and lazy evaluation results. If the abstractions are eager, then the actual parameters are evaluated eagerly as well—correspondence is forced upon the language.

3.9 The Parameterization Principle Is a Lambda Abstraction Principle

Section 3.3 showed that a parameterized abstraction is just an abstraction whose body is a parameterized phrase. We used the lambda abstraction notation, $\lambda I{:}\theta.\ U$, to make this point. The parameterization principle says that phrases of "any semantically meaningful syntactic class" may be parameters; that is, θ can take be any type attribute. Although the lambda abstraction notation is not crucial to this chapter, it makes clear that parameterization is distinct from abstraction. This is confirmed by the typing rules, which use a new type attribute, $\theta_1 \rightarrow \theta_2$, to state the typing of a parameterized phrase. Within the semantics, the meanings of parameterized phrases are functions.

The lambda abstraction notation also suggests that parameterized phrases need not be named. Though it is unlikely that a programmer would prefer to write, say, $(\lambda X{:}intexp.\ A{:}{=}X)(@A{+}1)$ instead of $A{:}{=}@A{+}1$, both commands should be syntactically legal. (This idea is developed in Chapter 5.) For this reason, the parameterization principle is in fact a "lambda abstraction principle," because parameterized phrase forms—lambda abstractions—are allowed in the language.

It is now worthwhile to review what has been developed in the first three chapters. Starting with a core language that had its own syntax, type attributes, typing rules, and denotational semantics, we first added abstraction forms and then added parameter forms.

Each addition augmented the core language with new syntax constructions, new type attributes, new typing rules, and new denotational semantics equations. But the structure of the core language stayed the same, because the additions were independent of the core language and each other—the additions were *orthogonal*. Abstraction and parameterization are perhaps the two most important orthogonal extensions, but others exist, and they will be seen in subsequent chapters. Although the abstraction and parameterization principles are orthogonal, they share the common tool of the identifier to implement their respective namings. The correspondence principle suggests that the commonly used identifier should have the same semantics, regardless of whether is it an abstraction identifier or a parameter identifier. Chapter 5 explores these ideas further.

3.10 Summary

Here is a summary of the application of the parameterization principle. For arbitrary syntax domains U and V, a U-abstraction with a V-parameter has the form

$$D ::= \cdots \mid \textbf{define } I_1(I_2:\theta_1)=U$$

and is invoked by the form

$$U ::= \cdots \mid \textbf{invoke } I(V)$$

The formal parameter may be referenced wherever a V-phrase may appear:

$$V ::= \cdots \mid I$$

The typing rules for definition, invocation, and parameter reference read as follows:

$$\frac{\pi \uplus \{I_2:\theta_1\} \vdash U:\theta_2}{\pi \vdash \textbf{define } I_1(I_2:\theta_1)=U:\{I_1:\theta_1 \to \theta_2\}dec} \qquad \frac{\pi \vdash V:\theta_1}{\pi \vdash \textbf{invoke } I(V):\theta_2} \text{ if } (I:\theta_1 \to \theta_2) \in \pi$$

$$\pi \vdash I:\theta, \quad \text{if } (I:\theta) \in \pi$$

where $\pi_1 \uplus \pi_2 = \pi_2 \cup (\pi_1 - \{(I:v) \mid (I:w) \in \pi_2 \text{ and } (I:v) \in \pi_1\})$. The addition of the new type attribute, $\theta_1 \to \theta_2$, brings the syntax of type attributes to read as follows:

$$\theta ::= \tau \mid \tau exp \mid comm \mid \delta \mid \delta class \mid \pi dec \mid \theta_1 \to \theta_2$$
$$\tau ::= int \mid bool$$
$$\delta ::= intloc \mid \pi$$
$$\pi ::= \{j:\theta_j\}_{j \in J} \text{ such that } J \subseteq \text{Identifier is a finite set}$$

In the case of lazy evaluation semantics, $[\![\theta_1 \to \theta_2]\!] = [\![\theta_1]\!] \to [\![\theta_2]\!]$; that is, it is the set of functions that take arguments from the set $[\![\theta_1]\!]$ and produce answers from the set $[\![\theta_2]\!]$. The lazy evaluation semantics is

$$[\![\pi \vdash \textbf{define } I_1(I_2:\theta_1) = U:\{I_1:\theta_1 \to \theta_2\}dec]\!]e \, s = (\{I_1 = p\}, s)$$

where $p\,f\,s = [\![\pi \uplus \{I_2:\theta_1\} \vdash U: \theta_2]\!](e \uplus \{I_2=f\})\,s$

and $e \uplus \{I=u\} = \{I=u\} \cup (e - \{(I=v) \mid (I=v) \in e\})$

$[\![\pi \vdash \text{invoke } I_1(V): \theta_2]\!]e\,s = p\,f\,s$

where $(I_1 = p) \in e$ and $f\,s' = [\![\pi \vdash V: \theta_1]\!]e\,s'$

$[\![\pi \vdash I_2: \theta]\!]e\,s = f\,s,$ where $(I_2=f) \in e$

A more explicit approach to parameterization introduces the lambda abstraction phrase. The syntax becomes

D ::= $\cdots$ | **define** $I_1 = A$

A ::= $\lambda I:\theta.\,U$

U ::= $\cdots$ | **invoke** $I(V)$

V ::= $\cdots$ | I

The typing rule from Chapter 2 for abstractions works alongside this rule for lambda abstraction:

$$\frac{\pi \uplus \{I:\theta_1\} \vdash E: \theta_2}{\pi \vdash (\lambda I:\theta_1.\,E): \theta_1 \to \theta_2}$$

and its semantics is

$[\![\pi \vdash \lambda I: \theta_1.\,E: \theta_1 \to \theta_2]\!]e = f$

where $f\,v = [\![\pi \uplus \{I: \theta_1\} \vdash E: \theta_2]\!](e \uplus \{I=v\})$

This admits a parameter copy rule for binding an actual parameter to a formal one:

$(\lambda I:\theta.\,U)V \;\Rightarrow\; [V/I]U$

where $[V/I]U$, the substitution of V for free occurrences of I in U, is defined in Section 3.3.

Suggested Reading

Parameterization arose as a consequence of the interaction of the correspondence and abstraction principles, as noted by Tennent (1977, 1981). The correspondence principle was stated by Tennent (1977), who built upon the efforts of Landin (1965, 1966). Parameterization as a principle per se was stated in Schmidt 1986, where its denotational semantics is given. Evaluation strategies for parameters is a classic topic; see Pratt 1984 for a long list of possibilities. Type equivalence also has a long history; see Ghezzi and Jazayeri 1987 and Tennent 1981 for historical examples and references. Interesting subtleties are discussed in Chapter 8 of Nelson 1991. Static parameters are introduced in

Tennent 1981, and a theory of binding times is documented in Nielson and Nielson 1987 and 1992. Applications of binding-time analysis are seen in Jones and Muchnick 1976, Jones, Sestoft, and Søndergaard 1989, Jones, et al. 1993, Consel and Danvy 1991 and 1993, and Launchbury 1992. The parameter copy rule and the definition of substitution stem from the lambda calculus, which will be studied in Chapter 6. Gentle introductions are found in Hindley and Seldin 1986 and Gordon 1991.

Exercises

1.1. Draw the attributed syntax trees for those well-formed programs that follow:

    a. **var** A: **newint**; **fun** $F(X: intexp) = X+1$;
       proc $P(X: boolexp) =$ **while** X **do** $A := F(@A)$ **od**
       in $A := 1$; **call** $P(@A=0)$; **call** $P((@A+1)=F(@A))$

    b. **fun** $F(X: intexp) = X+1$, **proc** $P(X:intexp) =$ **skip** **in call** $P(F)$

    c. **fun** $F(X:intexp) = X+1$;
       var A: **newint**;
       proc $P(G: intexp \rightarrow intexp) = A := G(0)$
       in call $P(F)$

1.2. Prove that the typing rules for expression parameters preserve the unicity of typing property.

1.3. a. Say that lazy evaluation is used for expression parameters. Therefore, if a variable name, I, appears within an actual parameter, then the corresponding formal parameter becomes an alias for I's location. Given this language

       P ::= D **in** C
       D ::= $D_1; D_2$ | **proc** $I_1(I_2:intexp) = C$ | **var** I: **newint**
       C ::= L:=E | $C_1;C_2$ | **call** I(E)
       E ::= N | E_1+E_2 | @L
       L ::= I

      write a set of typing rules that prevents the aliasing of a location by two different identifiers.

    b.* Extend your answer to Part a to arrays.

2.1. Calculate the semantics of the well-typed programs in Exercise 1.1 for eager evaluation of parameters; for lazy evaluation of parameters.

2.2. Explain why this typing rule is appropriate when expression parameters are eagerly evaluated. Consider the soundness of the rule.

$$\frac{\pi \vdash I: \tau \rightarrow \theta \quad \pi \vdash E: \tau exp}{\pi \vdash \textbf{invoke } I(E): \theta}$$

2.3. If you worked Exercise 2.3 from Chapter 2, proceed. Add eagerly (and lazily) evaluated expression parameters to procedures in the structural operational semantics (and natural semantics) of the language. Prove the soundness of your rules with respect to the denotational semantics.

2.4. As in the previous chapters, the denotational semantics can do double duty as an operational semantics. We extend the definition of Value by including those functions, f, defined as $f\,v\,s = \cdots$, that are the meanings of parameterized abstractions. Extend Figures 2.3 and 2.4 in Chapter 2 by lazily evaluated expression parameters and prove that the operational semantics is adequate with respect to the denotational semantics. Define $comp_{\theta_1 \to \theta_2} p$ iff for all v, $comp_{\theta_1} v$ implies $comp_{\theta_2} p\,v$. (Hint: When you work the proof, assume this lemma has been proved: $comp_\theta p$ and $p' \Rightarrow^* p$ imply $comp_\theta p'$. Once you complete the proof, prove the lemma.)

2.5. If you worked Exercise 10.1 from Chapter 2, proceed. Augment the definition of *size* by

$$size_{w,\theta_1 \to \theta_2} f \text{ iff for all } k \geq w, \text{ for all } a \in [\![\theta_1]\!], \; size_{k,\theta_1} a \text{ implies } size_{k,\theta_2} f(a)$$

Re-prove the results in Exercise 10.1 for the programming language with parameters.

2.6. Say that the language from Chapter 2 has eagerly evaluated abstractions and say that parameters are added. What is the denotational semantics of the parameterized abstractions?

3.1. Apply the parameter copy rule to the well-typed programs in Exercise 1.1.

3.2. a. Say that **fun** $F(A:intexp) = A + C$ and **proc** $P(B:intloc) = A := F(@B)$. Show how the copy rules let us deduce that **proc** $P = \lambda B:intloc.\ A := ((\lambda A:intexp.\ A + C)(@B))$.

   b. Show in complete detail the substitution steps in: $[loc_1/A]\ [B + 1/C]\ (\lambda B:intloc.\ A := ((\lambda A:intexp.\ A + C)(@B)))$

3.3.* If you worked Exercise 4.3 of Chapter 2, proceed. Prove, in the absence of recursively defined abstractions and variable name declarations, that if $\vdash D$ **in** C: *comm* holds, then a finite number of applications of the parameter copy rule and the copy rules from Chapter 2 suffice to rewrite D **in** C into a core language program.

3.4. Lambda abstractions make a good notational tool for the denotational semantics notation as well. For example, the semantics of assignment can be written in lambda-abstraction form as follows:

$$[\![\pi \vdash L := E: comm]\!]e = \lambda s:Store.\ update([\![\pi \vdash L:intloc]\!]e, [\![\pi \vdash E:intexp]\!]e\ s,\ s)$$

For $\pi_1 = \{A:intloc\}$ and $e_1 = \{A = loc_1\}$, the calculation $[\![\pi_1 \vdash A := 0:$

comm$\rrbracket e_1 s_1$ goes: $(\lambda s{:}Store.\ update(\llbracket \pi_1\ \vdash A{:}\ intloc \rrbracket e_1,\ \llbracket \pi_1 \vdash 0{:}\ intexp \rrbracket e_1\ s,$ $s))s_1\ =\ update(\llbracket \pi_1\ \vdash A{:}\ intloc \rrbracket e_1,\ \llbracket \pi_1\ \vdash 0{:}\ intexp \rrbracket e_1\ s_1,\ s_1)\ =\ update(loc_1,$ $(\lambda s{:}Store.\ 0)s_1,\ s_1) = update(loc_1,\ 0,\ s_1).$

a. Rewrite the denotational semantics of the imperative language with lambda abstractions; use them also for the semantics of parameter binding; and rework the semantics of the well-typed programs in Exercise 1.1.

b. The lambda abstraction notation impacts the operational semantics in a profound way, because operational semantics evaluation can proceed without the store, computing just upon environments. This resembles what a complier does when it processes a symbol table at compile time. Prove, for all commands, C, type assignments, π, and environment Values, $e_0 \in Env_\pi$, that $\llbracket \pi \vdash C{:}\ comm \rrbracket e_0 \Rightarrow^* p_1$, where p_1 has no occurrences of environment phrases.

c.* Prove that, if $\llbracket \pi \vdash C{:}\ comm \rrbracket e_0 \Rightarrow^* p_1$, as in Part b, then for all store Values, $s_0,\ p_1\ s_0 \Rightarrow^* s_1$ iff $\llbracket \pi \vdash C{:}\ comm \rrbracket e_0\ s_0 \Rightarrow^* s_1$, where s_1 is a store Value.

4.1. Prove there is no value for θ that makes this program well typed:

var $A{:}$**newint**; **proc** $P(Q{:}\theta) =$ **if** $@A{=}0$ **then skip else** $A{:=}@A{-}1$; **call** $Q(Q)$ **fi** **in call** $P(P)$

4.2. Write the syntax, typing rules, and semantics for identifier parameters.

4.3. a. If you worked Exercise 10.2 from Chapter 2, proceed. Say that the imperative language with arrays gets variable parameters. Define the eager evaluation semantics and the lazy evaluation semantics of variable parameters and apply both semantics to this example:

array var $A[3]$; **var** $B{:}$**newint**; **proc** $P(X{:}intloc) = X{:=}@X{+}1;\ X{:=}@X{+}1$ **in** $A[2]{:=}0;\ B{:=}0;$ **call** $P(B)$; **call** $P(A[@B])$; **call** $P(A[@A[@B]])$

For the case of lazy evaluation semantics, why might the type attribute *intloc exp* be more appropriate than *intloc* for X? (Hint: Consider $\llbracket intexp \rrbracket$ versus $\llbracket int \rrbracket$.)

b. If you worked Exercise 6.5 of Chapter 1, proceed. To that language, add procedures, expression parameters, and variable parameters. Give lazy evaluation semantics to the additions. Why is lazy evaluation suitable for variable parameters?

4.4. Verify that these programs are well typed. (Assume that modules can be indexed.)

a. **module** $M = \{$ **var** $A{:}$ **newint** $\}$; **module** $P(X{:} \{A{:}intloc\}) = \{$ **proc** $ZERO = X.A{:=}0 \}$; **module** $Q(Y{:} \{A{:}intloc\}) = \{$ **proc** $SUCC = Y.A{:=}@Y.A{+}1 \}$;

> **import** $P(M)$; **import** $Q(M)$
> **in call** *ZERO*; **call** *SUCC*

   b. **module** $M = \{ \textbf{var } A: \textbf{newint} \}$;
      module $N(X: \{ A:intloc \}) = \{ \textbf{var } B: \textbf{newint}; X \}$;
      class $K(Y: \{ A:intloc \}) = \textbf{record import } N(Y) \textbf{ end}$;
      var $C: K(M)$; **var** $D: K(\textbf{var } A: \textbf{newint})$; **import** $N(M)$
      in $C.A := @D.B$

   c. Explain the semantics of the two parts.

4.5. Give the syntax and typing rules for **proc** $I_1(I_2: T) = C$, that is, for the use of type structures as type attributes for formal parameters. How does your definition compare to, say, Pascal's? Is the following program well typed with your definition?

> **class** $K = \textbf{record var } A: \textbf{newint}; \textbf{var } B: \textbf{newint end}$;
> **var** $X: \textbf{record var } B: \textbf{newint}; \textbf{var } A: \textbf{newint end}$;
> **proc** $P(Y: K) = Y.A := 0$
> **in** $P(X)$

5.1. Write the complete set of typing rules for the imperative language with occurrence-equivalence typing.

5.2. Under occurrence-equivalence typing, can *any* variable at all be an actual parameter to this procedure: **proc** $P(X: \textbf{record var } A: \textbf{newint end}) = \cdots$?

5.3. Modula-3 uses structural type equivalence, but a user can attach "brands," which force a type to be unique. Consider

> **class** $K = \textbf{brand newint}$;
> **var** $A: \textbf{newint}$; **var** $B: K$; **var** $C: K$

The types of A and B are different, but B and C have the same type. Add brands to the imperative language and give the typing rules.

6.1. Write typing rules for Ada-style type-structure parameters.

6.2. Say that type attributes are allowed as parameters; that is, **define** $I_1(\theta$: *TypeAttribute*$)=U$ is allowed. Explain why this example would be well typed. (Assume that modules can be indexed.)

> **var** $A: \textbf{newint}$;
> **module** $M(T: TypeAttr) = \{ \textbf{define } ID(X: T) = X \}$
> **in** $M(intloc).ID(A) := M(intexp).ID(1+2)$

Draw an attributed syntax tree for the example and try to write some of the typing rules for type-attribute parameters.

7.1. a. Return to the language definition in Section 2.15. For each abstraction, create a corresponding parameter. Revise the syntax definition so that each abstraction can take any of the possible actual parameter forms. (Use Figure 3.4 as a guide.)

b. What combinations of actual parameters and abstractions seem worthless? Confusing? What additional parameters do you desire?

c. For each of the abstractions and parameter forms, consider the merits of eager and lazy evaluation. Is there any syntax domain where the abstraction form should be evaluated one way (for example, lazily) and the parameter form the other way (eagerly)? Do you know of any programming languages where this arises?

d. Say that all abstractions and parameters are evaluated eagerly. Add two new operators, **freeze** and **thaw**. The effect of **freeze** U is to delay U's evaluation, that is, to make it evaluate lazily. The effect of **thaw** V is to remove the freeze action and force the evaluation of V. Define the syntax, typing rules, and semantics for these constructs. If possible, define copy rules.

e. Say that all abstractions and parameters are evaluated lazily. Add the operator, **eval**, which forces a phrase to evaluate eagerly. Define the syntax, typing rules, and semantics.

7.2. a. *Call-by-need* parameter transmission is a variant of call-by-name, where the first time the actual parameter is evaluated, its result is remembered. Subsequent references to the parameter use the result of the initial evaluation. Define the semantics of call-by-need; show that call-by-need can yield results different from those given by call-by-name; and define the corresponding abstraction form.

b. *Call-by-result* parameter transmission can be used when the actual parameter is a variable: A newly allocated location is bound to the formal parameter, and when the abstraction finishes, the value in the formal parameter's location is copied into the actual parameter variable. Define the semantics of call-by-result and define the corresponding abstraction form.

c. *Call-by-value-result* can also be used when the actual parameter is a variable name: The value in the variable is placed in a newly allocated location, which is bound to the formal parameter. When the abstraction finishes, the value in the formal parameter's location is copied into the actual parameter variable. Define the semantics of call-by-value-result; show that call-by-value-result can yield results different from those given by call-by-reference; and define the corresponding abstraction form. (Recall that *call-by-reference* is the eager evaluation of a variable parameter.)

d. If you worked Exercise 4.3.b, proceed. Add acceptor parameters (*intacc* parameters—see Exercise 6.5, Chapter 1) to the language. Compare variable parameters, expression parameters, and acceptor parameters to call-by-reference, call-by-value, and call-by-result, respectively.

7.3. a. Say that we integrate static parameters into the imperative language, and we use square brackets to mark static parameters. (Dynamic parameters are enclosed in round brackets.) For the example below, mark those phrases in the bodies of F and P that can be evaluated statically, that is, evaluated at compile time.

> **fun** $F[A:intexp](B:intloc) = B:=A+2$
> **rec-proc** $P[X:intexp] = $ **if** $X=0$ **then skip**
>   **else** $Y:=X+2+F[X](@Y);$ **call** $P[X-1]$ **fi**

   b. Generate the specialized functions and procedures for **call** $P[2+1]$.

   c. Explain why this example is malformed:

> **rec-proc** $P[X:intexp](Y:intloc) = $ **call** $P[@Y](@Y+X)$

   d.* Give typing rules that enforce the well-formedness of abstractions with static parameters.

8.1. Calculate the semantics of this example:

> **var** A:**newint**; **proc** $P(X:intloc,P:comm,F:intexp) = X:=0;$ **call** $P;$ $A:=@X+F$
> **in call** P(**var** X: **newint**; **fun** $F = @X+1;$ **proc** $P = X:=F$)

8.2. Here is a well-known example that appears to speak against the use of lazy evaluation of parameters:

> **var** $TEMP$: **newint**;
> **proc** $SWAP(X:intloc, Y:intloc) = TEMP:=@X; X:=@Y; Y:=@TEMP;$
> **var** I: **newint**; **var** A: **array** $[\cdots]$ **of newint**
> **in** $\cdots$ **call** $SWAP(I, A[@I])$

   a. Read Exercise 7.2 and explain which forms of parameter transmission lead to a successful swap of I and $A[@I]$.

   b. Explain why parallel assignment, $I_1, I_2, \ldots, I_n := E_1, E_2, \ldots, E_n$, can be used to rewrite $SWAP$ so that it works correctly with lazy evaluation.

10.1. If you worked Exercise 15.1 from Chapter 2, proceed. Augment the language you developed in that exercise with parameters. State where the correspondence principle holds and fails. What interesting programs now become possible in your language?

10.2. Here is the syntax of a core language of boolean expressions; the semantics of the logical operators are the usual ones:

> $B\in$ Bool-expr
> $A\in$ Atom

$$B ::= A_1 = A_2 \mid B_1 \text{ or } B_2 \mid B_1 \text{ and } B_2 \mid \text{if } B_1 \text{ then } B_2 \text{ else } B_3 \text{ fi} \mid \text{true} \mid \text{false}$$
$$A ::= \text{mary} \mid \text{john} \mid \text{wine} \mid \text{cheese} \mid \cdots$$

a. Give the language its typing rules; then apply the abstraction and parameterization principles, to whatever degree you desire, to the language. Justify your design decisions.

b. Code the following statements as abstractions in your language:
   - Only bread and cheese are healthy. (Hint: code an abstraction named *is-healthy*(X), which returns a truth value.)
   - Mary likes soda and things that are healthy; John likes everything;
   - Persons A and B can eat food F together if both A and B like F.

   Now, evaluate the query, "Can Mary and John eat wine and cheese together?"

c. If you are familiar with Prolog, compare the language developed here to Prolog. In particular, what does Prolog possess that the present language does not?

4 The Qualification Principle

The abstraction principle introduced definitions to a program, but there was no consideration of the definitions' scope. Practice has proved that procedures, modules, classes, and so on, benefit from local definitions. The addition of local definitions is guided by

The Qualification Principle:

Any semantically meaningful syntactic class may admit local definitions.

We call a construct that admits local definitions a *block structure* (or *block*, for short) and call a language with blocks *block-structured*. For an arbitrary syntax domain, U, we use the following form of block:

$$U ::= \cdots \mid \textbf{begin } D \textbf{ in } U \textbf{ end}$$

The intended semantics is that the declarations, D, are visible only to U, the *body* of the block. The typing rule for blocks is:

$$\frac{\pi_1 \vdash D; \pi_2 \, dec \quad \pi_1 \uplus \pi_2 \vdash U: \theta}{\pi_1 \vdash \textbf{begin } D \textbf{ in } U \textbf{ end}: \theta}$$

Recall the definition of $\pi_1 \uplus \pi_2$ from Chapter 3: The type assignments π_1 and π_2 are combined, but the bindings in π_2 take precedence over bindings in π_1. Further, the bindings, π_2, made by D are visible no further than U.

There is a natural correspondence of parameters to local definitions: For every parameterized abstraction form, there may be a corresponding qualification form (and vice versa) such that $\textbf{define } I_1(I_2:\theta) = U \textbf{ in } I_1(V)$ is semantically equivalent to $\textbf{begin define } I_2 = V \textbf{ in } U \textbf{ end}$ (cf. Section 3.7). Although a "U-block" may appear anywhere a U-phrase may appear, we will emphasize blocks as the bodies of U-abstractions, thereby giving local definitions to procedures, modules, and the like.

(**begin**

   (**var** A :**newint**)$_{\varnothing}^{\pi_1 dec}$;

   (**proc** P = **begin** (**var** C :**newint**)$_{\pi_1}^{\pi_2 dec}$ **in** $(C:=@A)_{\pi_1 \uplus \pi_2}^{comm}$ **end**)$_{\pi_1}^{\pi_3 dec}$;

   (**proc** Q = **begin** (**var** B :**newint**; **var** A :**newint**)$_{\pi_1 \cup \pi_3}^{\pi_4 dec}$

        in $(A:=1;$ **call** $P)_{(\pi_1 \cup \pi_3) \uplus \pi_4}^{comm}$ **end**)$_{\pi_1 \cup \pi_3}^{\pi_5 dec}$

in $(A:=0;$ **call** P; **call** $Q)_{\pi_1 \cup \pi_3 \cup \pi_5}^{comm}$ **end**)$_{\varnothing}^{comm}$

where: $\pi_1 = \{A:intloc\}$, $\pi_2 = \{C:intloc\}$, $\pi_3 = \{P:comm\}$,

$\pi_4 = \{A:intloc,\ B:intloc\}$, and $\pi_5 = \{Q:comm\}$

Figure 4.1

4.1 Command Blocks

The command block is the centerpiece of the prototypical block-structured language, Algol-60. Its typing rule reads:

$$\frac{\pi_1 \vdash D:\pi_2 dec \qquad \pi_1 \uplus \pi_2 \vdash C: comm}{\pi_1 \vdash \textbf{begin } D \textbf{ in } C \textbf{ end}: comm}$$

Here is an example:

   begin

      var A: **newint**;

      proc P = **begin var** C: **newint in** $C:=@A$ **end**;

      proc Q = **begin var** B :**newint**; **var** A :**newint in** $A:=1$; **call** P **end**

   in $A:=0$; **call** P; **call** Q **end**

The typing of this program is depicted in Figure 4.1. If one reads the program in the figure from first line to last, one sees that the type assignment attributes grow and shrink like a stack. When a compiler type checks a block-structured program, it keeps a single, global, stack-based symbol table to simulate the type assignments.

The crucial feature of a command block is that it limits visibility of the definitions it contains to its own body. If the definitions include variable declarations, there is no need to allocate locations for the variables before block entry, nor is there a need to keep the

---

$Store = \{\, \langle n_1, n_2, \ldots, n_m \rangle \mid n_i \in Int, \; 1 \le i \le m, \; m \ge 0 \,\}$

$lookup\!:\! Location \times Store \rightarrow Int$

      $lookup\,(loc_i, \langle n_1, ,n_2, \ldots, n_i, \ldots, n_m \rangle) = n_i$

$update\!:\! Location \times Int \times Store \rightarrow Store$

      $update\,(loc_i, \, n, \, \langle n_1, n_2, \ldots, n_i, \ldots, n_m \rangle) = \langle n_1, n_2, \ldots, n, \ldots, n_m \rangle$

$allocate\!:\! Store \rightarrow Location \times Store$

      $allocate\ \langle n_1, n_2, \ldots, n_m \rangle = (loc_{m+1}, \ \langle n_1, n_2, \ldots, n_m, init \rangle),$

          where *init* is some designated integer, for example, 0

$size\text{-}of\!:\! Store \rightarrow Int$

      $size\text{-}of\ \langle n_1, n_2, \ldots, n_m \rangle = m$

$free\!:\! Int \rightarrow Store \rightarrow Store$

      $free\ i\ \langle n_1, n_2, \ldots, n_i, n_{i+1}, \ldots, n_m \rangle = \langle n_1, n_2, \ldots, n_i \rangle, \; \text{if } 0 \le i \le m$

Figure 4.2 _____

locations after block exit.* This observation motivates the stack-based storage management of block-structured imperative languages.

In the above example, two locations are allocated immediately for global variables A and B. When P is invoked the first time, a third location is allocated for P's variable, C. That location is freed upon P's completion. Then, the call to Q allocates the locations for Q's variables, B and A. If storage is managed as a stack, B reuses the location that was just allocated and freed for C. Then P is invoked again, and a location is allocated again for C—a different one than the one allocated for C the first time P was called. When P, and then Q, finish, the locations for their local variables are freed.

4.1.1 Semantics of the Command Block

The denotational semantics of the command block makes precise the ideas in the previous paragraph. We treat the storage vector as a stack and use the operations in Figure 4.2. The important operations are *allocate*, which creates a new location in the store, *size-of*, which remembers the size of the store, and *free*, which reduces the store to a smaller size. The semantics of a command block follows:

---

    * This claim fails under certain circumstances; see Section 4.3.

$$[\![\pi \vdash \textbf{begin } D \textbf{ in } C \textbf{ end}: comm]\!]e\ s = free\ (size\text{-}of\ s)\ s_2$$

$$\text{where } (e_1, s_1) = [\![\pi \vdash D: \pi_1 dec]\!]e\ s$$

$$\text{and } s_2 = [\![\pi \uplus \pi_1 \vdash C: comm]\!](e \uplus e_1)\ s_1$$

The command block controls the size of the store by allowing D to allocate locations for the body, C, and then freeing the locations at conclusion, reducing the store to its original size.

The semantics of a small example is calculated in Figure 4.3. The calculation shows the store behaving like a stack. Of course, the store need not be implemented as a stack—heap storage might be used—but whatever implementation that is chosen must maintain the correct lifetime of the storage locations.

Here is a final technical point: If declarations are eagerly evaluated, it is conceivable that $[\![\pi \vdash D: \pi_1 dec]\!]e\ s = \bot$. In this case, $e \uplus \bot = \bot$, and the meaning of the command block is $\bot$ as well.

$[\![\varnothing \vdash \textbf{begin var } A: \textbf{newint}; \textbf{proc } P=A:=0$

$\qquad \textbf{in begin var } A: \textbf{newint in call } P \textbf{ end end}: comm]\!]\varnothing\ s_0$

$= free\ n\ s_2, \quad \text{where } n = size\text{-}of\ s_0$

$\text{where } (e_1, s_1) = [\![\varnothing \vdash \textbf{var } A; \textbf{proc } P=A:=0: \{A:intloc, P:comm\}dec]\!]\varnothing\ s_0$

$\qquad\qquad = (\{A=loc_{n+1}, P=f\}, s_0@init)$

$\qquad\qquad\qquad \text{where } f s' = [\![\{A:intloc\} \vdash A:=0: comm]\!]\{A=loc_{n+1}\}\ s'$

$\qquad\qquad\qquad \text{and } s_0@init \text{ denotes store } s_0 \text{ with a new location}$

$\qquad s_2 = [\![\pi_1 \vdash \textbf{begin var } A:\textbf{newint in call } P \textbf{ end}: comm]\!]e_1\ s_1$

$\qquad\qquad \text{where } \pi_1 = \{A:intloc, P:comm\}$

$\qquad\qquad = free\ (n{+}1)\ s_{21}$

$\qquad\qquad\quad \text{where } (e_{11}, s_{11}) = [\![\pi_1 \vdash \textbf{var } A: \textbf{newint}: \{A:intloc\}dec]\!]e_1\ s_1$

$\qquad\qquad\qquad\qquad = (\{A=loc_{n+2}\}, s_0@init@init)$

$\qquad\qquad\qquad s_{21} = [\![\pi_1 \vdash \textbf{call } P: comm]\!]\{A=loc_{n+2}, P=f\}\ s_{11}$

$\qquad\qquad\qquad\qquad = f\ s_{11} = [\![\{A:intloc\} \vdash A:=0:comm]\!]\{A=loc_{n+1}\}\ s_{11}$

$\qquad\qquad\qquad\qquad = s_0@init@init$

$\qquad\qquad = s_0@0$

$= s_0$

Figure 4.3

4.2 Scope

Consider again the example in Figure 4.1. When P is invoked the second time, we expect that the location named by C gets the value 0. This occurs in the Algol-like languages, but if the program is evaluated in Lisp 1.5, APL, or Smalltalk, then C's location gets 1. Why does this happen? The answer lies in the answer to the question: How is an invocation associated with the definition that it invokes? The answer defines the scoping policy of the programming language.

The Algol-like languages have a *static scoping* policy, where an invocation of I is associated with the definition of I whose scope contains the invocation. The *scope of the definition of* I in: **begin define** I=V **in** U **end** is U, less any part of U that falls in the scope of a redefinition of I. In the previous example, the scope of the outer definition of A is the phrase

> **proc** P = **begin var** C: **newint in** C:=@A **end**
>   **proc** Q = **begin var** B: **newint; var** A: **newint in** [ ] **end**
> **in** A:=0; **call** P; **call** Q

where the "[ ]" marks the absence of the phrase that falls in the scope of the redefinition of A. Sometimes the missing phrase is called a "hole in the scope" of the definition.

An important feature of static scoping is that the associations between invocations and definitions can be calculated prior to evaluating the program. Indeed, the type assignment attribute in the typing rules does just this, and the corresponding environment argument in the denotational semantics holds the bindings of those identifiers whose scopes are in force. This is worth a second look:

> $[\![\pi \vdash \textbf{begin } D \textbf{ in } C \textbf{ end}: comm]\!]e\; s = free\;(size\text{-}of\; s)\; s_2$
>   where $(e_1, s_1) = [\![\pi \vdash D: \pi_1 dec]\!]e\; s$
>   and $s_2 = [\![\pi \uplus \pi_1 \vdash C: comm]\!](e \uplus e_1)\; s_1$

The environment, e, contains all identifiers whose scopes are in force for the block. The local declarations, D, create the bindings, e_1, whose scopes are the block body, C. The bindings in e_1 cancel the scopes for like-named identifiers in e, hence the correct environment for C is $e \uplus e_1$. The bindings in e_1 are used just for C.

The alternative to static scoping, *dynamic scoping*, cannot be so simply described. One might summarize it by stating that an interpreter for the language makes the association between an invocation and a definition. Further, the association between an invocation and its definition can change each time the invocation is evaluated. If the program in Figure 4.1 is evaluated with dynamic scoping, the invocation of A in procedure P's body evaluates twice, due to the two **call** P commands. The first time A evaluates, it is associated with the outer definition of A, whose scope contains the first **call** P. The second time A evaluates, it is associated with the inner definition of A, whose scope contains the second **call** P.

This behavior can be simulated with a naive version of copy rule that substitutes bodies of procedures for their invocations while ignoring name clashes. If one applies this technique to Figure 4.1, one sees that for the second invocation of P, the body of P is copied into the body of procedure Q, placing P's variable, A, within the scope of Q's definition of A.

Here is an example that looks well formed but evaluates improperly with dynamic scoping:

> **begin var** A: **newint; proc** $P = A:=0$
> **in begin fun** $A = 1$
> **in call** P **end end**

With dynamic scoping, the invocation of P causes its body, $A:=0$, to fall under the scope of **fun** $A=1$, causing a run-time incompatibility error. The example shows that dynamic scoping makes typing rules difficult or impossible to write.

4.2.1 Semantics of Dynamic Scoping

The crucial aspect of dynamic scoping can be formalized in a denotational-style semantics: A phrase's environment is not determined until the phrase is evaluated, just like the phrase's store is not determined until the phrase is evaluated. This impacts the definition and invocation constructs:

> $[\![\textbf{define I=U}]\!]e\ s = (\{\, \text{I}{=}f \,\}, s)$, where $f\ e'\ s' = [\![\text{U}]\!]e'\ s'$
> $[\![\textbf{invoke I}]\!]e\ s = f\ e\ s$, where $(\text{I}{=}f) \in e$

The environment used by an abstraction is fixed only when the abstraction is invoked—the environment behaves like a store. Notice that the type attributes have disappeared—we can no longer predict the types of phrases, so the semantics definition must be given for untyped phrases. This is a bad omen and calls into question the well-formedness of the semantics. Nonetheless, we proceed and rework the example in Figure 4.3 as an operational semantics calculation in Figure 4.4. The key stage in the calculation, marked by (**), is the updating of the local variable A by global procedure P.

Strange programs can be written in a dynamically scoped language, and their semantics are dubious. Consider:

$[\![\textbf{begin var } A\!:\textbf{newint; proc } P\!=\!A\!:=\!0 \textbf{ in begin var } A\!:\textbf{newint in call } P \textbf{ end end}]\!]\varnothing \; \langle \rangle$
$\Rightarrow free \; (\textit{size-of} \langle \rangle) \; s_2 \Rightarrow free \; 0 \; s_2$
where $(e_1, s_1) = [\![\textbf{var } A;\; \textbf{proc } P\!=\!A\!:=\!0]\!]\varnothing \; \langle \rangle$
$\qquad\qquad \Rightarrow^* (\{A\!=\!loc_1,\, P=f\},\, \langle \textit{init} \rangle),$ where $f \; e' \; s' = [\![A\!:=\!0]\!]e' \; s'$
$\quad s_2 = [\![\textbf{begin var } A\!:\!\textbf{newint in call } P \textbf{ end}]\!]e_1 \; s_1$
$\qquad\qquad \Rightarrow^* free \; (\textit{size-of} \langle \textit{init} \rangle) \; s_{21} \Rightarrow^* free \; 1 \; s_{21}$
$\qquad\quad$ where $(e_{11}, s_{11}) = [\![\textbf{var } A\!:\!\textbf{newint}]\!]e_1 \; \langle \textit{init} \rangle$
$\qquad\qquad\qquad \Rightarrow^* (\{A\!=\!loc_2\},\, \langle \textit{init}, \textit{init} \rangle)$
$\qquad\qquad s_{21} = [\![\textbf{call } P]\!](e_1 \uplus e_{11}) \; \langle \textit{init}, \textit{init} \rangle$
$\qquad\qquad\qquad \Rightarrow^* [\![\textbf{call } P]\!]\{A\!=\!loc_2,\, P\!=\!f\} \; \langle \textit{init}, \textit{init} \rangle$
$\qquad\qquad\qquad \Rightarrow f \; \{A\!=\!loc_2,\, P\!=\!f\} \; \langle \textit{init}, \textit{init} \rangle$
$\qquad\qquad\qquad \Rightarrow [\![A\!:=\!0]\!]\{A\!=\!loc_2,\, P\!=\!f\} \; \langle \textit{init}, \textit{init} \rangle \quad (**)$
$\qquad\qquad\qquad \Rightarrow^* \langle \textit{init}, 0 \rangle$
$\qquad\qquad \Rightarrow free \; 1 \; \langle \textit{init}, 0 \rangle \Rightarrow \langle \textit{init} \rangle$
$\Rightarrow free \; 0 \; \langle \textit{init} \rangle \Rightarrow \langle \rangle$

Figure 4.4 _____

    begin proc $P = $ **call** P **in call** P **end**

Apparently, the meaning of P is a function, $f \; e' \; s' = g \; e' \; s'$, where $(P\!=\!g) \in e'$. Next, we see that $[\![\textbf{begin proc } P = \textbf{call } P \textbf{ in call } P \textbf{ end}]\!]e_0 \; s_0$ is $f(e_0 \uplus \{P\!=\!f\}) \; s_0$, which means that f must be able to receive itself as an argument (via the environment). Under the usual definition of a function as a set of argument, answer pairs, this cannot be done. Thus, the mathematical foundations of the semantics have collapsed. We can resolve the problem with advanced techniques, but it is simplest here to treat the semantics equations as an operational semantics, where symbols are merely shifted about.

4.3 Extent

The lifetime of a variable is called its *extent*. The program in Figure 4.1 showed that the extent of a variable differs from its scope. (In that example, when P was called from Q, the scope of variables A and B in Q did not cover P's code, but their locations remained allocated while P evaluated.) In this section, we consider issues related to extent. We assume static scoping.

The command block controls the extent of local variables: it allocates locations for them on block entry, and it frees the locations upon block exit. Why are we assured that block exit is the correct time to free the locations for the variables? The answer is that, in the present language, no location bound to a local variable "escapes" from a command block. A local variable's location might escape from a block in several ways:

(i)   The answer produced by the block contains a local variable's location;
(ii) A value assigned to a nonlocal variable contains a local variable's location;
(iii) An actual parameter containing a local variable's location is transmitted to a nonlocal abstraction that saves the location.

At this point, we have no guarantee that this list is exhaustive, but it makes a good starting point for analysis (cf. Exercise 3.3).

Consider the first possibility. It can be realized when the type of a command block is not *comm*, but, say, $\theta \rightarrow comm$. Consider this slightly convoluted example:

begin proc P = **begin var** A: **newint; proc** $Q(X:intexp) = A:=X$ **in** Q **end**
  in (**call** P)(2) **end**

Procedure P takes no parameter, yet it has type $intexp \rightarrow comm$. When P is called, it returns as its answer a parameterized procedure. Say that loc_i is allocated (and deallocated) for local variable A when P is called. Then, the value returned by P is a procedure, q, that updates loc_i:

$$q\, v\, s = [\![\pi \uplus \{A:intloc, X:intexp\} \vdash A:=X: comm]\!](e \uplus \{A=loc_i, X=v\})\, s$$
$$= update(loc_i, v, s)$$

Location loc_i has escaped from the body of P, and when the actual parameter, 2, is bound to q and the assignment is undertaken, a dereferencing error arises.

The above variant of command block is disallowed in the present version of the imperative language. The only "answer" that can be produced by a command block is a store, which is a vector of integers. No locations are embedded in the store, so no locations can escape.

Next, consider the second possibility for locations to escape: Say that the imperative language is extended by *pointer variables*, that is, variables whose locations can contain location numbers. Thus, a store contains integers and location numbers. Say that A is a globally declared pointer variable; then **begin var** B: **newint in** $A:=B$ **end** saves B's location number in A's location, allowing it to escape from the block. (Notice that we did *not* write $A:=@B$.) Many general purpose imperative languages admit pointer variables, so additional restrictions must be imposed to prevent escapes. One possible restriction is to segregate to a heap those variables whose location numbers can be assigned to pointer variables.

The third possibility for escapes arises when an actual parameter containing a location number is transmitted to a nonlocal abstraction. If the nonlocal abstraction has a way of saving the actual parameter, say, in a nonlocal variable, then an escape is possible. Obviously, variable parameters are candidates for this treatment, but when actual parameters are evaluated lazily, any actual parameter that mentions a variable, for example, $@A+1$, might allow a location to escape. The key issue is whether or not the nonlocal abstraction can save the actual parameter. In the present version of the imperative language, this is impossible: There are no pointer variables, and unevaluated phrases, like $@A+1$, cannot be saved in the store. Issues related to escapes are treated further in the Exercises.

Issues about extent arise for other forms of blocks. Consider a module that contains a local variable. (This is a *declaration block*.)

module M = **begin var** A : **newint in**
  { **proc** *INIT* $= A := 0$,
  proc *SUCC* $= A := @A+1$,
  fun *VAL* $= @A$ } **end**

M's body is a declaration block. When M is evaluated, a location for A is allocated and the answer M produces is the set of bindings for *INIT*, *SUCC*, and *VAL*. Although the scope of A does not go beyond the module, A's location clearly *must* escape the declaration block. That is, A's extent must go beyond module M. Therefore, a declaration block must not free storage upon completion of the block. The semantics follows:

$\llbracket \pi \vdash \textbf{begin } D_1 \textbf{ in } D_2 \textbf{ end}: \pi_2 dec \rrbracket e\, s = \llbracket \pi \uplus \pi_1 \vdash D_2: \pi_2 dec \rrbracket (e \uplus e_1)\, s_1$
  where $(e_1, s_1) = \llbracket \pi \vdash D_1 : \pi_1 dec \rrbracket e\, s$

The locations allocated within D_1 and D_2 are retained. Although this semantics appears to ignore the notion of stack-based storage, the point is that the command block alone takes responsibility for the release of storage locations. Here is an example that uses M as above and K, a type-structure block:

begin module M = **begin var** A : **newint in**
      { **proc** *INIT* $= A := 0$, **proc** *SUCC* $= A := @A+1$, **fun** *VAL* $= @A$ } **end**;
    class K = **begin var** B : **newint in record proc** $Q(X : intexp) = B := X$ **end**;
    proc P = **begin import** M; **var** C : K **in call** *SUCC*; **call** $C.Q$ (*VAL*) **end**
  in call $M.INIT$; **call** P **end**

The program is a command block, and when module M is eagerly evaluated, A's location is allocated and stays allocated until the program finishes. When procedure P is called, storage for the variable B in C is allocated. B's location is freed, not when K's block finishes, but when *P*'s block, a command block, finishes. Since locations can not escape from command blocks, this policy is safe. Notice that the command block in *P* does not free the location for *A* in *M*—this location was allocated before *P*'s block was entered, so the location remains allocated after *P*'s block is exited.

4.4 Declaration Blocks

As suggested by the previous section, declaration blocks can hide details about the implementation of a structure. A user can reference only the declarations in the body of the block. An example is:

> **module** *GLOBAL-STACK*(*HOW-MANY*:*int*)=
> **begin var** *CTR* : **newint, var** *STACK* : **array** [1..*HOW-MANY*] **of newint in**
>   **proc** *PUSH*(*X* :*intexp*)
>   = **if** @*CTR*=*HOW-MANY* **then skip**
>   **else** *CTR* :=@*CTR*+1;*STACK* [@*CTR*]:=*X* **fi,**
>   **proc** *POP* = **if** @*CTR*=0 **then skip else** *CTR*:=@*CTR*−1 **fi,**
>   **fun** *TOP* = **if** @*CTR*=0 **then failure else** @ (*STACK* [@*CTR*]) **fi,**
>   **proc** *INIT* = *CTR* :=0 **end**

This module holds private copies of variables *CTR* and *STACK*. When the module is imported, the procedures and functions become visible, but the variables remain invisible. Thus, a simulated global stack is created:

> **import** *GLOBAL-STACK*(8)
> **in call** *INIT*; **call** *PUSH* (0); **call** *PUSH*(1); **call** *POP*; · · · *TOP* · · ·

Both Ada and Modula-2 allow their modules to expose some of the information in the local definitions. Here is a motivational example:

> **module** *RATIONAL-NUMBER*=
> **begin class** *RAT* = **record var** *NUM* :**newint, var** *DEN* :**newint end in**
>   **proc** *INIT-RAT*(*N* :*intexp*, *D* :*intexp*, *M* :*RAT*) = *M.NUM*:=*N* ; *M.DEN*:=*D*,
>   **proc** *MULT-RAT*(*M* :*RAT*, *N* :*RAT*, *P* :*RAT*)
>   = *P.NUM*:=@*M.NUM*∗@*N.NUM*; *P.DEN*:=@*M.DEN*∗@*N.DEN*,
>   **fun** *WHOLE-PART*(*M* :*RAT*) = @*M.NUM div* @*M.DEN*,
>   · · · **end**

A problem appears: In order to use the module's procedures, a user must declare variables of class *RAT*. (We assume name equivalence typing (cf. Section 3.5): Under structural equivalence, *RAT*'s type is merely {*NUM*:*intloc*, *DEN*:*intloc*}, which is a disappointment, because it means that a user can fabricate a *RAT*-value by constructing a record of two *intloc*s.)

Modula-2 and Ada let the name *RAT* be visible outside of the block, but the body of *RAT*'s definition is not exposed. In Modula-2, the above code is labeled the *implementation module*; a *definition module* lists the definitions that will be visible to a user:

> **definition module** *RATIONAL-NUMBER* =
> > **class** *RAT*,
> > **proc** *INIT-RAT*(*N*:*intexp*, *D*:*intexp*, *R*:*RAT*),
> > **proc** *MULT-RAT*(*M*:*RAT*, *N*:*RAT*, *P*:*RAT*),
> > **fun** *WHOLE-PART*(*M*:*RAT*):*intexp*,
> > $\cdots$ **end**

Class *RAT* is called *opaque*. Variables can be declared with opaque classes, for example,

> **var** *X*:*RAT* $\cdots$ **call** *INIT-RAT*(3,2,*X*); **call** *MULT-RAT*(*X*,*X*,*X*)

but the phrases *X.NUM* and *X.DEN* would be ill typed, since the body of *RAT* is invisible. The typing laws for opaque classes are left for the exercises.

Opaque classes allow modules to simulate *objects*. More will be said about objects in the next section.

4.5 Type-Structure Blocks

The semantics of a type-structure block looks like that for a declaration block:

$$[\![\pi \vdash \textbf{begin D in T end}: \pi_2 dec]\!]e\ s = [\![\pi \uplus \pi_1 \vdash T: \delta class]\!](e \uplus e_1)\ s_1$$
$$\text{where } (e_1, s_1) = [\![\pi \vdash D_1 : \pi_1 dec]\!]e\ s$$

Type-structure blocks whose bodies are record structures prove most useful. Here is an example:

> **class** *PERSONAL-STACK*=
> **begin var** *CTR*:**newint**, **var** *STACK*:**array** [1..100] **of newint**
> **in record**

proc *PUSH*(*X* :*intexp*) = **if** @*CTR* =100
    then skip else *CTR* :=@*CTR* +1; *STACK* [@*CTR*]:=*X* **fi**,
proc *POP* = **if** @*CTR* =0 **then skip else** *CTR* :=@*CTR* −1 **fi**,
fun *TOP* = **if** @*CTR* =0 **then failure else** @ (*STACK* [@*CTR*]) **fi**,
proc *INIT* = *CTR* :=0
  end end

The declaration   **var** *A* :*PERSONAL-STACK*   creates a record value for *A*, and in the process allocates storage for local variables *CTR* and *STACK*. We use *A*'s components to manipulate the local storage:

    call *A.INIT* ; **call** *A.PUSH* (0); **call** *A.POP* ; · · · *A.TOP* · · ·

If a second variable, say,   **var** *B* :*PERSONAL-STACK*,   is declared, new local storage is created for it. Thus, we can create as many instances of *PERSONAL-STACK*s as desired. As in the case of declaration blocks, type blocks hide local definitions and provide a well-defined interface to them.

We say that an *object* is a declared variable instance of a type-structure block. In the example, variables *A* and *B* are objects. Simula pioneered objects, and objects form the centerpiece of all object-oriented languages. Since Modula-2 and Ada lack type-structure blocks, they use opaque types to simulate objects. An object is almost always a record structure, and we call the fields of the record the *methods* of the object. For example, *PUSH* is a method of object *A*.

Classes make good units for system building. The standard way of using them is to embed the classes in one another:

class *EXTENDED-STACK* =
begin var *M* :*PERSONAL-STACK*, **var** *N* :*newint*, · · ·
 in record proc *P* = · · ·
      proc *PUSH-EXTENDED*(*X* :*intexp*) = **call** *M.PUSH* (*X*);
      · · · **end end**

Class *EXTENDED-STACK* builds on the structure of *PERSONAL-STACK* with additional local definitions (for example, *N*) and additional methods (for example, *P*). When an instance of an *EXTENDED-STACK* is declared, a copy of a *PERSONAL-STACK* is also created. But there is a problem: If we have   **var** *C* :*EXTENDED-STACK*, we must say **call** *C.PUSH-EXTENDED*(0), because we can not state **call** *C.PUSH* (0); the reason should be clear.

Procedures like *PUSH-EXTENDED*, which do no more than invoke procedures within nested classes, soon become irritating. One way to relieve the irritation is to allow an *inheritance* of class structure: When one class is embedded within another, the outer class can pretend that the operations of the inner class are its own. For example, when a *PERSONAL-STACK* is nested inside an *EXTENDED-STACK*, the operation *PUSH* can be used by an owner of an *EXTENDED-STACK*. That is, given **var** *D*:*EXTENDED-STACK*, we can say **call** *D.PUSH* (0). The syntax of inheritance might read as follows:

> **class** *EXTENDED-STACK* = **inherits** *PERSONAL-STACK* **with**
>> **begin var** *N*:**newint**, · · ·
>>> **in record proc** *P* = · · · **end end**

The clause **inherits** *PERSONAL-STACK* appends the *PERSONAL-STACK* structure to the structure defined in *EXTENDED-STACK*. We say that *EXTENDED-STACK* is a *subclass* of *PERSONAL-STACK*. An important question is: Should the declarations local to the *PERSONAL-STACK* class be made visible to the *EXTENDED-STACK* class (for example, can *SWAP* reference *CTR* and *STACK*)? Some languages that support inheritance allow this (or allow the programmer to control the degree of visibility), but this violates the usual static scoping laws. Other scoping questions arise with inheritance. In this example

> **class** *T* = **record proc** *P* = · · · **end**;
> **class** *U* = **inherits** *T* **with record proc** *P* = · · · **end**;
> **var** *X*:*U* **in call** *X.P*

we should worry about which copy of procedure *P* is invoked by *X.P*. The conflict is resolved by using the "most local" definition of *P*; that is, the version in class *U* is invoked. But a problem arises when there is no most local definition:

> **class** *T* = **record proc** *P* = · · · **end**;
> **class** *U* = **record proc** *P* = · · · **end**;
> **class** *R* = **inherits** *T*, **inherits** *U* **with** · · · ;
> **var** *X*:*R* **in call** *X.P*

Does *X.P* refer to the procedure in *T* or the one in *U*? This problem is caused by *multiple inheritance* of unrelated classes. Multiple inheritance can be disallowed, although some languages implement a specific lookup policy, say, first declaration to last. The typing of class inheritance (less multiple inheritance) is straightforward:

$$\frac{\pi \vdash T_1 : \pi_1 \, class \qquad \pi \uplus \pi_1 \vdash T_2 : \pi_2 \, class}{\pi \vdash \textbf{inherits } T_1 \textbf{ with } T_2 : (\pi_1 \uplus \pi_2) class}$$

The semantics is the union of the respective records built by the two type structures:

$$[\![\pi \vdash \textbf{inherits } T_1 \textbf{ with } T_2\!:\!(\pi_1 \uplus \pi_2)class]\!]e\ s = (f, s)$$
$$\text{where } f\,s' = [\![\pi \uplus \pi_1 \vdash T_2\!:\!\pi_2 class]\!](e \uplus e_1)\,s_1$$
$$\text{and } (e_1, s_1) = [\![\pi \vdash T_1\!:\!\pi_1\,class]\!]e\ s'$$

4.6 Object-Oriented Languages

Classes with inheritance are found in *object-oriented languages*. What exactly constitutes an object-oriented language? There is no consensus, although objects and inheritance are the central features. Another property often mentioned is the ability to redefine, via dynamic scoping, the methods of a class. This permits a high degree of code refinement and reuse. The concept is best introduced by examples. Say that we define a representation of natural number values

> **class** *NAT* = **record**
> > **var** *NUM* : **newint**;
> > **proc** *SUCC* = *NUM*:=@*NUM*+1;
> > **proc** *PLUSTWO* = **call** *SUCC*; **call** *SUCC* **end**

and say that we use *NAT* to develop a system of natural number-processing routines. (For the moment, please ignore that there is no way to initialize a *NAT*!) Next, we extend the system for integers, which we represent by embedding the *NAT* class into a new one:

> **class** *INT* = **inherits** *NAT* **with**
> > **record**
> > > **var** *ISNEG* : **newbool**;
> > > **proc** *SUCC* = **if** ¬*ISNEG* **then** *NUM*:=@*NUM*+1
> > > > **else** *NUM*:=@*NUM*−1; **if** @*NUM*=0 **then** *ISNEG*:=**false fi fi**
> > **end**

The new class, *INT*, uses a boolean variable, *ISNEG*, to remember if the simulated integer is negative or nonnegative. This is a silly representation of integers, but the idea is that a new class is built by augmenting another. (Local definitions are not crucial to the issues in this section, so we let *NUM* and *ISNEG* be visible to users of the classes.)

The operation *SUCC* was redefined for *INT*, but *PLUSTWO* should not require recoding, since it should be able to invoke the new version of *SUCC*. But recall that other routines in the system are using just the *NAT* class alone, which requires that *PLUSTWO* invoke the original coding of *SUCC*. How can the code for *PLUSTWO* refer to two different versions of *SUCC*? Static scoping will not support this behavior.

The answer lies with dynamic scoping, which allows an invocation of an identifier to refer to different definitions of it. To support dynamic scoping, most object-oriented languages use the moniker, *self*, to prefix invocations of a class's methods from within the class itself.* Using the *self* moniker, we recode the example as follows:

class *NAT* = **record**
        var *NUM*: **newint**;
        proc *SUCC* = *self*.*NUM*:=@*self*.*NUM*+1;
        proc *PLUSTWO* = **call** *self*.*SUCC*; **call** *self*.*SUCC* **end**
class *INT* = **inherits** *NAT* **with**
   record
      var *ISNEG*: **newbool**
      proc *SUCC* = **if** ¬*self*.*ISNEG* **then** *self*.*NUM*:=@*self*.*NUM*+1
               else *self*.*NUM*:=@*self*.*NUM*−1;
               if @*self*.*NUM*=0 **then** *self*.*ISNEG*:=*false* **fi fi**
   end

The *self* moniker is an unresolved identifier. When a class is invoked to declare an object, the *self* references are resolved to denote the object that is being declared. Say that we declare these two objects

    object *N*: *NAT*, **object** *I*: *INT*

(From here on, we use the syntax, **object** I_1:I_2, to create objects.) The first object, *N*, is a record where all instances of *self* are resolved to denote *N*, giving a kind of "recursive variable," that we *might* write as follows:

    rec-var *N*: **record** **var** *NUM*: **newint**;
              proc *SUCC* = *N*.*NUM*:=@*N*.*NUM*+1;
              proc *PLUSTWO* = **call** *N*.*SUCC*; **call** *N*.*SUCC* **end**

This technique binds the dynamically scoped *self* at the time of variable declaration.

---

* Actually, *self* reference arose in the language Smalltalk for implementational reasons: When a method of a class is invoked, a pointer to the object that invoked the method is passed to the component. This allows easy implementation of dynamic scoping. The name of the pointer is *self*.

Similarly, the second object, *I*, is a record where instances of *self* are resolved to *I*, giving a recursively defined variable like this:

rec-var *I*: **record var** *NUM*: **newint**;

           proc *PLUSTWO* = **call** *I.SUCC* ; **call** *I.SUCC* **end**

           var *ISNEG* : **newbool**

           proc *SUCC* = **if** $\neg I.ISNEG$ **then** $I.NUM:=@I.NUM+1$

                else $I.NUM:=@I.NUM-1$;

                if $@I.NUM=0$ **then** $I.ISNEG:=false$ **fi fi end**

In *I*'s declaration, the definition of *SUCC* in *NAT* is cancelled by the more local definition of *SUCC* in *INT*.

The recursion on the semantics of object declaration neatly handles method definition. But method redefinition has its hazards, since the dynamic scoping invalidates the typing rules of the previous section. Consider this example:

class *K1* = **record**   **proc** $P(X:intexp) = \cdots$;

              proc $Q = \cdots$ **call** $self.P(3) \cdots$ **end**

class *K2* = **inherits** *K1* **with record** **proc** $P(X:boolexp) = \cdots$ **end**;

object *A* :*K2*

The invocation **call** *A.Q* invokes *A.P*(3), which causes a run-time error. This is a foolish error, because we should not allow a method to be redefined with a typing different from the original's.

Those object-oriented languages that attempt to enforce a typing discipline also allow some version of *subtyping*. Consider again the example with *NAT* and *INT*; and say that we code

proc $P(X:NAT) = \cdots$ **call** *X.PLUSTWO* $\cdots$

The invocation **call** *P*(*N*) is clearly well formed, and there is good reason to allow **call** *P*(*I*) as well: *I* has at least as much structure as a *NAT*-class, so any *NAT*-named methods invoked in the body of *P* can be handled by *I*'s methods. It is tempting to state a general principle that, if C_1 is a subclass of C_2, then any context that requires an object of type C_2 can use an object of type C_1. But there are difficulties with this claim: First, it confuses the notion of type attribute (and subtype) with class (and subclass); second, it ignores problems that arise when a method is redefined in a subclass. Both difficulties come to the fore in the example that follows momentarily.

Yet another feature of an object-oriented language is that the primary syntactic (and semantic) concept is the class. All computation is conducted by invocations of one class's routines by another's. Even low-level computation steps, such as storage lookup and update, are performed by class calls. (The idea is that primary storage and its related operations form a class.) This philosophy requires objects to take one another as parameters, which can be implemented with the *self* reference and—if we cling to our hope of a typed language—a new type attribute, *selftype*. Consider another simulation of natural numbers and integers but with operations that take objects as arguments:

> **class** *NAT2* = **record**
> > **var** *NUM* : **newint**;
> > **fun** *EQ* (*X* :*selftype*) = (@*X.NUM* =@*self*.*NUM*) **end**
>
> **class** *INT2* = **inherits** *NAT2* **with record**
> > **var** *ISNEG* : **newbool**;
> > **fun** *EQ* (*Y* :*selftype*) = (@*Y.ISNEG* =@*self*.*ISNEG*)
> > > & (@*Y.NUM* =@*self*.*NUM*) **end**

The *EQ* operation takes an object as an argument and compares it for equality to the local one. Given the declarations

> **object** *N2*: *NAT2*; **object** *I2*: *INT2*

we see that the value of *selftype*, like the value of *self*, will be resolved when an object is declared. Thus, *N2.EQ* is typed *NAT2* $\rightarrow$ *boolexp*, and *I2.EQ* is typed *INT2* $\rightarrow$ *boolexp*. These typings use the class names as typing attributes.

An earlier example made clear that method redefinition must never alter the typing of the original method. Now, consider the typing of *EQ* in *NAT2*: It *appears* to be *selftype* $\rightarrow$ *boolexp*, which matches the typing of *EQ* in *INT2*. But the typing of *N2.EQ*, which fixes *selftype* to *NAT2*, differs from that of *I2.EQ*, which fixes *selftype* to *INT2*. Perhaps this is acceptable, since *INT2* is a subclass of *NAT2*. But ultimately, it is not; given this well-typed procedure

> **proc** *Q*(*Z* :*NAT2*) = $\cdots$ *Z.EQ* (*N2*) $\cdots$

we might try **call** *Q* (*I2*), since *INT2* is a subclass of *NAT2*, and disaster results! The correspondence between subclass and subtype is broken by the combination of method redefinition and objects-as-parameters. Indeed, the Trellis/Owl language disallows situations like the above. In Section 4.7, we clarify this problem and define "subtype" and relate it to "subclass."

4.6.1 Semantics of Dynamically Scoped Objects

The typing rules and semantics definition for inheritance in Section 4.5 support static scoping, so we must abandon them here. We will not present new typing rules yet—that is the topic of the next section—but we will attempt an operational semantics for the untyped language.

A key change to the semantics definition is that a class is parameterized on the unknown value of *self*:

$$[\![\textbf{class } I{=}T]\!]e \; s = (\{\,I{=}f\,\}, s), \text{ where } f\,s'\,m = [\![T]\!](e \uplus \{\,self{=}m\,\})\,s'$$

The meaning of *self* must be supplied when the class is activated by an object declaration. This is done *recursively*:

$$[\![\textbf{object } I_1 : I_2\,]\!]e \; s = (\{\,I_1{=}b\,\}, s'), \text{ where } (b, s') = f\,s\,b \text{ and } (I_2{=}f) \in e$$

Since *self* ultimately refers to the object being declared, that object, b, must be defined in terms of itself. The semantics equations for the syntax of type structures

$$T ::= \textbf{newint} \mid \textbf{record } D \textbf{ end} \mid \textbf{inherits } T_1 \textbf{ with } T_2 \mid I$$

are routine, but the equation for I, class invocation, requires the the value of *self*:

$$[\![\textbf{newint}]\!]e \; s = allocate \; s$$
$$[\![\textbf{record } D \textbf{ end}]\!]e \; s = [\![D]\!]e \; s$$
$$[\![\textbf{ inherits } T_1 \textbf{ with } T_2]\!]e \; s = (e_1 \uplus e_2, s_2)$$
$$\quad\quad \text{where } (e_1, s_1) = [\![T_1]\!]e \; s \text{ and } (e_2, s_2) = [\![T_2]\!](e \uplus e_1)\,s_1$$
$$[\![I]\!]e \; s = f\,s\,m, \text{ where } (I{=}f) \in e \text{ and } (self{=}m) \in e$$

Figure 4.5 shows the calculation of the object, I, in the above example. Notably, I binds to the record $b = \{\,NUM{=}loc_i, PLUSTWO{=}g_2, ISNEG{=}loc_j, SUCC{=}f_1\,\}$, so the invocation of *I.PLUSTWO* yields $g_2\,s \Rightarrow^* f_1(f_1\,s)$, where f_1 is the denotation of *self.SUCC*, namely, the version of *SUCC* in *INT*.

4.7 Subtyping

We now develop a typing system, essentially that of Trellis/Owl, that formalizes subtyping. Given type attributes θ_1 and θ_2, we write $\theta_1 \leq \theta_2$ to assert that θ_1 is a *subtype* of θ_2. The intuition is that a phrase of type θ_1 can be used in any context that demands a phrase of type θ_2. We assume that the subtyping relation, $\leq$, is *reflexive* and *transitive*; that is, for all θ, $\theta \leq \theta$, and for all θ_1, θ_2, and θ_3, $\theta_1 \leq \theta_2$ and $\theta_2 \leq \theta_3$ imply $\theta_1 \leq \theta_3$.

Let $e_2 = e_1 \uplus \{INT = f\}$

    where $e_1 = e_0 \uplus \{NAT = g\}$

    $f\,s\,m = [\![\,\textbf{inherits}\; NAT\; \textbf{with}\; \textbf{record}\; \cdots\; \textbf{end}]\!]\,(e_1 \uplus \{self{=}m\})\,s$

    $g\,s\,m = [\![\textbf{record var}\; NUM\!:\textbf{newint};\; \cdots\; \textbf{end}]\!]\,(e_0 \uplus \{self{=}m\})\,s$

$[\![\textbf{object}\; I\!:\!INT]\!]e_2\,s_0 \;\Rightarrow\; (\{I{=}b\},\, s')$

    where $(b,\, s') = f\,s_0\,b$

        $\Rightarrow\; [\![\,\textbf{inherits}\; NAT\; \textbf{with}\; \textbf{record}$

                    $\textbf{var}\; ISNEG\!:\textbf{newbool}$

                    $\textbf{proc}\; SUCC = \cdots\; \textbf{end}]\!](e_1 \uplus \{self{=}b\})\,s_0$

      $\Rightarrow\; (e_3 \uplus e_4,\, s_4)$

      where $(e_3, s_3) = [\![NAT]\!](e_1 \uplus \{self{=}b\})\,s_0$

          $\Rightarrow\; g\,s_0\,b$

          $\Rightarrow\; [\![\textbf{record var}\; NUM\!:\textbf{newint};\; \textbf{proc}\; SUCC = self.NUM{:=}@\,self.NUM{+}1;$

                $\textbf{proc}\; PLUSTWO = \cdots\;]\!](e_0 \uplus \{self{=}b\})\,s_0$

       $\Rightarrow^*\; (\{NUM{=}loc_i,\; SUCC{=}g_1,\; PLUSTWO{=}g_2\},\; s_1)$

            where $(loc_i, s_1) = allocate\; s_0$

            $g_1\,s = [\![self.NUM := @\,self.NUM{+}1]\!](e_0 \uplus \{self{=}b,\; NUM{=}loc_i\})\,s$

            $g_2\,s = [\![\textbf{call}\; self.SUCC;\; \textbf{call}\; self.SUCC]\!](e_0$

                              $\uplus \{self{=}b,\; NUM{=}loc_i,\; SUCC{=}g_1\})\,s$

      and $(e_4, s_4) \Rightarrow [\![\textbf{record var}\; ISNEG\!:\textbf{newbool};\; \textbf{proc}\; SUCC = \textbf{if}\; \neg self.ISNEG$

                              $\textbf{then}\; \cdots\;]\!](e_1 \uplus \{self{=}b\} \uplus e_3)\,s_3$

          $\Rightarrow^*\; (\{ISNEG{=}loc_j,\; SUCC{=}f_1\},\; s_2)$

             where $(loc_j, s_2) = allocate\; s_1$

             $f_1\,s = [\![\textbf{if}\; \neg self.ISNEG\; \textbf{then}\; \cdots\;]\!](e_1 \uplus \{self{=}b\} \uplus e_3$

                              $\uplus \{ISNEG{=}loc_j\})\,s$

    $\Rightarrow (b, s') = (\{NUM{=}loc_i,\; PLUSTWO{=}g_2,\; ISNEG{=}loc_j,\; SUCC{=}f_1\},\; s_2)$

Figure 4.5

The simplest example of subtyping arises in mixed mode arithmetic, so we study it first before we consider subtyping for objects. For the following example, we assume that $int \leq real$ and that $\tau_1 \leq \tau_2$ implies $\tau_1 exp \leq \tau_2 exp$. We work with these typing rules:

$$\frac{\pi \vdash E: \theta_1}{\pi \vdash E: \theta_2} \text{ if } \theta_1 \leq \theta_2 \qquad\qquad \frac{\pi \vdash E_1: \tau exp \quad \pi \vdash E_2: \tau exp}{\pi \vdash E_1 + E_2: \tau exp}$$

$$\pi \vdash N: int \qquad \pi \vdash N_1.N_2: real \qquad \frac{\pi \vdash E: \tau}{\pi \vdash E: \tau exp} \ \tau \in \{ int, real \}$$

The first rule, called the *coercion rule*, allows us to deduce, say, $\pi \vdash 2: real$ and so then $\pi \vdash 2 + 4.5: realexp$.

As noted in a similar example in Section 1.5, there can be distinct derivation trees for the same well-typed program, and a well-typed program can have different typings, for example, we can show both $\pi \vdash 2 + 3: intexp$ and $\pi \vdash 2 + 3: realexp$, where the latter has distinct derivation trees. The unicity of typing property, which states that a well formed phrase has at most one typing, is lost. Nonetheless, the subtyping system seen above is manageable, because every expression has a *minimal* type. For a type assignment π, we say that a phrase, U, has a minimal type if there is a type attribute, θ_1, such that $\pi \vdash U: \theta_1$ can be derived, and for all other derivations, $\pi \vdash U: \theta_2$, we have $\theta_1 \leq \theta_2$. The minimal typing property is a good substitute for unicity of typing, and it suggests an implementation for type attribute calculation: at each step of a typing derivation, attach the minimal type to a phrase, applying the coercion rule only when absolutely necessary.

The minimal typing property is not automatic. If we add the types *nonnegative* (the nonnegative integers), *nonpositive* (the nonpositive integers) and state just the laws, $nonnegative \leq int$ and $nonpositive \leq int$, then the phrase, 0, will have types *nonnegative*, *nonpositive*, *int*, and *real*, but it has no minimal type.

A denotational semantics for a language with subtyping hinges on the meaning of the subtyping relation. Whenever $\theta_1 \leq \theta_2$, we require a coercion map $[\![\theta_1 \leq \theta_2]\!]: [\![\theta_1]\!] \rightarrow [\![\theta_2]\!]$, which coerces θ_1-typed values into θ_2-typed values. We insist that $[\![\theta \leq \theta]\!]$ is the identity function, and when $\theta_1 \leq \theta_2$ and $\theta_2 \leq \theta_3$, that $[\![\theta_1 \leq \theta_3]\!] = [\![\theta_2 \leq \theta_3]\!] \circ [\![\theta_1 \leq \theta_2]\!]$.

In the mixed mode arithmetic example above, $[\![int \leq real]\!]$ is the usual conversion of an integer into a rational, and $[\![\tau_1 exp \leq \tau_2 exp]\!] = [\![\tau_1 \leq \tau_2]\!] \circ f$, where $f \in [\![\tau_1 exp]\!] = Store \rightarrow [\![\tau_1]\!]$. The semantics of the constructions are the usual ones; the only addition is the semantics of the coercion rule:

$$[\![\pi \vdash E: \theta_2]\!]e \ s = [\![\theta_1 \leq \theta_2]\!]([\![\pi \vdash E: \theta_1]\!]e \ s)$$

There can be distinct derivation trees for the same well-formed program, for example, for $\pi \vdash 2 + 3: realexp$, so it is important that the semantics is *coherent*, that is, the meaning of a well-typed program is independent of the derivation used to assert the well-typing.

Coherence proofs are nontrivial, and the proof of coherence for the above system of mixed mode arithmetic is left as a stimulating exercise.

We can extend subtyping to objects. The key addition is the subtyping relation:

$$\{I_1:\theta_1, \ldots, I_m:\theta_m, I_{m+1}:\theta_{m+1}, \ldots, I_n:\theta_n\} \le \{I_1:\theta_1', \ldots, I_m:\theta_m'\}$$
$$\text{if } 0\le m\le n \text{ and } \theta_j\le\theta_j', \text{ for all } 1\le j\le m$$

The subtyping law says that one object's type is a subtype of another's if the first has all the method names of the second and the types of the respective method names are related by subtyping. The associated coercion map is:

$$[\![\{I_1:\theta_1, \ldots, I_m:\theta_m, \ldots, I_n:\theta_n\}$$
$$\le \{I_1:\theta_1', \ldots, I_m:\theta_m'\}]\!] \{I_1=v_1, \ldots, I_m=v_m, \ldots, I_n=v_n\}$$
$$= \{I_1 = [\![\theta_1\le\theta_1']\!]v_1, \ldots, I_m = [\![\theta_m\le\theta_m']\!]v_m\}$$

Recall the example with *NAT* and *INT* from the previous section; the type attribute for object *N* is *NN* and for *I* is *II*, where *NN* = {*NUM*:*intloc*, *SUCC*:*comm*, *PLUSTWO*:*comm*} and *II* = {*NUM*:*intloc*, *ISNEG*:*boolloc*, *SUCC*:*comm*, *PLUSTWO*: *comm*}. So, *I* has a type that is a subtype of *N*'s. Given the procedure **proc** $P(X:NAT)= \cdots$, we can deduce $\pi\vdash\textbf{call } P(I):comm$, where $\pi = \{P: NN \rightarrow comm, I:II, \ldots\}$. The linearized version of the deduction follows:

$$((\textbf{call P})_\pi^{NN\rightarrow comm}(I_\pi^{II\le NN}))_\pi^{comm}$$

Given our early successes with subtyping, we might extend subtyping to other parts of the programming language. For example, it is tempting to add the law $\pi_1 dec \le \pi_2 dec$ if $\pi_1\le\pi_2$, which states the conditions under which a declaration of type $\pi_1 dec$ can be used where a declaration of type $\pi_2 dec$ is needed. In particular, a program that needs to import a module of type $\pi_2 dec$ can import one of type $\pi_1 dec$, because the latter has all the declarations that the program requires (plus some unneeded, extra ones). But this law has a surprising and disastrous consequence: For our present language, it permits the declaration **fun** $A=2$, **proc** $A=$**skip** to be well typed in two different, *incorrect* ways:

$$((\textbf{fun A=2})_\pi^{\{A:intexp\}dec}, (\textbf{proc A=skip})_\pi^{\{A:comm\}dec\le\{\}dec})_\pi^{\{A:intexp\}dec}$$

$$((\textbf{fun A=2})_\pi^{\{A:intexp\}dec\le\{\}dec}, (\textbf{proc A=skip})_\pi^{\{A:comm\}dec})_\pi^{\{A:comm\}dec}$$

Clearly, subtyping laws should never be added carelessly, so we delete this subtyping law for declarations.

So that we can study objects with parameterized methods, we include the following law for function types:

$$\theta_{11} \rightarrow \theta_{12} \leq \theta_{21} \rightarrow \theta_{22}, \quad \text{if} \quad \theta_{21} \leq \theta_{11} \quad \text{and} \quad \theta_{12} \leq \theta_{22}$$

The law seems contraintuitive, but an example shows that it is sensible. Consider an operation, $TRUNC : realexp \rightarrow intexp$, that truncates its real-typed argument into an integer. $TRUNC$ can pretend to be an operation of type $intexp \rightarrow realexp$, since $intexp$-typed arguments can be coerced to $realexp$-typed ones, and $TRUNC$'s $intexp$-typed answers can be coerced to $realexp$-typed ones. This can be proved with the subtyping laws; we deduce $realexp \rightarrow intexp \leq intexp \rightarrow realexp$, since $intexp \leq realexp$.

The subtyping law for function types proves crucial to resolving the pathological example at the end of the previous section. Here are the (minimal) types of the players in the example; we use an additional type constructor, rec, which is explained momentarily:

$NAT2 : NN2class$

$INT2 : II2class$

$N2 : rec\,n.\,[n/selftype]NN2$

$I2 : rec\,i.\,[i/selftype]II2$

$Q : (rec\,n.\,[n/selftype]NN2) \rightarrow comm$

where $NN2 = \{NUM:intloc,\ EQ:selftype \rightarrow boolexp\}$

and $II2 = \{NUM:intloc,\ ISNEG:boolloc,\ EQ:selftype \rightarrow boolexp\}$

The occurrences of *selftype* in the definitions of $NAT2$ and $INT2$ complicate the typing of the objects. Since *selftype* is unfixed until the declaration of an object, the typings for $NAT2$ and $INT2$ contain *selftype* as an unresolved name. The unresolved name allows $INT2$ to simply inherit $NAT2$, since it contains the same unresolved name. Resolution is reached at the declarations of $N2$ and $I2$, which fix the meaning of *selftype*.

But fixing *selftype* at the object declarations leads to *recursive* typings. The type of object $N2$ is a recursive type, n, such that

$$n = \{NUM:intloc,\ EQ:n \rightarrow boolexp\}$$

and the type of $I2$ is a type, i, such that

$$i = \{NUM:intloc,\ ISNEG:boolloc,\ EQ:i \rightarrow boolexp\}$$

We use the rec constructor to state the recursive typings more compactly, and we introduce these laws to unfold and fold a recursive type:

$$rec\,t.\delta \leq [rec\,t.\,\delta/t]\delta$$
$$[rec\,t.\,\delta/t]\delta \leq rec\,t.\delta$$

For example

$$rec\,n.\{NUM:intloc,\ EQ:n \rightarrow boolexp\}$$

$$\leq \{ NUM : intloc, \ EQ : (rec \, n. \, \{ NUM : intloc, \ EQ : n \to boolexp \}) \to boolexp \}$$
$$\leq rec \, n. \, \{ NUM : intloc, \ EQ : n \to boolexp \}$$

We can verify that the invocations $N2.EQ(N2)$ and **call** $Q(N2)$ are well typed. For the invocation **call** $Q(I2)$ to be well typed, we must derive that $I2$ can have type $rec \, n. \, [n/selftype]NN2$. We need this law to compare different recursive types:

$$rec \, t_1. \, \delta_1 \leq rec \, t_2. \, \delta_2, \quad \text{if} \ t_1 \leq t_2 \ \text{implies} \ \delta_1 \leq \delta_2$$

For example, we can show

$$(rec \, t. \, \{ A : intexp, \ B : intloc, \ C : intexp \to t \}) \leq ((rec \, u. \, \{ A : realexp, \ C : intexp \to u \})$$

but more significantly, we can *not* show that $rec \, i. \, [i/selftype]II2$ is a subtype of $rec \, n. \, [n/selftype]NN2$, since the assumption that $i \leq n$ does not suffice for showing that $i \to boolexp \leq n \to boolexp$. Thus, the invocation **call** $Q(I2)$ cannot be well typed.

The subtyping laws for function types and recursive types show us that a method that takes an object as a parameter can destroy the subtype relation between a subclass and its superclass. But the laws stated above enforce severe restrictions. Even an innocent example of subclasses, such as

> **class** $C1$ = **record**
>> **var** NUM : **newint**;
>> **proc** $ADD(X : selftype) = self.NUM := @X.NUM + @self.NUM$ **end**;
>
> **class** $C2$ = **inherits** $C1$ **with var** $BOOL$: **newbool**;
> **object** $A : C1$; **object** $B : C2$ **in call** $A.ADD(B)$

causes the typing system to complain about **call** $A.ADD(B)$, since the typing system does not monitor method redefinition. The subtyping laws can be modified to deal with such examples, but with pain. The formulation of proper notions of scoping, inheritance, subclassing and subtyping for typed object-oriented languages is a topic of current research.

4.8 The Copy Rule for Blocks

In Chapters 2 and 3, we saw that lazy evaluation of abstractions and parameters supported copy rules for program transformation. The advantage of the copy rules is that a program with abstractions and parameters can be understood with just the copy rules and the semantics definition of the core language.* Here, we note that the copy rule for lazily evaluated abstractions still applies when the abstractions are defined locally within a block.

Recall the copy rule for abstractions from Chapter 2:

define $I_1 = U_1, \ldots,$ **define** $I_n = U_n$ **in** C $\Rightarrow$ $[U_1/I_1, \ldots, U_n/I_n]$C

The bodies of the globally defined abstractions are copied for their invocations in the body of the program. The same rule applies for local definitions:

begin define $I_1 = U_1, \ldots,$ **define** $I_n = U_n$ **in** V **end** $\Rightarrow$ $[U_1/I_1, \ldots, U_n/I_n]$V

The copy rule preserves the proper scope of the local definitions, but care must be taken with the substitution in the presence of local redefinition of an I_j. Here is a small example, an expression block:

begin const $A = 2$, **const** $B = 3$
    in begin fun $F(X:intexp) = X + A + B$
        in begin const $A = 4$ **in** $F(A) + B$ **end**
      end
   end

Recall from Chapter 3 that a parameterized abstraction can be recoded as a lambda abstraction:

begin const $A = 2$, **const** $B = 3$
    in begin fun $F = (\lambda X. \, X + A + B)$
        in begin const $A = 4$ **in** $F(A) + B$ **end end end**

We can apply the copy rule to any of the three blocks in the expression. The most interesting choice is to copy the definition of F in the second block into that block's body:

$\Rightarrow$ **begin const** $A = 2$, **const** $B = 3$
    in $[(\lambda X. \, X + A + B)/F]$(**begin const** $A = 4$ **in** $F(A) + B$ **end**) **end**

Since identifier A is free in F's body, the definition of A in the innermost block must be renamed to avoid a clash. We get

---

* And with the semantics of the eagerly evaluated declarations like variables.

$=$ **begin const** $A=2$, **const** $B=3$
   in $[(\lambda X.\ X+A+B)\,/\,F\,]($**begin const** $Z=4$ **in** $F(Z)+B$ **end**$)$ **end**

$=$ **begin const** $A=2$, **const** $B=3$
   in begin $[(\lambda X.\ X+A+B)\,/\,F\,]($**const** $Z=4)$ **in** $[(\lambda X.\ X+A+B)\,/\,F\,](F(Z)+B)$ **end end**

$=$ **begin const** $A=2$, **const** $B=3$
   in begin const $Z=4$ **in** $(\lambda X.\ X+A+B)(Z)+B$ **end end**

and we finish with

$\Rightarrow$ **begin const** $A=2$, **const** $B=3$ **in** $(\lambda X.\ X+A+B)(4)+B$ **end**

$\Rightarrow$ $(\lambda X.\ X+2+3)(4)+3$ $\Rightarrow$ $(4+2+3)+3$

The formalization of substitution into a block is left for the exercises, and the proof of soundness of the copy rule is handled in Chapter 6.

Finally, we should remember that eagerly evaluated abstractions, like variable declarations, cannot be handled by the copy rule. Thus, an example like

begin var A: **newint; proc** $P(X:intexp) = A:=X+1$
 in begin var B: **newint; fun** $A=@A+@B$
    in call $P(A)$ **end end**

can be copied to

$\Rightarrow$ **begin var** A: **newint**
    in begin var B: **newint; fun** $Z=@A+@B$
       in $(\lambda X:intexp.\ A:=X+1)(Z)$ **end end**

$\Rightarrow$ **begin var** A: **newint**
    in begin var B: **newint**
       in $(\lambda X:intexp.\ A:=X+1)(@A+@B)$ **end end**

$\Rightarrow$ **begin var** A: **newint**
    in begin var B: **newint**
       in $A:=(@A+@B)+1$ **end end**

and no further. The semantics of the core language plus variables must be used at this point to determine the meaning of the program.

4.9 The Qualification Principle Is a Record Introduction Principle

The above section title is a restatement of the title for Section 2.14, because the qualification principle is a restatement of the abstraction principle restricted to local scope. This is evident in the statement of the qualification principle, which states that "any semantically meaningful syntactic class may admit local definitions." Now, not only may the body of a program have declarations, but so may the other phrase forms. Indeed, there is but one principle at work, but its presentation was split across Chapters 2 and 4 for a fuller exposition.

Like the abstractions in Chapter 2, the locally defined abstractions use type attributes that are record types and use semantic values that are records of bindings. But the development in the present chapter emphasizes that the scope of the bindings is a crucial concept. In the terminology in Section 2.14, a block, **begin** D **in** U **end**, is in fact the expression, *with* D *do* U, and the copy rule for blocks is in fact the indexing rule for *with*:

$$ \textit{with } \{I_1 = V_1, I_2 = V_2, \ldots, I_n = V_n\} \textit{ do } U \quad \Rightarrow \quad [V_1/I_1, V_2/I_2, \ldots, V_n/I_n]U $$

(And recall that *R.I* is an abbreviation for *with R do I*.) Chapter 5 systematizes this idea and shows that the programming language developed thus far consists of a core language uniformly extended by records and parameters.

4.10 Summary

For a syntax domain, U, a U-block has the following form:

$$ U ::= \ldots \mid \textbf{begin } D \textbf{ in } U \textbf{ end} $$

Here is a summary of the imperative programming language extended by the qualification principle. With the exception of procedures, we have omitted parameterized abstractions, but parameters can be included for the other abstraction forms with no difficulty. Inheritance for classes is omitted.

D ∈ Declaration	AL ∈ Actual-list
FL ∈ Formal-list	E ∈ Expression
T ∈ Type-structure	X ∈ Identifier-expr
C ∈ Command	I ∈ Identifier

$$ D ::= D_1, D_2 \mid \textbf{var } I{:}T \mid \textbf{proc } I(FL)=C \mid \textbf{class } I=T \mid \textbf{module } I=\{D\} $$
$$ \mid \textbf{import } X \mid \cdots \mid \textbf{begin } D_1 \textbf{ in } D_2 \textbf{ end} $$
$$ FL ::= I{:}\theta \mid FL_1, FL_2 $$

$$T ::= \textbf{newint} \mid \textbf{record } D \textbf{ end} \mid \textbf{begin } D \textbf{ in } T \textbf{ end} \mid X$$
$$C ::= \cdots \mid \textbf{call } X(AL) \mid \textbf{begin } D \textbf{ in } C \textbf{ end}$$
$$AL ::= D$$
$$E ::= \cdots \mid \textbf{begin } D \textbf{ in } E \textbf{ end}$$
$$X ::= I \mid X.I$$

The typing rule for a U-block reads as follows:

$$\frac{\pi_1 \vdash D : \pi_2 dec \qquad \pi_1 \uplus \pi_2 \vdash U : \theta}{\pi_1 \vdash \textbf{begin } D \textbf{ in } U \textbf{ end} : \theta}$$

The syntax of the type attributes remains the same from Chapter 3:

$$\theta ::= \tau \mid \tau exp \mid comm \mid \delta \mid \delta class \mid \pi dec \mid \theta_1 \to \theta_2$$
$$\tau ::= int \mid bool$$
$$\delta ::= intloc \mid \pi$$
$$\pi ::= \{j{:}\theta_j\}_{j \in J}, \quad \text{where } J \subseteq \text{Identifier is a finite set}$$

The typing rules follow:

For Declaration:

$$\frac{\pi \vdash D_1 : \pi_1 dec \qquad \pi \vdash D_2 : \pi_2 dec}{\pi \vdash D_1, D_2 : \pi_1 \cup \pi_2 dec} \qquad \qquad \frac{\pi \vdash T : \delta class}{\pi \vdash \textbf{var } I{:}T : \{I{:}\delta\} dec}$$

$$\frac{\pi \uplus \pi_1 \vdash C : comm}{\pi \vdash \textbf{proc } I(F) = C : \{I{:}\pi_1 \to comm\} dec} \quad \text{where } \pi_1 = type\text{-}attrs(F),$$

$$type\text{-}attrs(I{:}\theta) = \{I{:}\theta\} \quad \text{and} \quad type\text{-}attrs(F_1, F_2) = type\text{-}attrs(F_1) \cup type\text{-}attrs(F_2)$$

$$\frac{\pi \vdash T : \delta class}{\pi \vdash \textbf{class } I = T : \{I{:}\delta class\} dec} \qquad \frac{\pi \vdash D : \pi_1 dec}{\textbf{module } I = \{D\} : \{I{:}\pi_1 dec\} dec}$$

$$\frac{\pi \vdash X : \pi_1 dec}{\pi \vdash \textbf{import } X : \pi_1 dec} \qquad \frac{\pi \vdash D_1 : \pi_1 dec \qquad \pi \uplus \pi_1 \vdash D_2 : \pi_2 dec}{\pi \vdash \textbf{begin } D_1 \textbf{ in } D_2 \textbf{ end} : \pi_2 dec}$$

For Type-structure:

$$\pi \vdash \textbf{newint} : intloc \; class \qquad \qquad \frac{\pi \vdash D : \pi_1 dec}{\pi \vdash \textbf{record } D \textbf{ end} : \pi_1 class}$$

$$\frac{\pi \vdash D : \pi_1\, dec \quad \pi \uplus \pi_1 \vdash T : \delta class}{\pi \vdash \textbf{begin } D \textbf{ in } T \textbf{ end} : \delta class} \qquad \frac{\pi \vdash X : \delta class}{\pi \vdash X : \delta class}$$

For Command:

$$\frac{\pi \vdash X : \pi_1 \rightarrow comm \quad \pi \vdash AL : \pi_1}{\pi \vdash \textbf{call } X(AL) : comm} \qquad \frac{\pi \vdash D : \pi_1\, dec \quad \pi \uplus \pi_1 \vdash C : comm}{\pi \vdash \textbf{begin } D \textbf{ in } C \textbf{ end} : comm}$$

For Actual-list:

$$\frac{\pi \vdash D : \pi_1\, dec}{\pi \vdash D : \pi_1}$$

For Expression:

$$\frac{\pi \vdash D : \pi_1\, dec \quad \pi \uplus \pi_1 \vdash E : \tau exp}{\pi \vdash \textbf{begin } D \textbf{ in } E \textbf{ end} : \tau exp}$$

For Identifier-expression:

$$\pi \vdash I : \theta, \quad \text{if } (I : \theta) \in \pi \qquad \frac{\pi \vdash X : \pi_1}{\pi \vdash X.I : \theta} \quad \text{if } (I : \theta) \in \pi_1$$

The semantics of the language is carried over unaltered from Chapters 2 and 3, and this is the semantics of a command block:

$$[\![\pi \vdash \textbf{begin } D \textbf{ in } C \textbf{ end} : comm]\!]e\ s = free\ (size\text{-}of\ s)\ s_2$$
$$\text{where } (e_1, s_1) = [\![\pi \vdash D : \pi_1 dec]\!]e\ s,$$
$$\text{and } s_2 = [\![\pi \uplus \pi_1 \vdash C : comm]\!](e \uplus e_1)\ s_1,$$

The command block manages storage allocation and deallocation. Blocks that do not manage storage have this form of semantics:

$$[\![\pi \vdash \textbf{begin } D \textbf{ in } U \textbf{ end} : \theta]\!]e\ s = [\![\pi \uplus \pi_1 \vdash U : \theta]\!]e_1\ s_1$$
$$\text{where } (e_1, s_1) = [\![\pi \vdash D : \pi_1 dec]\!]e\ s$$

When abstractions are evaluated lazily, the copy rule from Chapter 2 is adapted to blocks:

$$\textbf{begin define } I_1 = V_1, \textbf{ define } I_2 = V_2, \ldots, \textbf{ define } I_n = V_n \textbf{ in } U \textbf{ end}$$
$$\Rightarrow [V_1/I_1, V_2/I_2, \ldots, V_n/I_n]U$$

Here is the complete denotational semantics of the language:

For Declaration:

$$\llbracket \pi \vdash D_1, D_2 : (\pi_1 \cup \pi_2) dec \rrbracket e\ s = (e_1 \cup e_2, s_2)$$

where $(e_1, s_1) = \llbracket \pi \vdash D_1 : \pi_1 dec \rrbracket e\ s$ and $(e_2, s_2) = \llbracket \pi \vdash D_2 : \pi_2 dec \rrbracket e\ s_1$

$$\llbracket \pi \vdash \textbf{var } I{:}T{:} \{I{:}\delta\} dec \rrbracket e\ s = (\{I{=}v\}, s')$$

where $(v, s') = \llbracket \pi \vdash T : \delta class \rrbracket e\ s$

$$\llbracket \pi \vdash \textbf{proc } I(F){=}C{:} \{I{:}\pi_1 \rightarrow comm\} dec \rrbracket e\ s = (\{I{=}p\}, s)$$

where $p\ e_1\ s' = \llbracket \pi \uplus \pi_1 \vdash C : comm \rrbracket (e \uplus e_1)\ s$, and $type\text{-}attrs(F) = \pi_1$

$$\llbracket \pi \vdash \textbf{class } I{=}T{:} \{I{:}\delta class\} dec \rrbracket e\ s = (\{I = f, s)$$

where $f\ s' = \llbracket \pi \vdash T{:}\delta class \rrbracket e\ s'$

$$\llbracket \pi \vdash \textbf{module } I{=}\{D\}{:} \{I{:}\pi_1 dec\} dec \rrbracket e\ s = (\{I{=}e_1\}, s_1)$$

where $(e_1, s_1) = \llbracket \pi \vdash D : \pi dec \rrbracket e\ s$

$$\llbracket \pi \vdash \textbf{import } X{:}\pi_1 dec \rrbracket e\ s = (e_1, s)$$

where $e_1 = \llbracket \pi \vdash X{:}\pi_1 dec \rrbracket e$, as defined by the semantics of Identifier-expr

. . .

$$\llbracket \pi \vdash \textbf{begin } D_1 \textbf{ in } D_2 \textbf{ end}{:}\pi_2 dec \rrbracket e\ s = \llbracket \pi \uplus \pi_1 \vdash D_2 : \pi_2 dec \rrbracket (e \uplus e_1)\ s_1$$

where $(e_1, s_1) = \llbracket \pi \vdash D_1 : \pi_1 dec \rrbracket e\ s$

For Type-structure:

$$\llbracket \pi \vdash \textbf{newint}{:} intloc\ class \rrbracket e\ s = allocate(s)$$

$$\llbracket \pi \vdash \textbf{record } D \textbf{ end}{:}\pi class \rrbracket e\ s = \llbracket \pi \vdash D : \pi dec \rrbracket e\ s$$

$$\llbracket \pi \vdash \textbf{begin } D \textbf{ in } T \textbf{ end}{:}\delta class \rrbracket e\ s = \llbracket \pi \uplus \pi_1 \vdash T : \delta class \rrbracket e_1\ s_1$$

where $(e_1, s_1) = \llbracket \pi \vdash D : \pi_1 dec \rrbracket e\ s$

$$\llbracket \pi \vdash X{:}\delta class \rrbracket e\ s = p(s)$$

where $p = \llbracket \pi \vdash X{:}\delta class \rrbracket e$, as defined by the semantics of Identifier-expr

For Command:

$$\llbracket \textbf{call } X(D){:} comm \rrbracket e\ s = p\ e_1\ s'$$

where $(e_1, s') = \llbracket \pi \vdash D : \pi_1 dec \rrbracket e\ s$

and $p = \llbracket \pi \vdash X : \pi_1 \rightarrow comm \rrbracket e$, as defined by the semantics of Identifier-expr

$$\llbracket \pi \vdash \textbf{begin } D \textbf{ in } C \textbf{ end}{:} comm \rrbracket e\ s = free\ (size\text{-}of\ s)\ s_2$$

where $(e_1, s_1) = \llbracket \pi \vdash D : \pi_1 dec \rrbracket e\ s$,

and $s_2 = \llbracket \pi \uplus \pi_1 \vdash C : comm \rrbracket (e \uplus e_1)\ s_1$,

For Expression:

$$\llbracket \pi \vdash \textbf{begin } D \textbf{ in } E \textbf{ end}{:} \tau exp \rrbracket e\ s = \llbracket \pi \uplus \pi_1 \vdash E : \tau exp \rrbracket e_1\ s_1$$

where $(e_1, s_1) = \llbracket \pi \vdash D : \pi_1 dec \rrbracket e\ s$

For Identifier-expr:

$$[\![\pi \vdash I \colon \theta]\!]e = v, \quad \text{where} \quad (I = v) \in e$$
$$[\![\pi \vdash X.I \colon \theta]\!]e = v, \quad \text{where} \quad r = [\![\pi \vdash X \colon \pi_1]\!]e \quad \text{and} \quad (I = v) \in r$$

Suggested Reading

The qualification principle was proposed by Tennent (1981). Implementation methods for blocks can be found in Pratt 1984 or any compiling text, for example, Aho, Sethi, and Ullman 1986. Scoping issues arose with the designs of Algol-60 and Lisp 1.5; see Dijkstra 1962 and Naur 1963 for information about the former, and McCarthy, et al. 1965, Allen 1978, and Winston and Horn 1984 for information about the latter. A careful discussion of scoping appears in Kamin 1990. Declaration blocks are best observed in action in languages like CLU (see Liskov, et al. 1977 and Liskov, et al. 1981); Modula-2 (see Gleaves 1984 and Wirth 1977 and 1982); and Ada (see Barnes 1982).

Classes and inheritance originate from Simula-67; Birtwistle, et al. 1973 is the standard reference. The area of object-oriented languages grew from work on Smalltalk; see Goldberg and Robson 1983. Subsequent developments have been fast and furious; the series of OOPSLA conference proceedings from 1986 onwards documents the situation. The first five papers in OOPSLA 1986 make a good starting point. Most object-oriented languages are dynamically typed, but the book by Meyer (1989) presents a good view of statically typed object-oriented languages, with emphasis on the Eiffel language. Good introductions to subtyping are Cardelli 1984, Cardelli and Wegner 1985, and Cardelli 1986a. The distinctions between subclasses and subtypes are spelled out by Cook, Hill, and Canning 1990, Mitchell 1990, and Bruce 1993. See also Gunter and Mitchell 1993. Pierce 1992 points out the dangers in mixing subtypes with generic procedures.

Exercises

1.1. Verify that these programs are well typed and calculate their denotational semantics:

a. **begin const** A=2; **var** B: **newint**;
    fun F=A+1;
    proc $P(X\colon intexp)$ = **begin fun** A=0 **in** B:=X+F **end**
  in call $P(A)$ **end**

b. **begin**
    module M = { **var** A: **newint**; **fun** F = @A+1 }
    proc P = **begin import** M **in** A:=F **end**;
  in call P; **call** P **end**

1.2. Explain why the typing rule for $D_1;D_2$ should be replaced by the following:

$$\frac{\pi \vdash D_1 : \pi_1 \, dec \quad \pi \uplus \pi_1 \vdash D_2 : \pi_2 \, dec}{\pi \vdash D_1;D_2 : (\pi_1 \cup \pi_2) \, dec}$$

1.3. a. Use structural induction to prove that a single, global, stack variable can replace the type assignment attributes in the building of an attributed syntax tree.

b.* Consider a language with unparameterized abstractions and command blocks, and use the denotational semantics of the language as an operational semantics. Prove that a program's operational semantics can be calculated where all occurrences of the environment arguments are replaced by a single, global stack variable. (Note: The stack variable must use ''static links''; see a compiling text for details.) Next, add parameters to the abstractions and prove that the result still holds. Ultimately, the global stack variable fails to suffice; see the next chapter and Chapter 7.

2.1. a. For the two programs in Exercise 1.1, specify the scopes of the definitions in the programs.

b. Calculate the semantics of the two programs with dynamic scoping.

2.2. Consider this core language:

$C \in$ Command
$K \in$ Completion
$\quad$ C ::= L:=E | $C_1;C_2$ | K | **exblock** C **end**
$\quad$ K ::= C;K | **exit**

The **exit** construct forces control to jump to the end of the nearest enclosing **exblock**.

a. Define the typing rules of the language.

b.* Write a denotational semantics.

c. Say that command abstractions and command blocks are added, and for convenience, command blocks are merged with **exblocks**.

$\quad$ D ::= **proc** I=C | $D_1;D_2$
$\quad$ C ::= L:=E | $C_1;C_2$ | K | **begin** D **in** C **end**
$\quad$ K ::= C;K | **exit**

Now, an **exit** forces control to jump to the end of the nearest enclosing command block. What is the path of control in this program; in particular, which block does **exit** exit?

$\quad$ **begin proc** P = **exit**
$\quad$ **in** $\cdots$ **begin** $\cdots$ **in call** P **end** $\cdots$ **end**

In what sense is this a question of static versus dynamic scoping?

  d. Augment the language by completion abstractions:

$$D ::= \textbf{proc } I{=}C \mid D_1;D_2 \mid \textbf{exception } I{=}K$$
$$C ::= L{:=}E \mid C_1;C_2 \mid K \mid \textbf{begin } D \textbf{ in } C \textbf{ end}$$
$$K ::= C;K \mid \textbf{exit} \mid \textbf{signal } I$$

Which block is exited in this example?

> **begin exception** E = **exit**;
>   **proc** P = $\cdots$ **signal** E $\cdots$
> **in** $\cdots$ **begin exception** E = **exit**
>   **in** $\cdots$ **call** P $\cdots$ **end end**

Why is this also a scoping question?

3.1. Describe the extent of the variables in the examples in Exercise 1.1 and explain why the variables' extents differ from their scopes.

3.2 Calculate the denotational semantics of this recursively defined procedure:

> **begin var** A: **newint**;
>   **rec-proc** P = **begin var** B: **newint**
>   **in if** $@A{=}0$ **then skip else** $A{:=}@A{-}1$; **call** P **fi end**
>   **in** $A{:=}2$; **call** P **end**

What is the "extent" of B?

3.3. a.* If you worked Exercise 2.5 in Chapter 3, proceed. Re-prove that result for the language augmented by command blocks. Then, explain why the result implies that no escaped location will ever be used by a well-typed program.

    b. The result in Part a, strictly speaking, is not a proof that locations cannot escape from well-typed programs. The notion of escaping is an operational one, and the proof of the impossibility of escapes must be done with the operational semantics.

        Say that a computation, $[\![\vdash C: comm]\!]e_0\ s_0 = p_0 \Rightarrow p_1 \Rightarrow \cdots \Rightarrow p_n = v$, a Value, is *escape free* if for all $0 \leq i \leq n$, if a store Value, s_i, that holds w integers appears in p_i, then no loc_k, $k>w$, appears in p_i. Prove that all computations starting from $[\![\varnothing \vdash C: comm]\!]\varnothing\ s_w$ are escape free.

    c. Add pointer variables to language and give their semantics. Show that the proof in Part b cannot be extended for pointer variables.

    d. Now, add this restriction: For pointer variable, A, $A{:=}B$ is allowed if B is declared no more globally than A. Formulate typing rules to enforce this property; prove that escapes are impossible. Is this restriction pragmatically useful?

4.1. a. Give the typing rule for opaque types; use this syntax:

$$D ::= \cdots \mid \textbf{begin opaque } I = T \textbf{ in } D \textbf{ end}$$

   b. Define the denotational semantics.

5.1. Contrast the typing, scoping, extents, and semantics of these three examples:

   a. **module** A = { **var** X: **newint** };
       class B = **begin import** A **in record proc** P := X:=0 **end**;
       var S:B; **var** T:B

   b. **class** A = **record var** X: **newint end**;
       class B = **begin var** X:A **in record proc** P = $X.X$:=0 **end**;
       var S:B; **var** T:B

   c. **class** A = **record var** X: **newint end**;
       class B = **inherits** A **with record proc** P = X:=0 **end**;
       var S:B; **var** T:B

5.2. Say that a programming language allows its record variables to be assigned entire records, and say that record variables are implemented as pointers to structures in heap storage. The assignment of one record variable to another is the copying of a pointer, which causes sharing.

   a. Explain how the sharing is useful to object-oriented data bases; consider this:

   class $AUTHOR$ = **record var** $NAME$: $\cdots$ **end** ;
   class $BOOK$ = **record** WHO: $AUTHOR$ $\cdots$ **end**;
   var $DOSTOYEVSKI$: $AUTHOR$;
   var $CRIME\text{-}AND\text{-}PUNISHMENT$: $BOOK$;
   var $BROTHERS\text{-}KARAMAZOV$: $BOOK$
     in $\cdots$ $CRIME\text{-}AND\text{-}PUNISHMENT.AUTHOR$:=$DOSTOYEVSKI$

   b. Why does assignment-as-sharing plus inheritance make modules largely redundant?

6.1. Using the dynamic scoping/static binding method described in Section 4.6, calculate the structures of the variables declared in these examples. (Use the denotational-style semantics, if you wish.)

   a. **class** A = **record var** X: **newint**;
          fun $EQ(Y$:$selftype)$ = $@Y.X$:=$@self.X$ **end**
       class B = **inherits** A **with record var** Y: **newint**;
          fun $EQ(Z$: $selftype)$ = $@Z.X$=$@self.X$ & $@Z.Y$=$@self.Y$ **end**
       object M :A; **object** N:B

   b. **class** A = **record var** X: **newint**;
          fun $EQ(Y$: $selftype)$ = $@Y.X$=$@self.X$;
          fun $TRUE$ = $self.EQ(self)$ **end**
       class B = **inherits** A **with record var** X: **newint**;

      fun *EQ*(*Z*:*selftype*) = @*Z.X*=@*self.X* **end**
      object *M*:*A*; **object** *N*:*B*

  c. In Part b, if the definition of *EQ* in *B* was dropped, would there be any difference in behavior?

  d. Redo Parts a and b with static scoping.

6.2. There are variations on inheritance.

  a. One form allows inheritance to be restricted to specific field names:

    class *POLYGON* = **record**
      var *CORNERS*: $\cdots$;
      var *EDGES*: $\cdots$;
      proc *ADD-EDGE* = $\cdots$; $\cdots$ **end**;
    class *RECTANGLE* =
      inherits from *POLYGON*:*CORNERS*, *EDGES* **with** $\cdots$

So, the *ADD-EDGE* method is not inherited by *RECTANGLE*. Give a typing rule and semantics for this form of inheritance with static scoping. What problems arise with dynamic scoping?

  b. Another form of inheritance allows reference to a redefined method by means of a *super* reference:

    class *A* = **record var** *X*:**newint**; **proc** *INIT* = *X*:=0 **end**
    class *B* = **inherits** *A* **with record var** *X*:**newint**;
      fun *EQ* = (@*self.X* = @*super.X*)
    end

Define a typing rule and semantics for the *super* reference with static scoping. Describe the semantics of *super* for dynamic scoping. Give applications of *super* with static scoping; with dynamic scoping.

  c.* Some object-oriented languages allow methods to be added dynamically:

    begin class *M* = $\cdots$
    in $\cdots$ **add-method-to** *M*:(**proc** *P* = $\cdots$) $\cdots$ **end**

Define a syntax and describe a semantics for dynamic method addition. Give examples of usefulness.

6.3. Many object-oriented languages treat objects as pointers to structures in heap storage; for example, **class** *C* = $\cdots$; **var** *S*:*C* **in** $\cdots$ *S*:=**new** *C* $\cdots$ allocates the storage for a *C*-object at run time and assigns a pointer to the storage to *S*. Write a semantics for dynamic allocation of objects.

6.4. a. Return to the semantics of objects in Section 4.6.1 and calculate the semantics of this example:

    class *A* = **record var** *X*:**newint end**;

> **class** B = **inherits** A **with record fun** EQ = $(@\,self.X=X)$;
>   **var** X: **newint end**;
> **object** M : B

How does the example compare to the one that uses *super* reference in Exercise 6.2.b?

    b. Add type structure blocks and give them the usual semantics. Can variables, I, local to a type structure block be referenced via *self.I*?

7.1. a. Use the subtyping rules for mixed mode arithmetic, given at the beginning of Section 4.7, to draw multiple proof trees for both of these examples: $\{\,\} \vdash 3+2 : realexp$; $\{\,\} \vdash (3+2)+1.5 : realexp$.

    b. Say that the programming language allows *real*-valued variables, for example, **var** X: **newreal**. Try to formulate typing rules for *intloc*, *realloc*, and in general, τloc, such that an example like

        var X: **newreal**, **var** Y: **newint in** $X := 2 + @Y$

is well typed, but

        var Y: **newint**, **proc** $P(Z:realloc)$ = $Z:=1.5$ **in call** $P(Y)$

is not. What is the difficulty?

    c. If you worked Exercise 6.5.f of Chapter 1, proceed. Re-work Part b, where a variable is an acceptor, expression pair, that is, $\tau var = \tau acc \times \tau exp$, and define subtyping laws for τacc and τexp. Is it possible to define a useful subtyping law for τvar?

    d. A Pascal-style subrange type defines a form of subtype, for example, **class** $SMALL$ = $0..9$ and $SMALL \leq int$. State subtyping laws for subrange types. Why does a compiler find such laws difficult to apply?

7.2. Use the subtyping laws for objects to type check the programs in Exercises 6.1a and b.

8.1. a. Define $[V/I]$**begin** D **in** U **end**. Why must we know the typing of D to define the substitution? Thus, it becomes crucial that substitution preserves the typing of a well-typed phrase. (The proof is given in Chapter 6.)

    b. Define $[V_1/I_1, V_2/I_2, \ldots, V_n/I_n]$**begin** D **in** U **end**.

10.1. For any core language that you have extended with abstractions and parameters, add blocks. Use the correspondence principle to judge your results.

10.2. For your favorite general purpose programming language, define its core, list its forms of abstractions, parameters, and blocks, and note its degree of compliance with the correspondence principle. What suggestions would you make to streamline the language?

5 Records and Lambda Abstractions

The previous chapters developed at length the applications of names and parameters. It is now time to place this work into perspective and see precisely what has been accomplished. In doing so, we will learn that records and lambda abstractions constitute the crucial components of a structured, parameterized language. We will also see that a natural "model" and "logic" are consequences of these components.

5.1 The Desugared Programming Language

We return to the core imperative programming language of Chapter 1 and "desugar" it by rewriting its syntax definition so that all the constructions reside within the same syntax rule:

$E \in$ Everything
$N \in$ Numeral
$L \in$ Location

$E ::= E_1 := E_2 \mid E_1; E_2 \mid$ **if** E_1 **then** E_2 **else** E_3 **fi** $\mid$ **skip** $\mid$ **while** E_1 **do** E_2 **od**
$\mid E_1 + E_2 \mid E_1 = E_2 \mid \neg E \mid @E \mid N \mid L$

The language appears to have lost its structure, but the typing annotations preserve it: See Figure 5.1. The types distinguish the command constructs from the expression constructs and from the location and numeral constructs, so the set of well-typed programs remains the same. Our reasons for collapsing the language are:

(i) We will momentarily introduce two structuring devices, and rather than define instances of each for a multitude of syntax domains, we can use just one instance for the entire language.

(ii) In subsequent chapters, we study additional language extensions, and we will find it convenient to work with a core language with just one syntax domain.

By no means are we abandoning the methodology of distinct syntax domains to organize and present a language, but the approach in this chapter is especially useful for language analysis.

$$\frac{E_1 : intloc \quad E_2 : intexp}{E_1 := E_2 : comm} \qquad \frac{E_1 : comm \quad E_2 : comm}{E_1 ; E_2 : comm}$$

$$\frac{E_1 : boolexp \quad E_2 : comm \quad E_3 : comm}{\textbf{if } E_1 \textbf{ then } E_2 \textbf{ else } E_3 \textbf{ fi}: comm} \qquad \textbf{skip}: comm \qquad \frac{E_1 : boolexp \quad E_2 : comm}{\textbf{while } E_1 \textbf{ do } E_2 \textbf{ od}: comm}$$

$$\frac{E_1 : intexp \quad E_2 : intexp}{E_1 + E_2 : boolexp} \qquad \frac{E_1 : \tau exp \quad E_2 : \tau exp}{E_1 = E_2 : intexp} \qquad \frac{E : boolexp}{\neg E : boolexp}$$

$$\frac{E : intloc}{@E : intexp} \qquad N : intexp \qquad L : intloc$$

Figure 5.1

5.2 Record Introduction

First, we apply the abstraction/qualification principle and augment the desugared programming language by these constructs

$$E ::= \cdots \mid I{=}E \mid E_1, E_2 \mid \textit{with } E_1 \textit{ do } E_2 \mid I$$

and the following typing rules:

$$\frac{\pi \vdash E : \theta}{\pi \vdash I{=}E : \{I{:}\theta\}} \qquad \frac{\pi \vdash E_1 : \pi_1 \quad \pi \vdash E_2 : \pi_2}{\pi \vdash E_1, E_2 : \pi_1 \cup \pi_2}$$

$$\frac{\pi \vdash E_1 : \pi_1 \quad \pi \uplus \pi_1 \vdash E_2 : \theta}{\pi \vdash \textit{with } E_1 \textit{ do } E_2 : \theta} \qquad \pi \vdash I : \theta \ \text{ if } (I{:}\theta) \in \pi$$

The construct, $I{=}E$, is a binding, and we follow convention and call it a *record*. (In the past, such a record was written $\{I{=}E\}$.) E_1, E_2 unions two records together; an example is $(A=2, \ B=\textbf{skip}), \ C=(A{=}@loc_1{+}1)$, which we write as $A=2, \ B=\textbf{skip}, \ C = (A{=}@loc_1{+}1)$ or with braces for clarity: $\{A=2, \ B=\textbf{skip}, \ C=\{A{=}@loc_1{+}1\}\}$. Records model definitions. The *with* E_1 *do* E_2 construction is the desugared form of **begin** E_1 **in** E_2 **end**, and I refers to a field in a record; that is, it is the invocation construct for definitions.

Since we have merged the language's syntax domains into one, the record construction allows phrases from all syntax domains to be named—this is the abstraction principle. The *with* construction ensures that phrases from all syntax domains may have local definitions—this is the qualification principle.

The introduction of records enriches the type system of the language: The type $\{i{:}\theta_i\}_{i \in I}$ is used as the type attribute for records. Since phrases can include identifiers, the typing of the phrases requires a type assignment attribute. All of the rules in Figure 5.1 are enriched in the expected way, for example,

$$\frac{\pi \vdash E_1 : intloc \quad \pi \vdash E_2 : intexp}{\pi \vdash E_1 := E_2 : comm}$$

Here is a well-typed program, with the type assignments written as subscripts and the type attributes written as superscripts:

$$(with \ (A{=}loc_1)_{\varnothing}^{\{A:intloc\}}$$
$$do \ (with \ (M = (P = A:={@}A{+}1)_{\pi_1}^{\{P:comm\}})_{\pi_1}^{\{M:\{P:comm\}\}}$$
$$do \ (with \ (M_{\pi_2}^{\{P:comm\}}, \ (F{=}0)_{\pi_2}^{\{F:intexp\}})_{\pi_2}^{\{P:comm, \ F:intexp\}}$$
$$do \ (A:=F; \ P)_{\pi_3}^{comm})_{\pi_2}^{comm})_{\pi_1}^{comm})_{\varnothing}^{comm}$$

where $\pi_1 = \{A{:}intloc\}$, $\pi_2 = \pi_1 \uplus \{M{:}\{P{:}comm\}\}$,

and $\pi_3 = \pi_2 \uplus \{P{:}comm, \ F{:}intexp\}$

The previous program is the desugared version of this one:

begin alias $A{=}loc_1$

    in begin module $M = \{$ **proc** $P = A{:}{=}{@}A{+}1 \}$

        in begin import M, **fun** $F{=}0$

            in $A{:}{=}F$; **call** P **end end end**

5.3 Lambda Abstraction Introduction

Next, we apply the parameterization principle by augmenting the language with these new constructions

$$E ::= \ \cdots \ | \ \lambda I{:}\theta. \ E \ | \ E_1 \ E_2 \ | \ I$$

and these typing rules:

$$\frac{\pi \uplus \{I{:}\theta_1\} \vdash E{:}\theta_2}{\pi \vdash \lambda I{:}\theta_1. \ E{:} \ \theta_1 \to \theta_2} \qquad \frac{\pi \vdash E_1{:}\theta_1 \to \theta_2 \quad \pi \vdash E_2{:}\theta_1}{\pi \vdash E_1 \ E_2{:}\theta_2} \qquad \pi \vdash I{:} \ \theta, \ \text{if} \ (I{:}\theta) \in \pi$$

The lambda abstraction, $\lambda I_2 : \theta. E$, was seen in Chapter 3 to be the desugared body of a parameterized abstraction, **define** $I_1(I_2 : \theta) = E$. The construction $E_1 E_2$ is the desugared form of abstraction invocation with an actual parameter, but here we allow an arbitrary expression, E_1, and not just an identifier, to be the abstraction that is invoked. Finally, I is parameter reference. The identifier looks identical to the identifier used to refer to a field of a record. It is traditional to merge the two identifier forms, but complications to the semantics arise if the semantics of definition binding differs from the semantics of parameter binding (cf. the correspondence principle in Section 3.7).

Since we have merged the language's syntax domains into one, the lambda abstraction allows phrases from all syntax domains to be parameters to phrases—this is the parameterization principle.

The introduction of parameters enriches the type system of the language: The type $\theta_1 \rightarrow \theta_2$ is used as the type attribute for lambda abstractions. Since the same identifier construct, I, is used for both record identifiers and parameter identifiers, the lone type assignment, π, suffices to resolve identifier references. Here is a well-typed program:

$$(with \ (M = (\lambda X \!:\! intloc. \ (A \!=\! loc_1, \ P \!=\! \lambda Y \!:\! intexp. \ X \!:=\! Y)_{\pi_1}^{\pi_2})_\varnothing^{intloc \rightarrow \pi_2})_\varnothing^{\pi_3}$$
$$do \ (with \ (M \ loc_1)_{\pi_3}^{\pi_2} \ do \ (P \ (@A\!+\!1))_{\pi_3 \,\uplus\, \pi_2}^{comm})_{\pi_3}^{comm})_\varnothing^{comm}$$

where $\pi_1 = \{X \!:\! intloc\}$, $\pi_2 = \{A \!:\! intloc, \ P \!:\! intexp \rightarrow comm\}$, and $\pi_3 = \{M \!:\! intloc \rightarrow \pi_2\}$

The previous program is the desugared version of this one:

> **begin module** $M(X \!:\! intloc) = \{$ **alias** $A \!=\! loc_1$, **proc** $P(Y \!:\! intexp) \!=\! X \!:=\! Y \}$
>   **in begin import** $M(loc_1)$ **in call** $P(@A\!+\!1)$ **end end**

Variables are momentarily ignored, but they will be considered in Sections 5.5 and 5.6.

5.4 Higher-Order Programming Languages

Figure 5.2 shows the imperative language with records and lambda abstraction. The language admits more well-formed programs than the one developed over Chapters 1–4. We have claimed that the abstraction principle is a record introduction principle, but in Chapter 2 we limited how records were used. In that chapter, we named and referenced records, for example,

> **alias** $A \!=\! loc_1$; **module** $M = \{$ **fun** $F \!=\! @A\!+\!1$, **proc** $P \!=\! A \!:=\! F \}$ **in call** $M.P$

but we did not write the records "in-line," as values in their own right:

$$E ::= E_1 := E_2 \mid E_1 ; E_2 \mid \textbf{if } E_1 \textbf{ then } E_2 \textbf{ else } E_3 \textbf{ fi} \mid \textbf{skip} \mid \textbf{while } E_1 \textbf{ do } E_2 \textbf{ od}$$
$$\mid E_1 + E_2 \mid E_1 = E_2 \mid \neg E \mid @E \mid N \mid L$$
$$\mid I = E \mid E_1, E_2 \mid with\ E_1\ do\ E_2 \mid I \mid \lambda I{:}\theta.\ E \mid E_1\ E_2$$

$$\theta ::= \tau exp \mid comm \mid intloc \mid \pi \mid \theta_1 \to \theta_2$$

$$\tau ::= int \mid bool$$

$$\pi ::= \{j{:}\theta_j\}_{j \in J}, \quad \text{where } J \subseteq \text{Identifier is a finite set}$$

$$\frac{\pi \vdash E_1 : intloc \quad \pi \vdash E_2 : intexp}{\pi \vdash E_1 := E_2 : comm} \qquad \frac{\pi \vdash E_1 : comm \quad \pi \vdash E_2 : comm}{\pi \vdash E_1 ; E_2 : comm}$$

$$\frac{\pi \vdash E_1 : boolexp \quad \pi \vdash E_2 : comm \quad \pi \vdash E_3 : comm}{\pi \vdash \textbf{if } E_1 \textbf{ then } E_2 \textbf{ else } E_3 \textbf{ fi} : comm}$$

$$\pi \vdash \textbf{skip} : comm \qquad \frac{\vdash E_1 : boolexp \quad \vdash E_2 : comm}{\vdash \textbf{while } E_1 \textbf{ do } E_2 \textbf{ od} : comm}$$

$$\frac{\pi \vdash E_1 : intexp \quad \pi \vdash E_2 : intexp}{\pi \vdash E_1 + E_2 : boolexp} \qquad \frac{\pi \vdash E_1 : \tau exp \quad \pi \vdash E_2 : \tau exp}{\pi \vdash E_1 = E_2 : intexp}$$

$$\frac{\pi \vdash E : boolexp}{\pi \vdash \neg E : boolexp} \qquad \frac{\pi \vdash E : intloc}{\pi \vdash @E : intexp} \qquad \pi \vdash N : intexp \qquad \pi \vdash L : intloc$$

$$\frac{\pi \vdash E : \theta}{\pi \vdash I = E : \{I{:}\theta\}} \qquad \frac{\pi \vdash E_1 : \pi_1 \quad \pi \vdash E_2 : \pi_2}{\pi \vdash E_1, E_2 : \pi_1 \cup \pi_2} \qquad \frac{\pi \vdash E_1 : \pi_1 \quad \pi \uplus \pi_1 \vdash E_2 : \theta}{\pi \vdash with\ E_1\ do\ E_2 : \theta}$$

$$\pi \vdash I : \theta \text{ if } (I{:}\theta) \in \pi \qquad \frac{\pi \uplus \{I{:}\theta_1\} \vdash E : \theta_2}{\pi \vdash \lambda I{:}\theta_1.\ E : \theta_1 \to \theta_2} \qquad \frac{\pi \vdash E_1 : \theta_1 \to \theta_2 \quad \pi \vdash E_2 : \theta_1}{\pi \vdash E_1\ E_2 : \theta_2}$$

Figure 5.2

alias $A=loc_1$ **in call** { **fun** $F=@A+1$, **proc** $P=A:=F$ }.P

The language in Figure 5.2 admits the second program. (Recall that $R.I$ is a shorthand for **with** R **do** I.)

Similarly, in Chapter 3 we claimed that the parameterization principle was a lambda abstraction principle. In that chapter, we parameterized abstractions, for example,

fun $F(X:intexp) = X+1$ **in** $A:=F(@A)+2$

but we did not parameterize arbitrary phrases:

$A:=((\lambda X:intexp.X+1)@A)+2$

Nor did we produce parameterized procedures as results from procedure calls, for example,

proc $R(X:intloc) = \lambda Y:intexp.X:=Y$

But these programs *are* allowed by Figure 5.2.

We say that a language is *higher order* if it lets lambda abstractions (and records) be full-fledged values, to be used in line, as components of records and other structures, and as arguments and results of abstraction invocations. A language that does not allow this free use of lambda abstractions is *first order*. Higher order programming languages encourage computation on structures—lambda abstractions and records—rather than on just primitive values like integers; see Bird and Wadler 1988 for examples.

5.5 The Semantics of Records and Lambda Abstractions

Since the denotational semantics of records and lambda abstractions have been studied in previous chapters, no surprises will be found in this section. Nonetheless, a restatement of the semantics is helpful, for it reveals an elegance that was obscured by the pragmatic concerns of earlier chapters.

We return to the language of Figure 5.2. The semantics of the core part of the language is given in Figure 5.3. As shown in Chapter 2, the addition of the environment argument to the core language's semantics does not affect the meaning of core language programs.

5.5.1 Lazy Evaluation Semantics

The semantics of lazily evaluated lambda abstractions and records is simple and beautiful. See Figure 5.4. The key feature of the semantics is that the store argument need not be mentioned, even though the extensions are added to an imperative language. This is

$\llbracket \pi \vdash L := E : comm \rrbracket e\, s = update(\llbracket \pi \vdash L : intloc \rrbracket e,\ \llbracket \pi \vdash E : intexp \rrbracket e\, s,\ s)$

$\llbracket \pi \vdash E_1 ; E_2 : comm \rrbracket e\, s = \llbracket \pi \vdash E_2 : comm \rrbracket e\ (\llbracket \pi \vdash E_1 : comm \rrbracket e\, s)$

$\cdots$

$\llbracket \pi \vdash E_1 + E_2 : intexp \rrbracket e\, s = plus(\llbracket \pi \vdash E_1 : intexp \rrbracket e\, s,\ \llbracket \pi \vdash E_2 : intexp \rrbracket e\, s)$

$\cdots$

$\llbracket \pi \vdash N : intexp \rrbracket e\, s = \llbracket N : int \rrbracket e$

$\llbracket \pi \vdash loc_i : intloc \rrbracket e = loc_i$

where $\llbracket comm \rrbracket = Store \rightarrow Store_\perp$ and $\llbracket \tau exp \rrbracket = Store \rightarrow \llbracket \tau \rrbracket$

Figure 5.3 _____

$\llbracket \pi \vdash I = E : \{ I : \theta \} \rrbracket e = \{ I = \llbracket \pi \vdash E : \theta \rrbracket e \}$

$\llbracket \pi \vdash E_1, E_2 : \pi_1 \cup \pi_2 \rrbracket e = (\llbracket \pi \vdash E_1 : \pi_1 \rrbracket e) \cup (\llbracket \pi \vdash E_2 : \pi_2 \rrbracket e)$

$\llbracket \pi \vdash with\ E_1\ do\ E_2 : \theta \rrbracket e = \llbracket \pi \uplus \pi_1 \vdash E_2 : \theta \rrbracket (e \uplus \llbracket \pi \vdash E_1 : \pi_1 \rrbracket e)$

$\llbracket \pi \vdash I : \theta \rrbracket e = v,\ \text{where}\ (I = v) \in e$

$\llbracket \pi \vdash \lambda I : \theta_1 . E : \theta_1 \rightarrow \theta_2 \rrbracket e = f,\ \text{where}\ f u = \llbracket \pi \uplus \{ I : \theta_1 \} \vdash E : \theta_2 \rrbracket (e \uplus \{ I = u \})$

$\quad\quad \text{and}\ e \uplus \{ I = u \} = \{ I = u \} \cup (e - \{ (I = v) \mid (I = v) \in e \})$

$\llbracket \pi \vdash E_1\ E_2 : \theta_2 \rrbracket e = (\llbracket \pi \vdash E_1 : \theta_1 \rightarrow \theta_2 \rrbracket e)\ (\llbracket \pi \vdash E_2 : \theta_1 \rrbracket e)$

where $\llbracket \{ i : \theta_i \}_{i \in I} \rrbracket = \{ i : \llbracket \theta_i \rrbracket \}_{i \in I}$ and $\llbracket \theta_1 \rightarrow \theta_2 \rrbracket = \llbracket \theta_1 \rrbracket \rightarrow \llbracket \theta_2 \rrbracket$

Figure 5.4 _____

because lazy evaluation never supplies a store to a record binding or to a lambda abstraction or to the argument of a lambda abstraction. Only a core language construct forces the store to participate in the calculation. Records and lambda abstractions constitute a "functional sublanguage" overlaid upon an imperative core. (Functional languages will be studied in Chapter 7.) The semantics of a simple example is presented in Figure 5.5. Notice how the store plays no role at all in the calculation of the meaning until the last line, when the update comes to the fore.

The lazy evaluation semantics makes the typing rules sound; the proof has been presented piecemeal in Chapters 2–4, and the assembly of the parts into a whole is left as an easy exercise. The semantics also makes sound the copy rules for records and lambda abstractions. The rules, which were first seen in Chapters 2 and 3, have the following form:

$[\![\varnothing \vdash with\ M = (\lambda X{:}intloc.\ X{:=}0)\ do\ (M\ loc_1){:}\ comm]\!]\varnothing\ s$

$= [\![\pi_1 \vdash M\ loc_1{:}\ comm]\!]e_1\ s,$ where $\pi_1 = \{M{:}\ intloc{\to}comm\},\ e_1 = \{M{=}f\},$

    and $f\ u = [\![\{X{:}intloc\} \vdash X{:=}0{:}comm]\!]\{X{=}u\}$

$= [\![\pi_1 \vdash M{:}\ intloc{\to}comm]\!]e_1\ ([\![\pi_1 \vdash loc_1{:}\ intloc]\!]e)\ s$

$= f\ loc_1 = [\![\{X{:}intloc\} \vdash X{:=}0{:}comm]\!]\{X{=}loc_1\}\ s$

$= update\ (loc_1,\ 0,\ s)$

Figure 5.5 _____

    $with\ (i{=}E_i)_{i \in I}\ do\ E\ \Rightarrow\ [E_i/i]_{i \in I}E,$ where $I \subseteq$ Identifier is a finite set

    $(\lambda I{:}\theta.\ E_1)E_2\ \Rightarrow\ [E_2/I]E_2$

Here, $(i{=}E_i)_{i \in I}$ abbreviates the record $(i_1{=}E_1,\ i_2{=}E_2,\ \dots,\ i_n{=}E_n),$ for $I = \{i_1,\ i_2,\ \dots,$ $i_n\}.$ $[E_i/i]_{i \in I}$ is a similar abbreviation for a simultaneous substitution. The definition of substitution was stated in Chapter 3, and we summarize it here for the language in Figure 5.2. For simplicity, we consider substitution for a single identifier:

    $[E/I](E_1{:=}E_2) = [E/I]E_1{:=}[E/I]E_2$

    $[E/I](E_1;E_2) = [E/I]E_1;\ [E/I]E_2$

    $\cdots$

    $[E/I]loc_i = loc_i$

    $[E/I](J{=}E_1) = (J{=}[E/I]E_1)$

    $[E/I](E_1,E_2) = [E/I]E_1,\ [E/I]E_2$

    $[E/I](with\ E_1\ do\ E_2) = with\ [E/I]E_1\ do\ E_2,$ if $\pi \vdash E_1{:}\pi_1$ holds and $(I{:}\theta) \in \pi_1$

    $[E/I](with\ E_1\ do\ E_2) = with\ [E/I]E_1\ do\ [E/I]E_2,$ if $\pi \vdash E_1{:}\pi_1$ holds and $(I{:}\theta) \notin \pi_1$

    $[E/I]I = E$

    $[E/I]J = J,$ and $J \neq I$

    $[E/I](\lambda I{:}\theta.\ E_1) = \lambda I{:}\theta.\ E_1$

    $[E/I](\lambda J{:}\theta.\ E_1) = \lambda J{:}\theta.\ [E/I]E_1,$ if $I \neq J$ and $J \notin FV(E)$ (cf. Section 3.3)

    $[E/I](\lambda J{:}\theta.\ E_1) = \lambda K{:}\theta.\ [E/I][K/J]E_1,$ if $I \neq J,\ J \in FV(E),$ and K is fresh

    $[E/I](E_1\ E_2) = [E/I]E_1\ [E/I]E_2$

Notice that the typing of the *with* expression is necessary for defining the substitution into it. This implies that we only work with well-typed phrases; it also implies that the copy rules should preserve the typing of phrases. (This is proved in Chapter 6.)

    The soundness of the copy rules lets us calculate the semantics of a program by first applying the copy rules to make all bindings and then using the semantics of the core language. In the example in Figure 5.5, one can reduce *with M* = $(\lambda X : intloc.\ X := 0)$ *do* $(M\ loc_1) \Rightarrow (\lambda X : intloc.\ X := 0)loc_1 \Rightarrow loc_1 := 0$ and calculate $[\![\varnothing \vdash X := 0 \colon comm]\!]\varnothing\ s$.

An issue that was implicit in Chapter 3 needs to be made explicit here: Function application, $E_1\ E_2$, is nonstrict in the meaning of E_2, that is, $[\![\pi \vdash E_1\ E_2 \colon \theta_2]\!]e$ need not be $\perp$ merely because $[\![\pi \vdash E_2 \colon \theta_1]\!]e = \perp$. In the imperative language, E_2's meaning is typically a function that requires the store, but this need not be the case. Consider a new numeral, **loop**, such that $[\![\pi \vdash \mathbf{loop} \colon int]\!]e = \perp$. Then, $[\![\pi \vdash (\lambda X : int.\ \mathbf{skip})\mathbf{loop} \colon comm]\!]e$ = $[\![\pi \vdash \lambda X : int.\ \mathbf{skip} \colon int \to comm]\!]e\ \perp$ = $[\![\pi \uplus \{X : int\} \vdash \mathbf{skip} \colon comm]\!]\ (e \uplus \{X = \perp\})$ = $[\![\pi \vdash \mathbf{skip} \colon comm]\!]e$. A similar derivation can be made for **with** X=**loop do skip**. This makes the copy rules sound.

Variable declarations can be added to the language, and the simplest way of preserving the elegant lazy evaluation semantics is to use a new block construction specifically for integer variables:

$$\frac{\pi \uplus \{V : intloc\} \vdash E \colon comm}{\pi \vdash new\ V\ in\ E \colon comm}$$

For the purpose of exposition, we use V to stand for a variable identifier, to distinguish it from an "ordinary" identifier, I. The block *new* V E allocates a location, binds it to V, and lets V be visible to command E. The denotational semantics follows:

$[\![\pi \vdash new\ V\ in\ E \colon comm]\!]e\ s = free\ (size\text{-}of\ s)\ s_2$
    where $(l, s_1) = allocate\ s$
    and $s_2 = [\![\pi \uplus \{V : intloc\} \vdash E \colon comm]\!](e \uplus \{V = l\})\ s_1$

The semantics is essentially that of the command block from Chapter 4, limited to a single integer variable. A program like: **begin var** A : **newint in begin proc** $P = A := 0$ **in call** P **end end** is desugared into: *new A in* (*with* $P = A := 0$ *do P*). A drawback of the *new* construction is that modules, classes, and objects do not naturally arise, but Tennent (1991) shows how to compensate. Here is a small example. Say that a program requires a module, M, that contains a private variable, $COUNT$, and public operations, VAL and ADD. The program is coded with M as a parameter, and likewise the module is coded as a procedure that takes the *program* as a parameter. Here is the result in the "sugared" language:

proc $START(P : \{VAL : intexp,\ ADD : intexp \to comm\} \to comm) =$
    begin var $COUNT$: **newint in** $COUNT := 0$;
        call P { **fun** $VAL = @COUNT$,
                proc $ADD(X : intexp) = COUNT := @COUNT + X$ } **end**;
    proc $PROGRAM(M : \{VAL : intexp,\ ADD : intexp \to comm\}) =$

begin import M **in** $\cdots$ *VAL* $\cdots$ **call** *ADD*(1) $\cdots$ **end**
in call *START(PROGRAM)*

The code is easily translated into the desugared notation of this section.

5.5.2 Eager Evaluation Semantics

Next, we consider the semantics of eagerly evaluated records and lambda abstractions. Without variable declarations, the denotational semantics is pleasant; see Figure 5.6. The eager evaluation semantics uses the store argument to force the evaluation of the phrases that bind to identifiers. The soundness of the typing rules are preserved, but the role of the store in the semantics invalidates the copy rules in Section 5.5.1.

Recall from Chapters 2 and 3 that eager evaluation semantics requires that the semantic binding operation is strict: $\{I=\bot\} = \bot$. Also, function application is strict: $f(\bot) = \bot$. As always, $\cup$ and $\uplus$ are strict as well; for example, $\bot \uplus e = \bot \cup e = \bot$. Finally, $[\![\pi \vdash E: \theta]\!] \bot\, s = \bot$, since no phrase with an improper environment can have a proper meaning.

These technical points are important because nontermination arises everywhere in the language; that is, $\bot \in [\![\theta]\!]$, for every θ. To see this, let $\vdash E_0: \theta_0$ hold for the E_0 and θ_0 of your choosing. Then $[\![\varnothing \vdash (\lambda X\!:\!comm.\,E_0)\;(\textbf{while }0{=}0\textbf{ do skip od}): \theta_0]\!]\varnothing\,s_0$ $= [\![\varnothing \vdash \lambda X\!:\!comm.\,E_0 : comm{\to}\theta_0]\!]\varnothing)\,\bot\,s_0 = \bot$, for every $s_0 \in Store$. The eager evaluation of the actual parameter, here, a looping command, causes the overall phrase to loop.

$[\![\pi \vdash I{=}E: \{I{:}\theta\}]\!]e\,s = \{I{=}[\![\pi \vdash E: \theta]\!]e\,s\}$

$[\![\pi \vdash E_1,E_2: \pi_1 \cup \pi_2]\!]e\,s = ([\![\pi \vdash E_1: \pi_1]\!]e\,s) \cup ([\![\pi \vdash E_2: \pi_2]\!]e\,s)$

$[\![\pi \vdash with\;E_1\;do\;E_2: \theta]\!]e\,s = [\![\pi \uplus \pi_1 \vdash E_2: \theta]\!](e \uplus ([\![\pi \vdash E_1: \pi_1]\!]e\,s))\,s$

$[\![\pi \vdash I: \theta]\!]e\,s = u,\;\;\text{where}\;(I{=}u) \in e$

$[\![\pi \vdash \lambda I{:}\theta_1.\,E: \theta_1{\to}\theta_2]\!]e\,s = f,\;\;\text{where}\;f\,u\,s' = [\![\pi \uplus \{I{:}\theta_1\} \vdash E: \theta_2]\!](e \uplus \{I{=}u\})\,s'$

$[\![\pi \vdash E_1\,E_2: \theta_2]\!]e\,s = ([\![\pi \vdash E_1: \theta_1{\to}\theta_2]\!]e)\,([\![\pi \vdash E_2: \theta_1]\!]e\,s)\,s$

where $[\![\{i{:}\theta_i\}_{i\in I}]\!] = (\{i{:}eval(\theta_i)\}_{i\in I})_\bot$ $\qquad$ $[\![comm]\!] = (Store \to Store)_\bot$

$\qquad$ $[\![\theta_1 \to \theta_2]\!] = (eval(\theta_1) \to [\![\theta_2]\!])_\bot$ $\qquad\qquad$ $[\![\tau exp]\!] = (Store \to [\![\tau]\!])_\bot$

and $eval(\{i{:}\theta_i\}_{i\in I}) = \{i{:}eval(\theta_i)\}_{i\in I}$ $\qquad\qquad$ $eval(comm) = Store$

$\qquad$ $eval(\theta_1 \to \theta_2) = eval(\theta_1) \to [\![\theta_2]\!]$ $\qquad\qquad\quad$ $eval(\tau exp) = [\![\tau]\!]$

Figure 5.6 _____

Of course, commands normally evaluate lazily, but the point is that if there is just one eagerly evaluated phrase that can loop, then all types have phrases that can loop.

The *new* V *in* E construction from the previous section can be used to add variables to the language in Figure 5.6.

5.6 Lazy and Eager Evaluation Combined

We now integrate lazy and eager evaluation along with the **newint** construction into the same language. The experiment summarizes the developments in Chapters 2-4 and presents a stimulating exercise in language design. The roadmap to the language is the structure of the type attributes:

$$\theta ::= \tau \mid \tau exp$$
$$\tau ::= int \mid bool \mid intloc \mid store \mid \pi \mid \theta_1 \to \theta_2$$
$$\pi ::= \{ i : \theta_i \}_{i \in I}$$

A type attribute, τ, is the type of an evaluated phrase, whereas τexp is the type of an unevaluated phrase that produces a τ-typed value when evaluated. Commands are by nature unevaluated phrases, since the run-time store is needed for their evaluation, so they have the type *store exp*. Similarly, the type-structure phrase **newint** is unevaluated and has type *intloc exp*. In contrast, a numeral is by nature evaluated and has type *int*. The evaluated declaration, **var** X: **newint**, has type $\{X:intloc\}$. Here are some equivalences to keep in mind:

$$comm \equiv store\ exp$$
$$\delta class \equiv \delta exp$$
$$\pi dec \equiv \pi exp$$

The syntax of the language consists of the core language, **newint,** and the following extensions:

$$E ::= E_1 := E_2 \mid E_1; E_2 \mid \cdots \mid \textbf{newint} \mid lazy\, I = E \mid eager\, I = E$$
$$\mid E_1, E_2 \mid with\ E_1\ do\ E_2 \mid I \mid \lambda I : \theta.\, E \mid E_1\ E_2$$

Here are some examples of the two forms of record binding: (i) **var** X: **newint** is coded *eager* X = **newint** to signify that the value bound to X must be eagerly evaluated to a location; (ii) **class** K = **record var** Y: **newint, proc** P = **skip end** is coded *lazy* K = (*eager* Y = **newint,** *lazy* P = **skip**) to signify that the value bound to K is an unevaluated record. The declaration **var** R:K is coded *eager* R = K. This forces the evaluation of K, creating a record variable; (iii) **module** M = { **var** X: **newint, proc** P = **skip** } is coded *eager M* = (*eager Y* = **newint**, *lazy P* = **skip**). In this manner, the varieties of abstractions detailed in Chapter 2 can be coded. The present notation makes clear that the differences between record variables and modules are insignificant and that the distinction between classes and modules is primarily a matter of evaluation time.

The lambda abstraction is, in fact, two constructions: $\lambda I{:}\tau exp. E$ accepts an unevaluated phrase as its argument, and $\lambda I{:}\tau. E$ demands an evaluated one. Thus, $(\lambda I{:}intexp. A{:=}X)(@A{+}1)$ allows $@A{+}1$ to bind, unevaluated, to X, whereas $(\lambda X{:}int. A{:=}X)(@A{+}1)$ demands that the *intexp*-typed phrase $@A{+}1$ evaluate to an integer before the binding occurs.

The interaction of unevaluated, evaluated, and side-effecting phrases makes assembly of a sound set of typing rules a fascinating exercise. To start, here are a few possibilities:

$$\pi \vdash \textbf{newint}: intloc\ exp \qquad \frac{\pi \vdash E{:}\,\theta}{\pi \vdash lazy\, I{=}E{:}\,\{I{:}\theta\}exp} \qquad \frac{\pi \vdash E{:}\,\tau exp}{\pi \vdash eager\, I{=}E{:}\,\{I{:}\tau\}exp}$$

One might argue that the succedents of the second and third rules should be $\pi \vdash lazy\, I{=}E{:}\,\{I{:}\theta\}$ and $\pi \vdash eager\, I{=}E{:}\,\{I{:}\tau\}$, respectively, and the justification of this argument is left as an exercise. The rule for identifiers is the usual one, but the *with* construction requires some thought. The evaluation of *with* E_1 *do* E_2 requires that E_1 be evaluated to a record before E_2 proceeds. This suggests (at least) these two rules:

$$\frac{\pi \vdash E_1{:}\,\pi_1 \qquad \pi \uplus \pi_1 \vdash E_2{:}\,\theta}{\pi \vdash with\ E_1\ do\ E_2{:}\,\theta}$$

$$\frac{\pi \vdash E_1{:}\,\pi_1\, exp \qquad \pi \uplus \pi_1 \vdash E_2{:}\,\tau exp}{\pi \vdash with\ E_1\ do\ E_2{:}\,\tau exp} \qquad \text{where } \tau \in \{\pi_2,\ store\}$$

The first states that an evaluated record, E_1, is acceptable; the second considers that the evaluation of E_1 may cause side effects (storage allocation), and the consequences must be managed by E_2; hence it has type τexp.

Similar issues arrise for function application: If storage is allocated as a side effect of evaluating E_1 in $(\lambda I{:}\tau. E_2)E_1$, then E_2 must deal with the consequences. This can be done, but we avoid the issue for the moment and suggest just these two simple rules:

$$\frac{\pi \vdash E_1{:}\,\theta_1 \rightarrow \theta_2 \qquad \pi \vdash E_2{:}\,\theta_1}{\pi \vdash E_1\ E_2{:}\,\theta_2} \qquad \frac{\pi \vdash E_1{:}\,\tau \rightarrow \theta \qquad \pi \vdash E_2{:}\,\tau exp}{\pi \vdash E_1\ E_2{:}\,\theta} \qquad \text{where } \tau \in \{int,\ bool\}$$

The first says that an exact match of actual to formal parameter is always acceptable; the second states that the actual parameter must be forced to evaluate when the formal parameter expects an evaluated value. The typing rule for lambda abstraction is the usual one.

$[\![\pi \vdash \textbf{newint}: intloc\ exp]\!]e\ s = allocate\ s$

$[\![\pi \vdash lazy\ \mathrm{I}{=}\mathrm{E}{:}\{\mathrm{I}{:}\theta\}exp]\!]e\ s = (\{\,\mathrm{I} = [\![\pi \vdash \mathrm{E}{:}\theta]\!]e\,\},\ s)$

$[\![\pi \vdash eager\ \mathrm{I}{=}\mathrm{E}{:}\{\mathrm{I}{:}\tau\}exp]\!]e\ s = (\{\mathrm{I}{=}v\},\ s'),\ \text{where}\ (v,\ s') = [\![\pi \vdash \mathrm{E}{:}\tau exp]\!]e\ s$

$[\![\pi \vdash \mathrm{I}{:}\tau exp]\!]e\ s = v\ s,\ \ \text{where}\ (\mathrm{I}{=}v) \in e$

$[\![\pi \vdash \mathrm{I}{:}\tau]\!]e\ s = v,\ \ \text{where}\ (\mathrm{I}{=}v) \in e$

$[\![\pi \vdash with\ \mathrm{E}_1\ do\ \mathrm{E}_2{:}\theta]\!]e\ s = [\![\pi \uplus \pi_1 \vdash \mathrm{E}_2{:}\theta]\!](e \uplus [\![\pi \vdash \mathrm{E}_1{:}\pi_1]\!]e)\ s$

$[\![\pi \vdash with\ \mathrm{E}_1\ do\ \mathrm{E}_2{:}\pi_2 exp]\!]e\ s = [\![\pi \uplus \pi_1 \vdash \mathrm{E}_2{:}\pi_2 exp]\!](e \uplus e_1)\ s_1$
$\qquad \text{where}\ (e_1,\ s_1) = [\![\pi \vdash \mathrm{E}_1{:}\pi_1 exp]\!]e\ s$

$[\![\pi \vdash with\ \mathrm{E}_1\ do\ \mathrm{E}_2{:}store\ exp]\!]e\ s = free\ (size\text{-}of\ s)\ s_2$
$\qquad \text{where}\ (e_1,\ s_1) = [\![\pi \vdash \mathrm{E}_1{:}\pi_1 exp]\!]e\ s$
$\qquad \text{and}\ s_2 = [\![\pi \uplus \pi_1 \vdash \mathrm{E}_2{:}store\ exp]\!](e \uplus e_1)\ s_1$

$[\![\pi \vdash \mathrm{E}_1\ \mathrm{E}_2{:}\theta_2]\!]e\ s = ([\![\pi \vdash \mathrm{E}_1{:}\theta_1 {\to} \theta_2]\!]e)\ ([\![\pi \vdash \mathrm{E}_2{:}\theta_1]\!]e)\ s$

$[\![\pi \vdash \mathrm{E}_1\ \mathrm{E}_2{:}\theta]\!]e\ s = ([\![\pi \vdash \mathrm{E}_1{:}\tau {\to} \theta]\!]e)\ ([\![\pi \vdash \mathrm{E}_2{:}\tau exp]\!]e\ s)\ s$

where $[\![\tau exp]\!] = Store \to [\![\tau]\!]$
$\qquad [\![int]\!] = Int_\perp,\ \ [\![bool]\!] = Bool_\perp$
$\qquad [\![\theta_1 \to \theta_2]\!] = (proper\ [\![\theta_1]\!] \to [\![\theta_2]\!])_\perp$
$\qquad [\![\{\,i{:}\theta_i\,\}_{i \in I}]\!] = (\{\,i{:}proper\ [\![\theta_i]\!]\,\}_{i \in I})_\perp$
$\qquad [\![intloc]\!] = Location_\perp,\ \ [\![store]\!] = Store_\perp$
and $proper\ D = D - \{\,\perp\,\}$

Figure 5.7 _____

These typing rules are a subset of the various possibilities. The multiple rules for *with* and function application are not only a consequence of the two kinds of evaluation but also of the complications introduced by **newint**, which allocates storage as a side effect. In the terminology of Section 5.8, **newint** is certainly not an orthogonal construction!

As noted earlier, the justification for the proposed typing rules comes from proving their soundness with respect to a denotational semantics. Figure 5.7 gives the semantics for the language defined in this section. The interaction of lazy and eager evaluation and the effects of the **newint** operator come clearly into focus. The semantics is essentially Figures 5.4 and 5.6 combined, modulo the troubles generated by **newint**. Figure 5.7 is essentially the semantics developed over Chapters 2-4.

5.7 Lambda Abstraction Alone

If we wish to extend a core language with naming and parameter devices but do not care about record structures, classes, and modules, then it is possible to use lambda abstraction alone as the foundation. The key idea is that a block of the form **begin define** $I=E$ **in** E_2 **end** is desugared into $((\lambda I:\theta. E_2)E_1)$, that is, parameter binding simulates definition binding. This simulation forces a correspondence between the semantics of definition binding and the semantics of parameter binding. Here is the desugaring technique, structured into three stages of translation:

(i)   Every parameterized abstraction

$$\textbf{define } I(I_1:\theta_1, I_2:\theta_2, \cdots, I_n:\theta_n) = U, \quad n \geq 0,$$

is translated as follows:

$$\textbf{define } I = (\lambda I_1:\theta_1. (\lambda I_2:\theta_2. \cdots (\lambda I_n:\theta_n. U) \cdots)))$$

The nested lambda abstraction binds the actual parameters to the formal parameters one at a time.

(ii)   Every block

$$\textbf{begin define } I_1=U_1, \textbf{define } I_2=U_2, \cdots, \textbf{define } I_n=U_n \textbf{ in } W \textbf{ end}, \quad n \geq 0$$

is translated as follows:

$$((\cdots (((\lambda I_1:\theta_1. (\lambda I_2:\theta_2. \cdots (\lambda I_n:\theta_n. W) \cdots))) U_1) U_2) \cdots) U_n)$$

The independently declared abstracts bind to their names one at a time.

(iii) Every invocation

$$\textbf{invoke } I(V_1, V_2, \ldots, V_n), \quad n \geq 0,$$

is translated as follows:

$$((\cdots ((I\ V_1) V_2) \cdots) V_n)$$

The actual parameter tuple is split into its individual components to match the format of the nested lambda abstraction denoted by I.

Here is an example. The program

$$\textbf{begin alias } A = loc_1$$
$$\textbf{in } A := 0;$$
$$\qquad \textbf{begin proc } P\,(X:intexp,\ Y:boolexp) = \textbf{begin alias } A = loc_2 \textbf{ in } A := X \textbf{ end}$$
$$\qquad\qquad \textbf{in call } P\,(@A,\ @A=0)\ \textbf{end};$$
$$\qquad A := @A + 1\ \textbf{end}$$

is translated in three stages. The result of the first stage, the translation of parameterized abstractions, follows:

> **begin alias** $A = loc_1$
> **in** $A := 0;$
> > **begin proc** $P = (\lambda X : intexp.\ (\lambda Y : boolexp.\ \textbf{begin alias}\ A = loc_2\ \textbf{in}\ A := X\ \textbf{end}))$
> > **in call** $P\ (@A,\ @A = 0)$ **end**;
> $A := @A + 1$ **end**

When the blocks in the program are translated, we have the following:

$$((\lambda A : intloc.\ A := 0;$$
$$((\lambda P : intexp \rightarrow (boolexp \rightarrow cmd).\ \textbf{call}\ P\ (@A,\ @A = 0)$$
$$)(\lambda X : intexp.\ (\lambda Y : boolexp.\ ((\lambda A : intloc.\ A := X)loc_2))));$$
$$A := @A + 1\ )loc_1)$$

When the invocations are translated, we obtain the result:

$$((\lambda A : intloc.\ A := 0;$$
$$((\lambda P : intexp \rightarrow (boolexp \rightarrow cmd).\ ((P\ @A)\ @A = 0)$$
$$)(\lambda X : intexp.\ (\lambda Y : boolexp.\ ((\lambda A : intloc.\ A := X)loc_2))));$$
$$A := @A + 1\ )loc_1)$$

Since the invocations of A (and X and Y) are parameter-free, they translate to themselves. If the lambda abstraction is evaluated lazily, the copy rule can be applied to the program, producing the core language program $loc_1 := 0;\ loc_2 := @loc_1$.

If variable declarations are added to the language, the *new* V *in* E construction from Section 5.5.1 should be used. The resulting language is essentially "idealized Algol," as introduced by Reynolds (1981a).

5.8 Orthogonality

The previous section noted that lambda abstractions can be added to a core language whether or not records are present. It is also clear that records can be added independently of lambda abstractions. The two concepts are *orthogonal* to each other and to the core language. A new construction is orthogonal to a programming language if

(i) The semantics of the original constructs in the language remain unchanged by the addition of the new construction.

(ii)   If the new construction uses component phrases from the original language, then the
        semantics of the new construction is uniformly defined with respect to the com-
        ponent phrases—there are no "special cases."

The record construction is an orthogonal construction, since its addition does not affect
the semantics of the existing language constructions. (Of course, the semantics is
extended by an environment argument—if one wasn't already present—but we saw in
Chapter 2 that the inclusion of the environment does not affect the meanings assigned to
core language programs.) Also, the semantics of a record, I=E, is uniform regardless of
E.

A consequence of the orthogonality of records is that the typing rules and semantics
equations for them can be added without affecting the typing rules and semantics equations of the existing language. (This is modulo the type assignment attribute and the
environment, of course.) A similar story can be told for the lambda abstraction construction, which is orthogonal to the language to which it is added. In contrast, the **newint**
construction of Section 5.6 is not an orthogonal addition to a language, because it forces a
revision of the language's semantics equations. But the *new* V *in* E construction of Section 5.5.1 is orthogonal.

Orthogonal features encourage a uniformity in language structure that makes a programming language look like a "toolkit" of standardized parts that connect together in
predictable ways. For this reason, orthogonality is promoted as a crucial property of a
well-designed programming language. But a slavish devotion to orthogonality, per se,
can lead to a baroque language with many unnecessary features. For example, does the
imperative language in Chapter 1 truly benefit from "numeral blocks" and "location
blocks"?

We will encounter additional orthogonal constructions in the chapters that follow.

5.9 The Model of the Programming Language

The record and lambda abstraction constructions are important to a modern programming
language, and the semantics given to them seems natural, but how do we know that the
versions of records and lambda abstractions presented here are the "right" ones? Questions like this are often asked in mathematics, and there is a branch of mathematics,
called *category theory*, which sets down precise criteria for judging whether or not a construction is the right one. In this section, we use the notions of *categorical product* and
categorical exponentiation to judge the appropriateness of records and lambda abstractions.

To begin, recall the notion of *cartesian product* from set theory: For sets A and B,
the cartesian product set, $A{\times}B$, is the set of ordered pairs $\{\langle a,b\rangle \mid a \in A, b \in B\}$. Pairs
are indexed by the operations $\downarrow 1$ and $\downarrow 2$, such that $\langle a,b\rangle\downarrow 1 = a$ and $\langle a,b\rangle\downarrow 2 = b$. It is
standard to generalize from binary cartesian products, $A{\times}B$, to ternary products,

$A \times B \times C$, and to n-ary products, $A_1 \times A_2 \times \cdots \times A_n$, for $n > 0$.

When we add records to a core programming language, we are adding products, where a record type, $\{I_1 : \theta_1, \ I_2 : \theta_2, \ \ldots, \ I_n : \theta_n\}$, is an n-ary product. In particular, $\theta_1 \times \theta_2$ is $\{fst : \theta_1, \ snd : \theta_2\}$ is the binary product type, an ordered pair, $\langle E_1, E_2 \rangle$ is $(fst = E_1, \ snd = E_2)$, and $e{\downarrow}1 = with \ e \ do \ fst$ and $e{\downarrow}2 = with \ e \ do \ snd$.

Now, records seem to be ordered pairs, but does the semantics of records support this? That is, we must validate that the semantics of records really is product-like. This is not necessarily trivial, since the semantics manipulates environments and stores. Category theory suggests a standard notion of product that we can use to validate our intuitions. In the definitions that follow, we write $E_1 \equiv E_2$ as an abbreviation for $[\![\pi \vdash E_1 : \theta]\!]e = [\![\pi \vdash E_2 : \theta]\!]e$, where $e \in Env_\pi$.

5.1 Definition

$\theta_1 \times \theta_2$ *is the* categorical product *of* θ_1 *and* θ_2 *iff the following equalities hold:*

(i) $\langle E_1, E_2 \rangle {\downarrow} 1 \equiv E_1$
(ii) $\langle E_1, E_2 \rangle {\downarrow} 2 \equiv E_2$
(iii) $\langle E{\downarrow}1, E{\downarrow}2 \rangle \equiv E$, *when* $\pi \vdash E : \theta_1 \times \theta_2$ *holds*

Clauses (i) and (ii) state that indexing behaves correctly, and clause (iii) states that the product type contains exactly pairs and nothing more. It is easy to prove:

5.2 Theorem

For the semantics in Figure 5.4, $\theta_1 \times \theta_2 = \{fst : \theta_1, \ snd : \theta_2\}$ *is the categorical product.*

Theorem 5.2 fails for the eager evaluation semantics in Figure 5.6. The problem is that the store becomes involved in the semantics, and "looping" phrases cause clauses (i) and (ii) to fail. For example, say that c_0 is a looping command, that is, $[\![\pi \vdash c_0 : comm]\!]e \ s = \perp$, for all possible values of e and s. Even though $[\![\pi \vdash 0 : intexp]\!]e \ s = 0$, we have that $[\![\pi \vdash (fst = 0, \ snd = c_0){\downarrow}1 : intexp]\!]e \ s = \perp$ with the eager evaluation semantics. The reason is that eager evaluation forces both components of the pair to be evaluated with the store before the pair can be built. Although the record construction in eager evaluation semantics is not the categorical product, it is still valuable because we can build tuples and index them most of the time. Without delving into technical details, we call this form of "almost" product a "tensor product."

Next, we study lambda abstractions. In set theory, a *function set*, $A \Rightarrow B$, is the set of single-valued mappings from arguments in set A to answers in set B. Functions are "indexed" by an *apply* operation: For $f \in A \Rightarrow B$, $apply\langle f, a \rangle = f(a)$. (Notice that $apply : (A \Rightarrow B) \times A \rightarrow B$ uses the categorical product.)

When we add lambda abstractions to a programming language, we are adding a form of function set to the language, where $\theta_1 \Rightarrow \theta_2$ is just $\theta_1 \to \theta_2$. A lambda abstraction of type $\theta_1 \to \theta_2$ is an element in this set, and the *apply* operation is coded $\lambda I:(\theta_1 \Rightarrow \theta_2) \times \theta_1 . (I\downarrow 1)(I\downarrow 2)$. But does the semantics support the view that a lambda abstraction is a function? Category theory defines a standard notion of function space, given the existence of a (categorical or tensor) product:

5.3 Definition

$\theta_1 \Rightarrow \theta_2$ *is the* categorical exponentiation *of* θ_1 *and* θ_2 *(with respect to a product* $\theta_1 \times \theta_2$*) iff the following equalities hold:*

(i) $apply\langle(\lambda I:\theta_1 . E), U\rangle \equiv subst(U, I, E)$, *where* $subst(U, I, E) \equiv$ *with* I=U *do* E
(ii) $(\lambda I:\theta_1 . apply\langle E, I\rangle) \equiv E$, *if* $\pi \vdash E: \theta_1 \Rightarrow \theta_2$ *holds*

The definition states that (i) function application is substitution-like in the sense that the binding I=U resolves the occurrences of I in E (note that the lazy evaluation semantics of *with* implies $subst(U, I, E) \equiv [U/I]E$.); (ii) the function type contains exactly lambda abstractions and nothing more. We have this result, showing that the lazy evaluation semantics of lambda abstraction is appropriate:

5.4 Theorem

For the semantics of Figure 5.4, $\theta_1 \Rightarrow \theta_2 = \theta_1 \to \theta_2$ *is the categorical exponentiation.*

Theorem 5.4 fails to hold for the eager evaluation semantics in Figure 5.7. Using the tensor product defined by the records in Figure 5.6, we find that Clause (ii) of Definition 5.3 fails. A counterexample is the expression $(\lambda X:comm.\lambda Y:comm.Y)c_0$, where c_0 is a looping command. This means $\theta_1 \to \theta_2$ contains looping phrases in addition to lambda abstractions. Clause (i) does hold, however, and for this reason, we say that $\theta_1 \to \theta_2$ in the eager evaluation semantics is ''weak exponentiation.''

Clause (i) of Definition 5.3 is phrased in a nonstandard way, but its point is that, for a function, $\lambda I:\theta_1 . E$, to produce a result from its application to an argument, U, the function's body, E, must evaluate within a context that binds I to U, the net result being the same as *with* I=U *do* E. A more direct way of putting it is: $(\lambda I:\theta. E)U \equiv$ *with* I=U *do* E, which is the desugared version of the correspondence principle of Chapter 3. In this light, the correspondence principle and (weak) exponentiation are intimately connected, and the moral is: The form of evaluation used for records (products) should match the form used for lambda abstractions (functions). Banerjee and Schmidt 1994 provides details.

5.10 The Logic of the Programming Language

The previous section focused on the semantical properties of records and lambda abstractions. Now we study the typing rules and consider their logical properties. The typing rules for the core programming language resemble a logic, and the derivation of a well-typed program resembles a proof in the logic. This idea is developed at length in Chapters 9 and 10, so we focus just on specific aspects of the typing rules for records and lambda abstractions.

Let's pretend that the set of type attributes for the core programming language are primitive propositions, as in a logic. Primitive propositions are combined by logical connectives, like conjunction, $\wedge$ ("and"), and implication, $\supset$ ("implies"). For example, if θ_1 and θ_2 are propositions, then $\theta_1 \wedge \theta_2$, $\theta_1 \supset \theta_2$, $(\theta_1 \wedge \theta_2) \supset \theta_1$, and so on, are propositions as well. Consider $\theta_1 \wedge \theta_2$; for it to be proved true, one must prove both θ_1 and θ_2. Then, the two proofs are combined by an inference rule:

$$\frac{\pi \vdash \theta_1 \quad \pi \vdash \theta_2}{\pi \vdash \theta_1 \wedge \theta_2}$$

Read $\pi \vdash \theta$ as saying, "based upon assumptions, π, there is a proof of θ." There are also inference rules for disassembling a conjunction proposition:

$$\frac{\pi \vdash \theta_1 \wedge \theta_2}{\pi \vdash \theta_1} \qquad \frac{\pi \vdash \theta_1 \wedge \theta_2}{\pi \vdash \theta_2}$$

These inference rules look like the typing rules we use, except that the program components are missing. Indeed, when we derive $\pi \vdash E : \theta$, we are saying, in some sense, that E is a "proof" of "proposition" θ. The typing rules for a programming language form a kind of logic.

When we use the type attributes of the core programming language as primitive propositions, we can synthesize inference rules for the primitive propositions by rewriting the core language's typing rules without the program components. For example, the typing rule for the assignment statement is revised to read as follows:

$$\frac{\pi \vdash intloc \quad \pi \vdash intexp}{\pi \vdash comm}$$

The rule is a bit artificial, but it asserts that if we can build (prove) an *intloc* and an *intexp*, we can build (prove) a *comm*.

This game becomes significant when we play it with the rules for records and lambda abstractions. Consider records, and for the moment, consider only binary records of the form $\{fst : \theta_1, snd : \theta_2\}$. The typing rules follow:

$$\frac{\pi \vdash E_1 : \theta_1 \qquad \pi \vdash E_2 : \theta_2}{\pi \vdash \{fst=E_1, \; snd=E_2\} : \{fst:\theta_1, \; snd:\theta_2\}}$$

$$\frac{\pi \vdash E_1 : \{fst:\theta_1, \; snd:\theta_2\} \qquad \pi \uplus \{fst:\theta_1, \; snd:\theta_2\} \vdash E_2 : \theta}{\pi \vdash with \; E_1 \; do \; E_2 : \theta} \qquad \pi \vdash I: \theta, \;\; \text{if } (I:\theta) \in \pi$$

When the program components are omitted, we obtain inference rules for conjunction—$\{fst:\theta_1, \; snd:\theta_2\}$ is $\theta_1 \wedge \theta_2$:

$$\frac{\pi \vdash \theta_1 \qquad \pi \vdash \theta_2}{\pi \vdash \{fst:\theta_1, \; snd:\theta_2\}} \qquad\qquad \frac{\pi \vdash \{fst:\theta_1, \; snd:\theta_2\} \qquad \pi \uplus \{\theta_1, \; \theta_2\} \vdash \theta}{\pi \vdash \theta}$$

$$\pi \vdash \theta, \;\; \text{if } (I:\theta) \in \pi$$

The first rule builds a conjunction, the second disassembles it for use, and the third references assumptions. The second and third rules can be combined to derive the traditional rules for conjunction (instantiate θ in the second rule by θ_1 and then by θ_2, respectively, and use the third rule both times to prove the second hypothesis of the second rule):

$$\frac{\pi \vdash \{fst:\theta_1, \; snd:\theta_2\}}{\pi \vdash \theta_1} \qquad\qquad \frac{\pi \vdash \{fst:\theta_1, \; snd:\theta_2\}}{\pi \vdash \theta_2}$$

We can repeat the above procedure with the typing rules for lambda abstraction, and we obtain the usual rules for logical implication; that is, the type $\theta_1 \rightarrow \theta_2$ is the implication $\theta_1 \supset \theta_2$:

$$\frac{\pi \uplus \{I:\theta_1\} \vdash \theta_2}{\pi \vdash \theta_1 \rightarrow \theta_2} \qquad\qquad \frac{\pi \vdash \theta_1 \rightarrow \theta_2 \qquad \pi \vdash \theta_1}{\pi \vdash \theta_2} \qquad\qquad \pi \vdash \theta \;\; \text{if } (I:\theta) \in \pi$$

The first rule builds an implication from an extra assumption, the second applies the implication, and the third is assumption reference.

In this way, the typing rules for records and lambda abstractions define a propositional logic with conjunction and implication. Since the inference rules that were derived for conjunction and implication are the traditional ones, we have evidence that the typing rules for the programming language are appropriate. The next, obvious step is to investigate other programming language extensions whose typing rules derive other logical connectives (for example, disjunction, negation, and quantifiers). This activity is developed at length in Chapters 9 and 10.

Suggested Reading

The starting points for the modeling of programming language features by lambda abstraction are Landin 1965 and 1966, Morris 1968, Strachey 1967, and Reynolds 1970. Extensions are found in Reynolds 1988, Tennent 1989, Friedman, Wand, and Haynes 1992, and Weeks and Felleisen 1993. The use of records is based on work by Cardelli and MacQueen, as realized in Amber and Standard ML; see MacQueen 1984, Cardelli 1986a, and Cardelli and Mitchell 1991. The modelling of storage allocation as a core language primitive is proposed in Reynolds 1981 and developed by Tennent 1991, where modules are encoded. Laws for storage allocation and assignment are studied in Felleisen and Friedman 1989, Felleisen and Hieb 1992, and Mason and Talcott 1991, 1992. A good introduction to category theory as applied to programming languages is Pierce 1991; see Lambek and Scott 1986 for its application to records and lambda abstraction. Nordström 1981 sets down the logical principles of records and lambda abstractions.

Exercises

1.1. Use Figure 5.1 to draw the attributed syntax tree for the following:

$loc_1 := 0$; **if** $\neg(@loc_1 = 0)$ **then skip else** $loc_2 := @loc_1 + 1$ **fi**

2.1. Propose a method to desugar declarations of the form $D_1; D_2$ into the record notation of Figure 5.2. Explain the difficulties that arise.

2.2. An alternative to the record construction is the tuple. The syntax is

$E ::= \cdots \mid (E_1, E_2, \ldots, E_n) \mid E.i$

with the computation rule $(E_1, \ldots, E_i, \ldots, E_n).i \Rightarrow E_i$. Tuples are just records with labels that are numerals. But records are just tuples, where each label maps to a numeral. Give an algorithm that translates a program with records and record indexing into one with tuples and tuple indexing. Also, propose a version of the *with* construct for tuples that matches the *with* construct for records.

3.1. Desugar this program into records and lambda abstractions and attach typing attributes:

begin module $M(X:intloc) = \{$ **alias** $Y=X \}$, **alias** $A = loc_1$
in begin import $M(A)$,
  begin import $M(loc_2)$ **in proc** $P(X:intexp) = (A:=1; Y:=X)$ **end**
in call $P(@Y)$ **end end**

4.1. a. Give arguments for why block-structured, imperative languages usually do not allow "in-line" records.

b. Why are lambda abstractions disallowed as results from functions? (See

Section 4.3.) But why are lambda abstractions allowed as actual parameters?

c.* Georgeff (1984) proposes a stack implementation that allows lambda abstractions as results from functions. Read Georgeff's paper and explain how (some of) the difficulties in Part b can be resolved.

5.1. Use the core semantics in Figure 5.3 plus the lazy evaluation semantics in Figure 5.4 to calculate the meaning of the (desugared) program in Exercise 3.1. Repeat the activity for the semantics in Figure 5.3 plus the eager evaluation semantics in Figure 5.6.

5.2. Apply the copy rules to the (desugared) program in Exercise 3.1 and reduce it to a core language program.

5.3. For the semantics in Figures 5.4 and 5.6, prove that E_1, E_2 is an associative operation; that is, for all E_1, E_2, E_3, $[\![\pi \vdash (E_1, E_2), E_3 : \pi_1]\!] = [\![\pi \vdash E_1, (E_2, E_3) : \pi_1]\!]$. Next, prove that E_1, E_2 is commutative. Finally, show that there is an identity, E_0, such that $[\![\pi \vdash E_0, E : \pi]\!] = [\![\pi \vdash E, E_0 : \pi]\!] = [\![\pi \vdash E : \pi]\!]$ for all records, E.

5.4. a. Define a denotational semantics where records are evaluated lazily and (arguments to) lambda abstractions are evaluated eagerly. What is the semantics of identifier reference?

   b. Change the semantics in Figure 5.4 so that *intexp* abstractions are evaluated eagerly but all other abstractions are evaluated lazily.

5.5. a. The typing of *new* V *in* E requires that E has type *comm*. Does any harm arise if E has the type τexp? *intloc*? π? $\theta \rightarrow comm$?

   b.* As it stands, *new* allocates just integer locations. Extend *new* to arbitrary classes:

$$\frac{\pi \uplus \{V : \delta\} \vdash E : comm}{\pi \vdash new\,(V : \delta)\,in\,E : comm} \quad \text{for } \delta ::= intloc \mid \pi$$

   What problems arise?

5.6. Prove that the usual operational semantics is adequate for the language in Figure 5.4; here are the key definitions:

$comp_{\{i : \theta_i\}_{i \in I}} p$ iff $p \Rightarrow^* \{i = v_i\}_{i \in I}$ and for all $i \in I$, $comp_{\theta_i} v_i$

$comp_{\theta_1 \rightarrow \theta_2} p$ iff for all v, $comp_{\theta_1} v$ implies $comp_{\theta_2} (p\,v)$

5.7. Consider the construct, *rec* I:θ. E, for recursion. Its semantics follows:

$[\![\pi \vdash rec\,I : \theta.\,E : \theta]\!]e = v$, where $v = [\![\pi \uplus \{I : \theta\} \vdash E : \theta]\!](e \uplus \{I = v\})$

   a. Imperative languages normally require that a parameterized abstraction specify all its formal parameter names, that is, the recursion must be in the following format:

$rec\,I\!:\theta_1\!\to\cdots\to\theta_n\!\to\theta.\lambda I_1\!:\!\theta_1.\cdots\lambda I_n\!:\!\theta_n.\,E,\;$ where $\;\theta\neq(\theta'\!\to\theta'')$

Give the denotational semantics of this format for *rec* with lazy evaluation semantics (Figure 5.4). Does this equality hold: $[\![\pi\vdash rec\,I\!:\theta_1\!\to\theta_2.$ $E\!:\theta_1\!\to\theta_2]\!]e = [\![\pi\vdash rec\,I\!:\theta_1\to\theta_2.\lambda I_1\!:\!\theta_1.\,(E\,I_1)\!:\theta_1\to\theta_2]\!]e$?

b. Repeat Part a, but for eager evaluation semantics (Figure 5.6).

c. Similar issues arise for records. Give the lazy and eager evaluation semantics for:

$$rec\,I\!:\{I_1\!:\!\theta_1,\,\ldots,\,I_n\!:\!\theta_n\,\}.\,\{I_1\!=\!E_1,\,\ldots,\,I_n\!=\!E_n\,\}$$

Does this equality hold: $[\![\pi\vdash rec\,I\!:\{J\!:\!\theta\}.\,E\;:\{J\!:\!\theta\}]\!]e \;=\; [\![\pi\vdash rec\,I\!:\{J\!:\!\theta\}.$ $\{J\!=\!with\;E\;do\;J\}:\{J\!:\!\theta\}]\!]e$?

7.1. a. Translate the following program into lambda abstraction form and draw its attributed syntax tree:

begin var A: **newint, fun** $F(X\!:\!intexp,\,Y\!:\!intexp) = X{+}Y$
in $A\!:=\!0;$
           begin proc $P(X\!:\!intloc) =$ **begin var** B: **newint in** $B\!:=\!F(@X,\,1)$ **end**
           in if $\neg(@A\!=\!0)$ **then skip else call** $P(A)$ **fi end**
end

b. What difficulty arises in translating this example into lambda abstraction form?

begin var A: **newint**
in begin module $M = \{$ **fun** $F = @A{+}1,$ **var** B: **newint** $\}$
      in begin import M **in** $B\!:=\!F$ **end**
end end

7.2. Arrays are sometimes modeled by lambda abstraction. An array, **var** A: **array** $[M..N]$ **of newint**, is modeled by $A = (\lambda I\!:\!M..N.\,loc_{k+(I-M)})$, where loc_k is the first location in the vector. How can this modeling be generalized to multidimensional arrays? Arrays of records?

8.1. Another structuring device is the *variant* construction, $\theta_1{+}\theta_2$, whose operations are tagging and **cases**:

$$E ::= \cdots \mid in_1\,E \mid in_2\,E \mid cases\,E_1\,of\,(I\!:\!\theta)E_2\,(I\!:\!\theta)E_3$$

$$\frac{\pi\vdash E\!:\theta_i}{\pi\vdash in_i E\!:\theta_1{+}\theta_2}\;\;i\in\{1,2\}$$

$$\frac{\pi\vdash E_1\!:\theta_1{+}\theta_2 \quad \pi\uplus\{I\!:\!\theta_1\}\vdash E_2\!:\theta_3 \quad \pi\uplus\{I\!:\!\theta_2\}\vdash E_3\!:\theta_3}{\pi\vdash \mathbf{cases}\,E_1\,\mathbf{of}\,(I\!:\!\theta_1)E_2\,;\,(I\!:\!\theta_2)E_3\!:\theta_3}$$

Here are some potential copy rules:

cases in$_1$ E$_1$ **of** (I:θ$_1$)E$_2$; (I:θ$_2$)E$_3$ ⇒ [E$_1$/I]E$_2$
cases in$_2$ E$_1$ **of** (I:θ$_1$)E$_2$; (I:θ$_2$)E$_3$ ⇒ [E$_1$/I]E$_3$

Add the variant construction to the language in Figure 5.1. Write a lazy evaluation semantics for the construction and prove that the typing rules and copy rules are sound. Write an eager evaluation semantics. Is the variant construction an "orthogonal" construction?

9.1. If you worked Exercise 8.1, proceed. A standard construction in category theory is the *coproduct*. A coproduct resembles a disjoint union construction in set theory, where sets A and B are disjointly unioned into $A{+}B = \{(1, a) \mid a \in A\} \cup \{(2, b) \mid b \in B\}$. There are "tagging" operations $in_1 : A \to A{+}B$ and $in_2 : B \to A{+}B$, such that $(in_1\ a) = (1, a)$, and $(in_2\ b) = (2, b)$, and a ternary *cases* construction, like the one described in Exercise 8.1, whose behavior is defined below. A type, $\theta_1{+}\theta_2$, is the categorical coproduct if the following equalities hold:

(i) *cases* $(in_i\ E_0)\ of\ (I{:}\theta_1)E_1$; $(I{:}\theta_2)E_2 \equiv subst(E_0, I, E_i)$, for $i \in \{1,2\}$;

(ii) for $\pi \vdash E_0 : \theta_1{+}\theta_2$ and $\pi \uplus \{I{:}\theta_1{+}\theta_2\} \vdash E : \theta_3$, $subst(E_0, I_0, E) \equiv$ *cases* $E_0\ of\ (I{:}\theta_1)subst\ ((in_1\ I), I_0, E)$; $(I{:}\theta_2)subst\ ((in_2\ I), I_0, E)$.

Prove that the lazy evaluation semantics of the variant construction is categorical coproduct, where $subst(U, I, E) \equiv$ *with* I=U *do* E. Under what conditions is the eager evaluation semantics of the variant the categorical coproduct?

10.1. If you worked Exercise 8.1, proceed. Use the technique in Section 5.10 to derive propositional logic inference rules from the typing rules for the variant construction. What logical connective is defined?

6 The Lambda Calculus

The lambda abstraction and its copy rule come from a system invented in the 1930s by Church, called the *lambda calculus*. Church developed the lambda calculus to study the foundations of mathematics and logic. At one time Church hoped that the lambda calculus would serve as a set-theoretic-like foundation for mathematics, but this goal proved unachievable. In the 1960s, Strachey, Landin, and others observed that the lambda calculus worked well as a notation for stating the semantic properties of computer programming languages. This application has proved fruitful, and the lambda calculus stands today as a fundamental tool for programming language design and analysis.

6.1 The Untyped Lambda Calculus

The lambda calculus is pleasant because it is so simple. Its syntax is in Figure 6.1. The first construct in the syntax rule is called a *lambda abstraction*, the second is an *application* (or *combination*), and the third is an *identifier* (or *variable*).

In the lambda abstraction $\lambda I_0.E$, the I_0 is called a *binding identifier*. The *scope* of λI_0 is E, less those lambda abstractions within E whose binding identifiers are also I_0. Occurrences of I_0 in E within λI_0's scope are said to be *bound*; an unbound identifier is *free*. The free identifiers in an expression, E, are denoted by $FV(E)$:

$$FV(\lambda I.E) = FV(E) - \{I\}$$
$$FV(E_1\ E_2) = FV(E_1) \cup FV(E_2)$$
$$FV(I) = \{I\}$$

An expression, E, is *closed* if $FV(E) = \varnothing$.

The free identifiers in an expression can be affected by substitution. We write $[E_1/I]E_2$ to denote the substitution of E_1 for all free occurrences of I in E_2. Substitution is defined as usual:

E ∈ Expression
I ∈ Identifier

$$E ::= (\lambda I. E) \mid (E_1\ E_2) \mid I$$

Figure 6.1 _____

$[E/I](\lambda I.E_1) = \lambda I.E_1$

$[E/I](\lambda J.E_1) = \lambda J.\,[E/I]E_1$, if $I \neq J$ and $J \notin FV(E)$

$[E/I](\lambda J.E_1) = \lambda K.\,[E/I][K/J]E_1$, if $I \neq J$, $J \in FV(E)$, and K is fresh

$[E/I](E_1\ E_2) = [E/I]E_1\ [E/I]E_2$

$[E/I]I = E$

$[E/I]J = J$, if $J \neq I$

Here are a few examples of lambda calculus expressions:

$(\lambda X. X)$

$(\lambda X. (X\ (Y\ X)))$

$((\lambda X. (X\ X))(\lambda Y. Z))$

$(\lambda X. (\lambda Y. (X\ (\lambda X. (\lambda Y. Y)))))$

The piles of brackets prove tiresome, so we drop the outermost set and abbreviate nested combinations $((E_1\ E_2)\ E_3)$ to $(E_1\ E_2\ E_3)$. We abbreviate $(\lambda I.(E))$ to $(\lambda I. E)$ as well. Here are the abbreviated forms of the previous expressions:

$\lambda X. X$

$\lambda X. X\ (Y\ X)$

$(\lambda X. X\ X)(\lambda Y. Z)$

$\lambda X. \lambda Y. X\ (\lambda X. \lambda Y. Y)$

With this abbreviation, the scope of a binding identifier, I, in $\lambda I. \cdots$ extends from the period that follows I to the first unmatched right parenthesis (or the end of the phrase, whichever comes first), less any lambda abstractions with the same binding identifier.

So far, it is not clear what the expressions *mean*. Don't worry—they don't mean anything, yet! For the moment, the lambda calculus is just a notation of identifiers.

These rewriting rules manipulate lambda expressions:

α-rule: $\lambda I. E \ \Rightarrow \ \lambda J.[J/I]E, \ \text{if } J \notin FV(E)$

β-rule: $(\lambda I. E_1) E_2 \ \Rightarrow \ [E_2/I]E_1$

η-rule: $\lambda I. E I \ \Rightarrow \ E, \ \ \text{if } I \notin FV(E)$

The α-rule suggests that the choice of binding identifier is unimportant; the β-rule says that binding of an argument to a binding identifier is just substitution; and the η-rule implies that all lambda calculus expressions represent functions. The α-, β-, and η-rules make good sense for a logic of functions, and a good intuition to have is that the lambda calculus is a language of purely functions.

We do not use the α- and η-rules for computation; for the moment, that leaves just the β-rule. Here is a sample computation, where the substitutions are displayed:

$(\lambda Y. (\lambda X. (Y X)) Y)(\lambda Z. X)$

$\Rightarrow [\lambda Z.X/Y](\lambda X. (Y X)) Y$

$= (\lambda A. [\lambda Z.X/Y][A/X](Y X))([\lambda Z.X/Y]Y)$

$= (\lambda A. [\lambda Z.X/Y](Y A))(\lambda Z.X)$

$= (\lambda A. (\lambda Z. X)A)(\lambda Z. X)$

$\Rightarrow [\lambda Z.X/A]((\lambda Z. X)A)$

$= (\lambda Z. X)(\lambda Z. X) \Rightarrow [\lambda Z.X/Z]X = X$

Say that an expression, E, contains the subexpression $(\lambda I. E_1)E_2$; the subexpression is called a (β-)*redex*; the expression $[E_2/I]E_1$ is its *contractum*; and the action of replacing the contractum for the redex in E, giving E', is called a *contraction* or a *reduction step*. A reduction step is written $E \Rightarrow E'$. A *reduction sequence* is a series of reduction steps $E_1 \Rightarrow E_2 \Rightarrow \cdots \Rightarrow E_i \Rightarrow \cdots$ that has finite or infinite length. If the sequence has finite length, starting at E_1 and ending at E_n, $n \geq 0$, we write $E_1 \Rightarrow^* E_n$. (Note that, for every E, $E \Rightarrow^* E$.) A lambda expression is in (β-)*normal form* if it contains no (β-)redexes.* An expression *has* normal form if it can be rewritten to an expression *in* normal form. A fun and time-consuming game is to rewrite lambda expressions into their normal forms. But beware—not all expressions have normal forms. Here is a famous example that does not:

$(\lambda X. X X)(\lambda X. X X) \ \Rightarrow \ (\lambda X. X X)(\lambda X. X X) \ \Rightarrow \ (\lambda X. X X)(\lambda X. X X) \ \Rightarrow \ \cdots$

Here is another example that you should try: $(\lambda X. X (X X))(\lambda X. X (X X))$; and yet another: $\lambda F. (\lambda X. F (X X))(\lambda X. F (X X))$. None of these has a normal form. It is no coincidence that all of them use *self-application*—the application of an expression to

---

* If both the β- and η-rules were used in reduction sequences, we would say an expression is in $\beta\eta$-normal form if it had no $\beta\eta$-redexes.

itself. It is through self-application that repetitive computation can be simulated in the lambda calculus. Indeed, the third of the previous three examples is famous because it can encode recursive function definitions. Call it **Y**; a definition **rec-define** $f = \cdots f \cdots$ is encoded **define** $f = \mathbf{Y}(\lambda f. \cdots f \cdots)$.

Arithmetic can be simulated in the lambda calculus. Although it is not our intention to use the lambda calculus in this way, it is interesting that we can define the following simulations of the natural numbers, called the "Church numerals":

$\bar{0}$: $\lambda S. \lambda Z. Z$

$\bar{1}$: $\lambda S. \lambda Z. S\, Z$

$\bar{2}$: $\lambda S. \lambda Z. S\,(S\, Z)$

   $\cdots$

$\bar{i}$: $\lambda S. \lambda Z. S\,(S\,(\cdots (S\, Z)\cdots))$, S repeated i times

Now we can encode numeric operations, such as the successor function, *succ* $= \lambda N. \lambda S. \lambda Z. S\,(N\, S\, Z)$, and addition, *add* $= \lambda M.\lambda N. M\, succ\, N$, and indeed, all of the general recursive functions, in the sense that, if $\bar{n}$ is the Church numeral for number n, then for every general recursive function $f : \mathbb{N} \to \mathbb{N}$, we can construct a lambda expression, F, such that, for all $n \in \mathbb{N}$, $(F\, \bar{n}) \Rightarrow^* \overline{f(n)}$ (when $f(n)$ is defined, otherwise $(F\, \bar{n})$ has no normal form). This means the lambda calculus is as powerful a computation system as any known. A consequence of this result is that it is impossible to mechanically decide whether or not an arbitrary expression has a normal form. (If we could decide this question, then we could solve the famous, undecidable "halting problem.")

The β-rule has several pleasing properties. The most important are these three:

6.1 Theorem (The Confluence Property)

For any lambda expression E, if $E \Rightarrow^* E_1$ and $E \Rightarrow^* E_2$, then there exists a lambda expression, E_3, such that $E_1 \Rightarrow^* E_3$ and $E_2 \Rightarrow^* E_3$ (modulo application of the α-rule to E_3).

This theorem implies that the order in which we reduce redexes is unimportant; all reduction sequences can be made to meet at a common expression (up to renaming of binding identifiers). But the confluence property does not say that all reduction sequences *must* meet, only that they can be made to meet; for example, let Δ be $(\lambda X.\, X\, X)$. For $E_0 = (\lambda Y.Z)(\Delta\, \Delta)$, we have $E_0 \Rightarrow Z$ and $E_0 \Rightarrow E_0$. By the confluence property, there must be some E_3 such that $Z \Rightarrow^* E_3$ and $E_0 \Rightarrow^* E_3$. Since Z is in normal form, E_3 must be Z, and indeed, $E_0 \Rightarrow^* Z$. But notice that the reduction sequence $E_0 \Rightarrow E_0 \Rightarrow \cdots \Rightarrow E_0 \Rightarrow \cdots$ never reaches Z, although the confluence property guarantees that a reduction sequence $E_0 \Rightarrow^* E_0$ can be extended to $E_0 \Rightarrow^* E_0 \Rightarrow^* Z$. Thus, the strategy for choosing redexes is significant. A key consequence of confluence is

6.2 Corollary (The Uniqueness of Normal Forms Property)

If E can be rewritten to some E′ in normal form, then E′ is unique (modulo application of the α-rule).

The proof of this property is easy: If expression E would, in fact, reduce to distinct normal forms E_1 and E_2, the confluence property tells us there is some E_3 such that $E_1 \Rightarrow^* E_3$ and $E_2 \Rightarrow^* E_3$. But this is impossible, since E_1 and E_2 cannot be further reduced.

Uniqueness of normal forms is crucial, because it gives a programmer a naive but useful semantics for the lambda calculus: The "meaning" of an expression is the normal form to which it rewrites.

The confluence property is sometimes called the *Church-Rosser property*, after the persons who first proved it. A proof of the confluence property is described in Section 6.8.

Finally, there is a particular rewriting strategy that always discovers a normal form, if one exists. Say that the *leftmost-outermost redex* in an expression is the redex whose λ-symbol lies to the leftmost in the expression. (The redex is "leftmost-outermost" in the sense that, when the expression is drawn as a tree, the redex is outermost—it is not embedded in another redex—and it is the leftmost of all the outermost redexes.) The leftmost-outermost rewriting strategy reduces the leftmost-outermost redex at each stage until no more redexes exist.

6.3 Theorem (The Standardization Property)

If an expression has a normal form, it will be found by the leftmost-outermost rewriting strategy.

Here is an example of a reduction by the leftmost-outermost strategy:

$(\lambda Y.\ Y\ Y)\ ((\lambda X.X)(\lambda Z.Z))$
$\Rightarrow\ ((\lambda X.X)(\lambda Z.Z))\ ((\lambda X.X)(\lambda Z.Z))$
$\Rightarrow\ (\lambda Z.Z)\ ((\lambda X.X)(\lambda Z.Z))\ \Rightarrow\ (\lambda X.X)(\lambda Z.Z)\ \Rightarrow\ (\lambda Z.Z)$

The leftmost-outermost strategy is a "lazy evaluation" strategy—an argument is not reduced until it finally appears as the leftmost-outermost redex in an expression. Other reduction strategies might arrive at a normal form in fewer steps. The previous reduction is done quicker if we reduce the rightmost-innermost redex each time:

$(\lambda Y.\ Y\ Y)((\lambda X.X)(\lambda Z.Z))$

$\Rightarrow\ (\lambda Y.\ Y\ Y)(\lambda Z.Z)$

$\Rightarrow\ (\lambda Z.Z)(\lambda Z.Z)\ \Rightarrow\ (\lambda Z.Z)$

The rightmost-innermost strategy roughly corresponds to "eager evaluation." But in some cases the strategy will not discover a normal form, whereas the leftmost-outermost strategy will, for example, $(\lambda Y.Z)((\lambda X.\ X\ X)(\lambda X.\ X\ X))$.

6.2 Call-by-Name and Call-by-Value Reduction

The β-rule in the previous section is sometimes titled the *call-by-name* β-rule because it places no restriction on the argument, E_2, of the redex $(\lambda I.E_1)E_2$. There is an alternative, the *call-by-value* β-rule (or β-*val* rule), which does restrict the form of E_2.

Say that identifiers, I, and lambda abstractions, $\lambda I.E$, are *Values*. The call-by-value β-rule reads as follows:

β-*val*: $(\lambda I.E_1)E_2\ \Rightarrow\ [E_2/I]E_1$, if E_2 is a Value

This roughly corresponds to call-by-value evaluation of actual parameters in programming languages. Here is a computation undertaken with the β-*val* rule:

$(\lambda W.A)((\lambda Y.\lambda Z.Z\ Z)((\lambda X.B)C)(\lambda X.X\ X))$

$\Rightarrow\ (\lambda W.A)((\lambda Y.\lambda Z.Z\ Z)C\ (\lambda X.X\ X))$

$\Rightarrow\ (\lambda W.A)((\lambda Z.Z\ Z)(\lambda X.X\ X))$

$\Rightarrow\ (\lambda W.A)((\lambda X.X\ X)(\lambda X.X\ X))$

$\Rightarrow\ (\lambda W.A)((\lambda X.X\ X)(\lambda X.X\ X))\ \Rightarrow\ \cdots$

At each stage there is only one redex, and the computation is nonterminating, since the argument to λW will never reduce to a Value. Contrast the above reduction sequence to one generated by the usual β-rule, which terminates in one step. Perhaps this suggests that the β-*val* rule is not as "useful" as the β-rule, but Section 6.7 will show that the β-*val* rule is often the appropriate one for specifying the operational semantics of programming languages.

A useful insight is that the β-*val* rule can be coded as *two* rules:

β-*val*$_1$: $(\lambda I.E_1)J\ \Rightarrow\ [J/I]E_1$

β-*val*$_2$: $(\lambda I.E_1)(\lambda J.E_2)\ \Rightarrow\ [(\lambda J.E_2)/I]E_1$

Here, the notion of "Value" is encoded within the patterns of the two rules. Another variant of the β-*val* rule is just β-*val*$_2$: Only lambda abstractions are Values. This variant works well with a lambda calculus of closed expressions. Yet another variant arises when additional phrases, such as arithmetic expressions, are added to the lambda calculus. In the case of arithmetic, the numerals 0, 1, 2, and so on, are Values, and we have:

$$\beta\text{-}val_3: \quad (\lambda I.E_1)n \;\Rightarrow\; [n/I]E_1, \text{ if } n \text{ is a numeral}$$

When the β-*val* rule is used, the purpose of a computation is to reduce an expression to a Value. But Values differ from normal forms: An expression—even one without a normal form—can reduce to more than one Value. An example is $(\lambda X. \lambda Y. (\lambda Z. Z\,Z\,Z)$ $(\lambda Z. Z\,Z\,Z))A$. Nonetheless, for typed programming languages, the notion of Value is useful because the inputs and outputs for programs are typically phrases of type *int*, *bool*, and the like. For these types, Values and normal forms coincide. Section 6.6 gives details.

6.3 An Induction Principle

Proofs of properties of programming languages are usually undertaken by structural induction. But structural induction often fails to work when properties about substitution must be proved. Let $E_1 \equiv E_2$ mean that E_1 and E_2 are identical, modulo use of the α-rule, and consider this example:

6.4 Proposition

For all identifiers, I, *and expressions,* E_1 *and* E_2, *if* $I \notin FV(E_1)$, *then* $[E_2/I]E_1 \equiv E_1$.

Attempted proof: We use induction on the structure of E_1. There are three cases:

(i) $E_1 = J$: Assume $I \notin FV(J)$. This implies $I \neq J$, so $[E_2/I]J = J$.

(ii) $E_1 = (E_{11}\,E_{12})$: Assume $I \notin FV(E_{11}\,E_{12})$; then $I \notin FV(E_{11})$ and $I \notin FV(E_{12})$. Since $[E_2/I](E_{11}\,E_{12}) = ([E_2/I]E_{11}\,[E_2/I]E_{12})$, the result follows immediately from the inductive hypotheses for E_{11} and E_{12}.

(iii) $E_1 = \lambda J.E_{11}$: Assume $I \notin FV(\lambda J.E_{11})$. If $I = J$, the result is immediate. If $I \neq J$ and $J \notin FV(E_2)$, then $[E_2/I](\lambda J.E_{11}) = (\lambda J.[E_2/I]E_{11})$. We have that $I \notin FV(E_{11})$, so the result follows from the inductive hypothesis for E_{11}. Finally, consider when $I \neq J$ and $J \in FV(E_2)$. Then, $[E_2/I](\lambda J.E_{11}) = (\lambda K.[E_2/I][K/J]E_{11})$. Now, we are stuck, because the inductive hypothesis applies only to E_{11} and *not* to $[K/J]E_{11}$, which may be a different expression!

The technical problem with substitution is frustrating, since the renaming of J to K in case (iii) is cosmetic and does not affect the structure of E_{11} at all. The problem has motivated some researchers to replace explicit substitution by an implicit form (where substitution always, automatically, correctly occurs) or even to abandon identifiers and substitution altogether and replace identifiers by numerical offsets, similar to the relative addresses for variables that a compiler calculates. The exercises introduce these alternatives. Here, we stick with substitution and sidestep the problem in the traditional way. We define the *rank* of a lambda calculus expression as follows:

$rank(I) = 0$

$rank(E_1 \ E_2) = max\{ rank(E_1), \ rank(E_2) \}+1$

$rank(\lambda I. E) = rank(E)+1$

The definition of *rank* admits a useful induction principle:

6.5 Theorem (Induction on Rank)

To prove that a property, P, holds for all lambda calculus expressions, it suffices to prove, for an arbitrary expression, E_0, with $rank(E_0) = j$, that
*   if (for all expressions, E, such that $rank(E)<j$, P(E) holds),*
*   then $P(E_0)$ holds.*

The soundness of induction on rank can be proved by means of mathematical induction; this is left as an exercise. The utility of induction on rank is enhanced by the following lemma.

6.6 Lemma

For all identifiers I and J and expressions E, $rank(E) = rank([J/I]E)$.

Proof: The proof is by induction on the rank of E. For arbitrary $j \geq 0$, we may assume, for all expressions E' such that $rank(E')<j$, that for all I and J, $rank(E') = rank([J/I]E')$. We must show, when $rank(E) = j$, that for all I and J, $rank(E) = rank([J/I]E)$. There are three cases:

(i)   E=K, an identifier: Then $rank([J/I]K) = 0 = rank(K)$, whether or not I equals K.

(ii) $E = (E_1 \ E_2)$: $[J/I](E_1 \ E_2) = ([J/I]E_1 \ [J/I]E_2)$. By the definition of *rank*, $rank(E_1) < rank(E)$ and $rank(E_2) < rank(E)$, and by the inductive hypothesis, $rank([J/I]E_1) = rank(E_1)$ and $rank([J/I]E_2) = rank(E_2)$; this implies the result.

(iii) $E=(\lambda K. E_1)$: the only interesting case to consider of $[J/I](\lambda K. E_1)$ is when $I \neq K$ but $J=K$. The resulting expression is $(lamL. [J/I][L/J]E_1)$. Since $rank(E_1) < rank(E)$, we have that $rank([L/J]E_1) = rank(E_1)$, by the inductive hypothesis. But this implies $rank([L/J]E_1) < rank(E)$, and by applying the inductive hypothesis again, we have $rank([J/I][L/J]E_1) = rank([L/J]E_1) = rank(E_1)$. This gives the result. □

With the aid of Lemma 6.6, we can view induction by rank as a form of structural induction that is unaffected by cosmetic substitutions. We return to this point momentarily, but first we perform the proof of Proposition 6.4.

Proof of Proposition 6.4: The proof is by induction on the rank of E_1. For arbitrary $j \geq 0$, we assume, for all expressions E' such that $rank(E') < j$, that $I \notin FV(E')$ implies $[E_2/I]E' \equiv E'$. We must show the same result for E_1, where $rank(E_1) = j$. Now, E_1 must have one of three forms:

(i) $E_1 = J$: The reasoning in the "attempted proof" applies.
(ii) $E_1 = (E_{11} E_{12})$: The reasoning in the "attempted proof" applies, since $rank(E_{11}) < rank(E_1)$ and $rank(E_{12}) < rank(E_1)$.
(iii) $E_1 = (\lambda J.E_{11})$: If $I = J$, the reasoning in the "attempted proof" applies. If $I \neq J$ and $J \notin FV(E_2)$, then the "attempted proof" reasoning applies, since $rank(E_{11}) < rank(E_1)$. Finally, if $I \neq J$ and $J \in FV(E_2)$, then $[E_2/I](\lambda J.E_{11}) = (\lambda K. [E_2/I] [K/J]E_{11})$. By Lemma 6.6, $rank([K/J]E_{11}) = rank(E_{11}) < rank(E_1)$. Since $I \notin FV(E_{11})$, it is easy to prove that $I \notin FV([K/J]E_{11})$. Therefore, the inductive hypothesis gives us $[E_2/I][K/J]E_{11} \equiv [K/J]E_{11}$. Since $(\lambda J.E_{11}) \equiv (\lambda K.[K/J]E_{11})$, this gives the result. $\square$

This proof looks almost exactly like a proof by structural induction where the only exception is when a cosmetic renaming of identifiers is necessary, so from here on, we write proofs that use induction on rank as if they are structural induction proofs. Thanks to Lemma 6.6, we obtain an additional inductive hypothesis for cosmetic substitutions like $[K/J]E_{11}$. Induction by rank will be essential to proofs of several standard results for the lambda calculus.

6.4 The Simply Typed Lambda Calculus

An important extension to the lambda calculus is a typing system. The *simply typed lambda calculus* is presented in Figure 6.2. Since the system is similar to the one in Chapter 5, we do not consider examples.

When we write type expressions of the form $\tau_1 \to (\tau_2 \to \tau_3)$, we usually drop the rightmost brackets and write $\tau_1 \to \tau_2 \to \tau_3$. The β-rule applies to the simply typed lambda calculus:

β-rule: $((\lambda I{:}\tau. E_1) E_2) \Rightarrow [E_2/I]E_1$

When the β-*val* rule is used, it reads as before, namely,

β-*val* rule: $((\lambda I{:}\tau. E_1) E_2) \Rightarrow [E_2/I]E_1$, if E_1 is a Value

where the notion of "Value" is defined recursively on the types in the language:

E ∈ Expression

I ∈ Identifier

τ ∈ Data-Type

ι ∈ Primitive-Data-Type (for example, *int*)

$$E ::= (\lambda I{:}\tau.\,E) \mid (E_1\ E_2) \mid I$$
$$\tau ::= \iota \mid \tau_1 \to \tau_2$$

$$\frac{\pi \uplus \{I{:}\tau_1\} \vdash E{:}\tau_2}{(\lambda I{:}\tau_1.\,E){:}\tau_1 \to \tau_2} \qquad \frac{\pi \vdash E_1{:}\tau_1 \to \tau_2 \quad \pi \vdash E_2{:}\tau_1}{\pi \vdash (E_1\ E_2){:}\tau_2} \qquad \pi \vdash I{:}\tau,\ \text{if } (I{:}\tau) \in \pi$$

Figure 6.2 _____

Value $(\iota) = $ a set of constants, for example, *Value*$(int) = \{\,0,\ 1,\ 2,\ \ldots\,\}$

Value $(\tau_1 \to \tau_2) = \{\,(\lambda I{:}\tau_1.E) \mid$ there exists π such that $\pi \vdash (\lambda I{:}\tau_1.E){:}\tau_1 \to \tau_2$ holds $\}$

The simply typed lambda calculus has the confluence, uniqueness of normal forms, and unicity of typing properties. Another notable property is that substitution preserves typing:

6.7 Lemma

For all π, τ_1, τ_2, I, E_1, *and* E_2, *if* $\pi \vdash E_2{:}\tau_2$ *and* $\pi \uplus \{I{:}\tau_2\} \vdash E_1{:}\tau_1$ *hold, then so does* $\pi \vdash [E_2/I]E_1{:}\tau_1$.

Proof: The proof is by induction on the rank of E_1, which has one of three forms:

(i) $E_1 = I$: If $I = J$, then $[E_2/I]I = E_2$, and since $\pi \vdash E_2{:}\tau_2$, the result holds. If $I \neq J$, then $[E_2/I]J = J$. We know that $\pi \uplus \{I{:}\tau_2\} \vdash J{:}\tau_1$, but this implies $(J{:}\tau_1) \in \pi$, by the typing rule for identifiers, implying $\pi \vdash J{:}\tau_1$.

(ii) $E_1 = (E_{11}\ E_{12})$: The typing rule for combinations implies that $\pi \uplus \{I{:}\tau_2\}$ $\vdash E_{11}{:}\tau_{12} \to \tau_1$ and $\pi \uplus \{I{:}\tau_2\} \vdash E_{12}{:}\tau_{12}$ both hold, for some type τ_{12}. The inductive hypothesis for E_{11} yields $\pi \vdash [E_2/I]E_{11}{:}\tau_{12} \to \tau_1$ and for E_{12} yields $\pi \vdash [E_2/I]E_{12}{:}\tau_{12}$. By the typing rule for combinations, we get the result.

(iii) $E_1 = (\lambda J{:}\tau_{11}.\,E_{11})$ for $\tau_1 = \tau_{11} \to \tau_{12}$: There are three subcases:

    (a) If $I = J$, we must show $\pi \vdash (\lambda I{:}\tau_{11}.\,E_{11}){:}\tau_{11} \to \tau_{12}$. By hypothesis, we have $\pi \uplus \{I{:}\tau_2\} \vdash (\lambda I{:}\tau_{11}.\,E_{11}){:}\tau_{11} \to \tau_{12}$, and by the typing rule for abstractions we know that $\pi \uplus \{I{:}\tau_1\} \uplus \{I{:}\tau_{11}\} \vdash E_{11}{:}\tau_{12}$ holds. But $\pi \uplus \{I{:}\tau_1\} \uplus \{I{:}\tau_{11}\} = \pi \uplus \{I{:}\tau_{11}\}$, so $\pi \uplus \{I{:}\tau_{11}\} \vdash E_{11}{:}\tau_{12}$ holds also, and this implies the result.

(b) If $I \neq J$ and J is not free in E_2, then we must show $\pi \vdash (\lambda J:\tau_{11}. [E_2/I]E_1):$
$\tau_{11} \to \tau_{12}$. By reasoning similar to that in case (a), we know that
$\pi \uplus \{I:\tau_1\} \uplus \{J:\tau_{11}\} \vdash E_{11}:\tau_{12}$ holds. Since $I \neq J$, we also have $\pi \uplus \{J:$
$\tau_{11}\} \uplus \{I:\tau_1\} \vdash E_{11}:\tau_{12}$. By the inductive hypothesis on E_{11} we get
$\pi \uplus \{J:\tau_{11}\} \vdash [E_2/I]:\tau_{12}$, which implies the result.

(c) If $I \neq J$, and J is free in E_2, we must show $\pi \vdash (\lambda K:\tau_{11}. [E_2/I] [K/J]E_{11}):$
$\tau_{11} \to \tau_{12}$, where K is fresh. By hypothesis, we have $\pi \uplus \{I:\tau_1\} \uplus \{J:\tau_{11}\}$
$\vdash E_{11}:\tau_{12}$. Since K is fresh, we can easily prove $\pi \uplus \{I:\tau_1\} \uplus \{J:\tau_{11}\}$
$\uplus \{K:\tau_{11}\} \vdash E_{11}:\tau_{12}$. (The proof is left as an exercise.) Since I, J, and K are
all distinct, $\pi \uplus \{K:\tau_{11}\} \uplus \{I:\tau_1\} \uplus \{J:\tau_{11}\} \vdash E_{11}:\tau_{12}$ holds also. The
rule for identifiers gives us $\pi \uplus \{K:\tau_{11}\} \uplus \{I:\tau_1\} \vdash K:\tau_{11}$, so we apply the
inductive hypothesis to E_{11}. This gives us $\pi \uplus \{K:\tau_{11}\} \uplus \{I:\tau_1\}$
$\vdash [K/J]E_{11}:\tau_{12}$. Next, we can apply the inductive hypothesis a second time,
this time to $[K/J]E_{11}$, and obtain $\pi \uplus \{K:\tau_{11}\} \vdash [E_1/I] [K/J]E_{11}:\tau_{12}$. The
typing rule for abstractions gives the result. $\square$

A consequence of the above lemma is that the β-rule does not change the typing of an
expression. As a result, we obtain this important theorem:

6.8 Theorem (The Subject Reduction Property)

If $\pi \vdash E_1:\tau$ holds and $E_1 \Rightarrow^* E_2$, then $\pi \vdash E_2:\tau$ holds as well.

Proof: It suffices to show the result for $E_1 \Rightarrow E_2$, a single reduction step. The proof is by
induction on the structure of E_1:

(i) $E_1 = I$: This case is impossible.

(ii) $E_1 = \lambda I:\tau_1. E_{11}$: Clearly, $E_{11} \Rightarrow E_{11}'$, and the inductive hypothesis for E_{11} implies
the result.

(iii) $E_1 = (E_{11}\ E_{12})$: If the reduction step is wholly within E_{11}, that is, $E_{11} \Rightarrow E_{11}'$, then
the inductive hypothesis for E_{11} implies the result. A similar argument holds if
$E_{12} \Rightarrow E_{12}'$. The only other possibility is that E_1 is $(\lambda I:\tau. E')E_{12}$ and E_1
$\Rightarrow [E_{12}/I]E'$. Then, the result follows from Lemma 6.7. $\square$

The Subject Reduction Property shows that the β-rule does not change the typing structure of an expression, hence type (re)checking is unnecessary during a reduction
sequence.

The next result about the simply typed lambda calculus is startling and crucial:

6.9 Theorem (The Strong Normalization Property)

If $\pi \vdash E:\tau$ holds, then every reduction sequence starting from E has finite length.

The proof is nontrivial and will not be shown here; a presentation can be found in Hindley and Seldin 1986 or Thompson 1991.

Two immediate consequences of the strong normalization property are: (i) every well-typed term has a normal form; (ii) any rewriting strategy will find it. The reason for strong normalization is that the typing system prevents the coding of self-application, the method for simulating repetition. A term $(X\ X)$ would have to be typed in a way that the first occurrence of X has type $\tau_1 \to \tau_2$ and the second occurrence of X has type τ_1. But this is impossible with the rules for a well-typed expression.

Another major benefit of the typing system is that it allows us to reintroduce a denotational semantics and easily prove two important soundness results. These are covered in the next section.

6.5 Denotational Semantics and Soundness

The usual semantics for the simply typed lambda calculus is the lazy evaluation semantics from Chapter 5:

$$[\![\pi \vdash \lambda I{:}\tau_1 . E{:}\tau_1 \to \tau_2]\!]e = f, \quad \text{where } f u = [\![\pi \uplus \{I{:}\tau_1\} \vdash E{:}\tau_2]\!](e \uplus \{I{=}u\})$$
$$\text{and } e \uplus \{I{=}u\} = \{I{=}u\} \cup (e - \{(I{=}v) \mid (I{=}v) \in e\})$$
$$[\![\pi \vdash E_1\ E_2{:}\tau_2]\!]e = ([\![\pi \vdash E_1 : \tau_1 \to \tau_2]\!]e)\,([\![\pi \vdash E_2 : \tau_1]\!]e)$$
$$[\![\pi \vdash I{:}\tau]\!]e = v, \quad \text{where } (I{=}v) \in e$$

As usual, let $[\![\iota]\!]$ be the set of values named by ι (for example, $[\![int]\!] = Int$), and let $[\![\tau_1 \to \tau_2]\!] = [\![\tau_1]\!] \to [\![\tau_2]\!]$, that is, the set of functions from arguments in $[\![\tau_1]\!]$ to answers in $[\![\tau_2]\!]$.

The first important result is soundness of typing. As before, an environment, e, is *consistent* with a type assignment, π, if $(I{:}\tau) \in \pi$ exactly when $(I{=}v) \in e$ and $v \in [\![\tau]\!]$. Let Env_π be the set of those environments that are consistent with π.

6.10 Theorem

If $e \in Env_\pi$, then $[\![\pi \vdash E{:}\tau]\!]e \in [\![\tau]\!]$.

Proof: The proof is an induction on the structure of E. The three cases are:

(i)   An identifier, I: We have $\pi \vdash I{:}\theta$ and $(I{:}\theta) \in \pi$. The result follows because e is consistent with π.

(ii) An application $(E_1\ E_2)$: By the typing rule for applications and the inductive hypothesis, we have $[\![\pi \vdash E_1 : \tau_1 \to \tau_2]\!]e \in [\![\tau_1 \to \tau_2]\!]$ and $[\![\pi \vdash E_2 : \tau_1]\!]e \in [\![\tau_1]\!]$. Thus, $([\![\pi \vdash E_1 : \tau_1 \to \tau_2]\!]e)\,([\![\pi \vdash E_2 : \tau_1]\!]e) \in [\![\theta_2]\!]$.

(iii) An abstraction $\lambda I{:}\tau_1 . E$: By the typing rule for abstractions, we have

$\pi \uplus \{I{:}\tau_1\} \vdash E{:}\tau_2$. Assume that $v \in [\![\tau_1]\!]$, for an arbitrary v. Then, $e \uplus \{I{=}v\}$ is consistent with $\pi \uplus \{I{:}\tau_1\}$. By the inductive hypothesis, we have $[\![\pi \vdash E{:}\tau_2]\!]$ $(e \uplus \{I{=}v\}) \in [\![\tau_2]\!]$. Since v is arbitrary, the function $f(v) = [\![\pi \vdash E{:}\tau_2]\!](e \uplus \{I{=}v\})$ is in the set $[\![\tau_1 \to \tau_2]\!]$. $\square$

The typing theorem gives a "road map" for the semantics of the typed lambda calculus, telling us what form of value a well-typed expression represents. If we attempt to use the above denotational semantics for the untyped lambda calculus (delete all typing information), we encounter a significant problem: An expression like $\lambda X.X$ apparently represents an identity function that can take all other functions—including itself, $(\lambda X.X)(\lambda X.X)$—as arguments. This implies that the set theoretic representation of the identity function is a set of argument, answer pairs of the form: $Id = \{\ldots, (Id, Id),$ $\ldots\}$. Such a set is outlawed by the foundation axiom of set theory, so the well definedness of the semantics for untyped lambda calculus falls into doubt. There is a way to repair the problem, due to Scott, and see a denotational semantics text for details.

The next important result, one that has been promised for several chapters, is the proof of soundness of the β-rule. The result is a corollary of the following:

6.11 Theorem (The "Substitution Lemma")

For all $e \in Env_\pi$, $[\![\pi \vdash [E_2/I]E_1{:}\tau_1]\!]e = [\![\pi \uplus \{I{:}\tau_2\} \vdash E_1{:}\tau_1]\!](e \uplus \{I = [\![\pi \vdash E_2{:}\tau_2]\!]e\})$.

Proof: The proof is by induction on the rank of E_1.

(i) $E_1 = J$: If $J \neq I$, the result is immediate. If $J = I$, then $[\![\pi \vdash [E_2/I]I{:}\tau_1]\!]e = [\![\pi \vdash E_2{:}\tau_1]\!]e = [\![\pi \uplus \{I{:}\tau_1\} \vdash I{:}\tau_1]\!](e \uplus \{I = [\![\pi \vdash E_2{:}\tau_1]\!]e\})$.

(ii) $E_1 = (E_{11} E_{12})$: Since $[E_2/I](E_{11} E_{12}) = ([E_2/I]E_{11} [E_2/I]E_{12})$, the result follows from the inductive hypotheses for E_{11} and E_{12}.

(iii) $E_1 = (\lambda J{:}\tau_{11}.E_{12})$: If $J = I$, the result is immediate. If $J \neq I$ and J is not free in E_2, then the result follows from the inductive hypothesis for E_{12}. Otherwise, $[\![\pi \vdash [E_2/I](\lambda J{:}\tau_{11}.E_{12}){:}\tau_{11} \to \tau_{12}]\!]e = [\![\pi \vdash \lambda K{:}\tau_{11}.[E_2/I][K/J]E_{12}{:}\tau_{11} \to \tau_{12}]\!]e = f$, such that $f(v) = [\![\pi_1 \vdash [E_2/I][K/J]E_{12}{:}\tau_{12}]\!]e_1$, where $\pi_1 = \pi \uplus \{K{:}\tau_{11}\}$ and $e_1 = e \uplus \{K{=}v\}$. Now, $[K/J]E_{12}$ has the same rank as E_{12}, so the inductive hypothesis says that the previous value equals $[\![\pi_1 \uplus \{I{:}\tau_2\} \vdash [K/J]E_{12}{:}\tau_{12}]\!](e_1 \uplus \{I = [\![\pi \vdash E_2{:}\tau_2]\!]e_1\}) = [\![\pi_1 \uplus \{I{:}\tau_2\} \vdash [K/J]E_{12}{:}\tau_{12}]\!](e_1 \uplus \{I = [\![\pi \vdash E_2{:}\tau_2]\!]e\})$, since K is not in E_2. Let $\pi_2 = \pi_1 \uplus \{I{:}\tau_2\}$ and $e_2 = e_1 \uplus \{I = [\![\pi \vdash E_2{:}\tau_2]\!]e\}$; by the inductive hypothesis on E_{12}, the previous value equals $[\![\pi_2 \uplus \{J{:}\tau_{11}\} \vdash E_{12}{:}\tau_{12}]\!](e_2 \uplus \{J = [\![\pi \uplus \{K{:}\tau_{11}, I{:}\tau_2\} \vdash K{:}\tau_{11}]\!]e_2\}) = [\![\pi_2 \uplus \{J{:}\tau_{11}\} \vdash E_{12}{:}\tau_{12}]\!](e_2 \uplus \{J{=}v\}) = [\![\pi \uplus \{I{:}\tau_2, J{:}\tau_{11}\} \vdash E_{12}{:}\tau_{12}]\!](e \uplus \{I = [\![\pi \vdash E_2{:}\tau_2]\!]e\} \uplus \{J{=}v\})$, since K does not appear in E_{12}. But this value is just $g(v)$, where $g = [\![\pi \uplus \{I{:}\tau_2\} \vdash (\lambda J{:}\tau_{11}.E_{12}){:}\tau_{11} \to \tau_{12}]\!](e \uplus \{r = [\![\pi \vdash E_2{:}\tau_2]\!]e\})$. $\square$

It follows immediately that $[\![\pi \vdash ((\lambda I{:}\tau_1 . E_2)E_1){:}\tau_2]\!]e = [\![\pi \vdash [E_1 / I]E_2{:}\tau_2]\!]e$, and then a proof like that of Theorem 6.8 yields

6.12 Theorem

For $e \in Env_\pi$, $\pi \vdash E_1{:}\tau$ and $E_1 \Rightarrow^* E_2$ imply $[\![\pi \vdash E_1{:}\tau]\!]e = [\![\pi \vdash E_2{:}\tau]\!]e$.

6.6 Lambda Calculus with Constants and Operators

To obtain facilities for repetition, arithmetic, and the like, we extend the simply typed lambda calculus by a set of constants and operators. For arithmetic, we might add:

$$E ::= \cdots \mid 0 \mid 1 \mid 2 \mid \cdots \mid (plus\ E_1\ E_2) \mid (minus\ E_1\ E_2)$$

along with the following typing rules:

$$\pi \vdash n{:}int, \text{ for all } n \ge 0 \qquad \frac{\pi \vdash E_1{:}int \quad \pi \vdash E_2{:}int}{\pi \vdash (plus\ E_1\ E_2){:}int} \qquad \frac{\pi \vdash E_1{:}int \quad \pi \vdash E_2{:}int}{\pi \vdash (minus\ E_1\ E_2){:}int}$$

Symbols like 0 and 1 that cannot be reduced are *constants*, and symbols like *plus* and *minus* that take arguments and can be reduced are *operators*. An expression that adds 1 to 3 and then subtracts 2 is written $(minus\ (plus\ 1\ 3)\ 2)$. If we prefer, we can define operators as constants of function type, for example, $\pi \vdash plus{:}int \to int \to int$ and code addition as $((plus\ 1)\ 3)$. The difference is often just a matter of style. In the terminology of Section 6.2, we say that $0, 1, 2, \ldots$, are the Values for the *int*-typed expressions; that is, $Value(int) = \{0, 1, 2, \ldots\}$. This particular set is special, and we call it the set of *numerals*.

Operators have little use without rewriting rules. For example, we want to show that $(minus\ (plus\ 1\ 3)\ 2)$ rewrites to $(minus\ 4\ 2)$, which rewrites to 2. Here are the rewriting rules for *plus* and *minus*:

$(plus\ m\ n) \Rightarrow m{+}n$, where m and n are numerals,
   and $m{+}n$ is the numeral that denotes the sum of m and n

$(minus\ m\ n) \Rightarrow m{-}n$, where m and n are numerals,
   and $m{-}n$ is the numeral that denotes the difference of m and n

(For simplicity, we use natural numbers and natural number subtraction: If $n > m$, then $(minus\ m\ n) \Rightarrow 0$.) The two rules are call-by-value rules, like the ones in Section 6.2, and they should be read as abbreviating two families of rewriting rules. For example, the rule for *plus* abbreviates this family:

$$(plus\ 0\ 0)\ \Rightarrow\ 0 \qquad\qquad (plus\ 1\ 1)\ \Rightarrow\ 2$$
$$(plus\ 0\ 1)\ \Rightarrow\ 1 \qquad\qquad (plus\ 1\ 2)\ \Rightarrow\ 3$$
$$(plus\ 1\ 0)\ \Rightarrow\ 1 \qquad\qquad \cdots$$

Rules like the ones above are called δ-*rules*, and we use the term δ–*redex* for an expression that can be reduced by a δ-rule. General properties of δ-rules are given in Section 6.8; for now, we take on faith that properties like confluence and subject reduction hold for the simply typed lambda calculus extended by δ-rules. We choose the leftmost-outermost redex in an expression by picking that redex whose λ-symbol or operator lies to the leftmost in the expression.

We can also add booleans, where *Value(bool)* = { *true, false* }:

$$\pi \vdash true : bool \qquad \pi \vdash false : bool \qquad \frac{\pi \vdash E : bool}{\pi \vdash (not\ E) : bool}$$

$$\frac{\pi \vdash E_1 : int \quad \pi \vdash E_2 : int}{\pi \vdash (equals\ E_1\ E_2) : bool} \qquad\qquad \frac{\pi \vdash E_1 : bool \quad \pi \vdash E_2 : \tau \quad \pi \vdash E_3 : \tau}{\pi \vdash (if\ E_1\ E_2\ E_3) : \tau}$$

We use these δ-rules:

$$(equals\ m\ m)\ \Rightarrow\ true, \quad \text{where } m \text{ is a numeral}$$
$$(equals\ m\ n)\ \Rightarrow\ false, \quad \text{where } m \text{ and } n \text{ are different numerals}$$
$$(not\ true)\ \Rightarrow\ false \qquad\qquad (not\ false)\ \Rightarrow\ true$$
$$(if\ true\ E_1\ E_2)\ \Rightarrow\ E_1 \qquad\qquad (if\ false\ E_1\ E_2)\ \Rightarrow\ E_2$$

Here is a leftmost-outermost reduction that uses the β-rule and the above δ-rules:

$$(\lambda X : bool.\ if\ X\ (minus\ 2\ 1)\ (plus\ 3\ 4))\ (equals\ 0\ 1)$$
$$\Rightarrow\ (if\ (equals\ 0\ 1)\ (minus\ 2\ 1)\ (plus\ 3\ 4))$$
$$\Rightarrow\ (if\ false\ (minus\ 2\ 1)\ (plus\ 3\ 4))\ \Rightarrow\ (plus\ 3\ 4)\ \Rightarrow\ 7$$

We now add an operator and δ-rule to express repetition:

$$\frac{\pi \vdash E : \tau \rightarrow \tau}{\pi \vdash (fix\ E) : \tau} \qquad\qquad (fix\ E)\ \Rightarrow\ (E\ (fix\ E))$$

The δ-rule for *fix* has canceled the strong normalization property, since it is now possible to write expressions that have no normal forms. We do an example; let *F* name the following expression:

$$\lambda FAC : int \rightarrow int.\lambda N : int.\ if\ (equals\ N\ 0)\ 1\ (times\ N\ (FAC\ (minus\ N\ 1)))$$

Thus, *(fix F)* is a representation of the factorial function. We put it to work on the argument 2 and do a leftmost-outermost reduction:

(fix F) 2

$\Rightarrow$ *F (fix F)* 2

= *(λFAC:int→int.λN:int. if (equals N 0) 1 (times N (FAC (minus N 1)))) (fix F)* 2

$\Rightarrow$ *(λN:int. if (equals N 0) 1 (times N ((fix F) (minus N 1)))) 2*

$\Rightarrow$ *if (equals 2 0) 1 (times 2 ((fix F) (minus 2 1)))*

$\Rightarrow$ *if false 1 (times 2 ((fix F) (minus 2 1)))*

$\Rightarrow$ *times 2 ((fix F) (minus 2 1))*

$\Rightarrow$ *times 2 ((F (fix F)) (minus 2 1))*

= *times 2*
   ((λFAC:int→int.λN:int. if (equals N 0) 1 (times N (FAC (minus N 1)))) (fix F)
   (minus 2 1))

$\Rightarrow$ *times 2 ((λN:int. if (equals N 0) 1 (times N ((fix F) (minus N 1))))(minus 2 1))*

$\Rightarrow$ *times 2 (if (equals (minus 2 1) 0) 1 (times (minus 2 1)*
   ((fix F) (minus (minus 2 1) 1))))

$\Rightarrow$ *times 2 (if (equals 1 0) 1 (times (minus 2 1) ((fix F) (minus (minus 2 1) 1))))*

$\Rightarrow$ *times 2 (if false 1 (times (minus 2 1) ((fix F) (minus (minus 2 1) 1))))*

$\Rightarrow$ *times 2 (times (minus 2 1) ((fix F) (minus (minus 2 1) 1)))*

$\Rightarrow$ *times 2 (times 1 ((fix F) (minus (minus 2 1) 1)))*

$\Rightarrow$ *times 2 (times 1 ((F (fix F)) (minus (minus 2 1) 1)))*

and so the reduction goes. You are invited to perform the remaining stages of rewriting; the Value uncovered is 2.

Since the example used leftmost-outermost reduction, a number of numerical expressions, like *(minus 2 1)*, were copied and reduced several times. We will address this efficiency question momentarily.

The β- and δ-rules for the arithmetic language form an operational semantics, since the rules show how to compute an arithmetic expression to a Value. But the specific strategy of applying the rewriting rules (for example, leftmost-outermost, rightmost-innermost) is unspecified by the rules themselves. The confluence property suggests that the order of reductions should not be important, but efficiency questions and the possibility of nontermination means that it is. In the above example, the rightmost-innermost reduction strategy might be tried to get a more efficient reduction sequence, but the reduction of *(fix F)*2 does not terminate. (Try it.)

Ideally, we should use a set of rewriting rules that are insensitive to reduction strategy, but this is rarely achievable. In the above example, if the efficiency of the reduction sequence is an issue, the β-rule can be replaced by the β-*val* rule. Since the numerals are the only *int*-typed phrases that are Values, the β-*val* rule would force $(\lambda N:int. \cdots N \cdots)(minus\,2\,1)$ to reduce to $(\lambda N:int. \cdots N \cdots)1$ before it reduces to $\cdots 1 \cdots$. But the β-*val* rule does not interact well with the previously stated rewriting rule for *fix*. (Try it on the above example.) A variant of *fix* that is sometimes used with the β-*val* rule is

$$fix'\,E \;\Rightarrow\; E\,(\lambda I{:}\tau_1 . fix'\,E\,I)$$

where E must be typed $(\tau_1 \rightarrow \tau_2) \rightarrow (\tau_1 \rightarrow \tau_2)$. Another possiblity is to use the *rec* operator and its rule from Chapter 2:

$$rec\,I{:}\tau.\,E \;\Rightarrow\; [(rec\,I{:}\tau.\,E)\,/\,I]E$$

A consequence of the latter rule is, either *rec* I:τ. E must be a Value or else the rule β-*val*$_1$ must be dropped because identifiers no longer stand for Values.

When the call-by-value rules are used for computation, the strategy for reduction changes from normal form discovery to Value discovery. In particular, reductions should not be performed within a lambda abstraction, since a lambda abstraction is already a Value. For the call-by-value reduction rules in this section, a leftmost-outermost strategy that does not reduce redexes within lambda abstractions always discovers Values, if they exist.

If the call-by-value rules are not desired, there is an implementation technique for the β-rule, known as *call-by-need*, which gives efficiency at least as good as the β-*val* rule. For a call-by-need implementation, a phrase is implemented as a graph, and the implementation of the β-rule upon $(\lambda I.E_1)E_2$ replaces all occurrences of I in E_1 by a pointer to E_2's subgraph. Since all occurrences of I point to the same subgraph, whenever any occurrence of I is computed, the sharing implies that all occurrences are computed. Details are given in Wadsworth 1971 and Peyton-Jones 1987.

6.7 Operational Semantics for a Source Language

Section 1.8 stated that a programming language's denotational semantics can do double duty as an operational semantics. In this section, we justify why this is so and demonstrate that such an operational semantics is a simply typed lambda calculus with constants and operators. The development is pedantic and can be skipped if the reader accepts these claims.

The metalanguage for the operational semantics definition is the simply typed lambda calculus with integers, booleans, locations, and stores. Integers and booleans were presented in the previous section. Locations are the usual: $loc_i : intloc$, for $i \geq 0$, and $Value(intloc) = \{ loc_i \mid i \geq 0 \}$. There are no operations upon locations. The store type has these constructions:

$$\frac{\pi \vdash E_1 : int \quad \pi \vdash E_2 : int \quad \cdots \quad \pi \vdash E_n : int}{\pi \vdash \langle E_1, E_2, \ldots, E_n \rangle : store}, \text{ for } n \geq 0$$

$$\frac{\pi \vdash E_1 : intloc \quad \pi \vdash E_2 : store}{\pi \vdash (lookup\ E_1\ E_2) : int} \qquad \frac{\pi \vdash E_1 : intloc \quad \pi \vdash E_2 : int \quad \pi \vdash E_3 : store}{\pi \vdash (update\ E_1\ E_2\ E_3) : store}$$

and $Value(store) = \{ \langle n_1, n_2, \ldots, n_m \rangle \mid m \geq 0$ and for all $1 \leq i \leq m,\ n_i \in Value(int) \}$. As usual, a store like $\langle 3, 1, 7 \rangle$ defines a store that has 3 in loc_1's location, 1 in loc_2's location, and 7 in loc_3's location. The rewriting rules for the store operators are the expected ones:

$$(lookup\ loc_i\ \langle n_1, n_2, \ldots, n_i, \ldots, n_m \rangle) \Rightarrow n_i$$
$$(update\ loc_i\ n\ \langle n_1, n_2, \ldots, n_i, \ldots, n_m \rangle) \Rightarrow \langle n_1, n_2, \ldots, n, \ldots, n_m \rangle$$

The arguments to *lookup* and *update* must be Values for the reductions to occur.

Now, we are ready to define the operational semantics of the source programming language; we use the typing rules in Figure 5.1 plus these two:

$$\frac{E_1 : \tau exp \quad \pi \vdash E_2 : store}{\pi \vdash [\![E_1 : \tau exp]\!]\ E_2 : \tau} \qquad \frac{E_1 : comm \quad \pi \vdash E_2 : store}{\pi \vdash [\![E_1 : comm]\!]\ E_2 : store}$$

The semantics definition is a set of rewriting rules:

$[\![E_1 := E_2 : comm]\!]s \ \Rightarrow \ (update\ E_1\ ([\![E_2 : intexp]\!]s)\ s)$

$[\![E_1 ; E_2 : comm]\!]s \ \Rightarrow \ [\![E_2 : comm]\!]([\![E_1 : comm]\!]s)$

$[\![\textbf{while}\ E_1\ \textbf{do}\ E_2\ \textbf{od} : comm]\!]s$
$\qquad \Rightarrow \ if\ ([\![E_1\ boolexp]\!]s)\ ([\![\textbf{while}\ E_1\ \textbf{do}\ E_2\ \textbf{od} : comm]\!]([\![E_2 : comm]\!]s))\ s$
$\qquad \cdots$

$[\![E_1 + E_2 : intexp]\!]s \ \Rightarrow \ (plus\ ([\![E_1 : intexp]\!]s)\ ([\![E_2 : intexp]\!]s))$

$[\![@L : intexp]\!]s \ \Rightarrow \ (lookup\ L\ s)$
$\qquad \cdots$

where, for all of the above rules, s is a Value

Computations with the rewriting rules proceed like the calculations seen in earlier chapters.

Since the metalanguage is the simply typed lambda calculus, we can reformat the above rules with lambda abstractions and compute with the β-*val* rule:

$$[\![E_1\!:=\!E_2\!:comm]\!] \;\Rightarrow\; \lambda s\!:store.\,(update\ E_1\ ([\![E_2\!:intexp]\!]s)\ s)$$

$$[\![E_1;\!E_2\!:comm]\!] \;\Rightarrow\; \lambda s\!:store.\,[\![E_2\!:comm]\!]([\![E_1\!:comm]\!]s)$$

$\cdots$

Now, the previous two typing rules are unneeded, because we can make the equivalences *comm* $\equiv$ *store* $\rightarrow$ *store* and $\tau exp \equiv store \rightarrow \tau$.

The next step is to add abstractions, parameters, and blocks to the source programming language. If we follow the lines of Chapter 5, then we add records and lambda abstraction to the source programming language, creating a simply typed lambda calculus of it. We focus upon lambda abstractions here, leaving records as an exercise. Once we add lambda abstractions to the source language, we may add the β-rule for rewriting them. The result is a *substitution semantics*, so named because the semantics of lambda abstraction in the source language is understood by means of syntactic substitution, as defined by the β-rule. In the terminomolgy of Chapter 2, a substitution semantics applies the copy rule to a program with lambda abstractions, reducing the program into one in the core language, and then uses the semantics of the core language to calculate the meaning.

Substitution semantics works fine, but insight can be gained from an *environment semantics*, where an environment argument and its operations are added to the metalanguage. The rewriting rules for the language are altered to include environments:

$$[\![\pi \vdash E_1\!:=\!E_2\!:comm]\!]$$
$$\Rightarrow\; \lambda e\!:env.\lambda s\!:store.\,(update\ ([\![\pi \vdash E_1\!:intloc]\!]e)\ ([\![\pi \vdash E_2\!:intexp]\!]e\ s)\ s)$$

$$[\![\pi \vdash E_1;\!E_2\!:comm]\!] \;\Rightarrow\; \lambda e\!:env.\lambda s\!:store.\,[\![\pi \vdash E_2\!:comm]\!]e\,([\![\pi \vdash E_1\!:comm]\!]e\,s)$$

$\cdots$

$$[\![\pi \vdash \lambda I\!:\!\theta_1.\,E\!:\theta_1\!\rightarrow\!\theta_2]\!] \;\Rightarrow\; \lambda e\!:env.\lambda u\!:\!\theta_1.\,[\![\pi \uplus \{I\!:\!\theta_1\} \vdash E\!:\theta_2]\!](bind\ I\ u\ e)$$

$$[\![\pi \vdash E_1 E_2\!:\theta_2]\!] \;\Rightarrow\; \lambda e\!:env.\,([\![\pi \vdash E_1\!:\theta_1\!\rightarrow\!\theta_2]\!]e)\,([\![\pi \vdash E_2\theta_1]\!]e)$$

$$[\![\pi \vdash I\!:\theta]\!] \;\Rightarrow\; \lambda e\!:env.\,find\ I\ e$$

bind and *find* are operations that insert and look up bindings in the environment; their definitions are left as exercises. A technical point is that the β-rule can be applied to the source language lambda abstractions, or the β-*val* rule can be applied to the metalanguage lambda abstractions and the end result is the same. In earlier chapters, this was called soundness of the copy rules; here, it becomes a confluence result.

6.8 Subtree Replacement Systems

When a lambda calculus is extended by δ-rules, one must verify that confluence, standardization, and other properties are preserved. The general version of a lambda calculus-like system is called a *subtree replacement system (SRS)*.* In this and the next section, we study subtree replacement systems and state general properties that imply confluence and standardization. These properties can be used to verify that an operational semantics for a programming language is worthwhile.

Say that a language, *L*, is defined by a single syntax rule:

$$L ::= construction_1 \mid \cdots \mid construction_n, \quad n > 0.$$

Languages defined by multiple syntax rules can also be studied, but it is simplest to work with just one rule. Next, let the syntax rule be augmented by a set of *variables* $V = \{X, Y, Z, \ldots\}$

$$L_V ::= construction_1 \mid \cdots \mid construction_n \mid V$$

and let L_V be the language that results. L_V is the language of *polynomials of L*. That is, a polynomial of *L* is an *L*-expression with zero or more variables in it. For *lhs, rhs* $\in L_V$, we say that *lhs*⇒*rhs* is a *rewriting rule* for *L* if *lhs* and *rhs* are polynomials of *L* and every variable that appears in *rhs* also appears in *lhs*. The rewriting rule is *linear* if no variable appears in *lhs* more than once.

6.13 Definition

A *(linear) subtree replacement system (SRS)* is a pair, (*L, R*), where *L* is a syntax rule and *R* is a set of linear rewriting rules for *L*.

An example of an SRS follows:

(E ::= *true* | *false* | *not* E | *if* E$_1$ E$_2$ E$_3$,
     { *not true* ⇒ *false*, *not false* ⇒ *true*, *if true X Y* ⇒ *X*, *if false X Y* ⇒ *Y* })

For simplicity, we work with systems whose operators are in prefix form.

The systems are called subtree replacement systems because the expressions are trees. We draw the trees so that the operators are at the roots. An example is

```
        if
      /  |  \
   not  not  true
    |    |
   true not
         |
        false
```

---

* Another name is *term rewriting system*, but we wish to emphasize the tree-like structure of the phrases in the system.

which depicts *if (not true) (not (not false)) true*. A polynomial expression is an incomplete tree, where variables mark the places where subtrees need insertion. Rewriting rules are tree transformers: When a tree matches the pattern defined by the left-hand side of a rewriting rule, the variables in the left-hand side mark subtrees in the tree, and the marked subtrees are used to build a new tree with the structure described by the right-hand side of the rule. These notions can be formalized.

A *substitution*, denoted by σ, is a set of variable, polynomial pairs. The application of a substitution, σ, to a polynomial, E, written σE, is the replacement of all occurrences of X in E by polynomials, E', for all $(X, E') \in \sigma$. An example, in terms of the SRS above, is $\sigma = \{(X, true), (Z, (not \ Y))\}$, E = *if true X (not Z)*, and σE = *if true true (not (not Y))*. An expression, E, *matches* a polynomial, p, if there is a substitution, σ, such that $\sigma p = E$. An expression is a *redex* if it matches *lhs* of a rewriting rule *lhs*⇒*rhs*, via a substitution σ; the *contractum* is the expression σ*rhs*. The replacement of the redex by its contractum is a *contraction* or *reduction*. These notions are the same as the ones used with the lambda calculus, and we continue to use terms such as "normal form," "reduction sequence," and so on.

Given a polynomial, p, we say that its *pattern* is p less its variables. For example, the pattern of *if true X Y* is *if true* [ ] [ ], where the brackets mark the missing variables. The pattern of a polynomial shows the structure necessary for an expression to match the polynomial. If an expression, E, is a redex by means of a rewriting rule, *lhs*⇒*rhs*, we say that the *pattern of the redex* is that subpart of E that matches the pattern of *lhs*. For example, for redex *if true false true*, the pattern of the redex is *if true* [ ] [ ].

Recall the *confluence property*: For all E, if E⇒*E₁ and E⇒*E₂, then there is some E₃ such that E₁⇒*E₃ and E₂⇒*E₃. Verifying that an arbitrary linear SRS has confluence is undecidable, so we will state a criterion that is sufficient for confluence. The notion behind the criterion is that rewriting rules should not "interfere" with one another.

Consider an SRS that contains this pair of rules:

$$f (g \ X) \ Y \ \Rightarrow \ Y$$
$$g \ a \ \Rightarrow \ a$$

The expression $f (g \ a) \ a$ can be reduced by the first rule to a and by the second rule to $f a \ a$. Can a and $f a \ a$ be reduced to the same expression? This cannot be done with the two rules here, so the question of confluence depends upon the other rules of the SRS. This situation is dangerous, and the danger arises because the two rules interfere with one another—reducing a redex by the second rule alters a redex by the first rule. In contrast, the rules

$$f X \ Y \ \Rightarrow \ Y$$
$$g \ a \ \Rightarrow \ a$$

do not interfere with each other, in the sense that, if an expression contains a redex by the first rule and a redex by the second rule, the two redexes can be reduced in either order, and the end result is the same. For example, $f a (g a) \Rightarrow g a$ and also $f a (g a) \Rightarrow f a a$, but then $g a \Rightarrow a$ and $f a a \Rightarrow a$. For the expression $f (g a) a$, we see that $f (g a) a \Rightarrow a$ and also $f (g a) a \Rightarrow f a a \Rightarrow a$. Also, a rewriting rule can interfere with itself; for $f (f X) \Rightarrow a$, and the expression $f (f (f a))$, we see that the expression can be reduced in two different ways that cannot be reconciled: $f (f (f a)) \Rightarrow f a$ and $f (f (f a)) \Rightarrow a$.

A precise definition of the above intuition is: A pair of rules $(lhs_1 \Rightarrow rhs_1, lhs_2 \Rightarrow rhs_2)$ *interfere* if there is a substitution σ such that σlhs_1 contains σlhs_2 as a subtree and the pattern of σlhs_2 overlaps the pattern of σlhs_1. For the substitution, σ, to be meaningful, we assume that the variables in the two rules are distinct (else we rename the variables to make them distinct). Also, since every rewriting rule trivially ''interferes'' with itself, we ignore trivial self interference.

In the first example above, the substitution $\sigma = \{(X,a), (Y,a)\}$ shows that the rules interfere. No substitution can be found for the second example, because the rules do not interfere. In the final example, after renaming the variable in the second occurrence of the rule, we find that the substitution $\sigma = \{(X, f a), (Y, a)\}$ makes the rule pair $(f (f X) \Rightarrow a, f (f Y) \Rightarrow a)$ interfere.

In practice, it is easy to see when a pair of rules interfere: Build a tree where the patterns of the left-hand sides of the two rules overlap in the tree. In the first example, such a tree has form $f (g a)$ E, and in the third example the tree has form $f (f (f E))$.

6.14 Definition

A linear SRS is *orthogonal* if no pair of its rewriting rules interfere.

Orthogonal systems are common and natural; the δ-rule sets in Section 6.6 are examples. The main result of this section is

6.15 Theorem

Every orthogonal SRS has the confluence property.

A core programming language is typically an orthogonal SRS, and the addition of lambda abstraction preserves orthogonality, so Theorem 6.15 implies that the languages we develop have semantics definitions that make the rewriting rules sound.

The remainder of this section is devoted to a proof of Theorem 6.15, and if you are disinterested in its development, you may proceed to the next section.

A key notion is that of *residual*. Let R_1 and R_2 be redexes in an expression, E, and say that R_1 is reduced, which we write as: $E \Rightarrow^{R_1} E'$. The residuals of R_2 are those copies of R_2, if any, remaining in E'. We formalize this as

6.16 Definition

For redexes R_1 and R_2 in E, and $E \Rightarrow^{R_1} E'$, *the residuals of R_2 in* E', written $res(R_2)$, are defined as

(i) If R_1 are R_2 are disjoint subtrees in E, then $res(R_2)$ is the single copy of R_2 in E'.

(ii) If R_1 is within R_2 in E, and the patterns of R_1 and R_2 are disjoint, then $res(R_2)$ is the single copy of R_2 in E'. (But note that the subpart of R_2 that contained R_1 is changed.)

(iii) If R_2 is within R_1 in E, and the patterns of R_1 and R_2 are disjoint, then $res(R_2)$ are those copies, if any, of R_2 in E' that were propagated by the rewriting rule.

(iv) If the patterns of R_1 and R_2 overlap, then $res(R_2)$ in E' is empty.

For example, for rules $f\,X\,Y \Rightarrow h\,Y\,Y$ and $g\,X \Rightarrow a$, expressions $E = f\,(g\,a)\,(f\,(g\,b)\,(g\,c))$ and $E' = f\,(g\,a)\,(h\,(g\,c)\,(g\,c))$, and reduction step $E \Rightarrow E'$, the residual of $g\,a$ is its single copy in E', $g\,b$ has no residuals, $g\,c$ has two residuals in E', $f\,(g\,b)\,(g\,c)$ has none (why?), and the residual of E in E' is E' itself.

A residual of a redex is itself a redex, and after several reduction steps, we say that the *descendants* of a redex are the residuals of the residuals of . . . the redex, that is, the "residual" definition is extended by transitivity. For example, for expression E above, the descendants of $g\,c$ in E_3, where

$$E = f\,(g\,a)\,(f\,(g\,b)\,(g\,c)) \Rightarrow f\,(g\,a)\,(h\,(g\,c)\,(g\,c))$$
$$\Rightarrow h\,(h\,(g\,c)\,(g\,c))\,(h\,(g\,c)\,(g\,c)) \Rightarrow h\,(h\,a\,(g\,c))\,(h\,(g\,c)\,(g\,c)) = E_3$$

are the three occurrences of $g\,c$ in E_3.

An excellent way to track the descendants of a redex is by "coloring" them: If we wish to monitor the descendants of a redex in a reduction sequence, we color the pattern of the original redex with a red pencil, and at each reduction step, any redexes with red-colored patterns that are copied into the next expression in the sequence are copied in red. (If the reduction step contracts a redex with a red pattern, the pattern of the contractum is not colored red.) In the above example, if we wish to monitor the residuals of $g\,c$ in $E \Rightarrow^* E_3$, we color the "g" part of $g\,c$ in E with red. Each reduction step copies red patterns into red patterns, so it is easy to locate the three residuals in E_3 (and note that the a in E_3 is not colored red).

An important game to play is reduction-of-colored-redexes-only. Given expression E, say that we color the patterns of some of the redexes in E and then generate a reduction sequence where only colored redexes are reduced. Stated formally, a *complete development* of a set of redexes S in an expression E is a reduction sequence that at each stage reduces a descendant of a redex in S until no more descendants exist. An intuitive and useful result is

```
        R                      R₂
   /    |    \      R'    /    |    \
        R'           ⇒         S'
```
                                                    where S' denotes the contractum of R'

```
   R ⇓                          ⇓  res(R)

        R₁                     R₃
   / /  \  \    res(R')  / /  \  \
      R'  R'        ⇒        S'  S'
```

Figure 6.3 _____

6.17 Proposition

Every complete development must terminate.

Proposition 6.17 lets us write $E \Rightarrow^S E'$ to denote a complete development of S. When S is a singleton set, $\{R\}$, we write $E \Rightarrow^R E'$, as usual.

An obvious question to ask is: Does the order of reduction in a complete development influence the final result? We will see that the answer is ''no,'' and the easiest way to get to the answer is by way of the proof of confluence. Here is the central property in our proof of confluence:

6.18 Definition

A subtree replacement system has the *closure property* if, for every redex R that contains another redex R', if $R \Rightarrow^R R_1$ and $R \Rightarrow^{R'} R_2$, then there exists some R_3 such that $R_1 \Rightarrow^{res(R')} R_3$ and $R_2 \Rightarrow^{res(R)} R_3$.

Figure 6.3 pictures the closure property. Closure formalizes the idea that rule pairs should not interfere with each other. You are left with the straightforward (but crucial) exercise of showing that every orthogonal SRS has the closure property.

Now, we show how confluence follows from closure. Say that an SRS has the *parallel moves property* if, for redex sets S_1 and S_2, $E \Rightarrow^{S_1} E_1$ and $E \Rightarrow^{S_2} E_2$ imply that there exists some E_3 such that $E_1 \Rightarrow^{res(S_2)} E_3$ and $E_2 \Rightarrow^{res(S_1)} E_3$. That is, the parallel moves property generalizes closure to sets of redexes. Momentarily, we show that closure and the parallel moves property are equivalent, but first we go to the main goal:

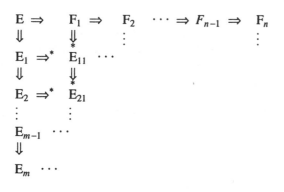

$$E \Rightarrow \quad F_1 \Rightarrow \quad F_2 \quad \cdots \Rightarrow F_{n-1} \Rightarrow \quad F_n$$

Figure 6.4

6.19 Theorem

If an SRS has the parallel moves property, then it has confluence.

Proof: Our job is to "tile the plane" bounded by E, E_m, and F_n at the corners, where $E \Rightarrow E_1 \Rightarrow E_2 \Rightarrow \cdots \Rightarrow E_m$ and $E \Rightarrow F_1 \Rightarrow F_2 \Rightarrow \cdots \Rightarrow F_n$, $m, n \geq 0$. See Figure 6.4. Each square in the figure will be filled by a "tile" created by the parallel moves property. For example, we could tile the plane column by column; the first two tiles of the first column would be (1) the tile whose edges are $E \Rightarrow E_1$, $E \Rightarrow F_1$, $E_1 \Rightarrow^* E_{11}$, and $F_1 \Rightarrow^* E_{11}$, where E_{11} is the name of the new corner; (2) the tile whose edges are $E_1 \Rightarrow E_2$, $E_1 \Rightarrow^* E_{11}$, $E_2 \Rightarrow^* E_{21}$, and $E_{11} \Rightarrow^* E_{21}$, where E_{21} is the new corner. The rest of the first column uses tiles similar to that of tile (2). Each tile has a format that matches the parallel moves property. The second (and subsequent) columns are covered with tiles of the form: $E_{ij} \Rightarrow^* E_{(i+1)j}$, $E_{ij} \Rightarrow^* E_{i(j+1)}$, $E_{(i+1)j} \Rightarrow^* E_{(i+1)(j+1)}$, and $E_{i(j+1)} \Rightarrow^* E_{(i+1)(j+1)}$. $\square$

To show the last, missing result, that closure and the parallel moves property are equivalent, we must introduce yet another version of confluence. An SRS is *weakly confluent* if $E \Rightarrow E_1$ and $E \Rightarrow E_2$ implies that there is some E_3 such that $E_1 \Rightarrow^* E_3$ and $E_2 \Rightarrow^* E_3$. Weak confluence looks like confluence, but it is indeed weaker; the following system is weakly confluent but *not* confluent:

$$a \Rightarrow b \qquad\qquad a \Rightarrow c$$
$$b \Rightarrow a \qquad\qquad b \Rightarrow d$$

The counter example to confluence is $a \Rightarrow^* c$ and $a \Rightarrow^* d$. But an important result is

6.20 Lemma

If an SRS is strongly normalizing (that is, it has no infinite reduction sequences) and weakly confluent, then it is confluent.

Proof: Our proof of this result is somewhat informal, but it gives the main intuition. (A precise proof is in Huet 1980.) As in the proof of Theorem 6.18, we tile the plane bounded by E, E_m, and F_n at the corners, where $E \Rightarrow E_1 \Rightarrow E_2 \Rightarrow \cdots \Rightarrow E_m$ and $E \Rightarrow F_1 \Rightarrow F_2 \Rightarrow \cdots \Rightarrow F_n$, $m, n \geq 0$. Clearly, we can lay the first tile, which is bounded at its corners by E, E_1, F_1, and there is some E_{11p}, $p \geq 0$, such that $E_1 \Rightarrow E_{111} \Rightarrow E_{112} \Rightarrow \cdots \Rightarrow^* E_{11p}$ and $F_1 \Rightarrow^* E_{11p}$. Now we wish to lay a tile underneath the first one, but we need p tiles, not just one! We can lay the p tiles, but to tile underneath them, we will need $q_{11} \times q_{12} \times \cdots \times q_{1p}$ tiles, where each q_{1i} represents the number of tiles needed underneath the ith tile in the row above. Figure 6.5 pictures the situation. There is danger of infinite regress: Perhaps the tiling underneath the initial tile can never complete because an infinite number of tiles are ultimately needed. But this would imply the existence of an infinite reduction sequence, which is impossible, since the SRS is strongly normalizing. Hence, the tiling, as tedious as it is, must complete. $\square$

We use Lemma 6.20 to prove the last result:

6.21 Lemma

An SRS has closure iff it has the parallel moves property.

Proof: The "if" part is easy: A system with the parallel moves property has closure, because closure is just the parallel moves property with redex sets that are singleton sets. For the "only if" part, assume that the SRS has closure. We build a new, "colored SRS" such that its rewriting rules reduce redexes only when they are colored red. By Proposition 6.17, the colored SRS has the strong normalization property. By the closure

---

$$E \Longrightarrow\!\Longrightarrow F_1$$

$$\Downarrow \qquad\qquad\qquad\qquad\qquad\qquad\qquad \Downarrow *$$

$$E_1 \Longrightarrow\quad E_{111} \Rightarrow E_{112} \Rightarrow \cdots \Rightarrow E_{11p}$$

$$\Downarrow \qquad\qquad \Downarrow *$$

$$E_2 \Rightarrow \Rightarrow \cdots \Rightarrow \quad E_{21q}$$

$$\vdots$$

Figure 6.5 _____

property, the colored SRS is weakly confluent, since the residuals of a colored redex are always colored. By Lemma 6.19, the SRS is confluent. But confluence in the colored SRS is just the parallel moves property in the original SRS, when the redexes in the sets S_1 and S_2 are exactly the ones colored red. $\square$

The "only if" part of Lemma 6.21 is sometimes called the "parallel moves lemma," hence our use of the term "parallel moves property."

Perhaps you have noted that the (untyped or simply typed) lambda calculus is not an SRS; in particular, the β-rule does *not* fit the format for a rewriting rule. The problem is, as usual, substitution. The closest we can come to formalizing the β-rule as a rewriting rule is

$$((\lambda I. \cdots I \cdots I \cdots) Y) \;\Rightarrow\; \cdots Y \cdots Y \cdots$$

but neither the left-hand nor the right-hand side of the rule is a polynomial expression. Apparently, what is needed is a form of variable that can match a tree whose leaves are labeled by free occurrences of an identifier, I. We write such a variable as $_IX$ and code the β-rule as

$$((\lambda I. _IX) Y) \;\Rightarrow\; _YX$$

where $_YX$ represents the tree that matches $_IX$ when its free occurrences of I are replaced by Y. (Note: We blithely ignore issues related to the clash of free and bound identifiers!) A variable like X is sometimes called a "higher-order variable," since it uses arguments like I and Y.

Now, the pattern of a β-redex is $((\lambda I._I[\,])\,[\,])$; that is, the pattern includes the combination, the $\lambda I.$, and the free occurrences of I. We see that patterns of nested β-redexes can intertwine, but they cannot overlap, and in this sense the lambda calculus is an orthogonal SRS. A crucial feature of this sense of orthogonality is that an outer β-redex remains a redex even if an inner redex is contracted and some of the outer redex's free identifiers are replicated or deleted.

An orthogonal SRS without lambda abstraction can be augmented by lambda abstraction and the β-rule, and the result is an orthogonal system. (This assumes that the syntax of lambda abstraction, combinations, and identifiers is new to the SRS; otherwise, patterns of rewriting rules might overlap.) Also, the lambda calculus with the β-*val* rule can be seen as orthogonal, since β-*val* can be written as a family of orthogonal rules, one rule for each form of Value, for example,

$(\lambda I._IX)\, n \;\Rightarrow\; _nX$, where n is a numeral

$(\lambda I._IX)\, true \;\Rightarrow\; _{true}X$

$(\lambda I._IX)\, (\lambda J.Y) \;\Rightarrow\; _{(\lambda J.Y)}X$

$\cdots$

We will not formalize higher-order variables here; details can be found in Klop 1980 and Khasidashvili 1993. But it is worthwhile to ponder their origin. Identifiers, as used in the lambda calculus, are not ordinary phrases—they are placeholders, or literally, "hole labels," because they label holes in a phrase where other phrases should be inserted. Imagine a phrase that contains a number of holes; it should be possible to match that phrase to a variable that remembers the locations of the holes. This is the idea behind the variable, $_IX$, where I marks the holes.

If we develop this idea, we naturally represent a phrase, E, with holes in it as $_IE$ (the traditional representation is (I)E) to state that E has holes and they are labeled by I. The purpose of the λ is to delimit or bind together the holes, so that when one hole is filled by a phrase, all of them are filled simultaneously by the same phrase. We write $\lambda(I)E$, a lambda abstraction, to do this. This suggests there might be additional delimiters for holes besides λ; the idea is explored in Chapters 8–10.

6.9 Standardization

A second major property of an SRS is strong normalization. Unfortunately, strong normalization is undecidable for an arbitrary SRS, and many natural systems lack the property, anyway. So, we concentrate on a standardization property, that is, we demonstrate a rewriting strategy that always finds an expression's normal form, if one exists.

We say that a redex, R, in an expression, E, is *outermost* if R is not properly contained in another redex within E. Notice that the residual of an outermost redex might not itself be outermost; for the rules

$$f X a \Rightarrow a$$
$$b \Rightarrow a$$
$$c \Rightarrow a$$

the expression $f c b$ contains c as an outermost redex, but the reduction of redex b, giving $f c a$, means that c's residual is not outermost.

An outermost redex, R, in E is *eliminated* by a reduction E⇒E′ if either (i) R has no residual in E, or (ii) R's residual is not outermost in E′. Notice that an outermost redex might be eliminated only after several reduction steps; for example, the (descendant of the) outermost redex b in the expression $f c b$ is eliminated in two reduction steps in this sequence: $f c b \Rightarrow f a b \Rightarrow f a a \Rightarrow a$. A reduction sequence is called *eventually outermost* if every outermost redex that appears in some expression in the reduction sequence is eventually eliminated. The previous example is an eventually outermost reduction sequence.

6.22 Theorem

If an SRS is orthogonal, then if an expression E has a normal form, then any eventually outermost reduction sequence starting from E will find it.

So, a proper rewriting strategy for an orthogonal SRS is one that computes eventually outermost reduction sequences. One such strategy, called *parallel outermost*, reduces all the outermost redexes in an expression at once, in parallel. Often the leftmost-outermost strategy computes eventually outermost reduction sequences—as it did in the previous section—but this is not guaranteed. Consider these rewriting rules:

if X Y true ⇒ *X*
loop ⇒ *loop*
not false ⇒ *true*

and the expression *if a loop (not false)*. The leftmost-outermost reduction strategy is inadequate in this case.

But there is a form of SRS for which leftmost-outermost reduction will discover normal forms if they exist. Say that a rewriting rule, *lhs*⇒*rhs*, is *left normal* if no variable in *lhs* precedes a constant or operator in *lhs*. The first rule in the above example violates this condition, because both *X* and *Y* precede the constant *true*. An orthogonal SRS is left normal if all its rules are. The example SRSs in the previous section are left normal. (The β-rule is discussed below.)

6.23 Theorem

If an SRS is left normal, then leftmost-outermost reduction generates eventually outermost reduction sequences.

Thus, leftmost-outermost reduction for a left normal SRS will discover a normal form for any expression that has one.

The intuition in the preceding development can be generalized to handle the β-rule, since the rule is left normal in the sense that, when we write its left-hand side as *apply* (λI.$_I$**X**) *Y* (*apply* is an explicit operator that stands for application), we see that no variable precedes the operators *apply* and λI. (The identifiers, I, in $_I$**X** are "hole markers" and not constants in the usual sense.) The β-*val* rule is problematic, however, because the goal of a reduction sequence that uses β-*val* is to reduce a phrase to a Value, which is not necessarily the same as a normal form. Also, when the β-*val* rule is written as a family of orthogonal rules, it is clear that β-*val* is not left normal.

Given a left normal SRS, where Values are also normal forms, say that we add lambda abstractions and the β-*val* rule. Then, the strategy of reducing the leftmost-outermost redex not contained within the body of a lambda abstraction suffices for computing a Value. The proof is nontrivial, but some intuition can be gained in terms of the development in this section. The body of a lambda abstraction should be invisible to the rewriting rules, so imagine that the bodies of lambda abstractions are covered by boxes, for example, λX. (λY.Y)A looks like λX.□ to the rewriting rules. The box is a kind of constant, and this makes the β-*val* rule left normal. Further, the lambda abstraction

$\lambda X.\Box$ is a kind of normal form. The leftmost-outermost reduction strategy on phrases with boxed lambda abstractions is exactly the strategy of reducing leftmost redexes not contained within lambda abstractions. Such a strategy suffices for finding normal forms and therefore Values.

Suggested Reading

Church 1941 remains a readable presentation of the lambda calculus, although a beginner might prefer Hindley and Seldin 1986, and the advanced reader might consult Barendregt 1984. Curry and Feys 1958 is a standard and important reference. The simply typed lambda calculus is described in Hindley and Seldin 1986, and extensions are covered in Barendregt and Hemerik 1990 and Barendregt 1992. Morris 1968 shows how to use δ-rules to model a core programming language. The approach led to denotational semantics; see Strachey 1966, 1968, and 1973 for evidence. The standard reference for the β-*val* rule is Plotkin 1975; see also Felleisen and Hieb 1992.

Fundamental concepts of subtree replacement systems can be found in Klop 1992 and Dershowitz and Jouannaud 1990; background can be found in Huet 1980, Huet and Oppen 1980, and Klop 1980. The standardization results in this chapter are based on O'Donnell 1977; another reference is Dershowitz 1987.

Exercises

1.1. Abbreviate these lambda expressions by removing all superfluous parentheses:

    a. $((\lambda Y. (\lambda X. ((Y\ Z)X)))(\lambda X.\ X))$

    b. $(\lambda X. ((\lambda Y. ((\lambda X.\ Y)Y))X))$

    c. $((\lambda Y. ((\lambda Z.\ A)(Y\ Y)))(\lambda X. (X\ X)))$

1.2. Reinsert all parentheses in these lambda expressions:

    a. $\lambda X. (\lambda Y.\ Y\ Y)Z\ X$

    b. $(\lambda Y.\ Y\ Y\ Y)(\lambda X.\ X\ X)$

1.3. a. Using just the β-rule, reduce the expressions in Exercises 1.1 and 1.2 to their β-normal forms. If an expression does not appear to have a normal form, explain why.

    b. Using the β- and η-rules, reduce the expressions in Exercises 1.1 and 1.2 to their $\beta\eta$-normal forms, if they exist.

1.4. Demonstrate that the α-rule is crucial to Theorem 6.1, that is, confluence cannot be strengthened to "for any lambda expression E, if $E\Rightarrow^* E_1$ and $E\Rightarrow^* E_2$, then there exists a lambda expression E_3 such that $E_1\Rightarrow^* E_3$ and $E_2\Rightarrow^* E_3$."

1.5. An important consequence of the standardization is that it can be used to prove that a lambda expression does *not* have a normal form. Use induction on the length of a leftmost-outermost reduction sequence to prove that these expressions do not have normal forms:

   a. $(\lambda X.\, X\, X)(\lambda X.\, X\, X)$

   b. $(\lambda X.\, F(X\, X))(\lambda X.\, F(X\, X))$

1.6. Using Church numerals and the encoding for the addition operation

   a. verify that $add\ \overline{2}\ \overline{3} \Rightarrow^* \overline{5}$.

   b. prove, by mathematical induction, for all m and n, that $add\ \overline{m}\ \overline{n} \Rightarrow^* \overline{m+n}$.

   c. let *true* be encoded by $(\lambda X.\lambda Y.\, X)$ and *false* be encoded by $(\lambda X.\lambda Y.\, Y)$. Code an operation, *not*, such that *not false* $\Rightarrow^*$ *true* and *not true* $\Rightarrow^*$ *false*. Similarly, encode *if* such that *if true* $E_1\ E_2 \Rightarrow^* E_1$ and *if false* $E_1\ E_2 \Rightarrow^* E_2$. Finally, encode logical conjunction and disjunction.

   d. let *eq0* be $\lambda N.\, N\, (\lambda X.\, false)\ true$. Verify that $eq0\ \overline{0} \Rightarrow^*$ *true* and $eq0\ \overline{n+1} \Rightarrow^*$ *false*.

   e. code the multiplication and exponentiation operations on Church numerals.

   f. The Church numerals simulate *simple recursion* on the natural numbers, namely, $\overline{n}\ k\ g$ implements $f(n)$, where: $f(0) = k$, and $f(n+1) = g(f(n))$. Now, consider primitive recursion, which takes the form: $f(0) = k$, and $f(n+1) = g(n, f(n))$. Show how to use Church numerals to encode primitive recursion. (Hint: Consider this form of simple recursive function

   $$f(0) = (0, k)$$
   $$f(n+1) = (n+1, g(f(n)))$$

   where f returns a pair, consisting of the argument value and its answer. Simulate pairs, and use them to simulate primitive recursion.) Use your construction to encode the predecessor ("minus one") function; the factorial function.

1.7. When β-reducibility is extended to a congruence relation, the result is *β-convertibility*. Let *cnv* be the reflexive, symmetric, transitive, substitutive closure of the (α- and) β-rule(s). That is, E_1 *cnv* E_n iff there exist $E_2, \ldots, E_{n-1}$ such that, for all $0 \le i \le n$, $E_i \Rightarrow E_{i+1}$ or $E_{i+1} \Rightarrow E_i$. The *Church-Rosser property* is: If E_1 *cnv* E_2, then there is some E_3 such that $E_1 \Rightarrow^* E_3$ and $E_2 \Rightarrow^* E_3$ (modulo application of the α-rule). Prove that the Church-Rosser property is equivalent to the confluence property.

1.8. Read Exercise 1.6. Now, let $\mathbf{Y} = \lambda F.\, (\lambda X.\, F(X\, X))(\lambda X.\, F(X\, X))$.

   a. Show that $\mathbf{Y}\, F$ *cnv* $F(\mathbf{Y}\, F)$.

   b. If you worked Exercise 1.6, proceed. Let *pred* be some lambda expression such that $pred\ \overline{0} \Rightarrow^* \overline{0}$ and $pred\ \overline{n+1} \Rightarrow^* \overline{n}$. Use **Y**, *pred*, and the expressions from Exercise 1.6 to encode the factorial function on Church numerals; to encode Ackermann's function on Church numerals. Note: Ackermann's function is defined as follows:

$$ack\ 0\ n = n+1$$
$$ack\ (m+1)\ 0 = ack\ m\ 1$$
$$ack\ (m+1)\ (n+1) = ack\ m\ (ack\ (m+1)\ n)$$

1.9. Here is a structural operational semantics for the lambda calculus and its β-rule. A computation step is a proof of $E_1 \triangleright E_2$, and a computation is a sequence of steps $E_1 \triangleright E_2, E_2 \triangleright E_3, \cdots, E_{n-1} \triangleright E_n$. Here are the rules:

$$(\lambda I.\ E_1)E_2 \triangleright [E_2/I]E_1 \qquad \frac{E_1 \triangleright E_1{}'}{E_1\ E_2 \triangleright E_1{}'\ E_2}$$

a. Calculate the semantics of the expressions in Exercises 1.1 and 1.2. What reduction strategy is encoded by the semantics?

b. Alter the semantics so that any redex whatsoever can be selected for a computation step. Prove that $E_1 \Rightarrow^* E_n$ iff $E_1 \triangleright E_2 \triangleright \cdots \triangleright E_n$.

1.10 Here is a natural semantics for the lambda calculus and its β-rule. A computation is a proof of $E_1 \triangleright E_2$. These are the rules:

$$\lambda I.\ E \triangleright \lambda I.\ E \qquad I \triangleright I \qquad \frac{E_1 \triangleright \lambda I.\ E_1{}' \quad [E_2/\ I]E_1{}' \triangleright E}{E_1\ E_2 \triangleright E}$$

a. Calculate the semantics of the expressions in Exercises 1.1 and 1.2. What reduction strategy is encoded by the semantics?

b.* Alter the semantics so that it encodes a leftmost-outermost reduction strategy; prove this.

1.11. Here is yet another logic for the lambda calculus, which we call the *theory of β-reducibility* (cf. Hindley and Seldin 1986). Its formulas are phrases of the form $E_1 \triangleright E_2$, and its axioms and rules follow:

$$\lambda I.E \triangleright \lambda I'.[I'/I]E, \text{ if } I' \notin FV(E) \qquad (\lambda I.\ E_1)E_2 \triangleright [E_2/\ I]E_1 \qquad E \triangleright E$$

$$\frac{E_1 \triangleright E_1{}' \quad E_2 \triangleright E_2{}'}{E_1\ E_2 \triangleright E_1{}'E_2{}'} \qquad \frac{E \triangleright E'}{\lambda I.E \triangleright \lambda I.E'} \qquad \frac{E_1 \triangleright E_2 \quad E_2 \triangleright E_3}{E_1 \triangleright E_3}$$

a. Prove that $E_1 \Rightarrow^* E_2$ (with the α- and β-rules) iff $E_1 \triangleright E_2$ holds.

b. The *theory of β-convertibility* is the theory of β-reducibility, where the "$\triangleright$" symbol is changed to the "$\equiv$" symbol and this rule is added:

$$\frac{E_1 \equiv E_2}{E_2 \equiv E_1}$$

Prove that E_1 *cnv* E_2 iff $E_1 \equiv E_2$ holds. (See Exercise 1.7 for the definition of *cnv*.)

1.12. An expression, E, is in *head normal form* if it has the form $(\lambda I_1.\lambda I_2. \cdots \lambda I_m. \, I \, E_1 \, E_2 \cdots E_n)$, $m, n \geq 0$. I may be an I_j, $1 \leq j \leq m$, but it is not necessary; for example, $\lambda X. \, Y \, X$ is in head normal form. (See Barendregt 1984.)

    a. Prove that $\Omega = (\lambda X. \, X \, X)(\lambda X. \, X \, X)$ has no head normal form but **Y** (see Exercise 1.8) does. Hence, an expression that has no normal form can have a head normal form.

The intuition is that expressions that have head normal forms are computationally useful. This can be formalized. A closed expression, E, is *solvable* iff there exist expressions, $E_1, E_2, \ldots, E_n$, $n \geq 0$, such that $(E \, E_1 \, E_2 \cdots E_n)$ *cnv* $(\lambda X.X)$.

    b. Prove that Ω is not solvable (hint: use Theorem 6.3) but that **Y** is solvable.

    c.* Prove, for every closed expression, E, that E is solvable iff E has a head normal form.

For an expression, $(\lambda I_1.\lambda I_2. \cdots \lambda I_m. \, (\lambda I.E_0) \, E_1 \, E_2 \cdots E_n)$, $m \geq 0$, $n > 0$, say that $(\lambda I.E_0)E_1$ is the *head redex* of the expression. The *head redex reduction strategy* reduces the head redex at each stage of a reduction sequence.

    d. Use Theorem 6.3 to prove that E has a head normal form iff the head redex reduction strategy applied to E terminates.

An expression, E, is in *weak head normal form* if it is in head normal form or it is a lambda abstraction. (See Abramsky 1990 or Peyton Jones 1987.)

    e. Give an example of an expression that has weak head normal form but not head normal form.

    f. Define a reduction strategy such that an expression, E, has weak head normal form iff the reduction strategy applied to E terminates. Prove this.

    g. If you understand the implementation of a functional language like Lisp, Scheme, or ML, comment as to which of the notions of normal form, head normal form, or weak head normal form is most suited to describing the implementation.

2.1. Apply the β-*val* rule to these examples:

    a. $(\lambda X. \, (\lambda Y. \, Y \, Y)(\lambda Y. \, X \, X))((\lambda Y. \, Y)(\lambda X. \, X \, X))$

    b. $(\lambda X. \, (\lambda Z. \, (\lambda Y. \, Y) \, X)(X \, X))(\lambda X. \, X \, X)$

2.2. Say that the β-*val* rule is altered to read as follows:

$$(\lambda I. \, E_1)E_2 \; \Rightarrow \; [E_2/I]E_1, \text{ if } E_2 \text{ is in normal form}$$

Show that the confluence property fails. (Hint: Consider when E_2 is $(X \, X)$.)

2.3. Define a reduction strategy for the β-*val* rule and prove that it discovers a Value for an expression, if one exists.

2.4. If you worked Exercises 1.9, 1.10, or 1.11, proceed. Alter those semantics definitions so that the β-*val* rule is used in place of the β-rule.

2.5. Here is another logistic system for the lambda calculus. Let e stand for an *environment* of the usual form $\{I_1=v_1, \ldots, I_n=v_n\}$. Configurations have the form $e \vdash E \Rightarrow v$. Here are the axioms and inference rules:

$$e \vdash (\lambda I. E) \Rightarrow \langle e, I, E \rangle \qquad e \vdash I \Rightarrow v, \text{ if } (I=v) \in e$$

$$\frac{e \vdash E_1 \Rightarrow \langle e', I, E \rangle \qquad e \vdash E_2 \Rightarrow v \qquad e' \uplus \{I=v\} \vdash E' \Rightarrow v'}{e \vdash (E_1\ E_2) \Rightarrow v'}$$

The system is another natural semantics of the lambda calculus.

a. Prove: If $\{I_1=v_1, \ldots, I_n=v_n\}$ $\vdash E \Rightarrow v$ can be proved, then $[v_1/I_1, \ldots, v_n/I_n]E \Rightarrow^* v$.

b. Show that the converse to Part a does not hold.

c. Describe the form of reduction strategy defined by the logistic system.

3.1. Let $E_1 \equiv E_2$ mean that E_1 and E_2 are the same expression, modulo application of the α-rule, and let $E_1 \Rightarrow^* E_2$ mean that E_1 reduces, by means of the β-rule, to E_2, modulo applications of the α-rule. Use induction on rank to prove the following:

a. If $J \notin FV(E_1)$, then $[E_2/J][J/I]E_1 \equiv [E_2/I]E_1$.

b. If $J \notin FV(E_2)$, then $[E_2/I][E_3/J]E_1 \equiv [([E_2/I]E_3)/J][E_2/I]E_1$.

c. $[E_2/I][E_3/I]E_1 \equiv [([E_2/I]E_3)/I]E_1$.

d. If $E_1 \Rightarrow^* E_2$, then $[E_1/I]E_3 \Rightarrow^* [E_2/I]E_3$.

e. If $E_1 \Rightarrow^* E_2$, then $[E_3/I]E_1 \Rightarrow^* [E_3/I]E_2$.

3.2. Following are three alternatives to the classic definition of substitution. For each, (i) reformulate the β-rule; (ii) re-prove Exercise 3.1.

a. From Barendregt 1984, the "expressions" of the lambda calculus are equivalence classes with respect to the α-rule. Let $[E]_\alpha$ represent an equivalence class. For example, the equivalence classes $[\lambda X.X]_\alpha$ and $[\lambda Y.Y]_\alpha$ are the same "expression." Substitution is defined as follows:

$$[[E]_\alpha/I]\ [I]_\alpha = [E]_\alpha$$
$$[[E]_\alpha/I]\ [J]_\alpha = [J]_\alpha, \text{ if } J \neq I$$
$$[[E]_\alpha/I]\ [E_1\ E_2]_\alpha = [E_1'\ E_2']_\alpha, \text{ where } [E_1']_\alpha = [[E]_\alpha/I]\ [E_1]_\alpha,$$
$$\quad \text{and } [E_2']_\alpha = [[E]_\alpha/I]\ [E_2]_\alpha$$
$$[[E]_\alpha/I]\ [\lambda J. E_1]_\alpha = [\lambda J. E_1']_\alpha$$
$$\quad \text{where } J \neq I, \ J \text{ is not free in } E, \text{ and } [E_1']_\alpha = [[E]_\alpha/I][E_1]_\alpha$$

Prove that the definition of substitution is well defined; that is: (i) for all expressions, E_1, $[[E]_\alpha/I][E_1]_\alpha$ is defined; (ii) if expressions E_1 and E_2 are α-convertible, then $[[E]_\alpha/I][E_1]_\alpha = [[E]_\alpha/I][E_2]_\alpha$. The proof method for the calculus is structural induction. Explain why structural induction is sound for expressions-as-equivalence-classes.

b. From Stoughton 1984b, the expressions for the lambda calculus are the traditional ones. A *substitution*, σ, is a mapping from identifiers to expressions. For convenience, we represent a substitution as a (finite) set of the form $\{I_1 = E_1, \ldots, I_n = E_n\}$. We write $\sigma.I = E$, when $(I = E) \in \sigma$, and write $\sigma.I = I$ otherwise. Application of a substitution, σ, to an expression, E, is written σE. It is defined as

$$\sigma I = \sigma.I$$
$$\sigma(E_1\ E_2) = (\sigma E_1\ \sigma E_2)$$
$$\sigma(\lambda I.E) = (\lambda J.(\sigma \uplus \{I=J\})E)$$

where J is the "first" identifier in an enumeration of all identifiers that do not appear free in any $\sigma.I'$, for all $I' \in FV(\lambda I.E)$. The proof method for the calculus is structural induction. Define $\sigma_2 \circ \sigma_1$ to be the mapping: $(\sigma_2 \circ \sigma_1).I = \sigma_2(\sigma_1.I)$. Prove that for all σ_1, σ_2, and E, $(\sigma_2 \circ \sigma_1)E = \sigma_2(\sigma_1 E)$.

c. From de Bruijn 1972 and Barendregt 1984, the expressions for the lambda calculus have the following syntax:

$$E ::= E_1\ E_2 \mid \lambda E \mid n, \text{ for } n > 0$$

The intuition is that a numeral stands for an identifier that binds to the nth enclosing lambda. For example, $(\lambda\ 1\ (\lambda\ 2\ 1\ 4))\ 1$ represents $(\lambda X.\ X\ (\lambda Y.\ X\ Y\ F_2))\ F_1$, where the free identifiers are enumerated as $F_1, F_2,$ .... Define $[E_1/n]E_2$. (Be careful about the "free identifiers" in E_1.) The proof method for the calculus is structural induction.

4.1. a. Prove the unicity of typing property for the simply typed lambda calculus: For all π, E, and τ, if $\pi \vdash E : \tau$ holds, then τ is unique.

b. Prove that if $\pi \uplus \{I:\tau\} \vdash E:\tau'$ holds, then $\pi \uplus \{J:\tau\} \vdash [J/I]E:\tau'$ holds.

c. Prove that if $\pi \vdash E:\tau$ holds and K is a fresh identifier, then $\pi \uplus \{K:\tau'\} \vdash E:\tau$ holds.

d. Prove the converse to Theorem 6.7: if $\pi \vdash E_2:\tau_2$ and $\pi \vdash [E_2/I]E_1:\tau_1$ hold, then so does $\pi \uplus \{I:\tau_2\} \vdash E_1:\tau_1$.

e. Prove that for all π, I, and τ, that $\pi \vdash (I\ I):\tau$ can*not* hold. Conclude from Part d that if $\pi \vdash E:\tau$ holds, then $\pi \vdash E\ E:\tau'$ cannot.

4.2. A useful tool for studying reduction strategies is the *evaluation context* (cf. Felleisen and Hieb 1992). An evaluation context is a phrase with a single "hole," into which a redex can fit. Here is a syntax rule for evaluation contexts:

$$X ::= [\,] \mid (X\ E)$$

E is a lambda calculus expression, as usual, and [] is a hole; we write $C[\,]$ to denote an evaluation context.

a. Prove that if E_0 contains a β-redex, R, then E_0 can be derived in the form $C[R]$ iff R is the leftmost redex in E_0 not contained within a lambda abstraction.

b. Say that a reduction step, $E \Rightarrow E'$, must match exactly this format:

$$C[(\lambda I.E_1)E_2] \Rightarrow C[[E_2/I]E_1]$$

What reduction strategy is encoded by this rewriting rule?

c. Consider this syntax for evaluation contexts:

$$X ::= [\,] \mid (XE) \mid (VX)$$
$$V ::= \lambda I.E \mid I$$

If the β-*val* rule is used in place of the β-rule (cf. Part b), what reduction strategy is defined?

d. We can perform simple proofs of reduction properties by induction on the structure of evaluation contexts. Re-prove the subject-reduction property for the reduction strategies in Parts b and c.

4.3. Add records to the simply typed lambda calculus, with the syntax and typing rules in Figure 5.2. The rewriting rule is

$$\textit{with } \{ I_1 = E_1, I_2 = E_2, \ldots, I_n = E_n \} \; \textit{do } E \;\; \Rightarrow \;\; [E_1/I_1, E_2/I_2, \ldots, E_n/I_n]E$$

So, parallel substitution is required.

a. Give a complete, formal definition of parallel substitution for the simply typed lambda calculus with records. (Take care with the definition of substitution into a *with* expression!)

b. Define the rank of a record expression and a *with* expression.

c. Reprove Theorem 6.4.

Confluence and strong normalization hold for this calculus.

5.1. Alter the lazy evaluation semantics of the lambda calculus in the following ways. First, for ground type, ι, add the constant, *loop*, such that $\pi \vdash loop: \iota$ holds. Say that $[\![\pi \vdash loop: \iota]\!]e = \bot$. Next, replace the semantics equations for lambda abstraction and application by these:

$$[\![\pi \vdash \lambda I:\tau_1.E:\tau_1 \rightarrow \tau_2]\!]e = f,$$
$$\text{where } f \bot = \bot$$
$$\text{and } f u = [\![\pi \uplus \{I:\tau_1\} \vdash E:\tau_2]\!](e \uplus \{I=u\}), \text{ if } u \neq \bot$$
$$[\![\pi \vdash E_1 E_2: \theta_2]\!]e = \bot, \text{ if } [\![\pi \vdash E_1:\tau_1 \rightarrow \tau_2]\!]e = \bot$$
$$[\![\pi \vdash E_1 E_2: \theta_2]\!]e = ([\![\pi \vdash E_1:\theta_1 \rightarrow \theta_2]\!]e)\,([\![\pi \vdash E_2:\theta_1]\!]e), \text{ otherwise}$$

Prove that the β-*val* rule is sound for this semantics but the β-rule is not.

6.1. Verify that the following expressions are well typed and reduce them to normal forms, if normal forms exist.

    a. *(equals (if (not(equals 3 2)) 4 (plus 5 (if true 6 7))) 8)*

    b. $(\lambda X{:}int.\lambda Y{:}int.\ plus\ X\ Y))((if\ true\ (\lambda X{:}int.\ plus\ X\ 1)\ (\lambda Y{:}int.\ Y))\ 3)$

    c. $(fix\ (\lambda F{:}int{\to}int.\lambda X{:}int.\ plus\ X\ (F\ (plus\ X\ 1))))\ 0$

6.2. Use the *fix* operator to encode the multiplication function in terms of the addition operator; use *fix* to encode exponentiation in terms of multiplication.

7.1. Calculate the substitution semantics and the environment semantics of these programs with the input store $\langle 0,1 \rangle$:

    a. $(\lambda X{:}intloc.\ (\lambda P{:}comm{\to}comm.\ X{:=}0;\ (P\ (X{:=}@X{+}1)))(\lambda Q{:}comm.\ Q))loc_1$

    b. **while** $loc_1{=}0$ **do** $(\lambda A{:}intexp.\ loc_2{:=}A)@loc_1$ **od**

7.2. Say that the β-rule is used in place of the β-*val* rule to reduce lambda abstractions in the metalanguage. Does this make any difference to the semantics of the source language?

8.1. Consider this SRS:

$$(\ E\ ::=\ a\ |\ b\ |\ fE\ |\ g\ E_1\ E_2,$$
$$\{fa \Rightarrow b,\ \ fb \Rightarrow a,\ \ g\ X\ (fY) \Rightarrow g\ (fY)\ (g\ X\ X)\}\ )$$

    a. Is the SRS orthogonal?

    b. Calculate the residuals of $(f\,a)$ at each stage in the leftmost outermost reduction sequence of $g\ (f\,a)\ (f\,b)$.

    c. Do a complete development of the redex set $\{(f\,a),\ (g\ (f\,a)\ (f\,b))\}$ for $g\ (f\,a)\ (f\,b)$. Is there more than one possible complete development?

    d. Does the SRS have the closure property? Confluence?

8.2. a. Give an example of an SRS that is not orthogonal but has the closure property.

    b. Give an example of an SRS that does not have closure but has confluence.

8.3. Verify that the rewriting rules in Section 6.6 form an orthogonal SRS.

8.4.* Prove Proposition 6.17.

8.5.* Without appealing to orthogonality, prove that the lambda calculus and its β-rule have the closure property.

8.6. There is a close relationship between certain orthogonal SRSs and natural semantics definitions. The intuition is that a natural semantics rule

$$\frac{E_1 \triangleright v_1 \quad \cdots \quad E_n \triangleright v_n}{op\,E_1 \cdots E_n \triangleright f_{v_1 \cdots v_n}}$$

corresponds to the rewriting rule $op\, E_1 \cdots E_n \Rightarrow f_{v_1 \cdots v_n}$, where $v_1, \ldots, v_n$ are Values.

   a. Define the class of orthogonal SRSs and natural semantics definitions that "correspond" and give translations between the two.

   b. An advantage of natural semantics definitions is that proofs about computations can be performed by induction on the structure of the proof trees. Based on your answer to Part a, state an induction principle for proofs of computations in orthogonal SRSs.

9.1. Which of these reduction strategies for orthogonal SRSs are eventually outermost? Justify your answer.

   a. Full reduction: At each stage, all redexes in an expression are reduced in parallel.

   b. Parallel innermost: At each stage, all redexes not containing other redexes are reduced in parallel.

   c. Rightmost outermost: At each stage, the rightmost redex is reduced.

   d. Round robin: A queue is kept of the redexes that were outermost at some stage. At each stage, the front element of the queue is selected, and all residuals of the redex are reduced. Any new outermost redexes are added to the queue. (The queue is initialized with all the outermost redexes in the initial expression.)

9.2. Say that an SRS is not orthogonal. Will an eventually outermost reduction strategy always discover a normal form?

7 Functional Programming Languages

In this chapter, we call a programming language *functional* if it is expression-based and lacks store. (Some functional languages, notably, Standard ML, CAML, Lisp, and Scheme, have store but make the operations on it subservient to expression evaluation.) We will develop a language based on a functional language core and during the process encounter issues significantly different from those in Chapters 2–5.

7.1 The Core Functional Language

The core language uses three data types: integers, booleans, and lists. Figure 7.1 displays the syntax and typing rules. The meanings of the integer- and boolean-typed phrases are the expected ones. For lists, **nil** represents the empty list; **cons** E_1 E_2 attaches E_1 to the front of a list, E_2; **hd** E represents the value of the front element of the list, E; **tl** E represents the list, E, without its front element; and **null** E states whether or not E is empty.

    The above summary leaves several questions unanswered. The first is, What is the value of **hd nil**? Perhaps such a program should be ill typed, but the current framework makes this difficult to enforce—consider **hd** (**if** $\cdots$ **then nil else cons** 1 **nil fi**). A similar situation arises in imperative languages when arrays are indexed: $A[I+1]$ might not represent a location in array A. We will say that the value of **hd nil** and similar phrases is *failure*. If a failure is encountered during a program's evaluation, we say that the result of the overall program is failure as well. Some languages are equipped with an exception-handler construction, which "traps" a failure and converts it into a default answer or an error message. Exception handlers are saved for the Exercises at the end of the chapter.

    A second semantic issue is the evaluation strategy for lists. Like actual parameters, the components of a list might be evaluated eagerly or lazily. With eager evaluation, all components of a list must be evaluated to Values for the list to be useful. With lazy evaluation, the components are not evaluated until they are extracted from the list and used. Consider **cons** (1+2) **nil**; if evaluated eagerly, this program evaluates to a list with a single element, 3. If evaluated lazily, the program evaluates to a structure containing the subphrases 1+2 and **nil**. Here is another example: With eager evaluation, the

---

$E \in$ Expression

$N \in$ Numeral

$E ::= N \mid \textbf{true} \mid \textbf{false} \mid E_1 + E_2 \mid E_1 = E_2 \mid \textbf{not } E \mid \textbf{if } E_1 \textbf{ then } E_2 \textbf{ else } E_3 \textbf{ fi}$
$\quad \mid \textbf{nil} \mid \textbf{cons } E_1 \ E_2 \mid \textbf{hd } E \mid \textbf{tl } E \mid \textbf{null } E$

$\tau ::= int \mid bool \mid \tau list$

$$N{:}int \qquad\qquad \textbf{true}{:}bool \qquad \textbf{false}{:}bool \qquad \frac{E_1 : int \quad E_2 : int}{E_1 + E_2 : int}$$

$$\frac{E_1 : int \quad E_2 : int}{E_1 = E_2 : bool} \qquad \frac{E : bool}{\textbf{not } E : bool} \qquad \frac{E_1 : bool \quad E_2 : \tau \quad E_3 : \tau}{\textbf{if } E_1 \textbf{ then } E_2 \textbf{ else } E_3 \textbf{ fi} : \tau} \qquad \textbf{nil}: \tau list$$

$$\frac{E_1 : \tau \quad E_2 : \tau list}{\textbf{cons } E_1 \ E_2 : \tau list} \qquad \frac{E : \tau list}{\textbf{hd } E : \tau} \qquad \frac{E : \tau list}{\textbf{tl } E : \tau list} \qquad \frac{E : \tau list}{\textbf{null } E : bool}$$

Figure 7.1 _____

program $4 + (\textbf{hd } (\textbf{cons } (1+2) \ (\textbf{cons } (\textbf{hd nil}) \ \textbf{nil})))$ evaluates to a failure, because the sub-phrase $\textbf{cons } (1+2) \ (\textbf{cons } (\textbf{hd nil}) \ \textbf{nil}))$ must be evaluated to a list of numbers from which the front number is extracted. Although $1+2$ evaluates to 3, the next element, $\textbf{hd nil}$, evaluates to a failure, and the overall list is a failure. But with lazy evaluation, the program evaluates to 7, because $\textbf{hd } (\textbf{cons } (1+2) \cdots)$ evaluates to $1+2$, and there is no need to evaluate the remainder of the list.

A third semantic issue is the meaning of **nil**, the empty list. Is **nil** an empty integer list, an empty boolean list, an empty integer list list, or what? Apparently, it must be all these things, since one can write $\textbf{cons } 0 \ \textbf{nil}$, $\textbf{cons true nil}$, $\textbf{cons } (\textbf{cons } 0 \ \textbf{nil}) \ \textbf{nil}$, and so on. This question originates from the typing system in Figure 7.1, which lacks unicity of typing: **nil** can be typed *int list*, *bool list*, *(int list)list*, and so on. If this is undesirable, we might replace **nil** by a family of constants, $\textbf{nil}_{int}$, $\textbf{nil}_{bool}$, $\textbf{nil}_{int\ list}$, and so on. This restores unicity of typing but is cumbersome. A second approach, which is developed at length in Section 7.8, gives **nil** the type attribute $\alpha list$, where α is a dummy value called a *placeholder* or *type variable*. As the overall program is type checked, α is instantiated based upon the context in which **nil** appears. Here is a small example where, as usual, the type attributes are written as superscripts. Instantiations of placeholders are presented also as superscripts:

$$(\textbf{cons } 0^{int} \ \textbf{nil}^{\alpha list})^{int\ list, \ \alpha = int}$$

A second example is

$$(\textbf{cons}\ (\textbf{cons}\ 2^{int}\ \textbf{nil}^{\alpha list})^{int\ list,\ \alpha=int}\ (\textbf{cons}\ \textbf{nil}^{\beta list}\ \textbf{nil}^{\gamma list})^{(\beta list)list,\ \gamma=\beta list})^{(int\ list)list,\ \sigma}$$

where σ is $\alpha=int$, $\beta=int$, $\gamma=int\ list$

This approach restores unicity of typing, but the precise meaning of programs like **(cons nil nil)** remains unclear, since placeholders appear in the type attribute of the overall program.

7.2 Rewriting Rules for the Core Language

Since functional languages lack store, we can define rewriting rules upon the core language by applying the ideas from Section 6.6. First, for integers and booleans, the respective Value sets are $Value(int) = \{\ 0, 1, 2, \dots\ \}$ and $Value(bool) = \{\ \textbf{true}, \textbf{false}\ \}$. Their rewriting rules follow:

$m+n \Rightarrow p$

> where m and n are Values and p denotes the sum of m and n

$m=m \Rightarrow \textbf{true}$,   where m is a Value

$m=n \Rightarrow \textbf{false}$,   where m and n are different Values

not true $\Rightarrow$ **false**

not false $\Rightarrow$ **true**

if true then E_1 **else** E_2 **fi** $\Rightarrow$ E_1

if false then E_1 **else** E_2 **fi** $\Rightarrow$ E_2

For lists, lazy evaluation or eager evaluation must be chosen. The rules for lazy evaluation follow:

hd $(\textbf{cons}\ E_1\ E_2) \Rightarrow E_1$

tl $(\textbf{cons}\ E_1\ E_2) \Rightarrow E_2$

null nil $\Rightarrow$ **true**

null $(\textbf{cons}\ E_1\ E_2) \Rightarrow$ **false**

Here is a simple example:

$1 + \textbf{if true then hd}\ (\textbf{cons}\ (4+5)\ (\textbf{cons}\ (6+7)\ \textbf{nil}))\ \textbf{else}\ 8+9\ \textbf{fi}$

$\Rightarrow 1 + \textbf{hd}\ (\textbf{cons}\ (4+5)\ (\textbf{cons}\ (6+7)\ \textbf{nil}))$

$\Rightarrow 1+(4+5) \Rightarrow 1+9 \Rightarrow 10$

The rewriting rules for eager evaluation of lists are a minor variation of the ones for lazy evaluation:

> **hd** (**cons** E_1 E_2) $\Rightarrow$ E_1, if E_1 and E_2 are Values
>
> **tl** (**cons** E_1 E_2) $\Rightarrow$ E_2, if E_1 and E_2 are Values
>
> **null nil** $\Rightarrow$ **true**
>
> **null** (**cons** E_1 E_2) $\Rightarrow$ **false**, if E_1 and E_2 are Values

We say that $Value(\tau list) = \{\,\mathbf{nil}\,\} \cup \{\,\mathbf{cons}\ E_1\ E_2 \mid E_1 \in Value(\tau)$ and $E_2 \in Value(\tau list)\,\}$. The inductive definition says that a list Value's elements are Values themselves. With these rules, the previous example is computed:

> $1 + \mathbf{if\ true\ then\ hd}$ (**cons** (4+5) (**cons** (6+7) **nil**)) **else** 8+9 **fi**
>
> $\Rightarrow$ $1 + \mathbf{hd}$ (**cons** (4+5) (**cons** (6+7) **nil**))
>
> $\Rightarrow$ $1 + \mathbf{hd}$ (**cons** 9 (**cons** (6+7) **nil**))
>
> $\Rightarrow$ $1 + \mathbf{hd}$ (**cons** 9 (**cons** 13 **nil**)) $\Rightarrow$ 1+9 $\Rightarrow$ 10

The rewriting rules for the core language form an operational semantics, since a program's Value can be calculated directly from the program itself. This lessens the importance of the language's denotational semantics, but the denotational semantics is valuable nonetheless for confirming our understanding of the core language and validating the soundness of the rewriting rules. It will be examined in Section 7.5.

7.3 The Abstraction and Qualification Principles

We follow the suggestion of Chapter 5 and introduce naming devices via records. Figure 7.2 shows the revised syntax and typing rules for the additions. As usual, a type assignment attribute must be added to the typing rules. **val** I=E is a "one field record," and E_1, E_2 concatenates two records together. **let** E_1 **in** E_2 is the block construct, which was represented by *with* in Chapter 5. Although not a record construction, a recursive definition construct, **rec** I:τ. E, is included.

The choice of lazy or eager evaluation of definitions must be made. Lazy evaluation has its usual copy rule:

> **let val** $I_1{=}E_1, \dots,$ **val** $I_n{=}E_n$ **in** E $\Rightarrow$ $[E_1/I_1, \dots, E_n/I_n]E$

This works well when the core language uses lazy evaluation for lists. But if lists are eagerly evaluated, then it is sensible to evaluate definitions eagerly, and the appropriate copy rule follows:

> **let val** $I_1{=}E_1, \dots,$ **val** $I_n{=}E_n$ **in** E $\Rightarrow$ $[E_1/I_1, \dots, E_n/I_n]E$
>
>   if $E_1, \dots, E_n$ are Values

Note that $Value\{I_1{:}\tau_1, \dots, I_n{:}\tau_n\} = \{(\mathbf{val}\ I_1{=}E_1, \dots, \mathbf{val}\ I_n{=}E_n) \mid$ for all $1 \le i \le n$, $E_i \in Value(\tau_i)\}$.

$$E ::= N \mid \textbf{true} \mid \textbf{false} \mid E_1 + E_2 \mid E_1 = E_2 \mid \textbf{not } E \mid \textbf{if } E_1 \textbf{ then } E_2 \textbf{ else } E_3 \textbf{ fi}$$
$$\mid \textbf{nil} \mid \textbf{cons } E_1 \, E_2 \mid \textbf{hd } E \mid \textbf{tl } E \mid \textbf{null } E$$
$$\mid \textbf{val } I = E \mid E_1, E_2 \mid \textbf{let } E_1 \textbf{ in } E_2 \mid I \mid \textbf{rec } I{:}\tau.\, E$$

$$\tau ::= \textit{int} \mid \textit{bool} \mid \tau\textit{list} \mid \pi$$
$$\pi ::= \{\, j{:}\tau_j \,\}_{j \in J} \quad \text{where } J \subseteq \text{Identifier is a finite set}$$

$$\frac{\pi \vdash E : \tau}{\pi \vdash \textbf{val } I = E : \{\, I{:}\tau \,\}} \qquad\qquad \frac{\pi \vdash E_1 : \pi_1 \quad \pi \vdash E_2 : \pi_2}{\pi \vdash E_1, E_2 : \pi_1 \cup \pi_2}$$

$$\frac{\pi \vdash E_1 : \pi_1 \quad \pi \uplus \pi_1 \vdash E_2 : \tau}{\pi \vdash \textbf{let } E_1 \textbf{ in } E_2 : \tau} \qquad \pi \vdash I : \tau, \;\; \text{if } (I{:}\tau) \in \pi \qquad \frac{\pi \uplus \{\, I{:}\tau \,\} \vdash E : \tau}{\pi \vdash \textbf{rec } I{:}\tau.\, E : \tau}$$

Figure 7.2 _____

Lazily evaluated lists and definitions can work together to define lists of infinite length. Consider what is apparently an infinite list of zeros: $\textbf{val } L = \textbf{rec } X{:}\textit{int list}.$ $\textbf{cons } 0\, X$. We use the usual unfolding rule

$$\textbf{rec } I{:}\tau.\, E \;\Rightarrow\; [(\textbf{rec } I{:}\tau.\, E)/\, I]E$$

and we can deduce the following:

$\textbf{val } L = \textbf{rec } X{:}\textit{int list}.\, \textbf{cons } 0\, X$
$\Rightarrow \textbf{val } L = \textbf{cons } 0\, (\textbf{rec } X{:}\textit{int list}.\, \textbf{cons } 0\, X)$
$\Rightarrow \textbf{val } L = \textbf{cons } 0\, (\textbf{cons } 0\, (\textbf{rec } X{:}\textit{int list}.\, \textbf{cons } 0\, X))$
$\Rightarrow^* \textbf{val } L = \textbf{cons } 0\, (\textbf{cons } 0\, (\,\cdots\, (\textbf{cons } 0\, (\textbf{rec } X{:}\textit{int list}.\, \textbf{cons } 0\, X)\,\cdots\,))$

That is, L contains an inexhaustible supply of zeros. Despite this apparently nonterminating behavior, the lazy evaluation rules for the list operations make good use of L. An example is:

$\textbf{let val } L = (\textbf{rec } X{:}\textit{int list}.\, \textbf{cons } 0\, X) \textbf{ in } 2 + (\textbf{hd } L)$
$\Rightarrow 2 + (\textbf{hd } (\textbf{rec } X{:}\textit{int list}.\, \textbf{cons } 0\, X))$
$\Rightarrow 2 + (\textbf{hd } (\textbf{cons } 0\, (\textbf{rec } X{:}\textit{int list}.\, \textbf{cons } 0\, X)))$
$\Rightarrow 2 + 0 \Rightarrow 2$

In contrast, the eager evaluation rules for lists would demand that L be calculated to a list of full length, and this causes a nonterminating computation.

Not so useful lists can be defined recursively as well. Two examples are: (**rec** *Y:int list. Y*), which is a "looping list" that produces no elements at all, and **cons** 0 (**rec** *Y:int list. Y*)), which is a partially defined list that yields an initial 0 and then loops.

7.4 The Parameterization Principle

It is simplest to add parameters in the manner suggested in Chapter 5, that is, via lambda abstractions. The resulting language is "unsugared," but its components are easy to understand. The language plus the typing rules for the additions are shown in Figure 7.3. The copy rule for parameters is of course the β-rule (for lazy evaluation), namely,

$$(\lambda I{:}\tau.E_1)E_2 \;\Rightarrow\; [E_2/I]E_1$$

or the β-*val* rule (for eager evaluation):

$$(\lambda I{:}\tau.E_1)E_2 \;\Rightarrow\; [E_2/I]E_1, \text{ if } E_2 \text{ is a Value}$$

Note that $Value(\tau_1 \to \tau_2) = \{\lambda I{:}\tau_1.E \mid \text{ for some } \pi, \pi \uplus \{I{:}\tau_1\} \vdash E{:}\tau_2 \text{ holds}\}.$

The **rec** construction from the previous section can be used to define recursively defined functions, for example,

$$\textbf{val } MAP = \lambda F{:}int \to bool.\textbf{rec } M{:}int\ list \to bool\ list.$$
$$\lambda L{:}int\ list. \textbf{ if null } L \textbf{ then nil else cons } (F\ (hd\ L))\ (M\ (tl\ L))$$

The absence of "sugaring" is noticeable, and the formulation of an appropriate sugared syntax is left as an interesting exercise.

E ::= N | **true** | **false** | E_1+E_2 | $E_1=E_2$ | **not** E | **if** E_1 **then** E_2 **else** E_3 **fi**
 | **nil** | **cons** $E_1\ E_2$ | **hd** E | **tl** E | **null** E | **rec** I:τ. E
 | **val** I=E | E_1,E_2 | **let** E_1 **in** E_2 | I | $\lambda I{:}\tau.E$ | $E_1\ E_2$

τ ::= *int* | *bool* | τ*list* | π | $\tau_1 \to \tau_2$

π ::= $\{j{:}\tau_j\}_{j\in J}$ where $J \subseteq$ Identifier is a finite set

$$\frac{\pi \uplus \{I{:}\tau_1\} \vdash E{:}\tau_2}{\pi \vdash (\lambda I{:}\tau_1.E){:}\tau_1 \to \tau_2} \qquad \frac{\pi \vdash E_1{:}\tau_1 \to \tau_2 \quad \pi \vdash E_2{:}\tau_1}{\pi \vdash (E_1\ E_2){:}\tau_2}$$

Figure 7.3 ———————————————————————

7.5 Denotational Semantics of the Functional Language

The absence of store from functional languages makes the denotational semantics simple. For starters, the semantics of the language core appears in Figure 7.4. The operations for integer- and boolean-typed phrases are taken from Figure 1.6; the operations for lists are defined presently.

As noted in Section 7.1, the issue of failure must be handled. We say that $[[\textbf{hd nil}: \tau]] = fail$, where *fail* is a new meaning that belongs to all meaning sets. Due to recursive bindings, $\perp$ appears everywhere as well. Therefore, $Bool = \{fail, \perp, true, false\}$ and $Int = \{fail, \perp, 0, 1, \ldots \}$. *fail* and $\perp$ are *improper meanings*, whereas *true*, *false*, 0, 1, . . . are *proper*. The operations on truth values and numbers are defined only on proper meanings—an improper argument causes an improper answer, for example, $plus(i, j) = i$ if i is improper, and $plus(n, i) = i$ if n is proper and i is not.

The decision to use eager or lazy evaluation for lists impacts the semantics. Figure 7.5 gives the meaning set and operations for eagerly evaluated lists. A proper, eagerly evaluated list has a finite number of elements, each of which is proper. The following are left as easy exercises: (i) The typing rules are sound; that is, $[[E: \tau]] \in [[\tau]]$, where $[[int]] = Int$, $[[bool]] = Bool$, and $[[\tau list]] = [[\tau]]List$. (ii) The rewriting rules for eager evaluation are sound with respect to the core language semantics; that is, if $E_1 \Rightarrow E_2$, then $[[E_1: \tau]] = [[E_2: \tau]]$.

The meaning set for lazy evaluation is more complex. Figure 7.6 presents it with its operations. *DList* contains: (i) finite, total lists of the form $cons\ d_1\ (cons\ d_2\ \cdots\ (cons\ d_n\ nil)\ \cdots)$; (ii) finite, partial lists of the form $cons\ d_1\ (cons\ d_2\ \cdots\ (cons\ d_n\ \perp)\ \cdots)$; (iii) lists ending in failure $cons\ d_1\ (cons\ d_2\ \cdots\ (cons\ d_n\ fail)\ \cdots)$; and (iv) lists of infinite length $cons\ d_1\ (cons\ d_2\ \cdots\ (cons\ d_i\ \cdots)\ \cdots)$. All of these are proper meanings. *nil* and *cons* are constructors and not operations in their own right. An example is: $[[\textbf{cons } 0\ (\textbf{tl nil}): int\ list]] = cons\ 0\ fail$, so $[[\textbf{hd (cons } 0\ (\textbf{tl nil})): int]] = 0$.

$[[N: int]] = N$ $[[E_1 + E_2: int]] = plus([[E_1: int]], [[E_2: int]])$

$[[\textbf{true}: bool]] = true$ $[[E_1 = E_2: int]] = equalint([[E_1: int]], [[E_2: int]])$

$[[\textbf{false}: bool]] = false$ $[[\textbf{not } E: bool]] = not[[E: bool]]$

$[[\textbf{if } E_1 \textbf{ then } E_2 \textbf{ else } E_3 \textbf{ fi}: \tau]] = if([[E_1: bool]], [[E_2: \tau]], [[E_3: \tau]])$

$[[\textbf{nil}: \tau list]] = nil$ $[[\textbf{cons } E_1\ E_2: \tau list]] = cons\ [[E_1: \tau]]\ [[E_2: \tau list]]$

$[[\textbf{hd } E: \tau]] = head[[E: \tau list]]$ $[[\textbf{null } E: \tau]] = null[[E: \tau list]]$

$[[\textbf{tl } E: \tau]] = tail[[E: \tau list]]$

Figure 7.4 _____

$DList = \{ [d_1, d_2, \ldots, d_n] \mid n \geq 0,\ and\ for\ 1 \leq i \leq n,\ d_i \in D,\ d_i\ is\ proper \} \cup \{fail,\ \bot \}$

> *nil*: *DList*
>> $nil = [\ ]$
>
> *cons*: $D \times DList \rightarrow DList$
>> $cons\ d_1\ [d_2, \ldots, d_n]) = [d_1, d_2, \ldots, d_n]$, if d_1 is proper
>>
>> $cons\ i\ l = i$, if i is improper; $cons\ d\ i = i$ if d is proper and i is not
>
> *head*: $DList \rightarrow D$
>> $head\ [d_1, d_2, \ldots, d_n] = d_1$
>>
>> $head\ [\ ] = fail;$ $head\ i = i$, if i is improper
>
> *tail*: $DList \rightarrow DList$
>> $tail[d_1, d_2, \ldots, d_n] = [d_2, \ldots, d_n]$
>>
>> $tail\ [\ ] = fail;$ $tail\ i = i$, if i is improper
>
> *null*: $DList \rightarrow Bool$
>> $null\ [\ ] = true$
>>
>> $null[d_1, \ldots, d_n] = false;$ $null\ i = i$, if i is improper

Figure 7.5 _____

$DList = \{ cons\ d\ l \mid d \in D,\ l \in DList \} \cup \{ nil,\ fail,\ \bot \}$
$\qquad \cup \{ cons\ d_1\ (cons\ d_2\ (\cdots (cons\ d_i\ \cdots)\cdots)) \mid for\ all\ i > 0,\ d_i \in D \}$

> *head*: $DList \rightarrow D$
>> $head\ (cons\ d\ l) = d$
>>
>> $head\ nil = fail;$ $head\ i = i$, if i is improper
>
> *tail*: $DList \rightarrow DList$
>> $tail\ (cons\ d\ l) = l$
>>
>> $tail\ nil = fail;$ $tail\ i = i$, if i is improper
>
> *null*: $DList \rightarrow Bool$
>> $null\ nil = true$
>>
>> $null\ (cons\ d\ l) = false;$ $null\ i = i$, if i is improper

Figure 7.6 _____

Unlike eagerly evaluated lists, lazily evaluated lists can contain improper values, and they can have infinite length; we saw examples of both in the previous sections. We also saw "looping" lists, that is, lists that have meaning $\bot$. With the definitions in Figure 7.6, one can prove that the typing rules and rewriting rules for lazy evaluation are sound.

There is a technical issue regarding *Dlist* that deserves mention. In a denotational semantics text, *Dlist* is defined merely as follows:

$$Dlist = \{ cons \; d \; l \mid d \in D, \; l \in Dlist \} \cup \{ nil, fail, \bot \}$$

The usual reading of the equation as an inductive definition generates a set, $Dlist_0$, that contains lists of finite length only. But we can define $Dlist_1$ to be

$$Dlist_1 = Dlist_0 \cup \{ (cons \; d_1 \; (cons \; d_2 \; \cdots \; (cons \; d_i \; \cdots) \cdots)) \mid d_i \in D \}$$

and this equality holds:

$$Dlist_1 = \{ (cons \; d \; t) \mid d \in D, \; t \in Dlist_1 \} \cup \{ nil, fail, \bot \}$$

In this sense, $Dlist_1$ is a "solution" to the inductive definition. It is not the least solution—$Dlist_0$ is—but if we require that the solution to the definition of *Dlist* contain limits of sequences of partial lists, then $Dlist_0$ does not suffice, and $Dlist_1$ is the smallest solution that does. Limits of sequences are crucial to calculating the meaning of recursively defined lists, like **rec** X:*int list*. **cons** $0X$, as we now see. The usual semantics of recursive binding follows:

$$[\![\pi \vdash \mathbf{rec}\, I{:}\tau.E{:}\tau]\!]e = v, \;\; \text{where} \;\; v = [\![\pi \uplus \{I{:}\tau\} \vdash E{:}\tau]\!](e \uplus \{I{=}v\})$$

The meaning, v, is the "limit" of a sequence of approximations that begins with $\bot \in [\![\tau]\!]$:

$$v_0 = \bot$$
$$v_{i+1} = [\![\pi \uplus \{I{:}\tau\} \vdash E{:}\tau]\!](e \uplus \{I{=}v_i\}), \;\; \text{for } i \geq 0$$

In the case of **rec** X:*int list*. **cons** $0X$, we see that the family of approximations is a sequence of partial lists such that the ith list in the sequence can emit i zeros before becoming exhausted:

$$[\![\varnothing \vdash \mathbf{rec}\, X{:}int\; list.\mathbf{cons}\; 0\, X{:}int\; list]\!]\varnothing = v$$
$$\text{where } v = [\![\{X{:}int\; list\} \vdash \mathbf{cons}\; 0\, X{:}int\; list]\!]\{X{=}v\}$$
$$v_0 \;\;= \bot$$
$$v_{i+1} \;\;= [\![\{X{:}int\; list\} \vdash \mathbf{cons}\; 0\, X{:}int\; list]\!]\{L{=}v_i\}$$
$$= cons\; 0\; (cons\; 0 \cdots (cons\; 0\; \bot) \cdots)), \; 0 \text{ repeated } i \text{ times}$$

The limit of this sequence is a list that contains all the partial lists as sublists, namely, the infinite list of zeros. The precise formalization of the notion of "limit" is beyond the scope of this book; consult any denotational semantics text.

Now, we consider records and lambda abstractions. Their semantics appears in Figure 7.7. Unlike the semantics definitions in Chapter 5, where the store acted as a "trigger" that "fired" computations, the distinction between lazy and eager evaluation is made by the way that the semantic binding operation, $\{I=v\}$, and the semantic function application, $f(v)$, are defined. The definition for eager evaluation goes as follows:

(i) $\{I=v\}$ is proper, when v is; $\{I=i\} = i$, when i is improper.
(ii) $f(v)$ is the answer from the function, f, when f and v are proper; $i(v) = i$, when i is improper; and $f(i) = i$, when f is proper and i is not.

The definition for lazy evaluation is as follows:

(i) $\{I=v\}$ is always proper.
(ii) $f(v)$ is the answer from the function, f, when f is proper; $i(v) = i$, when i is improper.

Thus, the operations are *strict* in the eager evaluation case and *nonstrict* (except for $i(v)$) in the lazy evaluation case. The distinctions noted above are crucial to the meanings of programs like **let val** $X=$ **hd nil in** 0 and $(\lambda X{:}int.\,0)\,(\textbf{hd nil})$, both of which fail for eager evaluation and terminate in 0 for lazy evaluation. But $(\textbf{hd nil})0$ fails for both eager and lazy evaluation.

The two semantic union operations, $\cup$ and $\uplus$, are defined in the usual way and are strict in their arguments: $i\cup e = i \uplus e = i$, if i is improper; $e\cup i = e \uplus i = i$, if e is proper and i is not. Finally, $[\![\pi\vdash E{:}\tau]\!]i = i$, because no phrase may have a proper meaning with an improper environment. Thus, **let** $(\textbf{hd nil})$, **val** $X{=}0$ **in** X fails for both eager and lazy evaluation.

$[\![\pi\vdash \textbf{val } I{=}E{:}\{I{:}\tau\}]\!]e = \{I = [\![\pi\vdash E{:}\tau]\!]e\}$

$[\![\pi\vdash E_1,E_2{:}\pi_1\cup\pi_2]\!]e = ([\![\pi\vdash E_1{:}\pi_1]\!]e)\cup([\![\pi\vdash E_2{:}\pi_2]\!]e)$

$[\![\pi\vdash \textbf{let } E_1 \textbf{ in } E_2{:}\tau]\!]e = [\![\pi \uplus \pi_1 \vdash E_2{:}\tau]\!](e \uplus ([\![\pi\vdash E_1{:}\pi_1]\!]e))$

$[\![\pi\vdash I{:}\tau]\!]e = v, \quad \text{where } (I{=}v)\in e$

$[\![\pi\vdash \lambda I{:}\tau_1.\,E{:}\tau_1{\to}\tau_2]\!]e = f, \quad \text{where } f\,u = [\![\pi \uplus \{I{:}\tau_1\}\vdash E{:}\tau_2]\!](e \uplus \{I{=}u\})$

$[\![\pi\vdash E_1\ E_2{:}\tau_2]\!]e = ([\![\pi\vdash E_1{:}\tau_1{\to}\tau_2]\!]e)\,([\![\pi\vdash E_2{:}\tau_1]\!]e)$

$\quad\quad \text{where } [\![\{i{:}\tau_i\}_{i\in I}]\!] = (\{i{:}[\![\tau_i]\!]\}_{i\in I})\cup\{fail,\ \bot\}$

$\quad\quad \text{and } [\![\theta_1{\to}\theta_2]\!] = ([\![\theta_1]\!]{\to}[\![\theta_2]\!])\cup\{fail,\ \bot\}$

Figure 7.7 _____

7.5.1 PCF and Computational Adequacy

The rewriting rules for the core language in Section 7.2 plus the copy rules for records, lambda abstraction, and **rec** form an operational semantics for the functional language. As always, the operational semantics should be validated for subject reduction, strong typing, soundness, and computational adequacy. In the present setting, subject reduction is stated as follows: If $\pi \vdash E_1 : \tau$ holds and $E_1 \Rightarrow^* E_2$, then $\pi \vdash E_2 : \tau$ holds. The proof is left as an exercise. Soundness is stated similarly: If $\pi \vdash E_1 : \tau$ holds and $E_1 \Rightarrow^* E_2$, then $[\![\pi \vdash E_1 : \tau]\!]e = [\![\pi \vdash E_2 : \tau]\!]e$, for $e \in Env_\pi$. Strong typing is a bit more interesting, because one must show that if $\pi \vdash E_1 : \tau$ holds and $E_1 \Rightarrow^* E_2$, then E_2 contains no operator-operand incompatibilities. Now, is (**hd nil**) an incompatibility? If so, then strong typing fails. Similar issues arise with array indexing operations and other situations that generate run-time failures. For this reason, some say that a language is strongly typed if its run-time implementation prevents an incompatibility like (**hd nil**) from executing and instead reports a failure.

The remaining property is adequacy, and we study it in detail because this particular example is well known. For the moment, we consider the sublanguage consisting of the integer and boolean constants and their operations, conditional, (lazy) lambda abstraction, and **rec**. This is essentially the PCF language of Plotkin 1975. The *programs* of PCF are those E such that $\varnothing \vdash E : \iota$ holds, where $\iota \in \{int, bool\}$. A *computation* is a reduction $E \Rightarrow^* V$, where E is a program, V is a Value (hereon we always use "V" to denote Values), and at each stage of the reduction, the leftmost redex not within a lambda abstraction is reduced. Given that soundness holds for this language, adequacy amounts to showing, if $[\![\varnothing \vdash E : \iota]\!]\varnothing = [\![\varnothing \vdash V : \iota]\!]\varnothing$, then $E \Rightarrow^* V$. This statement is appropriate because the integer and boolean Values are in one to one correspondence with the proper meanings in $[\![int]\!]$ and $[\![bool]\!]$, respectively.

To obtain the result, we prove, for all $\pi \vdash E : \tau$, that $comp_{\pi,\tau}E$ holds. The definition of *comp* is given in two stages. First, we define *comp* as a recursive function just on closed expressions. For $\varnothing \vdash E : \tau$

(i) $comp_\iota E$ holds iff $[\![\varnothing \vdash E : \iota]\!]\varnothing = [\![\varnothing \vdash V : \iota]\!]\varnothing$ implies $E \Rightarrow^* V$.
(ii) $comp_{\tau_1 \to \tau_2} E$ holds iff for all $\varnothing \vdash E_1 : \tau_1$, $comp_{\tau_1} E_1$ implies $comp_{\tau_2}(E E_1)$.

Next, for $\pi \vdash E : \tau$, $\pi = \{i:\tau_i\}_{i \in I}$, we define

(iii) $comp_{\pi,\tau}E$ holds iff for all $i \in I$ and $\varnothing \vdash E_i : \tau_i$ such that $comp_{\tau_i} E_i$ holds, $comp_\tau \sigma E$ holds, where σ is $[E_i/i]_{i \in I}$.

That is, $comp_{\pi,\tau}E$ holds iff the replacement of the free identifiers in E by closed expressions, E_i, such that $comp_{\tau_i} E_i$ holds, means that $comp_\tau[E_i/I]E$ holds also.

Adequacy follows from the proof, for all $\pi \vdash E : \tau$, that $comp_{\pi,\tau}E$ holds. We begin with a useful lemma:

7.1 Lemma

For $\varnothing \vdash E':\tau$ and $\varnothing \vdash E:\tau$, if $comp_\tau E$ holds and $E' \Rightarrow^* E$, then $comp_\tau E'$ holds as well.

Proof: The proof is by induction on the structure of τ.

(i) ι: This is trivial.

(ii) $\tau_1 \to \tau_2$: We must show $comp_{\tau_1} E_1$ implies $comp_{\tau_2}(E'E_1)$, for $\varnothing \vdash E_1 : \tau_1$. By hypothesis, $comp_{\tau_1 \to \tau_2} E$ holds, hence $comp_{\tau_2}(EE_1)$ holds also. But if $E' \Rightarrow^* E$, then $(E'E_1) \Rightarrow^* (EE_1)$ as well, since E' cannot be a lambda abstraction. (Remember, we do not reduce redexes within lambda abstractions.) By the inductive hypothesis for τ_2, we have that $comp_{\tau_2}(E'E_1)$. $\square$

7.2 Theorem

For all $\pi \vdash E : \tau$, $comp_{\pi, \tau} E$ holds.

Proof: Let $\pi = \{i : \tau_i\}_{i \in I}$, and say that $comp_{\tau_i} E_i$ holds, for all $i \in I$. The proof is by induction on the structure of E:

(i)   I: To show $comp_{\pi, \tau} I$, we must show $comp_\tau \sigma I$. But this is immediate.

(ii) N: Immediate.

(iii) $E_1 + E_2$: If $[\![\varnothing \vdash \sigma(E_1 + E_2) : int]\!]\varnothing = [\![\varnothing \vdash V_3 : int]\!]\varnothing$, then $[\![\varnothing \vdash \sigma(E_i) : int]\!]\varnothing = [\![\varnothing \vdash V_i : int]\!]\varnothing$, for $i \in \{1, 2\}$. By the inductive hypothesis, $\sigma E_i \Rightarrow^* V_i$; hence, $\sigma(E_1 + E_2) = \sigma E_1 + \sigma E_2 \Rightarrow^* V_1 + \sigma E_2 \Rightarrow^* V_1 + V_2 \Rightarrow^* V_3$. The result now follows from Lemma 7.1, since $comp_{int} V_3$ trivially holds. Proofs for the other core language operators are similar.

(iv) $(E_1 \, E_2)$: Immediate from the inductive hypotheses for E_1 and E_2.

(v) $\lambda I : \tau_1 . E_2$: We must show $comp_{\tau_1 \to \tau_2} \sigma(\lambda I : \tau_1 . E_2)$. Assume $comp_{\tau_1} E_1$ holds; we have that $\sigma(\lambda I : \tau_1 . E_2)E_1 = (\lambda I : \tau_1 . \sigma E_2)E_1 \Rightarrow [E_2/I]\sigma E_1$. By the inductive hypothesis, $comp_{\pi \cup \{I : \tau_1\}, \tau_2} E_2$ holds, hence, $comp_{\tau_2} \sigma[E_1/I]E_2$ holds. Since I is not in the domain of σ, $comp_{\tau_2}[E_1/I]\sigma E_2$ holds also, and the result follows from Lemma 7.1.

(vi) **rec** $I : \tau . E$: It is helpful to note that τ must have the form $\tau_1 \to \tau_2 \to \cdots \to \tau_n \to \iota$, where $n \geq 0$. Then, for an expression, E_0, $comp_\tau E_0$ holds iff $comp_\iota E_0 E_1 E_2 \cdots E_n$ does, where $comp_{\tau_i} E_i$ all hold. So, we will prove $comp_\iota \sigma(\textbf{rec } I : \tau . E)E_1 E_2 \cdots E_n$.

   Recall that $[\![\varnothing \vdash \sigma(\textbf{rec } I : \tau . E) : \tau]\!]\varnothing = v$, where v is the "limit" of the family consisting of $v_0 = \bot$ and $v_{i+1} = [\![\{I : \tau\} \vdash \sigma E : \tau]\!]\{I = v_i\}$. In particular, this means $v \, a_1 a_2 \cdots a_n = b$, a proper meaning, iff for some $k \geq 0$, $v_k \, a_1 a_2 \cdots a_n = b$.

   Now, let the expression e_0 be **rec** $I : \tau, I$; so, $[\![\varnothing \vdash e_0 : \tau]\!]\varnothing = v_0$, and

$comp_\tau e_0$ holds because $comp_\iota e_0 \, E_1 \, E_2 \cdots E_n$ does. Next, let e_{i+1} be $[e_i / \text{I}]\sigma \text{E}$; so, $[\![\varnothing \vdash e_{i+1} : \tau]\!]\varnothing = v_{i+1}$, and $comp_\tau e_{i+1}$ holds, by the inductive hypothesis on E. Say that $[\![\varnothing \vdash (\textbf{rec } \text{I}:\tau.\sigma \text{E}) \text{E}_1 \, \text{E}_2 \cdots \text{E}_n : \iota]\!]\varnothing = [\![\varnothing \vdash \text{V}: \iota]\!]\varnothing$. Therefore, there is some $k \geq 0$ such that $[\![\varnothing \vdash e_k \, \text{E}_1 \, \text{E}_2 \cdots \text{E}_n : \iota]\!]\varnothing = [\![\varnothing \vdash \text{V}: \iota]\!]\varnothing$. Hence, $e_k \, \text{E}_1 \, \text{E}_2 \cdots \text{E}_n \Rightarrow^* \text{V}$.

To finish, we need some syntactic information. We write $\text{E} \sqsubseteq \text{E}'$ to say that $\text{E} \, \text{E}_1 \, \text{E}_2 \cdots \text{E}_n \Rightarrow^* \text{V}$ implies $\text{E}' \text{E}_1 \, \text{E}_2 \cdots \text{E}_n \Rightarrow^* \text{V}$. Now, it is easy to show for all $\varnothing \vdash e' : \tau$, $e_0 \sqsubseteq e'$. By induction on the structure of E, we get that $e \sqsubseteq e'$ implies $[e / \text{I}]\sigma \text{E} \sqsubseteq [e' / \text{I}]\sigma \text{E}$. So, we deduce, for all $i \geq 0$, that $e_i \sqsubseteq [\textbf{rec } \text{I}:\tau. \sigma \text{E} / \text{I}]\sigma \text{E} \sqsubseteq \textbf{rec } \text{I}:\tau. \sigma \text{E}$. In particular, $e_k \sqsubseteq \textbf{rec } \text{I}:\tau. \sigma \text{E}$, implying that $comp_\iota (\textbf{rec } \text{I}: \tau. \sigma \text{E}) \, \text{E}_1 \, \text{E}_2 \cdots \text{E}_n$ holds. $\square$

When the language is extended by (lazy) records and (eager) lists, adequacy holds, but more advanced proof techniques are needed; see Gunter 1992, Chapter 6. Lazy lists pose even more difficult problems; see Mosses and Plotkin 1987.

7.6 Type Abstractions

The appearance of τ in the language's syntax motivates the abstraction of types. Unlike Chapter 2, where we distinguished between type structures (''classes'') and type attributes and we abstracted only type structures, here we confront the issue of type-attribute abstractions. We use the syntax

$$\text{E} ::= \cdots \mid \textbf{lettype } \text{I} = \tau \textbf{ in } \text{E}$$

as in: **lettype** $A = int$ **in** $\lambda x : A. \, x + 1$. Should this phrase be well formed? We might say ''yes'' because the A in $x : A$ refers to *int*, and $(\lambda x : int. \, x + 1)$ is well formed. But there is justification for a ''no'' answer: The above might be read as a ''sugared'' form of $(\lambda A : *. \lambda x : A. \, x + 1) int$, where ''*'' names the collection of all type attributes. If the abstraction part of this expression is truly well formed, it should take arbitrary types for arguments, for example, $(\lambda A : *. \lambda x : A. \, x + 1) bool$, but this is malformed.

If we accept the ''no'' answer, then the uses of a type identifier like A are limited to those expressions that make no assumptions about the structure of the type denoted by A. Examples of such expressions are $(\lambda x : A.x)$ and $(\lambda x : (A \, list) list. \, \textbf{tl} \, (\textbf{tl} \, x))$. These are examples of *parameteric polymorphic functions*—functions that behave the same way regardless of the instantiation of the type identifier. The *second-order lambda calculus*, described in Chapter 8, formalizes the notion of parametric polymorphic function.

Here, we develop the consequences of a ''yes'' answer to the above question and treat the example as well formed, since this is done in the ML-like languages. In order to type check expressions like the above, the binding ($A = int$) must be saved to validate the well-formedness of $(\lambda x : A. \, x + 1)$. We add a new attribute, a *type environment*, to the typing rules. A type environment, represented by ρ, is a set of identifier, type attribute pairs, written in the form $\{i = \tau_i\}_{i \in I}$, where $I \subseteq$ Identifier is a finite set. An example type environment is $\rho_0 = \{A=int, B=bool\ list\}$. For a type expression, τ, we write $\rho\tau$ to denote the simultaneous substitution of the type identifiers defined in ρ for the type identifiers in τ. That is, $\rho\tau = [\tau_i/i]_{i \in I}\tau$, where $\rho = \{i = \tau_i\}_{i \in I}$. An example is $\rho_0((B \to C)list) = [int/A,\ bool\ list/B](B \to C)list = (bool\ list \to C)list$.

Figure 7.8 presents the current version of the language. The **lettype** construct adds new bindings to the type environment, and the type environment is used when the type of an identifier must be calculated. The typing for **lettype** $A=int$ **in** $(\lambda x:A.\ x+1)$ is

$$\textbf{(lettype } A = int \textbf{ in } (\lambda x:A.\ (x_{\rho_1,\pi_1}^{int} + 1_{\rho_1,\pi_1}^{int})_{\rho_1,\pi_1}^{int})_{\rho_1,\pi_0}^{int \to int})_{\rho_0,\pi_0}^{int \to int}$$

$$\text{where } \rho_0 = \{\ \}, \quad \rho_1 = \rho_0 \uplus \{A=int\}, \quad \pi_0 = \{\ \}, \text{ and } \pi_1 = \pi_0 \uplus \{x:A\}$$

The changes to the typing rules for identifier reference and lambda abstraction are crucial to the well-typing of this example: x has type int (and not A), and $\lambda x:A.\ x+1$ has type $int \to int$ (and not $A \to int$). The typing rules neatly match the copy rule for **lettype** :

lettype I$=\tau$ **in** E $\Rightarrow$ $[\tau/I]$E

The restriction on the **letttype** construct that I not be free in π prevents ambiguous expressions like **lettype** $A=bool$ **in** $(\lambda x:A.$ **lettype** $A=int$ **in** $x)$. This expression should have type $bool \to bool$, but it is easy to misread it and conclude that it has type $bool \to int$, since x has type A. So we disallow it.*

Figure 7.8 allows identifiers to have type attributes that are themselves identifiers. The merit in this strategy becomes apparent when we add opaque types to the language. Say that we code a simulated stack module:

> **lettype** *Intstack* = *int list*
> **in val** *empty* = **nil**,
>   **val** *push* = $\lambda n:int.\ \lambda s:Intstack.$ **cons** $n\ s$

We wish it to have the following type:

> { *empty*:*Intstack*, *push*: *int* $\to$ *Intstack* $\to$ *Intstack* }

But Figure 7.8 gives the code the type $\{empty:int\ list,\ push:int \to int\ list \to int\ list\}$, so some adjustments must be made. Two problems are (i) How do we know when a type should be opaque, as *Intstack* is above? (ii) How do we handle an opaque type identifier outside the scope of its definition?

---

* Another solution is to alter the typing rule for lambda abstraction, so that $\{I:\rho\tau_1\}$ is added to π, but this obscures the relation of the typing rules to the laws of predicate logic as developed in Chapters 8 and 10.

$E ::= N \mid \cdots \mid \textbf{null } E$

$\quad \mid E_1, E_2 \mid \textbf{let } E_1 \textbf{ in } E_2 \mid \textbf{val } I{=}E \mid I \mid E_1 \; E_2 \mid \lambda I{:}\tau.\, E \mid \textbf{lettype } I{=}\tau \textbf{ in } E$

$\tau ::= int \mid bool \mid \tau list \mid \pi \mid \tau_1 \to \tau_2 \mid I$

$\pi ::= \{\, i{:}\tau_i \,\}_{i \in I} \quad \text{where } I \subseteq \text{Identifier is finite}$

$\rho ::= \{\, i{=}\tau_i \,\}_{i \in I} \quad \text{where } I \subseteq \text{Identifier is finite}$

The typing rules from Figure 7.2 now use a type environment attribute:

$$\rho, \pi \vdash N{:}int \qquad\qquad \cdots \qquad\qquad \frac{\rho, \pi \vdash E{:}\tau list}{\rho, \pi \vdash \textbf{null } E{:}bool}$$

The other rules are:

$$\frac{\rho, \pi \vdash E_1 : \pi_1 \quad \rho, \pi \vdash E_2 : \pi_2}{\rho, \pi \vdash E_1, E_2 : \pi_1 \cup \pi_2} \qquad \frac{\rho, \pi \vdash E_1 : \pi_1 \quad \rho, \pi \uplus \pi_1 \vdash E_2 : \tau}{\rho, \pi \vdash \textbf{let } E_1 \textbf{ in } E_2 : \tau}$$

$$\frac{\rho, \pi \vdash E : \tau}{\rho, \pi \vdash \textbf{val } I{=}E : \{\, I{:}\tau \,\}} \qquad \rho, \pi \vdash I : \rho\tau, \quad \text{if } (I{:}\tau) \in \pi$$

$$\frac{\rho, \pi \vdash E_1 : \tau_1 \to \tau_2 \quad \rho, \pi \vdash E_2 : \tau_1}{\rho, \pi \vdash E_1 \; E_2 : \tau_2} \qquad \frac{\rho, \pi \uplus \{\, I{:}\tau_1 \,\} \vdash E : \tau_2}{\rho, \pi \vdash \lambda I{:}\tau_1.\, E : \rho\tau_1 \to \tau_2}$$

$$\frac{\rho \uplus \{\, I{=}\rho\tau \,\}, \pi \vdash E : \tau_1}{\rho, \pi \vdash \textbf{lettype } I{=}\tau \textbf{ in } E : \tau_1} \quad \text{if } I \notin FV(\pi)$$

where $FV(\pi)$ is defined:

$FV(int) = \varnothing = FV(bool)$ $\qquad$ $FV(I) = \{\, I \,\}$

$FV(\tau list) = FV(\tau)$ $\qquad\qquad$ $FV(\tau_1 \to \tau_2) = FV(\tau_1) \cup FV(\tau_2)$

$FV(\pi) = \bigcup_{(I{:}\tau) \in \pi} FV(\tau)$

Figure 7.8

To handle problem (i), we introduce a special construction, **abstype** I=τ **in** E, which we use when we desire that I=τ be an opaque type definition. Within the body, E, of the **abstype** definition, we use coercion operations to manually convert a value of type τ to type I and back. We use

> **absI**, which coerces a value of type τ into one of type I
>
> **repI**, which coerces a value of type I into one of type τ

The **absI** and **repI** operations preserve unicity of typing and help us control encapsulation, since we should not automatically infer that every τ-typed expression that appears in the body of the **abstype** is also I-typed.

We redo the *Intstack* example with the new notation:

> **abstype** *Intstack* = *int list*
> **in** **val** *empty* = abs*Intstack* **nil**,
>   **val** *push* = λ*n* :*int*.λ*s* :*Intstack*. **abs***Intstack*(**cons** *n* (**rep***Intstack s*))

Now it is clear that *empty* is a constant that names an *Intstack* value, and *push* is an operation that maps an integer and an *Intstack* value into an *Intstack* result.

Problem (ii) is more difficult to resolve. For **abstype** I=τ **in** E, we state its type as *exists*(I, π), where E has type π. Read the type as saying that there is some type, I, whose definition we cannot see, but it is used by the definitions named in π. In the above example, the type of the abstype is *exists*(*Intstack*, { *empty* :*Intstack*, *push* :*int* →*Intstack* →*Intstack* }).

If we treat an abstype as a "package" that must be "opened" before it is used, then we must introduce a form of **let** expression that opens the abstype. The expression is **open** E₁ **in** E₂, where E₁ is an abstype. A simple example follows:

> **let val** *S* = (**abstype** *Intstack* = *int list*
>   **in val** *empty* = abs*Intstack* **nil**,
>   **val** *push* = λ*n* :*int*.λ*s* :*Intstack*.abs*Intstack*(**cons** *n* (**rep***Intstack s*)),
>   **val** *top* = λ*s* :*Intstack*. **hd** (**rep***Intstack s*))
> **in** 2+(**open** *S* **in** *top*(*push* 3 *empty*)+4)

The operations of *S* are not available until *S* is opened, which is done for the expression *top*(*push* 3 *empty*)+4.

These ideas are formalized by Figure 7.9, and some explanation of the (I≡τ) binding is necessary. When the body, E, of the abstype **abstype** I=τ **in** E is type checked, the binding of I to τ must be in the type environment, ρ. But this binding is unlike a **lettype** binding: As noted above, an identifier that has type I should not be coerced automatically to have type τ. Hence, the binding (I≡τ) is treated differently from a

---

$E ::= \cdots \mid$ **abstype** $I = \tau$ **in** $E \mid$ **repI** $\mid$ **absI** $\mid$ **open** E_1 **in** E_2

$\rho ::= \{ i = \tau_i \}_{i \in I} \cup \{ j \equiv \tau_j \}_{j \in J}$ where $I, J \subseteq$ Identifier are finite and $I \cap J = \varnothing$

$$\frac{\rho \uplus \{ I \equiv \rho\tau \}, \pi \vdash E : \pi_1}{\rho, \pi \vdash \textbf{abstype } I = \tau \textbf{ in } E : exists(I, \pi_1)} \quad \text{if } I \notin FV(\pi)$$

$$\frac{\rho, \pi \vdash E : I}{\rho, \pi \vdash \textbf{repI } E : \tau} \quad \text{if } (I \equiv \tau) \in \rho \qquad\qquad \frac{\rho, \pi \vdash E : \tau}{\rho, \pi \vdash \textbf{absI } E : I} \quad \text{if } (I \equiv \tau) \in \rho$$

$$\frac{\rho, \pi \vdash E_1 : exists(I, \pi_1) \qquad \rho_{-I}, \pi \uplus \pi_1 \vdash E_2 : \tau}{\rho, \pi \vdash \textbf{open } E_1 \textbf{ in } E_2 : \tau} \quad \text{if } I \notin FV(\pi) \text{ and } I \notin FV(\tau)$$

where ρ_{-I} denotes: $\rho - \{ (I = \tau), (I \equiv \tau) \}$

and the definition of FV in Figure 7.8 is extended by: $FV(exists(I, \pi)) = FV(\pi) - \{ I \}$

Figure 7.9 _____

binding $(I = \tau)$: The former will be ignored by a substitution, for example, for $\rho_0 = \{ A = int, B \equiv bool \}$, $\rho_0(A \to B) = int \to B$. But $(I \equiv \tau)$ is used for the typing of the **absI** and **repI** operations, for example, $\rho_0, \{ x : B \} \vdash \textbf{repB } x : bool$ holds.

The typing of the previous example reads as follows:

$\textbf{(let (val } S = (\textbf{abstype } Intstack = int \ list$

$\quad\quad\quad \textbf{in (val } empty = (\textbf{abs}Intstack \ \text{nil}^{int \ list}_{\rho_1, \pi_0})^{Intstack}_{\rho_1, \pi_0})^{\{ empty : Intstack \}}_{\rho_1, \pi_0}$,

$\quad\quad\quad\quad (\textbf{val } push = \lambda n : int. \lambda s : Intstack. \ \cdots)^{\{ push : int \to Intstack \to Intstack \}}_{\rho_1, \pi_0}$,

$\quad\quad\quad\quad (\textbf{val } top = (\lambda s : Intstack. \ (\text{hd} \ (\textbf{rep}Intstack \ s^{Intstack}_{\rho_1, \pi_1})^{int \ list}_{\rho_1, \pi_1})^{int}_{\rho_1, \pi_1})^{Intstack \to int}_{\rho_1, \pi_0}$

$\quad\quad\quad\quad)^{\{ top : Intstack \to int \}}_{\rho_1, \pi_0})^{exists(Intstack, \pi_2)}_{\rho_0, \pi_0})^{\{ S : exists(Intstack, \pi_2) \}}_{\rho_0, \pi_0}$

$\quad\quad \textbf{in } (2^{int}_{\rho_0, \pi_3} + (\textbf{open } S^{exists(Intstack, \pi_2)}_{\rho_0, \pi_3} \ \textbf{in } (((top(push \ 3 \ empty))^{int}_{\rho_0, \pi_4} + 4^{int}_{\rho_0, \pi_4})^{int}_{\rho_0, \pi_4})^{int}_{\rho_0, \pi_3}$

$\quad\quad)^{int}_{\rho_0, \pi_3})^{int}_{\rho_0, \pi_0}$

where $\rho_0 = \{ \}$, $\rho_1 = \rho_0 \uplus \{ Intstack \equiv int \ list \}$

$\pi_0 = \{ \}$, $\pi_1 = \pi_0 \uplus \{ s : Intstack \}$

$\pi_2 = \{ empty : Intstack, \ push : int \to Intstack \to Intstack, \ top : Intstack \to int \}$

$\pi_3 = \pi_0 \uplus \{ s : exists(Intstack, \pi_2) \}$, $\pi_4 = \pi_0 \uplus \pi_2$

The binding (*Intstack*≡*int list*) is used only for the typing of the **absI** and **repI** operations. Once the typing of the body of *Intstack* completes, the binding (*Intstack*≡*int list*) is forgotten, and *Intstack* becomes opaque.

Some examples clarify these ideas. If A is not free in π (that is, $A \notin FV(\pi)$), then

$$\rho, \pi \vdash (\textbf{abstype } A = int \textbf{ in val } id = \lambda x{:}A.\ x) : exists(A, \{ id{:}A \rightarrow A \})$$

holds. It is crucial that the type of x remains A and not *int*. Contrast the previous example with

$$\rho, \pi \vdash (\textbf{abstype } B = int \textbf{ in val } coerce = \lambda x{:}B.\ \textbf{rep}B\ x) : exists(B, \{ id{:}B \rightarrow int \})$$

where the underlying type of x is revealed. A third example is:

$$\rho, \pi \vdash \textbf{abstype } C = int \textbf{ in val } succ = \lambda x{:}C.\ \textbf{abs}C((\textbf{rep}C\ x)+1)$$
$$: exists(C, \{ succ{:}C \rightarrow C \})$$

When an expression, E_1, has type $exists(I, \pi)$, its use in **open** E_1 **in** E_2 makes the operations, π, contained in E_1 visible to E_2, but the binding to I is unknown, since the type environment is ρ_{-I}. Like the **lettype** construct, the **abstype** construct must be restricted so that the opaque type name is not already free in the type assignment. This prevents confusing examples like this one:

lettype $A = bool$ **in** ($\lambda y{:}A.$ **abstype** $A = int$ **in val** $f = (\lambda x{:}A.\ y)$)

An important restriction is that the overall type of the **open** construct does not mention the opaque type. This prevents

lettype $A = bool$
         in let val $f =$ **open** (**abstype** $A = int$ **in val** $g = (\lambda x{:}A.\ \textbf{rep}A\ x)$) **in** g
            in $f\ true$

where f's type, $A \rightarrow int$, might be read mistakenly as $bool \rightarrow int$. The rewriting rules for **abstype** are straightforward:

open abstype $I = \tau$ **in** $\{ I_1 = E_1, \ \cdots, \ I_n = E_n \}$ **in** $E_0 \ \Rightarrow \ [\tau / I][E_1 / I_1, \ldots, E_n / I_n]E_0$

repτ(**abs**τ E) $\ \Rightarrow \ $ E

7.7 Variations on Type Abstractions

The **open** construct correctly uses an abstype, but it is restrictive. For example, we might wish to declare an abstype, open it once to create a value, and open it later to process that value:

> **let val** T = (**abstype** $A = \cdots$ **in val** a=**abs**$A(\cdots)$, **val** f=(λx:A. $\cdots$))
> **in let** v = (**open** T **in** a)
> **in** $\cdots$ (**open** T **in** ($f\,v$)) $\cdots$

The idea appears reasonable—after all, we are using the same abstype both times—but the restriction placed on the typing rule for the **open** construct disallows the example.

The abstype with the **open** construct is sometimes called the "weak" form of abstype. There is also a "strong" form, where the abstype is indexed like a record. If we use the strong form of abstype, we can recode the above example as

> **let val** T = (**abstype** $A = \cdots$ **in val** a=**abs**$A(\cdots)$, **val** f=(λx:A. $\cdots$))
> **in let** v=$T.a$
> **in** $\cdots$ ($T.f\ v$) $\cdots$

and it is well formed, because v has type $T.A$ (even the opaque type can be indexed), and $T.f$ takes as its argument a value of type $T.A$. But still there is encapsulation; if there was a second copy of the abstype, as in

> **let val** T = (**abstype** $A = \cdots$ **in val** a=**abs**$A(\cdots)$, **val** f = (λx:A. $\cdots$)),
> **val** U = (**abstype** $A = \cdots$ **in val** a=**abs**$A(\cdots)$, **val** f = (λx:A. $\cdots$))
> **in** $\cdots$ ($T.f\ \ U.a$) $\cdots$

the attempt to mix the operations of the two abstypes would fail: ($T.f\ \ U.a$) is malformed.

The issue of weak versus strong abstype proves important when module-based systems are coded. Typically, a key abstype is coded and distributed to all of a system's modules. The modules must be able to build upon the abstype and interface correctly. This is awkward with the weak form of abstype but is easier with the strong abstype. We develop some examples to show the strong abstype in action.

Say that we code two parameterized modules, M and N, that use abstype parameters. For the following series of examples, let $Ttype = exists(A, \{a{:}A, f{:}A \to int\})$, and let T be an abstype with type $Ttype$. We begin with this example:

> **val** M = (λr:$Ttype$. **val** v = $r.a$)
> **val** N = (λs:$Ttype$. **val** g = $s.f$)

M takes an abstype, r, as a parameter and uses r to build a module that contains a binding for v. N works similarly. M and N are invoked with the same abstype—here, T—in the main program:

val *MAIN* = **let** (*M T*) **in let** (*N T*) **in** $\cdots$ (*g v*) $\cdots$

MAIN is well typed, since *g* has type *T.A*→*int*, and *v* has type *T.A*.

A significant question about the above example is, What are the types of *M* and *N*? This issue comes to the fore in a version of the *MAIN* program that is independent of modules *M* and *N* and abstype *T*:

val *MAIN2* = λ*t* :*Ttype*.
$\qquad$ λ*m* : (*r* :*Ttype*)→{ *v* :*r.a* }.
$\qquad\qquad$ λ*n* : (*s* :*Ttype*)→{ *g* :*s.A* →*int* }.
$\qquad\qquad\qquad$ **let** (*m t*) **in let** (*n t*) **in** $\cdots$ (*g v*) $\cdots$

Since *m* represents a module parameterized on an abstype, *m* has function type. But the codomain of *m* depends on the *value* of the argument to *m*, and as depicted by *m*'s typing, (*r* :*Ttype*)→{ *v* :*r.a* }. This is an example of a *dependent type*, which will be studied in Chapter 8.

The typing information attached to *MAIN2*'s formal parameters allows *MAIN2* to be type checked; in particular, (*g v*) is well typed, since *g* has type *t.A* →*int* and *v* has type *t.A*. (Why?) Finally, the invocation (*MAIN2 T M N*) is well typed.

A trickier example to type check is this one:

val *MAIN3* = λ*m*: { *v*:α }.λ*n*: { *g*:α→*int* }. **let** *m* **in let** *n* **in** $\cdots$ (*g v*) $\cdots$

Here, *m* and *n* must bind to modules whose components "match" on an unknown type attribute, α. The α is a type variable, and it is best to make α into an argument to *MAIN3*:

val *MAIN3* = λα: *. λ*m*: { *v* :α }. λ*n*: { *g* :α→*int* }. **let** *m* **in let** *n* **in** $\cdots$ (*g v*) $\cdots$

That is, α is a *type parameter* that tells *MAIN3* the relationship between *v* and *g*. Now, this invocation is well typed: (*MAIN3 T.A* (*M T*) (*N T*)), since (*M T*) has type { *v* :*T.A* } and (*N T*) has type { *g* :*T.A* →*int* }.

If we wish to avoid type parameters like α, we can use a technique due to Burstall (1989), which parameterizes *MAIN* on the abstype used to instantiate *M* and *N*:

val *MAIN4* = λ*t* : *Ttype*. λ*m*: *Mtype* (*t*). λ*n*: *Ntype* (*t*). **let** *m* **in let** *n* **in** $\cdots$ (*g v*) $\cdots$
$\qquad$ where *Mtype* = λ*r* : *Ttype*. { *v*:*r.A* }
$\qquad$ and *Ntype* = λ*s* : *Ttype*. { *g* :*s.A* →*int* }

Here, we parameterize type expressions on values, and the type checker must use the β-rule to calculate the type of (*MAIN4 T* (*M T*) (*N T*)). The relation of parameterized type expressions to dependent types is close, but we delay consideration to Chapter 8.

The above solution has the drawback that *MAIN4* must know the identity of the abstype that was used to build the values bound to *m* and *n*. Here is yet another solution, based on MacQueen's module language in Standard ML (MacQueen 1984):

> **let val** $M' = \lambda r: Ttype.$ (**val** $R=r$; **val** $v=R.a$),
>
> $\quad$ **val** $N' = \lambda s: Ttype.$ (**val** $S=s$; **val** $g=S.f$),
>
> $\quad$ **val** $MAIN5 = \lambda m: \{ R:Ttype ; v:R.A \}. \lambda n: \{ S:Ttype ; g :S.A \rightarrow int \}.$
>
> $\qquad\qquad\qquad\qquad$ **sharing** $m.R=n.S$ **in** $\cdots$ (*n.g* *m.v*) $\cdots$
>
> **in** $MAIN5$ (*M' T*) (*N' T*)

This solution requires that *M'* and *N'* carry with them the abstypes they use. This allows the types of the formal parameters to *MAIN5* to state precisely the contents of the modules. A special clause, "**sharing** $m.R=n.S$," allows the type checker to validate the well-typing of *MAIN5*'s code. The sharing clause is also consulted to validate the invocation (*MAIN5* (*M' T*) (*N' T*)).

The above example differs from codings in Standard ML, which use a "signature" construct to specify the typing of modules. The **sharing** clauses are specified in the signatures, giving a smoother treatment than that shown here (Paulson 1991).

There is a surprising consequence to the inclusion of strong abstypes in the functional language: When combined with a lambda abstraction that has the dependent typing $(x{:}\tau_1) \rightarrow \tau_2$, the strong abstype construction destroys the strong normalization property of the language, even if the language core is strongly normalizing. A corollary is that type checking is not terminating, so compile-time type checking is lost. We will study these results in the next chapter, but an overview is useful.

Let η be a type, and let *n* be a value of type η. Then, for any type, τ, **abstype** $X=\tau$ **in** $\{a=n\}$ has type $exists(X, \{a{:}\eta\})$; call this type, *B*. The strong abstype is merely a "container" for τ, since τ can be extracted by indexing:

> (**abstype** $X=\tau$ **in** $\{a=n\}$).X $\Rightarrow$ τ

If we build such abstypes for all $\tau \in PhraseType$, they all have type *B*; thus, *B* can be considered the set of all phrase types.

But *B* is itself a type, and we have $\rho, \pi \vdash$ **abstype** $X=B$ **in** $\{a=n\}{:}B$, suggesting that *B* represents a set that contains itself! It is not surprising that a consequence of this situation is that *B*-typed terms can code self-application and introduce nontermination into the language, even if it was not in the language core. Further, since we can embed value expressions into type expressions, for example, $((\lambda Z{:}B.\ Z)$ (**abstype** $X=B$ **in** $\{a=n\}$)).X, nontermination spreads to the language of type expressions, ruining compile-time type checking. The details of this development can be found in Coquand 1986, Meyer and Reinhold 1986, and Hook and Howe 1986.

Standard ML avoids the above problem with strong abstypes by a language split: Its *value sublanguage* allows (implicit) dependent typing but only weak abstypes. Standard ML's *module sublanguage* is built on top of its value sublanguage, and it allows a version of strong abstype where the τ in (**abstype** $X = \tau$ **in** $\cdots$) can range over all types in the value sublanguage but is limited in the types over which it can range in the module sublanguage. A type like B cannot be defined. Harper and Mitchell 1993 makes precise the structure of Standard ML.

We conclude this section by examining a number of miscellaneous issues related to type abstractions. The first is variant types. In Standard ML, a variant type is introduced by a **datatype** construct, and values of the variant type are processed by functions coded in pattern matching style. Here is an example:

> **datatype** *USAmoney* = *penny* | *nickel* | *dime* | *quarter* | *bill* **of** *int*;
> **val** *worth penny* = 1
> | *worth nickel* = 5
> | *worth dime* = 10
> | *worth quarter* = 25
> | *worth* (*bill n*) = *n* ∗ 100
> **in let val** *x* = *dime* , **val** *y* = *bill* 5 **in** (*worth x*) + (*worth y*)

The variant type, *USAmoney*, has five variants; the tags are *penny, nickel, dime, quarter*, and *bill*. Only the last tag labels a component. Function *worth* uses pattern matching to define its actions on each of the variants.

The **datatype** construct resembles an abstype, where the tags are operations that build elements of the type. Indeed, the coercion operations **absI** and **repI** of an opaque type, I, can be conveniently coded with variant tags. Here is a recoding of the *Intstack* example in ML-style:

> **abstype** *Intstack* = *st* **of** *int list*
> **in val** *empty* = *st* **nil**,
>   **val** *push n* (*st s*) = *st*(**cons** *n s*)

There is only one variant tag, *st*, in this simple example, and it replaces the **abs***Intstack* operation. The **rep***Intstack* operation is replaced by the pattern matching facility (cf. the second argument to *push*). Here is a more interesting example, where stacks are modeled by a recursively defined type and a set of operations:

```
rec-abstype Intstack = nil | cons of { hd : int, tl : Intstack }
in val empty = nil,
    val push n s = cons(val hd=n, val tl=s ),
    val isempty nil = true
    | val isempty (cons r ) = false
    val top (cons r ) = r.hd,
    val pop (cons r ) = r.tl
```

Stacks are modeled as records with *hd* and *tl* fields, and pattern matching guides the operations and converts values of opaque type into their representation type. Finally, *top* and *pop* are only partially defined, since Standard ML automatically generates a failure for missing cases like *top nil*.

7.8 Type Parameters

Type parameters let us create *parametric polymorphic functions*. Recall that a polymorphic function handles arguments from all types uniformly. We can code examples like this:

```
let val polyid = λt :*.λx :t. x,
    val twice = λt :*.λf :t→t.λx :t. f (f x )
in · · · (polyid bool true) · · · (polyid (int list) (cons 3 nil))
    · · · (twice int (polyid int) 0) · · ·
```

The functions *polyid* and *twice* can be instantiated to operate on arguments from any type, and the β-rule serves as the copy rule for the polymorphic functions, for example, $(\lambda t :*.\lambda x :t. x)bool\,true \Rightarrow (\lambda x :bool. x)true \Rightarrow true$. Polymorphic functions differ from the example at the beginning of Section 7.4: **lettype** $A=int$ **in** $\lambda x :A.x+1$. That example displayed a *monomorphic* (i.e., ''single-typed'') function, where the identifier A was merely an alias for type *int*. Also, polymorphic functions differ from *overloaded* operations. An operation is overloaded if it names several unrelated operations, one of which is selected based on the types of the arguments to the operation. For example, the + symbol is often overloaded to represent integer addition, real addition, logical disjunction, and set union: 3.4+2.0 represents an addition of reals, {}+{2} represents a set union, and so on.

An obvious question to ask is, What is the type of a polymorphic function? We might write $* \to t \to t$, but this will not do, since t is free. Instead, we write a dependent type, $(t :*) \to (t \to t)$, because the overall type depends on the value of the first argument. Indeed, the first argument acts as a "quantifier" to the rest, so a format that is commonly used is $\forall t:*.\, t \rightarrow t$, or just $\forall t.\, t \rightarrow t$. The last format is particularly relevant to the typing system in ML, which is explored in Section 7.8.

Types might also be parameters to other types:

> **lettype** *Fun* = $\lambda t:*.\, t \rightarrow t$
> **in let val** *twice* = $\lambda t:*.\, \lambda f:(Fun\; t).\, \lambda x:t.\; f(f\, x)$,
>   **val** *test* = $\lambda g:Fun\,(Fun\; int).\; g\,(\lambda x:int.x)$
>   **in** $\cdots$ (*twice int* $(\lambda y:int.y+1)$ 3) $\cdots$ (*test* (*twice int*)) $\cdots$

The "metatype" of *Fun* is $* \rightarrow *$, because it maps a type name into a new type name. In order to validate the well-formedness of the example, the metatype of *Fun* must be retained, and the β-rule must be applied to type attributes to uncover the types represented by (*Fun int*) and (*Fun* (*Fun int*)). This is developed at length in the next chapter.

We can use type parameters to define generic abstypes. The *Intstack* example of the previous section is generalized to this:

> **let** *stack* = $\lambda t:*.$ **abstype** *S* = *t list*
>   **in val** *empty* = **abs***S* **nil**,
>   **val** *push* = $\lambda n:t.\, \lambda s:S.$ **abs***S* (**cons** *n* (**rep***S s*))
> **in** (**open** (*stack int*) **in** $\cdots$ (*push* 3 *empty*) $\cdots$)

The type of *stack* is $(t:*) \rightarrow exists(S, \{\, empty:S, push:t \rightarrow S \rightarrow S \,\})$, that is, *stack* is a function from type names into abstypes, and the type of the abstype is dependent on the value of the argument to *stack*. When *stack* is opened, a type must be supplied, so that the operations of the abstype can be typed. In the example, *stack* is initialized by type *int*, and *push* gets type $int \rightarrow S \rightarrow S$.

The version of generic abstype in Standard ML allows the type parameter to be an argument to the operations of the abstype:

> **let** *stack'* = **abstype** *S* = $(\lambda t:*.\, t\; list)$
>   **in val** *empty* = $\lambda t:*.$ **abs**(*S t*) **nil**,
>   **val** *push* = $\lambda t:*.\lambda n:t.\, \lambda s:(S\; t).$ **abs**(*S t*) (**cons** *n* (**rep**(*S t*) *s*))
> **in** (**open** *stack'* **in** $\cdots$ (*push int* 3 (*empty int*))
> $\cdots$ (*push bool true* (*empty bool*)) $\cdots$)

The "type" that is encapsulated by the abstype is in fact a function on types, so the type of *stack'* is $exists(S: * \rightarrow *, \{\, empty: (t:*) \rightarrow (S\; t), push: (t:*) \rightarrow t \rightarrow (S\; t) \rightarrow (S\; t) \,\})$. The metatype of *S* is displayed so that it can be verified that the type expression (*S t*) is sensible. When opened, the abstype can be used in different ways within the scope of a single **open** construct, as seen in the example.

Given the complexity of this notation, Standard ML hides type parameters from the user and lets the implementation maintain them. In Section 7.8, we see how this is done.

7.9 Semantics of Type Abstractions and Type Parameters

It is nontrivial to give a mathematically well-founded denotational semantics to type abstractions and type parameters. A fundamental problem is self-containment—values can contain themselves. Here is the standard example of this phenomenon.

With type parameters, we are able to code $\lambda t{:}*.\lambda x{:}t.\, x$. A denotational semantics must therefore produce a meaning for this program such that

$$[\![\varnothing \vdash \lambda t{:}*.\lambda x{:}t.\, x : (t{:}*) \rightarrow t \rightarrow t]\!]\varnothing \in [\![(t{:}*) \rightarrow t \rightarrow t]\!]$$

The set-theoretical meaning of $(\lambda t{:}*.\lambda x{:}t.\, x)$ is apparently a set $S = \{(t, id_t) \mid t \in *\}$ of argument, answer pairs, where id_t is the set-theoretic representation of the identity function on elements of type t. Then, $((t{:}*) \rightarrow (t \rightarrow t), id_{(t{:}*)\rightarrow(t\rightarrow t)})$ is one of the pairs in S. But $id_{(t{:}*)\rightarrow(t\rightarrow t)}$ is itself a set of argument, answer pairs, one of which must be (S, S)! This development violates the foundation axiom of set theory, and indeed, Reynolds proved that no model of the second-order lambda calculus can use function sets as meanings of the terms (Reynolds 1984).

There are non–set-theoretic models for type abstractions, but their development goes well beyond the scope of this text. For this reason, from this point onward we will rely heavily upon the rewriting rules to describe the behavior of type abstractions and parameters.

Chapters 8 and 10 examine related issues.

7.10 Type Inference

Despite the insight they provide, type parameters soon become tedious to read and write. It is convenient to omit typing information from expressions and let the types be inferred from context. For example, for the definition of *polyid* in Section 7.6, since 3 has type *int*, the phrase (*polyid* 3) abbreviates (*polyid int* 3). The ML-like languages are defined so that type information is omitted, as a type checker (more precisely, a *type inference algorithm*) can infer it from context. In this section, we define the syntax of an ML-like language and give a brief description of the Hindley-Milner type inference algorithm for the language.

An *ML-like language* is a core functional language augmented by lambda abstraction and an expression block called a "**let** expression." Examples of ML-like languages

---

E ∈ Value-expression
I ∈ Identifier
op ∈ Primitive-operators-and-constants
    E ::= *op* | I | E$_1$ E$_2$ | λI. E | **let** I=E$_1$ **in** E$_2$

Figure 7.10 _____

---

are Standard ML, CAML, Miranda, and Haskell. Figure 7.10 gives the syntax. Although no type expressions appear in value expressions, the value expressions are *implicitly typed*, because data type compatibilities are still enforced.

    The successor function on integers can be coded (λ*x. plus x* 1), and the parametric polymorphic identity operation can be coded (λ*x.x*). The type inference algorithm deduces that the type of the former function is *int* → *int* (the type of *plus :int* → *int* → *int* is the key), and the type of the latter function is α → α. The symbol, α, is a *placeholder* or *type variable*. We will see that the quantified version, ∀α. α → α, is a more correct rendition of the type for the polymorphic identity function. We call such a quantified type a *polymorphic type*. Unquantified type expressions are called *monomorphic types*. The operations upon lists have polymorphic types:

    cons : ∀α. α × α*list* → α*list*
    hd : ∀α. α*list* → α
    tl : ∀α. α*list* → α*list*
    null : ∀α. α*list* → *bool*
    nil: ∀α. α*list*

The quantifiers read like the ones in logic and they allow a polymorphic operation to be used in different ways in the same expression. For example

    (**hd** (**cons** (λ*x.x*) **nil**)) (**cons** 3 **nil**)

is a well-formed expression; the second occurrence of **cons** has its type variable instantiated to *int*, and the first occurrence has its type variable instantiated to (*int list* → *int list*). The type variables for **nil** are similarly instantiated. If we recall the notation used in the previous section, we see that the example abbreviates this long-winded expression:

(**hd** (*int list* → *int list*) (**cons** (*int list* → *int list*) ((λ*t* :*.λx* :*t. x*) (*int list*)) (**nil** *int list*)))
        (**cons** *int* 3 (**nil** *int*))

Harper and Mitchell (1993) have defined an algorithm that translates any well-formed implicitly typed expression of the language of Figure 7.10 into its explicit typed form.

There is a marked difference in the typing assigned to the **let** expression versus the typing assigned to the lambda abstraction, implying that (**let** I=E_1 **in** E_2) does *not* correspond to ((λI. E_2)E_1). The **let** expression defines an operation, I, with polymorphic type, for use in E_2. In contrast, the binding identifier, I, in (*lam*I. E) binds only to arguments of monomorphic type. For example, the expression

> **let** *id* = ($\lambda x.x$) **in** (*id id*)

is well formed, because *id* has type $\forall \alpha. \alpha \rightarrow \alpha$, and the α can be instantiated in the first use of *id* by $\beta \rightarrow \beta$ and in the second use of *id* by β. So, the overall expression has type $\beta \rightarrow \beta$ (or $\forall \beta. \beta \rightarrow \beta$, if the the free variable, β, is quantified). But

> ($\lambda id.\ id\ id$)($\lambda x.x$)

is not well formed, because *id* must be given a monomorphic type, and there is no such type τ such that τ is identical to $\tau \rightarrow \tau$. The restriction on the type of the binding identifier of a lambda abstraction to a monomorphic type is an inherent feature of the type inference algorithm; Kfoury, Tiuryn, and Urzyczyn (1990b) proved that it is impossible to extend the algorithm to make binding identifiers polymorphic.

Now we consider the type inference algorithm, called the *Hindley-Milner algorithm* or *Algorithm W*. Figure 7.11 gives the syntax of the data types that the algorithm uses. We will continue to use the term "polymorphic type" to refer to an element of Type-scheme that has at least one quantifier. A key consequence of Figure 7.12 is that no element of Type-expression can contain a polymorphic type as a subexpression. This rules out type expressions like $(\forall \alpha. \alpha \rightarrow \alpha) \rightarrow (\forall \alpha. \alpha \rightarrow \alpha)$, which is a plausible typing for

---

$\sigma \in$ Type-scheme
$\tau \in$ Type-expression
$\alpha \in$ Placeholder
$p \in$ Primitive-type

$\sigma ::= \forall \alpha_1. \forall \alpha_2. \cdots \forall \alpha_n. \tau, \quad$ where $n \geq 0$

$\tau ::= p \mid \alpha \mid \tau_1 \rightarrow \tau_2$

$FV(\forall \alpha_1. \forall \alpha_2. \cdots \forall \alpha_n. \tau) = FV(\tau) - \{ \alpha_1, \alpha_2, \ldots, \alpha_n \}$,

$FV(p) = \{ \}, \quad FV(\alpha) = \{ \alpha \}, \quad$ and $\quad FV(\tau_1 \rightarrow \tau_2) = FV(\tau_1) \cup FV(\tau_2)$

Figure 7.11 _____

($\lambda id.\ id\ id$). The polymorphic types for an ML-like language are called "shallowly quantified types" for this reason: The quantifiers in a type scheme can appear only at the very left, or "shallow level," of the scheme.

The type inference algorithm makes crucial use of Robinson's unification algorithm. We require some definitions. A *substitution*, denoted by the letter, U, is a mapping from placeholders to type expressions. For example, $U_0 = \{ \alpha = int,\ \beta = (\gamma \rightarrow bool) \}$ is a substitution that maps placeholder α to type expression *int* and maps β to $\gamma \rightarrow bool$. We *apply* a substitution U to a type expression τ, written $U\tau$, by replacing all placeholders α in τ by τ' when $(\alpha = \tau') \in U$. An example is

$$U_0((\beta \rightarrow \delta) \rightarrow \gamma) = ((\gamma \rightarrow bool) \rightarrow \delta) \rightarrow \gamma$$

Given substitutions U_1 and U_2, we write $U_2 \circ U_1$ to represent the composition of the substitutions: $(U_2 \circ U_1)\tau = U_2(U_1\tau)$.

A substitution U is a *unifier* of two type expressions τ_1 and τ_2 if $U\tau_1 = U\tau_2$. For example, U_0 is a unifier of the two type expressions $\alpha \rightarrow \beta$ and $int \rightarrow \beta$. A unifier, U, is a *most general unifier* of type expressions τ_1 and τ_2 if it is a unifier of them, and for any other unifier, U', of τ_1 and τ_2, there is some substitution, V, such that $U' = V \circ U$. For example, a most general unifier of $\alpha \rightarrow \beta$ and $int \rightarrow \beta$ is the substitution $\{ \alpha = int \}$.

The intuition is that a substitution is used to make a type expression "more specific." For example, if we have deduced that $\alpha \rightarrow \alpha$ is an appropriate type expression for $(\lambda x.x)$, we can make the type expression more specific with a substitution, such as $\{ \alpha = bool \}$. The new type expression, $bool \rightarrow bool$, is another acceptable typing for $(\lambda x.x)$. Unifiers are used to combine the type expressions for two subexpressions into a type expression for an entire expression. Say that $\alpha \rightarrow \alpha$ is the type expression deduced for $(\lambda x.x)$, and $(int \rightarrow \beta) \rightarrow \beta$ is the type expression for $(\lambda f.f\ 2)$, and we wish to deduce the type of $(\lambda f.f\ 2)(\lambda x.x)$. The substitution $\{ \alpha = int,\ \beta = int \}$ is a unifier of $int \rightarrow \beta$ and $\alpha \rightarrow \alpha$. When we apply the unifier to the types of the two expressions, we deduce that $(int \rightarrow int) \rightarrow int$ is an acceptable typing for $(\lambda f.f\ 2)$, that $int \rightarrow int$ is an acceptable typing for $(\lambda x.x)$, and that *int* is an acceptable typing for $(\lambda f.f\ 2)(\lambda x.x)$. If the unifier is a most general unifier, we know that the minimum amount of substitution was performed to deduce an acceptable typing for the overall expression from the typings of its components. For the example, a most general unifier is indeed $\{ \alpha = int,\ \beta = int \}$.

Robinson defined an algorithm, which we call *mgu*, that calculates a most general unifier for two type expressions, if some unifier exists. Robinson's algorithm has been used in resolution-based theorem provers, Prolog implementations, and the type inference algorithm we give below. We do not present the unification algorithm here; it is an interesting exercise to derive it (think of it as a tree-matching algorithm, where type expressions are represented as trees), but you should ultimately consult Robinson's original paper (Robinson 1965) or any book on theorem proving for the correct algorithm.

As usual, we employ a type assignment, π, to bind identifiers to type schemes. We write $U\pi$ to represent the application of U to all the type expressions in π. For

$$\pi \vdash op : \{\ \}, \{\alpha_1 = \beta_1, \ldots, \alpha_n = \beta_n\}\tau$$

> where $\forall \alpha_1 \cdots \alpha_n.\tau$ is the type scheme for primitive operator op, $n \geq 0$, $\beta_1, \ldots, \beta_n$ are fresh placeholders, and $\{\ \}$ represents the empty substitution

$$\pi \vdash I : \{\ \}, \{\alpha_1 = \beta_1, \ldots, \alpha_n = \beta_n\}\tau$$

> if $(I: \forall \alpha_1 \cdots \forall \alpha_n.\tau) \in \pi$, $n \geq 0$, and $\beta_1, \ldots, \beta_n$ are fresh placeholders

$$\frac{\pi \vdash E_1 : U_1, \tau_1 \qquad (U_1 \pi) \vdash E_2 : U_2, \tau_2}{\pi \vdash E_1\ E_2\ :\ U_3 \circ U_2 \circ U_1, U_3 \alpha} \quad \text{if } U_3 = mgu(U_2 \tau_1, \tau_2 \to \alpha), \text{ where } \alpha \text{ is fresh}$$

$$\frac{\pi \uplus \{I : \alpha\} \vdash E : U, \tau}{\pi \vdash \lambda I.\ E\ :\ U, (U\alpha \to \tau)} \quad \text{where } \alpha \text{ is fresh}$$

$$\frac{\pi \vdash E_1 : U_1, \tau_1 \qquad (U_1 \pi) \uplus \{I : Clos\ (U_1 \pi)\ \tau_1\} \vdash E_2 : U_2, \tau_2}{\pi \vdash \textbf{let } I = E_1 \textbf{ in } E_2\ :\ U_2 \circ U_1, \tau_2}$$

Figure 7.12

example, for $U_1 = \{\alpha = int,\ \beta = \gamma \to bool\}$ and $\pi_1 = \{A: \beta \to int,\ B: \gamma,\ C: \alpha \to \beta\}$, we have $U_1 \pi_1 = \{A: (\gamma \to bool) \to int,\ B: \gamma,\ C: int \to (\gamma \to bool)\}$.

Finally, say that we have deduced that $\pi \vdash E: \tau$ holds, and we wish to force E to have a polymorphic type; that is, we wish to quantify all the placeholders in τ. We write $Clos\ \pi\ \tau$ to denote $\forall \alpha_1 \forall \alpha_2 \cdots \forall \alpha_n.\tau$, where $\alpha_1, \alpha_2, \ldots, \alpha_n$ are all the placeholders in τ that are not free in π. (A placeholder is *free in* π if it is in $FV(\tau)$, for some $(I:\tau) \in \pi$, where FV is defined in Figure 7.11.) For example, if we have deduced

$$\{x: \beta\} \vdash (\lambda f.\lambda y.\ f\ x\ y): (\beta \to \gamma \to \delta) \to \gamma \to \delta$$

then

$$Clos\ \{x: \beta\}\ (\beta \to \gamma \to \delta) \to \gamma \to \delta\ =\ \forall \gamma.\forall \delta.(\beta \to \gamma \to \delta) \to \gamma \to \delta$$

which is the "most polymorphic" type that is acceptable for $(\lambda f.\lambda y.f\ x\ y)$ in the type assignment $\{x: \beta\}$.

Algorithm W, the type inference algorithm for the ML-like language, is given in inference rule form in Figure 7.12. (The version given here is due to Tofte 1988.) Typings take the form $\pi \vdash E: U, \tau$, where π is a type assignment, U is a substitution, and τ is a type expression. Figure 7.13 gives the typing for the example **let** $id = (\lambda x.x)$ **in** $(id\ id)\ n$.

$\pi_0 = \{ n : \eta \}, \ \pi_1 = \pi_0 \uplus \{ x : \alpha \}, \ \pi_2 = \pi_0 \uplus \{ id : \forall \alpha. \ \alpha \to \alpha \}$

$U_1 = \{ \beta = \gamma \to \gamma, \ \delta = \gamma \to \gamma \}$

$U_2 = \{ \gamma = \eta, \ \varepsilon = \eta \} \circ U_1 = \{ \beta = \eta \to \eta, \ \gamma = \eta, \ \delta = (\eta \to \eta) \to (\eta \to \eta), \ \varepsilon = \eta \}$

$$\pi_0 \vdash E : U_2, \eta$$

$$\begin{array}{c}\qquad\qquad / \qquad\qquad\qquad\qquad\qquad \backslash \\ \textbf{let } id = \quad \pi_0 \vdash E : \{\ \}, \alpha \to \alpha \quad \textbf{in} \quad \pi_2 \vdash E : U_2, \eta \end{array}$$

$$\begin{array}{c}\qquad\qquad\qquad | \qquad\qquad\qquad\qquad\qquad / \qquad\qquad \backslash \\ (\lambda x. \quad \pi_1 \vdash E : \{\ \}, \alpha\ ) \quad \pi_2 \vdash E : U_1, \gamma \to \gamma \qquad \pi_2 \vdash E : \{\ \}, \eta \\ x \qquad\qquad\qquad\qquad / \qquad \backslash \qquad\qquad\qquad n \end{array}$$

$$\begin{array}{c}\pi_2 \vdash E : \{\ \}, \beta \to \beta \quad \pi_2 \vdash E : \{\ \}, \gamma \to \gamma \\ id \qquad\qquad\qquad\qquad id\end{array}$$

Figure 7.13 _____

Algorithm W never assigns a polymorphic type to an expression; for example, it deduces that $\pi \vdash (\lambda x.x) : U, \ \alpha \to \alpha$, rather than $\pi \vdash (\lambda x.x) : U, \forall \alpha. \alpha \to \alpha$; the user must "manually" compute *Clos* $\pi \ \alpha \to \alpha$ to obtain the polymorphic type of the overall expression.

In what sense does Algorithm W perform properly? For example, the expression $(\lambda x.x)$ might be typed $int \to int$, $bool \to bool$, and so on, but Algorithm W calculates $\alpha \to \alpha$, which seems to be the "best" choice. Hindley and Damas and Milner proved that Algorithm W always assigns the best, or *principal*, type to an expression. A bit of formalization is necessary to make the point.

Figure 7.14 gives typing rules for a typed version of the language in Figure 7.10. The rules define all the ways that an expression can be well typed. The rule set lacks unicity of typing; in particular, $(\lambda x.x)$ can be typed in all of the ways noted above. Given a type assignment, π, and an expression, E, we say that τ is the *principal type for* E *in* π, if $\pi \vdash E : \tau$, and for all other type-expressions τ' such that $\pi \vdash E : \tau'$, we have that *Clos* $\pi \ \tau \sqsubseteq \tau'$. ($\sqsubseteq$ is defined in Figure 7.14.) That is, the principal type is the "most general" in the sense that all other typings are substitution instances of it.

It can be proved that every expression, E, has a unique principal type in a given π, and it can also be shown that, if Algorithm W calculates $\pi \vdash E : U, \tau$ for E and π, then τ is the principal type for E in π. For details, see Hindley 1969 and Damas and Milner 1982.

$$\frac{(\forall \alpha_1 \cdots \forall \alpha_n . \tau') \sqsubseteq \tau}{\pi \vdash op : \tau} \quad \text{if } (\forall \alpha_1 \cdots \forall \alpha_n . \tau') \text{ is the type scheme for } op, \ n \geq 0$$

$$\frac{(\text{I}:\sigma) \in \pi \quad \sigma \sqsubseteq \tau}{\pi \vdash \text{I}:\tau} \qquad \frac{\pi \vdash \text{E}_1 : \tau_1 \rightarrow \tau_2 \quad \pi \vdash \text{E}_2 : \tau_1}{\pi \vdash (\text{E}_1 \ \text{E}_2) : \tau_2}$$

$$\frac{\pi \uplus \{ \text{I}:\tau_1 \} \vdash \text{E}:\tau_2}{\pi \vdash \lambda \text{I.E}: \tau_1 \rightarrow \tau_2} \qquad \frac{\pi \vdash \text{E}_1 : \tau_1 \quad \pi \uplus \{ \text{I}: Clos \ \pi \ \tau_1 \} \vdash \text{E}_2 : \tau_2}{\pi \vdash \textbf{let } \text{I}=\text{E}_1 \textbf{ in } \text{E}_2 : \tau_2}$$

where $(\forall \alpha_1 \cdots \forall \alpha_n . \tau') \sqsubseteq \tau$, $n \geq 0$,

if there is a substitution, $U = \{ \alpha_1 = \tau_1 , \ldots , \alpha_n = \tau_n \}$, such that $U\tau' = \tau$

Figure 7.14 _____

7.11 Prolog and Logic Programming Languages

In the previous section, we applied placeholders and unification to calculate types. Now we use these tools to calculate values. We will find that a particular core language with placeholders naturally develops into a Prolog subset.

Say that we design a core language of boolean expressions with placeholders. Given a boolean expression as input, the evaluator tries to find values for the placeholders that makes the expression true. For example, for the expression $X=john$ to be true, the evaluator would calculate that the placeholder, X, must get the value, $john$, and the output would be the substitution $\{X=john\}$. An expression like $X=john$ or $mary=X$ has more than one acceptable substitution, so the output is in fact a list of substitutions, $[\{X = john\}, \{X = mary\}]$. (We use the notation $[d_1, d_2, \ldots, d_n]$ to mean a list with n elements.)

The meaning sets and operations for such a language are given in Figure 7.15. There is a set of constant names and a set of placeholders; an atom is either a constant or a placeholder. A substitution is a finite mapping from placeholders to atoms, like the substitutions in the previous section. The key operation is *unify*, which unifies two input atoms after the input substitution has been applied to them. If the unification succeeds, the answer is the substitution generated by the unification composed with the input substitution. The operation *mgu* is the most general unifier operation from the previous section. For the moment, we unify only atoms, but later we extend unification to arbitrary terms.

The syntax of the language is presented in Figure 7.16. The typing rules for the language say little, which is typical for a Prolog-like language. We gain insight from the

Constant = { *john, mary, bread, cheese,* . . . }   (no operations)

Placeholder = { *X, Y, Z,* . . . }   (no operations)

Atom = *Constant* ∪ *Placeholder*   (no operations)

Subst = { { $i = a_i$ }$_{i \in I}$ | $I \subseteq Placeholder$ is finite, and for all $i \in I$, $a_i \in Atom$ }
    unify: *Atom* × *Atom* × *Subst* → *Subst* ∪ { *fail* }
        unify (a, b, σ) = *if*$(\sigma'=fail,\ fail,\ \sigma' \circ \sigma)$, where $\sigma' = mgu(\sigma a, \sigma b)$

Slist = { $[s_1, s_2, \ldots, s_n]$ | $n \geq 0$, $1 \leq i \leq n$, $s_i \in Subst$ }
    @: *Slist* × *Slist* → *Slist*
        $[s_1, \ldots, s_m]@[s_1', \ldots, s_n'] = [s_1, \ldots, s_m, s_1', \ldots, s_n']$

Figure 7.15 _____

_____

B ∈ Bool-expression
G ∈ Guarded-bool-expr
A ∈ Atom
    B ::= B_1, B_2 | **true** | **cases** A **of** G **end**
    G ::= A:B | G_1 [] G_2
    τ ::= *comm* | *guard* | *atom*

$$\frac{B_1: comm \quad B_2: comm}{B_1, B_2: comm} \qquad \textbf{true}: comm \qquad \frac{A: atom \quad G: guard}{\textbf{cases } A \textbf{ of } G \textbf{ end}: comm}$$

$$\frac{A: atom \quad B: comm}{A:B: guard} \qquad \frac{G_1: guard \quad G_2: guard}{G_1 \text{ [] } G_2: guard} \qquad a: atom, \text{ for all } a \in Atom$$

Figure 7.16 _____

core language's denotational semantics, which appears in Figure 7.17. Bool-expression constructs are functions on substitution lists. (Think of a substitution list as a form of store.) B_1, B_2 represents sequencing of commands, where the output substitution list from B_1 is given to B_2 as its input, and B_2 produces the final output substitution list. The bool expression **true** represents the identity mapping on substitution lists. The evaluation of **cases** A **of** G **end** goes as follows: One by one, the substitutions in the input substitution list are given as arguments to G. The atom, A, is passed as a

$$[\![B_1, B_2 : comm]\!]l = [\![B_2 : comm]\!]([\![B_1 : comm]\!]l)$$

$$[\![\textbf{true} : comm]\!]l = l$$

$$[\![\textbf{cases } A \textbf{ of } G \textbf{ end} : comm]\!][s_1, s_2, \dots, s_n] =$$

$$([\![G : guard]\!](A, s_1)) @ ([\![G : guard]\!](A, s_2)) @ \cdots @ ([\![G : guard]\!](A, s_n))$$

$$[\![A{:}B : guard]\!](a, s) = if(s' \neq fail, [\![B : guard]\!][s'], [\,]), \text{ where } s' = unify(A, a, s)$$

$$[\![G_1 \,[\!]\, G_2]\!](a, s) = [\![G_1 : guard]\!](a, s) @ [\![G_2 : guard]\!](a, s)$$

where $[\![comm]\!] = Slist \rightarrow Slist$ and $[\![guard]\!] = Atom \times Subst \rightarrow Subst$

Figure 7.17

companion argument. Each substitution given to G generates an output substitution list. The substitution lists are appended to together into one list, which is the output from the **cases** construct.

A guarded bool expression, G, takes an atom and a substitution as arguments and uses them to generate a substitution list. The real computational work in the language is done by the construct A:B, which uses the *unify* operation in Figure 7.15: A:B computes $unify(A, a, \sigma)$, where a is the atom at the head of the cases construct and σ is the input substitution. If *unify* succeeds in producing a new substitution, the substitution is given, as a singleton list, to B, and B generates an output substitution list. The construct $G_1 \,[\!]\, G_2$ gives the input substitution to both G_1 and G_2, and the two guarded bool expressions operate independently, producing output substitution lists. The output lists are appended.

The input to a program is a single, empty substitution. The output is a list of all the substitutions that make the program true. If no substitution can make a program true, then the output is an empty list. Figure 7.18 shows the meaning of an example.

From here on, we use the following abbreviations:

$A_1 \equiv A_2$ for **cases** A_1 **of** A_2:**true end**

B_1 **or** B_2 for **cases** z_0 **of** z_0:B_1 $[\!]$ z_0:B_2 **end**, where z_0 is some fixed constant

We now apply the abstraction and parameterization principles to the core language. For the moment, we limit abstraction to bool expressions and parameterization to tuples of atoms and keep the syntax as simple as possible. The result appears in Figure 7.19. Since all atoms have the same type, there is no need for the type of a formal parameter to be mentioned. The typing rules are left as an easy exercise; the copy rules are the usual ones (for lazy evaluation).

The resulting language resembles an "unsugared" Prolog. Here is a small example of its use. Say that we wish to encode the following information as declarations:

[[**cases** X **of** *john* :**true** [] *mary* :(**cases** *john* **of** X :**true end**) **end**: *comm*]][{ }]

= [[*john* :**true** [] *mary* :(**cases** *john* **of** X :**true end**): *guard*]](X, { })

= [[*john* :**true**: *guard*]](X, { }) @ [[*mary* :(**cases** *john* **of** X :**true end**): *guard*]](X, { })

= *if*($s_0 \neq fail$, [[**true**: *comm*]][s_0], []) @ [[*mary* :(**cases** *john* **of** X :**true end**): *guard*]](X, { })
    where $s_0 = unify(john, X, \{ \}) = \{X{=}john\}$

= [[**true**: *comm*]][s_0] @ [[*mary* :(**cases** *john* **of** X :**true end**): *guard*]](X, { })

= [s_0] @ [[*mary* :(**cases** *john* **of** X :**true end**): *guard*]](X, { })

= [s_0] @ *if*($s_1 \neq fail$, [[**cases** *john* **of** X :**true end**: *comm*]][s_1], [])
    where $s_1 = unify(mary, X, \{ \}) = \{mary{=}X\}$

= [s_0] @ [[**cases** *john* **of** X :**true end**: *comm*]][s_1]

= [s_0] @ [[X :**true end**: *guard*]](*john*, [s_1])

= [s_0] @ *if*($s_2 \neq fail$, [[**true**: *comm*]][s_2], []), where $s_2 = unify(X, john, s_1) = fail$

= [s_0] @ [] = [s_0]

Figure 7.18 _____

P ∈ Program   A ∈ Atom
D ∈ Declaration   I ∈ Identifier
B ∈ Bool-expression

    P ::= D **in** B
    D ::= $D_1.D_2$ | $I_0(I_1, I_2, \ldots, I_n)$=B,   for $n \geq 0$
    B ::= $\cdots$ | $I(A_1, A_2, \ldots, A_n)$,   for $n \geq 0$

Figure 7.19 _____

(i)   Juice and bread are healthy.
(ii) Mary likes something if it is cheese or if it is healthy; John likes everything.
(iii) X and Y can eat food F together if they both like F.

We write this:

    healthy (X) = $X \equiv juice$ **or** $X \equiv bread$.
    likes (X,Y) = **cases** X **of** *mary* :$Y \equiv cheese$ **or** *healthy* (Y) [] *john* :**true end**.
    eat (X,Y,Z) = *likes* (X,Z), *likes* (Y,Z)

Now we can ask questions like *eat* (*john*, *mary*, *bread*) and use the copy rule to guide our understanding of the abstractions:

> *eat (john, mary, bread)*
>
> $\Rightarrow$ *likes (john, bread), likes (mary, bread)*
>
> $\Rightarrow$ (**cases** *john* **of** *mary*:*bread*≡*cheese* **or** *healthy*(*bread*) [] *john*:**true end**),
>
>   (**cases** *mary* **of** *mary*:*bread*≡*cheese* **or** *healthy*(*bread*) [] *john*:**true end**)
>
> $\Rightarrow$ (**cases** *john* **of** *mary*:*bread*≡*cheese*
>
>   **or** (*bread*≡*juice* **or** *bread*≡*bread*) [] *john*:*true* **end**),
>
>   (**cases** *mary* **of** *mary*:*bread*≡*cheese*
>
>   **or** (*bread*≡*juice* **or** *bread*≡*bread*) [] *john*:**true end**)

The result is a core program whose meaning can be calculated with the assistance of Figure 7.17. With a starting substitution list of [{ }], the program outputs the substitution list [{ }]. Another example is *eat (john, mary, A)*, which succeeds with the substitution list [{$A = cheese$}, {$A = juice$}, $A = \{bread\}$]. A third example is *eat (mary, A, B)*, which succeeds with an output list of six substitutions:

> [{$A = mary, B = cheese$}, {$A = john, B = cheese$},
>
>   {$A = mary, B = juice$}, {$A = john, B = juice$},
>
>   {$A = mary, B = bread$}, {$A = john, B = bread$}]

The examples show that formal parameters behave like placeholders in that the binding of an actual parameter to a formal parameter behaves like a unification.

If we introduce pattern matching as an abbreviation for the **cases** construct, then

> $I_0(\ldots, A_1, \ldots) = B_1.$
>
> $I_0(\ldots, A_2, \ldots) = B_2.$
>
> $\cdots$
>
> $I_0(\ldots, A_n, \ldots) = B_n.$

is the abbreviation of

> $I_0(\ldots, I_j, \ldots) = $ **cases** I_j **of** A_1:B_1 [] A_2:B_2 [] $\cdots$ [] A_n:B_n **end**

And if we allow a sequence of disjunctions to be written one to a line, then

> $I_0(\cdots) = B_1.$
>
> $I_0(\cdots) = B_2.$
>
> $\cdots$
>
> $I_0(\cdots) = B_n.$

is the abbreviation of

> $I_0(\cdots) = B_1$ **or** B_2 **or** $\cdots$ **or** B_n

Then we obtain the usual Prolog syntax. Finally, those clauses of form $F(X)$=**true** are shortened to $F(X)$. The above example reads as follows:

> *healthy (juice).*
> *healthy (bread).*
> *likes (mary,cheese).*
> *likes (mary,Y) = healthy (Y).*
> *likes (john,Y).*
> *eat (X,Y,Z) = likes (X,Z), likes (Y,Z)*

Prolog's name abbreviates the phrase ''programming in logic'' and reflects its origins. In particular, a clause of the form

$$I_0(E_{01}, E_{02}, \ldots, E_{0n}) = I_1(E_{11}, E_{12}, \ldots, E_{1n}), \ldots, I_m(E_{m1}, E_{m2}, \ldots, E_{mn})$$

can be read as the logical formula

$$\forall X_1.\forall X_2.\cdots \forall X_p. \, I_1(E_{11}, E_{12}, \ldots, E_{1n}) \wedge \cdots \wedge I_m(E_{m1}, E_{m2}, \ldots, E_{mn})$$
$$\supset I_0(E_{01}, E_{02}, \cdots, E_{0n})$$

where $X_1, X_2, \ldots, X_p$ are the placeholders in the equation. Such formulas, called *Horn clauses*, can be neatly manipulated by a resolution-based theorem prover. The theorem prover serves as the Prolog interpreter. We will not delve into the details of Horn clauses and theorem proving here; you should consult a Prolog text.

Prolog uses data structures that are labeled tuples. A simple example is the structure *person* (NAME, *mother* (NAME), *father* (NAME)), where the occurrences of NAME are atoms. An example is *person* (*charles, mother* (*elizabethII*), *father* (*philip*)). Such values are processed by pattern matching:

> *siblings (person (I1, mother (I2), father (I3)), person (J1, mother (J2), father (J3)))*
> $= I2 \equiv J2, \, I3 \equiv J3.$
>
> **in** *siblings (person (charles, mother (elizabethII), father (philip)),*
>   *person (edward, mother (X), father (Y)))*

The obvious way to extend the core language in Figure 7.16 to data structures is to allow *terms*, rather than mere atoms, in the **cases** and guarded-bool expression constructs:

> B ::= $\cdots$ | **cases** T **of** G **end**
> G ::= T:B | G_1 [] G_2
> T ::= A | $C(T_1, T_2, \ldots, T_n)$, $n>0$, where C denotes a constant

and parameterize bool-expression abstractions on terms, rather than atoms.

If we are willing to deviate a bit from Prolog, we might introduce data structures as declaration abstractions—modules. For example, this module

    module *charles* = (*mother*=*elizabethII*. *father*=*philip*).

codes information about the person *charles*. The two entries in *charles* are atom abstractions. Bool-expression blocks and atom blocks, represented by **with** D **do** B and **with** D **do** A, respectively, might be added; let *R.I* abbreviate **with** *R* **do** *I*. Here is the previous example, recoded:

    module *edward* = (*mother*=*X*. *father*=*Y*).
    siblings (*P*,*Q*) = *P*.*mother* ≡ *Q*.*mother*, *P*.*father* ≡ *Q*.*father*
    in *siblings*(*charles*, *edward*)

The introduction of other forms of abstraction, parameter, and block is left as an interesting exercise.

Prolog is called a *logic programming language*. There is no consensus as to what features a logic programming language must have, but languages called by the name typically use unification to compute values and have a theorem prover as an interpreter.

The presentation of Prolog in this section is nontraditional; the language was originally developed as an application of a Horn clause theorem prover, and perhaps it is merely a pleasant coincidence that Prolog possesses a core like the one shown here. Nonetheless, the logic programming languages in current use have similar cores and extensions. The development in this section is intended to show that logic programming languages have more in common with their functional and imperative language counterparts than what is apparent at first glance.

Suggested Reading

Literature on functional programming languages abounds. Samples are Abelson and Sussman 1985, Bird and Wadler 1988, Darlington 1982, Field and Harrison 1988, Friedman, Wand, and Haynes 1992, Henderson 1980, Henson 1987, Michaelson 1989, Paulson 1991, Peyton Jones 1987, Reade 1989, Sokolowski 1991, Springer and Friedman 1989, Turner 1990, and Wikstrom 1987. The PCF language is studied in Plotkin 1977, Stoughton 1988, and Gunter 1992. The treatment of abstract types is discussed in Burstall 1989, Cardelli and Leroy 1990, Cardelli and Wegner 1985, Harper, Milner, and Tofte 1987 and 1990, Hudak and Wadler 1990, MacQueen 1984, 1986, and 1990, and Mitchell and Plotkin 1985. Languages that use such constructs are Standard ML (see Milner, Tofte, and Harper 1990); Haskell (see Hudak and Wadler 1990); Pebble (see Burstall and Lampson 1984); Russell (see Hook 1984); and Quest (see Cardelli 1989).

Robinson's efforts on unification can be found in Robinson 1965; a recent, comprehensive survey is Siekmann 1989. Type inference for ML-like languages is documented in Hindley 1969 and 1983, Milner 1978, Damas and Milner 1982, and Cardelli 1987. See Mairston 1990 and Kfoury, Tiuryn, and Urzyczyn 1990 for proof that the inference algorithm is, surprisingly, deterministically exponential-time complete. (In practice, linear-time behavior is the norm.)

Good starting points for learning about Prolog-like languages are Kowalski 1979, Clocksin and Mellish 1987, Robinson 1992, and Sterling and Shapiro 1986, but this short list is truly just the tip of the iceberg.

Exercises

1.1.* Write typing rules for the core language when **nil**'s rule reads: **nil**: $\alpha list$, where α is a placeholder.

2.1.   a. Add the constant, **fail,** to the core language along with rewriting rules like **hd nil** $\Rightarrow$ **fail**. Add enough rewriting rules so that a program that has a result of failure is computed by the copy rules to **fail.**

      b. Say that the exception-handler construct E_1 **trap** E_2 is added to the language. If E_1 evaluates to a failure, then the result is E_2. If E_1 evaluates to an answer, then E_2 is ignored. Write the typing rule for the construct and give a set of rewriting rules for **trap** that work with the rules in Part a such that the rules compute the correct Value for a program.

2.2.   Another form of exception handler lets a programmer explicitly signal an error and supply the recovery value:

        E ::= $\cdots$ | **fail** E | **trapblock** E **end**

The evaluation of **fail** E_1 causes the value of the nearest enclosing **trapblock** expression to be E_1. For example, **(trapblock** 2+**(fail** 1) **end)**+3 evaluates to 4. Give the typing rules and rewriting rules for the new constructs. Apply them to this example: **(trapblock (fail** 0)+**(fail** 1) **end)**+2.

3.1.   Combine the copy rules for lazily evaluated lists with the rules for eagerly evaluated abstractions and comment on the pragmatics of the results. Do the same with the copy rules for eagerly evaluated lists and the rules for lazily evaluated abstractions.

3.2.   If you worked Exercise 2.2, proceed. Say that we apply the qualification principle and merge **trapblock** with the expression block construct. The syntax is

        D ::= **val** I=E
        E ::= $\cdots$ | **fail** E | **lettrap** D **in** E **end**

Consider

> **lettrap val** $F = $ **fail** 0
>   **in** $1+$(**lettrap val** $G = 1$ **in** F **end**) **end**

Should the value of this program be 0 or 1? What does the copy-rule semantics suggest?

4.1 Use **rec**, lambda abstraction, and lazily evaluated lists to code the following:

a. an infinite list of the odd positive integers

b. an infinite list of $n!$, for all $n \geq 0$

c. a function that takes inputs an infinite list of integers and outputs an infinite list of the squares of the elements in the input list

5.1. a. Say that *fail* is removed from the meaning sets for records and functions:
$\llbracket \{ i{:}\tau_i \}_{i \in I} \rrbracket = (\{ i{:}\llbracket \tau_i \rrbracket \}_{i \in I})_\perp$ and $\llbracket \tau_1 \rightarrow \tau_2 \rrbracket = (\llbracket \tau_1 \rrbracket \rightarrow \llbracket \tau_2 \rrbracket)_\perp$. Redefine the lazy evaluation semantics of abstractions and parameters. Show that the copy rules for lazy evaluation are not an adequate operational semantics, and propose alternative copy rules.

b. Next, remove $\perp$ from $\llbracket \{ i{:}\tau_i \}_{i \in I} \rrbracket$ and $\llbracket \tau_1 \rightarrow \tau_2 \rrbracket$ and repeat Part a.

5.2. Prove adequacy for PCF with the β-*val* rule and the eager evaluation denotational semantics. (Hint: $comp_{\tau_1 \rightarrow \tau_2}$ iff if $\llbracket \varnothing \vdash E{:}\tau_1 \rightarrow \tau_2 \rrbracket \varnothing$ is proper, then for all E_1, $comp_{\tau_1} E_1$ implies $comp_{\tau_2}(E\, E_1)$.)

6.1. For these programs, attempt typings. If an example is well typed, apply the rewriting rules to it.

a. **lettype** $A{=}int$ **in lettype** $A{=}A$ **in** $\lambda x{:}A.\, x$

b. **lettype** $A{=}int$ **in** $\lambda x{:}A.$ **lettype** $A{=}bool$ **in** x

c. **lettype** $A{=}int$ **in lettype** $B{=}A$ **in** $\lambda x{:}A.$ **lettype** $A{=}bool$ **in** $\lambda x{:}B.\, x$

d. **lettype** $A{=}int$ **in** $\lambda A{:}A.\, A$

e. **let val** $T = ($**abstype** $A{=}int$ **in val** $A = \lambda A{:}int.\, \text{abs}A(A))$
   in open T **in** $A(1)$

f. **lettype** $A{=}int$ **in let val** $F = \lambda x{:}A.\, x$
   in open (**abstype** $A{=}bool$ **in val** $B = \text{abs}A(\textbf{true})$) **in** $F\, 2$

g. **lettype** $A{=}int$ **in** $\lambda x{:}A.$ **open** (**abstype** $A{=}bool$ **in val** $B = \text{abs}A(\textbf{true})$) **in** x

h. **open** (**abstype** $A{=}int$ **in val** $B{=}\text{abs}A(0)$, **val** $C{=}\lambda a{:}A.\text{rep}A(a)$)
   in $1+((\lambda x{:}A.\, x)B)$

i. **lettype** $Ttype = exists(A, \{ B{:}int{\rightarrow}A \})$
   in $(\lambda m{:}Ttype.\, m)($**abstype** $C{=}bool$ **in val** $B{=}\lambda x{:}int.\, \text{abs}C(x{=}0))$

6.2. The typing rules in Section 7.4 enforce structural type equivalence.

a. Alter the typing for **lettype** so that name type equivalence is enforced. With your rules, can you prove that **lettype** $A = int$ **in** $(\lambda x : A.x)2$ is well typed?

6.3. Remove the **lettype** $I = \tau$ **in** E construct and replace it by **val** $I = \tau$. Describe the complications that arise within the typing rules.

6.4. Prove the subject reduction property for the copy rules for **lettype**; for **abstype**.

7.1.* Write the typing rules for the strong abstype construct. (It is best to do the exercise in stages, handling the examples in Section 7.4 one by one.)

7.2. Say that we allow recursively defined types, **let-rec-type** $I = \tau$ **in** E, where occurrences of I in τ refer to the I being defined.

a. Code a type, *Intstream*, of infinite streams of integers, and code a function, $f : Intstream \to Intstream$, that inputs a stream as input and outputs a stream of squares of the elements in the input.

b. What problems arise in type checking the code for f?

8.1. a. Return to the core language in Figure 7.1 and extend it with lambda abstractions that allow value and type expressions to be arguments to value expressions:

$\tau \in$ Type-expression
$E \in$ Value-expression
$\quad \tau ::= int \mid bool \mid \tau list \mid \tau_1 \to \tau_2 \mid (I{:}*) \to \tau \mid I$
$\quad E ::= \cdots \mid \lambda I{:}\tau.\, E \mid (E_1\ E_2) \mid I \mid \lambda I{:}*.\, E \mid [E\ \tau]$

Define the typing rules and copy rules for the language.

b. Extend the language in Part a so that type expressions can be arguments for type expressions.

c. Add the **abstype** construction.

9.1.* Write a denotational semantics for the core language plus abstractions, type abstractions, and abstypes. (Hint: For abstypes, use $[\![exists(I, \pi)]\!] = \{ (\tau, r) \mid \tau \in *, r \in [\![[\tau/I]\pi]\!] \}$.)

9.2. Although it is not mathematically well founded, define an operational semantics based on $[\![\cdot]\!]$ and environments for type abstractions and type parameters.

10.1. For each expression, write the corresponding explicitly typed expression.

a. $(\lambda x.\, \textbf{hd}\ x)(\textbf{cons 3 nil})$

b. **tl (cons (null nil) nil)**

c. $(\lambda x.\, x)(\textbf{cons nil nil})$

10.2. For each of the examples that follow, verify that the stated substitution, U, is a unifier of the two type expressions, τ_1 and τ_2. If the unifier is not the most general unifier, give the most general unifier, U', and a substitution, V, such that $U = V \circ U'$.

a. $U = \{\alpha = int \rightarrow int,\ \beta = int\}$, $\tau_1 = \alpha \rightarrow \beta$, and $\tau_2 = (int \rightarrow \beta) \rightarrow int$

b. $U = \{\alpha = \beta\}$, $\tau_1 = \alpha$, and $\tau_2 = \beta$

c. $U = \{\alpha = \gamma,\ \beta = \gamma\}$, $\tau_1 = \alpha$, and $\tau_2 = \beta$

d. $U = \{\alpha = \delta,\ \beta = \delta \rightarrow bool,\ \delta = \gamma\}$, $\tau_1 = (\gamma \rightarrow \beta)list$, and $\tau_2 = (\alpha \rightarrow (\gamma \rightarrow bool))list$

e. $U = \{\alpha = bool,\ \beta = bool\}$, $\tau_1 = \alpha \rightarrow \beta$, $\tau_2 = \beta \rightarrow \alpha$

10.3. Explain why these pairs of type expressions have no unifiers.

a. $\alpha \rightarrow int$ and $\beta list$

b. $\alpha \rightarrow int$ and $bool \rightarrow \alpha$

c. α and $\alpha list$

d. $(bool \rightarrow \alpha)$ and α

10.4. Use Algorithm W (Figure 7.12) to calculate the types of these expressions:

a. **tl (cons 3 nil)**

b. **hd (cons nil nil)**

c. $\lambda f.\lambda x.\ f(f\ x)$

d. $\lambda x.$ **hd nil**

e. **let** $f = (\lambda x.\ x)$ **in** f **(cons** $(f\ 1)$ **nil)**

10.5.* Prove that Algorithm W (Figure 7.12) calculates the principal type for the logistic system of Figure 7.14. (Hint: Prove by induction on the structure of the proof trees built by Figure 7.14.)

10.6.* The principal typing property was originally proved for a logistic system developed by Damas and Milner. The system is

$$\pi \vdash I : \sigma,\ \text{if}\ (I : \sigma) \in \pi \qquad \frac{\pi \vdash E : \sigma}{\pi \vdash E : \sigma'}\ \text{if}\ \sigma \leq \sigma'$$

$$\frac{\pi \vdash E_1 : \tau_1 \rightarrow \tau_2 \quad \pi \vdash E_2 : \tau_1}{\pi \vdash E_1\ E_2 : \tau_2} \qquad \frac{\pi \uplus \{I : \tau_1\} \vdash E : \tau_2}{\pi \vdash \lambda I.E : \tau_1 \rightarrow \tau_2}$$

$$\frac{\pi \uplus \{I : \sigma\} \vdash E_1 : \tau \quad \pi \vdash E_2 : \sigma}{\pi \vdash \text{let}\ I = E_1\ \text{in}\ E_2 : \tau}$$

where $\sigma \leq \sigma'$ iff $\sigma = \forall \alpha_1 \cdots \forall \alpha_m. \tau$, $\sigma' = \forall \beta_1. \cdots \forall \beta_m. \tau'$, and there is a substitution, $U = \{\alpha_1 = \tau_1, \cdots, \alpha_m = \tau_m\}$, such that $U\tau = \tau'$, and no β_i is free in σ.

a. Prove that the Damas/Milner system is equivalent to the one in Figure 7.14 by showing that a proof of $\pi \vdash E : \tau$ by means of Figure 7.14 can be replicated in the Damas/Milner system and vice versa.

b. Add this rule to the Damas/Milner system:

$$\frac{\pi \uplus \{I{:}\tau\} \vdash E{:}\tau}{\pi \vdash \textbf{rec}\ I.\ E{:}\tau}$$

Extend Algorithm W for the language with **rec** and prove the principal typing property. What problems arise if the following rule is used instead (cf. Kfoury, et al. 1990b)?

$$\frac{\pi \uplus \{I{:}\sigma\} \vdash E{:}\sigma}{\pi \vdash \textbf{rec}\ I.\ E{:}\sigma}$$

10.7.* Extend the syntax of the ML-like language and Algorithm W for records; for abstypes.

11.1. Calculate the meaning of these core language programs:

a. $[\![\textbf{cases}\ X\ \textbf{of}\ john{:}\ \textbf{true}\ [\!]\ mary{:}\ \textbf{true}\ \textbf{end}),$
    $(\textbf{cases}\ X\ \textbf{of}\ mary{:}\ \textbf{true}\ \textbf{end}{:}\ comm]\!]\ [\{\ \}]$

b. $[\![X{\equiv}john\ \textbf{or}\ Y{\equiv}john{:}\ comm]\!]\ [\{\ \}]$

11.2 a. Augment Figure 7.17 with denotational semantics equations for $A_1{\equiv}A_2$ and $B_1\ \textbf{or}\ B_2$ so that the two operators can be treated as primitives. Prove that $[\![A_1{\equiv}A_2{:}\ comm]\!]\ =\ [\![\textbf{cases}\ A_1\ \textbf{of}\ A_2{:}\ \textbf{true}\ \textbf{end}{:}\ comm]\!]$, and prove that $[\![B_1\ \textbf{or}\ B_2{:}\ comm]\!] = [\![\textbf{cases}\ z_0\ \textbf{of}\ z_0{:}\ B_1\ [\!]\ z_0{:}\ B_2\ \textbf{end}{:}\ comm]\!]$.

b. Use the definitions in Part a to calculate the semantics of the example in Exercise 11.1.b.

11.3. a. What core language program is represented by this Prolog program?

$f(a).\ \ f(b) = f(a).$
$g(n, a).\ \ g(n, b) = f(b),\ f(Y).\ \ g(m, X) = f(X)$
$\textbf{in}\ g(m,b),\ g(n,b)$

b. The example in Part a used a recursively defined abstraction. Add recursively defined abstractions, an unfolding rule, and a semantics.

c. What form of abstraction is needed to code the following example?

$append(L1, nil) = L1.$
$append((\textbf{cons}\ A\ L1), L2) = \textbf{cons}\ A\ (append\ L1\ L2)$

Add it to the language.

11.4. Add linear lists to the programming language:

$$B ::= B_1, B_2 \mid \textbf{true} \mid \textbf{cases}\ T\ \textbf{of}\ G\ \textbf{end}$$
$$G ::= T{:}B \mid G_1\ [\!]\ G_2$$
$$T ::= A \mid \textbf{nil} \mid \textbf{cons}\ A\ T$$

a. Redefine the *unify* operation in Figure 7.16 to operate on terms, rather than atoms.

b. Introduce boolean-expression abstractions and pattern matching on formal parameters, so that we can code programs like:

append(**nil**, *L2*, *L3*) = *L3*≡*L2*.
append((**cons** *A L1*), *L2*, *L3*) = *append*(*L1*, *L2*, *X*), *L3*=(**cons** *A X*)

How does this compare to the usual way one codes *append* in Prolog?

11.5. Starting from the language in Figure 7.17, consider all possible forms of abstractions, parameters, and blocks. List the advantages, if any, of each. Are typing rules necessary?

11.6. Consider this example:

f1(*me*, *me*).
f2(*X*, *Z*) = *f1*(*X*, *Y*), *f1*(*Y*, *Z*).
g1(*me*, *you*).
g2(*X*) = *g1*(*X*, *Y*)
  in *f2*(*A*, *B*), *g2*(*A*)

a. Apply the copy rule to uncover the core language program. Why isn't the result what you expect? How does Prolog process this example?

b. The problem in Part a arises from the "careless" use of placeholders in the bodies of abstractions. Consider the addition of a "placeholder block" construct

B ::= ··· | **block**$_I$ B **end**
as it might be used in

f2(*X*, *Z*) = **block**$_Y$ *f1*(*X*, *Y*), *f1*(*Y*, *Z*) **end**

to control the scope of the placeholder *Y*. Give the typing rules, copy rule, and semantics of the placeholder block.

c. Consider this example:

f(*a*, *b*). *f*(*b*, *c*). *f*(*c*, *d*). *f*(*X*, *Z*) = *f*(*X*, *Y*), *f*(*Y*, *Z*)
  in *f*(*a*, *d*)

What value(s) must placeholder *Y* obtain to satisfy the goal? Adapt the placeholder block and its operational semantics to correctly handle this example.

11.7. a. How does backtracking arise as a suitable implementation for the core language semantics in Figure 7.17?

b.* Can we make backtracking into a control structure (in particular, **or**)? If so, why might this motivate a Prolog-style **cut** construct?

8 Higher-Order Typed Lambda Calculi

To properly analyze issues regarding named types and type parameters, we must extend the simply-typed lambda calculus. In this chapter we find that lambda abstraction lets us develop a family of "higher order" typed lambda calculi that formalize the use of types as values. The presentation is based on a paper by Barendregt and Hemerik (1990).

We begin with some review. The syntax of a core language boils down to constructions of the form $(op\ E_1\ E_2 \cdots E_n)$, where each well-formed construction has a type attribute, ι. An example is $0=0$, or in prefix form, $(=0\,0)$, which has type *bool*. In Chapter 5 we added lambda abstractions and the function type, $\tau_1 \to \tau_2$, making the language into a simply typed lambda calculus. In order to simplify the presentation, we treat the core language constructs as constants that are combined by function application; for example, 0 is a constant of type *int*, and $=$ is a constant of type $int \to int \to bool$, so $(=0\,0)$ is a phrase of type *bool*. This gives us

$\tau \in *$ (from here on, let "$*$" name the set of types)

$\iota \in$ Ground-type

$E \in$ Value-expression

$C \in$ Constant

$\qquad \tau ::= \iota \mid \tau_1 \to \tau_2$

$\qquad E ::= C \mid (\lambda I{:}\tau.\,E) \mid (E_1\ E_2) \mid I$

The typing rules are the ones from Chapter 6, and computation rules like the β-rule reduce expressions to normal forms. Recall that the confluence property, the strong normalization property, and the subject-reduction property all hold for the pure simply-typed lambda calculus and its β-rule, but the core language and its δ-rules can cancel any of the properties.

The above version of lambda abstraction lets value expressions be arguments for other value expressions. For reasons to be seen later, we call this form of lambda abstraction $(*,*)$ abstraction.

8.1 The Second-Order Lambda Calculus

The simply typed lambda calculus cannot bind type attributes to identifiers, so we cannot code examples like

lettype $t=int$ **in** $(\lambda x : t.\ x)$ and   **let val** $f\ (t:*) = (\lambda x : t.\ x)$ **in** $\cdots$

To do this, we add a version of lambda abstraction that lets type attributes be arguments to value expressions. Figure 8.1 shows the result.

The $*$ represents the set of type attributes, and the new abstraction form, $(\lambda I:*.E)$, takes a type attribute as an argument. This lambda abstraction requires a new form of function type, namely, $(I:*) \to \tau$, where I can appear in τ. A simple example is

$$\{\ \} \vdash (\lambda t : *.\lambda x : t.\ x) : (t:*) \to (t \to t)$$

which is a generic identity operation. Notice that the type that binds to t affects the type of the overall expression. When the above expression is used in a combination, such as $(\lambda t:*.\lambda x:t.x)\ int$, the type of the expression is $int \to int$, because the argument value,

---

$$\tau ::= \iota \mid \tau_1 \to \tau_2 \mid (I:*) \to \tau \mid I$$
$$E ::= C \mid (\lambda I:\tau.\ E) \mid (E_1\ E_2) \mid I \mid (\lambda I:*.\ E) \mid (E\ \tau)$$

$$\pi \vdash C : \tau \qquad \frac{\pi \uplus \{I:\tau_1\} \vdash E : \tau_2}{(\lambda I : \tau_1.\ E) : \tau_1 \to \tau_2} \qquad \frac{\pi \vdash E_1 : \tau_1 \to \tau_2 \quad \pi \vdash E_2 : \tau_1}{(E_1\ E_2) : \tau_2}$$

$$\pi \vdash I : \tau,\ \text{if } (I:\tau) \in \pi \qquad \frac{\pi \vdash E : \tau}{\pi \vdash (\lambda I:*.\ E) : (I:*) \to \tau}\ \text{if } I \notin FV(\pi) \qquad \frac{\pi \vdash E : (I:*) \to \tau_1}{\pi \vdash (E\ \tau_2) : [\tau_2/I]\tau_1}$$

where: $FV(\pi) = \bigcup_{(I:\tau) \in \pi} FV(\tau)$

$FV(\iota) = \{\ \}$ $FV((I:*) \to \tau) = FV(\tau) - \{I\}$

$FV(\tau_1 \to \tau_2) = FV(\tau_1) \cup FV(\tau_2)$ $FV(I) = \{I\}$

and $[\tau/I]\tau_2$ is defined:

$[\tau/I]\iota = \iota$ $[\tau/I]I = \tau$

$[\tau/I](\tau_1 \to \tau_2) = [\tau/I]\tau_1 \to [\tau/I]\tau_2$ $[\tau/I]J = J$, if $I \neq J$

$[\tau/I](I:*) \to \tau_1 = (I:*) \to \tau_1$ $[\tau/I](J:*) \to \tau_1 = (J:*) \to [\tau/I]\tau_1$, if $I \neq J$

Figure 8.1 _____

int, binds to t and affects the type, $[int/t](t \rightarrow t) = int \rightarrow int$, of the result. The β-rule reduces the combination to $(\lambda x{:}int.\,x)$.

The typing rules define a deterministic algorithm for decorating syntax trees. You should draw the syntax tree for the previous example, attach typing attributes to it, and then compare it to the corresponding proof tree:

$$\{x{:}t\} \vdash x{:}t$$

$$|$$

$$\{\,\} \vdash (\lambda x{:}t.\,x){:}t \rightarrow t$$

$$|$$

$$\{\,\} \vdash (\lambda t{:}*.\,\lambda x{:}t.\,x){:}(t{:}*) \rightarrow (t \rightarrow t)$$

$$|$$

$$\{\,\} \vdash (\lambda t{:}*.\,\lambda x{:}t.\,x)\;int{:}\;[int/t](t \rightarrow t) = int \rightarrow int$$

The penultimate step of the proof is counterintuitive, because no binding is removed from the type assignment. This point is addressed in the next section. The two sample programs from the beginning of this section are encoded:

$$(\lambda t{:}*.\lambda x{:}t.\,x)\,int \quad \text{and} \quad (\lambda f{:}(t{:}*) \rightarrow (t \rightarrow t).\;\cdots\;)(\lambda t{:}*.\lambda x{:}t.\,x)$$

Since identifiers can appear within types, the restriction on the typing rule for (λI:*.E), similar to the one for the **lettype** construct in Chapter 7, becomes necessary. Thus, $\lambda x{:}t.\lambda t{:}*.x$ is not well formed, because there is a misuse of t.

Naming issues also arise. Given

$$(\lambda x{:}(y{:}*) \rightarrow (y \rightarrow y).\,(x\;int\;0))\,(\lambda z{:}*.\lambda a{:}z.\,a)$$

we note that the type of the operator of the combination is $((y{:}*) \rightarrow (y \rightarrow y)) \rightarrow int$, but the type of the operand is $(z{:}*) \rightarrow (z \rightarrow z)$. Our intuitions tell us that the overall type should be well formed—the names of the binding identifiers are unimportant—so we will indeed use "α-equivalence" for the types and conclude that the type is well formed.

The β-rule again serves as the reduction rule for the new form of lambda abstraction. A sample application of it is

$$(\lambda t{:}*.\lambda x{:}t.\,x)\,int \;\Rightarrow\; [int/t](\lambda x{:}t.\,x) = (\lambda x{:}int.\,x)$$

where substitution for type identifiers is defined in Figure 8.1. The β-rule preserves the confluence, strong normalization, and subject-reduction properties.

The typing rule for $(E\,\tau_2)$ suggests that a β-reduction step was made on the type $(I{:}*) \rightarrow \tau_1$ "applied to" the type τ_2 to get the type $[\tau_2/I]\tau_1$. Indeed, it is tempting to represent $(I{:}*) \rightarrow \tau_1$ by $(\lambda I{:}*.\,\tau_1)$! Essentially this approach is taken in Curry's "G-calculus" (Curry and Feys 1958; Curry, Hindley, and Seldin 1972), Automath (de Bruijn 1980), and the Calculus of Constructions (Coquand and Huet 1988; Coquand 1990), but we have many more lambdas to introduce, so we refrain, for the moment, from doing this. A common representation for $(I{:}*) \rightarrow \tau_1$ is $(\forall I{:}*. \tau_1)$, considered later.

The strong normalization property of the β-rule implies that a compiler can safely perform β-reductions of redexes that have types as arguments. Indeed, we noted above that the calculation of the type for $(E\ \tau)$ mirrors the β-reduction of $(E\ \tau)$ itself, so no extra overhead is incurred by doing the β-reduction at compile time.

In its pure form (that is, without core language constructs), this version of the lambda calculus is called *F2* or the *second-order lambda calculus*. We call the new version of lambda abstraction $(\square,*)$ abstraction.

We now explain the rationale for naming the lambda abstractions $(*,*)$ and $(\square,*)$. A lambda abstraction, $(\lambda I{:}\tau_1. E)$, which maps τ_1-typed arguments to τ_2-typed results, has typing $\tau_1 \rightarrow \tau_2$. Since $\tau_1 \in *$ and $\tau_2 \in *$, the lambda abstraction has "arity" $(*,*)$ and we say that $(\lambda I{:}\tau_1.E)$ is a $(*,*)$ abstraction. In contrast, $(\lambda I{:}*. E)$ maps "*-typed" arguments to τ-typed results and has typing $(I{:}*) \rightarrow \tau$. If we say that $* \in \square$, then the lambda abstraction has arity $(\square,*)$, and it is a $(\square,*)$ abstraction. In the next section, we introduce additional members to the set $\square$, which we call the set of *kinds*.

The lambda abstraction defined in this section encodes *parametric polymorphic* functions, that is, functions that behave the same way, regardless of the instantiation of the type parameter. In Chapter 7 we saw type abstractions of the following form:

lettype $t{=}int$ **in** $(\lambda x{:}t.\ x{+}1)$

This example is not a parametric polymorphic function, since t is merely an alias for *int* and not a full-fledged parameter. In contrast, the abstraction $(\lambda x{:}t.\ x)$ behaves uniformly, regardless of the value of t, so it is parametric polymorphic. Although it is difficult to give a precise definition of parameteric polymorphism (Strachey 1968; Reynolds 1974, 1983, and 1985), there is consensus that the second-order lambda calculus captures the notion. Hence, the second-order lambda calculus has been used as a test bed for theories related to polymorphism.

The **abstype** construct of Chapter 7 can be simulated the following way:

open (**abstype** $I{=}\tau$ **in val** $op_1{=}E_1 \cdots$ **val** $op_n{=}E_n$) **in** E

is encoded as

$(\lambda I{:}*.\ \lambda op_1{:}\tau_1. \cdots \lambda op_n{:}\tau_n.\ E)\ \tau\ E_1 \cdots E_n$

where τ_i is the type of op_i, $1 \le i \le n$. The expression is structured so that the type of E relies on I and not on τ. In this sense, hiding is enforced. The β-rule inserts the implementations of the op_is into E, so that computation can be undertaken. But the encoding does not match exactly the original notion of abstype: The grouping of a type with its operations, into a "package," is lost.

The second-order lambda calculus is also of interest for computability reasons. Recall from Chapter 6 that the natural numbers and the partial recursive functions on them can be encoded in the pure untyped lambda calculus. That encoding did not carry over to the simply typed lambda calculus: The types prevented the self-application that is essential to simulating general recursion. But the (pure) second-order lambda calculus admits a coding of numbers and recursive functions. This is somewhat surprising in light of strong normalization, but here it is the *total* recursive functions that are encoded.

The codings of the natural numbers are

0: $(\lambda t\!:\!*.\lambda f\!:\!t\!\rightarrow\!t.\lambda x\!:\!t.\,x)$

1: $(\lambda t\!:\!*.\lambda f\!:\!t\!\rightarrow\!t.\lambda x\!:\!t.\,(f\,x))$

$\cdots$

i: $(\lambda t\!:\!*.\lambda f\!:\!t\!\rightarrow\!t.\lambda x\!:\!t.\,(f(f(\,\cdots\,(f\,x)\,\cdots\,))),\quad f$ applied i times

All of these encodings have type $(t\!:\!*)\!\rightarrow\!(t\!\rightarrow\!t)\!\rightarrow\!t\!\rightarrow\!t$, and we say that this is the type, *nat*, of natural numbers. It can be proved that all closed expressions of type *nat* can be $\beta\eta$-reduced to one of the above codings. Standard arithmetic functions can be coded, for example,

$$succ = \lambda n\!:\!nat.\lambda t\!:\!*.\lambda f\!:\!t\!\rightarrow\!t.\lambda x\!:\!t.\,f\,(n\;t\;f\;x)$$

The main result of the development is that any function that can be proved total recursive by the laws of second-order arithmetic can be coded in the second-order lambda calculus. In this way, the second-order lambda calculus expresses the total functions of "practical" interest. For more information, you should consult Girard 1972, Girard, Lafont, and Taylor 1989, Fortune, Leivant, and O'Donnell 1983, and Leivant 1981.

One might wonder how it is possible to simulate general recursion. The answer is that limited self-application is possible in the second-order lambda calculus; for example, the polymorphic identity, $\lambda t\!:\!*.\lambda x\!:\!t.\,x$, can take its own type, namely, $(t\!:\!*)\!\rightarrow\!(t\!\rightarrow\!t)$, and then itself, as arguments. The calculus is "circular" or *impredicative*. In an impredicative system, the definition of an object can refer to the collection to which the object belongs. The polymorphic identity does this: Its first argument is some $t\!:\!*$, but the polymorphic identity itself belongs to type $(t\!:\!*)\!\rightarrow\!(t\!\rightarrow\!t)$, which belongs to $*$. In contrast, a *predicative* system is structured into ordered "ranks" or "universes" so that an object is defined in terms of components that belong to ranks smaller than the one to which the defined object belongs. In a predicative system, the above polymorphic identity cannot be defined. At best, we can define a family of identities of the form $(\lambda t\!:\!*_i.\lambda x\!:\!t.\,x)$, $i\geq 0$, each of which has type $(t\!:\!*_i)\!\rightarrow\!(t\!\rightarrow\!t)$ and belongs to rank $*_{i+1}$.

The circularity in an impredicative system is exposed when we attempt to give mathematical meanings to its expressions; the set-theoretical meaning of $(\lambda t\!:\!*.\lambda x\!:\!t.\,x)$ is apparently the function set $S = \{(t,id_t)\mid t\in *\}$ of argument, answer pairs, where id_t is the set-theoretical representation of the identity function on elements of type t. Then,

$((t:*) \to (t \to t),\ id_{(t:*) \to (t \to t)})$ is one of the pairs in S. But $id_{(t:*) \to (t \to t)}$ is itself a set of argument, answer pairs, one of which must be (S, S)! This development violates the foundation axiom of set theory, and indeed, Reynolds (1984) proved that no model of the second-order lambda calculus can use function sets as meanings of the terms.

In contrast, predicative lambda calculus systems can use types as arguments and have function sets as meanings for terms. We examine a predicative system in Chapter 10.

8.2 Parameterized Data Types

The next step is to extend the second-order lambda calculus so that it can model parameterized types, for example

lettype $t1(t2) = t2 \to t2$ **in** $(\lambda f: (t1\ int).\ f)$

That is, we want a lambda abstraction that lets types be arguments to types. This lets us represent $t1$ as $(\lambda t2:*.\ t2 \to t2)$, and the entire expression is coded:

$$(\lambda t1: * \to *.\ (\lambda f: (t1\ int).\ f))\ (\lambda t2: *.\ t2 \to t2)$$

Since $t1$ is a parameterized type, it has a "metatype" of $* \to *$. A "fully instantiated" type, like *int*, has metatype $*$. The metatypes are called *kinds*.

Figure 8.2 gives the syntax rules for the augmented language. The key addition is to the syntax rule for types, where lambda abstraction now appears. The issue of well-formedness of types arises (for example, the type (*int int*) is clearly malformed), so *kinding rules*, namely, the first six inference rules in Figure 8.2, give kind attributes to types. The rules use a *kind assignment*, P, which maps type identifiers to kinds. With these rules, we can derive, say, $\{\ \} \vdash ((\lambda t2:*.t2 \to t2)\ int): *$, which attests that the type is well formed and is fully instantiated (also called *saturated*). We can also derive the kind of a parameterized type, such as $\{\ \} \vdash (\lambda t:*.\ t): * \to *$. It is helpful to think of the language of types as a lambda calculus in its own right. Hence, Figure 8.2 displays a lambda calculus of types built on top of a lambda calculus of value expressions.

The syntax of expressions has one generalization: The $(\Box, *)$ lambda abstraction now accepts as arguments types of all kinds (and not just $*$, as before).

The typing rules for value expressions must use a kind assignment and a type assignment to enforce well-formedness. Indeed, the kind assignment was implicit in the typing rules for the second-order lambda calculus: Compare the typing rule for $(\Box, *)$ lambda abstraction in Figure 8.1 with its sister rule in Figure 8.2. Since the kind assignment and type assignment work together, we require that the pair P, π satisfy the constraint that, for all $(I:\tau) \in \pi$, $P \vdash \tau:*$ holds. The constraint prevents nonsensical kind, type assignment pairs, like $(\{f:* \to *\}, \{x:f\})$ or $(\{\ \}, \{x:(\lambda y:*.y)\})$ from appearing in derivations. The last rule in Figure 8.2, namely,

$\kappa \in \square$ (kind expressions) $P \in$ Kind-assignment

$\tau \in *$ (type expressions) $\pi \in$ Type-assignment

$E \in$ Value-expression

$I \in$ Identifier

$C \in$ Constant

$$\kappa ::= * \mid \kappa_1 \to \kappa_2$$
$$\tau ::= \iota \mid \tau_1 \to \tau_2 \mid (I{:}\kappa) \to \tau \mid I \mid (\lambda I{:}\kappa.\,\tau) \mid (\tau_1\ \tau_2)$$
$$E ::= C \mid (\lambda I{:}\tau.\,E) \mid (E_1\ E_2) \mid I \mid (\lambda I{:}\kappa.\,E) \mid (E\ \tau)$$

$$P \vdash \iota : * \qquad \frac{P \vdash \tau_1 : * \quad P \vdash \tau_2 : *}{P \vdash \tau_1 \to \tau_2 : *} \qquad \frac{P \uplus \{I{:}\kappa\} \vdash \tau : *}{P \vdash (I{:}\kappa) \to \tau : *}$$

$$P \vdash I : \kappa, \;\; \text{if } (I{:}\kappa) \in P \qquad \frac{P \uplus \{I{:}\kappa_1\} \vdash \tau : \kappa_2}{P \vdash (\lambda I{:}\kappa_1.\,\tau) : \kappa_1 \to \kappa_2} \qquad \frac{P \vdash \tau_1 : \kappa_1 \to \kappa_2 \quad P \vdash \tau_2 : \kappa_1}{P \vdash (\tau_1\ \tau_2) : \kappa_2}$$

$$P, \pi \vdash C : \tau, \;\; \text{where } \tau : * \qquad \frac{P \vdash \tau_1 : * \quad P, \pi \uplus \{I{:}\tau_1\} \vdash E : \tau_2}{P, \pi \vdash (\lambda I{:}\tau_1.\,E) : \tau_1 \to \tau_2}$$

$$\frac{P, \pi \vdash E_1 : \tau_1 \to \tau_2 \quad P, \pi \vdash E_2 : \tau_1}{P, \pi \vdash (E_1\ E_2) : \tau_2} \qquad P, \pi \vdash I : \tau, \;\; \text{if } (I{:}\tau) \in \pi$$

$$\frac{P \uplus \{I{:}\kappa\}, \pi \vdash E : \tau}{P, \pi \vdash (\lambda I{:}\kappa.\,E) : (I{:}\kappa) \to \tau} \;\; \text{if } I \notin FV(\pi)$$

$$\frac{P, \pi \vdash E : (I{:}\kappa) \to \tau_1 \quad P \vdash \tau_2 : \kappa}{P, \pi \vdash (E\ \tau_2) : [\tau_2 / I]\tau_1} \qquad \frac{P, \pi \vdash E : \tau_1}{P, \pi \vdash E : \tau_2} \;\; \text{if } \tau_1 \Rightarrow^* \tau_2 \text{ (by the } \beta\text{-rule)}$$

where each pair P, π satisfies the constraint that, for all $(I{:}\tau) \in \pi$, $P \vdash \tau : *$ holds

Figure 8.2

$$\frac{P,\pi \vdash E:\tau_1}{P,\pi \vdash E:\tau_2} \quad \text{if } \tau_1 \Rightarrow^* \tau_2$$

states that the β-rule can be applied to a type. The rule plays a crucial role in typing examples like:

$$\{\ \}, \{\ \} \vdash (\lambda f{:}((\lambda t{:}*.\,t \rightarrow t)int).\,f\,3) : (int \rightarrow int) \rightarrow int$$

because the type of f is $((\lambda t{:}*.\,t \rightarrow t)int)$, which must be β-reduced to $int \rightarrow int$ to validate the well-formedness of the combination $(f\,3)$. Figure 8.3 gives an example proof tree. The inference steps marked (β) in the figure apply the β-rule.

Because of the β-rule, it might not be clear that the rules in Figure 8.2 define a deterministic algorithm for attaching kind and type attributes to an abstract syntax tree. Fortunately, both confluence and strong normalization properties hold for the language of types, so the β-rule can be applied any time in the type checking of a tree. A good strategy is to apply the β-rule whenever a derivation step $P,\pi \vdash E:\tau$ is completed and τ is not in normal form. In the example in Figure 8.3, the assignment of type attributes to the tree for $(\lambda f{:}((\lambda t{:}*.\,t \rightarrow t)int).\,(f\,3))$ goes as follows. (Trace the steps in Figure 8.3 as we go.) First, the inherited attributes P_0, π_0 are attached to the root of the tree; then the well formedness of $(\lambda t{:}*.\,t \rightarrow t)int$ and $(f\,3)$ must be checked. P_0 is passed to the former, and P_0, π_1 are passed to the latter. In the former case, P_0 is used in the expected way to validate that $(\lambda t{:}*.\,t \rightarrow t)int$ has kind *. As for $(f\,3)$, P_0, π_1 are

---

Let $P_0 = \{\ \}$, $P_1 = \{t{:}*\}$, $\pi_0 = \{\ \}$, $\pi_1 = \{f{:}((\lambda t{:}*.\,t \rightarrow t)int)\}$

```
P₁ ⊢ t: *        P₁ ⊢ t: *
       \        /
     P₁ ⊢ t → t: *                         P₀,π₁ ⊢ f: ((λt:*. t → t)int)
          |                                      | (β)
P₀ ⊢ (λt:*. t → t): *→→*   P₀ ⊢ int: *    P₀,π₁ ⊢ f: int → int      P₀,π₁ ⊢ 3: int
               \        /                          \         /
           P₀ ⊢ ((λt:*. t → t)int: *              P₀,π₁ ⊢ (f 3): int
                   \                                 /
           P₀,π₀ ⊢ (λf:((λt:*. t → t)int). f 3): ((λt:*. t → t)int) → int
                           | (β)
           P₀,π₀ ⊢ (λf:((λt:*. t → t)int). f 3): (int → int) → int
```

Figure 8.3 _____

passed to f and to 3. Calculation of the type attribute for f is easy: A lookup in π_1 gives the type $(\lambda t{:}*.\,t \to t)int$. Since the type expression is not in normal form, β-reduction is applied and $int \to int$ results. The type attribute for 3 is just int. These type attributes are used to synthesize the typing, int, for $(f\,3)$. The type attribute for the whole tree is $((\lambda t{:}*.\,t \to t)int) \to int$, which β-reduces to $(int \to int) \to int$. It is a good exercise to implement the rules in Figure 8.2 as a type-checking algorithm for abstract syntax trees.

The pure version of the system presented in this section is called $F\omega$, and the lambda abstraction introduced here is called $(\Box,\Box)$ abstraction. (Can you explain why?) The name $\Box$ denotes the set of all kinds: $*$, $* \to *$, $(* \to *) \to *$, and so on.

All functions that can be proved total recursive in nth-order arithmetic, for some $n \geq 0$, can be coded as terms in $F\omega$ (Fortune, Leivant, and O'Donnell 1983).

8.3 Generalized Type Systems

The language in Figure 8.2 is unwieldy: There are three forms of lambda abstraction and application, three forms of β-rule, and two forms of type-assignment attribute. Since lambda abstractions were introduced three times, there should be a single syntax format that can be instantiated three ways. We now see this is so.

In order to combine the three forms of lambda abstraction into one, we make one generalization: We uniformly use $(I{:}\tau_1) \to \tau_2$ as the type/kind attribute for a lambda abstraction. We ignore identifier I if it is not used in τ_2. For example, the type of the lambda abstraction $(\lambda x{:}int.\,x)$ is $(x{:}int) \to int$. Since x is not used in int, we read the type as just $int \to int$. Another example is $(\lambda f{:}(* \to *).\,f\,int)$, whose kind is $(f{:}(* \to *)) \to *$, that is, $(* \to *) \to *$.

The syntax format we use is a *Generalized Type System* (*GTS*), due to Barendregt and Hemerik (1990). It is parameterized on four sets:

1. A set of *constants*, **C**, which names the primitive operators, types, and kinds.
2. A set of *sorts*, **S**, such that $\mathbf{S} \subseteq \mathbf{C}$, which lists those constants that are names of collections.
3. A set of *axioms*, **A**, whose members have the form $(c{:}s)$, where $c \in \mathbf{C}$ and $s \in \mathbf{S}$. Each axiom generates a typing rule.
4. A set of *abstraction rules*, **R**, whose members have the form (s_1, s_2), where $s_1, s_2 \in \mathbf{S}$. Each abstraction rule generates a lambda abstraction construct with its associated typing rules and β-rule.*

---

* Barendregt (1991 and 1992) has also presented a version of GTS where **R** consists of a set of triples. We use the simpler version here, as it better suits the purposes of this chapter.

$E, \tau, \kappa \in$ Expression
$I \in$ Identifier
$c \in \mathbf{C}$
$\pi \in$ Type assignment, a linearly ordered set of Identifier, Expression pairs

$$E ::= c \mid (I{:}\tau_1) \to \tau_2 \mid (\lambda I{:}\tau.\, E) \mid (E_1\ E_2) \mid I$$

$$\pi \vdash c : \kappa, \quad \text{if } (c, \kappa) \in \mathbf{A}$$

$$\frac{\pi \vdash \tau_1 : \kappa_1 \qquad \pi \uplus \{I{:}\tau_1\} \vdash \tau_2 : \kappa_2}{\pi \vdash (I{:}\tau_1) \to \tau_2 : \kappa_2} \quad \text{if } (\kappa_1, \kappa_2) \in \mathbf{R} \text{ and } I \notin FV(\pi)$$

$$\frac{\pi \vdash (I{:}\tau_1) \to \tau_2 : \kappa \qquad \pi \uplus \{I{:}\tau_1\} \vdash E : \tau_2}{\pi \vdash (\lambda I{:}\tau_1.\, E) : (I{:}\tau_1) \to \tau_2} \qquad\qquad \frac{\pi \vdash E_1 : (I{:}\tau_1) \to \tau_2 \qquad \pi \vdash E_2 : \tau_1}{\pi \vdash (E_1\ E_2) : [E_2/I]\tau_2}$$

$$\pi \vdash I : \tau, \quad \text{if } (I{:}\tau) \in \pi \qquad\qquad \frac{\pi \vdash E : \tau_1}{\pi \vdash E : \tau_2} \quad \text{if } \tau_1 \Rightarrow^* \tau_2$$

where $\pi \uplus \{I{:}\tau\} = (\pi - \{I{:}\tau'\})\, concat\, \{I{:}\tau\}$, and $FV(\pi) = \bigcup_{(I{:}\tau)\in\pi} FV(\tau)$

$FV(\lambda I{:}\tau.\, E) = FV(\tau) \cup (FV(E) - \{I\})$

$FV(c) = \{\ \}$ $\qquad\qquad\qquad\qquad\qquad\qquad FV(E_1\ E_2) = FV(E_1) \cup FV(E_2)$

$FV((I{:}\tau_1) \to \tau_2) = FV(\tau_1) \cup (FV(\tau_2) - \{I\}) \qquad FV(I) = \{I\}$

and all occurrences of $\pi = \{I_1{:}\tau_1, \ldots, I_n{:}\tau_n\}$, $n \geq 0$, satisfy the following well formedness constraint: for all $0 \leq i < n$, $\{I_1{:}\tau_1, \ldots, I_i{:}\tau_i\} \vdash \tau_{i+1} : \kappa$, for some $\kappa \in \mathbf{S}$

Figure 8.4 _____

As a motivational example, for (pure) $F\omega$ we have

$\mathbf{C} = \{*, \Box\}$ $\qquad\qquad\qquad\qquad \mathbf{A} = \{\ (* :: \Box)\ \}$

$\mathbf{S} = \{*, \Box\}$ $\qquad\qquad\qquad\qquad \mathbf{R} = \{\ (*,*), (\Box,*), (\Box,\Box)\ \}$

Given the definitions of $\mathbf{C}$, $\mathbf{S}$, $\mathbf{A}$, and $\mathbf{R}$, we use the syntax of the generalized type system, given in Figure 8.4, to define a language.

The uses of E, τ, and κ in the figure are only suggestive; *all three symbols represent expressions:*

$$E ::= c \mid (I{:}E_1) \to E_2 \mid (\lambda I{:}E_1.\, E_2) \mid (E_1\ E_2) \mid I$$

The hierarchy of values, types, and kinds is defined by axiom set, $\mathbf{A}$. The clauses of the syntax rule list, in order, constant symbols (like 0, *int*, $*$, and $\Box$), generalized function type, generalized lambda abstraction, generalized application, and identifiers. The typing rule schemes in the figure are instantiated based upon the definitions of **A** and **R**. In order to eliminate dubious type assignments, such as $\{f:*\rightarrow*, x:f\}$ and $\{x:t, t:x\}$, the type assignment, π, must be restricted: π is now a linearly ordered set. This means $\{t:*, x:t\}$ is different from $\{x:t, t:*\}$—the former is well formed, but the latter is not. Also, the operation $\pi \uplus \{I:\tau\}$ removes any existing binding of I from π and appends $(I:\tau)$ to the end of the ordered sequence of bindings. This ensures that the well-formedness condition, stated at the bottom of Figure 8.4, is sensible.

The generalized type system gives a language designer great flexibility to define hierarchies of type structure. In addition to the examples seen in the earlier sections, one might define several primitive kinds:

$$\mathbf{C} = \{F, D, I, C, \Box\} \qquad \mathbf{A} = \{(F:\Box), (D:\Box), (I:\Box), (C:\Box)\}$$
$$\mathbf{S} = \{F, D, I, C, \Box\} \qquad \mathbf{R} = \{(F,F), \ldots, (D,F), \ldots\}$$

A structure similar to the above arises in the *action semantics* metalanguage developed by Mosses (1992) and Watt (1991). Or, one might establish a predicative hierarchy of kinds:

$$\mathbf{C} = \{t_i \mid i \geq 0\} \qquad \mathbf{A} = \{(t_i:t_{i+1}) \mid i \geq 0\}$$
$$\mathbf{S} = \{t_i \mid i > 0\} \qquad \mathbf{R} = \{(t_i, t_i) \mid i > 0\}$$

Or, one can study systems that lack strong normalization:

$$\mathbf{C} = \{*\} \qquad \mathbf{A} = \{(*:*)\}$$
$$\mathbf{S} = \mathbf{C} \qquad \mathbf{R} = \{(*,*)\}$$

This last example, called the "**type:type**" calculus, is notorious and deserves closer scrutiny. Figure 8.5 shows the calculus obtained when Figure 8.4 is instantiated by **C**, **S**, **A**, and **R**. The rationale for the name of the calculus comes from the first typing rule. The **type:type** calculus is especially "clean" because it uses one form of lambda abstraction for both value parameters and type parameters. The **type:type** calculus appears to be an improvement over $F\omega$, but this "improvement" comes at a steep price: A complicated construction, called "Girard's paradox," shows how to build an expression, $\mathbf{Y}: (t:*) \rightarrow (t \rightarrow t) \rightarrow t$, such that $\mathbf{Y} t f \Rightarrow f(\mathbf{Y} t f)$. Hence, strong normalization is lost. A significant consequence is that every type in the calculus has well-defined terms; indeed, we can code a "polymorphic constant" $(\lambda t:*. \mathbf{Y} t (\lambda x:t. x))$, which has type $(t:*) \rightarrow t$, that can generate values of any type whatsoever! (Of course, the values never have normal form.)

Since the calculus confuses values with types—$(\mathbf{Y} * (\lambda x:*.x))$ is a type *and* a value—type expressions can contain expressions that might not have normal forms, and decidable type checking is lost. Further information on these points is given in Meyer and Reinhold 1986 and Cardelli 1986b. Girard's paradox is described in Girard 1972,

$$*:* \qquad \frac{\pi \vdash \tau_1 : * \quad \pi \uplus \{I{:}\tau_1\} \vdash \tau_2 : *}{\pi \vdash (I{:}\tau_1) \to \tau_2 : *} \quad \text{if } I \notin FV(\pi)$$

$$\frac{\pi \vdash (I{:}\tau_1) \to \tau_2 : * \quad \pi \uplus \{I{:}\tau_1\} \vdash E : \tau_2}{\pi \vdash (\lambda I{:}\tau_1 . E) : (I{:}\tau_1) \to \tau_2} \qquad \frac{\pi \vdash E_1 : (I{:}\tau_1) \to \tau_2 \quad \pi \vdash E_2 : \tau_1}{\pi \vdash (E_1\ E_2) : [E_2/I]\tau_2}$$

$$\pi \vdash I : \tau, \text{ if } (I{:}\tau) \in \pi \qquad \frac{\pi \vdash E : \tau_1}{\pi \vdash E : \tau_2} \quad \text{if } \tau_1 \Rightarrow^* \tau_2$$

Figure 8.5 _____

Coquand 1986, and Barendregt 1992.

   Girard's paradox was originally derived for the typing system that extended $F\omega$ to "metakinds," called *System U*:

   $C= \{*, \square, \Delta\}$ $A= \{ (* : \square), (\square : \Delta) \}$
   $S= \{*, \square, \Delta\}$ $R= \{ (*,*), (\square,*), (\square,\square), (\Delta,\square), (\Delta,*) \}$

It is surprising that strong normalization is lost by extending the typing hierarchy to three levels, but impredicative systems are delicate. (Indeed, the last pair in **R** can be deleted, and strong normalization still fails.)

   Let us consider in what sense the loss of strong normalization is "paradoxical" in System *U*. Recall that the type $(I{:}*) \to \tau$ is often written as $(\forall I{:}*.\ \tau)$, as if it were a proposition in logic. Now, pretend that types are in fact propositions in a logic; then, $*$ becomes the set of all propositions. Next, pretend that a closed expression, E, of type τ is a "proof" of proposition τ. Then, System *U* defines a higher-order predicate calculus where functions on proofs and propositions can be coded. But since System *U* falls to Girard's paradox, every "proposition" has a "proof." By definition, this makes the logic inconsistent—paradoxical. Chapters 9 and 10 develop the concept of lambda calculus as logic further.

8.4 Dependent Product Types

A function has *dependent type* if the type of a function's result depends on the *value* of its argument. The second-order lambda calculus possesses functions with dependent types; for example, the type of the result from $(\lambda t{:}*.\lambda x{:}t.\ x)$ depends on the value of the argument bound to t. In this section, we study another version of dependent type, where arguments like numbers determine types. An example of a function with this form of dependent type is f, which maps a natural number, n, to an n-tuple of zeros: $f(n) = \langle 0, 0, \ldots, 0 \rangle$, the zeros repeated n times. Clearly, $f(n) \in nat^n$, so f is typed $(n{:}nat) \to nat^n$, where nat^n is $nat \times nat \times \cdots \times nat$, repeated n times. The format of a dependent type is $(I{:}\tau) \to \tau_I$, where occurrences of I appear in τ_I. Perhaps a better term is *quantified type*, since $(I{:}\tau)$ acts as a quantifier for τ_I.

Mathematicians often write a dependent type as $\prod_{I \in \tau} \tau_I$, which leads some to call it the *dependent product type*. The rationale is that a function from a set A to a set B can be represented as a tuple of B-values, where the components of the tuple are indexed by values from A. The dependent product type therefore represents those tuples, f, such that the vth component of f, where $v \in \tau$, is a value of type $[v / I]\tau_I$. Logicians prefer to write $\forall I \in \tau.\, \tau_I$ for dependent product types; we saw this notation used for types in the second-order lambda calculus.

It is natural to think of a dependent type as a "parameterized type," but care must be taken. For example, given a type expression, τ_I, that contains a free identifier, I, we might write the lambda abstraction $(\lambda I{:}\tau.\, \tau_I)$, which has kinding $\tau \to *$. The abstraction is a $(*, \square)$ abstraction. Is this a dependent type? The relationship between a dependent type and a $(*, \square)$ abstraction is close: In both examples τ_I is dependent on I, and in both examples once a value is bound to I, a type is produced. But the "flavor" of the two forms of binding differ. A dependent type, $(I{:}\tau) \to \tau_I$, has kinding $*$; that is, it is a saturated type and can label a value expression, whereas $(\lambda I{:}\tau.\, \tau_I)$ has kinding $\tau \to *$; that is, it needs an argument of type τ before it is saturated and can label a value expression. The two forms are not interchangable.

In the Automath and Calculus of Constructions systems, a $(*, \square)$ abstraction $(\lambda I{:}\tau.\, \tau_I)$ can be "coerced" into the dependent type $(I{:}\tau) \to \tau_I$ by writing $\Pi(\lambda I{:}\tau.\, \tau_I)$. Indeed, there are theories of "higher-order syntax" where there is a universal binder— call it λ—and the different flavors of binding are represented by different operators, such as Π for dependent product binding and Λ for lambda-abstraction binding. See Pfenning and Elliot 1988, Hannan 1990, Talcott 1991, and Tennent 1987 for examples.

Now we examine a concrete example of dependent types and $(*, \square)$ abstraction. Figure 8.6 presents a core language for tuples. Operation *init* builds a tuple of size E_1 such that all the elements have value E_2; operation *lookup* produces the element in tuple E_2 indexed by E_1; and operation *update* builds a tuple from E_3, except that the element indexed by E_1 has value E_2. The typing rules implicitly enforce that E has type *nat* when it is used in the type expression *tuple* E. The type assignment attribute, π, is included in the rules in preparation for lambda abstractions.

The type, *tuple n*, is dependent on the value of n. For example, *tuple* 3 represents the type of triples, and *(init 3 0)* represents the triple, $\langle 0,0,0 \rangle$; it has type *tuple* 3. Most all general purpose programming languages use a dependent type similar to *tuple*: The array structure, whose lower and upper bounds are set for each particular declaration.

The presence of value expressions in types can cause headaches for a type checker.

$\tau \in$ Type-expression
$E \in$ Value-expression

$\tau ::= nat \mid tuple\ E$
$E ::= N \mid (init\ E_1\ E_2) \mid (lookup\ E_1\ E_2) \mid (update\ E_1\ E_2\ E_3)$

$$\pi \vdash N : nat \qquad\qquad \frac{\pi \vdash E_1 : nat \qquad \pi \vdash E_2 : nat}{\pi \vdash (init\ E_1\ E_2) : tuple\ E_1}$$

$$\frac{\pi \vdash E_1 : nat \qquad \pi \vdash E_2 : tuple\ E_3}{\pi \vdash (lookup\ E_1\ E_2) : nat} \qquad\qquad \frac{\pi \vdash E_1 : nat \qquad \pi \vdash E_2 : nat \qquad \pi \vdash E_3 : tuple\ E_4}{\pi \vdash (update\ E_1\ E_2\ E_3) : tuple\ E_4}$$

Figure 8.6 _____

In general, the value of E might need calculation by the type checker when it appears in the type *tuple* E. This implies that the operational semantics for value expressions should be available to the type checker. The problem is side-stepped in Figure 8.6 by not checking the size of the tuple argument to the *lookup* and *update* operations, but this means that erroneous expressions like $(lookup\ 7\ (init\ 3\ 0))$ are well typed—the language is statically typed but not strongly typed. If the typing rule for *lookup* is changed to read

$$\frac{\pi \vdash E_1 : nat \qquad \pi \vdash E_2 : tuple\ E_3}{\pi \vdash (lookup\ E_1\ E_2) : nat} \quad \text{if } E_1 \leq E_3$$

then both E_1 and E_3 must be evaluated by the type checker to verify the well formedness of the expression. Similar problems arise in the type checking of array expressions in general purpose programming languages.

Our intuition tells us that the *tuple* type builder is inherently a dependent type, and when we apply $(*,*)$ abstraction to the language, the dependent types leap forwards. The additions to the syntax are the usual ones,

$\tau ::= \cdots \mid (I{:}\tau_1) \rightarrow \tau_2$
$E ::= \cdots \mid (\lambda I{:}\tau.\ E) \mid (E_1\ E_2) \mid I$

and the typing rules are the usual ones. Within the extended language, we can code the following examples:

(i) $\pi \vdash (\lambda m{:}nat.\lambda n{:}nat.\ init\ m\ n) : (m{:}nat) \rightarrow (nat \rightarrow (tuple\ m))$
      This example exposes the dependent typing of the *init* operator.

(ii) $\pi \vdash (\lambda n{:}nat.\lambda p{:}(tuple\ n).\ (lookup\ n\ p)) : (n{:}nat) \rightarrow ((tuple\ n) \rightarrow nat)$

This example is guaranteed to apply the *lookup* operation to extract the *last* element of its tuple argument, regardless of the size of the tuple. Call this expression *F*. In order to check the well-formedness of $((F\ E_1)\ E_2)$, we are forced to evaluate E_1 and the type of E_2. The extra work is required, even though it was not necessary in the core language, because the dependent type of *F* forces its two arguments to satisfy a logical "precondition." (Here, the precondition is that the second argument must be a tuple of the size stated by the first argument.) A clever programmer can use dependent types to make precise statements about the input and output properties of functions. This idea is exploited in Chapter 10, where dependent types, coded as formulas in the predicate calculus, are used to state pre- and postconditions of the functions they label.

(iii) $\pi \vdash \lambda n{:}nat.\lambda p{:}tuple\ (lookup\ 1\ (init\ 2\ n)).\ (lookup\ n\ p)$

           $:\ (n{:}nat) \rightarrow (tuple\ (lookup\ 1\ (init\ 2\ n))) \rightarrow nat$

Call this example *G*. *G* also applies the *lookup* operation to extract the last element of its tuple argument, but the typing is more complex, since the instance of *tuple* takes a complex value expression as its argument. Perhaps the type checker can apply an algebraic law to simplify *tuple* (*lookup* 1 (*init* 2 *n*)) to *tuple n*, but it is more likely that the type checker would leave the type expression as it is and simplify it only when *G* is given its arguments. For example, the type of (*G* 4) can be calculated to be $(tuple\ (lookup\ 1\ (init\ 2\ 4))) \rightarrow nat \Rightarrow (tuple\ (lookup\ 1\ \langle 4,4 \rangle)) \rightarrow nat \Rightarrow (tuple\ 4) \rightarrow nat$.

When $(*, \square)$ abstraction is added to the language, the user can write parameterized types that behave much like dependent types. The syntax of types becomes the following:

$$\kappa\ ::=\ *\ |\ (I{:}\tau) \rightarrow \kappa$$
$$\tau\ ::=\ nat\ |\ (tuple\ E)\ |\ (I{:}\tau_1) \rightarrow \tau_2\ |\ (\lambda I{:}\tau_1.\ \tau_2)\ |\ (\tau\ E)$$

$$\pi \vdash *{:}\square \qquad \frac{\pi \vdash \tau{:}* \quad \pi \uplus \{I{:}\tau\} \vdash \kappa{:}\square}{\pi \vdash (I{:}\tau) \rightarrow \kappa{:}\square}$$

$$\pi \vdash nat{:}* \qquad \frac{\pi \vdash E{:}nat}{\pi \vdash tuple\ E{:}*} \qquad \frac{\pi \vdash \tau_1{:}* \quad \pi \uplus \{I{:}\tau_1\} \vdash \tau_2{:}*}{\pi \vdash (I{:}\tau_1) \rightarrow \tau_2{:}*}$$

$$\frac{\pi \vdash \tau_1{:}* \quad \pi \vdash \kappa{:}\square \quad \pi \uplus \{I{:}\tau_1\} \vdash \tau_2{:}\kappa}{\pi \vdash (\lambda I{:}\tau_1.\ \tau_2){:}\tau_1 \rightarrow \kappa} \qquad \frac{\pi \vdash \tau_1{:}\tau_2 \rightarrow \kappa \quad \pi \vdash E{:}\tau_2}{\pi \vdash (\tau_1\ E){:}\kappa}$$

Since types can be parameterized, kind attributes become necessary. The syntax rule for types lacks an identifier construct, I, because identifiers represent only value expressions, not types, so the identifier for value expressions suffices.

A simple example of a $(*, \Box)$ abstraction is:

$$\pi \vdash (\lambda n : nat.\ tuple\ n) : (n{:}nat) \to *$$

which exposes the underlying kinding of the *tuple* constructor to be $(n{:}nat) \to *$ (or $nat \to *$). Call this type expression H; it can be used in the following value expression:

$$\pi \vdash (\lambda m : nat.\ \lambda p :(H\ m).\ lookup\ m\ p) : (m{:}nat) \to ((p{:}tuple\ m) \to nat)$$

The argument, p, has the type *tuple m*, since $(H\ m) \Rightarrow tuple\ m$. A more convoluted example of $(*, \Box)$ abstraction is seen in

$$\pi \vdash (\lambda n : nat.\ \lambda p :tuple\ n.\ tuple\ (lookup\ n\ p)) : (n{:}nat) \to ((p{:}tuple\ n) \to *)$$

Call this J; it might be used in $\pi \vdash (J\ 2\ (init\ 2\ 3)) : *$, which is a well-formed type that β-reduces to *tuple* 3. Another use of J is seen here:

$$\pi \vdash (\lambda m : nat.\ \lambda q :((J\ m\ (init\ m\ m)).\ (update\ m\ 0\ q))$$
$$: (m{:}nat) \to (q : ((J\ m)\ (init\ m\ m))) \to ((J\ m)\ (init\ m\ m))$$

When this abstraction is applied to the argument 1, the result has type $((J\ 1)\ (init\ 1\ 1)) \to ((J\ 1)\ (init\ 1\ 1))$, which reduces to *tuple* $1 \to$ *tuple* 1.

We can format the tuple language within a generalized type system. Figure 8.7 shows the language in this format. The first six typing rules define the language core, and the remaining rules are from Figure 8.4.

The pure form of a generalized typing system with $(*, *)$ and $(*, \Box)$ abstractions forms the heart of the *Logical Framework* (*LF*) system (Harper, Honsell, and Plotkin 1992). When $(\Box, *)$ and $(\Box, \Box)$ abstractions are added, one obtains the *Calculus of Constructions* system (Coquand and Huet 1988). Both systems have the confluence, strong normalization, and subject-reduction properties. The LF was designed for defining and analyzing programming logics. Because of Girard's paradox, the Calculus of Constructions may well be the most powerful and consistent, impredicative higher-order lambda calculus.

We finish the section with a brief summary of dependence in types and kinds. The tuple language used dependent types to label $(*, *)$ abstractions; an example is $(n{:}nat) \to (tuple\ n)$, which is the type of $(\lambda n{:}nat.\ init\ n\ 0)$. Earlier in the chapter, we saw that the second order lambda calculus used dependent types to label $(\Box, *)$ abstractions; an example is $(t{:}*) \to (t \to t)$, which is the type of $(\lambda t{:}*.\lambda x{:}t.\ x)$. We might consider what forms of dependency arise with the other two forms of abstraction that we studied. A *dependent kind* arises as the kinding attribute for a $(*, \Box)$ abstraction. The type expression J, seen previously, is a $(*, \Box)$ abstraction and has the dependent kind $(n{:}nat) \to ((p{:}tuple\ n) \to *)$. Another example might be a system with the primitive type *nat* and the following family of kinds:

$E, \tau, \kappa \in$ Expression
$N \in$ Numeral
$I \in$ Identifier

$\quad E ::= nat \mid tuple \mid N \mid init \mid lookup \mid update$
$\quad\quad \mid * \mid (I{:}E_1) \rightarrow E_2 \mid (\lambda I{:}E_1 . E_2) \mid (E_1 \ E_2) \mid I$

$$\pi \vdash nat{:}* \quad\quad \pi \vdash tuple{:}(n{:}nat) \rightarrow * \quad\quad \pi \vdash N{:}nat$$

$$\pi \vdash init{:}(n_1{:}nat) \rightarrow (n_2{:}nat) \rightarrow tuple \ n_1 \quad\quad \frac{\pi \vdash E{:}nat}{\pi \vdash lookup{:}(n_1{:}nat) \rightarrow (t{:}tuple \ E) \rightarrow nat}$$

$$\frac{\pi \vdash E{:}nat}{\pi \vdash update{:}(n_1{:}nat) \rightarrow (n_2{:}nat) \rightarrow (t{:}tuple \ E) \rightarrow tuple \ E}$$

$$\pi \vdash *{:}\Box \quad\quad \frac{\pi \vdash \tau_1{:}* \quad \pi \uplus \{I{:}\tau_1\} \vdash \tau_2{:}\kappa}{\pi \vdash (I{:}\tau_1) \rightarrow \tau_2{:}\kappa} \ \text{ if } \kappa \in \{*, \Box\} \text{ and } I \notin FV(\pi)$$

$$\frac{\pi \vdash (I{:}\tau_1) \rightarrow \tau_2{:}\kappa \quad \pi \uplus \{I{:}\tau_1\} \vdash E{:}\tau_2}{\pi \vdash (\lambda I{:}\tau_1 . E){:}(I{:}\tau_1) \rightarrow \tau_2} \quad\quad \frac{\pi \vdash E_1{:}(I{:}\tau_1) \rightarrow \tau_2 \quad \pi \vdash E_2{:}\tau_1}{\pi \vdash (E_1 \ E_2){:}[E_2/I]\tau_2}$$

$$\pi \vdash I{:}\tau, \ \text{if} \ (I{:}\tau) \in \pi \quad\quad \frac{\pi \vdash E{:}\tau_1}{\pi \vdash E{:}\tau_2} \ \text{ if } \tau_1 \Rightarrow^* \tau_2$$

Figure 8.7 _____

$*_0 = *$
$*_{i+1} = * \rightarrow *_i, \ i \geq 0$

Then, the dependent kind $(n{:}nat) \rightarrow *_n$ would arise in

$$\pi \vdash \lambda n{:}nat.\lambda \tau_1{:}*.\lambda \tau_2{:}* . \cdots \lambda \tau_n{:}* . \ \tau_1 \rightarrow \tau_2 \rightarrow \cdots \rightarrow \tau_n : (n{:}nat) \rightarrow *_n$$

Similar creativity might let us develop a dependent kind for $(\Box, \Box)$ abstraction. If we have a system where the type $t \rightarrow t$ has the kind $*_t$, then we might derive the following:

$$\pi \vdash (\lambda t{:}* . \ t \rightarrow t) : (t{:}*) \rightarrow *_t$$

Further examples are left as exercises.

8.5 Dependent Sum Types

In Chapter 7, we studied various encapsulation constructs ("abstypes") whose types had form *exists*(I, τ_I). We now write the type as $\exists I{:}\tau.\,\tau_I$, where occurrences of identifier I can appear in τ_I. Values of the type are pairs of the form (v, u_v), where v has type τ, and u_v, which can contain occurrences of v, has type τ_I.

Just like lambda abstraction can operate on values and types, encapsulation can also operate on values and types. Here are examples:

(i)   ($\square$,*) encapsulation: This is the form of encapsulation used in Chapter 7. The pair $(nat, \lambda x{:}nat.\,x)$ has type $\exists t{:}*.\,t \to t$. The first component of the pair, *nat*, has its identity hidden by the name t, and the second component has its usual type, $nat \to nat$, similarly masked. Note that the same pair, $(nat, \lambda x{:}nat.\,x)$, also can have type $\exists t{:}*.\,nat \to t$, as well as $\exists t{:}*.\,t \to nat$, as well as $\exists t{:}*.\,nat \to nat$. This explains the need for the **abs***t* and **rep***t* operations in Chapter 7 to maintain unicity of typing.

(ii) (*,*) encapsulation: The pair $(3, \langle 0,0,0 \rangle)$ has type $\exists n{:}nat.\,tuple\;n$. The value, 3, is hidden, and the type of $\langle 0,0,0 \rangle$ is similarly masked. This pair can also have type $\exists n{:}nat.\,tuple\;3$.

(iii) (*,$\square$) encapsulation: The pair $(3, tuple\;3)$ has kind $\exists n{:}nat.\,*$. A more interesting example is $(3, \lambda t{:}tuple\;3.\,tuple(lookup\;3\;t))$, which has kind $\exists n{:}nat.\,tuple\;n \to *$.

(iv) ($\square$,$\square$) encapsulation: The pair $(nat, nat \to nat)$ has kind $\exists t{:}*.\,*$. Another example is $(nat, \lambda t'{:}*.\,nat \to t')$, which has kind $\exists t{:}*.\,* \to *$. If dependent kinds were available (cf. the previous section), dependent kindings like the ones in (i), (ii), and (iii) could be defined.

The type $\exists I{:}\tau.\,\tau_I$ is sometimes called a *dependent sum type* because it can be viewed by a mathematician as the set $\sum_{I \in \tau} \tau_I$, that is, the set of all pairs (v, u_v) such that $v \in \tau$ and $u_v \in \tau_I$. Just as the type $(I{:}\tau) \to \tau_I$ (or $\forall I{:}\tau.\,\tau_I$, if you prefer) can be written $\tau \to \tau_I$ when τ_I contains no occurrences of I, the type $\exists I{:}\tau.\,\tau_I$ can be written $\tau \times \tau_I$ when τ_I has no occurrences of I. This is reasonable, since the elements of the type are ordered pairs.

In the previous chapter, we studied both weak and strong versions of the abstype construct. Here, we have versions of weak and strong dependent sum types. The definition of the weak sum is:

$$\frac{\pi \vdash E_1 : \tau \qquad \pi \vdash E_2 : [E_1 / I]\tau_I}{\pi \vdash (E_1, E_2) : \exists I{:}\tau.\,\tau_I} \qquad \frac{\pi \vdash E_1 : \exists I{:}\tau.\,\tau_I \qquad \pi \uplus \{I{:}\tau, J{:}\tau_I\} \vdash E_2 : \tau'}{\pi \vdash open\,(I, J) = E_1 \; in \; E_2 : \tau'}$$

$$\text{if I and J are not free in } \pi \text{ and } \tau'$$

This matches the weak abstype. An example is:

$$\pi \vdash (open\,(m,n) = (3, (init\;3\;0)) \; in \; (lookup\;m\;n)) : nat$$

where $\pi \vdash (3, (init\,3\,0))\colon \exists n\colon nat.\,tuple\ n$ holds. The computation rule for the weak sum is:

$open\ (I, J) = (v, u_v)\ in\ E \implies [v/I, u_v/J]E$

The syntax of the strong-sum operation uses the same pairing construct as weak sum, but the *open* construct is replaced by two indexing operations:

$$\frac{\pi \vdash E\colon \exists I\colon \tau.\ \tau_I}{\pi \vdash fst\ E\colon \tau} \qquad\qquad \frac{\pi \vdash E\colon \exists I\colon \tau.\ \tau_I}{\pi \vdash snd\ E\colon [fst\ E/I]\tau_I}$$

The computation rules follow:

$fst\ (v, u_v) \implies v$

$snd\ (v, u_v) \implies u_v$

In Chapter 7, we noted that strong sums combined with lambda abstraction generate a language where strong normalization fails. This can be proved by translating the "**type:type**" calculus from Figure 8.5 into a language with $(*,*)$ and $(\square,*)$ abstraction and strong $(\square,*)$ encapsulation and then showing that any computation in the former calculus is replicated in the latter. The key is simulating the axiom $*\colon*$. As outlined in Chapter 7, let N_1 be some type such that there is some element $0\colon N_1$. Let $U = \exists I\colon *.N_1$; elements of the form $(\tau, 0)$, where $\tau\colon *$, have type U. U can be considered the collection of all type names, since $fst(\tau, 0) = \tau$. Since $(U, 0)\colon U$, we can simulate $*\colon*$.

Given the **type:type** calculus in Figure 8.5, we define the translation, $[\![\cdot]\!]$, as follows:

$[\![*]\!] = (U, 0)$, which has type U

$[\![(x\colon A) \to B]\!] = ((x\colon fst[\![A]\!]) \to fst[\![B]\!], 0)$, which has type U

$[\![x]\!] = x$

$[\![\lambda x\colon A.\,E]\!] = \lambda x\colon fst[\![A]\!].\ [\![E]\!]$

$[\![E_1\ E_2]\!] = [\![E_1]\!]\ [\![E_2]\!]$

Hook and Howe (1986) used this translation to show that any computation in the **type:type** calculus is replicated in the language with lambda abstraction and strong sums. Hence, the latter is not strongly normalizable.

In Chapter 10, we see how the strong abstype can coexist with lambda abstraction in a predicative calculus.

Suggested Reading

The second-order lambda calculus is due to Girard 1972 and Reynolds 1974. A good introduction is Reynolds 1990, found in Huet 1990, which itself contains a variety of interesting papers. Model theoretic results are found in Gunter 1992, Mitchell 1990, and Odifreddi 1990. *F*ω was defined in Girard 1972, and Pierce, Dietzen, and Michaylov 1989 provides a pleasant introduction. See also Girard 1986. Generalized typing systems are described in Barendregt and Hemerik 1990 and Barendregt 1991 and 1992. Languages with dependent product types include Automath (see de Bruijn 1980); Calculus of Constructions (see Coquand and Huet 1988 and Coquand 1990); and the Edinburgh Logical Framework (see Harper, Honsell, and Plotkin 1992). See also Huet and Plotkin 1992.

Exercises

0.1. The simply typed lambda calculus can be extended by recursive types. The syntax of types becomes

$$\tau ::= \iota \mid \tau_1 \to \tau_2 \mid rec\,\mathrm{I}.\tau \mid \mathrm{I}$$

and we add the following typing rule:

$$\frac{\pi \vdash \mathrm{E}: \tau_1}{\pi \vdash \mathrm{E}: \tau_2} \quad \text{if } \tau_1 \equiv \tau_2$$

a. Say that we define $\tau_1 \equiv \tau_2$ to be the smallest equivalence relation such that $rec\,\mathrm{I}.\tau \equiv [rec\,\mathrm{I}.\tau/\mathrm{I}]\tau$ holds. Show that there is a type, τ, such that $(\lambda X{:}\tau.\,X\,X)(\lambda X{:}\tau.\,X\,X)$ is well typed. Thus, the system lacks normalization. Also show for any type, τ, that there is a type, σ, such that the expression

$$\mathbf{Y} = \lambda F{:}\tau \to \tau.\,(\lambda X{:}\sigma.\,F\,(X\,X))(\lambda X{:}\sigma.\,F\,(X\,X))$$

is well typed.

b. Can we use the definition of $\equiv$ in Part a to prove $rec\,\alpha.\beta \to \alpha \equiv rec\,\alpha.\beta \to (\beta \to \alpha)$? An alternative definition of $\equiv$ goes as follows: $\tau_1 \equiv \tau_2$ iff $tree(\tau_1) = tree(\tau_2)$, where

$$tree(\mathrm{C}) = \mathrm{C}$$
$$tree(\tau_1 \to \tau_2) = tree(\tau_1) \to tree(\tau_2)$$
$$tree(rec\,\mathrm{I}.\tau) = tree([rec\,\mathrm{I}.\tau/\mathrm{I}]\tau)$$

(note: if $tree([rec\,\mathrm{I}.\tau/\mathrm{I}]\tau)$ is undefined, the result is the "empty tree")

$$tree(\mathrm{I}) = \mathrm{I}$$

That is, type expressions are trees of potentially infinite depth. Show that $rec\,\alpha.\beta \to \alpha \equiv rec\,\alpha.\beta \to (\beta \to \alpha)$ under the new definition of $\equiv$ and use the equivalence in a derivation of a well-typed term.

c.* If we use the definition of $\equiv$ in Part b, can we still type check an expression in finite time? (Hint: Let a type expression define a finite state automaton, and use the result that equivalence of such automata is decidable.)

0.2 Yet another variation of the simply typed lambda calculus includes *intersection types*. The syntax of type expressions is

$$\tau ::= \iota \mid \tau_1 \rightarrow \tau_2 \mid \tau_1 \cap \tau_2$$

The intuition is that an intersection type expresses overloading, for example, we might have that $\pi \vdash +: (int \rightarrow int \rightarrow int) \cap (bool \rightarrow bool \rightarrow bool)$ to state that $+$ can operate upon integers (as addition) or upon booleans (as disjunction). The typing rules for expressions are augmented by

$$\frac{\pi \vdash E: \tau_1 \quad \pi \vdash E: \tau_2}{\pi \vdash E: \tau_1 \cap \tau_2} \qquad \frac{\pi \vdash E: \tau_1 \cap \tau_2}{\pi \vdash E: \tau_i} \text{ for } i \in \{1, 2\}$$

a. Show that there is a type, τ, such that $\lambda X{:}\tau. X\, X$ is well typed.

b. Explain why for any type, τ, that $(\lambda X{:}\tau. X\, X)(\lambda X{:}\tau. X\, X)$ cannot be typed.

Let us add a new type, *Top*, to the syntax of type expressions, along with the axiom

$$\pi \vdash E: Top$$

That is, *Top* is the "universal type," and all expressions have type *Top*.

c. Show that $(\lambda X{:}\tau. X\, X)(\lambda X{:}\tau. X\, X)$ is well typed.

If types are sets of expressions, then $\tau_1 \cap \tau_2$ should represent the intersection of the sets of expressions for τ_1 and τ_2. The notion of "subset" can be encoded by a version of "subtype." Say that τ_1 is a subtype of τ_2 if $\tau_1 \leq \tau_2$ can be deduced by the following rules:

$$\tau \leq \tau \qquad \tau \leq Top \qquad Top \leq Top \rightarrow Top$$

$$\tau_1 \cap \tau_2 \leq \tau_1 \qquad \tau_1 \cap \tau_2 \leq \tau_2 \qquad (\tau_1 \rightarrow \tau_2) \cap (\tau_1 \rightarrow \tau_3) \leq \tau_1 \rightarrow (\tau_2 \cap \tau_3)$$

$$\frac{\tau_1 \leq \tau_2 \quad \tau_2 \leq \tau_3}{\tau_1 \leq \tau_3} \qquad \frac{\tau_1 \leq \tau_2 \quad \tau_1 \leq \tau_3}{\tau_1 \leq \tau_2 \cap \tau_3} \qquad \frac{\tau_{21} \leq \tau_{11} \quad \tau_{12} \leq \tau_{22}}{\tau_{11} \rightarrow \tau_{12} \leq \tau_{21} \rightarrow \tau_{22}}$$

We also add one more inference rule:

$$\frac{\pi \vdash E: \tau_1}{\pi \vdash E: \tau_2} \text{ if } \tau_1 \leq \tau_2$$

d. Give an example of an expression that is well typed in the system with $\leq$ but is not well typed in the system without it.

A good reference for this exercise and the preceding one is Cardone and Coppo 1990.

1.1. Encode these ML-like programs in the second-order lambda calculus and draw their syntax trees. Reduce the programs to their normal forms.

a. **lettype** $t=int$ **in** $(\lambda x{:}t.\, x+(\textbf{let val}\, f\,(x{:}t){=}x\, \textbf{in}\, f\, 2))$

b. **let val** $twice(t{:}*)(f{:}t{\rightarrow}t) = \lambda x{:}t.\, f\,(f\, x)$ **in** $twice\, int\,(\lambda y{:}int.\, y{+}1)\, 2$

c. **let val** $f = \lambda t{:}*.\lambda x{:}t.x$ **in** $f\, intlist\,(cons\,(f\, int\, 0)\, nil)$

Explain why the following programs cannot be coded in an ML-like language (see Section 7.10); apply the β-rule to each.

d. $(\lambda x{:}(t{:}*)\rightarrow t\rightarrow(u{:}*)\rightarrow t.\, x\, int\, 3)$

e. $(\lambda f{:}(t{:}*)\rightarrow(t\rightarrow t\, list).\, f\, intlist\,(f\, int\, 0))\,(\lambda t{:}*.\lambda x{:}t.\, cons\, x\, nil)$

Explain why these programs are not well typed:

f. $\lambda t{:}*.\lambda x{:}t.\lambda t{:}*.\, x$

g. $(\lambda t{:}*.\lambda x{:}t.\, cons\, x\, nil)\, int\, intlist$

1.2 a. Try "improving" Figure 8.1 by replacing $(I{:}*)\rightarrow \tau$ by $(\lambda I{:}*.\tau)$ and replacing the rule for $(E\, \tau)$ by

$$\frac{\pi \vdash E{:}\, \tau_1}{\pi \vdash (E\, \tau_2){:}\,(\tau_1\, \tau_2)}$$

What other rules, constructions, and restrictions are needed?

b. Can the type, $\tau_1 \rightarrow \tau_2$ also be replaced by a lambda abstraction? If so, show the resulting language; if not, explain.

1.3 a. Justify, as best you can, why no closed expression has type $(t{:}*)\rightarrow t$ in the (pure) second-order lambda calculus.

b. Also, justify, as best you can, why the only closed, normal form expression of type $(t{:}*)\rightarrow(t\rightarrow t)$ in the (pure) second-order lambda calculus is $\lambda t{:}*.\lambda x{:}t.x$.

1.4. Say that the type, *bool*, is simulated in the second-order lambda calculus by expressions of type $(t{:}*)\rightarrow t\rightarrow t\rightarrow t$.

a. Give codings for *true* and *false*. (Hint: Consider these to be the typed, "polymorphic" versions of the codings for *true* and *false* from Exercise 1.6 of Chapter 6.) Code the operations *not*, *if*, and *and*.

b. Justify, as best you can, why the codings of *true* and *false* are the only closed, normal-form expression with type *bool*.

Say that the type, *nat*, is simulated in the second order lambda calculus by expressions of type $(t{:}*)\rightarrow t\rightarrow(t\rightarrow t)\rightarrow t$

c. Encode addition; multiplication; factorial (see Exercise 1.6f from Chapter 6).

Both *bool* and *nat* are examples of *inductive types*, and their encodings follow a standard pattern. See Pierce, et al. 1989 for details.

1.6. The second-order lambda calculus is sometimes extended by subtyping. (See

Section 4.7 for background.) Replace the last two typing rules in Figure 8.1 by the following:

$$\frac{\pi \uplus \{I \le \tau_1\} \vdash E : \tau_2}{\pi \vdash (\lambda I \le \tau_1 . E) : (I \le \tau_1) \to \tau_2} \quad \text{if } I \notin FV(\pi)$$

$$\frac{\pi \vdash E : (I \le \tau_1) \to \tau_2 \quad \pi \vdash \tau_1' \le \tau_1}{\pi \vdash (E \, \tau_1') : [\tau_1'/I]\tau_2} \qquad \frac{\pi \vdash E : \tau_1 \quad \pi \vdash \tau_1 \le \tau_2}{\pi \vdash E : \tau_2}$$

Now, the type assignment holds assertions of the form $\tau_1 \le \tau_2$, which states that τ_1 is a subtype of τ_2. The following subtyping rules are necessary:

$$\pi \vdash \tau \le \tau \qquad \frac{\pi \vdash \tau_1 \le \tau_2 \quad \pi \vdash \tau_2 \le \tau_3}{\pi \vdash \tau_1 \le \tau_3}$$

$$\pi \vdash \tau \le Top \qquad \pi \vdash I \le \tau, \text{ if } (I \le \tau) \in \pi$$

$$\frac{\pi \vdash \tau_{21} \le \tau_{11} \quad \pi \vdash \tau_{12} \le \tau_{22}}{\pi \vdash \tau_{11} \to \tau_{12} \le \tau_{21} \to \tau_{22}} \qquad \frac{\pi, I \le \tau_1 \vdash \tau_{12} \le \tau_{22}}{\pi \vdash (I \le \tau_1) \to \tau_{12} \le (I \le \tau_1) \to \tau_{22}}$$

Give example programs that make good use of these rules. Pierce (1992) shows that the last rule can *not* be generalized to:

$$\frac{\pi \vdash \tau_{12} \le \tau_{11} \quad \pi, I \le \tau_{11} \vdash \tau_{12} \le \tau_{22}}{\pi \vdash (I \le \tau_{11}) \to \tau_{12} \le (I \le \tau_{12}) \to \tau_{22}}$$

else static type checking is lost.

2.1. Draw attributed syntax trees for the following expressions, if possible. (Assume that the initial type and kind assignments are empty.) Reduce the well-typed expressions to their normal forms.

 a. $((\lambda x:((\lambda t:*.t)int).\, x)\, 0$

 b. $(\lambda f:* \to *.\lambda x:(f int).\, x)\,(\lambda t:*.t)\, 0$

 c. $((\lambda f:* \to *.\lambda g:(f int).\, g\, 3)\,(\lambda t:*.\, t \to t)\,(\lambda x:int.\, x+1)$

 d. $((\lambda f:* \to *.\lambda g:(f int).\, g)\,(\lambda t:*.\, t \to t)\,(\lambda x:int.\, x+1)\, 3$

 e. $(\lambda g:((\lambda t:*.t \to t)\, int).\, g\, 3)\,(\lambda x:int.\, x+1)$

2.2. Prove that if the pair P, π satisfy the well-formedness constraint in Figure 8.2, then $P, \pi \vdash E : \tau$ implies $P \vdash \tau : *$.

2.3. Reread Exercise 1.7 from Chapter 6. The usual typing rule for equivalence of types reads

$$\frac{P, \pi \vdash E : \tau_1}{P, \pi \vdash E : \tau_2} \quad \text{if } \tau_1 \, cnv \, \tau_2$$

Prove that this rule is equivalent to the one in Figure 8.2; that is, any proof tree built with one rule can be built with the other rule.

2.4. Say that the type expression $(I{:}\kappa){\to}\tau$ is replaced by $\forall\tau$, with the kinding rule

$$\frac{P\vdash\tau{:}\kappa\to *}{P\vdash\forall\tau{:} *}$$

a. Revise Figure 8.2 for the new construct.

b. If $\forall$ was treated as a "type constant," what would be its kind? That is, what would be Δ in $P\vdash\forall{:}\Delta$?

2.5. a. Add record types to Figure 8.2.

b.* Add record kinds to your answer in Part a.

2.6.* If you worked Exercise 1.4, proceed. Just as the second-order lambda calculus can simulate primitive types, $F\omega$ can simulate parameterized types. As an example, the simulation of the list constructor is

$$List = \lambda u{:} *.\ (F{:}*{\to}*) \to$$
$$((t{:}*) \to (F\ t))$$
$$\to ((t{:}*){\to}t{\to}(F\ t){\to}(F\ t))$$
$$\to (F\ u)$$

So, (*List bool*) is the simulated type of lists of booleans. The definitions of (polymorphic) *nil* and *cons* are

$$nil = \lambda u{:} *.\ \lambda F{:} *{\to}*.$$
$$\lambda n{:} ((t{:}*) \to (F\ t)).$$
$$\lambda c{:} ((t{:}*){\to}t{\to}(F\ t){\to}(F\ t)).$$
$$n\ u$$

$$cons = \lambda u{:} *.\lambda x{:} u.\lambda l{:} (List\ u).\ \lambda F{:} *{\to}*.$$
$$\lambda n{:} ((t{:}*) \to (F\ t)).$$
$$\lambda c{:} ((t{:}*){\to}t{\to}(F\ t){\to}(F\ t)).$$
$$c\ u\ x\ (l\ u\ n\ c)$$

So, (*nil bool*) and (*cons bool*) are the *nil* and *cons* operations for lists of booleans.

a. Verify that these definitions are well typed.

b. Define the *head* and *tail* operations

See Pierce, et al. 1989 for further information.

3.1. What are the values for **C**, **S**, **A**, and **R** for the (pure) simply typed lambda calculus? For the (pure) second-order lambda calculus?

3.2. For the representation of $F\omega$ as a GTS, rework Exercise 2.1.

3.3. If possible, calculate the types of these expressions in the **type:type** calculus. If possible, reduce the well-typed expressions to normal forms. Recall that $* \rightarrow *$ abbreviates $(I:*) \rightarrow *$.

a. $(\lambda a:((\lambda x:*.\ x \rightarrow x)*).\ a)\ (\lambda b:*.b)$

b. $(\lambda z:*.\lambda b:*.\ a)(((\lambda a:*.\ a)*) \rightarrow *)$

c. $(\lambda t:*.\lambda x:t.\ x)\ ((t:*) \rightarrow (t \rightarrow t))\ (\lambda t:*.\lambda x:t.\ x)$

d. $(\lambda a:*.a)\ (\lambda a:*.a)$

e. $(\lambda a:(\mathbf{Y} * (\lambda x:*.x)).\ a)\ *$

3.4. The original version of a GTS, in Barendregt and Hemerik 1990, differs somewhat from that in Figure 8.4. In the original version, first, a type assignment is a list of identifier, expression pairs, and $\uplus$ is list concatenation. Second, the well-formedness constraint on π is dropped, as are the restrictions on the rules for $\rightarrow$. Third, the rule for identifier lookup is replaced by these two rules:

$$\frac{\pi \vdash \tau : \kappa}{\pi \uplus \{I:\tau\} \vdash I:\tau} \quad \text{if } \kappa \in S \text{ and } I \text{ is fresh}$$

$$\frac{\pi \vdash I:\kappa \quad \pi \vdash E:\tau}{\pi \uplus \{I:\kappa\} \vdash E:\tau} \quad \text{if } \kappa \in S \text{ and } I \text{ is fresh}$$

Note: "I is fresh" means that I does not appear in π, τ, κ, and E

a.* Prove that the original version of GTS is equivalent to the one in Figure 8.4; that is, proofs of $\pi \vdash E:\tau$ in one version can be done in the other (modulo α-renaming of binding identifiers).

b. What problems arise in using the original version of GTS as the basis of a type-checking algorithm for a programming language?

3.5.* Add records to the GTS.

9 Propositional-Logic Typing

The previous chapter suggested ties between programming languages and predicate logic. In this and the next chapter, we develop the correspondence and observe the manner in which types are logical propositions and programs are logical proofs. The development is based on intuitionistic type theory (Martin-Löf 1984; Nordström, Petersson, and Smith 1990; Thompson 1991).

9.1 The Propositional Calculus

A *logistic system*, or *logic*, consists of (i) a syntax definition of the sentences of the logic, called the *well-formed formulas* (*wffs*); (ii) a set of axioms and inference rules for proving the "true" wffs; and (iii) a notion of proof. We now describe a logistic system for a propositional calculus. Wffs are built from an alphabet consisting of *propositional symbols*, $P, Q, R, \ldots$, *connectives*, $\supset$, $\wedge$, and *auxiliary symbols*, $\vdash$, (,). The syntax definition is

> $S \in$ Sequent (these are the wffs)
> $\Gamma \in$ Context
> $\phi \in$ Proposition
> $P \in$ Propositional-symbol

> $S ::= \Gamma \vdash \phi$
> $\Gamma ::= \phi_1, \phi_2, \ldots, \phi_n, \quad n \geq 0$
> $\phi ::= P \mid (\phi_1 \wedge \phi_2) \mid (\phi_1 \supset \phi_2)$

As usual, outermost parentheses on propositions are dropped, for example, $P \wedge (Q \supset R)$.

Propositions represent declarative statements about the world, for example, if P stands for "the sky is cloudy," and Q stands for "it is raining," then $P \wedge Q$ stands for "the sky is cloudy and it is raining," whereas $P \supset Q$ stands for "the sky is cloudy implies that it is raining." Any beginning logic text gives good examples. $\wedge$ is the *conjunction* connective and $\supset$ is the *implication* connective.

The basic units of proof are sequents. For a sequent, $\Gamma \vdash \phi$, we call Γ the *context*

---

axiom: $\Gamma \vdash \phi$,   if $\phi \in \Gamma$ (that is, $\phi \in \Gamma$ when Γ is $\phi_1, \phi_2, \ldots, \phi, \ldots, \phi_n$)

$$\wedge I: \frac{\Gamma \vdash \phi_1 \quad \Gamma \vdash \phi_2}{\Gamma \vdash \phi_1 \wedge \phi_2} \qquad \wedge E_1: \frac{\Gamma \vdash \phi_1 \wedge \phi_2}{\Gamma \vdash \phi_1} \qquad \wedge E_2: \frac{\Gamma \vdash \phi_1 \wedge \phi_2}{\Gamma \vdash \phi_2}$$

$$\supset I: \frac{\Gamma, \phi_1 \vdash \phi_2}{\Gamma \vdash \phi_1 \supset \phi_2} \qquad \supset E: \frac{\Gamma \vdash \phi_1 \supset \phi_2 \quad \Gamma \vdash \phi_1}{\Gamma \vdash \phi_2}$$

Figure 9.1 _____

---

or *assumptions* and call ϕ the *conclusion*. Read $\Gamma \vdash \phi$ as stating "from assumptions Γ, infer conclusion ϕ." An example is $P, P \supset Q \vdash Q$. Γ can be empty; for example, $\vdash P \supset P$. The symbol, $\vdash$, is called a *turnstile*; it behaves much like $\supset$, and once the axioms and inference rules are established, we can prove the *deduction theorem*, which states that $\Gamma \vdash \phi_1 \supset \phi_2$ is provable exactly when $\Gamma, \phi_1 \vdash \phi_2$ is.

The axiom and inference rules appear in Figure 9.1. The sequents above the line of an inference rule are called the *antecedents*; the one below is the *consequent*. (An axiom is just an inference rule with no antecedents.) The names of the inference rules are significant: They suggest that each connective, *op*, has an *introduction rule*, *op*I, which builds a proposition with the connective in it, and *elimination rules*, *op*E, which remove the connective from a proposition. (The analogy between a connective's introduction and elimination rules and a data structure's construction and destruction operations will become of prime importance.) The rules are called *natural-deduction rules*, due to their resemblance to common sense methods of reasoning.

A *sequent-proof tree* is a tree whose root is a sequent, $\Gamma \vdash \phi$, whose leaves are axioms and whose internal nodes are consequents of inference rules. Such a tree is a *proof of* $\Gamma \vdash \phi$. The sequent-proof trees are defined inductively:

(i)   If $\phi \in \Gamma$, then $\Gamma \vdash \phi$ is a sequent-proof tree.

(ii) If t_1 is a sequent-proof tree whose root is $\Gamma \vdash \phi_1$, and t_2 is a sequent-proof tree whose root is $\Gamma \vdash \phi_2$, then the tree

```
    t₁          t₂
     \         /  ∧I
      Γ ⊢ φ₁∧φ₂
```

is a sequent-proof tree.

(iii)–(iv) If t is a sequent-proof tree whose root is $\Gamma \vdash \phi_1 \wedge \phi_2$, then the trees

$$
\begin{array}{ccc}
t & \text{and} & t \\
\mid \wedge E_1 & & \mid \wedge E_2 \\
\Gamma \vdash \phi_1 & & \Gamma \vdash \phi_2
\end{array}
$$

are sequent-proof trees.

(v) If t is a sequent-proof tree whose root is $\Gamma, \phi_1 \vdash \phi_2$, then the tree

$$
\begin{array}{c}
t \\
\mid \supset I \\
\Gamma \vdash \phi_1 \supset \phi_2
\end{array}
$$

is a sequent-proof tree.

(vi) If t_1 is a sequent-proof tree whose root is $\Gamma \vdash \phi_1 \supset \phi_2$ and t_2 is a sequent-proof tree whose root is $\Gamma \vdash \phi_1$, then the tree

$$
\begin{array}{cc}
t_1 & t_2 \\
\backslash & / \supset E \\
\multicolumn{2}{c}{\Gamma \vdash \phi_2}
\end{array}
$$

is a sequent-proof tree.

Figure 9.2 shows a sequent-proof tree that proves $(Q \wedge R \supset S), P \wedge Q \vdash R \supset S$. It should be clear that the tree in the figure is well-formed, but it might not be clear how the tree was constructed. The derivation is best understood by reading the tree from the root to the leaves. To prove the goal $(Q \wedge R) \supset S, P \wedge Q \vdash R \supset S$, we should prove the subgoal $(Q \wedge R) \supset S, P \wedge Q, R \vdash S$, since the $\supset I$ rule then yields the result. The clue to the subgoaling step is that $\supset$ is the primary connective of the conclusion, $R \supset S$. Next, the conclusion, S, of the new subgoal has no primary connective, but a quick scan of the assumptions finds $(Q \wedge R) \supset S$. If we can prove the subgoal $(Q \wedge R) \supset S, P \wedge Q, R \vdash Q \wedge R$, then the $\supset E$ rule proves the result. The clue is that $\supset$ is the primary connective in the

---

$$
\begin{array}{c}
(Q \wedge R) \supset S, P \wedge Q, R \vdash P \wedge Q \\
\mid \wedge E_2 \\
(Q \wedge R) \supset S, P \wedge Q, R \vdash Q \qquad (Q \wedge R) \supset S, P \wedge Q, R \vdash R \\
\backslash \qquad\qquad / \wedge I
\end{array}
$$

$$
\begin{array}{cc}
(Q \wedge R) \supset S, P \wedge Q, R \vdash (Q \wedge R) \supset S & (Q \wedge R) \supset S, P \wedge Q, R \vdash Q \wedge R \\
\backslash & / \supset E
\end{array}
$$

$$
\begin{array}{c}
(Q \wedge R) \supset S, P \wedge Q, R \vdash S \\
\mid \supset I \\
(Q \wedge R) \supset S, P \wedge Q \vdash R \supset S
\end{array}
$$

Figure 9.2 _____

assumption $(Q \wedge R) \supset S$. The next subgoaling step is $\wedge$I, which produces two subgoals, one an axiom and the other easily proved by $\wedge E_2$.

A proved sequent of form $\vdash \phi$ is a *theorem*. Examples of theorems are $\vdash P \supset P$, $\vdash (P \wedge Q) \supset (Q \wedge P)$, and $\vdash ((P \supset Q) \supset R) \supset (Q \supset (P \supset R))$. A sequent-proof tree for the last theorem is displayed in Figure 9.3.

A theorem can be proved in infinitely many ways. (One trick is to add arbitrarily many extra $\wedge$I and $\wedge$E rules to the root of a proof tree: From $\vdash \phi$, infer $\vdash \phi \wedge \phi$ and then $\vdash \phi$ again.) We will not try to describe a "best" proof tree for a sequent, but we will describe later a technique for reducing a proof tree to a minimal form.

It is convenient to prove a sequent by a variant of proof tree that omits the contexts from the nodes of the tree. We call such a tree a *natural-deduction tree*. Natural-deduction trees for the sequent-proof trees in Figures 9.2 and 9.3 are shown in Figure 9.4. Draw the first tree in the figure—start by writing the conclusion, $R \supset S$, as the root and the assumptions, $(Q \wedge R) \supset S$ and $P \wedge Q$, as the leaves. Your job is to draw the middle of the tree, connecting the root and the leaves. Use the strategy described earlier and build the tree from the root to the leaves: Use $\supset$I to go from the goal $R \supset S$ to the subgoal S. This step creates a new leaf, R, which is a "local assumption" whose "scope" is indicated by the two occurrences of the symbol, ①. Next, apply $\supset$E to connect S to $(Q \wedge R) \supset S$, creating the new subgoal $Q \wedge R$. The final steps are $\wedge$I and $\wedge E_2$. The second example in Figure 9.4 has no assumption leaves at the start, but three local assumptions are introduced in the course of the proof.

The set of natural-deduction trees can be defined inductively, and this is left as an important exercise.

Natural-deduction trees are fun and easy to draw, but they must be verified as well formed. This is done by attaching the context information to the nodes, producing a

---

$$P \supset (Q \supset R), Q, P \vdash P \supset (Q \supset R) \qquad P \supset (Q \supset R), Q, P \vdash P$$
$$\backslash \qquad \qquad / \supset E$$
$$P \supset (Q \supset R), Q, P \vdash Q \supset R \qquad P \supset (Q \supset R), Q, P \vdash Q$$
$$\backslash \qquad \qquad / \supset E$$
$$P \supset (Q \supset R), Q, P \vdash R$$
$$| \supset I$$
$$P \supset (Q \supset R), Q \vdash P \supset R$$
$$| \supset I$$
$$P \supset (Q \supset R) \vdash Q \supset (P \supset R)$$
$$| \supset I$$
$$\vdash (P \supset (Q \supset R)) \supset (Q \supset (P \supset R))$$

Figure 9.3 _____

$$P\supset(Q\supset R) \;\; ① \quad P \;\; ③$$
$$\backslash \quad / \; \supset E$$

$$P\wedge Q$$
$$|\wedge E_2 \qquad\qquad\qquad Q\supset R \quad Q \;\; ②$$
$$\qquad\qquad\qquad\qquad\qquad \backslash \quad / \; \supset E$$
$$Q \qquad R \;\; ① \qquad\qquad R$$
$$\backslash \quad / \; \wedge I \qquad\qquad |\supset I \;\; ③$$
$$(Q\wedge R)\supset S \qquad Q\wedge R \qquad\qquad P\supset R$$
$$\backslash \quad / \; \supset E \qquad\qquad\qquad |\supset I \;\; ②$$
$$S \qquad\qquad\qquad\qquad Q\supset(P\supset R)$$
$$|\supset I \;\; ① \qquad\qquad\qquad |\supset I \;\; ①$$
$$R\supset S \qquad\qquad\qquad (P\supset(Q\supset R))\supset(Q\supset(P\supset R))$$

Figure 9.4

sequent-proof tree. The best way to insert the context information is to work from the root of the tree to the leaves. In the first example in Figure 9.4, the root is recoded $(Q\wedge R)\supset S, P\wedge Q \vdash R\supset S$. It is now clear that the node above the root is recoded $(Q\wedge R)\supset S, P\wedge Q, R \vdash S$, and so on. An example of an ill-formed natural-deduction tree is

$$S \qquad R\supset T \quad R \;\; ①$$
$$|\supset I \;\; ① \qquad \backslash \quad / \; \supset E$$
$$R\supset S \qquad\qquad T$$
$$\backslash \qquad\quad / \; \wedge I$$
$$(R\supset S)\wedge T$$

which purports to prove $S, R\supset T \vdash (R\supset S)\wedge T$, but the scope of the local assumption, R, is violated. This is detected when the attempt is made to attach context information to the tree's nodes.

Natural-deduction trees can be pasted together. For example, if we have the natural-deduction trees for $\Gamma \vdash (Q\wedge R)\supset S$ and $(Q\wedge R)\supset S, P\wedge Q \vdash R\supset S$, the two trees can be pasted together, root to leaf, at the "connection point" $(Q\wedge R)\supset S$, giving a natural-deduction tree for $\Gamma, P\wedge Q \vdash R\supset S$. The technique works because an assumption in a natural-deduction tree is merely a proposition whose proof is forthcoming. Pasting supplies the proof. Such proof pasting encourages "modular proof development."

9.2 Proofs as Programs

We make a startling discovery when we linearize a natural-deduction tree: It is an expression in a lambda calculus.

The linearization of a natural-deduction tree is simple enough: For example, if t_1 and t_2 are (the linear forms of) trees that prove ϕ_1 and ϕ_2, respectively, then $(\wedge I\ t_1\ t_2)$ is the linear form of the natural-deduction tree that proves $\phi_1 \wedge \phi_2$. The linearized forms for $\wedge E_1$, $\wedge E_2$, and $\supset E$ are similar. Since an assumption, ϕ, is a leaf that marks where a proof tree should be pasted, we use a dummy name, say, a, to stand for the forthcoming tree. Finally, $(\supset I\,(x \in \phi_1)\,t)$ is the linear form of a tree built by $\supset I$ that proves $\phi_1 \supset \phi_2$, where x is the hypothetical tree for the local assumption, ϕ_1, and t is the proof tree for ϕ_2. The local assumption has "scope" t.

Consider the first tree in Figure 9.4. Let a_1 stand for the assumption $(Q \wedge R) \supset S$, and let a_2 stand for $P \wedge Q$. This is the linear representation of the tree:

$$\supset I\ (x \in R)\ (\supset E\ a_1\ (\wedge I\ (\wedge E_2\ a_2)\ x)))$$

Notice how a_1, a_2, and x mark the places in the proof tree where assumptions are referenced. The second tree in Figure 9.4 is linearized as follows:

$$\supset I\ (x \in P \supset (Q \supset R))\ (\supset I\ (y \in Q)\ (\supset I\ (z \in P)\ (\supset E\ (\supset E\ x\ z)\ y))))$$

The scope of the three local assumptions, x, y, and z, are clear cut. Perhaps the linearized trees do not look like lambda calculus expressions, but the following reformatting makes it clear:

- $(\wedge I\ e_1\ e_2)$ is reformatted (e_1, e_2), that is, as an ordered pair.
- $(\wedge E_1\ e)$ is reformatted *fst e*, that is, as an indexing operation applied to a pair.
- $(\wedge E_2\ e)$ is reformatted *snd e*, that is, as an indexing operation applied to a pair.
- $(\supset I\ (x \in \phi)\ e)$ is reformatted $\lambda x \in \phi.\,e$, that is, as a lambda abstraction.
- $(\supset E\ e_1\ e_2)$ is reformatted $e_1 \cdot e_2$, that is, as the application of a lambda abstraction to its argument. (From now on, we represent the application of an operator, e_1, to an operand, e_2, by $e_1 \cdot e_2$, for clarity.)

The two reformatted trees are:

$$\lambda x \in R.\ a_1 \cdot (snd\,a_2, x) \qquad \text{and} \qquad \lambda x \in P \supset (Q \supset R).\ \lambda y \in Q.\ \lambda z \in P.\ (x \cdot z) \cdot y$$

The reformatting is purely syntactic; the expressions are still natural-deduction trees. But the lambda calculus notation suggests that the expressions are also functions—and they are. The first expression is a function that maps a natural-deduction tree, x, that proves R, into a natural-deduction tree that proves S. The second function maps a tree, x, that proves $P \supset (Q \supset R)$, into one that proves $Q \supset (P \supset R)$. Since trees are encoded as lambda-calculus expressions, the tree for $Q \supset (P \supset R)$ is itself a function, mapping trees for Q and P into a tree that proves R.

This interpretation of natural-deduction trees, called the *Heyting interpretation*, can be summarized as follows:

(i) A proof of a proposition, $\phi_1 \wedge \phi_2$, is a pair, consisting of a proof of ϕ_1 and a proof of ϕ_2.

(ii) A proof of a proposition, $\phi_1 \supset \phi_2$, is a function that transforms proofs of ϕ_1 into proofs of ϕ_2.

The terms "pair" and "function" used in (i) and (ii) refer to concrete constructions: a pair is a data structure holding two components, which can be indexed, and a function is a lambda abstraction that is applied to its argument by means of the β-rule.

The inference rules are *sound* with respect to the Heyting interpretation:

(a) The $\wedge I$ rule, applied to proofs, $e_1 \in \phi_1$ and $e_2 \in \phi_2$, constructs a pair, (e_1, e_2), which is a proof of $\phi_1 \wedge \phi_2$.

(b) The $\wedge E_1$ (respectively, the $\wedge E_2$) rule, applied to a proof, $e \in \phi_1 \wedge \phi_2$, extracts the first (resp., second) component of e, giving a proof, *fst e* (resp., *snd e*) of ϕ_1 (resp., ϕ_2).

(c) The $\supset I$ rule, applied to a proof, $e \in \phi_2$, that was built from a hypothetical proof, x, of ϕ_1, constructs a function, $\lambda x \in \phi_1 . e$, that constructs proofs of ϕ_2 from proofs of ϕ_1.

(d) The $\supset E$ rule, applied to proofs, $e_1 \in \phi_1 \supset \phi_2$ and $e_2 \in \phi_1$, applies function e_1 to e_2, giving a proof, $e_1 \cdot e_2$, of ϕ_2.

In parts (b) and (d) above, some computation steps may be necessary to compute the proof defined by the constructions *fst e*, *snd e*, and $e_1 \cdot e_2$ (see Section 9.4).

A natural-deduction tree that proves $\Gamma \vdash \phi$ is a "program" of "type" ϕ within "type assignment" Γ.

We can reformat the sequents and inference rules to emphasize that natural-deduction trees are typed programs. A *judgement* is a construct of the form $\Gamma \vdash e \in \phi$, where Γ is a list of items of the form $x_i \in \phi_i$, such that no identifier, x_i, appears twice in Γ. The identifiers represent the hypothetical proof trees for the assumptions. Read the judgement as saying, "within context Γ, e is a proof of ϕ," or, "within type assignment Γ, e is a program of type ϕ."

Next, we reformat the inference rules to look like typing rules. Figure 9.5 shows the results. The rules in Figure 9.5 can derive judgement-proof trees. But more importantly, when viewed as typing rules, *the rules attach context and typing information to natural-deduction trees*. The latter method is indeed how we plan to use the rules: Through design or accident, we draw a natural-deduction tree, and we apply the rules in Figure 9.5 to validate that the tree is a well-formed proof. Thus, Figure 9.6 is the validation of the natural-deduction tree (that is, the abstract syntax tree) $\lambda x \in R. a_1 \cdot (snd\, a_2, x)$.

The next step in merging the lines of development between propositional logic and

$$\text{axiom: } \Gamma \vdash x \in \phi, \quad \text{if } (x \in \phi) \in \Gamma$$

$$\land\text{I:} \quad \frac{\Gamma \vdash e_1 \in \phi_1 \quad \Gamma \vdash e_2 \in \phi_2}{\Gamma \vdash e_1, e_2 \in \phi_1 \land \phi_2} \qquad \land\text{E}_1: \quad \frac{\Gamma \vdash e \in \phi_1 \land \phi_2}{\Gamma \vdash fst\, e \in \phi_1} \qquad \land\text{E}_2: \quad \frac{\Gamma \vdash e \in \phi_1 \land \phi_2}{\Gamma \vdash snd\, e \in \phi_2}$$

$$\supset\text{I:} \quad \frac{\Gamma, x \in \phi_1 \vdash e \in \phi_2}{\Gamma \vdash \lambda x \in \phi_1.e \in \phi_1 \supset \phi_2} \qquad \supset\text{E:} \quad \frac{\Gamma \vdash e_1 \in \phi_1 \supset \phi_2 \quad \Gamma \vdash e_2 \in \phi_1}{\Gamma \vdash e_1 \cdot e_2 \in \phi_2}$$

Figure 9.5 _____

$$a_1 \in Q \land R \supset S, a_2 \in P \land Q, x \in R \vdash a_2 \in P \land Q$$
$$\mid \land\text{E}_2$$
$$a_1 \in Q \land R \supset S, a_2 \in P \land Q, x \in R \vdash snd\, a_2 \in Q \qquad a_1 \in Q \land R \supset S, a_2 \in P \land Q, x \in R \vdash x \in R$$
$$\setminus \qquad\qquad\qquad / \land\text{I}$$
$$a_1 \in Q \land R \supset S, a_2 \in P \land Q, x \in R \vdash a_1 \in Q \land R \supset S \qquad a_1 \in Q \land R \supset S, a_2 \in P \land Q, x \in R \vdash snd\, a_2, x \in Q \land R$$
$$\setminus \qquad\qquad\qquad / \supset\text{E}$$
$$a_1 \in Q \land R \supset S, a_2 \in P \land Q, x \in R \vdash a_1 \cdot (snd\, a_2, x) \in S$$
$$\mid \supset\text{I}$$
$$a_1 \in Q \land R \supset S, a_2 \in P \land Q \vdash \lambda x \in R.\, a_1 \cdot (snd\, a_2, x) \in R \supset S$$

Figure 9.6 _____

lambda calculus is noting that the logical connective, $\supset$, is just the function-type constructor, $\rightarrow$, and the logical connective, $\land$, is just the product-type constructor, $\times$. Alternatively, think of $\land$ as a binary-record constructor, where the two fields of the record are implicitly labeled by the identifiers *fst* and *snd*. Thus, the language of natural-deduction trees is just a simply typed lambda calculus with pairing/records. *For this reason, from this point onward we freely use the words "proposition" and "type" as synonyms and the words "proof," "program," "natural-deduction tree," and "expression" as synonyms.* This correspondence is called the *Curry-Howard isomorphism*, after two of its founders.

A concept useful for the future is that of *canonical expression*. The canonical expressions of a type are those (closed) expressions built by the type's introduction rules, that is, pairs for $\phi_1 \land \phi_2$ and lambda abstractions for $\phi_1 \supset \phi_2$. Canonical expressions represent the "values" of a type, as described by the Heyting interpretation.

9.3 Programming in the Logic

The previous chapters indicated that a programming language has a core of primitive types, which is then extended by lambda abstraction, records, and other structuring devices. The previous section showed that our propositional logic is a core logic of primitive propositions extended by implication, conjunction, and maybe other connectives. In this section, we consider the nature of the core logic and how it induces a core programming language.

We begin with two primitive propositions, *bool* and *nat*. The axioms and rules in Figure 9.7 define the data types. We can verify that expressions like 5, 3+2, and *if* (2=3) 5 (2+3) are natural-deduction trees that "prove" proposition *nat*. Since introduction rules create canonical expressions, we note that *true, false*, and the numerals are canonical.

One might wonder about the utility of distinct proofs of the same proposition, whether it be $P \wedge Q$ or *nat*, since only one proof suffices to show that a proposition is a theorem. But different proofs of the same proposition express different aspects of the proposition's "personality," for example, 0, 1, 2, ... are different aspects of *nat*'s personality. Finally, since every theorem can be proved in infinitely many different ways, there seems no need to artificially limit the number of its proofs.

We extend the core logic in Figure 9.7 with the rules for $\supset$ and $\wedge$ from Figure 9.5. Here are three example programs in the extended language:

$$\vdash \lambda x \in nat.\, x+1 \ \in nat \supset nat$$
$$\vdash \lambda x \in nat.\, \lambda y \in nat \wedge bool.\, x = fst\, y \ \in \ nat \supset ((nat \wedge bool) \supset bool)$$
$$f \in bool \supset (nat \supset nat),\, y \in bool \vdash if\, y\, (\lambda x \in nat.\, x)\, (f \cdot y) \ \in \ nat \supset nat$$

The third example shows that the *bool*E rule extends to propositions with connectives.

$$boolI_1: \ \Gamma \vdash false \in bool \qquad boolI_2: \ \Gamma \vdash true \in bool$$

$$boolE: \ \frac{\Gamma \vdash e_1 \in bool \quad \Gamma \vdash e_2 \in \phi \quad \Gamma \vdash e_3 \in \phi}{\Gamma \vdash if\, e_1\, e_2\, e_3 \in \phi} \qquad natI_n: \ \Gamma \vdash n \in nat, \text{ for } n \geq 0$$

$$natE_1: \ \frac{\Gamma \vdash e_1 \in nat \quad \Gamma \vdash e_2 \in nat}{\Gamma \vdash e_1 + e_2 \in nat} \qquad natE_2: \ \frac{\Gamma \vdash e_1 \in nat \quad \Gamma \vdash e_2 \in nat}{\Gamma \vdash e_1 = e_2 \in bool}$$

Figure 9.7 _____

This is how we program in the propositional logic. The task of constructing a function of a type, say, $nat \rightarrow nat$, becomes the job of proving the proposition $nat \supset nat$. Of course, there are infinitely many ways of proving the proposition, just as there are infinitely many ways of writing a program of type $nat \rightarrow nat$.

An important issue is decidability. We say that a question is *decidable* if there is a mechanical method—an algorithm—that can answer the question in finite time by "yes" or "no." There are two important questions that are decidable for the propositional logic. The first is, For a natural-deduction tree and a context, what proposition does the tree prove? The algorithm that decides the question checks the natural-deduction tree for well-formedness and calculates the proposition that the tree proves. In a programming language, such a tree checker is called a type checker. Indeed, the type checkers for Modula-like languages are merely proof tree checkers for varieties of propositional logics. A second decidable question is, Is a given proposition a theorem? Since a decision algorithm need only answer "yes" or "no," it need not build a natural-deduction tree in the case of a "yes" answer. The usual decision algorithm calculates a *truth table* for the proposition in question and sees if the truth table contains only *true* values. (See any beginning logic text for details.) But a decision algorithm can be built that generates a natural-deduction tree (Lemmon 1965).

Since propositional logic's fundamental purpose is the derivation of theorems, the decidability of theoremhood is an important result. But from the standpoint of the core language in this section, it is not so significant, since *any* proposition built with *bool*, *nat*, $\supset$, and $\wedge$ has a proof. The underlying issue is that the propositions are all-too-crude descriptors of the programs that they type. The statement that there is a program of type $(nat \wedge nat) \supset nat$ tells us virtually nothing about what the program *does*. Is it an addition program? A multiplication? Perhaps it is *fst*. All we know for certain is that the program takes a pair of numeric inputs and produces a number for its output. Although propositions are meant to be descriptors of program properties, the properties are too crude to be of much use.

This last point is crucial to the pragmatics of a programming language. Programmers expect a type checker to validate a program as trustworthy for execution. Beginning programmers naively believe that if a type checker validates a program, then the program must be "correct." Type checkers based on propositional logic do little validation, aside from guaranteeing the absence of operator-operand incompatibility errors. Type checkers can *not* report that a program computes, say, the addition function, because the logic that the type checker enforces—the propositional logic—is too crude to make such a statement. In the next chapter, we examine the predicate logic, which is rich enough that statements of a program's purpose *can* be encoded in the type and type checking *can* validate them.

9.4 Computing in the Logic

Programs must be computed by computation (rewriting) rules, and in our present development, computation rules are proof simplification rules. Consider this fragment of a natural-deduction tree and its simplification:

```
    . . .        . . .
  \e₁ /        \e₂ /
   φ₁           φ₂              ⇒        . . .
      \     / ∧I                       \e₁ /
       φ₁∧φ₂                            φ₁
        | ∧E₁
        φ₁
```

It is easy to verify that any tree that contains an application of the $\wedge$I rule, followed by an application of $\wedge E_1$, can be simplified this way without affecting the sequent that the complete tree proves. (We assume that the context for the complete tree remains the same.) The linear version of the simplification is

$$(\wedge E_1 \ (\wedge I \ e_1 \ e_2)) \ \Rightarrow \ e_1$$

which is stated in lambda-calculus form as the computation rule

$$\mathit{fst}(e_1, e_2) \ \Rightarrow \ e_1$$

that is, as the indexing rule for pairs. The analogous rule for $\wedge E_2$ is

$$\mathit{snd}(e_1, e_2) \ \Rightarrow \ e_2$$

The simplification for $\supset$ is a bit more interesting:

```
  . . . x ①. . .
   \   e₁   /
       φ₂
       |⊃I ①        . . .                           . . .
       φ₁⊃φ₂        \e₂ /                            \e₂ /
          \          φ₁            ⇒             . . . φ₁ . . .
              /  ⊃E                               \  e₁  /
           φ₂                                        φ₂
```

Here, the $\supset$I and $\supset$E rules cancel, and the e_2 tree is connected to all ①-labeled leaves in e_1. This is linearized as the β-rule for lambda abstraction:

$$(\lambda x \in \phi_1 . \, e_1) \cdot e_2 \ \Rightarrow \ [e_2/x] e_1$$

The computation rules are rewriting rules in an orthogonal subtree replacement system, and the confluence and subject reduction properties hold. The rules for $\supset$ and $\wedge$

are strongly normalizing, but as usual, the computation rules for the core language can destroy this property. In the case of the language in the previous section, they do not:

$$\textit{if true } e_1 \ e_2 \ \Rightarrow \ e_1$$

$$\textit{if false } e_1 \ e_2 \ \Rightarrow \ e_2$$

$$n_1 + n_2 \ \Rightarrow \ n_3, \quad \text{if } n_3 \text{ is the numeral denoting the sum of numerals } n_1 \text{ and } n_2$$

$$n = n \ \Rightarrow \ \textit{true}, \quad \text{if } n \text{ is a numeral}$$

$$n_1 = n_2 \ \Rightarrow \ \textit{false}, \quad \text{if } n_1 \text{ and } n_2 \text{ are different numerals}$$

Each of the above computation rules exhibits the same, important pattern: An operator created by an elimination rule operates upon a canonical expression, which is built by an introduction rule. This is not an accident: The elimination rule for a connective, *op*, tacitly assumes that a proof of $\phi_1 \ op \ \phi_2$ is a canonical expression, which is expected under the Heyting interpretation. Fortunately, a straightforward induction on the structure of a proof tree shows that every proof can be rewritten into one in canonical form.

Since the computation rules are normalizing and confluent, every expression has a unique normal form. It is convenient to claim that the underlying ''value'' of an expression is the normal form it rewrites to, but this notion has its limitations. For example, $\lambda x \in nat. \, x+1$ and $\lambda x \in nat. \, 1+x$ are distinct normal forms, but one can make the argument that they should be the same ''value.'' We sidestep this issue and concern ourselves only with canonical expressions. In the case of the primitive propositions *bool* and *nat*, the canonical expressions are exactly *true, false,* and the numerals.

9.5 Disjunction and Falsehood

A standard propositional logic contains disjunction and negation connectives. We introduce disjunction directly and define negation by means of a nullary connective, that is, a *logical constant*, for falsehood. The syntax of propositions is extended by

$$\phi ::= \ \cdots \ | \ \phi_1 \vee \phi_2 \ | \ \bot$$

and the inference rules in Figure 9.1 are augmented by those in Figure 9.8. The rules for disjunction match the usual pattern, but falsehood lacks an introduction rule because there should be no way to build a proof of $\bot$ in a consistent logic. (Of course, if a context, Γ, contains contradictory information, we can prove $\Gamma \vdash \bot$, but there is no way of proving $\vdash \bot$.)

Negation is defined in terms of falsehood. We write $\neg\phi$ as an abbreviation for $\phi \supset \bot$. This is sensible, since we can use $\supset$E to prove $\phi, \neg\phi \vdash \bot$.

Natural-deduction trees for the two sequents $P \vee Q, \neg P, (Q \vee R) \supset P \vdash R \wedge S$ and $\vdash (P \supset \neg P) \supset \neg P$ are shown in Figure 9.9. The first tree suggests that the $\vee$E rule comes into play whenever a sequent of form $\Gamma, \phi_1 \vee \phi_2 \vdash \phi_3$ must be proved: Prove

$$\vee I_1: \frac{\Gamma \vdash \phi_1}{\Gamma \vdash \phi_1 \vee \phi_2} \qquad \vee I_2: \frac{\Gamma \vdash \phi_2}{\Gamma \vdash \phi_1 \vee \phi_2}$$

$$\vee E: \frac{\Gamma \vdash \phi_1 \vee \phi_2 \quad \Gamma, \phi_1 \vdash \phi_3 \quad \Gamma, \phi_2 \vdash \phi_3}{\Gamma \vdash \phi_3} \qquad \bot E: \frac{\Gamma \vdash \bot}{\Gamma \vdash \phi}$$

Figure 9.8

```
                                    Q ②
                                    | ∨I₁
                   (Q∨R)⊃P  Q∨R          P⊃¬P ①   P ②
                       \   / ⊃E              \  / ⊃E
          ¬P  P ①  ¬P    P                  ¬P      P ②
           \  / ⊃E    \  / ⊃E                 \     / ⊃E
  P∨Q       ⊥          ⊥                        ⊥
    \       | ①       / ∨E ②                   | ⊃I ②
     ⊥                                          ¬P
     | ⊥E                                       |⊃I ①
    R∧S                                      (P⊃¬P)⊃¬P
```

Figure 9.9

$\Gamma, \phi_1 \vee \phi_2, \phi_1 \vdash \phi_3$ and $\Gamma, \phi_1 \vee \phi_2, \phi_2 \vdash \phi_3$ to get the result. Uses of $\vee I_1$ (and $\vee I_2$) appear on an ad hoc basis, since it is normally not a good strategy to try to transform a goal $\Gamma \vdash \phi_1 \vee \phi_2$ into the subgoal $\Gamma \vdash \phi_1$ (or $\Gamma \vdash \phi_2$). A subgoaling step from $\Gamma \vdash \phi$ to $\Gamma \vdash \bot$ should be attempted only when all else fails.

The second tree in the figure shows that reasoning about negation is done with the $\supset$I and $\supset$E rules. In particular, $\supset$I justifies the derived rule:

$$\frac{\Gamma, \phi \vdash \bot}{\Gamma \vdash \neg \phi}$$

which is a weak version of proof by contradiction.

We now follow the agenda set down by Section 9.2 and uncover the lambda-calculus representations of the new proof forms. The $\vee I_1$, $\vee I_2$, and $\bot E$ rules are linearized in the obvious way. Since $\vee E$ has two local assumptions, we use the format $(\vee E\ t_1\ (x \in \phi_1)\ t_2\ (y \in \phi_2)\ t_3)$ to indicate that x and y are the hypothetical trees for local assumptions ϕ_1 and ϕ_2, respectively.

Let a_1 be the hypothetical tree for $P \vee Q$, a_2 be the tree for $\neg P$, and a_3 be the tree for $(Q \vee R) \supset P$. The linearized form of the two trees in Figure 9.9 follow:

$$(\perp\!E_{R \wedge S} \ (\vee E \ a_1 \ (x \in P) \ (\supset\!E \ a_2 \ x) \ (y \in Q) \ (\supset\!E \ a_2 \ (\supset\!E \ a_3 \ (\vee I_{Q \vee R} \ y)))))$$

and

$$(\supset\!I \ (x \in P \supset \neg P) \ (\supset\!I \ (y \in P) \ (\supset\!E \ (\supset\!E \ x \ y) \ y)))$$

The subscripts to the $\vee$I and $\perp$E rules are needed to state precisely which propositions are proved by the rules. (We omit the subscripts when they can be inferred from context.)

The reformatting of the rules goes as follows:

- $(\vee I1_{\phi_1 \vee \phi_2} \ e)$ is reformatted $inl_{\phi_1 \vee \phi_2} \ e$, that is, as a tagged element of a disjoint union.
- $(\vee I2_{\phi_1 \vee \phi_2} \ e)$ is reformatted $inr_{\phi_1 \vee \phi_2} \ e$, that is, as a tagged element of a disjoint union.
- $(\vee E \ e_1 \ (x \in \phi_1) \ e_2 \ (y \in \phi_2) \ e_3)$ is reformatted $cases \ e_1 \ of \ isl(x \in \phi_1). \ e_2$ $[] \ isr(y \in \phi_2). \ e_3$, that is, as a cases statement.
- $(\perp\!E_\phi \ e)$ is reformatted $abort_\phi \ e$.

The operators for disjunction naturally correspond to the tagging and cases operations for a Pascal- or ML-variant data type. But the operator for $\perp$E has no corresponding operator in programming. We analyze this situation momentarily.

The lambda-calculus representations of the two trees in Figure 9.9 follow:

$$abort \ (cases \ a_1 \ of \ isl(x \in P). \ a_2 \cdot x \ [] \ isr(y \in Q). \ a_2 \cdot (a_3 \cdot (inl \ y))$$

and

$$\lambda x \in (P \supset \neg P). \lambda y \in P. \ (x \cdot y) \cdot y$$

The Heyting interpretation of the connectives goes as follows:

(i)   A proof of $\phi_1 \vee \phi_2$ is a proof of ϕ_1, labeled by *inl*, or a proof of ϕ_2, labeled by *inr*.

(ii) Proofs of $\perp$ do not exist.

The inference rules are sound with respect to this interpretation:

(a)   The $\vee I_1$ (respectively, the $\vee I_2$) rule, applied to a proof, e, of ϕ_1 (resp., ϕ_2), constructs the labeled value *inl e* (resp., *inr e*), which is a proof of $\phi_1 \vee \phi_2$.

(b)   The $\vee$E-rule, applied to (i) a proof, e_1, of $\phi_1 \vee \phi_2$, (ii) a proof, e_2, of ϕ_3, built with a hypothetical proof $x \in \phi_1$, and (iii) a proof, e_3, of ϕ_3, built with a hypothetical proof $x \in \phi_2$, constructs the proof *cases e_1 of isl($x \in \phi_1$). e_2* $[] \ isr(y \in \phi_2). \ e_3$, which computes a proof, $[e_1'/x]e_2$, of ϕ_3, when $e = inl \ e_1'$, and computes a proof, $[e_1'/y]e_3$, of ϕ_3, when $e = inr \ e_1'$.

(c)   The $\perp$E-rule constructs a proof, $abort_\phi \ e$, of ϕ from a proof, e, of $\perp$. But recall that there are no proofs of $\perp$.

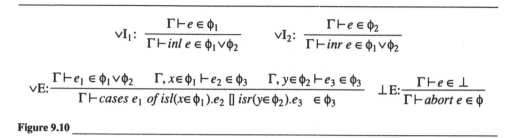

Figure 9.10

The inference rules for the judgement forms are presented in Figure 9.10. The canonical expressions for $\phi_1 \vee \phi_2$ are *inl e* and *inr e* (where *e* is closed), whereas $\perp$ has no canonical expressions. In part (b) above, some computation steps may be necessary to compute the proof defined by the *cases* construction. Also, notice how the structure of the $\vee$E rule is dictated by the tacit assumption that $e_1 \in \phi_1 \vee \phi_2$ should represent a canonical expression, either *inl x* or *inr y*; *x* and *y* must be identifiers, since the exact value of the canonical expression is unknown. In contrast, $\perp$E is formless, because there are no canonical forms to impose structure.

The computation rules for disjunction follow:

$$cases\ (inl\ e_1)\ of\ isl(x \in \phi_1).\,e_2\ [\!]\ isr(y \in \phi_2).\,e_3 \ \Rightarrow\ [e_1/x]e_2$$
$$cases\ (inr\ e_1)\ of\ isl(x \in \phi_1).\,e_2\ [\!]\ isr(y \in \phi_2).\,e_3 \ \Rightarrow\ [e_1/y]e_3$$

You should verify that the computation rules are sound tree simplifications. As usual, the rules show how an operator created by an elimination rule computes on a canonical expression. There are no computation rules for falsehood.

Although $\vdash \perp$ has no proof, $\phi, \neg\phi \vdash \perp$ does: $a_1 \in \phi, a_2 \in \neg\phi \vdash a_2 \cdot a_1 \in \perp$. Does this mean that $\perp$ has a proof? Recall that a_1 and a_2 are hypothetical natural-deduction trees—trees that have not been built (yet). Indeed, if one could construct trees for ϕ and $\neg\phi$, then the trees could be inserted for a_1 and a_2, respectively, and a proof of $\perp$ would indeed arise. But proofs for both $\vdash \phi$ and $\vdash \neg\phi$, for any ϕ, cannot be found.

A formal way of stating the above is that the propositional logic is *consistent*; that is, it is impossible to prove $\vdash \perp$; equivalently, it is impossible to prove $\vdash \phi$ and $\vdash \neg\phi$ for any $\phi \in$ Proposition. A context, Γ, is *consistent* if it is impossible to prove $\Gamma \vdash \perp$. The first proof in Figure 9.9 used a context that was inconsistent. Practical uses of propositional logic, for example, computer programming, work with consistent contexts.

9.6 Classical and Intuitionistic Logic

In the previous section, we noted that the $\supset I$ rule justified a weak principle of proof by contradiction; namely, from $\Gamma, \phi \vdash \bot$ we can infer $\Gamma \vdash \neg\phi$. (Notice the difference between this inference and the one justified by $\bot E$; namely, from $\Gamma, \phi \vdash \bot$, infer $\Gamma, \phi \vdash \neg\phi$.) There is a stronger version of proof by contradiction, known as the *reductio ad absurdum* (*RAA*) rule:

$$RAA: \quad \frac{\Gamma, \neg\phi \vdash \bot}{\Gamma \vdash \phi}$$

The *RAA* rule is not derivable from the existing rules. It allows us to prove new theorems, such as $\vdash (\neg\neg P) \supset P$, $\vdash (\neg(P \wedge Q)) \supset (\neg P \vee \neg Q)$, and $\vdash P \vee \neg P$, which are often taken for granted by users of propositional logic.

But we will *not* include the *RAA* rule in our logic, because it is incompatible with the Heyting interpretation of proofs as programs. We develop an example to see why this is so. Figure 9.11 shows the natural-deduction tree for the sequent $\vdash \phi \vee \neg\phi$ for arbitrary ϕ. The lambda-calculus form of the tree is

$$RAA \ (x \in \neg(\phi \vee \neg\phi)). (x \cdot (inr \ (\lambda y \in \phi. x \cdot (inl \ y))))$$

where "*RAA*" stands for itself, and x is the name of the local assumption that *RAA* introduces.

Call this expression e_0. Since e_0 serves as a proof for any instance of ϕ, consider

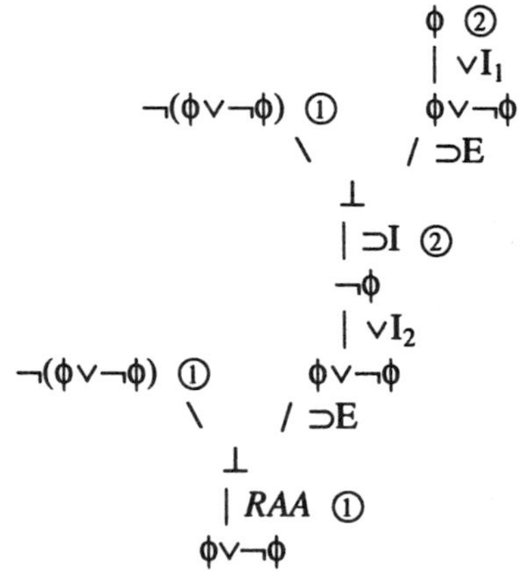

Figure 9.11

φ instantiated to *nat*; then e_0 proves $\vdash nat \vee \neg nat$. According to the Heyting interpretation, e_0 should be—or should rewrite to—a canonical expression of the form *inl n*, where $\vdash n \in nat$, or *inr m*, where $\vdash m \in \neg nat$. So, which is it?

We know that *nat* can be proved, and since this version of the propositional logic is known to be consistent, $\neg nat$ cannot be proved. Thus, e_0 apparently rewrites to *inl n*, where n apparently rewrites to a numeral. So, what numeral is lurking inside e_0? None is. Indeed, e_0 cannot be rewritten at all, since there is no computation rule for *RAA*, because there are no canonical expressions of type $\bot$.

The *RAA* rule causes trouble because it promises to create something from nothing. There is simply not enough information in the context $\Gamma, \neg\phi$ to build an expression of type φ. For example, the proof, e_0, of $\phi \vee \neg\phi$ promises to build an expression of type φ or one of type $\neg\phi$, for arbitrary φ. In effect, e_0 promises to decide theoremhood for φ. This promise is dubious, and when we extend the propositional logic to predicate logic, the theoremhood question becomes undecidable, even though e_0 still stands as a proof. So, there is no way that the *RAA* rule can be sound with respect to the Heyting interpretation.

The version of logic that includes the *RAA* rule is *classical* logic, and the version that omits it is *intuitionistic* logic. As outlined in this chapter, intuitionistic logic is based on the Heyting interpretation of propositions, and it effectively equates the truth of a proposition with computational evidence. Classical logic views the truth of a proposition as a notion separate from evidence. Every proposition *must* be either true or false, regardless of proof or disproof. In classical logic, negation is understood as Boolean complement, hence, if a proposition, P, is true, then $\neg P$ is false, and vice versa. Thus, $P \vee \neg P$ must be true, regardless of the underlying truth or falsehood of P. The *RAA* rule encodes the complementary nature of negation into the logistic system.

The classical understanding of negation appears reasonable, but it has its difficulties. Let P stand for "God has red hair." In classical logic, $P \vee \neg P$ is true and is even provable, despite the bizarre nature of the claim. In intuitionistic logic, the claim remains open until an angel arrives with evidence. But there is a result, due to Glivenko (cf. van Dalen 1983), that shows how results from classical propositional logic correspond to weaker results in intuitionistic propositional logic: φ can be proved in classical propositional logic exactly when $\neg\neg\phi$ can be proved in propositional intuitionistic logic.

9.7 Propositional Logic and Programming-Language Design

Section 9.3 noted that a core programming language can be designed as a logistic system and that language extensions arise as connectives in a propositional logic. This approach is considered here.

The core data types are the primitive propositions. Values in a core data type are defined by introduction rules, and operators upon the type are defined by elimination rules. Computation rules define how the operators compute on the canonical expressions. The structuring constructs are defined by rules for connectives: $\phi_1 \supset \phi_2$ introduces binding structures, and $\phi_1 \wedge \phi_2$ is a simplified version of record structure. (The labels of the record are *fst* and *snd*.) An *n*-ary conjunction gives the usual version of records, that is,

$$\wedge\text{I:}\quad \frac{\Gamma \vdash e_1 \in \phi_1 \quad \Gamma \vdash e_2 \in \phi_2 \quad \cdots \quad \Gamma \vdash e_n \in \phi_n}{\Gamma \vdash \{I_1 = e_1, I_2 = e_2, \dots, I_n = e_n\} \in \{I_1 : \phi_1, I_2 : \phi_2, \dots, I_n : \phi_n\}}$$

$$\wedge\text{E}_j:\quad \frac{\Gamma \vdash e \in \{I_1 : \phi_1, I_2 : \phi_2, \dots, I_n : \phi_n\}}{\Gamma \vdash e.I_j \in \phi_j} \quad \text{for all } 1 \le j \le n$$

or, alternatively

$$\wedge\text{E':}\quad \frac{\Gamma \vdash e_1 \in \{I_1 : \phi_1, I_2 : \phi_2, \dots, I_n : \phi_n\} \quad \Gamma, I_1 \in \phi_1, I_2 \in \phi_2, \dots, I_n \in \phi_n \vdash e_2 \in \psi}{\Gamma \vdash \textit{with } e_1 \textit{ do } e_2 \in \psi}$$

Although disjunction has not been studied in the earlier chapters, it fits the format of the variant data structure. Falsehood, being an empty type, gets scant attention in conventional languages, but no harm arises from its inclusion.

Other structuring devices/connectives might be added to the language. As long as the structuring device follows the usual pattern—introduction rules, elimination rules, and computation rules that show how operators compute on canonical expressions—the device will fit orthogonally into the language.

All of the examples in this chapter were for a functional language. We now define a core imperative language, which can be extended by the usual connectives. The result parallels the development in Chapters 1–5. The data types of *bool* and *nat* are defined as in Figure 9.7. The computation rules are the usual ones. Let *natloc* be the type with the introduction rule

$$\textit{natloc}\text{I:}\quad \Gamma \vdash n \in \textit{natloc} \quad \text{if } n \ge 0$$

and no elimination and computation rules. Possible rules for the *store* type follow:

$$\textit{store}\text{I}_1:\ \Gamma \vdash \textit{nil} \in \textit{store} \qquad \textit{store}\text{I}_2:\ \frac{\Gamma \vdash l \in \textit{natloc} \quad \Gamma \vdash n \in \textit{nat} \quad \Gamma \vdash s \in \textit{store}}{\Gamma \vdash \textit{update } l\ n\ s \in \textit{store}}$$

$$\textit{store}\text{E:}\quad \frac{\Gamma \vdash l \in \textit{natloc} \quad \Gamma \vdash s \in \textit{store}}{\Gamma \vdash \textit{lookup } l\ s \in \textit{nat}}$$

$$\textit{lookup } l\ \textit{nil} \ \Rightarrow\ 0$$
$$\textit{lookup } l\ (\textit{update } l\ n\ s) \ \Rightarrow\ n$$

lookup l (update m n s) $\Rightarrow$ *lookup l s,*   if *l* and *m* are distinct numerals

The *natexp* and *comm* types can be fashioned from scratch. The introduction rules resemble those in Figure 1.8, namely,

$$commI_1: \frac{\Gamma \vdash L \in natloc \quad \Gamma \vdash E \in natexp}{\Gamma \vdash L := E \in comm} \qquad commI_2: \frac{\Gamma \vdash C_1 \in comm \quad \Gamma \vdash C_2 \in comm}{\Gamma \vdash C_1 ; C_2 \in comm}$$

$$natexpI_1: \frac{\Gamma \vdash N \in nat}{\Gamma \vdash N \in natexp} \qquad natexpI_2: \frac{\Gamma \vdash E_1 \in natexp \quad \Gamma \vdash E_2 \in natexp}{\Gamma \vdash E_1 + E_2 \in natexp}$$

and so on. We add these two elimination rules:

$$commE: \frac{\Gamma \vdash C \in comm \quad \Gamma \vdash s \in store}{\Gamma \vdash (C \ s) \in store} \qquad natexpE: \frac{\Gamma \vdash E \in natexp \quad \Gamma \vdash s \in store}{\Gamma \vdash (E \ s) \in nat}$$

The computation rules for the types are the rewriting rules from Chapter 6:

$(L := E \ s) \Rightarrow update \ L \ (E \ s) \ s$

$(C_1 ; C_2 \ s) \Rightarrow (C_1 \ (C_2 \ s))$

(if E **then** C_1 **else** C_2 **fi** s) $\Rightarrow$ *if* $(E \ s) \ (C_1 \ s) \ (C_2 \ s)$

(while E **do** C **od** s) $\Rightarrow$ *if* $(E \ s) \ ($**while** E **do** C **od** $(C \ s)) \ s$

$(N \ s) \Rightarrow N$

$(@L \ s) \Rightarrow lookup \ L \ s$

$(E_1 + E_2 \ s) \Rightarrow (E_1 \ s) + (E_2 \ s)$

$(\neg E \ s) \Rightarrow if \ (E \ s) \ false \ true$

The computation rules reveal that the *commE* and *natexpE* rules build *store-* and *nat-*valued expressions, respectively. The rule for the **while**-loop loses normalization.

Our motivation for placing programming language design methodology within logic is to marry the concepts of program property and data type. Earlier in the chapter, we noted that a beginning programmer typically assumes, whenever a program is verified as well formed by a type checker, that the program is "correct"; that is, the program will do what the programmer intended. Perhaps we laugh at the programmer's naiveté, but the ultimate purpose of a type checker should be to verify the correctness of a program. The typing language of a programming language should be rich enough that program properties can be expressed in it (for example, that a program computes the factorial function) and that program verification can be conducted within it. Any programmer who has used a programming logic (for example, Hoare logic, *wp*-logic, or dynamic logic) to verify a program knows that verification is type checking.

Since we are working within a propositional logic of types, we are presently unable to satisfy the goal of type checking as program verification. But the groundwork has been laid, and in the next chapter the goal will be achieved, by means of predicate logic. This implies an even stronger result: If a natural-deduction tree proves a program specification—a type—ϕ, the code of a program satisfying specification ϕ can be synthesized from the natural-deduction tree—indeed, it *is* the tree. Programming becomes theorem proving.

9.8 Summary

Our version of propositional logic is defined as follows:

(i)   Well formed formulas are built from an alphabet of propositional symbols, P, Q, R, $\ldots$, connectives , $\supset$, $\wedge$, $\vee$, and $\neg$, a logical constant, $\perp$, and the auxiliary symbols, $\vdash$, (,).

(ii)   The syntax is

$$S \in \text{Sequent}$$
$$\Gamma \in \text{Proposition-list}$$
$$\phi \in \text{Proposition}$$
$$P \in \text{Propositional-symbol}$$
$$S ::= \Gamma \vdash \phi$$
$$\Gamma ::= \phi_1, \phi_2, \cdots, \phi_n, \ n \geq 0$$
$$\phi ::= P \mid (\phi_1 \wedge \phi_2) \mid (\phi_1 \supset \phi_2) \mid (\phi_1 \vee \phi_2) \mid \perp$$

The proposition $\neg\phi$ abbreviates $\phi \supset \perp$.

(iii) The axiom and inference rules are

axiom: $\Gamma \vdash \phi$, if $\phi \in \Gamma$ (that is, $\phi \in \Gamma$ if Γ is $\phi_1, \phi_2, \ldots, \phi, \ldots, \phi_n$)

$$\wedge I: \frac{\Gamma \vdash \phi_1 \quad \Gamma \vdash \phi_2}{\Gamma \vdash \phi_1 \wedge \phi_2} \qquad \wedge E_1: \frac{\Gamma \vdash \phi_1 \wedge \phi_2}{\Gamma \vdash \phi_1} \qquad \wedge E_2: \frac{\Gamma \vdash \phi_1 \wedge \phi_2}{\Gamma \vdash \phi_2}$$

$$\supset I: \frac{\Gamma, \phi_1 \vdash \phi_2}{\Gamma \vdash \phi_1 \supset \phi_2} \qquad \supset E: \frac{\Gamma \vdash \phi_1 \supset \phi_2 \quad \Gamma \vdash \phi_1}{\Gamma \vdash \phi_2}$$

$$\vee I_1: \frac{\Gamma \vdash \phi_1}{\Gamma \vdash \phi_1 \vee \phi_2} \qquad \vee I_2: \frac{\Gamma \vdash \phi_2}{\Gamma \vdash \phi_1 \vee \phi_2}$$

$$\vee E: \frac{\Gamma \vdash \phi_1 \vee \phi_2 \quad \Gamma, \phi_1 \vdash \phi_3 \quad \Gamma, \phi_2 \vdash \phi_3}{\Gamma \vdash \phi_3} \qquad \perp E: \frac{\Gamma \vdash \perp}{\Gamma \vdash \phi}$$

(iv) A *sequent-proof tree* that proves $\Gamma \vdash \phi$ is a tree whose leaves are axioms, whose root is $\Gamma \vdash \phi$, and whose internal nodes are consequents of inference rules. The notion is formalized by an inductive definition in Section 9.1.

A *natural-deduction tree* is a sequent-proof tree where the context information is omitted from the nodes. When represented in linear form, natural-deduction trees are defined by the following syntax rules:

$e \in$ Natural-deduction-tree

$x \in$ Identifier

$e ::= e_1, e_2 \mid fst\ e \mid snd\ e \mid \lambda x \in \phi.e \mid e_1 \cdot e_2$
$\quad \mid inl_\phi\ e \mid inr_\phi\ e \mid cases\ e_1\ of\ isl(x_1 \in \phi_1).e_2\ [\![\ isr(x_2 \in \phi_2).e_3 \mid abort_\phi\ e$

The well-formedness of a natural-deduction tree can be verified by the following axiom and inference rules. (Note: Γ is now a list of $(x_i \in \phi_i)$ pairs, where no x_i is repeated.)

axiom: $\Gamma \vdash x \in \phi$, if $(x \in \phi) \in \Gamma$

$\wedge I: \dfrac{\Gamma \vdash e_1 \in \phi_1 \quad \Gamma \vdash e_2 \in \phi_2}{\Gamma \vdash e_1, e_2 \in \phi_1 \wedge \phi_2}$

$\wedge E_1: \dfrac{\Gamma \vdash e \in \phi_1 \wedge \phi_2}{\Gamma \vdash fst\ e \in \phi_1}$

$\wedge E_2: \dfrac{\Gamma \vdash e \in \phi_1 \wedge \phi_2}{\Gamma \vdash snd\ e \in \phi_2}$

$\supset I: \dfrac{\Gamma, x \in \phi_1 \vdash e \in \phi_2}{\Gamma \vdash \lambda x \in \phi_1.e \in \phi_1 \supset \phi_2}$

$\supset E: \dfrac{\Gamma \vdash e_1 \in \phi_1 \supset \phi_2 \quad \Gamma \vdash e_2 \in \phi_1}{\Gamma \vdash e_1 \cdot e_2 \in \phi_2}$

$\vee I_1: \dfrac{\Gamma \vdash e \in \phi_1}{\Gamma \vdash inl\ e \in \phi_1 \vee \phi_2}$

$\vee I_2: \dfrac{\Gamma \vdash e \in \phi_2}{\Gamma \vdash inr\ e \in \phi_1 \vee \phi_2}$

$\vee E: \dfrac{\Gamma \vdash e_1 \in \phi_1 \vee \phi_2 \quad \Gamma, x \in \phi_1 \vdash e_2 \in \phi_3 \quad \Gamma, y \in \phi_2 \vdash e_3 \in \phi_3}{\Gamma \vdash cases\ e_1\ of\ isl(x \in \phi_1).e_2\ [\![\ isr(y \in \phi_2).e_3 \in \phi_3}$

$\perp E: \dfrac{\Gamma \vdash e \in \perp}{\Gamma \vdash abort\ e \in \phi}$

A *judgement* is a construct, $\Gamma \vdash e \in \phi$. These computation rules simplify natural-deduction trees:

$fst\ (e_1, e_2) \Rightarrow e_1$
$snd\ (e_1, e_2) \Rightarrow e_2$
$(\lambda x \in \phi_1.e_1) \cdot e_2 \Rightarrow [e_2/x]e_1$
$cases\ (inl\ e_1)\ of\ isl(x \in \phi_1).e_2\ [\![\ isr(y \in \phi_2).e_3 \Rightarrow [e_1/x]e_2$
$cases\ (inr\ e_1)\ of\ isl(x \in \phi_1).e_2\ [\![\ isr(y \in \phi_2).e_3 \Rightarrow [e_1/y]e_3$

Suggested Reading

There are many good introductions to symbolic logic; two are Lemmon 1965 and Suppes 1957. Van Dalen 1989 gives a gentle introduction to intuitionistic logic; see Heyting 1956 and Dummett 1977 for more thorough presentations. Natural deduction and proof normalization is covered in depth in Prawitz 1965 and Dragalin 1988. The correspondence between data types and logical propositions, sometimes called the *Curry-Howard isomorphism*, is documented in Curry and Feys 1958, Girard, Lafont, and Taylor 1989, Howard 1980, and Scott 1980.

The logistic systems in this chapter are based on Martin-Löf's intuitionistic type theory, which is documented in Backhouse 1989, Backhouse, Chisholm, Malcolm, and Saaman 1989, Martin-Löf 1973, 1984, and 1985, Nordström 1981, Nordström, Petersson, and Smith 1990, and Thompson 1991.

Exercises

1.1. For each of the following, construct sequent-proof trees and natural-deduction trees.

    a. $P \wedge Q \vdash Q \wedge P$

    b. $P \supset (Q \supset R) \vdash (P \wedge Q) \supset R$

    c. $(P \wedge Q) \supset R \vdash P \supset (Q \supset R)$

    d. $\vdash P \supset (Q \supset P)$

    e. $Q \vdash P \supset ((Q \supset R) \supset R)$

    f. $\vdash P \supset (P \wedge P)$

    g. $Q \supset R \vdash (P \wedge Q) \supset (P \wedge R)$

1.2. For the logistic system of Figure 9.1, prove

    a. the substitution theorem: If $\Gamma \vdash \phi$ holds, then for all $\phi' \in$ Proposition, $[\phi'/P]\Gamma \vdash [\phi'/P]\phi$ holds. (Note: for $\Gamma = \psi_1, \psi_2, \ldots, \psi_n$, $[\phi'/P]\Gamma = [\phi'/P]\psi_1, [\phi'/P]\psi_2, \ldots, [\phi'/P]\psi_n$.)

    b. the deduction theorem: $\Gamma, \phi_1 \vdash \phi_2$ holds exactly when $\Gamma \vdash \phi_1 \supset \phi_2$ holds.

1.3. a. Using an inductive definition, formalize the notion of "natural-deduction tree" and formalize the notion, "natural-deduction tree, t, proves the sequent, $\Gamma \vdash \phi$."

    b. Formalize the notion of the "scope of an assumption" in a natural-deduction tree.

    c.* Prove that if t_1 is a natural-deduction tree that proves $\Gamma \vdash \phi_1$, and t_2 is a natural-deduction tree that proves $\Delta, \phi_1 \vdash \phi_2$, then t_1 pasted to t_2 at the leaf, ϕ_1, is a natural-deduction tree that proves $\Gamma, \Delta \vdash \phi_2$.

    d. Here is a simplified version of the *cut* rule:

$$\frac{\Gamma \vdash \phi_1 \quad \Gamma, \phi_1 \vdash \phi_2}{\Gamma \vdash \phi_2}$$

    The "cut elimination theorem" says if *cut* is used in the sequent-proof tree for $\Gamma_1 \vdash \phi_1$, then there is a sequent-proof tree for $\Gamma_1 \vdash \phi_1$ that does not contain *cut*. Adapt your proof of Part c to a proof of the cut elimination theorem. (Note: This is not the true cut elimination theorem. It properly belongs to the *sequent calculus*; see Gallier 1988 and Girard, Lafont, and Taylor 1989.)

2.1. If you worked Exercise 1.1, proceed. For each natural-deduction tree in your answer to Exercise 1.1

    a. write the lambda calculus expression that encodes the tree.

    b. use the rules in Figure 9.5 to validate the well-formedness of tree; that is, draw the corresponding judgement proof tree.

2.2 a. Recall from Exercise 4.4 from Chapter 5 that records are just tuples. Remove the $\wedge$I and $\wedge$E rules from Figure 9.5 and replace them by rules for record formation and record indexing.

    b. Return to Figure 9.5, and replace the $\wedge$E rules by this rule:

$$\wedge\text{E}': \quad \frac{\Gamma \vdash e \in \phi_1 \wedge \phi_2 \quad \Gamma, x \in \phi_1, y \in \phi_2 \vdash e_3 \in \phi_3}{\Gamma \vdash let\,(x, y) = e\ in\ e_3\ \in\ \phi_3}$$

    This is reminiscent of the *with* construct in Chapter 5. Prove that $\Gamma \vdash e_1 \in \phi$ holds with the rules in Figure 9.5 (that is, with the usual $\wedge$E rules) exactly when there is some e_2 such that $\Gamma \vdash e_2 \in \phi$ holds with the rules in Figure 9.5, less the usual $\wedge$E rules, plus the $\wedge$E' rule.

2.3. a. Explain why $\vdash \lambda x \in bool.\lambda x \in int.\,x\ \in\ bool \supset (int \supset int)$ can *not* be derived.

    b. Why does the addition of the *weakening rule*

$$\frac{\Gamma \vdash e \in \phi}{\Gamma, x \in \phi' \vdash e \in \phi}$$

    let us derive the judgement in Part a?

    c. How does a type checker for a functional language deal with the lambda expression in Part a? If the type checker is built from a set of typing rules, what trouble does the weakening rule cause for a type-checking algorithm?

    d.* Prove, that with the addition of the weakening rule, that the axiom in Figure 9.5 can be replaced by $x \in \phi \vdash x \in \phi$, and the new set of rules prove the same sequents, $\Gamma \vdash \phi$, as do the original rules in Figure 9.5.

3.1. Use the rules in Figures 9.5 and 9.7 to prove that these programs are well typed:

    a. $\lambda x \in nat.\ if\ (x = 0)\ (x{+}x)\ fst(x, 0)$

b. $\lambda f \in nat \supset (nat \supset nat).\lambda n \in nat. f \cdot n \cdot (f \cdot n \cdot n)$

3.2. Prove for all propositions, ϕ, defined by the syntax rule

$$\phi ::= nat \mid bool \mid \phi_1 \wedge \phi_2 \mid \phi_1 \supset \phi_2$$

that $\vdash \phi$ is a theorem.

4.1. For each of the following expressions, draw the natural-deduction tree that it represents and use the computation rules to rewrite the tree into its minimal (normal) form:

a. $(\lambda x \in nat \wedge nat. fst\ x) \cdot (0, 1)$

b. $(\lambda x \in nat.\ if\ (x = 0)\ (\lambda y \in nat.\ y{+}2)\ (\lambda y \in nat.\ x)) \cdot 1$

4.2. a. For the system defined by Figure 9.5 and 9.7, prove that every closed expression rewrites into a canonical expression. (Hint: Show, if $\Gamma = x_1 \in \phi_1, \ldots,$ $x_n \in \phi_n$, $\Gamma \vdash e \in \phi$ holds, and all $e_i \in \phi_i$ are canonical expressions, $1 \le i \le n$, then $[e_1/x_1, \ldots, e_n/x_n]e$ can be rewritten into a canonical expression.)

b. Must every closed expression rewrite to one in normal form? If so, define an extension to the system where every expression has a canonical form, but some expression does not have a normal form. (Hint: Add a *rec* operator.)

4.3. The judgement form of the cut rule from Exercise 1.3 might read

$$\frac{\Gamma \vdash e_1 \in \phi_1 \qquad \Gamma, x \in \phi_1 \vdash e_2 \in \phi_2}{\Gamma \vdash paste\ e_1\ (x \in \phi_1).e_2 \in \phi_2}$$

with the computation rule

$$paste\ e_1\ (x \in \phi_1).e_2 \;\Rightarrow\; [e_1/x]e_2$$

Justify that the cut rule is sound with respect to the Heyting interpretation.

5.1. For each of the following, write natural-deduction and sequent-proof trees. (Note: $\phi \dashv\vdash \psi$ abbreviates $\phi \vdash \psi$ and $\psi \vdash \phi$.)

a. $P \vee Q \dashv\vdash Q \vee P$

b. $P \vee (Q \wedge R) \dashv\vdash (P \vee Q) \wedge (P \vee R)$

c. $P \wedge (Q \vee R) \dashv\vdash (P \wedge Q) \vee (P \wedge R)$

d. $P \vdash \neg \neg P$

e. $P \vdash ((\neg P) \supset Q)$

f. $\neg (P \vee Q) \dashv\vdash (\neg P) \wedge (\neg Q)$

g. $(\neg P) \vee Q \vdash P \supset Q$

h. $P \supset Q \vdash (\neg Q) \supset (\neg P)$

i. $\bot \dashv\vdash P \wedge \neg P$

5.2. Extend any of the results in Exercises 1.2–1.4 for the system with disjunction and falsehood.

5.3. Another extension to the logic is the logical constant, $\top$, for truth. The inference rule is

$$\top\text{I:} \quad \Gamma \vdash () \in \top$$

There is no elimination rule.

   a. Show that the primitive type, *bool*, can be simulated by $\top \vee \top$; that is, show that if $\Gamma \vdash \phi$ holds in the original system, then $[\top \vee \top / bool]\Gamma \vdash [\top \vee \top / bool]\phi$ holds in the system with $\top$.

   b. In general, an enumeration type, $E = (a_1, a_2, \cdots, a_n)$, $n \geq 0$, can be simulated by $\top \vee \top \vee \cdots \vee \top$, $\top$ repeated n times. Explain.

5.4. Add these computation rules to the system:

$$fst\,(abort_{\phi_1 \wedge \phi_2} p) \;\Rightarrow\; abort_{\phi_1} p$$
$$snd\,(abort_{\phi_1 \wedge \phi_2} p) \;\Rightarrow\; abort_{\phi_2} p$$
$$(abort_{\phi_1 \supset \phi_2} p) \cdot q \;\Rightarrow\; abort_{\phi_2} p$$
$$cases\,(abort_{\phi_1 \vee \phi_2} p)\ of\ isl(x \in \phi_1).e_1\ [\,]\ isr(y \in \phi_2).e_2 \;\Rightarrow\; abort_{\phi_3} p$$

Do these rules preserve confluence? Existence of canonical forms? How do they correspond to proof reduction? Are there any bad aspects of the rules?

5.5. Consider the logistic system consisting of Figures 9.5, 9.7, and 9.8. Are there any elements of type $\neg nat$; that is, does $\vdash \neg nat$ hold? Are there any elements of type $\neg \neg nat$? Do such elements have "computational value"?

6.1. Prove the following with classical logic. (Note: $\phi \dashv\vdash \psi$ abbreviates $\phi \vdash \psi$ and $\psi \vdash \phi$.)

   a. $\vdash (\neg \neg P) \supset P$

   b. $(\neg Q) \supset (\neg P) \dashv\vdash P \supset Q$

   c. $\neg (P \vee Q) \dashv\vdash (\neg P) \wedge (\neg Q)$

   d. $(\neg P) \vee Q \dashv\vdash P \supset Q$

6.2. An alternative to the *RAA* rule is the double negation rule:

$$DN: \frac{\Gamma \vdash \neg \neg \phi}{\Gamma \vdash \phi}$$

Prove that *DN* is equivalent to *RAA* in the sense that if $\Gamma \vdash \phi$ can be proved in the system with *RAA*, then it can be proved in the system with *DN*, and vice versa.

6.3. Sometimes beginners propose that $\neg \phi$ be interpreted as the set of expressions that do *not* have type ϕ. Why is this incompatible with the Heyting interpretation?

7.1. An alternative version of the *store* type goes as follows:

$$m\text{-store}\mathrm{I}: \frac{\Gamma \vdash e_i \in nat, \quad 1 \leq i \leq m}{\Gamma \vdash \langle e_1, e_2, \dots, e_m \rangle \in store} \qquad m\text{-store}\mathrm{E}: \frac{\Gamma \vdash e \in store}{\Gamma \vdash lookup_i\ e \in nat} \quad 1 \leq i \leq m$$

$$lookup_i \langle e_1, \ldots, e_i, \ldots, e_m \rangle \;\Rightarrow\; e_i$$

a. Show that the usual updating operation, $update_i\; e_1\; e_2$, where $e_1 \in nat$, $e_2 \in store$, can be coded in terms of *m-store*I and *m-store*E. Prove that this rule is sound:

$$update_i\; e \langle e_1, \ldots, e_i, \ldots, e_m \rangle \;\Rightarrow\; \langle e_1, \ldots, e, \ldots, e_m \rangle$$

b. Perhaps a better elimination rule is

$$m\text{-}storeE'\text{:}\quad \frac{\Gamma \vdash e_1 \in store \qquad \Gamma,\, x_1 \in nat,\, \ldots,\, x_m \in nat \vdash e_1 \in \phi}{\Gamma \vdash let\; (x_1, \ldots, x_m) = e_1\; in\; e_2 \in \phi}$$

$$let\; (x_1, \ldots, x_m) = \langle v_1, \ldots, v_m \rangle\; in\; e \;\Rightarrow\; [v_1/x_1, \ldots, v_m/x_m]e$$

This defines a parallel lookup. Define parallel assignment in terms of *m-store*I and *m-store*E'. Give its computation rule.

c. Since the computation rules in Section 9.7 and the ones in this exercise place no restrictions upon the evaluation strategy, lazy evaluation is natural. Give a pragmatic reason why eager evaluation of *store*-typed expressions is desirable. If eager evaluation is used, does this cause any problems?

7.2. An alternative version of the imperative language goes as follows. We begin with the usual *nat* and *bool* data types and use the *store* type from the previous exercise. A context, Γ, is *store sequential* if Γ contains exactly one *store*-typed assumption. A context, Δ, is *store free* if it contains no *store*-typed assumptions. From here on, we use only *store*-sequential and *store*-free contexts. For the moment, we restrict the rule for *lookup* to read

$$\Delta,\, s \in store \vdash lookup_i\; s \in nat$$

Next, we use a variant of the *cut* rule from Exercise 4.3, where θ is specialized to *store*, namely,

$$\frac{\Delta,\, s \in store \vdash e_1 \in store \qquad \Delta,\, s \in store \vdash e_2 \in store}{\Delta,\, s \in store \vdash e_1;\, (s \in store).e_2 \in store}$$

with the computation rule:

$$e_1;\, (s \in store).\, e_2 \;\Rightarrow\; [e_1/s]e_2$$

When we prove $\Gamma \vdash p \in store$ with the restricted version of the *lookup* rule and the new cut rule, we say that p is an *imperative program*.

a. Apply the computation rules to these imperative programs plus their argument stores:

  (i) $\langle 0,0 \rangle;\, (s \in store).\, update_1\; 3\; s;\, (s \in store).\, update_2\; ((lookup_1\; s)+1)\; s$

  (ii) $\langle 0,0 \rangle;\, (s \in store).\, if\; ((lookup_1\; s)=0)$
        $(update_1\; 1\; s)\; (if\, false\; (update_2\; 2\; s)\; (update_2\; 2\; s))$
        $;\, (s \in store).\, update_2\; (lookup_1\; s)\; s$

b. Explain why the constructs, L:=E, $C_1;C_2$, **if** E **then** C_1 **else** C_2 **fi**, @L, etc., are just "syntactic sugar." Define a desugaring translation.

c. Add records, that is, conjunction, from the beginning of Section 9.7. Show the proof of

$$s \in store \vdash with \{A=lookup_1 \, s\} \, do \, update_1 \, 0 \, s; \, (s \in Store). update_2 \, A \, s \in store$$

Apply the computation rule for *with* to the example. Then compute the result with the input store, $\langle 0,0 \rangle$.

d. Next, add lambda abstractions, that is, implication. (Note: You will probably want to add the weakening rule from Exercise 2.3.b as well.) Show the proof of

$$s \in store \vdash with \{A = (\lambda s \in store.lookup_1 \, s)\} \, do \, update_1 \, 0 \, s$$
$$; (s \in Store). update_2 \, (A \cdot s) \in store$$

Apply the computation rule for lambda abstraction to the example. Then compute the result with the input store, $\langle 0,0 \rangle$.

e. One way of introducing iterative control into the language is by means of a proper elimination rule for *nat*. Here is a simplified version of the *nat*E rule, to be seen in Chapter 10:

$$nat\text{E}': \quad \frac{\Gamma \vdash e_1 \in nat \quad \Gamma \vdash e_2 \in \phi \quad \Gamma, x \in \phi \vdash e_3 \in \phi}{\Gamma \vdash upto \, e_1 \, do \, e_2 \, and \, (x \in \phi). e_3 \, \in \phi}$$

$$upto \, 0 \, do \, e_2 \, and \, (x \in \phi). e_3 \; \Rightarrow \; e_2$$
$$upto \, n{+}1 \, do \, e_2 \, and \, (x \in \phi). e_3 \; \Rightarrow \; [upto \, n \, do \, e_2 \, and \, (x \in \phi). e_3 \, / \, x]e_3$$

This defines a "**for** $i:=0$ **to** e_1" loop. Compute the normal forms of these examples:

(i) $(\lambda m \in nat.\lambda n \in nat. upto \, m \, do \, 0 \, and \, (x \in nat. n{+}x) \cdot 3 \cdot 2$

(ii) $(\lambda m \in nat. upto \, m \, do \, 1 \, and \, (x \in nat. m{*}x) \cdot 3$

Let θ be *store* in the *nat*E' rule. Simulate the Pascal-style "**for** $i:=0..e$" loop; simulate the "**for** $i:=e_1..e_2$" loop. Why can't the usual **while**-loop be simulated?

10 Predicate-Logic Typing

We now enrich the propositional logic so that we can reason about individuals like numbers. We wish to write propositions like, "for all natural numbers, x, $x+1$ is greater than x," and then use the proposition to deduce "2 is greater than 1." The resulting logistic system is a *predicate calculus*.

10.1 The Predicate Calculus

The well-formed formulas of the predicate calculus are built from an alphabet of *function symbols*, $+, \times, -, 0, 1, \ldots$; *predicate symbols*, $<, >, =, \ldots$; identifiers, $x, y, z, a, b,$ $\ldots$; connectives, $\forall, \exists, \wedge, \supset, \vee$; a logical constant, $\bot$; and auxiliary symbols $., \vdash, ($, $)$. The new connectives, $\forall$ and $\exists$, are called *quantifiers*. The syntax rules are

$S \in$ Sequent $\qquad\qquad f \in$ Function-symbol
$\Gamma \in$ Context $\qquad\qquad P \in$ Predicate-symbol
$\phi \in$ Proposition $\qquad\quad\; x \in$ Identifier
$t \in$ Term

$\quad S ::= \Gamma \vdash \phi$
$\quad \Gamma ::= \phi_1, \phi_2, \ldots, \phi_n, \quad n \geq 0$
$\quad \phi ::= \forall x. \phi \mid \exists x. \phi \mid \phi_1 \wedge \phi_2 \mid \phi_1 \supset \phi_2 \mid \phi_1 \vee \phi_2 \mid \bot \mid P(t_1, t_2, \ldots, t_n), \quad n \geq 0$
$\quad t ::= x \mid f(t_1, t_2, \ldots, t_n), \quad n \geq 0$

The quantifiers let us discuss individuals. The $\forall$ symbol, called the *universal quantifier*, lets us state, say, $\forall x. x+1 > x$; that is, for all x, $x+1$ is greater than x. (For the moment, assume the individuals are natural numbers.) The *existential quantifier*, $\exists$, lets us state $\exists x. x > 1$; that is, there exists some x that is greater than 1. Of course, both quantifiers can be used in the same proposition, as in $\forall x. \exists y. y > x$.

Quantifiers bind identifiers, and notions of *free* and *bound* identifier arise. We define the free identifiers in a proposition in the expected way:

$$FV(\forall x. \phi) = FV(\phi) - \{x\} = FV(\exists x. \phi)$$

$$\forall I: \frac{\Gamma \vdash \phi(x)}{\Gamma \vdash \forall x.\, \phi(x)} \quad \text{if } x \notin FV(\Gamma) \qquad \forall E: \frac{\Gamma \vdash \forall x.\, \phi(x)}{\Gamma \vdash \phi(t)}$$

$$\exists I: \frac{\Gamma \vdash \phi(t)}{\Gamma \vdash \exists x.\, \phi(x)} \qquad \exists E: \frac{\Gamma \vdash \exists x.\, \phi_1(x) \quad \Gamma, \phi_1(a) \vdash \phi_2}{\Gamma \vdash \phi_2} \quad \text{if } a \notin FV(\Gamma) \text{ and } a \notin FV(\phi_2)$$

Figure 10.1 _____

$$FV(\phi_1 \wedge \phi_2) = FV(\phi_1) \cup FV(\phi_2) = FV(\phi_1 \supset \phi_2) = FV(\phi_1 \vee \phi_2)$$
$$FV(\bot) = \{\,\}$$
$$FV(P(t_1, t_2, \ldots, t_n)) = FV(t_1) \cup FV(t_2) \cup \cdots \cup FV(t_n) = FV(f(t_1, t_2, \ldots, t_n))$$
$$FV(x) = \{x\}$$

The set of free identifiers in a context is $FV(\Gamma) = \{ x \mid x \in FV(\phi),\ \phi \in \Gamma \}$.

The substitution of a term, t, for an identifier, x, in ϕ, written $[t/x]\phi$, is the replacement of all free occurrences of x in ϕ by t. An example is $[1/x]((x>0)\wedge(\forall x.\, x>0)) = (1>0)\wedge(\forall x.\, x>0)$. The recursive definition of substitution is left as an easy exercise. It is traditional and convenient to use a special notation for substitution. We write $\phi(x)$ to represent a proposition, ϕ, that contains zero or more free occurrences of x. Then, we write $\phi(t)$ to denote $[t/x]\phi$. This notation will also be used for multiple identifiers and multiple substitutions, for example, $P(x, y)$ and $P(0, z+1)$. As seen above, we use infix notation, for example, $x>0$ instead of $>(x, 0)$, for readability. Constants like 0 are just nullary function symbols.

The axiom and inference rules for the predicate calculus are the ones for the propositional calculus plus the rules in Figure 10.1. The $\forall I$ rule states that any claim, $\phi(x)$, proved about a purely hypothetical individual, x, holds for all individuals. The restriction on the rule enforces that x is hypothetical. For example, the restriction prevents a proof of $x<1 \vdash \forall x.\, x<1$. The $\forall I$ rule should be compared to the typing rules for polymorphism in Chapters 7 and 8, where similar restrictions were enforced. The $\forall E$ rule instantiates a proposition that holds for all individuals to a proposition that holds for a specific individual.

The $\exists I$ rule converts a proposition that holds for a specific individual into one that holds for an individual whose identity is secret. Compare this rule with the typing rules for the **abstype** construct in Chapter 7. The $\exists E$ rule proves a proposition, ϕ_2, that depends on $\phi_1(a)$, where the identity of identifier a is unimportant. The restrictions on the rule enforce that a's identity is unimportant; they prevent such proofs as $\exists x.\, P(x), P(a)\supset Q(a) \vdash Q(a)$.

A sequent-proof tree is defined as in Chapter 9. Figure 10.2 presents a sequent-proof tree and the natural-deduction tree for $\vdash (\forall x.\forall y.\, P(x, y)) \supset (\forall y.\forall x.\, P(x, y))$. The

$\forall x. \forall y. P(x, y) \vdash \forall x. \forall y. P(x, y)$
   |$\forall$E
$\forall x. \forall y. P(x, y) \vdash \forall y. P(x, y)$
   |$\forall$E
$\forall x. \forall y. P(x, y) \vdash P(x, y)$
   |$\forall$I
$\forall x. \forall y. P(x, y) \vdash \forall x. P(x, y)$
   |$\forall$I
$\forall x. \forall y. P(x, y) \vdash \forall y. \forall x. P(x, y)$
   |$\supset$I
$\vdash (\forall x. \forall y. P(x, y)) \supset (\forall y. \forall x. P(x, y))$

$\forall x. \forall y. P(x, y)$ ①
   |$\forall$E
$\forall y. P(x, y)$
   |$\forall$E
$P(x, y)$
   |$\forall$I
$\forall x. P(x, y)$
   |$\forall$I
$\forall y. \forall x. P(x, y)$
   |$\supset$I   ①
$(\forall x. \forall y. P(x, y)) \supset (\forall y. \forall x. P(x, y))$

Figure 10.2 _____

$\forall y. P(a, y)$ ①
   |$\forall$E
$P(a, y)$
   |$\exists$I
$\exists x. P(x, y)$
   |$\forall$I

$\forall x. P(x)$ ①
   |$\forall$E
$P(a)$
   |$\exists$I
$\exists y. P(y)$
   |$\supset$I   ①
$(\forall x. P(x)) \supset (\exists y. P(y))$

$\exists x. \forall y. P(x, y)$ $\forall y. \exists x. P(x, y)$
   \   / $\exists$E   ①
   $\forall y. \exists x. P(x, y)$

Figure 10.3 _____

proof shows routine applications of the $\forall$E and $\forall$I rules. Figure 10.3 shows natural-deduction trees for $\vdash (\forall x. P(x)) \supset (\exists y. P(y))$ and $\exists x. \forall y. P(x,y) \vdash \forall y. \exists x. P(x, y)$, respectively. The first proof in Figure 10.3 implies that the universe of individuals must be nonempty. (Later we relax this condition.) The second tree displays an application of the $\exists$E rule. The rule introduces a local assumption, $\forall y. P(a, y)$, where a stands for the individual whose identity is a secret.

As usual, the proofs are best drawn from the root to the leaves. When a goal of the form $\forall x. \phi(x)$ must be proved, the $\forall$I rule is typically used to justify the subgoal $\phi(x)$. When a goal of the form $\exists x. \phi(x)$ must be proved, the $\exists$I rule can be used to justify the subgoal $\phi(?)$, where the "?" is instantiated later. Another useful strategy is to search the assumptions for a proposition of the form $\exists y. \phi(y)$. If located, assume $\phi(a)$, where a is a new identifier. This step is justified by the $\exists$E rule. Finally, use the $\forall$E rule, as necessary, on assumptions of the form $\forall x.\phi(x)$. A bit of experience building such proofs will show that the form of reasoning used with the conjunction connective also applies to the universal quantifier, and reasoning appropriate for disjunction applies as well to the existential quantifier. This is because $\forall x.\phi(x)$ is a form of "abbreviation" for $\phi(0)\wedge\phi(1)\wedge\phi(2)\wedge\cdots$, where $0, 1, 2, \ldots$ are the individuals in the universe, and $\exists x.\phi(x)$ is a form of abbreviation for $\phi(0)\vee\phi(1)\vee\phi(2)\vee\cdots$.

As in Chapter 9, we gain new insights from linearizing natural-deduction trees and coding them in a lambda-calculus notation. The linearized forms of the four rules follow:

(i) $(\forall I\ (x \in V)\ e)$, which states that x is quantified in $\phi(x)$, the proposition proved by proof tree e. For the moment, we say that all individuals belong to a universe set, V.

(ii) $(\forall E\ e\ t)$, which states that $\forall x.\phi(x)$, proved by e, is instantiated to $\phi(t)$.

(iii) $(\exists I_{\exists x.\phi(x)}\ t\ e)$, which states that t is the individual in $\phi(t)$, proved by e, that is quantified. The subscript is necessary to clarify which proposition is proved. For example, $(\supset I\ (p \in 0{\geq}0)\ (\exists I\ 0\ p))$ might prove $\vdash 0{\geq}0 \supset (\exists x.\,x{\geq}0)$ or $\vdash 0{\geq}0 \supset (\exists x.\,x{\geq}x)$. Often, we omit the subscript when it can be inferred from context.

(iv) $(\exists E\ e_1\ (a{\in}V, b{\in}\phi_1(a))\ e_2)$, which states that a is the name chosen for the unknown individual in the proof, e_1, of $\exists x.\phi_1(x)$; b is the name of the hypothetical proof tree for the local assumption, $\phi_1(a)$; and e_2 is the proof tree for ϕ_2.

The linear representations of the natural-deduction trees in Figures 10.2 and 10.3 are

$$(\supset I\ (p \in \forall x \in V.\forall y \in V.\,P(x,y))\ (\forall I\ (y \in V)\ (\forall I\ (x \in V)\ (\forall E\ (\forall E\ p\ x)\ y))))$$

$$(\supset I\ (p \in \forall x \in V.\,P(x))\ (\exists I_{\exists y.P(y)}\ a\ (\forall E\ p\ a)))$$

$$(\exists E\ q\ (a \in V, s \in \forall y \in V.\,P(a,y))\ (\forall I\ (y \in V)\ (\exists I_{\exists x.P(x,y)}\ a\ (\forall E\ s\ y))))$$

where q is the hypothetical proof tree for the assumption $\exists x.\forall y.P(x,y)$

The reformatting of the linear forms into lambda-calculus expressions is straightforward:

(i) $(\forall I\ (x \in V)\ e)$ is reformatted $\lambda x \in V.\,e$, a lambda-abstraction.

(ii) $(\forall E\ e\ t)$ is reformatted $e \cdot t$, a combination.

(iii) $(\exists I_{\exists x.\phi(x)}\ t\ e)$ is reformatted $pair_{\exists x.\phi(x)}\ t\ e$, an ordered pair.

(iv) $(\exists E\ e_1\ (a \in V, b \in \phi(a))\ e_2)$ is reformatted $open\ e_1\ as\ (a \in V, b \in \phi(a)).\,e_2$, an indexing construct that indexes the pair of values in e_1 and binds them to the names a and b within the expression e_2.

The lambda-calculus representations of the three natural-deduction trees follow:

$\lambda p \in (\forall x \in V. \forall y \in V. P(x,y)). \lambda y \in V. \lambda x \in V. (p \bullet x) \bullet y$

$\lambda p \in (\forall x \in V. P(x)). \ pair \ a \ (p \bullet a)$

$open \ q \ as \ (a \in V, \ s \in (\forall y \in V. P(a,y)). \lambda y \in V. \ pair \ a \ (s \bullet y)$

where q names the assumption $\exists x \in V. \exists y \in V. P(x,y)$

The new representations show that proof trees are functions from proof trees and individuals to proof trees. The Heyting interpretation of the quantified propositions follows:

(i)   A proof of a proposition, $\forall x \in V. \phi(x)$, is a function, able to transform an individual, $x \in V$, into a proof of $\phi(x)$.

(ii)   A proof of a proposition, $\exists x \in V. \phi(x)$, is a pair, consisting of an individual, $t \in V$, called a *witness*, and a proof for $\phi(t)$.

As in Section 9.2., the terms "pair" and "function" refer to concrete constructions. The inference rules are sound with respect to the Heyting interpretation:

(a)   The $\forall$I rule, applied to a proof, $p(x)$, of $\phi(x)$, where x is an hypothetical individual, constructs a function, $\lambda x \in V. p(x)$, that maps an individual, a, to a proof, $p(a)$, of $\phi(a)$.

(b)   The $\forall$E rule, applied to a proof, p, of $\forall x \in V. \phi(x)$ and an individual, a, applies p to a, giving a proof, $p \bullet a$, of $\phi(a)$.

(c)   The $\exists$I rule, applied to a proof, $p(t)$, of $\phi(t)$, constructs the pair $pair_{\exists x \in V. \phi(x)} \ t \ p$, a proof of $\exists x \in V. \phi(x)$.

(d)   The $\exists$E rule, applied to a proof, p, of $\exists x \in V. \phi(x)$, and a proof, $q(a,b)$, of ϕ_2, which was built with a hypothetical witness, $a \in V$, and a hypothetical proof, $b \in \phi(a)$, produces a proof, $open \ p \ as \ (a \in V, b \in \phi(a)). b$, of ϕ_2.

As in Section 9.2, the constructions in (b) and (d) require computation; the computation rules are

$(\lambda x \in V. p(x)) \bullet a \ \Rightarrow \ p(a)$

$open \ (pair \ t \ p) \ as \ (a \in V, b \in \phi(a)). \ q(a, b) \ \Rightarrow \ q(t, p)$

The first rule is just a β-rule, and the second is a *with*-style computation rule.

As in Chapter 9, the introduction rules define the canonical expressions for a type: Here, $\lambda x \in V. p(x)$ for $\forall x \in V. \phi(x)$ and *pair t r* for $\exists x \in V. \phi(x)$. As usual, the computation rules show how the operators created by the elimination rules operate upon canonical forms. The calculus remains strongly normalizing, and every closed expression rewrites to one in canonical form.

From here on, we work with the typed predicate calculus, since we are interested in writing propositions like $\forall x \in nat.\, x{+}1{>}x$ as well as $\exists l \in natlist.\, tail(l){=}nil$. As in Chapter 9, propositions are data types, so the former proposition names a data type of functions that map input numbers, x, to proofs of $x{+}1{>}x$. The latter proposition names a data type of lists paired with proofs that the lists have length one.

The type $\forall x \in nat.\exists y \in nat.\, y{>}x$ holds far more interest. The proposition looks like a *specification* of a computer program; indeed, a proof of the proposition must be a program that maps an input number, x, to a pair consisting of an output number, y, and a proof that $y{>}x$, that is, a proof that y satisfies the specification. We now have these important correspondences:

Propositions are types are specifications.

Proofs are values are programs.

A program that satisfies a specification of the form $\forall x \in In.\exists y \in Out.\, \phi(x,y)$ is guaranteed correct, because it maps an input, $x \in In$, to an output, $y \in Out$, and a proof that the output satisfies $\phi(x,y)$. The proof is a "warranty" that comes with the output and ensures that the output is proper. Compare this with the real-life situation, say, of buying a television set. When you give money to the salesclerk, you receive in return a television set and a warranty that the television operates properly. Warranties are common to everyday life and should appear more often in computing. The predicate calculus makes such warranties an integral part of a program's type.

Another consequence of "propositions are types are specifications" is that type checking becomes program verification. This achieves the ideal of the naive programmer: If the type checker says that the program is well formed, then the program will operate correctly. The price paid for this wonderful result is that the programmer must encode more information into a program than what is traditionally expected. For example, a type checker cannot discover that the program $\lambda x \in nat.\, x$ is the identity function on numbers; that is, that the program satisfies the specification $\forall x \in nat.\exists y \in nat.\, y{=}x$. Instead, the program must be coded $\lambda x \in nat.\, pair\, x\, p$, where p is the proof of $x{=}x$. The programmer has the burden of writing the proof—the "warranty"—for the program's output. It is not surprising that *someone* must write the proof; perhaps the type checker can be enriched to a theorem prover and do the proof itself. But the predicate calculus is undecidable; that is, there can be no algorithm for deciding theoremhood, so any attempt to build a type checker that writes all its own proofs is doomed.

If programs produce outputs paired with correctness proofs, then such programs may well demand inputs that come with correctness proofs. For example, the proposition $\forall x \in nat.\, (x{>}1)\supset(\exists y \in nat.\, y{<}x \wedge y{\neq}0)$ can be read as a specification of a program that demands a number, x, and a proof that $x{>}1$ holds. Then, the output is a pair, namely, a number, y, and a proof that $y{<}x \wedge y{\neq}0$.

Propositions of the form $\forall x \in In.\, \phi_1(x)\supset(\exists y \in Out.\, \phi_2(x,y))$ are commonly used as program specifications. $\phi_1(x)$ is the *precondition* and $\phi_2(x,y)$ is the *postcondition* of the program. Preconditions prove crucial to the building of correct, modular systems. Each program in the system can be developed separately, because its precondition states restrictions under which the program is designed to operate. When a program is linked into a system, the program's precondition must be satisfied. Postconditions become important, because the output from one program typically becomes the input to another program. The postcondition states the properties that an output possesses, and the postcondition is used to validate the precondition for that program that uses the output as its input.

This method of system building demands that proofs become active values in a system. But in practice, precondition and postcondition proofs are not passed about as run-time values, no more than data-type tags are passed about as run-time values. Just as a compile-time type checker can "precompute" a system's data-type tags so that they need not appear as run-time values, a link-time precondition checker might "precompute" precondition and postcondition proofs, so that they need not appear as run-time values. Present day precondition checking is conducted by pencil and paper, rather than by an automated tool like a linker. But the situation is changing.

The "proofs are values are programs" correspondence permits propositions about the structure of proofs. One example is $\forall x \in nat.\ \forall p \in (x{+}1{>}x).\ \exists q \in (\exists y \in nat.\ y > x).$ $q = (pair\ x\ p)$, which states a fact about the *pair* constructor. Note that $x{+}1{>}x$ is a data type of proof trees, as is $\exists y \in nat.y > x$. Since programs are proofs, this implies that we can reason about program structure within the typing system.

10.2 The Typed Predicate Calculus with Natural Numbers

We now formalize the concepts in the previous section as a typed predicate calculus, where the basic units of proof are judgements of the form $\Gamma \vdash e \in \phi$. The alphabet contains the usual connectives, auxiliary symbols, and symbols for lambda-calculus expressions. The syntax for judgements, propositions, and terms follows:

$S \in$ Judgement $P \in$ Predicate-symbol
$\Gamma \in$ Context $e \in$ Term
$\phi \in$ Proposition $x \in$ Identifier

$$S ::= \Gamma \vdash e \in \phi$$
$$\Gamma ::= x_1 \in \phi_1, x_2 \in \phi_2, \cdots, x_n \in \phi_n,\ \ n \geq 0$$
$$\phi ::= \forall x \in \phi_1.\phi_2 \mid \exists x \in \phi_1.\phi_2 \mid \phi_1 \wedge \phi_2 \mid \phi_1 \supset \phi_2 \mid \phi_1 \vee \phi_2 \mid \bot$$
$$\mid nat \mid P(e_1, e_2, \ldots, e_n),\ \ n \geq 0$$
$$e ::= \lambda x \in \phi.\, e \mid e_1 \bullet e_2 \mid pair_\phi\ e_1\ e_2 \mid open\ e_1\ as\ (x \in \phi_1, y \in \phi_2).\, e_2$$
$$\mid e_1, e_2 \mid fst\ e \mid snd\ e \mid \lambda x \in \phi.\, e \mid e_1 \cdot e_2 \mid x$$
$$\mid inl_\phi\ e \mid inr_\phi\ e \mid cases\ e_1\ of\ isl(x_1 \in \phi_1).\, e_2\ [\!]\ isr(x_2 \in \phi_2).\, e_3 \mid abort_\phi\ e$$
$$\mid 0 \mid succ\ e \mid natrec\ e_1\ of\ is0.\, e_2\ [\!]\ is(succ\ x)(recx \in \phi(x)).\, e_3$$

$\Gamma \vdash \textit{nat IsProp}$ $\qquad \dfrac{\Gamma \vdash e_1 \in \textit{nat} \quad \Gamma \vdash e_2 \in \textit{nat}}{\Gamma \vdash e_1 < e_2 \ \textit{IsProp}}$ and similarly for $>, =, \ldots$

$\dfrac{\Gamma \vdash \phi_1 \ \textit{IsProp} \quad \Gamma, x \in \phi_1 \vdash \phi_2 \ \textit{IsProp}}{\Gamma \vdash \forall x \in \phi_1 . \phi_2 \ \textit{IsProp}}$ and similarly for $\exists x \in \phi_1 . \phi_2$

$\dfrac{\Gamma \vdash \phi_1 \ \textit{IsProp} \quad \Gamma \vdash \phi_2 \ \textit{IsProp}}{\Gamma \vdash \phi_1 \wedge \phi_2 \ \textit{IsProp}}$ and similarly for $\phi_1 \supset \phi_2$ and $\phi_1 \vee \phi_2$

$\Gamma \vdash \bot \ \textit{IsProp}$

Figure 10.4

Since individuals are typed, there is danger of ill-formed propositions, for example, $\forall p \in (\exists x \in \textit{nat}.\, x > 0).\, p > 0$, so we must provide rules that define when propositions are well formed. A proposition, ϕ, is well formed with respect to a context, Γ, if the judgement $\Gamma \vdash \phi \ \textit{IsProp}$ can be derived with the rules in Figure 10.4.

Since a proposition's well-formedness is established with respect to a context, we must state how contexts are well formed. A context, $x_1 \in \phi_1, x_2 \in \phi_2, \ldots, x_n \in \phi_n$, $n \geq 0$, is well formed if (i) all identifiers x_i are distinct from one another; (ii) for all i, $0 \leq i < n$, $x_1 \in \phi_1, \ldots, x_i \in \phi_i \vdash \phi_{i+1} \ \textit{IsProp}$ can be derived. Condition (ii) orders the members of a context, which is crucial to contexts like $x \in \textit{nat}, p \in x > 0$, where one assumption depends on another. The rules for well-formedness of propositions, contexts, and terms are interdependent, so an induction is necessary to prove that the notions of well-formedness are noncircular. This is left as an exercise. We always work with well-formed contexts and propositions, so the rules in Figure 10.4 are hereafter taken for granted.

The inference rules for the propositional connectives are exactly the rules in Figures 9.5 and 9.10; the rules for the quantifiers are presented in Figure 10.5. The rules are the expected ones; in particular, the $\exists$E rule uses the tacit assumption that $e_1 \in \exists x \in \phi_1 . \phi_2(x)$ represents some canonical expression *pair a b*, where a and b are identifiers since the exact value of the canonical expression is unknown.

For the moment, we will assume that predicates such as $<, >, =, \ldots$ and operations such as $+, \times, \ldots$ are given. Later, we will formally define them in terms of a general equality operator, but now it is convenient to move to examples. Here is the first: We want a program that satisfies the specification $\forall n \in \textit{nat}. \exists m \in \textit{nat}.\, m > n$, under the

$\forall$I: $\dfrac{\Gamma, x \in \phi_1 \vdash e \in \phi_2(x)}{\Gamma \vdash \lambda x \in \phi_1 . e \ \in \ \forall x \in \phi_1 . \phi_2(x)}$ $\forall$E: $\dfrac{\Gamma \vdash e_1 \in \forall x \in \phi_1 . \phi_2(x) \quad \Gamma \vdash e_2 \in \phi_1}{\Gamma \vdash e_1 \cdot e_2 \in \phi_2(e_2)}$

$\exists$I: $\dfrac{\Gamma \vdash e_1 \in \phi_1 \quad \Gamma \vdash e_2 \in \phi_2(e_1)}{\Gamma \vdash pair_{\exists x \in \phi_1 . \phi_2(x)} \ e_1 \ e_2 \ \in \ \exists x \in \phi_1 . \phi_2(x)}$

$\exists$E: $\dfrac{\Gamma \vdash e_1 \in \exists x \in \phi_1 . \phi_2(x) \quad \Gamma, a \in \phi_1, b \in \phi_2(a) \vdash e_2 \in \phi_3}{\Gamma \vdash open \ e_1 \ as \ (a \in \phi_1, b \in \phi_2(a)). e_2 \ \in \ \phi_3}$ if $a \notin FV(\phi_3)$ and $b \notin FV(\phi_3)$

Figure 10.5 _____

assumption that $\forall x \in nat. \ succ \ x > x$.* This judgement displays such a program:

$$a_1 \in (\forall x \in nat. \ succ \ x > x) \vdash \lambda n \in nat. \ pair \ (succ \ n) \ (a_1 \cdot n) \ \in \ \forall n \in nat. \exists m \in nat. \ m > n$$

The program is a function that maps an input, n, to an output, $succ \ n$, and a proof that $succ \ n > n$, for example, $(\lambda n \in nat. \ pair \ succ \ n \ (a_1 \cdot n)) \cdot 3 \ \Rightarrow \ pair \ succ \ 3 \ (a_1 \cdot 3)$. The heart of the judgement is the (linearized and reformatted) natural-deduction tree, $\lambda n \in nat. \ pair \ (succ \ n) \ (a_1 \cdot n)$. When a programmer needs to code a program that satisfies a specification like $\forall n \in nat. \exists m \in nat. \ m > n$, she should draw the natural-deduction tree that proves the specification. Then, the typing rules in Figures 9.5, 9.10, and 10.5 are used to validate the well formedness of the tree, and in effect, synthesize the program code from the tree. The latter step can be done automatically, as it is in the NuPRL proof system (Constable, et al. 1986). In this way, programming verified code is theorem proving.

The second example uses another assumption about $>$ to prove a specification with pre- and postconditions:

$$a_2 \in \forall x \in nat. \forall y \in nat. \forall z \in nat. \ x > y \supset x + z > z + y$$
$$\vdash \lambda m \in nat. \lambda n \in nat. \lambda p \in m > n. \ pair \ m + n \ (a_2 \cdot m \cdot n \cdot m \cdot p, \ a_2 \cdot m \cdot n \cdot n \cdot p)$$
$$\in \ \forall m \in nat. \forall n \in nat. \ m > n \supset (\exists q \in nat. \ m + m > q \land q > n + n))$$

The program accepts two numbers, m and n, and a proof that $m > n$ as inputs and builds a proof that $m + m > m + n > n + n$; it outputs $m + n$ and the proof. The proof of the

_____

* Of course, this assumption is just a law of arithmetic. Later in the chapter, we will state Peano's axioms, which are the standard laws of arithmetic, and we will outline how the axioms are proved within the calculus.

precondition is essential to deriving the correct output.

Now we construct a third example. It is coded independently of the two programs above, but it relies on the specifications of the two programs to get its result:

$f_1 \in \forall n \in nat.\exists m \in nat.\, m>n,$

$f_2 \in \forall m \in nat.\forall n \in nat.\, m>n \supset (\exists q \in nat.\, m+m>q \land q>n+n))$

$\vdash \lambda x \in nat.\, open\ (f_1 \bullet x)\ as\ (c_1 \in nat,\, b_1 \in c_1>x).$

$\quad open\ (f_2 \bullet c_1 \bullet x \cdot b_1)\ as\ (c_2 \in nat,\, b_2 \in (c_1+c_1>c_2 \land c_2>x+x)).$

$\quad\quad pair\ c_2\ (snd\ b_2)$

$\in \forall x \in nat.\exists z \in nat.\, z>x+x$

When the programs that correspond to f_1 and f_2 are linked to the above program, the result is a system that maps input numbers, x, to outputs, z, such that $z>x+x$. We have taken a roundabout way to satisfy the specification—$\lambda x \in nat.\, pair\ succ(x+x)\ (a_1 \bullet x+x)$ would work as well—but we wanted to observe the different forms of specifications and inference rules in action.

The third program is noteworthy in its use of the $\exists E$ rule, represented by the *open* construct. Since $f_1 \bullet x$ has type $\exists n \in nat.\, n>x$, the $\exists E$ rule lets us "open" $f_1 \bullet x$ by assuming that it represents the canonical expression $pair\ c_1\ b_1$, where c_1 is the number greater than x and b_1 is the proof of it. This information lets us deduce that $f_2 \bullet c_1 \bullet x \cdot b_1$ has the type $\exists q \in nat.\, c_1+c_1>q \land q>x+x$. Again, the $\exists E$ rule lets us assume that $c_2 \in nat$ and $b_2 \in c_1+c_1>c_2 \land c_2>x+x$. With this information, we build the program $pair\ c_2\ (snd\ b_2)$. With this style, we program intelligently and hierarchically.

If we suppress the proof parts in the above code and use the ML-style *let* construct from Chapter 7 in place of *open*, the program takes a familiar and simple form:

$\lambda x \in nat.\, let\ c_1,\, \cdots\, = (f_1 \bullet x)\ in$

$\quad let\ c_2,\, \cdots\, = (f_2 \bullet c_1 \bullet x\ \cdots\,)$

$\quad in\ pair\ c_2\ \cdots$

As noted in Chapter 9, the natural-deduction trees for the three above examples can be pasted together. This is just the linking of the three programs into one system, and it yields the following judgement:

$a_1 \in \forall x \in nat.\, succ\ x>x,$

$a_2 \in \forall x \in nat.\forall y \in nat.\forall z \in nat.\, x>y \supset x+z>z+y,$

$\quad \vdash \lambda x \in nat.$

$\quad\quad open\ (\lambda n \in nat.\, pair\ (succ\ n)\ (a_1 \bullet n)) \bullet x$

$\quad\quad\quad as\ (c_1 \in nat,\, b_1 \in c_1>x).$

$\quad\quad\quad\quad open\ (\lambda m \in nat.\lambda n \in nat.\lambda p \in m>n.$

$$pair \ m+n \ \ (a_2 \bullet m \bullet n \bullet m \cdot p, \ a_2 \bullet m \bullet n \bullet n \cdot p)) \bullet c_1 \bullet x \cdot b_1$$
$$as \ (c_2 \in nat, \ b_2 \in (c_1+c_1>c_2 \land c_1>x+x)).$$
$$pair \ c_2 \ \ (snd \ b_2)$$
$$\in \forall x \in nat. \exists z \in nat. \ z>x+x$$

The computation rules can be applied to the system, reducing the proof parts. We obtain

$$\Rightarrow \lambda x \in nat.$$
$$open \ pair \ (succ \ x) \ (a_1 \bullet x)$$
$$as \ (c_1 \in nat, \ b_1 \in a_1>x).$$
$$open \ pair \ c_1+x \ \ (a_2 \bullet c_1 \bullet x \bullet c_1 \cdot b_1, \ a_2 \bullet c_1 \bullet x \bullet x \cdot b_1)$$
$$as \ (c_2 \in nat, \ b_2 \in (c_1+c_1>c_2 \land c_1>x+x)).$$
$$pair \ c_2 \ \ (snd \ b_2)$$

$$\Rightarrow \lambda x \in nat.$$
$$open \ pair \ (succ \ x)+x \ \ (a_2 \bullet (succ \ x) \bullet x \bullet (succ \ x) \cdot (a_1 \bullet x), \ a_2 \bullet (succ \ x) \bullet x \bullet x \cdot (a_1 \bullet x))$$
$$as \ (c_2 \in nat, \ b_2 \in ((succ \ x)+(succ \ x)>c_2 \land (succ \ x)>x+x)).$$
$$pair \ c_2 \ \ (snd \ b_2)$$

$$\Rightarrow \lambda x \in nat. \ pair \ (succ \ x)+x \ \ (a_2 \bullet (succ \ x) \bullet x \bullet x \cdot (a_1 \bullet x))$$

The result is a program whose pre- and postconditions have been validated at link time and is now ready for its run-time input.

Now that we have examined the fundamentals of programming in the logic, it is time for a closer study of the type of natural numbers, *nat*. The fundamental introduction and elimination rules for *nat* are given in Figure 10.6. The introduction rules define the obvious canonical expressions. The elimination rule states the mathematical induction principle: If one can prove a property, $\phi(0)$, and show that $\phi(x)$ implies $\phi(succ \ x)$, then, for

---

$$natI_1: \ \Gamma \vdash 0 \in nat \qquad natI_2: \ \frac{\Gamma \vdash e \in nat}{\Gamma \vdash succ \ e \in nat}$$

$$natE: \ \frac{\Gamma \vdash e_1 \in nat \quad \Gamma \vdash e_2 \in \phi(0) \quad \Gamma, x \in nat, y \in \phi(x) \vdash e_3(x,y) \in \phi(succ \ x)}{\Gamma \vdash natrec \ e_1 \ of \ is0. \ e_2 \ [] \ issucc(x)(recx \in \phi(x)). \ e_3(x, recx) \ \in \ \phi(e_1)}$$

Figure 10.6 _____

any number, e_1, $\phi(e_1)$ holds. As usual, the elimination rule is structured around the canonical expressions for *nat*. When read as a program, the induction proof is a primitive recursive function. It might be helpful to read *natrec* e_1 *of* $is0$. e_2 [] $issucc(x)(recx \in \phi(x))$. $e_3(x, recx)$ as follows:

$$f(e_1), \quad \text{where } f(0) = e_2 \quad \text{and} \quad f(succ\ x) = e_3(x, f(x))$$

The inductive hypothesis, $y \in \phi(x)$, in the *nat*E rule is interpreted as the result of the recursive function call, $f(x)$. This is confirmed by the following computation rules:

$$natrec\ 0\ of\ is0.\ e_2\ [\,]\ issucc(x)(recx \in \phi(x)).\ e_3(x, recx) \implies e_2$$

$$natrec\ (succ\ e)\ of\ is0.\ e_2\ [\,]\ issucc(x)(recx \in \phi(x)).\ e_3(x, recx)$$
$$\implies e_3(e, (natrec\ e\ of\ is0.\ e_2\ [\,]\ issucc(x)(recx \in \phi(x)).\ e_3(x, recx)))$$

The *nat*E rule creates repetitive programs on the natural numbers. The programs appear to be merely primitive recursive, but they can do more, namely, produce functions as answers. This permits the coding of nonprimitive recursive functions, such as Ackermann's function, and indeed all functions that are provably total in Peano arithmetic.

Figure 10.7 shows the natural-deduction tree that proves $\forall x \in nat.x+0=x$, $\forall x \in nat.\forall y \in nat.succ(x+y) = x+(succ\ y) \vdash \forall n \in nat.\ n+0 = 0+n$. As usual, the tree is best read from the root to the leaves. To prove the main goal, it suffices to show $n+0 = 0+n$, for an arbitrary $n \in nat$. We do this by mathematical induction (the *nat*E rule), showing (i) $0+0 = 0+0$, that is, the base case, and (ii) $(succ\ x)+0 = 0+(succ\ x)$,

$$\begin{array}{l}
\qquad\qquad\qquad\qquad\qquad\qquad\qquad \forall x \in nat.\forall y \in nat.succ(x+y) = x+(succ\ y) \\
\qquad\qquad\qquad\qquad\qquad\qquad\qquad\qquad |\ \forall E,\ \forall E \\
\qquad\qquad\qquad \forall x \in nat.x+0=x \qquad x+0=0+x\ \textcircled{1} \qquad succ(0+x)=0+succ\ x \\
\qquad\qquad\qquad\qquad |\ \forall E \qquad\qquad\qquad \backslash \qquad\qquad / \text{ subst} \\
\forall x \in nat.x+0=x \qquad x+0=x \qquad\qquad succ(x+0)=0+succ\ x \\
\quad |\ \forall E \qquad\qquad\qquad \backslash \qquad\qquad\quad / \text{ subst} \\
succ\ x+0=succ\ x \qquad\qquad succ\ x=0+succ\ x \\
\qquad\qquad \backslash \qquad\qquad\qquad\qquad / \text{ trans} \\
0+0 = 0+0\ \ refl \quad (succ\ x)+0 = 0+(succ\ x) \\
\qquad\qquad \backslash \qquad\qquad / \ nat\text{E}\ \textcircled{1} \\
\qquad\qquad n+0 = 0+n \\
\qquad\qquad\quad |\ \forall I \\
\qquad\qquad \forall n \in nat.\ n+0 = 0+n
\end{array}$$

Figure 10.7 _____

the induction case, where we are allowed the inductive hypothesis $x+0 = 0+x$. The judgement form of the proof is

$p_3 \in \forall x \in nat.x+0=x,$

$p_4 \in \forall x \in nat.\forall y \in nat.succ(x+y) = x+(succ\ y)$

$\vdash \lambda n \in nat.\ natrec\ n\ of\ is0.\ refl\ 0$

$[]\ issucc(x)(recx \in x+0=0+x).$

$trans\ (p_3 \bullet succ\ x)\ \ (subst\ (p_3 \bullet x)\ (subst\ recx\ (p_4 \bullet 0 \bullet x)))$

$\in \forall n \in nat.\ n+0=0+n.$

where *refl*, *trans*, and *subst* stand for the reflexivity, transitivity, and substitutivity rules, respectively, for equality. (These will be formally defined momentarily.) The lambda-calculus coding of the proof is a function that builds, for an argument, n, a proof tree of $n+0 = 0+n$ that contains one use of the base case proof followed by n uses of the induction case proof. You can see this yourself—apply the function to an argument, say, 3, and use the computation rules for *nat*; the result is a proof that $3+0 = 0+3$.

A simple example of program development with the *nat*E rule is the proof of the factorial function from its classic specification:

$a_1 \in 0!=1,\ \ a_2 \in \forall x \in nat.\ (succ\ x)!=(succ\ x)\times x!$

$\vdash \lambda n \in nat.\ natrec\ n\ of\ is0.\ pair\ 1\ a_1$

$[]\ is\ succ(x)(recx \in (\exists m \in nat.\ x!=m)).$

$open\ recx\ as\ (a \in nat,\ b \in x!=a).$

$pair\ (succ\ x)\times a\ \ (subst\ b\ (a_2 \bullet x))$

$\in \forall n \in nat.\exists m \in nat.\ n!=m$

The context states the properties we demand of the arithmetic operator, !. It is not our job to prove assumptions a_1 and a_2 but to use them to derive the factorial function. If we reformat the proof into ML-like code, ignoring the proof parts, we obtain

$fac(0)\ =\ 1, \cdots$

$fac(succ\ x)\ =\ let\ a, \cdots\ =fac(x)\ in\ (succ\ x)\times a, \cdots$

A crucial point is that the recursive call, $fac(x)$, in the second equation, returns a value, a, and a proof that the value is correct. The value and its proof are used to build a new value and *its* proof of correctness. The Exercises give more examples that use the *nat*E rule.

Other connectives can be added to the logic. Figure 10.8 shows the list constructor, encoded as a logical connective. The rules follow the usual pattern; notably, the elimination rule defines an induction principle for lists and the computation rules show how

---

$$\frac{\Gamma \vdash \phi \; IsProp}{\Gamma \vdash \phi list \; IsProp} \qquad listI_1 : \; \Gamma \vdash nil_\phi \in \phi list \qquad listI_2 : \; \frac{\Gamma \vdash e_1 \in \phi \qquad \Gamma \vdash e_2 \in \phi list}{\Gamma \vdash cons \; e_1 \; e_2 \in \phi list}$$

*list*E:

$$\frac{\Gamma \vdash e_1 \in \phi_1 list \qquad \Gamma \vdash e_2 \in \phi_2(nil) \qquad \Gamma, \, a \in \phi_1, \, b \in \phi_1 list, \, x \in \phi_2(b) \vdash e_3(a,b,x) \in \phi_2(cons \; a \; b)}{\Gamma \vdash listrec \; e_1 \; of \; isnil. \; e_2 \; [] \; is(cons \; a \; b)(recb \in \phi_2(b)). \; e_3(a,b,recb) \; \in \; \phi_2(e_1)}$$

listrec nil of isnil. e_2 *[] is(cons a b)(recb* $\in \phi(b)$*).* $e_3(a,b,recb)$ $\Rightarrow$ e_2

listrec (cons e_0 e_1*) of isnil.* e_2 *[] is(cons a b)(recb* $\in \phi(b)$*).* $e_3(a,b,recb)$
$\quad \Rightarrow \; e_3(e_0, \, e_1, \, (listrec \; e_1 \; of \; isnil. \; e_2 \; [] \; is(cons \; a \; b)(recb \in \phi(b)). \; e_3(a,b,recb)))$

Figure 10.8 _____

proofs with the elimination rule cause repetitive computations.

Here is one example of program development for lists: The proof of a sorting specification. For the moment, we consider the type of lists of natural numbers, *natlist*. For $l,m \in natlist$, read the predicate *ord(l)* as saying, "*l* is an ordered list," and read *perm(l,m)* as saying, "lists *l* and *m* are permutations of one another." Here is (a not necessarily minimal) set of assumptions about *ord* and *perm*:

$z_1 \in \forall l \in natlist. \, perm(l, l)$

$z_2 \in \forall l \in natlist. \forall m \in natlist. \, perm(l, m) \supset perm(m, l)$

$z_3 \in \forall l \in natlist. \forall m \in natlist. \forall n \in natlist. \, (perm(l, m) \wedge perm(m, n)) \supset perm(l, n)$

$z_4 \in \forall a \in nat. \forall l \in natlist. \forall m \in natlist. \, perm(l, m) \supset perm(cons \; a \; l, \, cons \; a \; m)$

$z_5 \in \forall a \in nat. \forall b \in nat. \forall l \in natlist. \, perm(cons \; a \; (cons \; b \; l), \, cons \; b \; (cons \; a \; l))$

$z_6 \in ord(nil)$

$z_7 \in \forall a \in nat. \, ord(cons \; a \; nil)$

$z_8 \in \forall a \in nat. \, \forall l \in natlist. \, ord(cons \; a \; l) \supset ord(l)$

$z_9 \in \forall a \in nat. \forall b \in nat. \forall l \in natlist. \, (ord(cons \; a \; l) \wedge b \leq a) \supset ord(cons \; b \; (cons \; a \; l))$

$z_{10} \in \forall a \in nat. \forall b \in nat. \forall l \in natlist. \forall m \in natlist.$
$\quad (ord(cons \; a \; l) \wedge a \leq b \wedge perm(cons \; b \; l, m) \wedge ord(m)) \supset ord(cons \; a \; m)$

Say that someone uses the above assumptions to prove the following judgement:

$z_1 \cdots z_{10} \vdash insert \in (\forall l \in natlist. \, ord(l) \supset (\forall a \in nat. \exists m \in natlist. \, perm(cons \; a \; l, m) \wedge ord(m)))$

That is, *insert* is a program that inserts a number, *a*, into its proper place in an ordered list, *l*. *insert* can be used to derive an insertion sort. Here is the strategy: We wish to prove $\forall l \in natlist.\exists m \in natlist. perm(l,m) \wedge ord(m)$, so we show, for an arbitrary $l \in natlist$, that $\exists m \in natlist. perm(l,m) \wedge ord(m)$. The proof is by list induction, that is, by the *natlistE* rule. There are two cases:

(i)   List *l* is *nil*: Since $z_1 \cdots z_{10} \vdash (z_1 \bullet nil, z_6) \in perm(nil, nil) \wedge ord(nil)$ holds, we have that $z_1 \cdots z_{10} \vdash pair\ nil\ (z_1 \bullet nil, z_6) \in \exists m \in natlist. perm(nil, m) \wedge ord(m)$.

(ii) List *l* is *cons a b*: So, let $a \in nat$, $b \in natlist$, and $recb \in \exists m \in natlist. perm(b,m) \wedge ord(m)$. The last assumption is the inductive hypothesis for *b*. We must prove $\exists m \in natlist. perm(cons\ a\ b, m) \wedge ord(m)$. By the $\exists E$ rule we can assume that the proof, *recb*, of the inductive hypothesis has the canonical form *pair m′ y′*, where $m' \in natlist$ and $y' \in perm(b,m') \wedge ord(m')$; that is, *m′* is the sorted version of *b*, and *y′* is the proof that *m′* is sorted. Now we can use *insert* and prove

$$z_1 \cdots z_{10} \vdash insert \bullet m' \cdot (snd\ y') \bullet a \in \exists m \in natlist. perm(cons\ a\ m', m) \wedge ord(m)$$

We can use the $\exists E$ rule to assume that $insert \bullet m' \cdot (snd\ y') \bullet a$ has a canonical form *pair m″ y″*, where $m'' \in natlist$ and $y'' \in perm(cons\ a\ m', m'') \wedge ord(m'')$.

Now we are ready to build a proof of $\exists m \in natlist. perm(cons\ a\ b, m) \wedge ord(m)$; it will have the form *pair m″, proof-part*, since *m″* is the sorted version of *b* with *a* inserted at the appropriate place. The "proof-part" must be an ordered pair. The first component is built from instantiations of assumptions z_3 and z_4:

$$z_1 \cdots z_{10} \vdash z_3 \bullet (cons\ a\ b) \bullet (cons\ a\ m') \bullet m'' \cdot (z_4 \bullet a \bullet b \bullet m' \cdot (fst\ y'), (fst\ y''))$$
$$\in perm(cons\ a\ b, m'')$$

The second component is easily proved: $z_1 \cdots z_{10} \vdash snd\ y'' \in ord(m'')$. This completes the proof of the inductive step.

The complete judgement for the insertion sort reads as follows:

$$z_1 \cdots z_{10} \vdash \lambda l \in natlist.\ listrec\ l\ of\ isnil.\ pair\ nil\ (z_1 \bullet nil, z_6)$$
$$[]\ is(cons\ a\ b)(recb \in (\exists m \in natlist. perm(b,m) \wedge ord(m))).$$
$$open\ recb\ as\ (m' \in natlist, y' \in perm(b,m') \wedge ord(m')).$$
$$open\ insert \bullet m' \cdot (snd\ y') \bullet a$$
$$as\ (m'' \in natlist, y'' \in perm(cons\ a\ m',m'') \wedge ord(m'')).$$
$$pair\ m''$$
$$(z_3 \bullet (cons\ a\ b) \bullet (cons\ a\ m') \bullet m'' \cdot (z_4 \bullet a \bullet b \bullet m' \cdot (fst\ y'),$$
$$(fst\ y'')),\ snd\ y'')$$
$$\in \forall l \in natlist.\exists m \in natlist. perm(l,m) \wedge ord(m)$$

The code is a bit overwhelming, but remember that the program is just the natural-deduction tree for the proof of the sorting specification. If a programmer can write the natural-deduction tree that proves the sorting specification, the code therein can be automatically synthesized. If we suppress the proof parts in the above code, the usual version of insertion sort emerges:

$$insertion\text{-}sort(nil) = nil, \; \cdots$$
$$insertion\text{-}sort(cons\; a\; b) = let\; m', \cdots = insertion\text{-}sort(b)\; in$$
$$let\; m'', \cdots = insert\; m' \cdots a$$
$$in\; m'', \; \cdots$$

The insertion sort example plus those seen earlier suggest that programming in a typed language is just theorem proving. A program's specification serves as its data type, and a programming logic for a language is just its typing system.

In general, other structured types, such as trees, stacks, and files, can be defined the same way as numbers and lists: Introduction rules define the canonical expressions, and the elimination rule states an induction principle. But there are a variety of possible induction principles. In the case of lists, the induction defined above might be replaced by a course-of-values induction or even an induction on the length of lists. This suggests that a type might use a variety of elimination rules. The form of induction used to prove a specification provides a distinct style of programming. Although space prevents a complete exposition here, use of course-of-values induction in the proof of the sorting specification leads to a merge-sort algorithm, and a similar well-founded induction generates a quick-sort algorithm. The exercises develop these examples; see also Turner 1991.

10.3 Universes

In the terminology of Chapter 8, the present typing system admits $(*,*)$ abstraction and encapsulation. We can extend this to a form of $(\Box,*)$ abstraction and encapsulation by adding universes to the syntax of propositions. The result is a higher-order predicate calculus.

We call U_0 *the universe of small types*; think of U_0's members as being the well formed propositions. We formalize this by revising Figure 10.4, replacing every occurrence of *IsProp* by "$\in U_0$." Two examples follow:

$$\Gamma \vdash nat \in U_0 \qquad \frac{\Gamma \vdash \phi_1 \in U_0 \qquad \Gamma, x \in \phi_1 \vdash \phi_2 \in U_0}{\Gamma \vdash \forall x \in \phi_1 . \phi_2 \in U_0}$$

In this way, the rules in Figure 10.4 become the introduction rules for the new type, U_0. Judgements such as $\vdash nat \in U_0$, $x \in nat \vdash x{>}0 \in U_0$, $x \in nat \vdash (\exists y \in nat. x{>}y) \in U_0$, and so on, are valid. The rules for well-formedness of contexts and sequents are as before.

Our plan is to write "polymorphic" programs, such as polymorphic identity:

$$\vdash (\lambda t \in U_0.\lambda x \in t.\, x) \;\in\; \forall t \in U_0.\, t \supset t$$

Like the polymorphic identity from Chapter 8, the function takes two arguments: The type, t, and a value, x, of type t. But we can do even better. Here is a polymorphic identity that satisfies a specification that demands identity behavior:

$$\vdash (\lambda t \in U_0.\lambda x \in t.\, pair \; x \; ``proof\text{-}of \, x{=}x") \;\in\; \forall t \in U_0.\forall x \in t.\exists y \in t.\, y{=}x$$

In order to write such judgements, we must state how U_0 itself can appear within propositions; that is, we must justify why a form such as $\forall t \in U_0.\, t \supset t$ is a well-formed proposition. The obvious, but disastrous, approach is to introduce an axiom $\Gamma \vdash U_0 \in U_0$, but this causes Girard's paradox, and the predicate calculus becomes inconsistent; that is, we can prove $\vdash \bot$. It is better to establish yet another universe, U_1, that contains propositions that contain occurrences of U_0. We modify Figure 10.5 into Figure 10.9.

The new set of formation rules lets us prove, say, $\vdash (\forall t \in U_0.\, t \supset t) \in U_1$, and it lets us define well-formed contexts and sequents with respect to U_1. We can use the usual introduction and elimination rules to construct polymorphic programs. In particular, the two judgements of the polymorphic identity shown above are valid.

Since we have kept the universe of small types, U_0, separate from the propositions that it contains, self-application is impossible. For example, we cannot apply

---

$$\Gamma \vdash nat \in U_0 \qquad \dfrac{\Gamma \vdash e_1 \in nat \quad \Gamma \vdash e_2 \in nat}{\Gamma \vdash e_1 < e_2 \in U_0} \quad \text{and similarly for } >, =, \ldots$$

$$\dfrac{\Gamma \vdash \phi_1 \in U_i \quad \Gamma, x \in \phi_1 \vdash \phi_2 \in U_j}{\Gamma \vdash \forall x \in \phi_1.\, \phi_2 \in U_{max(i,j)}} \quad \text{and similarly for } \exists x \in \phi_1.\, \phi_2$$

$$\dfrac{\Gamma \vdash \phi_1 \in U_i \quad \Gamma \vdash \phi_2 \in U_j}{\Gamma \vdash \phi_1 \wedge \phi_2 \in U_{max(i,j)}} \quad \text{and similarly for } \phi_1 \supset \phi_2 \text{ and } \phi_1 \vee \phi_2$$

$$\Gamma \vdash \bot \in U_0 \qquad\qquad \Gamma \vdash U_i \in U_{i+1}$$

where $i, j \geq 0$

Figure 10.9 _____

polymorphic identity to itself; this code is not well formed

$$(\lambda t \in U_0.\lambda x \in t.\, x) \cdot (\forall t \in U_0.\, t \supset t) \cdot (\lambda t \in U_0.\lambda x \in t.\, x)$$

because the proposition $\forall t \in U_0.t \supset t$ cannot be proved an element of U_0. In the terminology of Chapter 8, our calculus is *predicative*—it has a well-defined hierarchy of universes that allow objects to be defined without reference to the sets to which they belong. Since $\vdash (\forall t \in U_0.t \supset t) \in U_1$ is valid, we can apply the polymorphic identity that operates upon propositions in U_1 to the one that operates upon propositions in U_0:

$$\vdash (\lambda t \in U_1.\lambda x \in t.\, x) \cdot (\forall t \in U_0.t \supset t) \cdot (\lambda t \in U_0.\lambda x \in t.\, x) \;\in\; \forall t \in U_0.t \supset t$$

There exists a countable hierarchy of universes, U_i, $i \geq 0$, and there also exists a hierarchy of polymorphic identity functions.

The form of polymorphism in the ML-like languages is impredicative, but this might be due to historical accident—the unification-based type-inference algorithm naturally supports impredicativity. But the form of self-application permitted by the ML typing system is restrictive, and virtually all ML programs can be type checked within a predicative typing system (Harper and Pollack 1991).

Universes also allow creative uses of the existential quantifier. The judgement

$$\vdash pair\ natlist\ (nil, \lambda x \in nat.\lambda l \in natlist.\ cons\ n\ l) \;\in\; \exists t \in U_0.\, t \wedge (nat \supset t \supset t)$$

resembles the coding of an abstype for stacks of numbers. Of course, the stack can be parameterized as

$$\vdash \lambda t \in U_0.\ pair\ t\ list\ (nil, \lambda x \in t.\lambda l \in t\ list.\ cons\ n\ l)$$
$$\in \forall t \in U_0.\exists st \in U_0.\ st \wedge (t \supset st \supset st)$$

but even better, the logical properties of the stack can be encoded in its type:

$$\vdash \lambda t \in U_0.\ pair\ t\ list$$
$$pair\ nil$$
$$pair\ \lambda n \in t.\lambda l \in t\ list.\ cons\ n\ l$$
$$pair\ \lambda l \in t\ list.\ listrec\ l\ of\ isnil.\ nil\ []\ is(cons\ a\ l')(rec\ l').\ l'$$
$$proof\text{-}part$$
$$\in \forall t \in U_0.\exists st \in U_0.$$
$$\exists empty \in st.$$
$$\exists push \in t \supset st \supset st.$$
$$\exists pop \in st \supset st.$$
$$\forall n \in t.\forall l \in st.\ (pop((push\ n)l)) = l \;\wedge\; pop(empty) = empty$$

10.4 The Equality Type

In earlier sections, we used arithmetic predicates like $=$ and $<$ and operators like $+$ and $\times$. These predicates and operators can be defined by means of the *natE* rule and the rules for a new type, the general equality type. Figure 10.10 defines the general equality type.

We will usually write $a=b$, rather than $a=_\phi b$. The introduction rule is the reflexivity property of equality, and the elimination rules express the symmetry, transitivity, and substitutivity properties. Strictly speaking, the expression *subst* e_1 e_2 should be annotated with information regarding which parts of e_2 should be replaced; for example, it is not clear whether the type of *subst* $(id\ 2\ 1+1)$ $(id\ 2\ 2)$ should be $1+1=1+1$ or $1+1=2$ or even $2=2$. We rely on the context to make this clear. From reflexivity and substitution, one can derive symmetry and transitivity, but because the derived rules are useful, we include them in the figure.

We wish to use the equality type to prove properties like $\forall n \in nat.\,0+n=n$, where the equality symbol in the proposition is the general equality operator just defined. First, we note that "$+$" is just an abbreviation for the program

$$\lambda m \in nat \wedge nat.\ natrec\ (fst\ m)\ of\ is0.\ snd\ m\ []\ is(succ\ x)(recx \in nat).\ succ(recx)$$

which is a proof of $(nat \wedge nat) \supset nat$. The computation rules for *nat* tell us that $0+n \Rightarrow^* n$. Surely, we should be able to use this information to prove $\forall n \in nat.\,0+n=n$. To do so, we introduce the notion of convertibility from Chapter 6.

Recall that an expression, a, is *convertible* to an expression, b, written $a\ cnv\ b$, if the pair (a, b) is found in the reflexive, symmetric, transitive, substitutive closure of $\Rightarrow$,

---

$$\frac{\Gamma \vdash a \in \phi \quad \Gamma \vdash b \in \phi}{\Gamma \vdash a=_\phi b\ IsProp} \qquad =\text{I:}\ \frac{\Gamma \vdash a \in \phi}{\Gamma \vdash id\ a\ a \in a=_\phi a} \qquad =\text{E}_1:\ \frac{\Gamma \vdash e \in a=_\phi b}{\Gamma \vdash symm\ e \in b=_\phi a}$$

$$=\text{E}_2:\ \frac{\Gamma \vdash e_1 \in a=_\phi b \quad \Gamma \vdash e_2 \in b=_\phi c}{\Gamma \vdash trans\ e_1\ e_2 \in a=_\phi c} \qquad =\text{E}_3:\ \frac{\Gamma \vdash e_1 \in a=_\phi b \quad \Gamma \vdash e_2(a) \in \phi(a)}{\Gamma \vdash subst\ e_1\ e_2(a) \in \phi(b)}$$

$symm\ (id\ a\ b) \Rightarrow id\ b\ a$

$trans\ (id\ a\ b)\ (id\ b\ c) \Rightarrow id\ a\ c$

$subst\ (id\ a\ b)\ e(a) \Rightarrow e(b)$

Figure 10.10 _____

treated as a relation. Since $\Rightarrow$ has the confluence property, $a\ cnv\ b$ holds exactly when there is some expression, c, such that $a\Rightarrow^* c$ and $b\Rightarrow^* c$. We use a new form of judgement, $\Gamma\vdash a\ cnv\ b\in\phi$, to assert that

(i) $\Gamma\vdash a\in\phi$
(ii) $\Gamma\vdash b\in\phi$
(iii) $a\ cnv\ b$

and we replace the $=$I rule in Figure 10.10 by

$$=\text{I:}\quad \frac{\Gamma\vdash a\ cnv\ b\in\phi}{\Gamma\vdash id\ a\ b\in a=_\phi b}$$

The new $=$I rule permits the desired proof about addition:

$$\vdash\boldsymbol{\lambda}n\in nat.\ id\ (0+n)\ n\ \in\ \forall n\in nat.\ 0+n=n$$

Say that multiplication, $\times$, is exposed as the code

$$\lambda m\in nat\wedge nat.\ natrec\ (fst\ m)\ of\ is0.\ 0\ []\ is(succ\ x)(recx\in nat).\ (snd\ m)+recx$$

Then, we can prove all of Peano's axioms of arithmetic:

$\forall m\in nat.\ \neg(0=succ\ m)$
$\forall m\in nat.\forall n\in nat.\ (succ\ m=succ\ n)\supset m=n$
$\forall m\in nat.\ 0+m=m$
$\forall m\in nat.\forall n\in nat.\ m+succ\ n=succ(m+n)$
$\forall m\in nat.\ 0\times m=0$
$\forall m\in nat.\forall n\in nat.\ m\times succ\ n=(m\times n)+m$
$(\phi(0)\wedge(\forall m\in nat.\ \phi(m)\supset\phi(succ\ m)))\supset(\forall n\in nat.\ \phi(n))$, for every $\phi\in$ Proposition

As one can learn from any text on mathematical logic, the other predicates and operations of arithmetic can be coded in terms of the ones used in Peano's axioms. For example, $a\leq b$ is an abbreviation for $\exists m\in nat.\ a+m=b$. Thus, the rules for nat and general equality in Figures 10.6 and 10.10 (plus the new $=$I rule) suffice for proving specifications about natural numbers.

The substitution rule for general equality has one important consequence: The unicity of typing property holds only modulo convertibility. Here is an example. We can easily show

$$a_1\in\forall m\in nat.\ m\geq 0\vdash subst\ (id\ 0+0\ 0)\ (a_1\cdot 2)\ \in\ 2\geq 0+0$$

because

$$a_1\in\forall m\in nat.\ m\geq 0\vdash 0+0\ cnv\ 0\ \in nat$$

$$a_1 \in \forall m \in nat.\, m \geq 0 \vdash a_1 \cdot 2 \in 2 \geq 0$$

both hold. The computation rule for *subst* allows us to simplify the first proof, giving us the following judgement:

$$a_1 \in \forall m \in nat.\, m \geq 0 \vdash a_1 \cdot 2 \in 2 \geq 0+0$$

Thus, $a_1 \cdot 2$ can be typed in at least two different ways. This result is not surprising; indeed, it is natural, since $0+0=0$, and we generally accept results "up to equality." A type checker copes with this situation by assigning an expression a type whose expression subphrases are in normal form. For example, a type checker would calculate $a_1 \cdot 2$'s type as $2 \geq 0$, which is also $a_1 \cdot (1+1)$'s type. This strategy works since the calculus is strongly normalizing and confluent, so expressions always map to unique normal forms.

Our version of general equality is *intensional* (or *weak*) *equality*—equality that is verified by finitary application of the computation rules. Intensional equality is well behaved but somewhat weak. For example, we cannot prove $\lambda x \in nat.\, x + (succ\ 0) = \lambda x \in nat.\, (succ\ 0) + x$. A stronger form of equality, called *extensional equality*, may be used instead. Extensional equality proves the claim above but brings with it loss of normalization of the computation rules. Since proofs can appear as terms within propositions, the loss of normalization implies that type checking might not terminate. Strong equality and its properties are examined in the Exercises.

10.5 General Forms of Elimination Rules

The examples with numbers and lists show how proofs, that is, values, can appear within propositions. We should be able to state and prove properties of other proof forms. One example is

$$\forall p \in (\exists x \in A.\, B(x)).\exists a \in A.\exists b \in B(a).\, p = (pair\ a\ b)$$

which says that every proof of an existential claim is convertible to a canonical expression.

The present form of $\exists$E rule is too weak to prove the above claim, because the rule does not allow mention of proofs in the proposition that is proved. This is easily remedied:

$$\exists E: \quad \frac{\Gamma \vdash e_1 \in \exists x \in \phi_1.\, \phi_2(x) \qquad \Gamma,\, a \in \phi_1,\, b \in \phi_2(a) \vdash e_2(a,b) \in \phi_3(pair\ a\ b)}{\Gamma \vdash open\ e_1\ as\ (a \in \phi_1,\, b \in \phi_2(a)).\, e_2(a,b) \in \phi_3(e_1)}$$

Now, this judgement is valid:

$\vdash \boldsymbol{\lambda} p \in (\exists x \in A.\, B(x)).\ open\ p\ as\ (m \in A,\, n \in B(m)).$

$$pair\ m\ (pair\ n\ (id\ (pair\ m\ n)\ (pair\ m\ n)))$$

$$\in\ \forall p \in (\exists x \in A.\, B(x)).\exists a \in A.\exists b \in B(a).\, p = (pair\ a\ b)$$

The judgement holds because we are able to show, for $\Gamma_0 = p \in \exists x \in A.\, B(x),\ m \in A,$ $n \in B(m),$ that

$\Gamma_0 \vdash p_1 \in (pair\ m\ n) = (pair\ m\ n),$ where p_1 is $id\ (pair\ m\ n)\ (pair\ m\ n)$

and

$\Gamma_0 \vdash p_2 \in \exists b \in B(m).\ pair\ m\ n = pair\ m\ b,$ where p_2 is $pair\ n\ p_1$

and then

$\Gamma_0 \vdash p_3 \in \exists a \in A.\exists b \in B(a).\ pair\ m\ n = pair\ a\ b,$ where p_3 is $pair\ m\ p_2$

The $\exists E$ rule gives the result.

The new version of the $\exists E$ rule forces a type checker to work harder. If a type checker is analyzing the program fragment *open p as* $(m \in A,\ n \in B(m)).\ p_3$, it calculates the type of p_3 as $\exists a \in A.\exists b \in B(a).\ pair\ m\ n = pair\ a\ b.$ Next, it must calculate the type of the *open* expression. Since m and n are free in the type of p_3, there appears to be a violation of the usual restriction on the $\exists E$ rule. But here, the m and n appear in the expression *pair m n*, which can be replaced by p, which gives a correct typing. The type checker now has the responsibility to do such replacements.

Similar changes to the elimination rules for other connectives can be made. The changes necessitate reformatting of the rules; see Figure 10.11. The traditional elimination rules can be derived from the ones in the figure. (This is an easy exercise.) The rules are "induction-like": To prove a property, $\phi_2(p)$, for some $\Gamma \vdash p \in \phi_1$, one must prove $\phi_2(e)$ for all forms of canonical expression, e, that can be constructed by the introduction rules for ϕ_1. Since all proofs, p, can be rewritten into canonical expressions, the induction implies that $\phi(p)$ holds.

General forms of elimination rules for the $\supset$ and $\forall$ connectives also exist, but they are not easily expressed in our sequent-based calculus; see Nordström, Petersson, and Smith (1990).

An important consequence of the new version of $\exists E$ rule is that one can derive the "strong existential" of Chapter 8 from the "weak" version. Figure 10.12 shows the derived rules for the strong existential. The derivation of $\exists E_1{}'$ from $\exists E$ is easy. The soundness of $\exists E_2{}'$ is justified starting from this judgement:

$e \in \exists x \in \phi_1.\, \phi_2(x) \vdash open\ e\ as\ (a \in \phi_1,\, b \in \phi_2(a)).\ subst\ (id\ a\ (first\ (pair\ a\ b)))\ b\ \in\ \phi_2(first\ e)$

That is, from $b \in \phi_2(a)$ and $a\ cnv\ first(pair\ a\ b)$, we get $b \in \phi_2(first(pair\ a\ b))$, and we apply the $\exists E$ rule. Next, the computation rule for *subst* lets us deduce

$\exists$E: $$\dfrac{\Gamma \vdash e_1 \in \exists x \in \phi_1 . \phi_2(x) \quad \Gamma, a \in \phi_1, b \in \phi_2(a) \vdash e_2(a,b) \in \phi_3(\textit{pair } a \, b)}{\Gamma \vdash \textit{open } e_1 \textit{ as } (a \in \phi_1, b \in \phi_2(a)) . \, e_2(a,b) \in \phi_3(e_1)}$$

$\wedge$E: $$\dfrac{\Gamma \vdash e_1 \in \phi_1 \wedge \phi_2 \quad \Gamma, a \in \phi_1, b \in \phi_2 \vdash e_2 \in \phi_3(a,b)}{\Gamma \vdash \textit{andsplit } e_1 \textit{ as } (a \in \phi_1, b \in \phi_2) . \, e_2 \in \phi_3(e_1)}$$

$\vee$E: $$\dfrac{\Gamma \vdash e_1 \in \phi_1 \vee \phi_2 \quad \Gamma, x \in \phi_1 \vdash e_2(x) \in \phi_3(\textit{inl } x) \quad \Gamma, y \in \phi_2 \vdash e_3(y) \in \phi_3(\textit{inr } y)}{\Gamma \vdash \textit{orsplit } e_1 \textit{ as } \textit{isl}(x \in \phi_1) . e_2(x) \textit{ oras } \textit{isr}(y \in \phi_2) . e_3(y) \in \phi_3(e_1)}$$

=E: $$\dfrac{\Gamma \vdash e_1 \in a =_{\phi_1} b \quad \Gamma, x \in \phi_1, y \in \phi_1 \vdash e_2 \in \phi_2(\textit{id } x \, y)}{\Gamma \vdash \textit{idsplit } e_1 \textit{ as } (\textit{id } x \, y) . \, e_2 \in \phi_2(e_1)}$$

*bool*E: $$\dfrac{\Gamma \vdash e_1 \in \textit{bool} \quad \Gamma \vdash e_2 \in \phi(\textit{true}) \quad \Gamma \vdash e_3 \in \phi(\textit{false})}{\Gamma \vdash \textit{boolsplit } e_1 \textit{ as } \textit{true} . e_2 \textit{ oras } \textit{false} . e_3 \in \phi(e_1)}$$

$\quad$ *open* (*pair* $e_1 \, e_2$) *as* $(a \in \phi_1, b \in \phi_2(a)) . \, e_3(a,b) \Rightarrow e_3(e_1, e_2)$

$\quad$ *andsplit* ($e_1 \, e_2$) *as* $(x, y) . \, e_3(x,y) \Rightarrow e_3(e_1, e_2)$

$\quad$ *idsplit* (*id* $e_1 \, e_2$) *as* (*id* $x \, y$) . $e_3(x,y) \Rightarrow e_3(e_1, e_2)$

$\quad$ *orsplit* (*inl* e_1) *as* $\textit{isl}(x \in \phi_1) . e_2(x)$ *oras* $\textit{isr}(y \in \phi_2) . e_3(y) \Rightarrow e_2(e_1)$

$\quad$ *orsplit* (*inr* e_1) *as* $\textit{isl}(x \in \phi_1) . e_2(x)$ *oras* $\textit{isr}(y \in \phi_2) . e_3(y) \Rightarrow e_3(e_1)$

$\quad$ *boolsplit true as true* . e_2 *oras false* . $e_3 \Rightarrow e_2$

$\quad$ *boolsplit false as true* . e_2 *oras false* . $e_3 \Rightarrow e_3$

Figure 10.11 _____

$\exists$E$_1$′: $$\dfrac{\Gamma \vdash e \in \exists x \in \phi_1 . \phi_2(x)}{\Gamma \vdash \textit{first } e \in \phi_1}$$ $\qquad$ $\exists$E$_2$′: $$\dfrac{\Gamma \vdash e \in \exists x \in \phi_1 . \phi_2(x)}{\Gamma \vdash \textit{second } e \in \phi_2(\textit{first } e)}$$

$\quad$ where *first e* abbreviates *open e as* $(a \in \phi_1, b \in \phi_2(a)) . \, a$

$\quad$ and *second e* abbreviates *open e as* $(a \in \phi_1, b \in \phi_2(a)) . \, b$

Figure 10.12 _____

$$open\ e\ as\ (a \in \phi_1, b \in \phi_2(a)).\ subst\ (id\ a\ first\ (pair\ a\ b))\ b$$
$$\Rightarrow\ open\ e\ as\ (a \in \phi_1, b \in \phi_2(a)).\ b$$

so we have

$$e \in \exists x \in \phi_1.\ \phi_2(x) \vdash open\ e\ as\ (a \in \phi_1, b \in \phi_2(a)).\ b \in \phi_2(first\ e)$$

This derivation might be surprising in light of the result of Chapter 8, which stated that Girard's paradox arises when the strong existential is mixed with the universal quantifier, but remember that the present system is predicative, so Girard's paradox cannot be coded in it.

The new forms of elimination rules cause headaches for a type checker. Consider the type checking of the program just seen, $open\ e\ as\ (a \in \phi_1, b \in \phi_2(a)).\ b$, within the type assignment $e \in \exists x \in \phi_1.\ \phi_2(x)$. The type checker calculates the type of b to be $B(a)$. But this type is not a proper one for application of the $\exists E$ rule, and further, the occurrence of the a does not appear within the expression *pair a b*, so the type checking strategy outlined earlier in this section fails. Apparently, the type checker must discover, within the type assignment $p \in \exists x \in \phi_1.\ \phi_2(x)$, $a \in A$, $b \in B(a)$, that a is convertible to *first*(*pair a b*) and use that expression in place of a; a solution is to replace the occurrence of a by *first*(p) automatically.

10.6 Technical Results

The calculus we have developed thus far is essentially Martin-Löf's 1973 version of intuitionistic type theory (less its rules for definitional equality of types), of which we review the main properties here.

Call e a *closed expression* if there is a type, ϕ, such that $\vdash \phi\ IsProp$ and $\vdash e \in \phi$ hold. Clearly, closed expressions are well formed and contain no free identifiers. The results that follow are stated in terms of closed expressions. Results regarding expressions with free identifiers, that is, expressions e such that $\Gamma \vdash e \in \phi$ holds, where Γ is $x_1 \in \phi_1, x_2 \in \phi_2, \ldots, x_n \in \phi_n$, $n > 0$, can be obtained from results regarding the "closure":

$$\vdash \lambda x_1 \in \phi_1.\lambda x_2 \in \phi_2.\ \cdots\ \lambda x_n \in \phi_n.\ e \in \forall x_1 \in \phi_1.\forall x_2 \in \phi_2.\ \cdots\ \forall x_n \in \phi_n.\ \phi$$

As always, a closed expression is in normal form if no computation rule can rewrite it.

The most significant result is strong normalization: Every closed expression must rewrite to a closed normal form. (Also, every closed expression rewrites to a canonical expression.) Further, the normal form is unique (up to renaming of binding identifiers). The rewriting rules have the confluence property. In the complete system with type equivalence rules, the proof of confluence by appealing to the usual proof in an orthogonal SRS fails, so confluence is proved as a consequence of strong normalization.

The convertibility relation is well behaved: For closed expressions e_1 and e_2 we can decide if e_1 *cnv* e_2 holds. (Thanks to strong normalization and confluence, we decide the question by rewriting e_1 and e_2 to normal forms and checking for identity.) As noted earlier, we also have equivalences under convertibility: If $\vdash e_1 \in \phi$ and e_1 *cnv* e_2, then $\vdash e_2 \in \phi$; and if $\vdash e \in \phi_1$ and ϕ_1 *cnv* ϕ_2, then $\vdash e \in \phi_2$.

When universes are added to the system, we have that $\vdash e \in \phi$ implies $\vdash \phi \in U_n$, for some $n \geq 0$. An important result regarding general equality is that it is *intensional*: $e_1 =_\phi e_2$ can be proved if and only if e_1 *cnv* e_2.

Finally, questions regarding type checking can be decided. We can decide if a type, ϕ, is well formed, that is, if $\vdash \phi$ *IsProp* holds, and so then, if a context is well formed. Finally, for an expression, e, and a type, ϕ, we can decide if $\vdash e \in \phi$ holds.

10.7 Predicate Logic and Programming-Language Design

Section 9.7 pointed out that a core programming language begins as a "core logic" and is extended by rules for the propositional connectives, which incorporate structuring devices into the language. Quantifiers, general equality, and universes can also be included, giving a language that supports polymorphism, encapsulation, and a verification logic.

The development in this chapter is essentially that for a functional language. Many of the constructions are reminiscent of the ones in Chapter 8, although they are stated here in their predicative forms. The development here goes beyond that of Chapter 8 because of the general equality type, which allows dependent typing of (∗,∗) abstraction and encapsulation constructs. This makes the typing system into a useful programming logic.

Keep in mind that a programmer need not use all of the capabilities of the typing system when programming. Within the same language, one can code a "secure" identity function, such as $\lambda t \in U_0.\lambda x \in t. pair\ x\ proof\text{-}part$, or an "insecure" one, like $\lambda t \in U_0.\lambda x \in t.\ x$. The degree of precision of typing is left to the programmer. Of course, automated tools, like NuPrl (Constable, et al. 1986), can be of assistance in making programs "secure," but substantial programmer effort will always be required for secure software development.

As suggested in Section 9.7, we can repeat the language development experiment for a core imperative language. Say that we augment the core logic in that section by the rules for quantifiers and equality. The resulting typing system allows one to state properties of programs in terms of input and output storage vectors. For example, the judgement

$\vdash \lambda in \in store.\ pair\ ((loc_1:=@loc_2+1)\cdot in)\ \textit{proof-part}$

$\quad \in\ \forall in \in store.\exists out \in store.\ lookup\ loc_1\ out = (lookup\ loc_2\ in)+1$

is valid, and it verifies that the program $loc_1:=@loc\,2+1$ assigns the successor of the value in loc_2 to loc_1.

The addition of quantifiers also exposes some weaknesses in the core language. For example, we can prove

$\forall C_1 \in comm.\forall C_2 \in comm.\forall C_3 \in comm.\forall s \in store.\ (((C_1;C_2);C_3)\ s) = (C_1;((C_2;C_3)\ s))$

but we can*not* prove

$\forall C_1 \in comm.\forall C_2 \in comm.\forall C_3 \in comm.\ (C_1;C_2);C_3 = C_1;(C_2;C_3)$

The problem is that the *comm*E rule is ad hoc; rather than stating an induction principle for commands, it makes the understanding of a command dependent on the application of it to a store. Another weakness is the inability to prove

$\forall E \in natexp.\forall C \in comm.\forall s \in store.$

$\quad ((\textbf{while E do C od};(\textbf{if E then C else skip}))\ s) = (\textbf{while E do C od}\ s)$

The absence of an induction rule for **while E do C od** is the problem.

We will not attempt to repair the core imperative language—this is a topic of current research—but we should imagine how the quality of the imperative language would improve if its core can be defined in a way that natural program properties can be specified and proved in the predicate logic version of the language. Even those programmers who do not write "secure" code would benefit from the improvements.

Once universes are added, we can write generic code. The format of an array-sorting procedure, parameterized on the bounds and component elements of its array argument, would appear as

$\lambda low \in nat.\ \lambda hi \in nat.\ \lambda t \in U_0.$

$\quad \lambda a \in array[low,hi]\ of\ t\ loc.\ \lambda lesseq \in (t \wedge t)\supset t.\ \textit{"code for sorting"}$

Type structure parameters can also be precisely coded and typings precisely stated:

$\lambda t \in U_0.\lambda T \in (t\ loc)class.\lambda v \in t.\ \textbf{begin var}\ X{:}T\ \textbf{in}\ X{:=}v\ \textbf{end}$

The type parameter, $t \in U_0$, was implicit in the presentation in Chapter 3, but an explicit form is necessary to the well-formedness of the code here. A similar treatment is possible for opaque types. Here is an "abstype":

abstype *P* = *pair intloc* (*pair* **newint** (λ*x* ∈ *intloc*. *x*:=0, λ*m* ∈ *intloc*. @*m*=0))

P's type is ∃*t* ∈ *U₀*.∃*T* ∈ *t class*. (*t*⊃*comm*)∧(*t*⊃*boolexp*). *P*'s opaque type and operations might be used in

> *open P as* (*t*, *p*).
> > *open p as* (*T*, *ops*).
> > > **begin var** *X*:*T*,
> > > > **proc** *P*(*Z*:*t*) = **if** (*snd ops*)·*Z* **then** · · ·
> > > **in call** (*fst ops*)·*X*;**call** *P*(*X*) **end**

A bit of syntactic "sugar" (for example, using *init* and *empty* for (*fst ops*) and (*snd ops*), respectively), makes the result easy to swallow. This treatment of opaque types is more systematic than the one in Chapter 4, which is based on an ad hoc extension of propositional logic. Once again, the design of the imperative language benefits from the treatment demanded by the rules for quantifiers. The programmer need not be aware of the quantifier rules; a sugared syntax and hardworking type checker can hide the work.

Although the presentation in Chapters 9 and 10 has emphasized intuitionistic predicate logic, other candidate logics exist for programming languages. Examples are modal and temporal logics, and most recently, intuitionistic linear logic.

Finally, we should consider what is gained by expressing programming languages and design methodology within logic. The main benefit is that the structure and theory of logistic systems tell us how to define a language and what questions to ask about it.

When one defines a logic, one is immediately committed to asking about its proof theory, What is a proof? Is the logic consistent? How does one normalize a proof? What are the normal (canonical) expressions? Is the system strongly normalizing? confluent? Are any inference rules redundant? Is there a cut-elimination theorem? Is the well formedness of a proof decidable? Does each proof prove exactly one proposition? Is theoremhood decidable? These questions are relevant to programming languages, because their answers state fundamental properties about a language's appearance, its computational behavior, and the nature of its typing system.

Although the presentation in the previous two chapters has emphasized proof theory, results from model theory are also significant. A person with a grounding in basic model theory will remember to ask, What is an interpretation of the language? What are its models? What are the cardinalities of the models? Is the logic sound with respect to its models? Is it complete? Questions related to model theory describe issues about a language's ability to express programming concepts correctly and completely.

This is not meant to suggest that language design be performed from mathematical logic texts, in isolation from reality. The design of a programming language is driven by the needs of its users, and experience, intuition, and creativity play crucial roles. But there is need for tools to organize and analyze the definition. Mathematical logic is a promising candidate.

10.8 Summary

The well-formed formulas of the predicate calculus are built from an alphabet of *function symbols*, $+$, $\times$, $-$, 0, 1, $\ldots$; *predicate symbols*, $<$, $>$, $=$, $\ldots$; identifiers, *x, y, z, a, b,* $\ldots$; connectives, $\forall$, $\exists$, $\wedge$, $\supset$ and $\vee$, a logical constant, $\perp$, and auxiliary symbols ., $\vdash$, (, and). The syntax rules are

$$S \in \text{Sequent} \qquad\qquad f \in \text{Function-symbol}$$
$$\Gamma \in \text{Context} \qquad\qquad P \in \text{Predicate-symbol}$$
$$\phi \in \text{Proposition} \qquad\qquad x \in \text{Identifier}$$
$$t \in \text{Term}$$

$$S ::= \Gamma \vdash \phi$$
$$\Gamma ::= \phi_1, \phi_2, \ldots, \phi_n, \quad n \geq 0$$
$$\phi ::= \phi_1 \wedge \phi_2 \mid \phi_1 \supset \phi_2 \mid \phi_1 \vee \phi_2 \mid \perp \mid \forall x.\, \phi \mid \exists x.\, \phi \mid P(t_1, t_2, \ldots, t_n), \quad n \geq 0$$
$$t ::= x \mid f(t_1, t_2, \ldots, t_n), \quad n \geq 0$$

The axiom and inference rule schemes are:

$$\text{axiom:}\ \ \Gamma \vdash \phi \ \ \text{if}\ \ \phi \in \Gamma$$

$$\wedge\text{I:}\ \frac{\Gamma \vdash \phi_1 \qquad \Gamma \vdash \phi_2}{\Gamma \vdash \phi_1 \wedge \phi_2} \qquad \wedge\text{E}_1:\ \frac{\Gamma \vdash \phi_1 \wedge \phi_2}{\Gamma \vdash \phi_1} \qquad \wedge\text{E}_2:\ \frac{\Gamma \vdash \phi_1 \wedge \phi_2}{\Gamma \vdash \phi_2}$$

$$\supset\text{I:}\ \frac{\Gamma, \phi_1 \vdash \phi_2}{\Gamma \vdash \phi_1 \supset \phi_2} \qquad \supset\text{E:}\ \frac{\Gamma \vdash \phi_1 \supset \phi_2 \qquad \Gamma \vdash \phi_1}{\Gamma \vdash \phi_2}$$

$$\vee\text{I}_1:\ \frac{\Gamma \vdash \phi_1}{\Gamma \vdash \phi_1 \vee \phi_2} \qquad \vee\text{I}_2:\ \frac{\Gamma \vdash \phi_2}{\Gamma \vdash \phi_1 \vee \phi_2}$$

$$\vee\text{E:}\ \frac{\Gamma \vdash \phi_1 \vee \phi_2 \qquad \Gamma, \phi_1 \vdash \phi_3 \qquad \Gamma, \phi_2 \vdash \phi_3}{\Gamma \vdash \phi_3} \qquad \perp\text{E:}\ \frac{\Gamma \vdash \perp}{\Gamma \vdash \phi}$$

$$\forall\text{I:}\ \frac{\Gamma \vdash \phi(x)}{\Gamma \vdash \forall x.\, \phi(x)}\ \ \text{if}\ x \notin FV(\Gamma) \qquad \forall\text{E:}\ \frac{\Gamma \vdash \forall x.\, \phi(x)}{\Gamma \vdash \phi(t)}$$

$$\exists I: \frac{\Gamma \vdash \phi(t)}{\Gamma \vdash \exists x.\, \phi(x)} \qquad \exists E: \frac{\Gamma \vdash \exists x.\, \phi_1(x) \quad \Gamma, \phi_1(a) \vdash \phi_2}{\Gamma \vdash \phi_2} \quad \text{if } a \notin FV(\Gamma) \text{ and } a \notin FV(\phi_2)$$

A sequent-proof tree is as defined in Chapter 9, and as before, a natural-deduction tree is a sequent-proof tree where the context information is omitted from the nodes. The linear form of a natural-deduction tree is defined by the following abstract syntax rules:

$e \in$ Natural-deduction-tree

$x \in$ Identifier

$$
\begin{aligned}
e ::= {} & e_1, e_2 \mid fst\ e \mid snd\ e \mid \lambda x \in \phi.\, e \mid e_1 \cdot e_2 \mid x \\
& \mid inl_\phi\ e \mid inr_\phi\ e \mid cases\ e_1\ of\, isl(x_1 \in \phi_1).\, e_2\ [\,]\ isr(x_2 \in \phi_2).\, e_3 \mid abort_\phi\ e \\
& \mid \lambda x \in \phi.\, e \mid e_1 \cdot e_2 \mid pair_\phi\ e_1\ e_2 \mid open\ e_1\ as\ (x \in \phi_1, y \in \phi_2).\, e_2 \\
& \mid 0 \mid succ\ e \mid natrec\ e_1\ of\, is0.\, e_2\ [\,]\ is(succ\ x)(recx \in \phi(x)).\, e_3 \\
& \mid nil_\phi \mid cons\ e_1\ e_2 \mid listrec\ e_1\ of\, isnil.\, e_2\ [\,]\ is(cons\ a\ l)(recl \in \phi(l)).\, e_3 \\
& \mid id\ e_1\ e_2 \mid symm\ e_1\ e_2 \mid trans\ e_1\ e_2 \mid subst\ e_1\ e_2
\end{aligned}
$$

The last three lines of the syntax definition state the proof constructs for *nat*, the type of natural numbers, for $\phi list$, the type of lists of elements of ϕ, and for $e_1 =_\phi e_2$, the general equality type.

The Heyting interpretation of the predicate calculus is expressed by the following inference rules, which deduce judgements in a typed predicate calculus with natural numbers, lists, and general equality:

$$\text{axiom: } \Gamma \vdash x \in \phi, \text{ if } (x \in \phi) \in \Gamma$$

$$\wedge I: \frac{\Gamma \vdash e_1 \in \phi_1 \quad \Gamma \vdash e_2 \in \phi_2}{\Gamma \vdash (e_1, e_2) \in \phi_1 \wedge \phi_2} \qquad \wedge E_1: \frac{\Gamma \vdash e \in \phi_1 \wedge \phi_2}{\Gamma \vdash fst\ e \in \phi_1} \qquad \wedge E_2: \frac{\Gamma \vdash e \in \phi_1 \wedge \phi_2}{\Gamma \vdash snd\ e \in \phi_2}$$

$$\supset I: \frac{\Gamma, x \in \phi_1 \vdash e \in \phi_2}{\Gamma \vdash \lambda x \in \phi_1.\, e \in \phi_1 \supset \phi_2} \qquad \supset E: \frac{\Gamma \vdash e_1 \in \phi_1 \supset \phi_2 \quad \Gamma \vdash e_2 \in \phi_1}{\Gamma \vdash e_1 \cdot e_2 \in \phi_2}$$

$$\vee I_1: \frac{\Gamma \vdash e \in \phi_1}{\Gamma \vdash inl\ e \in \phi_1 \vee \phi_2} \qquad \vee I_2: \frac{\Gamma \vdash e \in \phi_2}{\Gamma \vdash inr\ e \in \phi_1 \vee \phi_2}$$

$$\vee E: \frac{\Gamma \vdash e_1 \in \phi_1 \vee \phi_2 \quad \Gamma, x \in \phi_1 \vdash e_2 \in \phi_3 \quad \Gamma, y \in \phi_2 \vdash e_3 \in \phi_3}{\Gamma \vdash cases\ e_1\ of\, isl(x \in \phi_1).\, e_2\ [\,]\ isr(y \in \phi_2).\, e_3 \in \phi_3} \qquad \bot E: \frac{\Gamma \vdash e \in \bot}{\Gamma \vdash abort\ e \in \phi}$$

$$\forall I: \frac{\Gamma, x \in \phi_1 \vdash e \in \phi_2(x)}{\Gamma \vdash \lambda x \in \phi_1.\, e \in \forall x \in \phi_1.\, \phi_2(x)} \qquad \forall E: \frac{\Gamma \vdash e_1 \in \forall x \in \phi_1.\, \phi_2(x) \quad \Gamma \vdash e_2 \in \phi_1}{\Gamma \vdash e_1 \cdot e_2 \in \phi_2(e_2)}$$

$$\exists\text{I}: \quad \frac{\Gamma \vdash e_1 \in \phi_1 \qquad \Gamma \vdash e_2 \in \phi(e_1)}{\Gamma \vdash pair_{\exists x \in \phi_1.\phi_2(x)}\ e_1,\ e_2 \in \exists x \in \phi_1.\phi_2(x)}$$

$$\exists\text{E}: \quad \frac{\Gamma \vdash e_1 \in \exists x \in \phi_1.\phi_2(x) \qquad \Gamma, a \in \phi_1, b \in \phi_2(a) \vdash e_2 \in \phi_3}{\Gamma \vdash open\ e_1\ as\ (a \in \phi_1, b \in \phi_2(a)).\ e_2 \in \phi_3} \quad \text{if}\ a \notin FV(\phi_3)\ \text{and}\ b \notin FV(\phi_3)$$

$$nat\text{I}_1: \quad \Gamma \vdash 0 \in nat \qquad\qquad nat\text{I}_2: \quad \frac{\Gamma \vdash e \in nat}{\Gamma \vdash succ\ e \in nat}$$

$$nat\text{E}: \quad \frac{\Gamma \vdash e_1 \in nat \qquad \Gamma \vdash e_2 \in \phi(0) \qquad \Gamma, x \in nat, y \in \phi(x) \vdash e_3(x, y) \in \phi(succ\ x)}{\Gamma \vdash natrec\ e_1\ of\ is0.\ e_2\ [\!]\ issucc\ (x)(recx \in \phi(x)).\ e_3(x, recx) \in \phi(e_1)}$$

$$list\text{I}_1: \quad \Gamma \vdash nil_\phi \in \phi list \qquad\qquad list\text{I}_2: \quad \frac{\Gamma \vdash e_1 \in \phi \qquad \Gamma \vdash e_2 \in \phi list}{\Gamma \vdash cons\ e_1\ e_2 \in \phi list}$$

$list\text{E}:$

$$\frac{\Gamma \vdash e_1 \in \phi_1 list \qquad \Gamma \vdash e_2 \in \phi_2(nil) \qquad \Gamma, a \in \phi_1, b \in \phi_2 list, x \in \phi_2(b) \vdash e_3(a, b, x) \in \phi_2(cons\ a\ b)}{\Gamma \vdash listrec\ e_1\ of\ isnil.\ e_2\ [\!]\ is(cons\ a\ b)(recb \in \phi_2(b)).\ e_3 \in \phi_2(e_1)}$$

$$=\text{I}: \quad \frac{\Gamma \vdash a\ cnv\ b \in \phi}{\Gamma \vdash id\ a\ b \in a =_\phi b} \qquad\qquad =\text{E}_1: \quad \frac{\Gamma \vdash e \in a =_\phi b}{\Gamma \vdash symm\ e \in b =_\phi a}$$

$$=\text{E}_2: \quad \frac{\Gamma \vdash e_1 \in a =_\phi b \qquad \Gamma \vdash e_2 \in b =_\phi c}{\Gamma \vdash trans\ e_1\ e_2 \in a =_\phi c} \qquad\qquad =\text{E}_3: \quad \frac{\Gamma \vdash e_1 \in a =_\phi b \qquad \Gamma \vdash e_2(a) \in \phi(a)}{\Gamma \vdash subst\ e_1\ e_2(a) \in \phi(b)}$$

As in Chapter 9, a context, Γ, takes the form $x_1 \in \phi_1, x_2 \in \phi_2, \ldots, x_n \in \phi_n$. Since free identifiers can appear within propositions, the following rules are necessary to validate the well-formedness of a proposition:

$$\frac{\Gamma \vdash \phi_1\ IsProp \qquad \Gamma \vdash \phi_2\ IsProp}{\Gamma \vdash \phi_1 \wedge \phi_2\ IsProp} \quad \text{and similarly for}\ \phi_1 \supset \phi_2\ \text{and}\ \phi_1 \vee \phi_2$$

$$\Gamma \vdash \bot\ IsProp$$

$$\frac{\Gamma \vdash \phi_1\ IsProp \qquad \Gamma, x \in \phi_1 \vdash \phi_2\ IsProp}{\Gamma \vdash \forall x \in \phi_1.\phi_2\ IsProp} \quad \text{and similarly for}\ \exists x \in \phi_1.\phi_2$$

$$\Gamma \vdash nat \ IsProp \qquad \frac{\Gamma \vdash \phi \ IsProp}{\Gamma \vdash \phi list \ IsProp} \qquad \frac{\Gamma \vdash a \in \phi \quad \Gamma \vdash b \in \phi}{\Gamma \vdash a =_\phi b \ IsProp}$$

A context, $x_1 \in \phi_1, x_2 \in \phi_2, \ldots, x_n \in \phi_n$, $n \geq 0$, is well formed if (i) all identifiers x_i are distinct from one another; (ii) for all $1 \leq i < n$, $x_1 \in \phi_1, \ldots, x_i \in \phi_i \vdash \phi_{i+1} \ IsProp$ can be proved. These computation rules simplify natural-deduction trees:

$fst(e_1, e_2) \Rightarrow e_1, \qquad snd(e_1, e_2) \Rightarrow e_2$

$(\lambda x \in \phi_1 . e_1(x)) \cdot e_2 \Rightarrow e_1(e_2)$

$cases \ inl(e_1) \ of \ isl(x \in \phi_1). e_2(x) \ [] \ isr(y \in \phi_2). e_3(y) \Rightarrow e_2(e_1)$

$cases \ inr(e_1) \ of \ isl(x \in \phi_1). e_2(x) \ [] \ isr(y \in \phi_2). e_3(y) \Rightarrow e_3(e_1)$

$(\lambda x \in \phi . e_1(x)) \bullet e_2 \Rightarrow e_1(e_2)$

$open \ (pair \ t \ p) \ as \ (a \in \phi_1, b \in \phi_2(a)). q(a, b) \Rightarrow q(t, p)$

$natrec \ 0 \ of \ is0. e_2 \ [] \ issucc(x)(recx \in \phi(x)). e_3(x, recx) \Rightarrow e_2$

$natrec \ (succ \ e) \ of \ is0. e_2 \ [] \ issucc(x)(recx \in \phi(x)). e_3(x, recx)$

$\qquad\qquad \Rightarrow e_3(e, (natrec \ e \ of \ is0. e_2 \ [] \ issucc(x)(recx \in \phi(x)). e_3(x, recx)))$

$listrec \ nil \ of \ isnil. e_2 \ [] \ is(cons \ a \ b)(recb \in \phi(b)). e_3(a,b,recb) \Rightarrow e_2$

$listrec \ (cons \ e_0 \ e_1) \ of \ isnil. e_2 \ [] \ is(cons \ a \ b)(recb \in \phi(b)). e_3(a,b,recb)$

$\qquad \Rightarrow e_3(e_0, e_1, (listrec \ e_1 \ of \ isnil. e_2 \ [] \ is(cons \ a \ b)(recb \in \phi(b)). e_3(a,b,recb)))$

$symm \ (id \ a \ b) \Rightarrow id \ b \ a$

$trans \ (id \ a \ b) \ (id \ b \ c) \Rightarrow id \ a \ c$

$subst \ (id \ a \ b) \ e(a) \Rightarrow e(b)$

When universes are added to the system, the type-formation rules are converted into introduction rules for the family of universe types, U_i, $i \geq 0$:

$$\Gamma \vdash nat \in U_0 \qquad \frac{\Gamma \vdash \phi \in U_i}{\Gamma \vdash \phi list \in U_i} \qquad \frac{\Gamma \vdash \phi \in U_i \quad \Gamma \vdash e_1 \in \phi \quad \Gamma \vdash e_2 \in \phi}{\Gamma \vdash e_1 =_\phi e_2 \in U_i}$$

$$\frac{\Gamma \vdash \phi_1 \in U_i \quad \Gamma, x \in \phi_1 \vdash \phi_2 \in U_j}{\Gamma \vdash \forall x \in \phi_1 . \phi_2 \in U_{max(i,j)}} \quad \text{and similarly for } \exists x \in \phi_1 . \phi_2$$

$$\frac{\Gamma \vdash \phi_1 \in U_i \quad \Gamma \vdash \phi_2 \in U_j}{\Gamma \vdash \phi_1 \wedge \phi_2 \in U_{max(i,j)}} \quad \text{and similarly for } \phi_1 \supset \phi_2 \text{ and } \phi_1 \vee \phi_2$$

$$\Gamma \vdash \bot \in U_0 \qquad \Gamma \vdash U_i \in U_{i+1} \qquad \text{where } i, j \geq 0$$

There is no elimination rule for universe types, nor are there computation rules.

Suggested Reading

A good introduction to natural deduction-style predicate logic is van Dalen 1983; additional background is found in Church 1956, Enderton 1972, Mendelson 1987, Gallier 1988, 1991a, and 1991b. Papers that describe algorithm development in Martin-Löf type theory include Bjerner 1985, Chisholm 1987, Nordström 1981, Nordström and Petersson 1983, Nordström and Smith 1984, and Petersson and Smith 1986. Related useful materials are Constable 1989, Dybjer, et al. 1985, 1987, and 1989, Goto 1979, Manna and Waldinger 1980 and 1981, and Turner 1991. Constable (1991) comments on the relationship of type theory to programming language design.

Foundations of intuitionistic systems are described in Beeson 1985, Bishop 1967, and Troelstra and van Dalen 1988. Automated systems for algorithm development include AUTOMATH (see de Bruijn 1980); Calculus of Constructions (see Coquand and Huet 1988, Calculus 1989a and 1989b, Paulin-Mohring 1989); TK (see Henson 1989); PL/CV (see Constable and O'Donnell 1978); NuPRL (see Constable, et al. 1986); and PX (see Hayashi and Nakano 1988);

Exercises

1.1. Draw natural-deduction proof trees for the following, and then write the corresponding lambda calculus expressions for the trees. (Note: $\phi_1 \dashv\vdash \phi_2$ abbreviates $\phi_1 \vdash \phi_2$ and $\phi_2 \vdash \phi_1$.)

a. $\forall x.(\phi_1(x) \wedge \phi_2(x)) \dashv\vdash (\forall x.\phi_1(x)) \wedge (\forall x.\phi_2(x))$

b. $\exists x.(\phi_1(x) \vee \phi_2(x)) \dashv\vdash (\exists x.\phi_1(x)) \vee (\exists y.\phi_2(y))$

c. $\neg\exists x.\phi(x) \dashv\vdash \forall x.\neg\phi(x)$

d. $\exists x.\neg\phi(x) \vdash \neg\forall x.\phi(x)$

e. $\forall x.(\phi_1 \supset \phi_2(x)) \dashv\vdash \phi_1 \supset (\forall x.\phi_2(x))$ (note: x does not appear free in ϕ_1)

f. $\exists x.(\phi_1 \supset \phi_2(x)) \vdash \phi_1 \supset (\exists x.\phi_2(x))$ (note: x does not appear free in ϕ_1)

g. $\exists x.(\phi_1(x) \supset \phi_2) \vdash (\forall x.\phi_1(x)) \supset \phi_2$ (note: x does not appear free in ϕ_2)

h. $\forall x.(\phi_1(x) \supset \phi_2) \dashv\vdash (\exists x.\phi_1(x)) \supset \phi_2$ (note: x does not appear free in ϕ_2)

1.2. Given these laws of arithmetic
$$ax_1 \in \forall x \in nat.(x+1) > x$$
$$ax_2 \in \forall x \in nat.\forall y \in nat.\forall z \in nat.(x > y \wedge y > z) \supset (x > z)$$
$$ax_3 \in \forall x \in nat.\forall y \in nat.\forall z \in nat.(x > y) \supset (x+z > y+z)$$
$$ax_4 \in \forall x \in nat.(x > 0) \supset (x > x-1)$$

prove the following. Write the natural-deduction trees and the corresponding lambda-calculus expressions.

a. $\forall x \in nat.x+2 > x$ (note: $x+2$ abbreviates $x+1+1$)

b. $3>2$

c. $\exists x \in nat. \, x > 2$

d. $\forall x \in nat. \exists y \in nat. \, y > x$

e. $\forall x \in nat. \, (x > 0) \supset nat$

f. $\forall x \in nat. \, (x > 0) \supset (\exists y \in nat. x > y)$

g. $(\exists x \in nat.x > 1) \supset (\exists y \in nat. \, y > 0)$

h. $\forall x \in nat. \forall y \in nat. \, (x > y + 1) \supset (\exists z \in nat. \, x > z \land z > y)$

i. $\forall x \in nat. \, (x > 1) \supset (\exists z \in nat. \, x + x > z \land z > x)$

j. $\forall x \in nat. \, (x > 1) \supset (\exists y \in nat. \exists z \in nat. \, x > z \land z > y)$

k. $\exists x \in nat. \forall y \in nat. \, (y > 0) \supset (y > x)$

l. $(\forall x \in nat. \exists y \in nat. \, y > x + 1) \supset (\forall x \in nat. \exists y \in nat. \, y > x)$

m. $\forall x \in nat. \forall p \in (x > 0). \exists q \in (x > x - 1). \, q = ax_4 \bullet p$

 (note: use the identity axiom scheme: $id_e \in e = e$, for all $e \in Expression$)

1.3. If you worked Exercise 1.2, proceed.

a. Apply the $\forall E$ rule to the proof of 1.2.d to get a proof of $\exists y \in nat. \, y > 2$. Apply the computation rules to simplify the proof. Draw the resulting natural-deduction tree.

b. Build a proof that $2 > 1$. Use it with the proof of 1.2.i to get a proof of $\exists z \in nat. \, 4 > z \land z > 2)$. Apply the computation rules to the proof.

c. Repeat Part b but for $\exists z \in nat. \, 4 > z$.

2.1. Use the inference rules in Figure 10.6 to derive the following judgements:

a. $\vdash 2 \in nat$

b. $\vdash \lambda n \in nat. \, natrec \, n \, of \, is0. \, 0 \, [] \, isssucc(x)(recx \in nat). \, x \, \in \, nat \supset nat$

c. $\vdash \lambda p \in nat \land nat. \, natrec \, (fst \, p) \, of \, is0. \, (snd \, p) \, [] \, isssucc(x)(recx \in nat). \, succ(recx)$
 $\in (nat \land nat) \supset nat$

d. $ax_5 \in \forall x \in nat. \, x + 0 = x,$
 $ax_6 \in \forall x \in nat. \forall y \in nat. \, x + succ(y) = succ(x + y)$
 $\vdash \lambda x \in nat. \lambda y \in nat. \, natrec \, n \, of \, is0. \, pair \, m \, (ax_5 \bullet m)$
 $[] \, isssucc(x)(recx \in \exists p \in nat.m + x = p).$
 $open \, recx \, as \, (a \in nat, \, b \in m + x = a).$
 $pair \, (succ \, a) \, (subst \, b \, (ax_6 \bullet m \bullet x))$
 $\in \forall m \in nat. \forall n \in nat. \exists p \in nat. \, m + n = p)$
 where *subst* is taken from Figure 10.7.

2.2. Use $ax_1 - ax_4$ in Exercise 1.2 plus Figure 10.6 to prove the following:

a. $\forall m \in nat. \forall n \in nat. \, (n > 0) \supset (n + m > m)$

b. $\forall m \in nat. \exists n \in nat. \, n + n > m$

Use the *refl*, *trans*, and *subst* rules from Figure 10.7 plus these axioms:

$ax_7 \in \forall x \in nat.\, x \times 0 = 0$

$ax_8 \in \forall x \in nat.\forall y \in nat.\, x \times (y+1) = (x \times y) + x$

to prove the following:

c. $\forall m \in nat.\forall n \in nat.\exists p \in nat.\, m \times n = p$

d. $\forall m \in nat.\, (n > 0) \supset (\exists q \in nat.\exists r \in nat.\, ((q \times n) + r) = m \land n > r)$

     Hint: use the axiom $\forall x \in nat.\forall y \in nat.\, (x > y) \supset ((x > y + 1)$ **or** $(x = y + 1))$

2.3.   The example in Section 10.2 of the specification of the factorial function shows that a "specification" can be just primitive recursive equations.

  a.   Show that, from axioms of the form

$$op(0) = k$$
$$op(succ\ n) = g(n, op(n))$$

for $k \in \phi$, $g \in nat \land \phi \supset \phi$, we can always prove $\forall x \in nat.\exists y \in \phi.\, op(x) = y$

  b.   Extend the result in Part a to equations of the form

$$op(0, m) = f(m)$$
$$op((succ\ n), m) = g(n, m, op(n,m))$$

for $f \in \phi_1 \supset \phi_2$, $g \in nat \land \phi_1 \supset \phi_2$. Use just 0 and *succ* and show how addition can be specified by primitive recursive equations; show the lambda calculus form of the corresponding proof. Repeat the exercise for multiplication, using 0, *succ*, and addition.

  c.*   Note that ϕ in Part a can be a function type, for example, $\phi = nat \supset nat$. Ackermann's function is a famous example of a non-(first order) primitive recursive function. Its definition is

$$ack\ 0\ n = succ\ n$$
$$ack\ (succ\ m)\ 0 = 1$$
$$ack\ (succ\ m)\ (succ\ n) = ack\ m\ (ack\ (succ\ m)\ n)$$

Use the primitive recursive format in Part a to specify Ackermann's function.

2.4.   An alternative induction for the natural numbers is *course of values induction*. Its rule is

$$natE': \frac{\Gamma \vdash e_1 \in nat \quad \Gamma, m \in nat, f \in (\forall n \in nat.\, (n < m) \supset \phi(n)) \vdash e_2(m,f) \in \phi(m)}{\Gamma \vdash covrec\ e_1\ of\ (m \in nat, f \in \forall n \in nat.(n < m) \supset \phi(n)).\, e_2(m,f) \in \phi(e_1)}$$

The computation rule is

$$covrec\ e_1\ of\ (m \in nat, f \in \forall n \in nat.(n < m) \supset \phi(n)).\, e_2(m,f)$$
$$\Rightarrow\ e_2(e_1, (\lambda n \in nat.\lambda p \in (n < e_1).$$
$$covrec\ n\ of\ (m \in nat, f \in \forall n \in nat.(n < m) \supset \phi(n)).\, e_2(m,f)))$$

Use the induction rule to prove the following:

a. $\forall m \in nat. \forall n \in nat. (m<n) \supset ismod(m, n, m),$
   $\forall m \in nat. \forall n \in nat. \forall p \in nat. ismod(m-n, n, p) \supset ismod(m, n, p),$
   $\forall m \in nat. \forall n \in nat. (n>0) \supset (m<n) \lor (m \geq n)$
   $\vdash \forall x \in nat. \forall y \in nat. (y>0) \supset (\exists z \in nat. ismod(x,y,z))$
   Apply the proof to the arguments 8 and 3.

b. $iseven(0),\ isodd(1),$
   $\forall n \in nat. iseven(n-2) \supset iseven(n),$
   $\forall n \in nat. isodd(n-2) \supset isodd(n),$
   $\forall n \in nat. (n>1) \supset (n-2<n),$
   $\forall m \in nat. (m=0) \lor (m=1) \lor (m>1),$
   $\forall m \in nat. (m=0) \lor (m=1) \lor (m>1)$
   $\vdash \forall x \in nat. iseven(x) \lor isodd(x)$

c.* $\forall m \in nat. isgcd(m,m,m),$
   $\forall m \in nat. isgcd(m,0,0),$
   $\forall m \in nat. \forall n \in nat. \forall p \in nat. isgcd(m,n,p) \supset isgcd(n,m,p),$
   $\forall m \in nat. \forall n \in nat. \forall p \in nat. isgcd(m-n,n,p) \supset isgcd(m,n,p),$
   $\forall m \in nat. \forall n \in nat. (m<n) \lor (m=n) \lor (m>n)$
   $\vdash \forall x \in nat. \forall y \in nat. \exists z \in nat. isgcd(x,y,z)$

2.5. Use axioms $z_1 - z_{10}$ in Section 10.2 to derive the *insert* function; that is, prove the following:

$$\forall l \in natlist. ord(l) \supset (\forall a \in nat. \exists m \in natlist. perm(cons\ a\ l, m) \land ord(m))$$

2.6. Use axioms $z_1 - z_{10}$ plus these axioms about list membership:

$ax_1 \in \forall a \in nat. \forall l \in natlist. member(a, cons\ a\ l)$
$ax_2 \in \forall a \in nat. \forall b \in nat. \forall l \in natlist. member(a, l) \supset member(a, cons\ b\ l)$
$ax_3 \in \forall a \in nat. \neg member(a, nil)$
$ax_4 \in \forall a \in nat. \forall b \in nat. \forall l \in natlist. (\neg member(a,l) \land (a \neq b)) \supset \neg member(a, cons\ b\ l)$

to prove the following:

a. $\forall a \in nat. \forall b \in nat. \forall l \in natlist. (\neg member(a,l) \land member(a, b\ cons\ l)) \supset a=b$
   Hint: Use $\forall a \in nat. \forall b \in nat. (a=b) \lor (a \neq b)$

b. $\forall a \in nat. \forall l \in natlist. member(a,l) \lor \neg member(a, l)$
   Note that the proof is a boolean test function.

c. $\forall a \in nat. \forall l \in natlist. member(a,l) \supset (\exists m \in natlist. perm(l, cons\ a\ m))$

d. $\forall a \in nat. \forall l \in natlist. (ord(l) \land member(a,l))$
   $\supset (\exists m \in natlist. ord(m) \land perm(l, cons\ a\ m))$

e. $\forall a \in nat. \forall l \in natlist. \exists m \in natlist. \neg member(a,m)$
   $\land (\forall b \in nat. (b \neq a \land member(b,l)) \supset member(b,m))$

2.7. Here are "Horn clause" (Prolog-like) axioms for list append:

$\forall m \in \phi list.\ isapp(nil, m, m)$

$\forall a \in \phi.\forall l \in \phi list.\forall m \in \phi list.\forall n \in \phi list.\ isapp(l, m, n) \supset isapp(cons\ a\ l,\ m,\ cons\ a\ n)$

a. Prove that $\forall x \in \phi list.\forall y \in \phi list.\exists z \in \phi list.\ isapp(x, y, z)$.

b. Like in Exercise 2.3, show that a certain format for Horn clause axioms about a predicate, $P(x, y)$, on lists must always lead to a proof for $\forall x \in \phi list.\exists y \in \phi'.\ P(x, y)$.

c. Use the format for Horn clauses you gave in Part b to specify and derive the *reverse* function for lists; the *length* function for lists; the *map* function for lists.

2.8. Say that these axioms hold: (i) *null(nil)*; (ii) $\forall a \in \phi.\forall l \in \phi list.\ \neg null(cons\ a\ l)$.

    a. Derive the operations $head \in \forall l \in \phi list.\ \neg null(l) \supset \phi$ and $tail \in \forall l \in \phi list.\ \neg null(l) \supset \phi list$, which extract the head and tail components, respectively, from a nonempty list.

    b. Describe the canonical expressions in the type $\exists l \in \phi list.\ \neg null(l)$. Define the operations $head \in (\exists l \in \phi list.\ \neg null(l)) \supset \phi$ and $tail \in (\exists l \in \phi list.\ \neg null(l)) \supset \phi list$.

    c. Use the proof of Exercise 1.1.h to transform the functions derived in Part a into the functions derived in Part b and vice versa.

2.9. The version of lists defined in Section 10.2 is sometimes called a "cons list." Here are the inference rules for an "append list":

$$AlistI_1:\ \frac{\Gamma \vdash e \in \phi}{\Gamma \vdash [e] \in \phi list} \qquad AlistI_2:\ \frac{\Gamma \vdash e_1 \in \phi list \qquad \Gamma \vdash e_2 \in \phi list}{\Gamma \vdash e_1 @ e_2 \in \phi list}$$

$$AlistE:\ \frac{\begin{array}{c}\Gamma \vdash e_1 \in \phi_1 list \qquad \Gamma,\ a \in \phi_1 \vdash e_2(a) \in \phi_2([a]) \\ \Gamma,\ l_1 \in \phi_1 list,\ l_2 \in \phi_1 list,\ x_1 \in \phi_2(l_1),\ x_2 \in \phi_2(l_2) \vdash e_3(l_1, l_2, x_1, x_2) \in \phi_2(l_1 @ l_2)\end{array}}{\begin{array}{c}\Gamma \vdash Alistrec\ e_1\ of\ is[a].\ e_2(a)\ [\!]\ is(l_1 @ l_2)(recl_1 \in \phi_2(l_1),\ recl_2 \in \phi_2(l_2)). \\ e_3(l_1, l_2, recl_1, recl_2) \in \phi_2(e_1)\end{array}}$$

    a. Define the computation rules for append lists.

    b. Assume that someone has derived

$merge \in \forall l \in \phi list.\forall m \in \phi list.\ (ord(l) \wedge ord(m)) \supset (\exists n \in \phi list.\ perm(l @ m, n) \wedge ord(n))$

    Use the inference rules to prove the sorting specification:

$\forall l \in \phi list.\exists m \in \phi list.\ perm(l, m) \wedge ord(m)$

    What version of sorting algorithm results?

    c. Derive the *merge* function in Part b. (You will need some axioms about *ord* and *perm* with respect to @, like axioms z_1-z_{10} in Section 10.2.)

2.10. For a set, S, a binary relation $\ll\ \subseteq S \times S$ is a *well-founded ordering* iff it is *irreflexive*, that is, $a \ll b$ and $b \ll a$ imply that $a = b$; *transitive*, that is, $a \ll b$ and $b \ll c$ imply that $a \ll c$; and *finitely decreasing*, that is, every sequence $a_1 \gg a_2 \gg \cdots \gg a_i \gg \cdots$ terminates with a minimal value, b ($a \gg b$ is just $b \ll a$ inverted).

  a. Verify that the length of lists defines a well-founded ordering: For $l, m \in \phi list$, $l \ll m$ iff $length(l) < length(m)$. Verify that "sublist" is a well-founded ordering: For $l, m \in \phi list$, $l \ll m$ iff there exist $p, q \in \phi list$ such that $m = p @ l @ q$. ("@" is the list-append operation; see Exercise 2.9.) Verify that the usual inductive definition of lists defines a well-founded ordering: For all $a \in \phi$, $l \in \phi list$, $nil \ll l$ and $l \ll cons\, a\, l$.

  Explain how the list elimination rules seen in Section 10.2 and in Exercises 2.9 and 2.4 are special cases of the following rule:

$$OlistE: \frac{\Gamma \vdash e_1 \in \phi_1 list \qquad \Gamma, l \in \phi_1 list, f \in (\forall m \in \phi_1 list.\, (m \ll l) \supset \phi_2(m)) \vdash e_2(l,f) \in \phi_2(l)}{\Gamma \vdash wforec\ e_1\ of\ (l \in \phi_1 list, f \in (\forall m \in \phi_1 list.\, (m \ll l) \supset \phi_2(m))).\, e_2(l,m) \in \phi_2(e_1)}$$

  The computation rule is like the one in Exercise 2.4.

  b. Let $\ll$ be the well-founded ordering on lists by length. Say that someone has derived

$$split \in \forall l \in \phi list.\, (length\ l > 1) \supset (\exists (front, back) \in \phi list \wedge \phi list.$$
$$front \ll l \wedge back \ll l \wedge perm(front @ back, l)$$

  Use this and the inference rule in Part a to rederive merge sort from the usual specification of sorting.

  c. Derive *split*.

2.11. Using the elimination rule in the previous exercise, quicksort can be derived. Use this lemma to do so:

$$filter \in \forall n \in nat. \forall l \in natlist. \exists (m,n) \in natlist \wedge natlist.$$
$$(\forall a \in nat.\, member(a,m) \supset a \leq n) \wedge (\forall a \in nat.\, member(a,n) \supset n < a) \wedge perm(m @ n, l)$$

2.12. Define a data type, $\phi tree$, of binary trees whose nodes hold elements from ϕ. That is, define the introduction, elimination, and computation rules. Use the type to specify and derive preorder tree traversal; inorder tree traversal; a function for building an ordered tree from an unordered list of ϕ-elements; a sorting function using the previous two functions.

2.13. Data types, like natural numbers, lists, and trees, are examples of *inductive types*. Here is a format for defining inductive types. To define a type, ψ, first, define a family of constructors, $\{cons_i\}_{1 \leq i \leq n}$; each $cons_i$ has an introduction rule of the form:

$$\frac{\Gamma \vdash e_{i1} \in \phi_{i1} \quad \cdots \quad \Gamma \vdash e_{im} \in \phi_{im}}{\Gamma \vdash (cons_i\ e_{i1} \cdots e_{im}) \in \psi}$$

where some of the ϕ_{ij} can be ψ. For simplicity, say that ϕ_{ik} is ψ. Next, define an elimination rule of the form:

$$\frac{\Gamma \vdash e \in \Psi \quad \{\Gamma, a_{i1} \in \phi_{i1}, \ldots, a_{im} \in \phi_{im}, recik \in \phi'(a_{ik}) \vdash e_i(a_{i1}, \ldots, a_{im}, recik) \in \phi'(cons_i\, a_{i1} \cdots a_{im})\}_{1 \le i \le n}}{\Gamma \vdash rec\ e\ of\ \{is(cons_i\, a_{i1} \cdots a_{im})(recik \in \phi'(a_{ik})).\, e_i(a_{i1}, \ldots, a_{im}, recik)\}_{1 \le i \le n}\ \in\ \phi'(e)}$$

a. Define the corresponding computation rule for this type.

b. Use the format to define *nat*; ϕ*list*; ϕ*tree* from Exercise 2.12.

c. What data type is defined if $n = 0$? If $n = 1$ and $1m = 0$? If $n = 2$, $1m = 0$, and $2m = 0$?

2.14.* There is a more general definition of inductive type. An inductive type is specified by a recursively defined proposition, for example, $natlist = \top \vee (nat \wedge natlist)$. ($\top$, read "true," is the type with the single canonical expression, $()$; see Exercise 5.3, Chapter 9.)

If we prove $t\ IsProp \vdash F(t)\ IsProp$, then μF is an inductive type. For example, $t\ IsProp \vdash L(t)\ IsProp$ holds, where $L(t) = \top \vee (nat \wedge t)$. An important restriction is that t occurs only *positively* in $F(t)$, that is, all occurrences of t are embedded in an even number of argument positions of $\supset$ and $\forall$, for example, t occurs positively in $L(t)$ and in $F(t) = (\forall x \in t.nat) \supset t$ but not positively in $G(t) = (t \supset nat) \vee \top$ nor in $H(t) = (\forall x \in nat.\, t) \supset nat$.

The intuition is that $\mu F = F(\mu F)$ such that μF is the smallest such set that satisfies the equality. For example, μL is the set of finite lists of natural numbers.

The rules for an inductive type are

$$\frac{\Gamma, t\ IsProp \vdash F(t)\ IsProp}{\Gamma \vdash \mu F\ IsProp} \qquad ind_F I: \frac{\Gamma \vdash e \in F(\mu F)}{\Gamma \vdash make_F\ e \in \mu F}$$

$$ind_F E: \frac{\Gamma \vdash e_1 \in \mu F \quad \Gamma, x \in F(t), f \in (\forall x \in t.\, \phi(x)) \vdash e_2(x,f) \in \phi(x)}{\Gamma \vdash rec_F\ e_1\ of\ (x \in F(\mu F), f \in \forall x \in \mu F.\phi(x)).\, e_2(x,f) \in \phi(e_1)}$$

$$rec_F\ (make_F\ e_1)\ of\ (x \in F(\mu F), f \in \forall x \in \mu F.\phi(x)).\, e_2(x,f)$$
$$\Rightarrow\ e_2(e_1,\ (\lambda y \in \mu F.rec_F\ y\ of\ (x \in F(\mu F), f \in \forall x \in \mu F.\phi(x)).\, e_2(x,f)))$$

For the $ind_F E$ rule, the intuition is that $x \in F(\mu F)$ represents e_1 when its internal canonical form is made visible, and $f \in \forall x \in \mu F.\phi(x)$ encodes the inductive hypotheses for all μF-typed components of e_1.

a. For $N(t) = \top \vee t$ (that is, $nat = \mu N$), write the specific versions of $ind_N I$ and $ind_N E$. Justify why $1 \in nat$ is encoded $make_N(inr(make_N(inl\ ())))$, where $() \in \top$. Justify why $identity \in nat \supset nat$ is encoded

$$identity = \lambda n \in nat.\, rec_{nat}\ n\ of\ (x \in N(nat), f \in \forall x \in nat.\, nat),$$
$$cases\ x\ of\ isl(a \in \top).\, make_N(inl\ ())$$

$[]\ isr(b\in nat).\ make_N(inr(f\cdot b))$

Use the computation rules on *identity*·1. Finally, define *addition* $\in (nat\wedge nat)\supset nat$.

b. For $L(t) = \top\vee(nat\wedge t)$, write the $ind_L\mathrm{I}$ and $ind_L\mathrm{E}$ rules. Let $natlist = \mu L$. Justify why $(cons\ 1\ nil)$ is encoded $make_L(inr(1, make_L(inl\ ())))$. Justify why $length \in natlist\supset nat$ is encoded

$length = \lambda l\in natlist.$
$\quad rec_{natlist}\ l\ of\ (x\in L(natlist),\ f\in \forall x\in natlist.nat).$
$\quad\quad cases\ x\ of\ isl(a\in \top).\ 0$
$\quad\quad [] \ isr(b\in nat\wedge natlist).\ succ(f\cdot(snd\ b))$

Apply the computation rule to the expression $length\cdot(cons\ 1\ nil)$. Finally, define $append \in (natlist\wedge natlist)\supset natlist$; $reverse \in natlist\supset natlist$.

c. Explain why μT, where $T(t) = \top\vee(\phi\wedge(bool\supset t))$ defines a data type of binary ϕ-trees of finite depth. Why doesn't $U(t) = \phi\wedge(bool\supset t)$ define a data type of binary ϕ trees of infinite depth?

d. In the $ind_F\mathrm{E}$ rule, $\phi(x)$ is used three times, where $x\in t$, $x\in F(t)$, and $x\in\mu F$. Why is this not problematic?

e. The $ind_F\mathrm{E}$ rule can be coded more tersely as

$$\frac{\Gamma\vdash e\in (\forall x\in t.\phi(x))\supset(\forall y\in F(t).\phi(y))}{\Gamma\vdash fix\ e\in (\forall z\in\mu F.\phi(z))}$$

with the computation rule

$\quad (fix\ e)\bullet(make_F e') \ \Rightarrow\ e\cdot(fix\ e)\bullet e'$

Explain how this rule is "equivalent" to the one above.

References on inductive data types include Backhouse et al. 1989, Dybjer 1991, Greiner 1992, Mendler 1987 and 1991, Paulson 1986, Pfenning and Paulin-Mohring 1989, Pierce, et al. 1989, and Thompson 1991.

2.15.* If you worked Exercise 2.14, proceed. The "dual" of an inductive type is a *coinductive type*. (The duality can be formalized in a category-theoretic way, see Manes and Arbib 1986, for example.) As in the previous exercise, let $t\ IsProp\vdash F(t)\ IsProp$ hold, where t occurs only positively in $F(t)$. νF is a coinductive type, and the intuition is that $\nu F = F(\nu F)$, where νF is the "largest" such set that satisfies the equality. The standard example of a coinductive type is the type of (infinite) streams, νS, where $S(t) = nat\wedge t$. Another example is the type of finite and infinite lists, νL, where $L(t) = \top\vee(nat\wedge t)$.

The rules for coinductive types are

$$coind_F\mathrm{I}: \quad \frac{\Gamma\vdash e_1\in\phi \qquad \Gamma, x\in\phi, f\in\phi\supset t\vdash e_2(x,f)\in F(t)}{\Gamma\vdash corec_F\ e_1\ of\ (x\in\phi, f\in\phi\supset\nu F).\ e_2(x,f)\in\nu F}$$

$$coind_F \text{E}: \quad \frac{\Gamma \vdash e \in \nu F}{\Gamma \vdash unmake_F\ e \in F(\nu F)}$$

$$unmake_F(corec_F\ e_1\ of\ (x \in \phi,\ f \in \phi \supset \nu F).\ e_2(x,f))$$
$$\Rightarrow\ e_2(e_1,\ (\lambda y \in \phi.\ corec_F\ y\ of\ (x \in \phi,\ f \in \phi \supset \nu F).\ e_2(x,f)))$$

The intuition for $corec_F$I is that e_1 is a "seed" that generates a coinductive value, e_2 is the "top level" of the value, and f is the coinductive hypothesis that generates the remainder of the value. Since coinductive values are data structures of potentially infinite depth, a seed value is necessary for their effective generation.

a. For *stream* = νS, write the specific versions of $coind_S$I and $coind_S$E. Justify why the stream of even natural numbers, *evens*, is encoded

$$evens = corec_S\ 0\ of\ (x \in nat,\ f \in nat \supset stream).\ (x,\ f \cdot (x+2))$$

Show that $fst(unmake_S(snd(unmake_S\ evens)))$ is 2. Finally, write a function $sum \in (nat \wedge stream) \supset nat$ such that $sum \cdot n \cdot s$ adds together the first n elements in s.

b. Consider $I(t) = \top$ **or** $(nat \wedge t \wedge t)$; what is νI? Consider $T(t) = nat \wedge (nat \supset t)$; what is νT?

c. Despite the presence of potentially infinite data values due to coinductive types, the system retains strong normalization. Explain why.

Reference on coinductive types include Aczel and Mendler 1989, Greiner 1992, Hagino 1989, Manes and Arbib 1986, and Thompson 1991.

2.16. Why are the usual restrictions on the $\forall$I and $\exists$E rules unnecessary in Figure 10.5?

3.1. Prove the following:

a. $\forall t \in U_0.\ t\ list \supset nat$

b. $\forall t \in U_0.\ (t\ list) \wedge ((t \wedge t) \supset bool) \supset t\ list$

c. $\forall t \in U_0. \forall le \in (t \wedge t) \supset bool. \forall l \in t\ list. \exists m \in t\ list.\ ord(m,le) \wedge perm(l,m)$
     Note: You will need to revise axioms $z_1 - z_{10}$ in Section 10.2.

d. $\exists t \in U_0.\ t \wedge (t \supset t) \wedge (t \supset t)$

e. $\exists t \in U_0.\ \exists zero \in t.\ \exists succ \in t \supset t.\ \exists pred \in t \supset t.\ (\forall n \in t.\ pred(succ\ n) = n) \wedge (pred\ zero = zero)$ Note: Use the rule

$$equal\text{I}: \quad \frac{e_1 \Rightarrow^* e_2}{e_1 = e_2}$$

3.2. The rules in Figure 10.9 are "introduction rules" for the universe hierarchy. Speculate on "elimination rules." (See Nordström, et al. 1990.)

3.3. Why can't one prove $\forall t \in U_0.\ (\forall x \in t.\ \phi(x)) \supset (\exists x \in t.\ \phi(x))$?

4.1. Let *reverse* ∈ *natlist⊃natlist*

   reverse = λ*l*∈ *natlist.*
   listrec l of isnil. nil
   [] *is(cons a b)(recb∈ natlist). append·recb·(cons a nil)*

and: *append* ∈ *(natlist∧natlist)⊃natlist*

   append = λ*l*∈ *natlist.*λ*m*∈ *natlist.*
   listrec l of isnil.m
   [] *is(cons a b)(recb∈ natlist). cons a recb*

Use Figure 10.10 plus the new version of =I to prove the following:

a. ∀*l*∈ *natlist. append·(cons 0 nil)·l = (cons 0 l)*

b. ∀*l*∈ *natlist.*∀*m*∈ *natlist. perm(append·l·m, append·m·l)*

c. ∀*l*∈ *natlist. reverse·(reverse·l) = l*

d. ∀*l*∈ *natlist.*∀*m*∈ *natlist. reverse(append·l·m) = append·(reverse·m)·(reverse·l)*

4.2. Use the definitions of "+" and "×" from Section 10.4 to prove Peano's axioms:

a. ∀*m*∈ *nat.* 0+*m*=*m*

b. ∀*m*∈ *nat.*∀*n*∈ *nat. m+succ n = succ(m+n)*

c. ∀*m*∈ *nat.* 0×*m*=0

d. ∀*m*∈ *nat.*∀*n*∈ *nat. m×succ n = (m×n)+m*

e. ∀*m*∈ *nat.*∀*n*∈ *nat. (succ m=succ n) ⊃ m=n*
    Hint: Use the definition of *pred* and consider *pred(succ m)*.

f. ∀*m*∈ *nat.* ¬(0=*succ m*)
    Hint: Define *iszero*∈ *nat⊃U$_0$* to be
    iszero = λ*n*∈ *nat. natrec n of is0.⊤* [] *issucc(x)(recx∈ U$_0$). ⊥*.
    Then prove that () ∈ *iszero(0)* and () ∈ *iszero(succ m)*.

g. (φ(0) ∧ (∀*m*∈ *nat.* φ(*m*)⊃φ(*succ m*))) ⊃ (∀*n*∈ *nat.* φ(*n*)),   for every φ ∈ Proposition

4.3. A stronger equality elimination rule gives "strong" (or *extensional*) equality. Replace rules =E$_1$, =E$_2$, and =E$_3$ by

   =*strong*E: $\dfrac{\Gamma \vdash e \in a=_\phi b}{\Gamma \vdash a\ cnv\ b \in \phi}$

Use this rule to derive the following judgements:

a. ⊢ *e$_0$* ∈ (λ*x*∈ *nat. x*+1) = (λ*x*∈ *nat.* 1+*x*), for some *e$_0$*

b.* *f*∈ φ$_1$⊃φ$_2$ ⊢ *e$_0$* ∈ (λ*x*∈ φ$_1$.*f·x*) =*f*, for some *e$_0$*

c. ⊢ λ*x*∈ ⊥. (λ*y*∈ *nat. y·y*)·(λ*y*∈ *nat. y·y*) ∈ ⊥⊃*nat*
    Hint: Prove *x*∈ ⊥ ⊢ *abort x* ∈ *nat = nat⊃nat*
    Thus, normalization is lost in a system with the strong equality rule. Can

$\vdash (\lambda y \in nat. \, y \cdot y) \cdot (\lambda y \in nat. \, y \cdot y) \in nat$ be proved with the strong equality rule?

5.1. Use the rules in Figure 10.11 to prove the following:

    a. $\forall b \in bool. \, b{=}true \vee b{=}false$

    b. $\forall n \in nat. \exists p \in (bool \vee nat). \, ((n{=}0) \supset (p{=}inl(true))) \wedge ((n{>}0) \supset (\exists m \in nat. \, p{=}inr(m)))$

    c. $\forall p \in (\exists m \in nat. \, m{>}0). \, \exists a \in nat. \exists b \in a{>}0. \, (p{=}pair\ a\ b) \wedge (a{>}pred\ a)$
        Note: use the axiom: $\forall x \in nat. \, (x{>}0) \supset (x{>}pred\ x)$

    d. $\forall p \in nat \wedge nat. \, (fst\ p{>}0) \supset (sum \cdot p{>}0)$
        where $sum \cdot (m,n) = m{+}n$

5.2.* Prove the axiom of choice:

$$(\forall x \in \phi_1. \exists y \in \phi_2. \, \phi_3(x,y)) \supset (\exists f \in \phi_1 \supset \phi_2. \forall x \in \phi_1. \, \phi_3(x, f \cdot x))$$

The proof of the converse is easy.

    Thompson (1990) remarks that the axiom of choice allows the "usual" program specification of the form $\forall x \in \phi_1. \exists y \in \phi_2. \, \phi_3(x,y)$ to be transformed into $\exists f \in \phi_1 \supset \phi_2. \forall x \in \phi_1. \, \phi_3(x, f \cdot x)$. Give the pragmatics of the two formats.

5.3. Use the rules in Figure 10.12 to prove the following:

    a. $\forall p \in (\exists m \in nat. m{>}0). \, (first\ p){>}0$

    b. $\forall n \in nat. \exists p \in (\exists m \in nat. \, m{>}n). \, (first\ p{=}succ\ n) \wedge (\exists q \in nat. \, second\ p{=}ax\ 1 \cdot q)$
        where $ax_1 \in \forall x \in nat. \, succ\ x{>}x$

Bibliography

Abelson, H., and Sussman, G. Structure and Interpretation of Computer Programs. MIT Press, Cambridge, MA, 1985.

Abramsky, S. The lazy lambda calculus. In D. Turner, ed. *Research Topics in Functional Programming.* Addison-Wesley, Reading, MA, 1990, pp. 65–116.

Aczel, P., and Mendler, N. A final coalgebra theorem. In D. Pitt, D. Rydeheard, P. Dybjer, A. Pitts, and A. Poigne, eds. *Category Theory and Computer Science.* LNCS 389, Springer, Berlin, 1989, pp. 357–365.

Aho, A., Sethi, R., and Ullman, J. *Compilers: Principles, Techniques, and Tools.* Addison Wesley, Reading, MA, 1986.

Amadio, R., and Cardelli, L. Subtyping recursive types. *ACM Transactions on Programming Languages and Systems* 15 (1993): 575–631.

Appel, A. A critique of Standard ML. Technical Report CS-TR-364-92, Princeton University, 1992.

Apt, K. Ten years of Hoare's logic: a survey. *ACM Transactions on Programming Languages and Systems* 3 (1981): 431–83.

Backhouse, R. Constructive type theory: an introduction. In M. Broy, ed. *Constructive Methods in Computing Science.* Springer, Berlin, 1989, pp. 9–62.

———, Chisholm, P., Malcolm, G., and Saaman, E. Do-it-yourself type theory. *Formal Aspects of Computing* 1 (1989): 19–84.

Barendregt, H. *The Lambda Calculus: Its Syntax and Semantics 2d. ed.* North-Holland, Amsterdam, 1984.

———. Introduction to generalized type systems. *J. Functional Programming* 1 (1991): 125–154.

———. Lambda calculi with types. In S. Abramsky, D. Gabbay, and T. Maibaum, eds. *Handbook of Logic in Computer Science.* Vol. 2. Oxford University Press, 1992, pp. 118–310.

————, and Dekkers, W. *Typed Lambda Calculi: Syntax and Semantics*. To appear.

————, and Hemerik, K. Types in lambda calculi and programming languages. In N.D. Jones, ed. *3d. European Symposium on Programming*. LNCS 432, Springer, Berlin, 1990, pp. 1–35.

Barrett, W., Bates, R., Gustafson, D., and Couch, J. *Compiler Construction: Theory and Practice*. 2d ed. SRA Press, Chicago, 1986.

Beeson, M. *Foundations of Constructive Mathematics*. Springer, Berlin, 1985.

Berry, G., Curien, P.-L., and Levy, J.-J. Full abstraction of sequential languages: the state of the art. In J. Reynolds and M. Nivat, eds. *Algebraic Methods in Semantics*. Cambridge University Press, Cambridge, 1985, pp. 89–131.

Bird, R., and Wadler, P. *Introduction to Functional Programming*. Prentice-Hall International, London, 1988.

Bishop, E. *Foundations of Constructive Analysis*. McGraw-Hill, New York, 1967.

Bjerner, B. Verifying some efficient sorting strategies in type theory. PMG Memo 26, Chalmers University, Gothenburg, 1985,

Bjørner, D., Ershov, A., and Jones, N., eds. *Partial Evaluation and Mixed Computation*. North-Holland, Amsterdam, 1988.

Bruce, K. Safe type checking in a statically-typed object-oriented programming language. In *20th ACM Symposium on Principles of Programming Languages*, ACM Press, New York, 1993, pp. 285–298.

Bruijn, N.G. de. Lambda calculus notation with nameless dummies. *Indag. Mathematica* 34 (1972): 381–92.

————. A survey of the project AUTOMATH. In J.P. Seldin and J.R. Hindley, eds. *To H.B. Curry: Essays on Combinatory Logic, Lambda Calculus, and Formalism*. Academic Press, New York, 1980, pp. 589–606.

Burstall, R. Programming with modules as typed functional programming. In *International Conference on Fifth Generation Computing Systems,* ICOT, Tokyo, 1989.

————, and Lampson, B. A kernel language for abstract data types and modules. In G. Kahn, D. MacQueen, and G. Plotkin, eds. *Semantics of Data Types*. LNCS 173, Springer, Berlin, 1984, pp. 1–50.

The calculus of constructions: collected papers. Version 4.0, Projet Formel, INRIA-ENS, May, 1989a.

————: documentation and user's guide. Version 4.10, Projet Formel, INRIA-ENS, July, 1989b.

Cardelli, L. A semantics of multiple inheritance. In G. Kahn, D. MacQueen, and G. Plotkin, eds. *Semantics of Data Types*. LNCS, Springer, Berlin, 1984, pp. 51–69.

———. Basic polymorphic type checking. *Science of Computer Programming* 8 (1987): 147–72.

———. Amber. In G. Cousineau, P.-L. Curien, and B. Robinet, eds. *Combinators and Functional Programming Languages*. LNCS 242, Springer, Berlin, 1986a, pp. 21–47.

———. A polymorphic lambda calculus with type:type. Research Report 10, DEC Systems Research Center, Palo Alto, CA, 1986b.

———. Typeful programming. Research Report 45, DEC Systems Research Center, Palo Alto, CA, 1989. Also appears in *IFIP State of the Art Seminar on Formal Description of Programming Concepts,* North-Holland, Amsterdam, 1989.

———, and Leroy, X. Abstract types and the dot notation. In M. Broy and C. Jones, ed. *Programming Concepts and Methods*. North-Holland, Amsterdam, 1990, pp. 479–504.

———, and Mitchell, J. Operations on records. *Mathematical Structures in Computer Science* 1 (1991): 3–48.

———, and Wegner, P. On understanding types, data abstraction, and polymorphism. *Computing Surveys* 17 (1985): 471–522.

Cardone, F., and Coppo, M. Two extensions of Curry's type inference system. In P. Odifreddi, ed. *Logic and Computer Science*. Academic Press, New York, 1990, pp. 19–76.

Cartwright, R., and Fagan, M. Soft typing. In *ACM SIGPLAN '91 Conference on Programming Language Design and Implementation,* ACM Press, New York, 1991, pp. 278–92.

Cartwright, R., and Felleisen, M. Observable Sequentiality and Full Abstraction. In *19th ACM Symposium on Principles of Programming Languages,* ACM Press, New York, 1992, pp. 328–341.

Chisholm, P. Derivation of a parsing algorithm in Martin-Löf's type theory. *Science of Computer Programming* 8 (1987): 1–42.

Church, A. *Introduction to Mathematical Logic*. Vol. 1. Princeton University Press, Princeton, NJ, 1956.

Clocksin, W., and Mellish, C. *Programming in Prolog*. 3d ed. Springer, Berlin, 1987.

Consel, C., and Danvy, O. Static and dynamic semantics processing. In *18th ACM*

Symposium on Principles of Programming Languages, ACM Press, New York, 1991, pp. 14–24.

————. Tutorial notes on partial evaluation. In *20th ACM Symposium on Principles of Programming Languages,* 1993, pp. 493–501.

Constable, R. Assigning meaning to proofs. In M. Broy, ed. *Constructive Methods in Computing Science.* Springer, Berlin, 1989, pp. 63–94.

————. Type theory as a foundation for computer science. In T. Ito and A. Meyer, eds. *Theoretical Aspects of Computer Software.* LNCS 526, Springer, Berlin, 1991, pp. 226-243.

————, and O'Donnell, M. *A Programming Logic.* Winthrop, Cambridge, MA, 1978.

————, Allen, S., Bromley, H., Cleaveland, R., Cremer, J., Harper, R., Howe, D., Knoblock, T., Mendler, N., Panangaden, P., Sasaki, J., and Smith, S. *Implementing Mathematics with the NuPRL Proof Development System.* Prentice-Hall, Englewood Cliffs, NJ, 1986.

Cook, W., Hill, W., and Canning, P. Inheritance is not subtyping. In *17th ACM Symposium on Principles of Programming Languages,* ACM Press, New York, 1990, pp. 125–136.

Coquand, T. Analysis of Girard's paradox. In *1st IEEE Symposium on Logic in Computer Science,* IEEE Computer Society Press, Los Alamitos, CA, 1986, pp. 227–36.

————. Metamathematical investigations of a calculus of constructions. In Odifreddi, P., ed. *Logic and Computer Science.* Academic Press, New York, 1990, pp. 91–122.

————, and Huet, G. The calculus of constructions. *Information and Computation* 76 (1988): 95–120.

Curry, H., and Feys, R. *Combinatory Logic.* Vol. 1. North-Holland, Amsterdam, 1958.

————, Hindley, R., and Seldin, J. *Combinatory Logic.* Vol. 2. North-Holland, Amsterdam, 1972.

Dalen, D. van. *Logic and Structure.* 2d. ed. Springer, Berlin, 1983.

Damas, L., and Milner, R. Principal type schemes for functional programs. In *9th ACM Symposium on Principles of Programming Languages,* 1982, ACM Press, New York, pp. 207–12.

Danforth, S., and Tomlinson, C. Type theories and object-oriented programming. *Computing Surveys* 20 (1988): 29–72.

Darlington, J., ed. *Functional Programming and its Applications.* Cambridge University Press, Cambridge, 1982.

Denransert, P., Jourdan, M., and Lorho, B. *Attribute Grammars.* LNCS 323, Springer, Berlin, 1988.

Dershowitz, N. Termination of rewriting. *Journal of Symbolic Computation* 3 (1987): 69–116.

——, and Jouannaud, J.P. Rewrite systems. In J. van Leeuwen, ed. *Handbook of Theoretical Computer Science.* Vol. 2. North-Holland, Amsterdam, 1990, pp. 243–320.

Donohue, J. Locations considered unnecessary. *Acta Informatica* 8 (1977): 221–42.

Dragalin, A.G. *Mathematical Intuitionism: Introduction to Proof Theory.* American Mathematical Society, Providence, RI, 1988.

Dummett, M. *Elements of Intuitionism.* Oxford University Press, Oxford, 1977.

Dybjer, P. Inductive sets and families in Martin-Löf's type theory and their set-theoretic semantics. Technical report 62, Programming Methodology Group, Chalmers University and University of Gothenburg, February 1991.

——, Hallnäs, L., Nordström, B., Petersson, K., and Smith, J., eds. Proceedings of the Workshop on Programming Logic. Report 54, Programming Methodology Group, University of Gothenburg, 1989.

——, Nordström, B., Petersson, K., and Smith, J., eds. Proceedings of the Workshop on Specification and Derivation of Programs. Report 18, Programming Methodology Group, University of Gothenburg, 1985.

——, Nordström, B., Petersson, K., and Smith, J., eds. Proceedings of the Workshop on Programming Logic. Report 37, Programming Methodology Group, University of Gothenburg, 1987.

Enderton, H. *A Mathematical Introduction to Logic.* Academic Press, New York, 1972.

Even, S., and Schmidt, D. Category-sorted algebra-based action semantics. *Theoretical Computer Science* 77 (1990): 73–96.

Felleisen, M. On the Expressive Power of Programming Languages. *Science of Computer Programming* 17 (1991): 35–75.

——, and Friedman, D. A syntactic theory of sequential state. *Theoretical Computer Science* 69 (1989): 243–287.

——, and Hieb, R. The revised report on the syntactic theories of sequential control and state. *Theoretical Computer Science* 102 (1992).

Field, A., and Harrison, P. *Functional Programming*. Addison-Wesley, Reading, MA, 1988.

Fokkinga, M. On the notion of strong typing. In J. de Bakker and J. van Vliet, eds. *International Symposium on Algorithmic Languages*. North-Holland, Amsterdam, 1981, pp. 305–320.

Fortune, S., Leivant, D., and O'Donnell, M. The expressiveness of simple and second order type structures. *Journal of the ACM* 30 (1983): 151–185.

Fradet, P., and Le Metayer, D. Compilation of Functional Languages by Program Transformation. *ACM Transactions on Programming Languages and Systems* 13 (1991): 21–51.

Friedman, D., Wand, M., and Haynes, C. *Essentials of Programming Languages*. MIT Press, Cambridge, MA, 1992.

Gallier, J. *Logic for Computer Science*. Wiley, New York, 1988.

————. Constructive logics. Part 1: a tutorial on proof systems and typed λ-calculi. Report 8, Digital Paris Research Lab, May 1991. Also, *Theoretical Computer Science* 110 (1993): 249–339.

————. Constructive logics. Part 2: linear logic and proof nets. Report 9, Digital Paris Research Lab, May 1991.

Gelernter, D., and Jagannathan, S. *Programming Linguistics*. M.I.T. Press, Cambridge, MA, 1990.

Georgeff, M. Transformations and Reduction Strategies for Typed Lambda Expressions. *ACM Transactions on Programming Languages and Systems* 6 (1984): 603–631.

Ghezzi, C., and Jazayeri, M. *Programming Language Concepts*. 2d ed. Wiley, New York, 1987.

Girard, J.-Y. Interprétation fonctionelle et élimination des compures de l'arithmétic d'ordre supérieur. Thèse d'état, Université Paris VII, 1972.

————. The system F of variable types, fifteen years later. *Theoretical Computer Science* 45 (1986): 159–192.

————, Lafont, Y., and Taylor, P. *Proofs and Types*. Cambridge University Press, Cambridge, 1989.

Gordon, M. J. C. *Programming Language Theory and Its Implementation*. Prentice-Hall International, London, 1991.

Goto, S. Program synthesis from natural deduction proofs. In *International Joint Conference on Artificial Intelligence,* Tokyo, 1979.

Greiner, J. Programming with inductive and co-inductive types. Technical Report 92-109, Computer Science Department, Carnegie Mellon University, Pittsburgh, 1992.

Gunter, C. *Foundations of Programming Languages.* MIT Press, Cambridge, MA, 1992.

————, and Mitchell, J., eds. *Semantics of Object-Oriented Programming Languages.* MIT Press, Cambridge, MA, 1993.

Hagino, T. Codatatypes in ML. *Journal of Symbolic Computation* 8 (1989): 629–650.

Hannan, J. Investigating a proof theoretic metalanguage for functional programs. Ph.D. dissertation, University of Pennsylvania, 1990.

Harland, D. *Polymorphic Programming Languages.* Ellis-Horwood, Chicester, 1984.

Harper, R., Honsell, F., and Plotkin, G. A framework for defining logics. *Journal of the ACM* 39 (1992).

Harper, R., Milner, R., and Tofte, M. A type discipline for program modules. In H. Ehrig, R. Kowlaski, G. Levi, and U. Montanari, eds. *TAPSOFT '87.* LNCS 250, Springer, Berlin, 1987, pp. 308–319.

Harper, R., and Mitchell, J. On the type structure of Standard ML. *ACM Transactions Programming Languages and Systems* 15 (1993): 211–252.

Harper, R., and Pollack, R. Type checking with universes. *Theoretical Computer Science* 89 (1991): 107–136.

Hayashi, S., and Nakano, H. *PX: A Computational Logic.* MIT Press, Cambridge, MA, 1988.

Henderson, P. *Functional Programming: Application and Implementation.* Prentice-Hall International, London, 1980.

————, and Morris, J. A lazy evaluator. In *3rd ACM Symposium on Principles of Programming Languages,* ACM Press, New York, 1976, pp. 95–103.

Hennessy, M. *The Semantics of Programming Languages: An Elementary Introduction Using Structured Operational Semantics.* Wiley, New York, 1991.

Henson, M. *Elements of Functional Programming.* Blackwell, Oxford, 1987.

————. Program development in the constructive set theory TK. *Formal Aspects of Computing* 1 (1989): 173–192.

Heyting, A. *Intuitionism: An Introduction.* North-Holland, Amsterdam, 1956.

Hindley, J. The principal type scheme of an object in combinatory logic. *Transactions American Mathematical Society* 146 (1969): 29–60.

————. The completeness theorem for typing λ-terms. *Theoretical Computer Science* 22 (1983): 1–17, 127–133.

————, and Seldin, J. *Introduction to Combinators and Lambda-calculus.* Cambridge University Press, Cambridge, 1986.

Hoare, C. A. R. Hints on programming language design. In *1st ACM Symposium on Principles of Programming Languages,* ACM Press, New York, 1973. Also in Horowitz 1983.

Hook, J. Understanding Russell—a first attempt. In G. Kahn, D. MacQueen, and G. Plotkin, eds. *Semantics of Data Types.* LNCS 173, Springer, Berlin, 1984, pp. 69–86.

————, and Howe, D. Impredicative strong existential equivalent to type:type. Technical report TR 86-760, Computer Science Department, Cornell University, Ithaca, NY, 1986,

Horowitz, E., ed. *Programming Languages: A Grand Tour.* Computer Science Press, Rockville, MD, 1983.

Howard, W. A. The formulae-as-types notion of construction. In J.P. Seldin and J.R. Hindley, eds. *To H.B. Curry: Essays on Combinatory Logic, Lambda Calculus, and Formalism.* Academic Press, New York, 1980.

Hudak, P., and Jones, N. D., eds. *Proceedings Symposium on Partial Evaluation and Semantics-Based Program Manipulation. SIGPLAN Notices* 26-9 (1991).

Hudak, P., and Wadler, P., eds. Report on the Programming Language Haskell, Version 1.0. Report DCS-RR-777, Yale University, New Haven, CT, 1990.

Huet, G. Confluent Reductions: abstract properties and applications to term rewriting systems. *Journal of Association for Computing Machinery* 27 (1980): 797–821.

————, ed. *Logical Foundations of Functional Programming.* Addison-Wesley, Reading, MA, 1990.

————, and Oppen, D. Equations and rewrite rules: a survey. In R. Book, ed. *Formal Language Theory.* Academic Press, New York, 1980.

————, and Plotkin, G., eds. *Logical Frameworks.* Cambridge University Press, Cambridge, 1992.

Hughes, J. Why functional programming matters. In D.A. Turner, ed. *Research Topics in Functional Programming.* Addison-Wesley, Reading, MA, 1990.

Ito, T., and Meyer, A., eds. *Theoretical Aspects of Computer Software.* LNCS 526, Springer, Berlin, 1991.

Jones, N. D., and Muchnick, S. Binding time optimization in programming languages. In *Proceedings 3rd ACM Symposium on Principles of Programming Languages,* ACM Press, New York, 1976, pp. 77–94.

————. *TEMPO: A Unified Treatment of Binding Time and Parameter Passing Concepts.* LNCS 66, Springer, Berlin, 1978.

Jones, N. D., Sestoft, P., and Gomard, C. *Partial Evaluation.* Prentice-Hall, Englewood Cliffs, NJ, 1993.

Jones, N. D., Sestoft, P., and Sondergaard, H. Mix: a self-applicable partial evaluator for experiments in compiler generation. *Lisp and Symbolic Computation* 2 (1989): 9–50.

Kahn, G. Natural semantics. In F. Brandenburg, G. Vidal-Naquet, and M. Wirsing, eds. *STACS '87.* LNCS 247, Springer, Berlin, 1987, pp. 22–39.

Kamin, S. *Programming Languages: An Intepreter-Based Approach.* Addison-Wesley, Reading, MA, 1990.

Kfoury, A., Tiuryn, J., and Urzyczyn, P. ML typability is Dexptime complete. In A. Arnold, ed. *15th. Coolq. on Trees in Algebra and Programming.* LNCS 431, Springer, Berlin, 1990a, pp. 206–220.

————. The undecidability of the semi-unification problem. In *22nd ACM Symposium on Theory of Computing,* ACM Press, New York, 1990b, pp. 468–476.

Khasidashvili, Z. The Church-Rosser theorem in orthogonal combinatory reduction systems. Research Report 1825, INRIA, Rocquencourt, France, 1993.

Klop, J.W. *Combinatory Reduction Systems.* Mathematical Centre Tracts 127, Mathematisch Centrum, Amsterdam, 1980.

————. Term rewriting systems. In S. Abramsky, D. Gabbay, and T. Maibaum, eds. *Handbook of Logic in Computer Science.* Vol. 2. Oxford University Press, Oxford, 1992, pp. 2–117.

Knuth, D. The semantics of context free languages. *Mathematical Systems Theory* 2 (1968): 127–145. (Corrigenda, vol. 5, p. 95, 1971).

Kohlbecker, E. Syntactic extensions in the programming language Lisp. Ph.D. dissertation, Indiana University, 1986.

————, Friedman, D. P., Felleisen, M., and Duba, B. Hygienic macro expansion. In *Proceedings ACM Conference on Lisp and Functional Programming,* ACM Press, New York, 1986, pp. 151–161.

Kowalski, R. *Logic for Problem Solving.* North-Holland, Amsterdam, 1979.

Lambek, J., and Scott, P. *Introduction to Higher Order Categorical Logic.* Cambridge University Press, Cambridge, 1986.

Landin, P. A correspondence between ALGOL60 and Church's lambda notation. *Communications of the ACM* 8 (1965): 89–101, 158–165.

———. The next 700 programming languages. *Communications of the ACM* 9 (1966): 157–164.

Launchbury, J. *Projection Factorizations in Partial Evaluation.* Cambridge University Press, Cambridge, 1992..

Lee, S.-D., and Friedman, D. Quasi-Static Scoping. In *20th Symposium Principles of Programming Languages,* ACM Press, New York, 1993, pp. 479–492.

Leivant, D. Reasoning about functional programs and complexity classes associated with type disciplines. In *13th Symposium Foundations of Computer Science,* IEEE Computer Society Press, Los Alamitos, CA, 1983, pp. 460–469.

Lemmon, E.J. *Beginning Logic.* Thomas Nelson and Sons, London, 1965.

Louden, K. *Programming Languages: Principles and Practice.* PWS-Kent Publishing, Boston, 1993.

Lucassen, J., and Gifford, D. Polymorphic effect systems. In *15th ACM Symposium on Principles of Programming Languages,* ACM Press, New York, 1988, pp. 47–57.

MacQueen, D. Modules for Standard ML. In *ACM Symposium on Lisp and Functional Programming,* ACM Press, New York, 1984, pp. 198–207.

———. Using dependent types to express modular structure. In *13th ACM Symposium on Principles of Programming Languages,* ACM Press, New York, 1986, pp. 277–286.

———. A higher-order type system for functional programming. In D. Turner, ed. *Research Topics in Functional Programming.* Addison-Wesley, Reading, MA, 1990, pp. 353–367.

MacLennan, B. Principles of Programming Languages. 2d ed. Holt, Reinhart, and Winston, New York, 1987.

Mairston, H. Deciding ML typability is complete for deterministic exponential time. In *17th ACM Symposium on Principles of Programming Languages,* ACM Press, New York, 1990, pp. 382–401.

Manes, E., and Arbib, M. Algebraic Approaches to Program Semantics. Springer, New York, 1986.

Manna, Z., and Waldinger, R. A deductive approach to program synthesis. *ACM Transactions on Programming Languages and Systems* 2 (1980): 90–121.

————. Deductive synthesis of the unification algorithm. *Science of Computer Programming* 1 (1981): 5–48.

Marcotty, M., and Ledgard, H. *The Programming Language Landscape.* 2d ed. SRA Press, Chicago, 1986.

Martin-Löf, P. An intuitionistic theory of types: predicative part. In H.E. Rose and J.C. Shepherdson, eds. *Logic Colloquium 1973.* North-Holland, Amsterdam, 1973.

————. *Intuitionistic Type Theory.* Bibliopolis, Naples, 1984.

————. Constructive mathematics and computer programming. In C. A. R. Hoare, ed. *Mathematical Logic and Programming Languages.* Prentice-Hall, Englewood Cliffs, NJ, 1985.

————. Mathematics of infinity. In P. Martin-Löf and G. Mints, eds. *COLOG-88.* LNCS 417, Springer, Berlin, 1988, pp. 146–197.

Mason, I., and Talcott, C. Equivalence in functional programming languages with effects. *Journal of Functional Programming* 1–3 (1991): 287–327.

————. Inferring the equivalence of functional programs that mutate data. *Theoretical Computer Science* 105 (1992): 167–215.

Mendelson, E. *Introduction to Mathematical Logic. 3d ed.* Wadsworth, 1987.

Mendler, N. Recursive types and type constraints in second-order lambda calculus. In *2d IEEE Symposium on Logic in Computer Science,* IEEE Computer Society Press, Los Alamitos, CA, 1987, pp. 30–36.

————. Predicative type universes and primitive recursion. In *6th IEEE Symposium on Logic in Computer Science,* IEEE Computer Society Press, Los Alamitos, CA, 1991, pp. 173–184.

Meyer, A., and Cosmadakis, C. Semantical paradigms: notes for an invited lecture. In *3d IEEE Symposium on Logic in Computer Science,* IEEE Computer Society Press, Los Alamitos, CA, 1988, pp. 236–253.

Meyer, A., and Reinhold, M. "Type" is not a type. In *13th ACM Symposium on Principles of Programming Languages,* ACM Press, New York, 1986, pp. 287–295.

Meyer, B. *Object-Oriented Software Construction.* Prentice-Hall International, London, 1988.

————. *Introduction to the Theory of Programming Languages.* Prentice-Hall International, London, 1990.

Michaelson, G. An Introduction to Functional Programming Through Lambda Calculus. Addison-Wesley, Reading, MA, 1989.

Milne, G., and Strachey, C. *A Theory of Programming Language Semantics.* Chapman and Hall, London, 1976.

Milner, R. Fully abstract models of typed lambda calculi. *Theoretical Computer Science* 4 (1977): 1–22.

———. A theory of type polymorphism in programming. *Journal Computing and System Sciences* 17 (1978): 348–75.

———, and Tofte, M. Commentary on Standard ML. MIT Press, Cambridge, 1990.

———, and Harper, R. *The Definition of Standard ML.* MIT Press, Cambridge, 1990.

Mitchell, J. Towards a typed foundation for method specialization and inheritance. In *17th ACM Symposium on Principles of Programming Languages,* ACM Press, New York, 1990, pp. 109–124.

———. Type Systems for Programming Languages. In J. van Leeuwen, ed. *Handbook of Theoretical Computer Science.* Vol. 2. North-Holland, Amsterdam, 1990,

———. *Introduction to Programming Language Theory.* MIT Press, Cambridge, to appear.

———, and Plotkin, G. Abstract types have existential types. In *12th ACM Symposium on Principles of Programming Languages,* ACM Press, New York, 1985, pp. 37–51.

Morris, J.H. Lambda calculus models of programming languages. Ph.D. dissertation, Massachusetts Institute of Technology, 1968.

Mosses, P.D. Abstract semantic algebras. In D. Bjørner, ed. *Formal Description of Programming Concepts II.* North-Holland, Amsterdam, 1983, pp. 45–72.

———. Unified algebras and action semantics. In *STACS '89,* LNCS 349, Springer, Berlin, 1989.

———. *Action Semantics.* Cambridge University Press, Cambridge, 1992.

———, and Plotkin. G. On proving limiting completeness. *SIAM Journal of Computing* 16 (1987): 179–194.

———, and Watt, D. The use of action semantics. In M. Wirsing, ed. *Formal Description of Programming Concepts III.* North-Holland, Amsterdam, 1987.

Naur, P. ed. Revised report on the algorithmic language ALGOL-60. *Communications ACM* 6 (1963): 1–17.

Nelson, G., ed. *Systems Programming with Modula-3*. Prentice-Hall, Englewood Cliffs, NJ, 1991.

Nielson, F., and Nielson, H.-R. Automatic binding time analysis for a typed lambda calculus. In *Proceedings 14th ACM Symposium Principles of Programming Languages,* ACM Press, New York, 1987, pp. 120–131.

———. *Semantics with Applications*. Wiley, Chicester, 1991.

———. *Two Level Functional Languages*. Cambridge University Press, Cambridge, 1992.

Nordström, B. Programming in constructive set theory: some examples. In *ACM Conference on Functional Languages and Computer Architecture,* ACM Press, New York, 1981, pp. 141–153.

———, and Petersson, K. Types and specfications. In R.E.A. Mason, ed. *IFIP 83*. North-Holland, Amsterdam, 1983, pp. 915–920.

———, Petersson, K., and Smith, J. *Programming in Martin-Löf's Type Theory*. Oxford University Press, Oxford, 1990.

Odifreddi, P., ed *Logic and Computer Science*. Academic Press, New York, 1990,

O'Donnell, M. *Computing in Systems Described by Equations*. LNCS 58, Springer, Berlin, 1977.

———. *Equational Logic as a Programming Language*. MIT Press, 1985.

O'Hearn, P., and Tennent, R. Relational parametricity and local variables. In *20th ACM Symposium on Principles of Programming Languages,* ACM Press, New York, 1993, pp. 171–184.

Paulin-Mohring, C. Extracting Fω's programs from proofs in the calculus of constructions. In *16th ACM Symposium on Principles of Programming Languages,* ACM Press, New York, 1989, pp. 89–104.

Paulson, L. Constructing recusion operators in intuitionistic type theory. *Journal of Symbolic Computation* 2 (1986):

———. *Logic and Computation: Interactive Proof with Cambridge LCF*. Cambridge University Press, Cambridge, 1987.

———. *Standard ML for the Working Programmer*. Cambridge University Press, Cambridge, 1991.

Petersson, K., and Smith, J. Program derivation in type theory: a partitioning problem. *Computer Languages* 11 (1986): 161–172.

Peyton Jones, S. *The Implementation of Functional Programming Languages.* Prentice-Hall International, London, 1987.

Pfenning, F., and Elliot, C. Higher-order abstract syntax. In *SIGPLAN 88 Conference on Programming Language Design and Implementation, SIGPLAN Notices* 23, no. 7 (1988): 199–208.

Pfenning, F., and Paulin-Mohring, C. Inductively defined types in the calculus of constructions. In M. Main, A. Melton, M. Mislove, and D. Schmidt, ed. *5th Conference Mathematical Foundations of Programming Language Semantics.* LNCS 442, Springer, Berlin, 1989, pp. 209–228.

Pierce, B. *Basic Category Theory for Computer Scientists.* MIT Press, Cambridge, MA, 1991.

———. Bounded quantification is undecidable. In *19th ACM Symposium on Principles of Programming Languages,* ACM Press, New York, 1992, pp. 305–315.

———, Dietzen, S., and Michaylov, S. Programming in higher order typed lambda calculi. Report CMU-CS-89-111, Computer Science Department, Carnegie-Mellon University, 1989.

Pittman, T., and Peters, J. *The Art of Compiler Design.* Prentice-Hall, Englewood Ciffs, NJ, 1991.

Plotkin, G. Call-by-name, call-by-value, and the lambda calculus. *Theoretical Computer Science* 1 (1975): 125–159.

———. LCF considered as a programming language. *Theoretical Computer Science* 5 (1977): 223–255.

———. Structured operational semantics. Report DAIMI FN-19, Aarhus University, Denmark, 1981.

Pratt, T. *Programming Languages: Design and Implementation. 2d ed.* Prentice-Hall, Englewood Cliffs, NJ, 1984.

Prawitz, D. *Natural Deduction: A Proof Theoretical Study.* Almqvist and Wiksell, Stockholm, 1965.

Reade, C. *Elements of Functional Programming.* Addison-Wesley, Reading, MA, 1989.

Reynolds, J.C. GEDANKEN—a simple typeless language based on the principle of completeness and the reference concept. *Communications of the ACM* 13 (1970): pp. 308–319.

———. Towards a theory of type structure. In *Colloque sur la Programmation,* LNCS 19, Springer, Berlin, 1974, pp. 408–425.

————. The essence of Algol. In J. de Bakker and J. van Vliet, eds. *International Symposium on Algorithmic Languages*. North-Holland, Amsterdam, 1981a, pp. 345–372.

————. *The Craft of Programming*. Prentice-Hall International, Englewood Cliffs, NJ, 1981b,

————. Types, abstraction, and parametric polymorphism. In R. E. A. Mason, ed. *Information Processing 83*. North-Holland, Amsterdam, 1983, pp. 513–23.

————. Polymorphism is not set-theoretic. In G. Kahn, D. MacQueen, and G. Plotkin, eds. *Semantics of Data Types*. LNCS 173, Springer, Berlin, 1984, pp. 145–156.

————. Three approaches to type structure. In H. Ehrig, C. Floyd, M. Nivat, and J. Thatcher, ed. *Colloquium on Trees in Algebra and Programming: CAAP'85*. LNCS 185, Springer, Berlin, 1985, pp. 97–138.

————. Preliminary design of the programming language Forsythe. Technical Report CMU-CS-88-159, Carnegie-Mellon University, Pittsburgh, 1988.

————. Introduction to polymorphic lambda calculus. In G. Huet, ed. *Logical Foundations of Functional Programming*. Addison-Wesley, Reading, MA, 1990, pp. 77–86.

Riecke, J. Fully abstract translations between functional languages. In *18th ACM Symposium on Principles of Programming Languages,* ACM Press, New York, 1991, pp. 245–254.

Robinson, J. A machine-oriented logic based on the resolution principle. *Journal of the ACM* 12 (1965): 23–41.

————. Logic and logic programming. *Communications ACM* 35 (1992): 40–65.

Schmidt, D.A. *Denotational Semantics*. W.C. Brown, Dubuque, Iowa, 1986.

Scott, D.S. Relating theories of the lambda calculus. In J. P. Seldin and J. R. Hindley, eds. *To H. B. Curry: Essays on Combinatory Logic, Lambda Calculus, and Formalism*. Academic Press, New York, 1980.

————. Domains for denotational semantics. In M. Nielsen and E. M. Schmidt, eds. *9th Conference on Automata, Languages and Programming*. LNCS 140, Springer, Berlin, 1982, pp. 577–613.

Sethi, R. *Programming Languages: Concepts and Constructs*. Addison-Wesley, Reading, MA, 1989.

Siekmann, J. Unification theory. *Journal of Symbolic Computation* 7 (1989): 207–274.

Sokolowski, S. *Applicative Higher Order Programming.* Chapman and Hall, London, 1991.

Springer, G., and Friedman, D. *Scheme and the Art of Programming.* McGraw-Hill, New York, 1989.

Statman, R. Logical relations and the typed lambda-calculus. *Information and Control* 65 (1985): 85–97.

Sterling, L., and Shapiro, E. *The Art of Prolog.* MIT Press, Cambridge, 1986.

Stoughton, A. *Fully Abstract Models of Programming Languages.* Pitman, London, 1988a.

———. Substitution revisited. *Theoretical Computer Science* 59 (1988b): 317–325.

Stoy, J.E. *Denotational Semantics: The Scott-Strachey Approach to Programming Language Theory.* MIT Press, Cambridge, MA, 1977.

Strachey, C. Towards a formal semantics. In T.B. Steele, ed. *Formal Language Description Languages.* North-Holland, Amsterdam, 1966, pp. 198–220.

———. Fundamental concepts in programming languages. Unpublished manuscript, Programming Research Group, Oxford University, 1968.

———. The varieties of programming languages. Technical Monograph PRG-10, Programming Research Group, Oxford University, 1973.

Suppes, P. *Introduction to Logic.* Van Nostrand, Princeton, 1957.

Talcott, C. Towards a theory of binding structures: extended abstract. In T. Rus, ed. *2d Conference on Algebraic Methodology and Software Methodology.* Iowa City, Iowa, 1991, pp. 135–138.

Tennent, R.D. Language design methods based on semantic principles. *Acta Informatica* 8 (1977a): 97–112.

———. On a new approach to representation-independent data classes. *Acta Informatica* 8 (1977b): 315–324.

———. *Principles of Programming Languages.* Prentice-Hall International, London, 1981.

———. Quantification in Algol-like languages. *Information Processing Letters* 25 (1987): 133–137.

———. Elementary data structures in Algol-like languages. *Science of Computer Programming* 13 (1989): 73–110.

————. *Semantics of Programming Languages.* Prentice-Hall International, London, 1991.

Thatte, S. Quasi-static typing. In *17th ACM Symposium on Principles of Programming Languages,* ACM Press, New York, 1990, pp. 367–381.

Thompson, S. *Type Theory and Functional Programming.* Addison-Wesley, Reading, MA, 1991.

Tofte, M. Operational semantics and polymorphic type inference. Ph.D. thesis, Report CST-52-88, Computer Science Department, University of Edinburgh, 1988.

Troelstra, A.S., and Dalen, D. van *Constructivism in Mathematics: An Introduction.* 2 vols. North-Holland, Amsterdam, 1988.

Turner, D., ed. *Research Topics in Functional Programming.* Addison-Wesley, Reading, MA, 1990.

Turner, R. *Constructive Foundations for Functional Languages.* McGraw Hill, New York, 1991.

Wadsworth, C. Semantics and Pragmatics of the Lambda-calculus. D.Phil. thesis, Oxford University, 1971.

Watt, D. A. *Programming Language Concepts and Paradigms.* Prentice-Hall International, London, 1990.

————. *Programming Language Syntax and Semantics.* Prentice-Hall International, London, 1991.

Weeks, S., and Felleisen, M. On the Orthogonality of Assignments and Procedures in Algol. In *20th ACM Symposium on Principles of Programming Languages,* ACM Press, New York, 1993, pp. 57–70.

Wegner, P. Programming Language Semantics. In R. Rustin, ed. *Formal Semantics of Programming Languages.* Prentice-Hall, Englewood Cliffs, NJ, 1972, pp. 149–248.

Wexelblat, R.L., ed. *History of Programming Languages.* Academic Press, New York, 1980.

Wikstrom, A. *Functional Programming Using Standard ML.* Prentice-Hall International, London, 1987.

Winskel, G. *Formal Semantics of Programming Languages.* MIT Press, Cambridge, MA, 1993.

Wirth, N. On the design of programming languages. In *IFIP Congress 74,* North-Holland, Amsterdam, 1974. Also in Horowitz (1983).,

————. Programming languages: what to demand and how to assess them. In R. H. Perrott, ed. *Software Engineering*. Academic Press, New York, 1977.

Index